A New Zealand Prayer Book

He Karakia Mihinare o Aotearoa

A New Zealand Prayer Book

He Karakia Mihinare o Aotearoa

The Anglican Church in Aotearoa,
New Zealand and Polynesia

Te Haahi Mihinare ki Aotearoa ki Nui Tireni,
ki Nga Moutere o te Moana Nui a Kiwa

HarperSan Francisco
A Division of HarperCollins*Publishers*

Originally published in 1989 by William Collins Publishers Ltd. first HarperCollins edition Published in 1997

Library of Congress Cataloging-in-Publication Data

Anglican Church in Aotearoa, New Zealand and Polynesia.
A New Zealand prayer book = He Karakia Mihinare o Aotearoa.
    p. cm.
Originally published: U.K. : W. Collins Publishers, 1989.
ISBN 0-06-060199-X (hardcover)
1. Anglican Church in Aotearoa, New Zealand and Polynesia— Liturgy and ritual. 2. Anglican Communion—New Zealand—Liturgy and ritual. 3. Lord's Supper. I. Title.
BX5720.5.C48   1997
264'.03—dc21   97-3716

    99 00 01 RRD 10 9 8 7 6 5 4 3

Contents

Preface

One of the treasures of Anglican spirituality has been its authorised Book of Common Prayer, helpful both for personal devotion and public liturgical worship. The prayer book of 1662 has served Anglicans well, and for longer than its English authors might have imagined. Now, all over the Anglican world, prayer books more suitable to local and contemporary needs are finding favour.

Though new in language and content, *A New Zealand Prayer Book, He Karakia Mihinare o Aotearoa*, preserves the ethos of Anglican spirituality and incorporates the best liturgical insights modern scholarship provides. It is also more faithful to the earliest liturgical traditions of the Church and allows more flexibility than the book of 1662.

More importantly, the New Zealand Prayer Book has been created in our own Pacific cultural setting, and shaped by our own scholarship. It belongs to our environment and our people.

We are thankful for the many hours of dedicated work done by the Prayer Book Commission since 1965. The result is a lively book, inclusive in language, comprehensive in purpose and rich in content.

I commend *A New Zealand Prayer Book, He Karakia Mihinare o Aotearoa*, as a God inspired taonga. As we use it in our homes and in the congregations of our churches, we will find the spiritual nourishment we need for our journey in Christ.

The Most Reverend Brian Davis,
Primate and Archbishop of New Zealand,
Wellington

Feast of St Barnabas,
11 June 1989

Introduction

A Multitude of Voices

A Prayer Book for the Church of the Province of New Zealand, including as it does Te Pihopatanga o Aotearoa, and the island nations of the South Pacific in the Diocese of Polynesia, must be a deliberate attempt to allow a multitude of voices to speak.

When the General Synod of 1964 established an initial Commission on Prayer Book Revision '...to plan and prepare a revised Book of Common Prayer, either in stages, or as a whole, in the light of the needs of the Province and of contemporary liturgical development,' that may have seemed a relatively straightforward task of liturgical revision. Since then successive Commission members have realised that it was indeed a major undertaking.

In the last twenty-five years the fabric of New Zealand society has changed. We live in a different, and to many, a strange world. There has been an increasing awareness of the delicate ecological balance within our country, interdependent with others. New Zealand has adopted an anti-nuclear stance. The basis of our economy has radically changed. The re-emergence of a sense of identity within the Maori people has seen the Maori language approved as an official language of the nation.

These words are still true:

> "We are living in a new world: it is ours, if we are true to the faith that is in us, to seek to make it a better world. ...New knowledge and new ways of life bring with them new customs and forms of speech unknown before."
>
> (Preface to the 1928 Book of Common Prayer)

Within the Church there have also been profound changes since 1964. Women have been ordained as priests within this Province since 1977, and this has ensured a continuing dialogue on the equal partnership of women and men within the Church. Thus there has been an increasing need to choose language which is inclusive in nature and which affirms the place of each gender under God.

Through the decisions of General Synod the Province is committed to affirming the partnership between Maori and Pakeha, and has maintained that the life and governance of the Church stand upon our Constitution, and the fundamental principles of the Treaty of Waitangi.

There have been other shifts as well. There has been an increasing recognition of the ministry of all the baptised people of God ministering in God's name. We know that we can function as more effective disciples in the world when there is no sharp division between those with different functions within the Church.

Through all these insights we have come to new understandings of who God is, and how God acts, among us in our world.

Many of these movements in Church and society are reflected within the services contained in this Prayer Book. This is now the context in which we seek to worship God.

We are fortunate that liturgical change in this country does not begin with the publication of this volume. We have experience in renewing liturgy over many years.

The first experimental *New Zealand Liturgy* issued in 1966, broke new ground in being one of the first Anglican eucharistic liturgies to address God as 'You'. This represented an attempt to close the gap between liturgical language and the words of everyday experience.

This was followed by the more definitive *The New Zealand Liturgy 1970* which gained wide acceptance within the worshipping congregations of the Province. An edition of this in both Maori and English languages was produced in 1977. The New Zealand Liturgy remained in place until the adoption in 1984 of *Liturgies of the Eucharist*. This was produced as a result of widespread experimentation around the dioceses, and is the basis for the present work.

Other separate booklets of services were produced for the Church's use during the decade 1970-1980. *Orders of Services*, containing Morning and Evening Prayer, canticles and Psalms for Worship, *Christian Initiation*, and *Marriage Services* (containing three forms), *Funeral Services*, *The New Zealand Calendar*, and *Services for use with the Sick and on other Pastoral Occasions*, were all produced, some with a number of expanded editions.

This steady flow of liturgical material from the Commission means that the Anglican Church in New Zealand does not now have to undergo a radical change with the introduction of *A New Zealand Prayer Book, He Karakia Mihinare o Aotearoa.* We are not in the situation where the normative worship of the Church has been that of the *Book of Common Prayer*, and where the shift to an alternative prayer book involves a massive dislocation for the parish worshipper. Those dissonances have already occurred during the last twenty years.

Many parishes are already familiar with the style and content developed within the Commission's previous work, and a variety of usage now prevails around the Province.

With the exception of the Commination the services in the 1662 Book, and all alternative services approved by the Church since then, remain fully authorised for public worship by those congregations who wish to use them.

The publication of this Prayer Book, now presented for use by the Church, is the result of over twenty years experimentation, usage, evaluation and criticism by many individuals and groups. Diocesan liturgical committees and parish groups have all contributed through their insights and drafts. The fruit of their labours has been gathered together and incorporated by the Commission.

Thus this Prayer Book is a gift from the Church to itself.

Since the establishment of the Commission over fifty individuals, women and men, ordained and lay, have served on it, contributing their energy and skills. We have been continually enriched by the attendance of observers from other Churches at our meetings.

We have also gained great benefit from the liturgical revisions of other parts of the Anglican communion, particularly those Provinces which have already published alternative service books.

In more recent years we have had to wrestle with the issues of justice and mutuality. Social assumptions are critical in writing liturgy, for we are apt to ascribe to God attitudes and prejudices which are ours alone. These become embedded within, and perpetuated by our liturgical usage. The dialogue about inclusive language has now moved beyond merely referring to humanity. Like the early Commission we are back to exploring ways in which it is possible to address God. This issue was there long before we faced it. We have gradually been compelled in our pilgrimage to start searching for ways to address God in language which is other than masculine and triumphal.

The purpose of liturgy is not to protect particular linguistic forms. It is to enable a community to pray. We know that some people will consider we have moved too far in the language we have chosen: others will insist that we have not gone far enough. What we present is one fragile moment in the relentless on-going process of liturgical change.

Liturgy describes the People of God. Liturgy expresses who we believe we are in the presence of God. Liturgy reveals the God whom we worship. Liturgy reflects our mission. Since the earlier experimental orders the imagery describing God has become more vivid, and more personal.

For members of the Commission, the experience of writing these services has been an intensely personal experience, representing immense spiritual growth. We discovered together that the material we were handling had the effect of enlarging our vision and experience. As a result, our work has steadily become less 'formal' and more devotional, both in breadth and in intensity. New voices are emerging.

Earlier work shows that the task before the Commission then seemed to be 'to provide revised services for the Church'. Later work reflects an attempt to provide deliberately for those private moments of prayer, for devotional experiences of a more intimate nature beyond what is common in New Zealand.

Whereas earlier services provided relatively fixed forms, the later liturgies offer more variety and options, encouraging flexibility in their use.

There is freedom within the heritage. Continuity is always in tension with liturgical change, but continuity there is. The intention is to extend, not break, the richness of our heritage.

New words and new voices encourage the exploration of new ways of acting liturgically.

It would be a tragic temptation to imagine that liturgy comprises words alone. Liturgy is not primarily what we say, but what we do, and the provision of new services will never by themselves renew the worship of the congregation.

Even new words are only a vehicle for the worship of God, so that we might reach for the things beyond the words in the language of the heart.

If worship is the response of the people of God to the presence of God, then the first function of liturgy is to provide conditions in which that presence may be experienced.

Musical settings, the sensitive use of silence, and careful imaginative preparation by the leaders of worship will be necessary if the words in this Prayer Book are to be allowed to speak so that an experience of God results.

Some services will seem very familiar. This should not discourage the exploration of new modes of expression which might now be the most appropriate. The very freshness of others might invite new paths to be explored, and new songs to be sung.

The Lord's song has been sung in this twice-discovered land since before Samuel Marsden first preached the Gospel on that Christmas Day in 1814 in Oihi Bay.

With the publication of *A New Zealand Prayer Book, He Karakia Mihinare o Aotearoa* the song is continued, the task of the Provincial Commission on Prayer Book Revision is completed, and new voices begin to be heard.

It is our hope that the use of these services will enable us to worship God in our own authentic voice, and to affirm our identity as the people of God in Aotearoa - New Zealand.

R.G. McCullough

College House, Christchurch.
Feast of St Augustine,
26 May, 1989

For the Provincial Commission
on Prayer Book Revision

Lift your hearts to heaven
where Christ in glory reigns.

Kia whakapaingia te Atua!

Welcome to you as you come to worship.

Worship is the highest activity of the human spirit. In this book you will find the means to express all the hopes and vision, common purpose and emerging love of which we are capable.

In each service, in a variety of ways, we experience God and respond to the eternal, following different threads and strands of spirituality.

As Christians, whether we are engaged in the Church's daily round of prayer and thanksgiving or being touched by God at the turning points of our lives, we worship in response to the love of God and out of love for one another. In worship we celebrate and make real that love and it strengthens our commitment to Christ, each other, and those who stand in need. It is only as we care for each other and care for our neighbours that our regular worship makes sense. Love of God becomes love of neighbour.

Worship is a skill to be learned and a creative art to practise. Whether you use this book as a leader or participant you will need to make your own contribution to the worship in which you are involved. Suggestions are given on how the service should be conducted but it is left open to each congregation to decide whether to sit, stand or kneel at the various parts of the service.

Where the service requires that action or words belong to a deacon, priest or bishop, this is stated. The term minister, however, denotes any authorised person who is leading the worship at that point.

In this book BOLD type indicates the words to be used for the people's part.

The Calendar

Te Maramataka

Concerning the Calendar

In its liturgy the Church remembers and celebrates the whole drama of God's revelation, with special focus on

- *the life, death and resurrection of Jesus Christ*
- *the many people and events with a special place in the Scriptures and the continuing life of the Church.*

These celebrations are not just a looking back into history. Their liturgical commemoration provides a way for the Church today to participate, through memory and imagination, in the work of the Holy Spirit in times past, and so be strengthened in its own life and witness.

As the Letter to the Hebrews reminds us

'*With so many witnesses in a great cloud on every side of us, we too, then, should throw off everything that hinders us, especially the sin that clings so easily, and keep running steadily in the race we have started. Let us not lose sight of Jesus, who leads us in our faith and brings it to perfection...*'

The Church Year

Seasons, Sundays, Principal Feasts and Holy Days

Advent

The season of preparation for Christmas

First Sunday in Advent
Second Sunday in Advent
Third Sunday in Advent
Fourth Sunday in Advent

Christmas

The celebration of the birth of Jesus Christ

The Birth of our Lord Jesus Christ: Christmas Day, 25 December
First Sunday after Christmas
Second Sunday after Christmas

Epiphany

The revelation of Christ

The Epiphany of our Lord Jesus Christ, 6 January
The Baptism of the Lord. First Sunday after the Epiphany
(Second Sunday to the Sixth Sunday after the Epiphany)*

Seventh Sunday after the Epiphany (Septuagesima)
Eighth Sunday after the Epiphany (Sexagesima)
Ninth Sunday after the Epiphany (Quinquagesima)

Lent

A time of preparation for Holy Week and Easter

First day of Lent: Ash Wednesday
First Sunday in Lent
Second Sunday in Lent
Third Sunday in Lent
Fourth Sunday in Lent
Fifth Sunday in Lent: Passion Sunday

Holy Week

The passion of our Lord

Palm Sunday: Sixth Sunday in Lent
Monday in Holy Week
Tuesday in Holy Week
Wednesday in Holy Week
Maundy Thursday
Good Friday
Holy Saturday

Easter

The resurrection and ascension of Jesus Christ

Easter Eve
Easter Day: the Day of Resurrection
Monday in Easter Week
Tuesday in Easter Week
First Sunday after Easter: Low Sunday
Second Sunday after Easter
Third Sunday after Easter
Fourth Sunday after Easter
Fifth Sunday after Easter
Ascension Day
Sunday after Ascension Day
The Day of Pentecost: Whitsunday

*Pentecost celebrates the coming of the Holy Spirit
and the birth of the Church.*

The Sundays after Pentecost

Trinity Sunday: First Sunday after Pentecost
Second Sunday to the Twenty-Third Sunday after Pentecost
(Twenty-Fourth Sunday to the Twenty-Seventh Sunday after
    Pentecost)*
Sunday before Advent

* The number of Sundays after Epiphany or Pentecost depends upon the date of Easter.
See Table on pages 944-945.

The Calendar

1 Principal Feasts and Holy Days

In the Church these days take precedence over any other observance.

Principal Feasts

Christmas Day
The Epiphany
Easter Day
Ascension Day
The Day of Pentecost (Whitsunday)
Trinity Sunday

Holy Days

Ash Wednesday
Good Friday

2 Other Feasts and Holy Days

*The following Holy Days are regularly observed throughout the year. Those in **bold type** take precedence over Sundays and all other days of commemoration or of special observance. Those Holy Days in light type occurring on a Sunday after Epiphany or after Pentecost may take precedence over the Sunday, or may be transferred as in the **Table to Regulate Observances** (page 944).*

A   Of our Lord

All Sundays are feasts of our Lord Jesus Christ
The Naming of Jesus, 1 January
The Baptism of the Lord, First Sunday after the Epiphany
The Presentation of Jesus in the Temple, 2 February
**The Annunciation of our Saviour to the Blessed Virgin Mary,
    25 March**
The Transfiguration of the Beloved Son, 6 August

B   Of the Saints

In the commemoration of saints, the Church celebrates the victory of Christ in the lives of particular individuals. The Calendar of Saints' Days varies considerably among Christian Churches and among the various churches of the Anglican Communion.

The Conversion of St Paul, 25 January
St Matthias the Apostle, 24 February
St Mark the Evangelist, 25 April
St Philip and St James, Apostles, 1 May
St Barnabas the Apostle, 11 June
St John the Baptist, 24 June
St Peter and St Paul, Apostles, Martyrs, 29 June
The Visitation of Mary to Elizabeth, 2 July
St Mary Magdalene, 22 July
St James and St John, Apostles, 25 July
St Mary, the Mother of Jesus, 15 August
St Bartholomew (Nathanael), Apostle, 24 August
St Matthew, Apostle, Evangelist, 21 September
St Michael and All Angels, 29 September
St Luke the Evangelist, 18 October
St James of Jerusalem, 23 October
St Simon and St Jude, Apostles, 28 October
All Saints' Day, 1 November
St Andrew, Apostle, Martyr, 30 November
St Thomas the Apostle, 21 December (3 July)
St Stephen, the first Christian Martyr, 26 December (3 August)
St John the Evangelist, 27 December (6 May)
The Holy Innocents, 28 December (16 February)

C   Of the Anglican Church in Aotearoa, New Zealand and Polynesia

The commemoration of all those who have built up this Church, 1 September

D   Local Feasts

The Feast of the Consecration or Dedication of a church
The Feast of the Patron or Title of a church

These local feasts may be observed on, or be transferred to, a Sunday, except in the seasons of Advent, Lent and Easter.

3   Other Commemorations

A   Of our Lord

Thanksgiving for Holy Communion (Corpus Christi),
    Thursday after Trinity Sunday
The Holy Name of Jesus, 7 August
Holy Cross Day, 14 September

B   Regional Commemorations

The Saints and Martyrs of Africa, 20 February
The Saints and Martyrs of the Americas, 8 April
The Saints and Martyrs of Europe, 30 July
The Saints and Martyrs of the Pacific, 7 September
The Saints and Martyrs of Asia, 6 October
The Saints and Martyrs of the Anglican Communion,
    8 November

C Commemorations particularly associated with Aotearoa – New Zealand

We remember many people who have provided inspiration and an example of Christian living in the history of this country, or who have contributed to the development of Christianity in this country.

These commemorations may be celebrated on other appropriate days according to local custom.

Carl Sylvius Volkner, Priest and Mokomoko, Rangatira, 2 March.
Kereopa and Manihera of Taranaki, 13 March
George Augustus Selwyn, 11 April
Heni Te Kirikaramu, 30 April
Ruatara, 11 May
Samuel Marsden, 12 May
Ihaia Te Ahu, 13 May
Ngakuku, 14 May
Piripi Taumataakura, 15 May
Te Wera Hauraki, 16 May
Wiremu Te Tauri, 17 May
Tamihana Te Rauparaha, 18 May
Rota Waitoa, 22 May
Frederick Augustus Bennett, 23 May
Mother Edith, 24 May
Henare Wiremu Taratoa, 21 June
Wiremu Tamihana, 23 June
Henry Williams, 16 July
Churchill Julius, 23 September
Mother Marie-Joseph Aubert, 1 October
Tarore of Waharoa, 19 October
Te Whiti o Rongomai, 6 November
Octavius Hadfield, 11 December
Marianne Williams, 16 December

D   Other names particularly associated with the Pacific

We remember some of the people who have dedicated their lives to the spread of the gospel in our part of the world.

Gladys Aylward, 3 January
The Martyrs of Japan, 5 February
Toyohiko Kagawa, 24 April
Rose of Lima, 23 August
The Martyrs of Papua New Guinea, 2 September
Charles Fox, 6 September
John Coleridge Patteson, 20 September
The Martyrs of Melanesia, 27 September
Martin of Porres, 3 November
Francis Xavier, 3 December

E   Other Commemorations in the Calendar

We include in the Calendar the names of people whose lives and work give special encouragement to others of all ages, and to those engaged in various aspects of the Church's life and witness. They are not all from remote history.

Modern times have also produced men and women whose lives have excited other people to sanctity and deeper discipleship.

These names are recorded in the Calendar on pages 14-25.

F   Diocesan, Tribal, Local or other Commemorations

Commemorations of people of local significance whom the community wishes to celebrate.

4 Days of Discipline, Self-Denial and Days of Special Devotion

(i)   Ash Wednesday   Good Friday

(ii) The other weekdays in Lent

(iii) All the Fridays in the year except those falling between 25 December and 1 January, 6 and 13 January inclusive; and the Friday following after Easter Day and Ascension Day.

5 Days of Optional Observance

Days of Prayer

(i)   *For the Ministry of the Church and Ordinands [Ember Days]*

Prayers are offered on the weekdays following the Day of Pentecost and the week preceding St Andrew's Day.

(ii) *For Work and Conservation [Rogation Days]*

The days on either side of the commemoration of St Francis of Assisi (4 October) provide opportunities for prayers to be offered for God's blessing on the fruits of the earth and the labours of all in farming and fisheries, industry and commerce.

(iii) *For Preparation before Feasts [Vigils]*

Special prayers and readings may be used in preparation on the day before

The Birth of our Lord Jesus Christ: Christmas Day
Day of Pentecost
St John the Baptist
St Mary, the Mother of Jesus
All Saints' Day
St Andrew's Day

Vigils may also be kept of: The Presentation of Jesus, St Matthias, The Annunciation, St Peter and St Paul, The Visitation, St James and St John, St Bartholomew (Nathanael), The Builders of the Anglican Church in Aotearoa, New Zealand and Polynesia, St Matthew, St Simon and St Jude, and St Thomas.

Note that if any of these Feasts falls on a Monday, then the Fast of the Vigil shall be kept on the Saturday, and not on the Sunday next before it.

6 Other Special Days

(i) *Harvest Thanksgiving*

may be observed on a Sunday as determined by local custom.

(ii) *Mothering Sunday*

may be observed on the fourth Sunday in Lent, but the proper for Mothering Sunday may not take precedence over that set for the Sunday unless there is more than one celebration of the Eucharist. The collect for Mothering Sunday may be added after the collect for the day.

(iii) Those Sundays designated by resolution of General Synod from time to time may be observed.

Aotearoa Sunday – Sunday before Advent
Sea Sunday – Second Sunday in July
Social Services Sunday – Fourth Sunday in July

(iv) *National Days of Remembrance*

should be celebrated in the same manner as the commemorations particularly associated with Aotearoa - New Zealand.

Waitangi Day, 6 February
Anzac Day, 25 April
United Nations Day, 24 October

January

1	**The Naming of Jesus**
	New Year's Day
2	Seraphim of Sarov, Mystic, Russia, 1833
3	Gladys Aylward, Missionary, China, 1970
4	
5	The Eve of the Epiphany
6	**The Epiphany of our Lord Jesus Christ**
	or The Revelation of Christ to the Gentiles
7	
8	
9	
10	
11	
12	
13	Hilary, Bishop of Poitiers, Teacher of the Faith, c.367
14	Sava, the Founder and first Archbishop of the Serbian Church, 1235
15	
16	
17	Antony of Egypt, Abbot, 356
18	
19	
20	
21	Agnes, Child-Martyr at Rome, c.304
22	Vincent, Spanish Deacon and Martyr, Saragossa, c.304
23	
24	
25	**The Conversion of St Paul**
26	Timothy and Titus, Companions of St Paul
27	John Chrysostom, Bishop of Constantinople, Teacher of the Faith, 407
28	Thomas Aquinas, Teacher of the Faith, 1274
29	
30	King Charles of England, 1649
31	

The Feast of **The Baptism of the Lord** is observed on **The First Sunday after the Epiphany**

February

1 Brigid of Ireland, Abbess, c.525
2 **The Presentation of Jesus in the Temple**
3 Anskar, Archbishop of Hamburg,
   Missionary to Denmark and Sweden, 865
4
5 The Martyrs of Japan, 1597
6 Waitangi Day
7
8
9
10
11
12
13
14 Cyril, 869 and Methodius, 885, Missionaries to the Slavs
15
16 Alternative date for The Holy Innocents (28 December)
17 Janani Luwum, Archbishop, Martyr of Uganda, 1977
18 Martin Luther, 1546, and other Reformers of the Church
19
20 The Saints and Martyrs of Africa
21
22 The Confession of St Peter
23 Polycarp, Bishop of Smyrna, Martyr, c.156
24 **St Matthias the Apostle**
25
26
27 George Herbert, 1633, and all saintly Parish Priests
28
29

March

1   David, Bishop, Patron Saint of Wales, c.601
2   Carl Sylvius Volkner, Priest and Mokomoko, Rangatira,
      Opotiki, 1865, symbols for reconciliation
3   John Wesley, Preacher, 1791, and Charles Wesley, Poet, 1788
4
5
6
7   Perpetua and her Companions, Martyrs at Carthage, 203
8
9
10
11
12 Gregory the Great, Bishop of Rome, Teacher of the Faith, 604
13 Kereopa and Manihera of Taranaki, Martyrs at Turangi, 1847
14
15
16
17 Patrick, Bishop, Patron Saint of Ireland, 461
18 Cyril of Jerusalem, Bishop, Teacher of the Faith, 386
19 Joseph of Nazareth
20 Cuthbert, Bishop of Lindisfarne, Missionary, 687
21 Thomas Cranmer, Archbishop of Canterbury,
      Liturgist and Martyr, 1556
22 Thomas Ken, Bishop of Bath and Wells, Poet, 1711
23
24 Gabriel, Archangel
25 **The Annunciation of our Saviour
      to the Blessed Virgin Mary**
26
27
28
29 John Keble of Oxford, Priest and Poet, 1866
30
31

April

1   Frederick Denison Maurice, Priest, Theologian, 1872
2
3   Richard of Chichester, Bishop, 1253
4   Martin Luther King, Prophet, 1968
5
6
7
8   The Saints and Martyrs of the Americas
9   Dietrich Bonhoeffer, Pastor, Theologian, Germany, 1945
10   William Law, Priest, Mystic, 1761
11   George Augustus Selwyn, Bishop of New Zealand, 1878
12
13
14
15
16
17
18
19
20
21   Anselm, Archbishop of Canterbury,
      Teacher of the Faith, 1109
22
23   George, Martyr, Patron Saint of England, c.304
24   Toyohiko Kagawa, Teacher, Evangelist, Japan, 1960
25   **St Mark the Evangelist**
    Anzac Day
26
27
28
29   Catherine of Siena, Teacher of the Faith, 1380
30   Heni Te Kirikaramu of Gate Pa, 1864

May

1   **St Philip and St James, Apostles**
2   Athanasius, Bishop of Alexandria, Teacher of the Faith, 373
3
4
5
6   Alternative date for St John the Evangelist (27 December)
7
8   Dame Julian of Norwich, Mystic, 1417
9   Gregory of Nazianzus, Bishop of Constantinople,
      Teacher of the Faith, 389
10
11   Ruatara, Te ara mo te Rongopai ' The gateway for the
      Gospel'
12   Samuel Marsden, Priest and Missionary,
      the Apostle of New Zealand, 1838
13   Ihaia Te Ahu, Missionary, Priest in Te Arawa
14   Ngakuku, Missionary in Mataatua
15   Piripi Taumataakura, Missionary in Ngati Porou
16   Te Wera Hauraki, Missionary in Ngati Kahungunu
17   Wiremu Te Tauri, Missionary in Wanganui
18   Tamihana Te Rauparaha,
      Missionary to Te Wai Pounamu, 1876
19   Dunstan, Archbishop of Canterbury and Reformer, 988
20
21
22   Rota Waitoa, Te matamua o nga minita Maori. The first
      Maori ordained in New Zealand, 1853
23   Frederick Augustus Bennett, Te matamua o nga pihopa
      Maori. The first Maori Bishop, 1950
24   Mother Edith, Founder of the Community
      of the Sacred Name, Christchurch, 1922
25   The Venerable Bede of Jarrow, Teacher of the Faith, 735
26   Augustine, first Archbishop of Canterbury, Missionary, 605
27
28
29
30   Apolo Kivebulaya of Uganda, Priest and Missionary, 1933
31

June

1   Justin, Martyr at Rome, c.165
2
3   The Martyrs of Uganda, 1886
4
5   Boniface, Bishop of Mainz, Missionary, Martyr, 754
6
7
8
9   Columba of Iona, Abbot, Missionary, 597
10
11 **St Barnabas the Apostle**
12
13 Antony of Padua, Missionary, Preacher,
        Teacher of the Faith, 1231
14 Basil the Great, Bishop of Caesarea in Cappadocia,
        Teacher of the Faith, 379
15 Evelyn Underhill, Mystic, 1941
16
17
18
19 Sadhu Sundar Singh, Teacher, Evangelist, India, 1929
20
21 Henare Wiremu Taratoa of Te Ranga, 1864
22 Alban, first Martyr of Britain, c.304
23 Wiremu Tamihana, Prophet, Kingmaker, 1866
24 **St John the Baptist**
25
26
27
28 Irenaeus, Bishop of Lyons, Teacher of the Faith, c.200
29 **St Peter and St Paul, Apostles, Martyrs**
30

For May and June
Thanksgiving for Holy Communion – Corpus Christi –
is observed on the Thursday after Trinity Sunday
Days of Prayers for the Ministry of the Church and Ordinands
are observed on the days of the week following the Day of Pentecost

July

1
2 **The Visitation of Mary to Elizabeth**
3 Alternative date for St Thomas, Apostle, Martyr
   (21 December)
4 Samuel Azariah, Bishop, Ecumenist, 1945
5
6 Thomas More, Scholar, 1535
7
8
9
10
11 Benedict of Nursia, Abbot of Monte Cassino, c.550
12
13 Silas, Companion of St Paul
14
15 Swithun, Bishop of Winchester, c.862, Translated 971
16 Henry Williams, Missionary, 1867
17
18
19
20
21
22 **St Mary Magdalene**
23
24
25 **St James and St John, Apostles**
   Christopher, Martyr, c.250
26 Anne, Mother of the Blessed Virgin Mary
27
28 Mary and Martha of Bethany
29 William Wilberforce, 1833, and All Social Reformers
30 The Saints and Martyrs of Europe
31 Joseph of Arimathea

August

1
2 Chad, Bishop of Lichfield, Missionary, 672
3 Alternative date for St Stephen the First Martyr
   (26 December)
4 John Baptist Vianney, Curé d'Ars, Priest, 1859
5 Oswald, King of Northumbria, Martyr, 642
6 **The Transfiguration of the Beloved Son**
7 The Holy Name of Jesus
8 Dominic, Priest, 1221
9 Mary Sumner, Founder of the Mothers' Union, 1921
10 Laurence, Deacon and Martyr at Rome, 258
11 Clare of Assisi, Abbess, 1253
12
13 Florence Nightingale, Nurse, Social Reformer, 1910
14 Maximilian Kolbe, Priest, Martyr, Auschwitz, 1941
15 **St Mary, the Mother of Jesus**
16 Holy Women of the Old Testament
17
18
19
20 Bernard of Clairvaux, Abbot, Poet, 1153
21
22
23 Rose of Lima, Mystic, 1617
24 **St Bartholomew (Nathanael) the Apostle**
25
26
27 Monnica, Mother of Augustine of Hippo, 387
28 Augustine, Bishop of Hippo, Teacher of the Faith, 430
29 The Beheading of St John the Baptist
30
31 Aidan, Bishop of Lindisfarne, Missionary, 651

September

1 **The Builders of the Anglican Church in Aotearoa, New Zealand and Polynesia**
2 The Martyrs of Papua New Guinea, 1942
3
4 Albert Schweitzer, Medical Missionary, Theologian, 1965
5
6 Charles Fox, Scholar, Missionary, 1977
7 The Saints and Martyrs of the Pacific
8 The Birth of the Blessed Virgin Mary, Mother of our Lord
9
10
11
12
13 Cyprian, Bishop of Carthage, Martyr, 258
14 Holy Cross Day
15
16 Ninian, Bishop in Galloway, Missionary, c.432
17 Hildegarde of Bingen, Mystic, Religious, 1179
18
19 Theodore of Tarsus, Archbishop of Canterbury, 690
20 John Coleridge Patteson,
   first Bishop of Melanesia, Martyr, 1871
21 **St Matthew, Apostle, Evangelist**
22
23 Churchill Julius, Bishop,
   first Archbishop of New Zealand, 1938
24
25 Sergius of Radonezh,
   Abbot of Holy Trinity, Moscow, 1392
26 Lancelot Andrewes, Bishop of Winchester, 1626
27 The Martyrs of Melanesia
28
29 **St Michael and All Angels**
30 Jerome, Priest, Teacher of the Faith,
   Translator of the Scriptures, 420

October

1   Mother Marie-Joseph Aubert, Religious,
        Social Reformer, 1926
2   The Holy Guardian Angels
3
4   Francis of Assisi, Friar, 1226
5
6   The Saints and Martyrs of Asia
7   William Tyndale, Translator of the Scriptures, Martyr, 1536
8   Bridget (Birgitta) of Sweden, Mystic, Religious,
        Patron Saint of Sweden, 1373
9   Robert Grosseteste, Bishop of Lincoln, 1253
10
11
12 Elizabeth Fry, Prison Reformer, England, 1845
13
14
15 Teresa of Avila, Teacher of the Faith, 1582
16 The English Reformers and Martyrs, 1555
17 Ignatius, Bishop of Antioch, Martyr, c.107
18 **St Luke the Evangelist**
19 Tarore of Waharoa, 1836
20 Henry Martyn, Missionary, 1812
21
22

23 **James of Jerusalem, Brother of the Lord, Martyr, c.62**
24 Raphael, Archangel
    United Nations Day
25
26 Alfred, King of the West Saxons, 899
27
28 **St Simon and St Jude, Apostles**
29
30 Holy Women of the New Testament
31

Days of Prayer for Work and Conservation are observed on 3 and 5 October

November

1   **All Saints' Day**
2   All Souls' Day
3   Martin of Porres, Monk, Peru, 1639
4   Richard Hooker, Priest, Theologian, 1600
5
6   Te Whiti o Rongomai, Prophet, 1907
7   Willibrord, Archbishop of Utrecht, Missionary, 739
8   The Saints and Martyrs of the Anglican Communion
9
10 Leo the Great, Bishop of Rome, Teacher of the Faith, 461
11 Martin, Bishop of Tours, 397
12 Charles Simeon of Cambridge, Priest, 1836
13
14
15
16 Margaret, Queen of Scotland, 1093
17 Hilda, Abbess of Whitby, 680
18 Hugh, Bishop of Lincoln, 1200
19 Elizabeth of Hungary, Princess, 1231
20 Mechtild of Magdeburg, Mystic, Prophet, 1280
21
22 Cecilia, Martyr at Rome, c.230
23 Clement, Bishop of Rome, Martyr, c.100
24
25
26
27
28
29
30   **St Andrew, Apostle, Martyr**

Days of Prayer for the Ministry of the Church and Ordinands
are observed on the days of the week preceding St Andrew's Day

December

1
2
3   Francis Xavier, Missionary, 1552
4
5
6   Nicholas, Bishop of Myra, c.342
7   Ambrose, Bishop of Milan, Teacher of the Faith, 397
8   Richard Baxter, Priest, Theologian, 1691
9   Holy Men of the Old Testament
10
11   Octavius Hadfield, Bishop, 1904
12
13   Lucy, Martyr, Syracuse, c.304
14
15
16   Marianne Williams, Missionary, 1879
17
18
19
20
21   **St Thomas, Apostle, Martyr** (or 3 July)
22
23
24   The Eve and Vigil of Christmas
25   **The Birth of our Lord Jesus Christ – Christmas Day**
26   **St Stephen, the first Christian Martyr** (or 3 August)
27   **St John the Evangelist** (or 6 May)
28   **The Holy Innocents** (or 16 February)
29   Thomas of Canterbury, Bishop, Martyr, 1170
30   Josephine Butler, Worker among Women, 1905
31   John Wycliffe, Theologian and Reformer, 1384

Liturgies of the Word

Concerning these Services

Our Christian life is a pilgrimage of growth into the stature of Christ. That growth is fostered above all by a regular pattern of prayer and reflection on the biblical story, especially the gospel. Our faith has been shaped by that story, and our patterns of worship have been enriched by passages and verses from the Bible as part of our praise and prayer before God.

In these services extensive provision is made for patterns of worship that provide for regular reflection on central elements of the gospel.

Morning and Evening Worship is a full Liturgy of the Word that is most suitable for use with a congregation or group.

Daily Services provide a simpler pattern of reading, psalms, praise and prayer for each day of the week, morning and evening, and are suitable for small groups and individuals.

Daily Devotions may be used as self-contained acts of reflection and prayer, based on the New Testament, but may also be added to by the use of appointed readings.

Midday Prayer, Night Prayer and **Family Prayer** provide brief services of praise and prayer that are suitable for groups, for families or for individual use.

Psalms for Worship. Together with biblical readings, the Psalms are the most common feature of regular patterns of worship, and provision is made for their use in the above services.

The Lectionary. A lectionary, offering a cycle of readings, psalms and other material for every day of the year, provides a helpful aid for use with the various services. A duly authorised table of readings and psalms shall be followed.

> Worship is the highest activity of the human spirit. In worship we contemplate the truth, mercy and power of God shown to us in Jesus Christ. We respond with adoration, we acknowledge our failures, and we seek to amend our lives in the strength of the Holy Spirit.

Morning and Evening Worship

This service provides for those occasions of public worship when there is a need for a Service of the Word. The service is modelled on Morning and Evening Prayer (Mattins and Evensong) from the Book of Common Prayer, and follows a pattern of

Praise of God
Confession and Absolution
Psalms
Readings from the Old and New Testaments
with appropriate response in Songs of Praise
and opportunity for preaching and prayers.

*The service, except for the **Absolution** and **Blessing**, may be conducted by any authorised lay person.*

***Additional Directions** are to be found on page 53.*

Introductory Scripture Sentences

For Seasonal Use

ADVENT

The glory of the Lord shall be revealed, and all people shall see it together.

Isaiah 40:5

Repent, for the kingdom of heaven is at hand.

Matthew 3:2

The Son of man is to come with the angels in the glory of the Father.

Matthew 16:27a (adapted)

CHRISTMAS

To us a child is born: O come, let us adore him. Alleluia.

Isaiah 9:6 (adapted)

Behold I bring you good news of a great joy; for to you is born in the city of David a Saviour, who is Christ the Lord.   *Luke 2:10,11*

In this, O God, your love was made manifest among us, that you sent your only Son into the world so that we might live through him.   *1 John 4:9 (adapted)*

EPIPHANY

From the rising of the sun to its setting my name is great among the nations, and in every place incense is offered to my name, and a pure offering; for my name is great among the nations, says the Lord of hosts.   *Malachi 1:11*

It is the God who said, 'Let light shine out of darkness,' who has shone in our hearts to give the light of the knowledge of the glory of God in the face of Christ.   *2 Corinthians 4:6*

LENT

Jesus told his disciples, 'If any of you would come after me you must deny yourself and take up your cross and follow me.'

Matthew 16:24 (adapted)

The sacrifice acceptable to God is a broken spirit: a broken and contrite heart, O God, you will not despise.   *Psalm 51:17*

HOLY WEEK

God shows such love for us in that while we were yet sinners Christ died for us.   *Romans 5:8*

Christ himself bore our sins in his body on the tree, that we might die to sin and live to righteousness. By his wounds you have been healed.   *1 Peter 2:24*

EASTER

It is true: the Lord has risen.

Luke 24:34

Christ has been raised from the dead, the first fruits of those who have fallen asleep.

1 Corinthians 15:20

Blessed be the God and Father of our Lord Jesus Christ, by whose great mercy we have been born anew to a living hope through the resurrection of Jesus Christ from the dead.

1 Peter 1:3

ASCENSION

Since we have a great high priest who has passed through the heavens, Jesus, the Son of God, let us with confidence draw near to the throne of grace, that we may receive mercy and find grace when we are in need of help.

Hebrews 4:14,16

PENTECOST

You shall receive power when the Holy Spirit has come upon you, and you shall be my witnesses.

Acts 1:8

God's love has been poured into our hearts through the Holy Spirit which has been given to us.

Romans 5:5

TRINITY

Round the throne of God, day and night they never cease to sing, 'Holy, holy, holy is the Lord God Almighty, who was and is and is to come!'

Revelation 4:8

ALL SAINTS

Since we are surrounded by so great a cloud of witnesses, let us also lay aside every weight, and sin which clings so closely, and let us run with perseverance the race that is set before us, looking to Jesus the pioneer and perfecter of our faith.

Hebrews 12:1,2

A SAINT'S DAY

The righteous will be remembered for ever: the memory of the righteous is a blessing.

Psalm 112:6; Proverbs 10:7

DAYS OF PRAYER FOR WORK AND CONSERVATION, AND HARVEST THANKSGIVING

God said, 'While the earth remains, seedtime and harvest, cold and heat, summer and winter, day and night, shall not cease.'

Genesis 8:22

The earth is the Lord's and all that is in it. *Psalm 24:1*

TIMES OF THANKSGIVING

Let the nations be glad and sing for joy, for you O Lord judge the peoples righteously and guide the nations on earth. *Psalm 67:4*

TIMES OF TROUBLE

God is our refuge and strength, a very present help in trouble.

Psalm 46:1

Have no anxiety about anything, but in everything by prayer and supplication with thanksgiving let your requests be made known to God. *Philippians 4:6*

DEDICATION FESTIVAL OF A CHURCH

Come to Christ, to that living stone, which people have rejected, but in God's sight chosen and precious; and like living stones be yourselves built into a spiritual house, to be a holy priesthood, to offer spiritual sacrifices acceptable to God through Jesus Christ.

1 Peter 2:4

For General Use

God is spirit, and those who worship God must worship in spirit and in truth.

John 4:24

Alleluia! For the Lord our God the Almighty reigns. Let us rejoice and exult and give God the glory.

Revelation 19:6,7

Worship the Lord in the beauty of holiness; let the whole earth stand in awe.

Psalm 96:9

Through Jesus let us continually offer up a sacrifice of praise to God, the fruit of lips that acknowledge God's name.

Hebrews 13:15

Rejoice always, pray constantly, give thanks in all circumstances; for this is the will of God for you in Christ Jesus.

1 Thessalonians 5:16-18 (adapted)

You are worthy, our Lord and God, to receive glory and honour and power, for you created all things, and by your will they existed and were created.

Revelation 4:11

When anyone is united to Christ, there is a new world; the old order has gone, and a new order has already begun.

2 Corinthians 5:17

Morning and Evening Worship

The Preparation

The minister may greet the people.

*The **Sentence of the Day** or one of the **Introductory Sentences** is read .*

Then the minister says to the people

Great is the Lord and worthy of all praise.

**Amen! Praise and glory and wisdom,
thanksgiving and honour, power and might,
be to our God for ever and ever! Amen.**

*The theme of praise may continue with the following or some other **Song of
Praise.***

Great and Wonderful

1   Great and wonderful are your deeds‿
     O Lord ' God · the al'mighty:
  just and true are your ways‿
     O ' Sovereign ' of the ' nations.

2   Who shall not revere and praise your ' name O ' Lord?:
    for ' you a'lone are ' holy.

3   All nations shall come and worship ' in your ' presence:
    for your just ' dealings · have ' been re'vealed.

4   To the One who is seated on the throne and ' to the ' Lamb:
    be blessing and honour, glory and might‿
      for ever and ' ever. ' A'men.
                          Revelation 15:3b-4; 5:13

E te whanau a te Karaiti / Brothers and sisters in Christ,
let us praise and worship God who has called us together.
Let us celebrate God's majesty,
and delight in the wonder of God's love.
Together we shall confess our sins
and receive assurance that we are forgiven.

As the scriptures are read,
we can allow God's word to speak to us,
and ponder its meaning for our lives.
In our prayers, we give thanks for God's goodness,
we pray for others as well as for ourselves,
and we offer our lives anew in Christ's service.

All this we do,
because we believe in the presence among us
of our Saviour Jesus Christ,
and in the mighty power of the Holy Spirit.

The minister says

Hear these words of scripture.

One of the following sentences is read.

As God who called you is holy,
be holy yourselves in all your conduct.
Spirit of God, search our hearts.

Or

If we claim to be sinless,
we are self-deceived and strangers to the truth.
If we confess our sins,
God is just and may be trusted to forgive our sins
and cleanse us from every kind of wrong.
Spirit of God, search our hearts.

Or

Love one another,
for love is of God,
and whoever loves is born of God and knows God.
Spirit of God, search our hearts.

The minister then says

Let us kneel and, in silence,
remember our need for God's forgiveness.

Silence

Let us confess our sins to God.

One of the following is used.

**Almighty and merciful God,
we have sinned against you,
in thought, word and deed.
We have not loved you with all our heart.
We have not loved others
as our Saviour Christ loves us.
We are truly sorry.
In your mercy forgive what we have been,
help us to amend what we are,
and direct what we shall be;
that we may delight in your will
and walk in your ways,
through Jesus Christ our Saviour. Amen.**

Or

**God of mercy,
we have sinned against you and against others.
We have sinned in what we have done,
and in what we have failed to do.
We are truly sorry.
For the sake of your Son Jesus Christ,
who died for our sins,
forgive us all that is past
and raise us to newness of life. Amen.**

A priest says

Almighty God, who pardons all who truly repent,
forgive your sins, strengthen you by the Holy Spirit,
and keep you in life eternal;
through Jesus Christ our Redeemer.
Amen.

(A deacon or layperson says 'us' and 'our' instead of 'you' and 'your'.)

The Ministry of the Word

O come, let us sing to the Lord,
    Tena kia waiata tatou ki a Ihowa,
let us rejoice in the rock of our salvation.
    kia hari tatou ki te toka o to tatou whakaoranga.

We sing to you, O God, and bless your name;
    Waiata atu ki a Ihowa, whakapaingia tona ingoa;
and tell of your salvation from day to day.
    korerotia tona whakaoranga i ia ra, i ia ra.

We proclaim your glory to the nations,
    Panuitia tona kororia ki nga iwi.
your praise to the ends of the earth.
    Tona whakanui ki nga topito o te ao.

*Then follows the **Psalm** (or **Psalms**) appointed.*

At the end of the psalm is said

Glory to the Father, and to the Son,
    and to the Holy Spirit:
as it was in the beginning, is now,
    and shall be for ever. Amen.

    Kororia ki te Matua, ki te Tama,
        ki te Wairua Tapu;
    mai i te timatanga, ki tenei wa,
        a, haere ake nei. Amine.

or one of the other forms in Maori on page 56 or 197.

*The **Reading** from the Old Testament*

Silence may follow the reading.

The reader may say

Hear what the Spirit is saying to the Church.
Thanks be to God.

One of the following or another Song of Praise is said or sung.

MORNING WORSHIP

The Song of Zechariah

Benedictus

1   Blessèd are you O ' Lord our ' God:
     you have come to your ' people · and ' set them ' free.

2   You have raised up for us a ' mighty ' Saviour:
     born of the ' house · of your ' servant ' David.

3   Through your holy prophets you ' promised · of ' old:
     that you would save us from our enemies,
       from the ' hands of ' all who ' hate us.

4   You promised to show ' mercy · to our ' forbears:
     and to re'member · your ' holy ' covenant.

5   This was the oath you swore to our ' father ' Abraham:
     to set us ' free · from the ' hands of · our ' enemies,

6   free to worship you with'out ' fear:
     holy and righteous in your sight '‿
     all the ' days of · our ' life.

7   And you, child, shall be called ‿
     the prophet of the ' Most ' High:
     for you will go before the ' Lord · to pre'pare the ' way,

8   to give God's people knowledge ' of sal'vation:
     through the for'giveness ' of their ' sins.

9   In the tender compassion ' of our ' God:
     the dawn from on ' high shall ' break up'on us,

10   to shine on those who dwell in darkness⌣
        and the ' shadow · of ' death:
    and to guide our feet ' into · the ' way of ' peace.

Luke 1: 68-79 (adapted)

    Glory to the Father and ' to the ' Son:
        and ' to the ' Holy ' Spirit;
    as it was in the be'ginning · is ' now:
        and shall be for ' ever. ' A'men.

Or

Te Waiata a Hakaraia

Kia whakapaingia te Ariki, te Atua o Iharaira: kua titiro mai
    hoki ia, kua hoko i tana iwi,
A kua whakaarahia ake e ia he haona whakaora mo tatou:
    i roto i te whare o Rawiri, o tana pononga;
Ko tana hoki ia, i korerotia e te mangai o ana poropiti tapu:
    no te timatanga iho ano o te ao:
Hei whakaora i a tatou i o tatou hoa-whawhai: i te ringaringa
    ano hoki o te hunga katoa e kino ana ki a tatou;
Hei whakaputa mo te mahi tohu ki o tatou tupuna:
    hei whakamahara ki tana kawenata tapu;
Ki te oati i oati ai ia ki a Aperahama: ki to tatou tupuna.
Kia tukua mai e ia ki a tatou he oranga i te ringaringa o tatou
    hoa-whawhai: a kia mahi wehi kore atu ki a ia,
I runga i te tapu, i te tika, ki tona aroaro: i nga ra katoa e ora ai
    tatou.
A ko koe, e tama, ka karangatia ko te poropiti a te Runga rawa:
    e haere hoki koe i te aroaro o te Ariki, hei whakapai i ona ara:
Hei whakamatau i tona iwi ki te whakaoranga: i o ratou hara e
    murua ana;
He mea hoki na te aroha, na te mahi tohu a to tatou Atua:
    na reira hoki i puta mai ai te puaotanga o runga ki a tatou,
Hei whakamarama i te hunga e noho ana i te pouri, i te atarangi
    hoki o te mate: hei whakatika i o tatou waewae ki te huarahi o
    te rangimarie.

Ruka 1:68-79

Kia whakakororiatia te Matua, te Tama: me te Wairua Tapu;
Ko te ritenga ia i te timatanga, a tenei ano inaianei: a ka mau
    tonu iho, a ake ake ake. Amine.

Or

The Steadfast Love of the Lord

1   The steadfast love of the Lord ' never ' ceases:
    God's mercies ' never ' come · to an ' end;

2   they are new ' every ' morning:
    your ' faithfulness · O ' Lord is ' great.

3   You are ' all · that I ' have:
    and ' therefore ' I will ' wait for you.

4   You O Lord are good to ' those who ' wait for you:
    to ' all ' those who ' seek you.

5† It is good to ' wait in ' patience:
    for the sal'vation ' of the ' Lord.   *Lamentations 3:22-26*

    Glory to the Father and ' to the ' Son:
    and ' to the ' Holy ' Spirit;
    as it was in the be'ginning · is ' now:
    and shall be for ' ever. ' A'men.

EVENING WORSHIP

The Song of the Blessed Virgin Mary   *Magnificat*

1   My soul proclaims the ' greatness · of the ' Lord:
    my spirit re'joices · in ' God my ' saviour,

2   for you Lord have looked with favour⌣
        on your ' lowly ' servant:
    and from this day all gener'ations · will ' call me ' blessèd.

3† You O Most Mighty have done ' great things ' for me:
    and ' holy ' is your ' name.

4   You have mercy on ' those who ' fear you:
    from gener'ation · to ' gener'ation.

5   You have shown the ' strength · of your ' arm:
    you have scattered the ' proud in ' their con'ceit.

6　You have cast down the mighty ' from their ' thrones:
　　　and have ' lifted ' up the ' lowly.

7　You have filled the hungry with ' good ' things:
　　　and the rich you have ' sent a'way ' empty.

8　You have come to the help ' of your ' people:
　　　for you have re'membered · your ' promise · of ' mercy,

9　the promise you ' made · to our ' forbears:
　　　to Abraham ' and his ' children · for ' ever.

Luke 1:46-55 (adapted)

　　Glory to the Father and ' to the ' Son:
　　　and ' to the ' Holy ' Spirit;
　　as it was in the be'ginning · is ' now:
　　　and shall be for ' ever. ' A'men.

Or

Te Waiata a te Puhi Tapu, a Meri

Ka whakanui toku wairua i te Ariki: a e hari ana toku wairua ki
　te Atua, ki toku Kai-whakaora;

Mona i titiro ki te iti o tana pononga: ta te mea hoki katahi ahau
　ka kiia e nga whakatupuranga katoa e haere ake nei,
　　he wahine hari.

He nui hoki nga mahi a te Mea Kaha ki ahau :
　a e tapu ana tona ingoa.

He mahi tohu tana ki te hunga e wehi ana ki a ia: ki tenei
　whakatupuranga, ki tenei whakatupuranga.

Kua whakaputaina he kaha e ia, ara, e tona ringaringa: nana te
　hunga whakakake i marara ai i te whakaaro o o ratou ngakau.

Kua whakataka e ia te hunga kaha i nga nohoanga: a
　whakateiteitia ake ana te hunga iti.

Kua whakakiia e ia te hunga mate hiakai ki nga mea pai: a tonoa
　kautia atu ana te hunga taonga.

Kua tautokona e ia a Iharaira tana pononga:
　he whakamaharatanga hoki ki tana mahi tohu.

Ki a Aperahama, ratou ko tana whanau ake tonu atu: pera hoki
　me tana i korero ai ki o tatou matua.　　　　　*Ruka 1:46-55*

Kia whakakororiatia te Matua, te Tama: me te Wairua Tapu;
Ko te ritenga ia i te timatanga, a tenei ano inaianei: a ka mau
　tonu iho, a ake ake ake. Amine.

Or

God is My Salvation

1   Behold God is ' my sal'vation:
     I will trust and ' will not ' be a'fraid,

2   for the Lord God is my ' strength · and my ' song:
     and has be'come ' my sal'vation.

3   With joy you will draw water from the ' wells · of sal'vation:
     and in that day ' all of ' you will ' say,

4   ' Give thanks and call upon the ' name · of the ' Lord:
     make known among the nations what the Lord has done,
      proclaim that the ' name · of the ' Lord is · ex'alted.

5   ' Sing praises for the Lord has ' triumphed ' gloriously:
     let this be ' known in ' all the ' earth.

6   ' Shout and sing for joy you ' people · of ' God:
     for great in your ' midst ' is the ' Holy One.'   *Isaiah 12:2-6*

Glory to the Father and ' to the ' Son:
   and ' to the ' Holy ' Spirit;
as it was in the be'ginning · is ' now:
   and shall be for ' ever. ' A'men.

The Reading from the New Testament

Silence may follow the reading.

The reader may say

Hear what the Spirit is saying to the Church.
Thanks be to God.

*One of the following or another **Song of Praise** is said or sung.*

The Song of the Church   *Te Deum Laudamus*

1   We praise ' you O ' God:
          we ac'claim you ' as the ' Lord.

2   All creation ' worships ' you:
          the ' Father ' ever'lasting.

3   To you all angels, all the ' powers · of ' heaven:
          cherubim and seraphim, ' sing in ' endless ' praise,

4   'Holy, holy, holy Lord, God of ' power · and ' might:
          heaven and ' earth are ' full of · your ' glory.'

5   The glorious company of a'postles ' praise you:
          the noble fellowship of prophets praise you,
               the white-robed ' army · of ' martyrs ' praise you.

6   Throughout the world the holy ' Church ac'claims you:
          Father, of ' majes'ty un'bounded,

7†   your true and only Son, worthy of ' all ' worship:
          and the Holy Spirit, our ' advo'cate and ' guide.

8   You Christ are the ' king of ' glory:
          the e'ternal ' Son · of the ' Father.

9   When you became incarnate to ' set us ' free:
          you humbly ac'cepted · the ' Virgin's ' womb.

10   You overcame the ' sting of ' death:
          and opened the kingdom of ' heaven · to ' all be'lievers.

11   You are seated at God's right ' hand in ' glory:
          we believe that you will ' come to ' be our ' judge.

12   Come then Lord and ' help your ' people:
          bought with the ' price of ' your own ' blood,

13   and bring us ' with your ' saints:
          to ' glory ' ever'lasting.

*The **Song of the Church** may end with the following verses*

14   Save your people Lord, and ' bless · your in'heritance:
          govern and up'hold them ' now and ' always.

15   Day by ' day we ' bless you:
       we ' praise your ' name for ' ever.

16   Keep us today Lord from ' all ' sin:
       have mercy ' on us ' Lord, have ' mercy.

17   Lord show us your ' love and ' mercy:
       for we ' put our ' trust in ' you.

18   In you Lord ' is our ' hope:
       let us not be con'founded ' at the ' last.

Or

Te Waiata a te Haahi

E whakapai atu ana matou ki a koe, e te Atua; e whakaae
   ana matou ko koe ano a Ihowa.
E koropiko ana te whenua katoa ki a koe: e te Matua ora tonu.
E kaha ana te karanga a nga Anahera katoa ki a koe:
   a nga Rangi, me o reira Kaha katoa.
Hono tonu te karanga a nga Kerupima: a nga Herapima,
   ki a koe,
Tapu, Tapu, Tapu rawa: e Ihowa, e te Atua o nga mano
   tuauriuri, whaioio;
Ki tonu te rangi me te whenua: i te Nui o tou Kororia.
E whakapai ana ki a koe nga Apotoro: te hunga ingoa nui.
E whakapai ana ki a koe: te huihuinga pai o nga Poropiti.
E whakapai ana ki a koe te ope ingoa nui: nga tangata i patua
   mo te whakapono.
E whakaae ana ki a koe: te Haahi tapu puta noa i te ao;
Ki te Matua: e hira rawa nei te kororia;
Ki tau Tama kotahi: he pono ia, he ingoa nui;
Ki te Wairua Tapu ano hoki: ki te Kai-whakamarie.
Ko koe te Kingi ingoa nui: e te Karaiti.
Ko koe te Tama ora tonu: a te Matua.
I a koe i anga ki te whakaora i te tangata: kihai koe i kino kia
   whanau i te Puhi.
Ano ka taea e koe te wero o te mate: ka tuwhera i a koe te
   Rangatiratanga o te Rangi ki te hunga whakapono katoa.

Kei te ringa matau o te Atua koe e noho ana:
    kei te Kororia o te Matua.
E whakapono ana matou, tera koe e haere mai: hei
    Kai-whakarite whakawa mo matou.
Koia matou ka inoi nei ki a koe kia whakakahangia au pononga:
    i hokoa e koe ki ou toto utu nui.
Whakaurua ratou ki roto ki au Tangata tapu: ki te kororia
    mutunga kore.
E Ihowa, whakaorangia tau hunga: whakapaingia tau Haahi.
Kawanatia ratou: whakaarahia, a, ake ake ake.
I tenei ra, i tenei ra: e whakanui ana matou i a koe;
E karakia ana matou ki tou Ingoa: aianei, ake ake ake.
Whakaae mai, e Ihowa: kia tiakina matou aianei kei hara.
E Ihowa, tohungia matou: tohungia matou.
E Ihowa, kia tau tou atawhai ki runga ki a matou: e whaka-
    whirinaki atu nei hoki matou ki a koe.
E Ihowa, e whakawhirinaki atu ana ahau ki a koe: aua ahau e
    tukua kia whakama.

Or

You are Worthy

1   You are worthy, our ' Lord and ' God:
        to receive ' glory · and ' honour · and ' power,

2   for you have cre'ated ' all things:
        and by your will⌣
            they were cre'ated · and ' have their ' being.

3   You are worthy O Christ, for ' you were ' slain:
        and by your blood have ' ransomed ' us for ' God,

4   ransomed us from every tribe and ' people · and ' nation:
        and made us a royal ' house of ' priests · to our ' God.

5† To the One who is seated on the throne and ' to the ' Lamb:
        be blessing and honour, glory and might,
            for ever and ' ever. ' A'men.

based on Revelation 4:11;5:9,10,13

The Song of Simeon
Nunc Dimittis

1   Lord now you let your servant ' go in ' peace:
   ' your ' word has ' been ful'filled.

2   My own eyes have ' seen the · sal'vation:
   which you have prepared in the ' sight of ' every ' people,

3† a light to reveal you ' to the ' nations:
   and the ' glory · of your ' people ' Israel.   *Luke 2:29-32*

Glory to the Father and ' to the ' Son:
   and ' to the ' Holy ' Spirit;
as it was in the be'ginning · is ' now:
   and shall be for ' ever. ' A'men.

Or

Te Waiata a Himiona

Katahi, e te Ariki, ka tukua tau pononga kia haere i runga i te
   rangimarie: ka pera me tau i korero ai:
Ka kite nei hoki oku kanohi: i tau whakaoranga.
Ka whakatakotoria nei e koe: ki te aroaro o nga iwi katoa;
Hei whakamarama e kite ai nga tauiwi: hei kororia hoki mo tau
   iwi, mo Iharaira.   *Ruka 2: 29-32*

Kia whakakororiatia te Matua, te Tama: me te Wairua Tapu;
Ko te ritenga ia i te timatanga, a tenei ano inaianei: a ka mau
   tonu iho, a ake ake ake. Amine.

Or

The Exalted Lord

1   Christ Jesus was in the ' form of ' God:
      yet he did not think to ' grasp · at e'quality · with ' God,

2   but emptied himself, taking the ' form · of a ' servant:
      and was ' born · in our ' human ' likeness.

3   Being found in our human state he ' humbled · him'self:
      and became obedient unto death,
         even ' death ' on a ' cross.

4   Therefore God has ' highly · ex'alted him:
      and bestowed on him the ' Name a·bove ' every ' name;

5   that at the name of Jesus every ' knee should ' bow:
      in heaven and on ' earth and ' under · the ' earth,

6   and every tongue confess that Jesus ' Christ is ' Lord:
      to the glory of God the ' Father. ' A'men.   *Philippians 2:6-11*

*The **Sermon** may be preached here, or after the **Collects**.*

*The Apostles' Creed or **Te Whakapono a nga Apotoro** (page 496) may be said, all standing.*

**I believe in God, the Father almighty,
   creator of heaven and earth.**

**I believe in Jesus Christ, God's only Son, our Lord,
   who was conceived by the Holy Spirit,
   born of the Virgin Mary,
   suffered under Pontius Pilate,
   was crucified, died, and was buried;
   he descended to the dead.
   On the third day he rose again;
   he ascended into heaven,
   is seated at the right hand of the Father,
   and will come again to judge the living and the dead.**

**I believe in the Holy Spirit,
   the holy catholic Church,
   the communion of saints,
   the forgiveness of sins,
   the resurrection of the body,
   and the life everlasting.   Amen.**

The Lord be with you.
The Lord bless you.

*The **Lord's Prayer** is said here or after the **Thanksgivings and Intercessions**.*

As our Saviour Christ has taught us, we pray

Our Father in heaven,
hallowed be your name,
your kingdom come,
your will be done,
on earth as in heaven.
Give us today our daily bread.
Forgive us our sins
as we forgive those who sin against us.
Save us from the time of trial
and deliver us from evil.

For the kingdom, the power, and the glory are yours
now and for ever.   Amen.

Kua akona nei tatou e to tatou Ariki,
ka inoi tatou

E to matou Matua i te rangi
Kia tapu tou Ingoa.
Kia tae mai tou rangatiratanga.
Kia meatia tau e pai ai
ki runga ki te whenua,
kia rite ano ki to te rangi.
Homai ki a matou aianei
he taro ma matou mo tenei ra.
Murua o matou hara,
Me matou hoki e muru nei
i o te hunga e hara ana ki a matou.
Aua hoki matou e kawea kia whakawaia;
Engari whakaorangia matou i te kino:
Nou hoki te rangatiratanga, te kaha,
me te kororia,
Ake ake ake.   Amine.

Make your ways known upon earth, O God,
>E Ihowa, meinga o tikanga kia mohiotia ki te ao,

your saving power among all peoples.
>**tou mana whakaora ki nga tauiwi katoa.**

Renew your Church in holiness,
>Whakahoungia to Haahi i runga i te tapu.

and help us to serve you with joy.
>**A awhinatia matou ki te mahi ki a koe i runga i te hari.**

Guide the leaders of this and every nation,
>E Ihowa, arahina nga iwi o tenei whenua.

that justice may prevail throughout the world.
>**Kia riro mai ai i nga tangata katoa nga mea e tika ana ki a ratou.**

Let not the needy, O God, be forgotten,
>E Ihowa, kaua e warewaretia te rawakore.

nor the hope of the poor be taken away.
>**Kaua ano te tumanako o te rawakore e whakakorea.**

Make us instruments of your peace,
>E Ihowa, meinga matou hei karere mo tou rangimarie.

and let your glory be over all the earth.
>**A tukua tou kororia kia horapa ki te ao katoa.**

Thanksgivings and Intercessions may follow here, or at the point indicated later in the service.

A Collect of the Day shall be said here, followed by the *Collect for Morning* or *Evening*.

MORNING

Holy and everliving God,
by your power we are created
and by your love we are redeemed;
guide and strengthen us by your Spirit,
that we may give ourselves to your service,
and live each day in love to one another and to you,
through Jesus Christ our Lord.
Amen.

EVENING

Gracious God,
you have given us much today;
grant us also a thankful spirit.
Into your hands we commend ourselves
and those we love.
Be with us still, and when we take our rest
renew us for the service of your Son Jesus Christ.
Amen.

**In darkness and in light,
in trouble and in joy,
help us, heavenly Father,
to trust your love,
to serve your purpose,
and to praise your name,
through Jesus Christ our Lord. Amen.**

*An **Anthem** may be sung here or at some other suitable place.*

*The **Sermon** may be preached here.*

***Thanksgivings and Intercessions** and the **Lord's Prayer** follow if they have
not already been said.*

During the service the Gifts of the People may be presented.

The Dismissal

One of the following conclusions is used.

Let us bless the Lord.
Thanks be to God.

**The almighty and merciful God bless us
and keep us now and for ever. Amen.**

Or

The grace of our Lord Jesus Christ,
and the love of God,
and the fellowship of the Holy Spirit
be with us all. Amen.

Or a priest may give a blessing.

The congregation is sent out with these words.

Go now to love and serve the Lord. Go in peace.
> Haere i runga i te rangimarie i runga i te aroha me te ngakau
> hihiko ki te mahi ki te Ariki.

Amen. We go in the name of Christ.
> **Amine. Ka haere matou i runga i te ingoa o te Karaiti.**

Additional Directions

Hymns or other songs may be sung at any appropriate point of the services.

The Readings *should be announced in the order: book, chapter, verse. At the end of each reading may be said*

Either   Here ends the reading.

Or   Hear what the Spirit is saying to the Church.
Thanks be to God.

Notes on pointing of **Psalms** *and* **Songs of Praise:**

(a)   *Breath is to be taken at the end of lines, except where the sign ⌣ indicates a 'carry-over'.*

(b)   *The inverted dot (·) is used to indicate how the syllables are to be divided between the notes of the bar when there are more than two syllables between the bar marks.*

(c)   *An obelus (†) indicates that the second half of a double chant is to be sung to the verse.*

(d)   *A double space between verses and the division of some psalms into parts indicates sections of psalms that may be used independently, or that a change of chant may be appropriate.*

(e)   *The final 'ed' should be pronounced as a separate syllable when it is marked with an accent (e.g. blessèd).*

The words of the traditional canticles as given in the Book of Common Prayer may be used for choral settings.

Daily Services

From early in the history of the Church, Christians have developed forms of daily prayer and worship, centred on the regular reading of Scripture and the recital of the psalms. Such regular spiritual discipline is commended to all, and especially when it is possible for groups of Christians to meet together.

Clergy in particular are expected to follow a personal spiritual discipline and to provide opportunities for other people to join in daily worship where possible. Such a scheme of regular spirituality is provided here.

Individuals or groups may adapt the pattern found here to their own needs. The following are examples of the kind of changes that can be made.

1 Seasonal Variations

In addition to the 'Alleluia' provided for use in Eastertide, the seasons of the Church's year and other festivals may be marked by the use of seasonal sentences at the beginning and end of the service, by a special selection of the **Songs of Praise** or from the **Additional Songs of Praise**, or by the insertion of appropriate hymns or other songs.

2 Simplification

(i) When said by one person alone, the opening and closing verse and response may be omitted.

(ii) The material provided may be used to construct a simple pattern: an **opening sentence**, a **New Testament reading**, a **Song of Praise** in a weekly or monthly cycle, and informal prayer.

3 One Service in the Day

The general pattern of the services may be followed in a single service for the day, using either the morning or evening Songs of Praise as set in a fortnightly cycle, or one song of praise in a monthly cycle, as a response to the Psalms and Readings. If the service is said in the middle of the day, the morning or evening collect is omitted, or replaced by an appropriate midday prayer.

4 The following are common texts for use in the Daily Services

Confession and Absolution

Almighty and merciful God,
we have sinned against you,
in thought, word and deed.
We have not loved you with all our heart.
We have not loved others
as our Saviour Christ loves us.
We are truly sorry.
In your mercy forgive what we have been,
help us to amend what we are,
and direct what we shall be;
that we may delight in your will
and walk in your ways,
through Jesus Christ our Saviour. Amen.

A priest says

Almighty God,
who pardons all who truly repent,
forgive your sins,
strengthen you by the Holy Spirit,
and keep you in life eternal;
through Jesus Christ our Redeemer.
Amen.

(A deacon or layperson says 'us' and 'our' instead of 'you' and 'your'.)

Gloria

At the end of the Psalm is said

Glory to the Father and ' to the ' Son:
and ' to the ' Holy ' Spirit;
as it was in the be'ginning · is ' now:
and shall be for ' ever. ' A'men.

Or

Kia whakakororiatia te Matua, te Tama:
  me te Wairua Tapu;
ko te ritenga ia i te timatanga, a tenei ano inaianei:
  a ka mau tonu iho, a ake ake ake. Amine.

Or

Kororia ki a koe, e te Ariki.

Or

Kororia ki te Matua, ki te Tama,
  ki te Wairua Tapu;
mai i te timatanga, ki tenei wa,
  a, haere ake nei. Amine.

The Apostles' Creed

I believe in God, the Father almighty,
  creator of heaven and earth.

I believe in Jesus Christ, God's only Son, our Lord,
  who was conceived by the Holy Spirit,
  born of the Virgin Mary,
  suffered under Pontius Pilate,
  was crucified, died, and was buried;
  he descended to the dead.
  On the third day he rose again;
  he ascended into heaven,
  is seated at the right hand of the Father,
  and will come again to judge the living and the dead.

I believe in the Holy Spirit,
  the holy catholic Church,
  the communion of saints,
  the forgiveness of sins,
  the resurrection of the body,
  and the life everlasting.   Amen.

The Lord's Prayer

Our Father in heaven,
   hallowed be your name,
   your kingdom come,
   your will be done,
      on earth as in heaven.
Give us today our daily bread.
Forgive us our sins
   as we forgive those who sin against us.
Save us from the time of trial
   and deliver us from evil.

For the kingdom, the power, and the glory are yours
   now and for ever.   Amen.

E to matou Matua i te rangi
   Kia tapu tou Ingoa.
   Kia tae mai tou rangatiratanga.
   Kia meatia tau e pai ai
      ki runga ki te whenua,
         kia rite ano ki to te rangi.
Homai ki a matou aianei
   he taro ma matou mo tenei ra.
Murua o matou hara,
      Me matou hoki e muru nei
         i o te hunga e hara ana ki a matou.
Aua hoki matou e kawea kia whakawaia;
   Engari whakaorangia matou i te kino:
Nou hoki te rangatiratanga, te kaha,
   me te kororia,
      Ake ake ake.   Amine.

Sunday Morning

The minister reads this sentence.

Awake sleeper;
rise from the dead, and Christ will shine upon you.

Open our lips, O Lord;
and our mouth shall proclaim your praise.
(In Eastertide: **Alleluia.***)*

This **Song of Praise** *follows.*

The Spirit of the Lord

1 The Spirit of the Lord God ' is up'on me:
        because the Lord has anointed me⌣
            to bring good ' tidings ' to the · af'flicted.

2 The Lord has sent me to bind up the ' broken-'hearted:
        to proclaim liberty for the captives,
            and re'lease for ' those in ' prison,

3 to comfort ' all who ' mourn:
        to bestow on them a crown of ' beauty · in'stead of ' ashes,

4 the oil of gladness in'stead of ' mourning:
        a garment of ' splendour · for the ' heavy ' heart.

5† They shall be called ' trees of ' righteousness:
        planted for the ' glory ' of the ' Lord.

6 Therefore I will greatly re'joice · in the ' Lord:
        my soul shall ex'ult ' in my ' God,

7 for God has robed me with salvation ' as a ' garment:
        and clothed me with in'tegri·ty ' as a ' cloak.

8 For as the earth brings ' forth its ' shoots:
        and as a garden causes the ' seeds to ' spring ' up,

9 so the Lord God will cause ' righteousness · and ' praise:
        to spring ' forth be·fore ' all the ' nations.   *Isaiah 61:1-3,10,11*

Glory to the Father and ' to the ' Son:
    and ' to the ' Holy ' Spirit;
as it was in the be'ginning · is ' now:
    and shall be for ' ever. ' A'men.

*The **Psalm** (or **Psalms**) appointed are said or sung.*

*Then follow **Readings** from the Bible as appointed.*

Silence is kept after the Readings.

*This **Song of Praise** follows.*

The Song of our Adoption

1   Blessèd are you, God and Father of our Lord ' Jesus ' Christ:
        you have blessed us in Christ with every⌣
           spiritual ' blessing · in the ' heaven·ly ' realms.

2   Even before the world was made⌣
        you chose us to be ' yours in ' Christ:
        that we should be holy and ' blameless ' in your ' sight.

3   In love you destined us for adoption⌣
        as your children ' through Christ ' Jesus:
        such was your ' pleasure ' and your ' purpose,

4   to the praise of your ' glori·ous ' grace:
        which you have freely given us in ' your be'lovèd ' Son.

Ephesians 1:3-6

Glory to the Father and ' to the ' Son:
    and ' to the ' Holy ' Spirit;
as it was in the be'ginning · is ' now:
    and shall be for ' ever. ' A'men.

Then follow   **The Apostles' Creed**
                    The Lord's Prayer
                    A Collect of the Day
                    Thanksgivings and Intercessions

*The following **Morning Collect** is said.*

God our creator,
yours is the morning and yours is the evening.
Let Christ the sun of righteousness
shine for ever in our hearts
and draw us to that light
where you live in radiant glory.
We ask this for the sake of Jesus Christ our Redeemer.
Amen.

The service concludes

Let us bless the Lord.
Thanks be to God.

The grace of our Lord Jesus Christ,
and the love of God,
and the fellowship of the Holy Spirit
be with us all.
Amen.
(In Eastertide: **Alleluia, Amen.)**

Sunday Evening

The minister reads this sentence.

Christ has been raised from the dead,
the first fruits of those who have fallen asleep.

You are in the midst of us, O Lord;
and we are called by your name.
(In Eastertide: **Alleluia.)**

Your Light has Come

1   Arise shine for your ' light has ' come:
       and the glory of the ' Lord has ' risen · up'on you.

2   Behold darkness ' covers · the ' earth:
       and thick ' darkness · is ' over · the ' peoples.

3   But upon you the ' Lord shall ' rise:
       and the glory of the ' Lord · will ap'pear up'on you.

4   Nations will ' come · to your ' light:
       and kings to the ' brightness ' of your ' rising.

5   No longer will violence be ' heard · in your ' land:
       nor ruin or des'truction · with'in your ' borders.

6   But you will call your ' walls 'Sal'vation':
       and ' all your ' gates ' 'Praise'.

7   No more shall the sun be your ' light by ' day:
       nor by night will you need the ' brightness ' of the ' moon,

8   for the Lord will be your ever'lasting ' light:
       and your ' God will ' be your ' glory.   *Isaiah 60:1-3,18,19*

       Glory to the Father and ' to the ' Son:
          and ' to the ' Holy ' Spirit;
       as it was in the be'ginning · is ' now:
          and shall be for ' ever. ' A'men.

*Then follows a time of **Self-examination** and **Penitence**.*

*The **Psalm** (or **Psalms**) appointed are said or sung.*

*Then follow **Readings** from the Bible as appointed.*

Silence is kept after the Readings.

*This **Song of Praise** follows.*

The Mystery of our Religion

1   Christ Jesus our Lord was manifested ' in the ' flesh:
      and was ' vindi·cated ' in the ' Spirit;

2   he was ' seen by ' angels:
      and pro'claimed a'mong the ' nations;

3   he was believed on ' in the ' world:
      and was ' taken ' up in ' glory.

4   He will be revealed in due ' time by ' God:
      the blessèd and only ruler,
            the ' sovereign ' Lord of ' all,

5   who alone has ' immor'tality:
      and dwells in ' unap'proacha·ble ' light,

6   whom no one has ever ' seen or ' can see:
      to whom alone be honour and might‿
            for ever and ' ever. ' A'men.   *1 Timothy 3:16; 6:15,16*

Then follow   **The Lord's Prayer**
                      A Collect of the Day
                      Thanksgivings and Intercessions

*The following **Evening Collect** is said.*

Loving creator of all,
watch over us this night
and keep us in the light of your presence.
May our praise continually blend
with the song of all creation,
until we come to those eternal joys
which you promise in your love;
through Jesus Christ our Saviour.
Amen.

Let us bless the Lord.
Thanks be to God.

To God, who is able to do far more abundantly
than all we ask or think,
be glory in the Church and in Christ Jesus,
from generation to generation for ever.
Amen.
(In Eastertide: **Alleluia, Amen.***)*

Monday Morning

The minister reads this sentence.

Our help comes from the Lord,
who has made heaven and earth.

Open our lips, O Lord;
and our mouth shall proclaim your praise.
(In Eastertide: **Alleluia.***)*

*This **Song of Praise** follows.*

Benedicite Aotearoa

*(Verses 10 and 11 of the following may be omitted in daily use.
A version of the traditional **Song of Creation (Benedicite)**
will be found on page 102.)*

1   O give thanks to our God ' who is ' good:
         whose ' love en'dures for ' ever.

2   You sun and moon, you stars of the ' southern ' sky:
         give to our ' God your ' thanks and ' praise.

3   Sunrise and sunset, ' night and ' day:
         give to our ' God your ' thanks and ' praise.

4   All mountains and valleys, grassland and scree,
        glacier, avalanche, ' mist and ' snow:
        give to our ' God your ' thanks and ' praise.

5   You kauri and pine, rata and kowhai, ' mosses · and ' ferns:
        give to our ' God your ' thanks and ' praise.

6   Dolphins and kahawai, sealion and crab,
        coral, anemone, ' pipi · and ' shrimp:
        give to our ' God your ' thanks and ' praise.

7   Rabbits and cattle, moths and dogs,
        kiwi and sparrow and ' tui · and ' hawk:
        give to our ' God your ' thanks and ' praise.

8   You Maori and Pakeha, women and men,
        all who inhabit the ' long white ' cloud:
        give to our ' God your ' thanks and ' praise.

9   All you saints and martyrs of the ' South Pa'cific:
        give to our ' God your ' thanks and ' praise.

10 All prophets and priests, all cleaners and clerks,
        professors, shop workers, typists and teachers,
        job-seekers, invalids, ' drivers · and ' doctors:
        give to our ' God your ' thanks and ' praise.

11 All sweepers and diplomats, writers and artists,
        grocers, carpenters, students and stock-agents,
        seafarers, farmers, ' bakers · and ' mystics:
        give to our ' God your ' thanks and ' praise.

12 All children and infants, all ' people · who ' play:
        give to our ' God your ' thanks and ' praise.

*The **Psalm** (or **Psalms**) appointed are said or sung.*

*Then follow **Readings** from the Bible as appointed.*

Silence is kept after the Readings.

*This **Song of Praise** follows.*

A Joyful Assembly

1   We have come before God's ' holy ' mountain:
        the heavenly Jerusalem, the ' city · of the ' living ' God;

2   we have come before myriads of angels⌣
           in ' festal ' gathering:
        before the assembly⌣
           of the ' first-born ' citizens · of ' heaven;

3†   we have come before God the ' judge of ' all:
        before the spirits of the righteous made perfect,
           and Jesus the mediator ' of a ' new ' covenant.

4   We are receiving a kingdom that ' cannot · be ' shaken:
        let us ' therefore · give ' thanks to ' God,

5   thus offering acceptable worship with ' reverence · and ' awe:
        for our ' God is · a con'suming ' fire.   *Hebrews 12:22-24,28,29*

    Glory to the Father and ' to the ' Son:
        and ' to the ' Holy ' Spirit;
  as it was in the be'ginning · is ' now:
        and shall be for ' ever. ' A'men.

Then follow   **The Apostles' Creed**
                  The Lord's Prayer
                  A Collect of the Day
                  Thanksgivings and Intercessions

*The following **Morning Collect** is said.*

Almighty and everlasting God,
we thank you that you have brought us safely
to the beginning of this day.
Keep us from falling into sin or running into danger,
and guide us to do always what is right in your eyes;
through Jesus Christ our Saviour.
Amen.

Let us bless the Lord.
Thanks be to God.

May the God of hope
fill us with all joy and peace in believing,
so that by the power of the Holy Spirit
we may abound in hope.
Amen.
(In Eastertide: **Alleluia, Amen.***)*

Monday Evening

The minister reads this sentence.

God's love has been poured into our hearts
through the Holy Spirit who has been given to us.

You are in the midst of us, O Lord;
and we are called by your name.
(In Eastertide: **Alleluia.***)*

*This **Song of Praise** follows.*

The Song of Judith

1   I will sing a new song ' to my ' God:
     Lord you are great and glorious, '
       wonderful · in ' strength, in'vincible.

2   Let the whole cre'ation ' serve you:
     for you spoke, and ' all things ' came · into ' being.

3   You sent out your ' breath · and it ' formed them:
     no one is ' able · to re'sist your ' voice.

4   Mountains and seas are ' stirred · to their ' depths:
     rocks ' melt like ' wax · at your ' presence.

5† But to ' those · who re've're you:
　　you will con'tinue · to ' show ' mercy.

Judith 16:13-15

Glory to the Father and ' to the ' Son:
　　and ' to the ' Holy ' Spirit;
as it was in the be'ginning · is ' now:
　　and shall be for ' ever. ' A'men.

*Then follows a time of **Self-examination** and **Penitence**.*

The Psalm (or Psalms) appointed are said or sung.

Then follow Readings from the Bible as appointed.

Silence is kept after the Readings.

*This **Song of Praise** follows.*

The Prologue of John

1　In the beginning ' was the ' Word:
　　and the ' Word ' was with ' God;

2　and the ' Word was ' God:
　　he was ' in the · be'ginning · with ' God.

3　All things were ' made through ' him:
　　and without him‿
　　　　was not anything ' made that ' was ' made.

4　In ' him was ' life:
　　and the life was the ' light · of the ' human ' race.

5　The light ' shines · in the ' darkness:
　　and the darkness has ' never ' over'come it.

6　He was in the world,
　　and the world was ' made through ' him:
　　yet the ' world ' knew him ' not.

7　He came to his ' own ' home:
　　and his own ' people · would ' not re'ceive him.

8   But to all who received him,
        who be'lieved · on his ' name:
        he has given power to be'come ' children · of ' God.

9   They were born not of blood, nor of the ' will · of the ' flesh:
        nor of any ' human · will, ' but of ' God.

10 And the ' Word be·came ' flesh:
        and dwelt among us, ' full of ' grace and ' truth.

11 We have ' seen his ' glory:
        glory as of the ' only ' Son · from the ' Father.

12 And from his fulness we have ' all re'ceived:
        even ' grace up'on ' grace.   *John 1:1-5,10-14,16*

    Glory to the Father and ' to the ' Son:
        and ' to the ' Holy ' Spirit;
    as it was in the be'ginning · is ' now:
        and shall be for ' ever. ' A'men.

Then follow   **The Lord's Prayer**
                A Collect of the Day
                Thanksgivings and Intercessions

The following **Evening Collect** *is said.*

God the source of eternal light,
shed forth your unending day on us who watch for you;
that our lips may praise you,
our hearts bless you and our lives glorify you;
through our Saviour Jesus Christ.
Amen.

The service concludes

Let us bless the Lord.
Thanks be to God.

May the God of peace sanctify us wholly,
and may our spirit, soul and body
be kept sound and blameless
at the coming of our Lord Jesus Christ.
Amen.
(In Eastertide: **Alleluia, Amen.**)

Tuesday Morning

The minister reads this sentence.

We will praise the name of the Lord;
ascribe greatness to our God.

Open our lips, O Lord;
and our mouth shall proclaim your praise.
(In Eastertide: **Alleluia.***)*

*This **Song of Praise** follows.*

The Steadfast Love of the Lord

1   The steadfast love of the Lord ' never ' ceases:
       God's mercies ' never ' come · to an ' end;

2   they are new ' every ' morning:
       your ' faithfulness · O ' Lord is ' great.

3   You are ' all · that I ' have:
       and ' therefore ' I will ' wait for you.

4   You Lord are good to ' those who ' wait for you:
       to ' all ' those who ' seek you.

5†   It is good to ' wait in ' patience:
       for the sal'vation ' of the ' Lord.   *Lamentations 3:22-26*

    Glory to the Father and ' to the ' Son:
       and ' to the ' Holy ' Spirit;
    as it was in the be'ginning · is ' now:
       and shall be for ' ever. ' A'men.

*The **Psalm** (or **Psalms**) appointed are said or sung.*

*Then follow **Readings** from the Bible as appointed.*

Silence is kept after the Readings.

The Song of the Church

Te Deum Laudamus

1 We praise ' you O ' God:
   we ac'claim you ' as the ' Lord.

2 All creation ' worships ' you:
   the ' Father ' ever'lasting.

3 To you all angels, all the ' powers · of ' heaven:
   cherubim and seraphim, ' sing in ' endless ' praise,

4 'Holy, holy, holy Lord, God of ' power · and ' might:
   heaven and ' earth are ' full of · your ' glory.'

5 The glorious company of a'postles ' praise you:
   the noble fellowship of prophets praise you,
       the white-robed ' army · of ' martyrs ' praise you.

6 Throughout the world the holy ' Church ac'claims you:
   Father, of ' majes'ty un'bounded,

7† your true and only Son, worthy of ' all ' worship:
   and the Holy Spirit, our ' advo'cate and ' guide.

8 You Christ are the ' king of ' glory:
   the e'ternal ' Son · of the ' Father.

9 When you became incarnate to ' set us ' free:
   you humbly ac'cepted · the ' Virgin's ' womb.

10 You overcame the ' sting of ' death:
   and opened the kingdom of ' heaven · to ' all be'lievers.

11 You are seated at God's right ' hand in ' glory:
   we believe that you will ' come and ' be our ' judge.

12 Come then Lord and ' help your ' people:
   bought with the ' price of ' your own ' blood,

13 and bring us ' with your ' saints:
   to ' glory ' ever'lasting.

The Song of the Church may end with the following verses.

14 Save your people Lord, and ' bless · your in'heritance:
   govern and up'hold them ' now and ' always.

15 Day by ' day we ' bless you:
  we ' praise your ' name for ' ever.

16 Keep us today Lord from ' all ' sin:
  have mercy ' on us ' Lord, have ' mercy.

17 Lord show us your ' love and ' mercy:
  for we ' put our ' trust in ' you.

18† In you Lord ' is our ' hope:
  let us not be con'founded ' at the ' last.

Then follow **The Apostles' Creed**
  The Lord's Prayer
  A Collect of the Day
  Thanksgivings and Intercessions

The following **Morning Collect** *is said.*

Holy and everliving God,
by your power we are created
and by your love we are redeemed;
guide and strengthen us by your Spirit,
that we may give ourselves to your service
and live this day in love to one another and to you;
through Jesus Christ our Saviour.
Amen.

The service concludes

Let us bless the Lord.
Thanks be to God.

May we continue to dwell in Christ,
so that when he appears,
we may be confident and unashamed before him
at his coming.
Amen.
(In Eastertide: **Alleluia, Amen.***)*

Tuesday Evening

The minister reads this sentence.

Sing praises, sing praises to the Lord;
tell of all the wonderful things God has done.

You are in the midst of us, O Lord;
and we are called by your name.
(In Eastertide: **Alleluia.***)*

This **Song of Praise** *follows.*

Great and Wonderful

1   Great and wonderful are your deeds‿
         O Lord ' God · the al'mighty:
      just and true are your ways‿
         O ' Sovereign ' of the ' nations.

2   Who shall not revere and praise your ' name O ' Lord?:
      for ' you a'lone are ' holy.

3   All nations shall come and worship ' in your ' presence:
      for your just ' dealings · have ' been re'vealed.

4   To the One who is seated on the throne and ' to the ' Lamb:
      be blessing and honour, glory and might‿
         for ever and ' ever. ' A'men.   *Revelation 15:3b,4; 5:13*

Then follows a time of **Self-examination** *and* **Penitence**.

The **Psalm** *(or* **Psalms***) appointed are said or sung.*

Then follow **Readings** *from the Bible as appointed.*

Silence is kept after the Readings.

This **Song of Praise** *follows.*

The First-born of All Creation

1   Christ is the image of the in'visi·ble ' God:
      the ' first-born · of ' all cre'ation.

2   In him all things in heaven and on earth ' were cre'ated:
      all that is ' seen and ' all · that is ' unseen,

3   thrones and dominions, princi'palities · and ' powers:
      through him and for him ' all things ' were cre'ated.

4   He ex'ists be·fore ' everything:
      and all things are ' held to'gether · in ' him.

5   He is the head of the ' body · the ' Church:
      he is its beginning, the first-born from the dead,
       to be in ' all · things a'lone sup'reme.

6   For in Christ O God⌣
      you were pleased to have all your ' fulness ' dwell:
      and through him to reconcile the ' uni·verse ' to your'self.

7†   You made peace by the ' blood · of his ' cross:
      and brought back to yourself '⌣
      all · things in ' heaven · and ' earth.   *Colossians 1:15-20*

    Glory to the Father and ' to the ' Son:
      and ' to the ' Holy ' Spirit;
    as it was in the be'ginning · is ' now:
      and shall be for ' ever. ' A'men.

Then follow   **The Lord's Prayer**
               A Collect of the Day
               Thanksgivings and Intercessions

*The following **Evening Collect** is said.*

Remember, merciful God,
what you have made of us and not what we deserve;
and as you have called us to your service,
make us worthy of our calling;
through Jesus Christ our Saviour.
Amen.

Let us bless the Lord.
Thanks be to God.

Now the God of peace
give us peace at all times and in all ways.
Amen.
(In Eastertide: **Alleluia, Amen.***)*

Wednesday Morning

The minister reads this sentence.

Rejoice always, pray constantly; in everything give thanks,
for this is the will of God in Christ Jesus.

Open our lips, O Lord;
and our mouth shall proclaim your praise.
(In Eastertide: **Alleluia.***)*

*This **Song of Praise** follows.*

The Song of Tobit

1 Blessèd be God who ' lives for ' ever:
    blessèd be God who ' rules ' over ' all.

2 We give thanks to you O Lord be'fore the ' nations:
    for you have ' scattered ' us a'mong them.

3 There we make your ' greatness ' known:
    and exalt you in the ' presence · of ' all the ' living,

4 because you are the ' Lord our ' God:
    you ' are our ' Father · for ' ever.

5 When we turn to you with all our ' heart and ' soul:
    to ' do · what is ' true be'fore you,

6 then you will ' turn to ' us:
    and hide your ' face from ' us no ' longer.

7   Consider now the deeds that ' God has ' done for you:
      and give thanks to ' God with ' full ' voice.

8   Praise the ' Lord of ' righteousness:
      and exalt the ' ruler ' of the ' ages.   *Tobit 13:1,3,4,6*

    Glory to the Father and ' to the ' Son:
      and ' to the ' Holy ' Spirit;
  as it was in the be'ginning · is ' now:
      and shall be for ' ever. ' A'men.

*The **Psalm** (or **Psalms**) appointed are said or sung.*

*Then follow **Reading**s from the Bible as appointed.*

Silence is kept after the Readings.

*This **Song of Praise** follows.*

A Living Hope

1   Blessèd be the God and Father of our Lord ' Jesus ' Christ:
      by whose great mercy ' we · have been ' born a'new,

2   born to a ' living ' hope:
      by the resurrection of Jesus ' Christ ' from the ' dead;

3   born to an inheritance_
      which will never perish or ' wither · a'way:
      one that is ' kept in ' heaven · for ' us.

4   By God's power we are ' guarded · through ' faith:
      for a salvation ready to be re'vealed · at the ' end of ' time.

5   We rejoice in this, though now we suffer ' vari·ous ' trials:
      so that the genuineness of our faith,
        more precious than ' gold · that is ' tested · by ' fire,

6   may result in praise and ' glory · and ' honour:
      at the reve'lation · of ' Jesus ' Christ.   *1 Peter 1:3-7*

    Glory to the Father and ' to the ' Son:
      and ' to the ' Holy ' Spirit;
  as it was in the be'ginning · is ' now:
      and shall be for ' ever. ' A'men.

Then follow   **The Apostles' Creed**
                The Lord's Prayer
                A Collect of the Day
                Thanksgivings and Intercessions

*The following **Morning Collect** is said.*

O God,
the author of peace and lover of concord;
to know you is eternal life,
to serve you is perfect freedom.
Defend us your servants in every stress and danger,
that we may trust in your defence
and not fear the power of any adversaries;
through Jesus Christ our Redeemer.
Amen.

The service concludes

Let us bless the Lord.
Thanks be to God.

May the God of steadfastness and encouragement
grant us to live in such harmony with one another
in accord with Christ Jesus,
that we may with one voice glorify our God and Father.
Amen.
(In Eastertide: **Alleluia, Amen.***)*

Wednesday Evening

The minister reads this sentence.

Grace, mercy and peace to us
from God our Father and Christ Jesus our Lord.

You are in the midst of us, O Lord;
and we are called by your name.
(In Eastertide: **Alleluia.***)*

*This **Song of Praise** follows.*

God is My Salvation

1   Behold God is ' my sal'vation:
      I will trust and ' will not ' be a'fraid,

2   for the Lord God is my ' strength · and my ' song:
      and has be'come ' my sal'vation.

3   With joy you will draw water from the ' wells · of sal'vation:
      and in that day ' all of ' you will ' say,

4   ' Give thanks and call upon the ' name · of the ' Lord:
      make known among the nations what the Lord has done,
        proclaim that the ' name · of the ' Lord is · ex'alted.

5   ' Sing praises for the Lord has ' triumphed ' gloriously:
      let this be ' known in ' all the ' earth.

6   ' Shout and sing for joy you ' people · of ' God:
      for great in your ' midst ' is the ' Holy One.'   *Isaiah 12:2-6*

Glory to the Father and ' to the ' Son:
    and ' to the ' Holy ' Spirit;
as it was in the be'ginning · is ' now:
    and shall be for ' ever. ' A'men.

*Then follows a time of **Self-examination** and **Penitence**.*

*The **Psalm** (or **Psalms**) appointed are said or sung.*

*Then follow **Readings** from the Bible as appointed.*

Silence is kept after the Readings.

This **Song of Praise** follows.

The Song of Simeon   *Nunc Dimittis*

1   Lord now you let your servant ' go in ' peace:
    your ' word has ' been ful'filled.

2   My own eyes have ' seen the · sal'vation:
    which you have prepared in the ' sight of ' every ' people,

3† a light to reveal you ' to the ' nations:
    and the ' glory · of your ' people ' Israel.   *Luke 2:29-32*

    Glory to the Father and ' to the ' Son:
    and ' to the ' Holy ' Spirit;
    as it was in the be'ginning · is ' now:
    and shall be for ' ever. ' A'men.

Or

The Love of God

1   E te whanau, let us ' love · one an'other:
    for ' love ' is from ' God.

2   Those who love are born of God and ' know ' God:
    but those who do not love‿
        know nothing of ' God; for ' God is ' love.

3   Those who ' dwell in ' love:
    are dwelling in ' God and ' God in ' them.

4   There is no room for ' fear in ' love:
    love which is per'fected ' banish·es ' fear.

5   We love because God ' first loved ' us:
    if anyone who hates another‿
        says, 'I love God,' that ' person ' is a ' liar.

6   If we do not love those whom ' we have ' seen:
    it cannot be that we love ' God whom ' we have ' not seen.

7† This commandment we ' have from ' God:
    that those who love God must ' also ' love their ' neighbour
                                            1 John 4:7,8,16,18-21

Glory to the Father and ' to the ' Son:
    and ' to the ' Holy ' Spirit;
as it was in the be'ginning · is ' now:
    and shall be for ' ever. ' A'men.

Then follow   **The Lord's Prayer**
            A Collect of the Day
            Thanksgivings and Intercessions

The following **Evening Collect** *is said.*

Be our light in the darkness, Lord we pray,
and in your great mercy
defend us from all perils and dangers of this night;
for the love of your only Son, our Saviour Jesus Christ.
Amen.

The service concludes

Let us bless the Lord.
Thanks be to God.

May our Lord Jesus Christ himself,
and God our Father,
who loved us and graciously gave us
unfailing encouragement and good hope,
comfort our hearts
and establish them
in every good word and deed.
Amen.
(In Eastertide: **Alleluia, Amen.***)*

Thursday Morning

The minister reads this sentence.

When Christ who is our life appears,
then we also will appear with him in glory.

Open our lips, O Lord;
and our mouth shall proclaim your praise.
(In Eastertide: **Alleluia.***)*

*This **Song of Praise** follows.*

Rich in Mercy

1 You O God are ' rich in ' mercy:
   out of the great ' love with ' which you ' loved us,

2 even when we were dead ' through our ' sins:
   you made us a'live to'gether · with ' Christ.

3 You raised us up in ' union · with ' him:
   and made us sit with him͜
   in the heavenly ' places · in ' Christ ' Jesus,

4 so that you might show the immeasurable riches '͜
   of your ' grace:
   in kindness to'wards us · in ' Christ ' Jesus.

5 By your Spirit at ' work with'in us:
   you do far more abundantly than ' all we ' ask or ' think.

6 To you be glory in the Church and in ' Christ ' Jesus:
   through all generations for ever and ' ever. ' A'men.

Ephesians 2:4-7; 3:20,21

*The **Psalm** (or **Psalms**) appointed are said or sung.*

*Then follow **Readings** from the Bible as appointed.*

Silence is kept after the Readings.

*This **Song of Praise** follows.*

The Beatitudes

1   Blessèd are the ' poor in ' spirit:
      for the ' kingdom · of ' heaven · is ' theirs.

2   Blessèd ' are the ' sorrowful:
      for they shall ' find ' consol'ation.

3   Blessèd are those of a ' gentle ' spirit:
      for they shall have the ' earth for ' their pos'session.

4   Blessèd are those who hunger and thirst to see ' right pre'vail:
      for ' they ' shall be ' satisfied.

5   Blessèd are ' those · who show ' mercy:
      for mercy ' shall be ' shown to ' them.

6   Blessèd are those whose ' hearts are ' pure:
      for ' they shall ' see ' God.

7   Blessèd ' are the ' peacemakers:
      for ' they · shall be ' called God's ' children.

8   Blessèd are those who have suffered persecution⌣
      for the ' cause of ' right:
        for the ' kingdom · of ' heaven · is ' theirs.   *Matthew 5:3-10*

      Glory to the Father and ' to the ' Son:
        and ' to the ' Holy ' Spirit;
      as it was in the be'ginning · is ' now:
        and shall be for ' ever. ' A'men.

Then follow   **The Apostles' Creed**
              The Lord's Prayer
              A Collect of the Day
              Thanksgivings and Intercessions

*The following **Morning Collect** is said.*

Holy and eternal God,
in you we live and move and have our being.
In all our cares and occupations,
guide and govern us by your Spirit,
that we may both remember and reveal your presence;
through our Saviour Jesus Christ.
Amen.

Let us bless the Lord.
Thanks be to God.

May the Lord direct our hearts
into God's love and Christ's perseverance.
Amen.
(In Eastertide: **Alleluia, Amen.***)*

Thursday Evening

The minister reads this sentence.

The Lord our God, the almighty reigns;
let us rejoice and exult
and give God the glory.

You are in the midst of us, O Lord;
and we are called by your name.
(In Eastertide: **Alleluia.***)*

*This **Song of Praise** follows.*

The Song of Hannah

1   My heart ex'ults · in the ' Lord:
       my strength is ex'alted ' in my ' God.

2   There is none holy ' like the ' Lord:
       there is none beside you, ' no rock ' like our ' God.

3   For you O Lord are a ' God of ' knowledge:
       and by ' you our ' actions · are ' weighed.

4   The bows of the ' mighty · are ' broken:
       but the ' feeble ' gird on ' strength.

5   You Lord make ' poor · and make ' rich:
       you bring ' low · and you ' also · ex'alt.

6   You raise up the ' poor · from the ' dust:
    and lift the ' needy ' from the ' ash-heap.

7   You make them ' sit with ' princes:
    and in'herit · a ' seat of ' honour.

8   For yours O Lord are the ' pillars · of the ' earth:
    and on them ' you have ' set the ' world.   *1 Samuel 2:1-4,7,8*

    Glory to the Father and ' to the ' Son:
    and ' to the ' Holy ' Spirit;
    as it was in the be'ginning · is ' now:
    and shall be for ' ever. ' A'men.

*Then follows a time of **Self-examination** and **Penitence**.*

*The **Psalm** (or **Psalms**) appointed are said or sung.*

*Then follow **Readings** from the Bible as appointed.*

Silence is kept after the Readings.

*This **Song of Praise** follows.*

The Exalted Lord

1   Christ Jesus was in the ' form of ' God:
    yet he did not think to ' grasp · at e'quality · with ' God,

2   but emptied himself, taking the ' form · of a ' servant:
    and was ' born · in our ' human ' likeness.

3   Being found in our human state, he ' humbled · him'self:
    and became obedient unto death,
        even ' death ' on a ' cross.

4   Therefore God has ' highly · ex'alted him:
    and bestowed on him the ' Name a·bove ' every ' name;

5   that at the name of Jesus every ' knee should ' bow:
    in heaven and on ' earth and ' under · the ' earth,

6   and every tongue confess that Jesus ' Christ · is ' Lord:
    to the glory of God the ' Father. ' A'men.   *Philippians 2:6-11*

The Lord's Prayer
A Collect of the Day
Thanksgivings and Intercessions

The following **Evening Collect** *is said.*

Living God,
in you there is no darkness;
shed upon us through this night the light of your forgiveness,
your healing and your peace,
that when we wake from sleep
we may know once more the brightness of your presence;
through our Saviour Jesus Christ.
Amen.

The service concludes

Let us bless the Lord.
Thanks be to God.

May we grow in the grace and knowledge
of our Lord and Saviour Jesus Christ;
to whom be glory both now and to the day of eternity.
Amen.
(In Eastertide: **Alleluia, Amen.***)*

Friday Morning

The minister reads this sentence.

Through Jesus
let us continually offer up a sacrifice of praise to God,
the fruit of lips that acknowledge God's name.

Open our lips, O Lord;
and our mouth shall proclaim your praise.
(In Eastertide: **Alleluia.***)*

The Song of Zechariah

Benedictus

1   Blessèd are you O ' Lord our ' God:
       you have come to your ' people · and ' set them ' free.

2   You have raised up for us a ' mighty ' Saviour:
       born of the ' house · of your ' servant ' David.

3   Through your holy prophets you ' promised · of ' old:
       that you would save us from our enemies,
          from the ' hands of ' all who ' hate us.

4   You promised to show ' mercy · to our ' forbears:
       and to re'member · your ' holy ' covenant.

5   This was the oath you swore to our ' father ' Abraham:
       to set us ' free · from the ' hands of · our ' enemies,

6   free to worship you with'out ' fear:
       holy and righteous in your sight ' ‿
          all the ' days of · our ' life.

7   And you, child, shall be called ‿
       the prophet of the ' Most ' High:
       for you will go before the ' Lord · to pre'pare the ' way,

8   to give God's people knowledge ' of sal'vation:
       through the for'giveness ' of their ' sins.

9   In the tender compassion ' of our ' God:
       the dawn from on ' high shall ' break up'on us,

10   to shine on those who dwell in darkness ‿
       and the ' shadow · of ' death:
       and to guide our feet ' into · the ' way of ' peace.

Luke 1:68-79 (adapted)

Glory to the Father and ' to the ' Son:
       and ' to the ' Holy ' Spirit;
as it was in the be'ginning · is ' now:
       and shall be for ' ever. ' A'men.

*The **Psalm** (or **Psalms**) appointed are said or sung.*

*Then follow **Readings** from the Bible as appointed.*

*This **Song of Praise** follows.*

Saviour of the World

Salvator Mundi

1 Jesus, Saviour of the world, come to us ' in your ' mercy:
   we look to ' you to ' save and ' help us.

2 By your cross and your life laid down⌣
      you set your ' people ' free:
   we look to ' you to ' save and ' help us.

3 When they were ready to perish⌣
      you ' saved · your dis'ciples:
   we look to ' you to ' come to · our ' help.

4 In the greatness of your mercy loose us ' from our ' chains:
   forgive the ' sins of ' all your ' people.

5 Make yourself known⌣
      as our Saviour and ' mighty · de'liverer:
   save and ' help us · that ' we may ' praise you.

6 Come now and dwell with us, ' Lord Christ ' Jesus:
   hear our ' prayer · and be ' with us ' always.

7 And when you ' come in · your ' glory:
      make us to be one with you⌣
      and to ' share the ' life of · your ' kingdom.

8 Thanks be to ' you O ' Lord:
   Alle'luia. ' A'men.

Then follow   **The Apostles' Creed**
              The Lord's Prayer
              A Collect of the Day
              Thanksgivings and Intercessions

*The following **Morning Collect** is said.*

Loving God,
your Son willingly endured agony and shame for us.
Give us grace to take up our cross
and follow him in newness of life and hope;
for he is our Redeemer.
Amen.

Let us bless the Lord.
Thanks be to God.

Peace be to us all and love with faith,
from God the Father and the Lord Jesus Christ.
Amen.
(In Eastertide: **Alleluia, Amen.***)*

Friday Evening

The minister reads this sentence.

In Christ Jesus, we who were once far away,
have been brought near through the blood of Christ.

You are in the midst of us, O Lord;
and we are called by your name.
(In Eastertide: **Alleluia.***)*

*This **Song of Praise** follows.*

Seek the Lord

1   Seek the Lord who is ' still · to be ' found:
     call upon ' God · who is ' yet at ' hand.

2   Return to the Lord, who will ' have com'passion:
     to our God, who ' will a'bundant·ly ' pardon.

3   'For my thoughts ' are not ' your thoughts:
     nor are your ways ' my ways,' ' says the ' Lord.

4   'For as the heavens are higher ' than the ' earth:
     so are my ways higher than your ways‿
        and ' my ' thoughts than ' your thoughts.

5   'For as the rain and snow come ' down from ' heaven:
     and return not a'gain but ' water · the ' earth,

6   'causing the earth to bring ' forth and ' sprout:
       giving seed to the ' sower · and ' bread · to the ' hungry;

7   'so shall my word be that goes ' forth · from my ' mouth:
       it shall ' not re'turn to · me ' empty,

8   ' but it shall accomplish that which ' I de'sire:
       and achieve the ' purpose · for ' which I ' sent it.'

Isaiah 55:6-11

Glory to the Father and ' to the ' Son:
    and ' to the ' Holy ' Spirit;
as it was in the be'ginning · is ' now:
    and shall be for ' ever. ' A'men.

*Then follows a time of **Self-examination** and **Penitence.***

*The **Psalm** (or **Psalms**) appointed are said or sung.*

*Then follow **Readings** from the Bible as appointed.*

Silence is kept after the Readings.

*This **Song of Praise** follows.*

You are Worthy

1   You are worthy, our ' Lord and ' God:
       to receive ' glory · and ' honour · and ' power,

2   for you have cre'ated ' all things:
       and by your will_
       they were cre'ated · and ' have their ' being.

3   You are worthy O Christ, for ' you were ' slain:
       and by your blood have ' ransomed ' us for ' God,

4   ransomed us from every tribe and ' people · and ' nation:
       and made us a royal ' house of ' priests · to our ' God.

5†   To the One who is seated on the throne and ' to the ' Lamb:
       be blessing and honour, glory and might,
         for ever and ' ever. ' A'men.

based on Revelation 4:11; 5:9,10,13

Then follow **The Lord's Prayer**
A Collect of the Day
Thanksgivings and Intercessions

The following **Evening Collect** *is said.*

Gracious God,
you have given us much today;
grant us also a thankful spirit.
Into your hands we commend ourselves
and those we love.
Be with us still,
and when we take our rest,
renew us for the service of your Son Jesus Christ.
Amen.

The service concludes

Let us bless the Lord.
Thanks be to God.

May the God of all grace
who has called us to eternal glory in Christ,
restore, establish and strengthen us.
To the one true God be the dominion for ever and ever.
Amen.
(In Eastertide: **Alleluia, Amen.***)*

Saturday Morning

The minister reads this sentence.

God has caused light to shine in our hearts,
to give us the light of the knowledge of the glory of God
in the face of Christ.

Open our lips, O Lord;
and our mouth shall proclaim your praise.
(In Eastertide: **Alleluia.***)*

*This **Song of Praise** follows.*

Peace for the Nations

1 In days to come the mountain of the ' Lord's ' house:
      will be established as the ' highest ' of the ' mountains.

2 It will be raised a'bove the ' hills:
      and ' all the ' nations · will ' flock to it.

3 Many peoples will come and ' they will ' say:
      'Let us go up to the mountain of the Lord,
         to the ' house · of the ' God of ' Jacob,

4 'that we may be taught the ' ways · of the ' Lord:
      and may ' walk · in the ' right ' paths.'

5 From the mountain of the Lord shall go ' forth the ' law:
      and the word of the ' Lord ' from Je'rusalem.

6 The Lord will judge be'tween the ' nations:
      and settle dis'putes for ' many ' peoples.

7 They shall beat their ' swords · into ' ploughshares:
      and their ' spears ' into ' pruning hooks.

8 Nation shall not lift up ' sword a·gainst ' nation:
      nor ever a'gain pre'pare for ' war.

9† Come O ' house of ' Jacob:
      let us walk in the ' light ' of the ' Lord.   *Isaiah 2:2-5*

   Glory to the Father and ' to the ' Son:
      and ' to the ' Holy ' Spirit;
   as it was in the be'ginning · is ' now:
      and shall be for ' ever. ' A'men.

*The **Psalm** (or **Psalms**) appointed are said or sung.*

*Then follow **Reading**s from the Bible as appointed.*

Silence is kept after the Readings.

*This **Song of Praise** follows.*

A New Heaven and a New Earth

1   I saw a new heaven and a ′ new ′ earth:
      for the first heaven and earth had passed away,
        and there was no ′ longer ′ any ′ sea.

2   I saw the holy city ′ new Je′rusalem:
      coming ′ down · out of ′ heaven · from ′ God.

3   I saw no temple ′ in the ′ city:
      for its temple is the Lord God⌣
        the Al′mighty ′ and the ′ Lamb.

4   The city has no need of sun or moon to ′ shine up′on it:
      for the glory of God illuminates it,
        and the ′ Lamb ′ is its ′ light.

5   The throne of God and of the Lamb will be ′ in the ′ city:
      and the servants of God⌣
        shall ′ worship · be′fore the ′ throne.

6   They shall see God ′ face to ′ face:
      and bear the name of their ′ God up′on their ′ foreheads.

7   There shall be ′ no more ′ night:
      nor will they need the ′ light of ′ lamp or ′ sun,

8   for the Lord God will ′ give them ′ light:
      and they shall ′ reign for ′ ever · and ′ ever.

9† To the One who is seated on the throne and ′ to the ′ Lamb:
      be blessing and honour, glory and might⌣
        for ever and ′ ever. ′ A′men.

Revelation 21:1, 2, 22, 23; 22:3-5; 5:13

Then follow   **The Apostles' Creed**
                The Lord's Prayer
                A Collect of the Day
                Thanksgivings and Intercessions

O God,
the well-spring of life,
pour into our hearts the living water of your grace,
that refreshed by you,
we may live this day in steadfast reliance
on the strength you give;
through our Saviour Jesus Christ.
Amen.

The service concludes

Let us bless the Lord.
Thanks be to God.

May the peace of God
which passes all understanding
keep our hearts and minds in Christ Jesus.
Amen.
(In Eastertide: **Alleluia, Amen.***)*

Saturday Evening

The minister reads this sentence.

Give thanks to the Lord who is good;
whose steadfast love endures for ever.

You are in the midst of us, O Lord;
and we are called by your name.
(In Eastertide: **Alleluia.***)*

*This **Song of Praise** follows.*

The Song of the Blessed Virgin Mary   *Magnificat*

1   My soul proclaims the ' greatness · of the ' Lord:
        my spirit re'joices · in ' God my ' saviour,

2   for you Lord have looked with favour
            on your ' lowly ' servant:
        and from this day all gener'ations · will ' call me ' blessèd.

3† You O Most Mighty have done ' great things ' for me:
        and ' holy ' is your ' name.

4   You have mercy on ' those who ' fear you:
        from gener'ation · to' gener'ation.

5   You have shown the ' strength · of your ' arm:
        you have scattered the ' proud in ' their con'ceit.

6   You have cast down the mighty ' from their ' thrones:
        and have ' lifted ' up the ' lowly.

7   You have filled the hungry with ' good ' things:
        and the rich you have ' sent a'way ' empty.

8   You have come to the help ' of your ' people:
        for you have re'membered · your ' promise · of ' mercy,

9   the promise you ' made · to our ' forbears:
        to Abraham ' and his ' children · for ' ever.

Luke 1:46-55(adapted)

Glory to the Father and ' to the ' Son:
        and ' to the ' Holy ' Spirit;
as it was in the be'ginning · is ' now:
        and shall be for ' ever. ' A'men.

*Then follows a time of **Self-examination** and **Penitence**.*

*The **Psalm** (or **Psalms**) appointed are said or sung.*

*Then follow **Readings** from the Bible as appointed.*

Silence is kept after the Readings.

*This **Song of Praise** follows.*

The Easter Anthems

1   Christ our passover lamb ' has been ' sacrificed:
       therefore ' let us ' keep the ' feast,

2   not with the old leaven,
       the leaven of cor'ruption · and ' wickedness:
       but with the unleavened ' bread · of sin'cerity · and ' truth.

3   Christ being raised from the dead will never ' die a'gain:
       death no ' longer · has do'minion ' over him.

4   The death he died, he died to sin ' once for ' all:
       but the life he ' lives, he ' lives to ' God.

5   So you also must consider yourselves ' dead to ' sin:
       and alive to ' God in ' Jesus ' Christ.

6   Christ has been ' raised · from the ' dead:
       the first fruits of ' those · who have ' fallen · a'sleep.

7   For as by a ' man came ' death:
       by a man has come also the resur'rection ' of the ' dead.

8   For as in ' Adam · all ' die:
       so also in Christ shall ' all be ' made a'live.

1 Corinthians 5:7,8; Romans 6:9-11; 1 Corinthians 15:20-22

Glory to the Father and ' to the ' Son:
       and ' to the ' Holy ' Spirit;
as it was in the be'ginning · is ' now:
       and shall be for ' ever. ' A'men.

Then follow   **The Lord's Prayer**
               A Collect of the Day
               Thanksgivings and Intercessions

Abide with us, O Lord,
for it is toward evening and the day is almost over;
abide with us,
for the days are hastening on
and we hasten with them;
abide with us and with all your faithful people,
until the daystar rises and the morning light appears,
and we shall abide with you for ever.
Amen.

The service concludes

Let us bless the Lord.
Thanks be to God.

May the God of peace,
who brought again from the dead our Lord Jesus,
equip us with everything good
that we may do God's will,
to whom be glory for ever.
Amen.
(In Eastertide: **Alleluia, Amen.***)*

Additional Songs of Praise

At the discretion of the minister, any of the following may be used in place of the **Song of Praise** *appointed.*

The Desert shall Blossom
(especially suitable in Advent)

1   The desert shall re'joice and ' blossom;
       it shall re'joice with ' gladness · and ' singing.

2   The glory of the Lord shall ' be re'vealed:
       and the ' majes·ty ' of our ' God.

3   Then shall the eyes of the ' blind be ' opened:
       and the ' ears · of the ' deaf un'stopped;

4   then shall the lame ' leap · like the ' hart:
       and the tongue of the ' dumb shall ' sing for ' joy.

5†   For waters shall break ' forth · in the ' wilderness:
       and ' streams ' in the ' desert.

6   The ransomed of the ' Lord · shall re'turn:
       and come with singing,
          with everlasting ' joy up'on their ' heads.

7   They shall obtain ' joy and ' gladness:
       and sorrow and ' sighing · shall ' flee a'way.

Isaiah 35:1,2,5,6,10

Glory to the Father and ' to the ' Son:
    and ' to the ' Holy ' Spirit;
as it was in the be'ginning · is ' now:
    and shall be for ' ever. ' A'men.

God's Chosen One
(especially suitable at Christmas)

1   There shall come forth a shoot from the ' stump of ' Jesse:
     and a ' branch · shall grow ' out of · its ' roots,

2   and the Spirit of the Lord shall ' rest up'on him:
     the spirit of ' wisdom · and ' under'standing,

3   the spirit of ' counsel · and ' might:
     the spirit of knowledge and the ' fear ' of the ' Lord.

4   He shall not judge by what his ' eyes ' see:
     or decide by ' what his ' ears ' hear,

5   but with righteousness he shall ' judge the ' poor:
     and decide with ' equity · for the ' meek of · the ' earth.

6   The wolf shall ' dwell · with the ' lamb:
     and the leopard shall ' lie down ' with the ' kid,

7   and the calf and the ' lion cub · to'gether:
     and a ' little ' child shall ' lead them.

8   They shall not hurt or destroy in all my ' holy ' mountain:
     for the earth shall be full of the knowledge of the Lord⌣
         as the ' waters ' cover · the ' sea.

Isaiah 11:1-4,6,9

Glory to the Father and ' to the ' Son:
    and ' to the ' Holy ' Spirit;
as it was in the be'ginning · is ' now:
    and shall be for ' ever. ' A'men.

The Time of God's Favour
(especially suitable at Epiphany)

1   Listen to ' me you ' islands:
     and hearken you ' peoples ' from a'far.

2   My servant, in the time of my favour ' I will ' answer you:
     and in the day of sal'vation ' I will ' help you;

3   to re'store the ' land:
     and share out a'fresh its ' deso·late ' fields;

4   to say to the ' captives · ' Go ' free':
     and to those in darkness, ' ' Come forth ' into ' light.'

5   They will feed be'side the ' way:
     and find pasture on ' every ' barren ' hill.

6   They will neither ' hunger · nor ' thirst:
     nor will the desert heat or the ' sun ' beat up'on them,

7†   for the One who ' loves them · will ' guide them:
     and lead them be'side the ' springs of ' water.

8   Shout for joy O heavens and ex'ult O ' earth:
     break forth O ' mountains ' into ' song;

9   for I the Lord will ' comfort · my ' people:
     and will have compassion on my ' own in ' their dis'tress.

Isaiah 49:1,8-10,13

Glory to the Father and ' to the ' Son:
     and ' to the ' Holy ' Spirit;
as it was in the be'ginning · is ' now:
     and shall be for ' ever. ' A'men.

Prayer of Manasseh *(abridged)*
(especially suitable in Lent)

1   O Lord almighty and ' God · of our ' ancestors:
     you made the heavens and the earth '‿
       in their ' glorious · ar'ray.

2   All things quake with fear ' at your ' presence:
     and ' tremble · be'cause · of your ' power.

3   But your merciful promise is be'yond all ' measure:
     it surpasses ' all · that our ' minds can ' fathom.

4   Lord you are ' full · of com'passion:
     long-suffering, ' and a'bounding · in ' mercy.

5   And now O Lord I ' humble · my ' heart:
     and make my appeal, ' sure · of your ' gracious ' goodness.

6   For you O Lord are the ' God · of the ' penitent:
     and in me you will ' show ' forth your ' goodness.

7 Unworthy as I am ' you will ' save me:
 and so I will praise you continually, '
  all the ' days · of my ' life.

8 For all the host of heaven ' sing your ' praises:
 and your ' glory · is for ' ever · and ' ever.

Glory to the Father and ' to the ' Son:
 and ' to the ' Holy ' Spirit;
as it was in the be'ginning · is ' now:
 and shall be for ' ever. ' A'men.

He was Despised and Rejected
(especially suitable in Passiontide)

1 Who would have believed what ' we have ' heard:
 and to whom has the power of the ' Lord ' been re'vealed?

2 He grew up before the Lord like a ' tender ' plant:
 like a ' root · out of ' arid ' ground.

3 He had no beauty, no majesty to ' draw our ' eyes:
 no grace to ' make us · de'light in ' him.

4 He was des'pised · and re'jected:
 a man of ' sorrows · and fa'miliar · with ' suffering.

5 Like one from whom people ' hide their ' faces:
 he was despised, and ' we es'teemed him ' not.

6 Surely he has borne our griefs and ' carried · our ' sorrows:
 yet we considered him stricken,
  smitten by ' God, ' and af'flicted.

7 But he was wounded for ' our trans'gressions:
 he was ' bruised for ' our in'iquities.

8 The punishment that brought us peace was ' laid up·on ' him:
 and by his ' wounds ' we are ' healed.   *Isaiah 53:1-5*

Glory to the Father and ' to the ' Son:
 and ' to the ' Holy ' Spirit;
as it was in the be'ginning · is ' now:
 and shall be for ' ever. ' A'men.

The Song of Moses

(especially suitable at Easter)

1   I will sing to the Lord,
        for the Lord has ' triumphed ' gloriously:
    the horse and its rider‿
        have been ' thrown ' into · the ' sea.

2   The Lord is my ' strength · and my ' song:
    and has be'come ' my sal'vation.

3   This is my God, whom ' I will ' praise:
    the God of my ' forbears · whom ' I · will ex'alt.

4   Who is like you O Lord a'mong the ' gods:
    who is like ' you ma'jestic · in ' holiness?

5   Who is like you O Lord a'mong the ' gods:
    terrible in glorious ' deeds and ' doing ' wonders?

6   In your unfailing love you will lead‿
        the people ' you · have re'deemed:
    in your strength you will‿
        guide them ' to your ' holy ' dwelling.

7   You will bring them in and plant them‿
        on the mountain of ' your in'heritance:
    the place O Lord that '‿
        you have ' made for · your ' dwelling,

8   the sanctuary O Lord that your ' hands · have e'stablished:
    you Lord will ' reign for ' ever · and ' ever.

Exodus 15:1,2,11,13,17

Glory to the Father and ' to the ' Son:
    and ' to the ' Holy ' Spirit;
as it was in the be'ginning · is ' now:
    and shall be for ' ever. ' A'men.

Our Great High Priest

(especially suitable at Ascension)

1   In you, Jesus, Son of God, we have a ' great high ' priest:
          you have passed through the heavens,
               and are seated at the right ' hand of ' God on ' high.

2   Therefore we hold fast to the faith that ' we pro'fess:
          for you are not a high priest who is unable‿
               to ' sympath·ise ' with our ' weaknesses.

3   In every respect you have been ' tempted · as ' we are:
          and ' yet you ' did not ' sin.

4   Although a Son, you learned obedience‿
          through ' what you ' suffered:
               and being made perfect, you have become the source‿
                    of eternal sal'vation · for ' all · who o'bey you.

5   This gives us ' every ' confidence:
          to draw ' near · to the ' throne of ' grace.

6   There we re'ceive ' mercy:
          and find grace to ' help in ' time of ' need.

based on Hebrews 4:14-16; 5:8,9; 8:1

Glory to the Father and ' to the ' Son:
     and ' to the ' Holy ' Spirit;
as it was in the be'ginning · is ' now:
     and shall be for ' ever. ' A'men.

Life in the Spirit

(especially suitable at Pentecost)

1   In Christ the life-giving ' law · of the ' Spirit:
          has set us free from the ' law of ' sin and ' death.

2   All who are led by the Spirit of God are ' children · of ' God:
          it is the Spirit that enables us to ' cry, ' Abba, ' Father.

3   The Spirit confirms that ' we are · God's ' children:
          and if ' children · then ' we are ' heirs.

4　　We are heirs of God, and fellow-'heirs with ' Christ:
　　　　if we share his suffering now,
　　　　　　in order to ' share his ' splendour · here'after.

5　　The sufferings we ' now en'dure:
　　　　bear no comparison with the ' splendour '‿
　　　　　　to be ' shown to us.

6　　The created universe itself waits with ' eager ' longing:
　　　　for the children of ' God to ' be re'vealed.

based on Romans 8:2,14-19

Glory to the Father and ' to the ' Son:
　　and ' to the ' Holy ' Spirit;
as it was in the be'ginning · is ' now:
　　and shall be for ' ever. ' A'men.

A Song of Creation　　　　　　　　　　　　*Benedicite*

1　　Let the whole creation ' bless the ' Lord:
　　　　praise and ex'alt our ' God for ' ever.

2　　Bless the ' Lord you ' heavens:
　　　　praise and ex'alt our ' God for ' ever.

3　　Bless the Lord you ' angels · of the ' Lord:
　　　　bless the ' Lord · all you ' heaven·ly ' hosts;

(verses 4 - 17 may be omitted)

4　　bless the Lord you waters a'bove the ' heavens:
　　　　praise and ex'alt our ' God for ' ever.

5　　Bless the Lord ' sun and ' moon:
　　　　bless the ' Lord you ' stars of ' heaven;

6　　bless the Lord all ' rain and ' dew:
　　　　praise and ex'alt our ' God for ' ever.

7　　Bless the Lord all ' winds that ' blow:
　　　　bless the ' Lord you ' fire and ' heat;

8　　bless the Lord scorching wind and ' bitter ' cold:
　　　　praise and ex'alt our ' God for ' ever.

9 Bless the Lord dews and ' falling ' snow:
   bless the ' Lord you ' nights and ' days;

10 bless the Lord ' light and ' darkness:
   praise and ex'alt our ' God for ' ever.

11 Bless the Lord ' frost and ' cold:
   bless the ' Lord you ' ice and ' snow;

12 bless the Lord ' lightnings · and ' clouds:
   praise and ex'alt our ' God for ' ever.

13 O let the earth ' bless the ' Lord:
   bless the ' Lord you ' mountains · and ' hills;

14 bless the Lord all that ' grows · in the ' soil:
   praise and ex'alt our ' God for ' ever.

15 Bless the Lord you ' springs of ' water:
   bless the ' Lord you ' seas and ' rivers;

16 bless the Lord you whales⌣
      and all that ' swim · in the ' waters:
   praise and ex'alt our ' God for ' ever.

17 Bless the Lord all ' birds · of the ' air:
   bless the ' Lord you ' beasts and ' cattle;

18 bless the Lord all you ' dwellers · on ' earth:
   praise and ex'alt our ' God for ' ever.

19 Bless the Lord you ' people · of ' God:
   bless the ' Lord you ' priests · of the ' Lord;

20 bless the Lord you ' servants · of the ' Lord:
   praise and ex'alt our ' God for ' ever.

21 Bless the Lord all you that are ' upright · in ' spirit:
   bless the Lord you that are ' holy · ⌣
      and ' humble · in ' heart.

22 Let us bless the Father, the Son and the ' Holy ' Spirit:
   praise and ex'alt our ' God for ' ever.

Song of the Three Young Men, 35-65

Daily Devotions

These daily devotions are for those who wish to base their worship on the New Testament, and whose time for prayer may be limited.

This order may be used by itself or as a brief form of daily worship, with the inclusion of a Scripture reading or readings.

Each week the seven sections of the Lord's Prayer are covered, with a morning and evening devotion for each day.

The same pattern is followed throughout:

- *a short opening, followed by a Gospel reflection, based on one or more Gospel sayings;*
- *after a brief meditation, a reflection on the epistles;*
- *the daily reading of Scripture may follow;*
- *the order concludes with prayer.*

Sunday Morning

Theme

The kingdom, the power, and the glory are yours
now and for ever.
Nou te rangatiratanga, te kaha, me te kororia ake ake ake.

Call to Worship

Sleeper awake! Rise from the dead,
and Christ will shine upon you. Alleluia.

Gospel Reflection

How blest are those who are poor in spirit:
  the kingdom of heaven is theirs.
How blest are the sorrowful:
  they shall find consolation.
How blest are those of a gentle spirit:
  they shall have the earth for their possession.
How blest are those who hunger and thirst to see right prevail:
  they shall be satisfied.
How blest are those who show mercy:
  mercy shall be shown to them.
How blest are those whose hearts are pure:
  they shall see God.
How blest are the peacemakers:
  they shall be called children of God.
How blest are those who have suffered persecution
    for the cause of right:
  the kingdom of heaven is theirs.

**How blest are those who follow Jesus
  and the Saviour's command to love.**

Silence for meditation.

Epistle Reflection

We set our hearts on heaven,
where Christ is at God's right hand.
Christ is our life, and when he appears,
we too will share his glory.
Christ lives in us.
Though our bodies will die,
yet for us the Spirit is life;
the Spirit of God who raised Jesus from death.
This is our secret.
Christ is in us;
we will share the glory of God.

The reading or readings may follow here.

Prayers

Our Father in heaven,
the kingdom, the power, and the glory are yours
now and for ever.

> **E to matou Matua i te rangi,**
> **nou te rangatiratanga, te kaha, me te kororia,**
> **ake ake ake.**

God,
you are our beginning and you will be our end;
we are made in your image and likeness.
We praise and thank you for this day.
This is the day on which you created light
and saw that it was good.
This is the day in whose early morning light
we discovered the tomb was empty,
and encountered Christ, the world's true light.
This is the day you have made;
we shall rejoice and be glad in it.

Lord, make us instruments of your peace;
where there is hatred, let us sow love;
where there is injury, pardon;
where there is discord, union;
where there is doubt, faith;
where there is despair, hope;
where there is darkness, light;
where there is sadness, joy.

Eternal God,
grant to us this day and every day
such readiness and delight in following Christ,
that whether our lives are short or long
we shall have lived abundantly.
Amen.

Sunday Evening

Theme

The kingdom, the power, and the glory are yours
now and for ever.

> Nou te rangatiratanga, te kaha, me te kororia, ake ake ake.

Call to Worship

Great beyond all question is the mystery of our religion;
Christ was manifested in the body,
vindicated in the spirit,
seen by angels.

**Christ was proclaimed among the nations,
believed in throughout the world,
glorified in heaven.**

Gospel Reflection

A grain of wheat is a solitary grain
till it falls to the ground and dies.
A grain of wheat is a solitary grain,
but dead it bears a mighty harvest.

Praise to Jesus, the resurrection and the life.
All who have faith in Christ,
though they die, they will come to life;
and no one who is alive in faith will ever die.

For the Son of Man was raised up
so that everyone who believes in Jesus
may have eternal life.

**Look on Jesus, lifted up,
lifted high to redeem the world.**

Silence for meditation.

Epistle Reflection

All we long for is to know the Christ
and the power of his resurrection,
to share in the sufferings of Christ
and become like him in his death.

For anyone united to Christ
the world is new.
The old order has gone;
the new has already begun.

So we press eagerly towards the goal
in order to win the prize,
the call that comes from God
to life with Christ in glory.

The reading or readings may follow here.

Prayers

Our Father in heaven,
the kingdom, the power, and the glory are yours
now and for ever.
> **E to matou Matua i te rangi,**
> **nou te rangatiratanga, te kaha, me te kororia,**
> **ake ake ake.**

God,
you are our beginning and you will be our end;
we are made in your image and likeness.
We praise and thank you for this day.
This is the day on which you created light
and saw that it was good.
This is the day in whose early morning light
we discovered the tomb was empty,
and encountered Christ, the world's true light.
For us your acts are gracious
and your love endures for ever.

O divine Master,
grant that we may not so much seek to be consoled,
as to console;
to be understood, as to understand;
to be loved, as to love.
For it is in giving that we receive;
it is in pardoning that we are pardoned;
it is in dying that we are born to eternal life.

Jesus our inspiration,
you come in the evening as our doors are shut,
and bring peace.
Grant us sleep tonight,
and courage tomorrow to go wherever you lead.
Amen.

Monday Morning

Theme

Hallowed be your name on earth as in heaven.
> Kia tapu tou ingoa ki runga ki te whenua,
> kia rite ano ki to te rangi.

Call to Worship

Always be joyful, pray continually;
give thanks, whatever happens.

Gospel Reflection

Hear Jesus' words:

When you do a kindness,
hide from your left hand what your right is doing.
Your good deed must be secret.

When you pray, pray privately alone,
when you fast, don't make a show of it,
don't do it to be seen;
and your Father who sees in secret
will reward you.

Would any of you who are parents
give your child a weta when asked for a fish?
Bad as you are, you know what to give your children;
how much more will the heavenly Father
give to those who ask.

Believe what Jesus says,
God is generous; God is good.

Silence for meditation.

Epistle Reflection

E te whanau, let us love one another,
because love is from God.
We love because God loved us first,
and everyone who loves is a child of God and knows God.
If we do not love the people we have seen,
it cannot be that we love God, whom we have not seen.
God is love;
those who dwell in love are dwelling in God,
and God in them.

The reading or readings may follow here.

Prayers

Our Father,
hallowed be your name
on earth as in heaven.
> **E to matou Matua,**
> **kia tapu tou ingoa**
> **ki runga ki te whenua,**
> **kia rite ano ki to te rangi.**

Holy One, holy and eternal,
awesome, exciting and delightful in your holiness;
make us pure in heart to see you;
make us merciful to receive your kindness,
and to share our love with all your human family;
then will your name be hallowed on earth as in heaven.

Lord God,
when you give to us your servants any great matter to do,
grant us also to know that it is not the beginning,
but the continuing of it, until it is thoroughly finished
which yields the true glory.

God of work and rest and pleasure,
grant that what we do this week may be for us an offering
rather than a burden;
and for those we serve, may it be the help they need.
Amen.

Monday Evening

Theme

Hallowed be your name on earth as in heaven.
>   Kia tapu tou ingoa ki runga ki te whenua,
>   kia rite ano ki to te rangi.

Call to Worship

There is nothing in death or life,
in the realm of spirits or superhuman powers,
in the world as it is or the world as it shall be,
in the forces of the universe, in heights or depths -
nothing in all creation
which can separate us from the love of God
which is in Jesus Christ our Lord.
Love never comes to an end.

Gospel Reflection

God of the scriptures, you said,
'I am the God of Abraham, of Isaac and of Jacob.'
We praise your holy name.

God our life, you are God of the living, not of the dead.
You are the only God,
and we love you with all our heart.
We love our neighbour as ourselves.

God of Sarah, Rebecca and Rachel,
in helping the least important,
we help you in your need,
and enter into your joy.

You are the living God;
Jesus is your name,
and the glory is yours.

Silence for meditation.

Epistle Reflection

We have come to the holy mountain
and to the city of the living God,
the heavenly Jerusalem;
before myriads of angels,
before the full assembly of the first-born citizens of heaven.

We have come to God who is the judge of all,
and the spirits of the good, made perfect;
we have come to Jesus, mediator of the new covenant.

Let us give thanks,
and worship God with reverence and awe,
for our God is a consuming fire.

The reading or readings may follow here.

Prayers

**Our Father, hallowed be your name,
on earth as in heaven.**

    **E to matou Matua,
kia tapu tou ingoa
ki runga ki te whenua,
kia rite ano ki to te rangi.**

Holy One, holy and eternal,
awesome, exciting and delightful in your holiness;
make us pure in heart to see you;
make us merciful to receive your kindness
and to share our love with all your human family;
then will your name be hallowed on earth as in heaven.

Support us, Lord, all the day long,
until the shadows lengthen, and the evening comes,
the busy world is hushed, the fever of life is over,
and our work done;
then Lord, in your mercy, give us safe lodging,
a holy rest and peace at the last.

God our judge and our companion,
we thank you for the good we did this day
and for all that has given us joy.
Everything we offer as our humble service.
Bless those with whom we have worked,
and those who are our concern.
Amen.

Tuesday Morning

Theme

Your kingdom come on earth as in heaven.
> Kia tae mai tou rangatiratanga
> ki runga ki te whenua,
> kia rite ano ki to te rangi.

Call to Worship

Arise, shine, for your light has come.
The glory of the Lord is risen upon us.

Gospel Reflection

The time has come; the kingdom of God is upon us.
Let us repent and believe the gospel.

The kingdom of God is like yeast:
a woman takes it and mixes it with flour until the dough is risen.
The kingdom of God is like a buyer looking for fine pearls.
When he finds one exceptional pearl,
he sells everything he has, and buys it.

When we set our minds on God's reign,
our hearts on God's justice,
everything else will be ours as well.

Listen to Jesus who proclaims good news,
which he alone fulfills.

Silence for meditation.

Epistle Reflection

Who are we whom God has called?
Few of us are wise, few are powerful.
Yet to shame the wise
God has chosen what the world counts folly;
to shame the strong
God has chosen what the world counts weakness.

In union with Christ Jesus, we are all children of God.
Baptised into union with Christ,
we have put on Christ like a garment.
There is no such thing as Jew or Greek,
slave or free, male or female;
we are all one in Jesus Christ.

The reading or readings may follow here.

Prayers

Our Father,
your kingdom come
on earth as in heaven.
> **E to matou Matua,**
> **kia tae mai tou rangatiratanga**
> **ki runga ki te whenua,**
> **kia rite ano ki to te rangi.**

Ruler of the everlasting kingdom,
prince of peace, champion of the despised:
you are the king;
you make a cross your throne;
you wear a crown of thorns;
you call your subjects friends.
Help us to take up our cross,
to hunger and thirst for all that is good;
then will your kingdom come on earth as in heaven.

God,
grant us the serenity
to accept the things we cannot change,
the courage to change the things we can,
and the wisdom to know the difference.

God our life,
be with us through this day,
whether or not it brings us joy.
Help us when evening comes
to recall one benefit,
for which to give you thanks.
Amen.

Tuesday Evening

Theme

Your kingdom come on earth as in heaven.
> Kia tae mai tou rangatiratanga
> ki runga ki te whenua,
> kia rite ano ki to te rangi.

Call to Worship

Now that we have been justified through faith,
let us continue at peace with God through our Lord Jesus Christ.
**Through Christ we have been allowed to enter
the sphere of God's grace where now we stand.**

Gospel Reflection

Kings lord it over their subjects,
but with us the highest must be like the lowest,
the chief like a servant.

Who is greater - the one who sits at table
or the servant who waits?
Surely the one at table.

Yet Jesus is among us like a servant.
He came not to be served but to serve,
and to give his life as a ransom for many.

So when we have done all that we have to do,
we shall simply be servants who have done our duty.
Come to Jesus, all those whose work is hard,
whose load is heavy,
and you will be renewed.

Silence for meditation.

Epistle Reflection

Praise to the God and Father of our Lord Jesus Christ.
We have been given new birth into a living hope
by the raising of Jesus Christ from the dead.

We are a chosen race, a royal priesthood,
a dedicated nation;
we are a people claimed by God
to proclaim the triumphs of Christ.

Christ has called us from darkness into his marvellous light.
We who were not a people at all, are now God's people.
We were outside God's mercy once,
but now we are blessed and forgiven.

The reading or readings may follow here.

Prayers

Our Father,
your kingdom come
on earth as in heaven.

**E to matou Matua,
kia tae mai tou rangatiratanga
ki runga ki te whenua,
kia rite ano ki to te rangi.**

Ruler of the everlasting kingdom,
prince of peace, champion of the despised:
you are the king;
you make a cross your throne;
you wear a crown of thorns;
you call your subjects friends.
Help us to take up our cross,
to hunger and thirst for all that is good;
then will your kingdom come on earth as in heaven.

Look down, Lord, from your heavenly throne.
Illuminate the darkness of this night
with your celestial brightness,
and from us, the children of light,
banish for ever the deeds of darkness.

God our judge and our teacher,
let us not waste time when the day is done
in guilt or self-reproach.
Give us rather the courage
to face whatever has been,
accept forgiveness, and move on to something better.
Amen.

Wednesday Morning

Theme

Your will be done on earth as in heaven.
Kia meatia tau e pai ai
ki runga ki te whenua,
kia rite ano ki to te rangi.

Call to Worship

Make full use of the present opportunity.
Give thanks every day for everything.

Gospel Reflection

We cannot serve God and money;
we cannot be slave to two masters.

So we shall enter by the narrow gate.
The gate is wide that leads to perdition, and many go that way.
But the gate to life is small, the road is narrow,
and those who find it are few.

If we want to be with Jesus,
we must forget ourselves, carry our cross and follow.
If we want to save our life we will lose it
but if we lose our life for Christ and for the gospel,
we will save it.

With us it is impossible, but not for God.
Only God can save us.

Silence for meditation.

Epistle Reflection

In everything we do,
in our troubles, difficulties and hardships
we show we are God's servants.
By purity, patience and kindness,
by the Spirit and by our love,
and by our message of truth,
we show ourselves for what we are.
We may seem poor, but we make many rich;
we seem to have nothing,
but we possess all that there is to have.

The reading or readings may follow here.

Prayers

Our Father,
your will be done
on earth as in heaven.

> **E to matou Matua,**
> **kia meatia tau e pai ai**
> **ki runga ki te whenua,**
> **kia rite ano ki to te rangi.**

Creator of the universe, infinite and glorious,
you give us laws to save us from our folly;
give us eyes to see your plan unfolding,
your purpose emerging as the world is made;
give us courage to follow the truth
courage to go wherever you lead;
then we shall know blessings beyond our dreams;
then will your will be done.

Almighty and everlasting God,
we thank you that you have brought us safely
to the beginning of this day;
keep us from falling into sin or running into danger,
and guide us to do always what is right in your eyes.

Holy and enabling Spirit,
give wings to our morning prayers.
May those we support and cherish with our love
receive your grace to help them in their need.
Amen.

Wednesday Evening

Theme

Your will be done on earth as in heaven.
> Kia meatia tau e pai ai
> ki runga ki te whenua,
> kia rite ano ki to te rangi.

Call to Worship

Kneel in prayer to the Father,
from whom every family in heaven and on earth
takes its name;
that out of the treasures of glory
God may grant us strength and power
through the Spirit in our inmost being;

that Christ, through faith,
may dwell in our hearts in love.

Gospel Reflection

Jesus, friend of sinners,
you call us to love our enemies,
to do good to those who hate us,
to bless those who curse us,
and pray for those who treat us badly.

Jesus, reconciler,
when someone slaps us on the cheek,
you call us to offer the other;
when someone takes our coat,
you bid us give our shirt as well;
when someone takes what is ours,
we may not demand it back.

Jesus, Son of God, our friend and brother,
when we love our enemies and do good
we are children of God,
who is kind to the wicked and ungrateful.

**Jesus, teacher without peer,
you have turned the world upside down.**

Silence for meditation.

Epistle Reflection

Blessed be the God and Father of our Lord Jesus Christ,
by whose loving kindness we have been born anew;
born to a living hope
by the resurrection of Jesus Christ from the dead;
born to an inheritance which will never perish
or be frittered away,
but is kept for us in heaven.

We rejoice, though now we suffer trials,
so that our faith, tested by fire,
may resound to the praise and glory and honour of God.

The reading or readings may follow here.

Prayers

**Our Father,
your will be done
on earth as in heaven.**

    **E to matou Matua,
kia meatia tau e pai ai
ki runga ki te whenua,
kia rite ano ki to te rangi.**

Creator of the universe, infinite and glorious,
you give us laws to save us from our folly;
give us eyes to see your plan unfolding,
your purpose emerging as the world is made;
give us courage to follow the truth,
courage to go wherever you lead;
then we shall know blessings beyond our dreams;
then will your will be done.

Thanks to you, Lord Jesus Christ,
for all the cruel pains and insults you have borne for us;
for all the many blessings you have won for us.
Holy Jesus, most merciful Redeemer, friend and brother,
may we know you more clearly, love you more dearly,
and follow you more nearly, day by day.

God of peace,
be with us through this night which waits for us;
bless us if it brings us sleep;
support us if it brings us pain or anxiety,
till we come once more to the morning light of another day.
Amen.

Thursday Morning

Theme

Give us today our daily bread.
> Homai ki a matou aianei
> he taro ma matou mo tenei ra.

Call to Worship

None of us lives and none of us dies for ourselves alone.
Living or dying we belong to the Lord.

Gospel Reflection

Jesus, you are the bread of life;
those who come to you will never be hungry;
those who believe in you will never thirst.
You are the living bread from heaven;
the bread you give is your own flesh,
and you give it for the life of the world.

All who eat your flesh and drink your blood
live in you and you in them;
for your flesh is the food we need,
your blood is our salvation;
all who eat your flesh and drink your blood have eternal life.

Look to Jesus in the wilderness,
breaking bread and feeding the multitude.

Silence for meditation.

Epistle Reflection

E te whanau.
Sparse sowing, meagre reaping;
but if we are generous, bountiful will be the harvest.
So let us give what we can,
not with regret, nor from a sense of duty.
God loves a cheerful giver.

And when we help others, we will not just meet their needs,
we will unleash a flood of gratitude to God.
Many will give glory to God
for our loyalty to the gospel and for our generosity.
God loves a cheerful giver.

The reading or readings may follow here.

Prayers

Our Father,
give us today our daily bread.
> **E to matou Matua,**
> **homai ki a matou aianei**
> **he taro ma matou mo tenei ra.**

God of seed and growth and harvest,
creator of need, creator of satisfaction;
give us, we pray, our daily bread,
sufficient and assured for all.
Give us also, we pray, the bread of life,
and we shall have a care to feed the hungry,
and to seek for peace and justice in the world.
Help us, then, to remember and to know
that you are our life today and every day;
you are the food we need, now and for ever.

God,
give us work till our life shall end,
and life till our work is done.

Look kindly on our world, our God,
as we suffer and struggle with one another.
Look kindly on your Church,
driven by the same necessity;
and may the light we have seen in Jesus
illuminate and brighten all the world.
Amen.

Thursday Evening

Theme

Give us today our daily bread.
> Homai ki a matou aianei
> he taro ma matou mo tenei ra.

Call to Worship

Now my friends, all that is true, all that is noble,
all that is just and pure,
all that is lovable and gracious,
whatever is excellent and admirable:
with these let us fill our hearts,
and the God of heaven will be with us.

Gospel Reflection

Jesus,
you are the vine;
your Father is the gardener,
who breaks off every branch that bears no fruit
and prunes each one that does.
We cannot bear fruit, unless we remain in you.

You are the vine, we are the branches.
If we remain in you, and your words remain in us,
whatever we ask, we shall have.

Your commandment is this:
Love one another, just as I love you.
You can have no greater love for your friends
than to give your life for them.

Jesus is the vine: Jesus makes us one.
Jesus is our life.

Silence for meditation.

Epistle Reflection

We must be like newborn babes,
always thirsty for spiritual milk,
so that we may grow up to be saved.

Our hearts and minds must be made completely new;
we must get rid of that old self, which made us live as we did;
we must put on the new self, created in God's likeness,
revealed in the true life which is upright and holy.

The reading or readings may follow here.

Prayers

**Our Father,
give us today our daily bread.**
> **E to matou Matua,
> homai ki a matou aianei
> he taro ma matou mo tenei ra.**

God of seed and growth and harvest,
creator of need, creator of satisfaction;
give us, we pray, our daily bread,
sufficient and assured for all.
Give us also, we pray, the bread of life,
and we shall have a care to feed the hungry,
and to seek for peace and justice in the world.
Help us, then, to remember and to know
that you are our life today and every day;
you are the food we need, now and for ever.

Look kindly, all-seeing God,
on all who spend this night in anxiety or pain.
Be with those who will die tonight.
Look kindly on those who are without food or shelter,
on those who have no love.
Your will is that we should have life, and share it.

Be present, merciful God,
and protect us through the silent hours of this night,
that we, who are wearied
by the changes and chances of this fleeting world,
may rest upon your eternal changelessness.
Amen.

Friday Morning

Theme

Forgive us our sins, as we forgive those who sin against us.
> Murua o matou hara,
> me matou hoki e muru nei
> i o te hunga e hara ana ki a matou.

Call to Worship

Never forget to show kindness,
to share what you have with others.
These are the sacrifices which God approves.

Gospel Reflection

Jesus, you are the good shepherd,
you are willing to die for the sheep.
You are the good shepherd;
as the Father knows you and you know the Father,
in the same way you know your sheep,
and your sheep know you;
you are willing to die for us.

The Father loves you because you are willing to give your life;
no one takes your life from you;
you give it up of your own free will;
you are the good shepherd.

**Jesus is the good shepherd who understands our frailty,
and knows each one of us by name.**

Silence for meditation.

Epistle Reflection

When we were still helpless,
Christ died for the wicked at the time God chose.
One of us might dare to die for someone good.
But now we see God's love;
while we were still sinners, Christ died for us.
God rescued us from the power of darkness
and brought us safe into the kingdom of his dear Son,
by whom we are set free and our sins are forgiven.
So we rejoice in the hope we have of sharing in God's glory.
By the Holy Spirit
God has poured into our hearts the love of Christ.

The reading or readings may follow here.

Prayers

**Our Father,
forgive us our sins
as we forgive those who sin against us.**

> **E to matou Matua,
> murua o matou hara,
> me matou hoki e muru nei
> i o te hunga e hara ana ki a matou.**

Saviour, hanging on the cross, declaring God's love to us,
you are forgiveness.
Beside you hangs a thief,
beneath you waits Mary the forgiven,
and all around watch those many people
to whom you give new life and hope.
To us you give new life and hope.
Forgiven sinners become your body and your Church;
may the reconciliation we share
bring your gospel to all the world.

Eternal God,
by your power we are created
and by your love we are redeemed;
guide and strengthen us by your Spirit,
that we may give ourselves to your service
and live this day in love to one another and to you.

Jesus, you knew rejection and disappointment;
help us if our work seems distasteful;
help us to decide what best to do,
what next to do,
or what to do at all.
Give us courage and cheerfulness to go the second mile,
and all the miles ahead.
Amen.

Friday Evening

Theme

Forgive us our sins, as we forgive those who sin against us.
> Murua o matou hara,
> me matou hoki e muru nei
> i o te hunga e hara ana ki a matou.

Call to Worship

Well we know that it was no perishable stuff,
like gold or silver, that bought our freedom.
The price was paid in precious blood, the blood of Christ.

Gospel Reflection

Why do we look at the speck in someone else's eye
but ignore the log in our own?
The measure we use for others, God will use for us.

If we do not judge others, God will not judge us;
if we do not condemn others, God will not condemn us;
if we forgive, God forgives us even more;
so let us give, and God will give to us a full measure,
a generous helping, poured into our hands,
more than we can hold.
The measure we use for others,
God will use for us.

Jesus, you are the giver and the gift.

Silence for meditation.

Epistle Reflection

Once we were God's enemies, far away from God;
but now by the Son's death, God has made us friends.

Through the Son,
God has reconciled and won back the universe;
God made peace through Jesus' death on the cross.

God has reconciled all things on earth and in heaven;
so we preach Christ to all the world.

The reading or readings may follow here.

Prayers

Our Father,
forgive us our sins
as we forgive those who sin against us.
> **E to matou Matua,**
> **murua o matou hara,**
> **me matou hoki e muru nei**
> **i o te hunga e hara ana ki a matou.**

Saviour, hanging on the cross declaring God's love to us,
you are forgiveness.
Beside you hangs a thief,
beneath you waits Mary the forgiven,
and all around watch those many people
to whom you give new life and hope.
To us you give new life and hope.
Forgiven sinners become your body and your Church;
may the reconciliation we share
bring your gospel to all the world.

God,
you call us to serve you with all the strength we have:
you are faithful to those you call;
may Jesus' resurrection raise us if we stumble,
the Christlight beckon us if we lose our way,
and we shall have strength once more
to walk with you to the cross.

Preserve us, O God, while waking,
and guard us while sleeping,
that awake we may watch with Christ,
and asleep may rest in your peace.
Amen.

Saturday Morning

Theme

Save us from the time of trial, and deliver us from evil.
    Aua hoki matou e kawea kia whakawaia,
        engari whakaorangia matou i te kino.

Call to Worship

The time has come for the judgment to begin;
it is beginning with God's own household.

Gospel Reflection

We must be on our guard.
We could be taken to court;
we could be summoned to appear
before the authorities, to testify for Jesus.
The gospel must be proclaimed to everyone.

If we are arrested and taken away,
we should not worry beforehand what to say;
when the time comes, say what is given;
we shall not be the speakers, but the Holy Spirit.

Jesus asked in the garden that the cup might pass from him;
Jesus drank the cup and walked the way of the cross.

Silence for meditation.

Epistle Reflection

E te whanau, if Christ's name is flung in our teeth
we should count ourselves happy,
because that glorious Spirit,
the Spirit of God, is resting upon us.

If we suffer, let it not be for murder, theft or sorcery,
nor for infringing the rights of others;
but if we suffer as Christians
we should feel no disgrace,
but confess that name to the honour of God.
It gives us a share in Christ's sufferings.
That is cause for joy!

The reading or readings may follow here.

Prayers

Our Father,
save us from the time of trial,
and deliver us from evil.

> **E to matou Matua,**
> **aua hoki matou e kawea kia whakawaia,**
> **engari whakaorangia matou i te kino.**

Giver of the present, hope for the future:
save us from the time of trial.
When prophets warn us of doom,
of catastrophe and of suffering beyond belief,
then, God, free us from our helplessness,
and deliver us from evil.
Save us from our arrogance and folly,
for you are God who created the world;
you have redeemed us and you are our salvation.

Almighty God,
you see that we have no power of ourselves
to help ourselves;
keep us both outwardly in our bodies
and inwardly in our souls,
that we may be defended from all adversities
which may happen to the body,
and from all evil thoughts
which may assault and hurt the soul.

God of opportunity and change,
praise to you for giving us life at this critical time.
As our horizons extend, keep us loyal to our past;
as our dangers increase, help us to prepare the future;
keep us trusting and hopeful,
ready to recognise your kingdom as it comes.
Amen.

Saturday Evening

Theme

Save us from the time of trial, and deliver us from evil.
Aua hoki matou e kawea kia whakawaia,
engari whakaorangia matou i te kino.

Call to Worship

So far you have faced no trial beyond what you can bear.
God keeps faith, and will not allow you
to be tempted beyond your power.
**When the test comes,
God will at the same time provide a way out,
enabling us to endure it.**

Gospel Reflection

Stay awake !
Happy those servants who are alert and ready
when their master comes.

When much is given, more will be demanded.
When a great deal is given on trust,
a great deal more is expected.
Stay awake!

Your master is coming.
Stand ready!

The Son of Man comes at the least expected hour.
The kingdom of God is upon us.

**'Why are you sleeping?' Jesus said.
'Rise and pray, that you may be spared the test.'**

Silence for meditation.

Epistle Reflection

Love is patient, love is kind and envies no one.
Love is not boastful, never conceited,
never rude nor selfish;
love is not quick to take offence.

Love keeps no score of wrongs;
love delights in the truth;
there is no limit to its faith,
its hope and its endurance.
Love never gives up.

Love never comes to an end.
There are three things that last for ever:
faith, hope and love,
but the greatest of them all is love.

The reading or readings may follow here.

Prayers

Our Father,
save us from the time of trial,
and deliver us from evil.
> **E to matou Matua,**
> **aua hoki matou e kawea kia whakawaia,**
> **engari whakaorangia matou i te kino.**

Giver of the present, hope for the future:
save us from the time of trial.
When prophets warn us of doom,
of catastrophe and of suffering beyond belief,
then, God, free us from our helplessness,
and deliver us from evil.
Save us from our arrogance and folly,
for you are God who created the world;
you have redeemed us and you are our salvation.

Dear Lord,
watch with those who wake or watch or weep tonight,
and give your angels charge over those who sleep;
tend your sick ones,
rest your afflicted ones, shield your joyous ones,
and all, for your love's sake.

God, we go into this night
confident that the dawn will break tomorrow;
grant that when we come to die,
we may go gladly and in hope,
confident in the resurrection.
Amen.

Prayers for Various Occasions

Each prayer may end with

We make this prayer through Jesus Christ. **Amen.**

or with a versicle and response familiar to the congregation.

FOR THE QUEEN

God, the source of all authority,
bless our queen, Elizabeth, her family
and the family of nations she upholds;
may she remain a worthy focus of our loyalty,
and point us unfailingly to a higher commonwealth,
the true humanity
to which she and all her subjects owe allegiance;
for you are the God of nations; you are our God.

FOR GOOD GOVERNMENT

Spirit of justice, creator Spirit;
help us to make and keep this country
a home for all its different peoples,
and grant to our government and all its representatives
imagination, skill and energy
that there may grow amongst us aroha and peace.

FOR OUR COUNTRY

God of the southern sea
and of these islands,
of Maori, Pakeha *
and of all who dwell in our land;
we give you thanks and praise for our country,
and for what we have achieved together.
Increase our trust in one another;
strengthen our quest for justice,
and bring us to unity and a common purpose.
You have made us of one blood;
make us also of one mind.

* This may be adapted in Polynesia

E te Atua o te Moana-nui-a-Kiwa,
me enei motu, o te iwi Maori, te iwi Pakeha,
me ratou katoa e noho nei i tenei wahi.
Ka whakamoemiti,
ka whakawhetai ki a koe mo tenei whenua o matou;
mo nga mea pai katoa kua whiwhi tahi nei matou.
Whakanuia to matou aroha tetahi ki tetahi,
whakakahangia to matou whai i te tika
kia kotahi ai matou i runga i te whakaaro kotahi.
Kua hanga matou e koe hei toto kotahi;
i raro i tenei whakaaro kotahi.
Amine.

FOR THOSE WHO GOVERN

Eternal God, Fount of wisdom;
we ask you to bless the representatives we have elected;
grant that through their discussions and decisions
we may solve our problems effectively,
enhance the well-being of our nation,
and achieve together a fairer and more united society.

FOR THE JUDICIARY AND POLICE

God of truth and justice;
we ask you to help the men and women
who administer and police our laws;
grant them insight, courage and compassion,
protect them from corruption and arrogance
and grant that we, whom they seek to serve,
may give them the support and affection they need;
so may our people be strengthened more and more
in respect and concern for one another.

FOR THE ARMED FORCES

God our stronghold and defence;
we commend to you those whose task it is
to defend us in danger;
inspire them in war to serve our country well;
in peace, hold them ready and alert.
In their lives may they bring honour to our country's name.

FOR TEACHERS AND EDUCATORS

God the source of all our inspiration,
help us to understand ourselves, our world and you;
and grant to those who teach us and our children
respect for others' inventiveness and questioning,
and for themselves commitment to truth.

FOR EDUCATIONAL INSTITUTIONS

O Eternal God,
bless all schools, colleges and universities
(especially ...),
that they may be lively centres for sound learning,
new discovery and the pursuit of wisdom;
grant that those who teach
and those who learn
may find you to be the source of all truth.

HARVEST THANKSGIVING

Blessed are you, God of all creation,
for you give us abundantly, thirty, sixty and a hundredfold;
we praise you for harvest
and for the assurance of food and drink for another year;
strengthen us, as we enjoy what we are given,
to help the hungry and intolerably poor.

FOR THE MISSION OF THE CHURCH

Draw your Church together, O God,
into one great company of disciples,
together following our Lord Jesus Christ
into every walk of life,
together serving him in his mission to the world,
and together witnessing to his love
on every continent and island.

KARAKIA BEFORE A MEETING

God our Creator,
when you speak there is light and life,
when you act there is justice and love;
grant that your love may be present in our meeting,
so that what we say and what we do
may be filled with your Holy Spirit.

E te Atua to matou Kai-hanga,
ka tiaho te maramatanga me te ora, i au kupu korero,
ka timata au mahi, ka mau te tika me te aroha;
meatia kia u tonu ki a matou
tou aroha i roto i tenei huihuinga.
Whakakii a matou whakaaro a matou mahi katoa,
e tou Wairua Tapu.
Amine.

AN OFFERING PRAYER

Almighty God;
you give seed for us to sow,
and bread for us to eat;
make us thankful for what we have received;
make us rich to do those generous things
which supply your people's needs;
so all the world may give you thanks and glory.

FOR PEACE

O God,
it is your will to hold both heaven and earth
in a single peace.
Let the design of your great love
shine on the waste of our wraths and sorrows,
and give peace to your Church,
peace among nations,
peace in our homes, and peace in our hearts.

FOR GOOD USE OF LEISURE

O God,
you rested the seventh day and are still at work;
in the course of this busy life
give us times of refreshment and peace;
and grant that we may so use our leisure
to rebuild our bodies and renew our minds,
that our spirits may be opened
to the goodness of your creation.

A THANKSGIVING FOR OUR COUNTRY

Blessed are you, God of the universe.
You have created us, and given us life.

Blessed are you, God of the planet earth.
You have set our world like a radiant jewel in the heavens,
and filled it with action, beauty, suffering, struggle and hope.

Blessed are you, God of Aotearoa New Zealand *
in all the peoples who live here,
in all the lessons we have learned,
in all that remains for us to do.

Blessed are you because you need us;
because you make us worthwhile,
because you give us people to love
and work to do
for your universe, for your world and for ourselves.

* This may be adapted in Polynesia

Prayers on Various Subjects
from the Collects of the Church's Year
[pages 550-641, as indicated]

The letters A, B and C refer to the first, second and third prayers for each Sunday or holy day.

Bereavement
590 Easter Eve A, B

Caring
635 Pentecost 23 B, C

The Church
559 Christmas 2 B, C
587 Good Friday A, C
613 Pentecost 6 B

567 Epiphany 5 B
604 Day of Pentecost B
615, 616 Pentecost 8

Communion of Saints
601 Ascension Day A

The Community
560 Epiphany B

637 Pentecost 25 C

Courage
567 Epiphany 5 C
583 Tuesday in Holy Week A
596 Easter 2 B

582 Monday in Holy Week B
595 Easter 1 A
632 Pentecost 21 C

Dedication and a Sense of Commitment
561, 562 Epiphany 1 A, B
600 Easter 5 A
621 Pentecost 13 A
628 Pentecost 18 B
640 Pentecost 27 A, B

587 Good Friday B
618 Pentecost 10
627 Pentecost 17 A, B
632 Pentecost 21 A, B

Faith
563 Epiphany 2 B
610 Pentecost 4 A
628 Pentecost 18 A, B

609 Pentecost 3 B
622 Pentecost 13 B, C
632 Pentecost 21 A

Family Life
633 Pentecost 22

Forgiveness
576, 577 Lent 3

624 Pentecost 15 A, B

Fulfilment of Our Potential
557 Christmas 1 A, C
608 Pentecost 2 C

569 Epiphany 7 A

Generosity
584 Wednesday in Holy Week C

616 Pentecost 8 C

Holy Communion
585, 586, Maundy Thursday A, C
619 Pentecost 11

595 Easter 1 B

Hope
623 Pentecost 14 B

Humility
580 Lent 6 B
586 Maundy Thursday D

584 Wednesday in Holy Week B

The Hungry
578 Lent 4 A, C

The Lonely
609 Pentecost 3 A

Love and Acceptance
579 Lent 5 C
624 Pentecost 15 C
634 Pentecost 23 A

614 Pentecost 7 A
627 Pentecost 17 C

Mission
564 Epiphany 3
606 Pentecost 1 B
613 Pentecost 6 A, B

604 Day of Pentecost
611 Pentecost 5 A

Self-discipline
573 Ash Wednesday A

Service
620 Pentecost 12
635 Pentecost 23 B, C

627 Pentecost 17 A

Sharing
616 Pentecost 8 C

Support in Trouble
568 Epiphany 6 B

Vocation
612 Pentecost 5 B, C

Watchfulness
550 Advent 1 A

641 Sunday before Advent

The World
558 Christmas 2 A
637 Pentecost 25 B

613 Pentecost 6 A
638 Pentecost 26 A

Midday Prayer

The Church lives in time and with time, and this truth is borne out by the observance of prayer even in the midst of a busy day.

Prayer at midday provides a way to consecrate the day at its centre and to realise the presence of God in the heart of life.

The admonition of Jesus that we pray and not be weary is fulfilled in this way, and we identify with him on the cross, the centre of his work.

Midday Prayer *is one among many opportunities for God's people, laity, religious orders, or clergy to extend the range of daily prayer.*

Invocation

E te whanau / My brothers and sisters,
our help is in the name of the eternal God,
who is making the heavens and the earth.

Eternal Spirit,
flow through our being and open our lips,
that our mouths may proclaim your praise.

Silence

Let us worship the God of love.
Alleluia. Alleluia.

Psalm

The following or some other psalm is said.

Sunday

Walking in God's path

Blessèd are those who are honest in their ways,
  who walk in the paths of God's law.

Blessèd are those who treasure God's wisdom,
  who seek God with all their heart.

Those who do no evil deeds
  are those who tread the way of justice.

Dear God, you have given command
  that we diligently hold to your word.

May my ways be kept steadfast
  on the narrow road of your love.

So shall I not be confounded
  while I respect the whole of your counsel.

I shall thank you with unfeigned heart
  as I learn to be guided by your Spirit.

I shall hold fast to your truths:
  do not utterly abandon me.

Psalm 119: 1-7

Monday

Desiring life in God's Spirit

Teach me, dear God, the way of your truth,
  and I shall follow it to the end.

Give me understanding, and I shall keep your law,
  I shall keep it with my whole heart.

Lead me in the path of your wisdom;
  to do your will is my deepest desire.

Incline my heart to your love,
  and not to envious greed.

Turn away my eyes from vanity,
  and give me life in your Spirit.

Establish me in your promise,
be faithful to those who are in awe of you.

Take away from me the rejection that I fear,
for your justice is good.

See, my delight is in your commandment:
quicken me in the power of your word.

Psalm 119: 33-40

Tuesday

Resting in God's hands

Your hands have made me and fashioned me:
give me understanding that I may know your mind.

Those who fear you will be glad when they see me,
because I have put my trust in your word.

I know that your judgments are right,
that in your faithfulness you have caused me to be troubled.

Let your merciful kindness be my comfort,
according to your promise to your servant.

Let your loving mercies come to me, that I may live,
for your law is my delight.

Let the proud be confounded, who twist us with deceit,
and I will meditate on your wisdom.

Let those who fear you turn to me,
that they may know your truth.

Psalm 119: 73-79

Wednesday

Trusting in God's purpose

Dear God, your eternal word of love
endures for ever in the universe.

Your truth stands fast from one generation to another.
You have laid the foundations of the earth, and it abides.

In fulfilment of your purpose it continues to this very day,
for all things serve you.

If my delight had not been in your wisdom,
I should have perished in my trouble.

I shall never forget your truths,
  for with them you have given me life.

I belong to you: save me,
  for I have sought your counsel.

The ungodly laid wait for me to destroy me,
  but I will meditate on your law.

I see that all things come to an end,
  but your commandment is exceeding broad. *Psalm 119: 89-96*

Thursday   *Being guided by God's light*

Your word is a lantern for my feet,
  a light searching out all my ways.

I have sworn, and am steadfastly purposed
  to keep the way of your justice.

I am troubled beyond measure:
  give me life, dear God, according to your promise.

Accept my offerings of praise,
  and teach me your truths.

My life is always in your hand,
  and I do not forget your law.

The ungodly have laid a snare for me:
  may I not swerve from your commandment.

Your wisdom have I claimed as my heritage for ever,
  it is the very joy of my heart.

I incline my heart to your counsel,
  always, even to the end. *Psalm 119: 105-112*

Friday   *Standing firm in God's counsel*

The powerful oppress me without cause,
  but my heart stands firm in awe of your word.

I rejoice in your love
  more than one who finds great spoils.

As for lies, I hate and abhor them,
  but your law do I love.

Seven times a day do I praise you,
  because of the justice of your way.

Great is the peace of those who treasure your wisdom,
  nothing can make them stumble.

Dear God, I have looked for your saving health,
  and followed your counsel.

Guide me in the path of your truth,
  all the ways of my heart are open before you.   *Psalm 119: 161-168*

Saturday   *Rejoicing in God's love*

Your steadfast love is wonderful:
  therefore I treasure your wisdom.

When your word goes forth
  it gives light and understanding to the simple.

I opened my mouth and drew in my breath,
  for my delight was in your counsel.

Look upon me and show me kindness,
  as is your joy for those who love your name.

Keep my steps steady in your word,
  and so shall no wickedness get dominion over me.

Relieve me from the weight of oppression,
  and so shall I keep your commandments.

Show the light of your face upon your servant,
  and teach me your way.   *Psalm 119: 129-135*

Reading

One of the following or some other passage of scripture is read.

Silence may follow the reading.

Sunday

For anyone who is in Christ, there is a new creation; the old creation has gone, and now the new one is here. It is all God's work. It is God who through Christ has won us back and given us a share in this work of reconciliation.   *2 Corinthians 5: 17-18*

Monday

The fruit of the Spirit is love, joy, peace, patience, kindness, goodness, faithfulness, gentleness, self-control. If we live by the Spirit, let us also walk by the Spirit.   *Galatians 5: 22, 23a,25*

Tuesday

From the rising of the sun to its setting my name shall be great among the nations, and in every place incense shall be offered to my name, and a pure offering; for my name shall be great among the nations, says the Lord of hosts.   *Malachi 1:11*

Wednesday

As servants of God we commend ourselves in every way: through great endurance, in afflictions, hardships, calamities, beatings, imprisonments, tumults, labours, watching, hunger; by purity, knowledge, forbearance, kindness, the Holy Spirit, genuine love, truthful speech, and the power of God; with the weapons of righteousness for the right hand and for the left; in honour and dishonour, in ill repute and good repute. We are treated as impostors, and yet are true; as unknown, and yet well known; as dying, and behold we live; as punished, and yet not killed; as sorrowful, yet always rejoicing; as poor, yet making many rich; as having nothing, and yet possessing everything.

2 Corinthians 6: 4-10

Thursday

Be kind to one another, tender-hearted, forgiving one another as God in Christ forgave you. Therefore be imitators of God, as beloved children. And walk in love, as Christ loved us and gave himself up for us, a fragrant offering and sacrifice to God.

Ephesians 4: 32 - 5:2

Friday

Put on then, as God's chosen ones, holy and beloved, compassion, kindness, lowliness, meekness, and patience, forbearing one another and, if one has a complaint against another, forgiving each other; as the Lord has forgiven you, so you also must forgive. And above all these put on love, which binds everything together in perfect harmony. And let the peace of Christ rule in your hearts, to which indeed you were called in the one body. And be thankful.

Colossians 3: 12-15

Saturday

Finally, whatever is true, whatever is honourable, whatever is just, whatever is pure, whatever is lovely, whatever is gracious, if there is any excellence, if there is anything worthy of praise, think about these things.

Philippians 4: 8

Canticle

One of the following or some other hymn or canticle may be said or sung.

1 A Hymn for Midday

O God, creation's secret force,
Thyself unmoved, all motion's source;
Who, from the morn till evening's ray,
Through all its changes guid'st the day.

Come, Holy Ghost, with God the Son,
And God the Father ever one;
Shed forth thy grace within our breast,
And dwell with us a ready guest.

By every power, by heart and tongue,
By act and deed thy praise be sung;
Inflame with perfect love each sense
That others' souls may kindle thence.

O Father, that we ask be done
Through Jesus Christ thine only Son.
Who, with the Holy Ghost and thee,
Doth live and reign eternally. Amen.

2 Poi

Kingi Ihaka

*The poi chant offered here as a canticle may be chanted on one note or
expressed in group action, in accordance with its original form.
The translation is provided for information only.*

Kia mau!
Titiro e nga iwi!
Te kapu taku ringa
He taonga tenei na
nga tupuna;
He poi, he poi, he poi, hei!

Be ready!
Take a look all people
at what is in the cup of my hand
for this is a treasure from
    our forebears;
a poi, a poi, a poi, hei!

Poi puritia!	Hold the poi!
Poi takawiri!	Quiver the poi!
Taupatupatu, taupatupatu,	Twirl and strike,
Taupatupatu, ko te tau!	and now the chant!
Patupatu taku poi,	I strike my poi,
Ka rere taku poi,	my poi flies,
Rere tika atu ana	and flies direct,
Ka tau ki Ngapuhi	landing in Ngapuhi country,
Kei reira te toka	for there stands the rock
Kei Rangihoua,	at Rangihoua,
Kei Oihi ra,	even at Oihi,
Ko te toka tena	that is the rock
I poua iho ai	on which was established
Te Rongopai ra e - Ka mau!	The gospel - and became fixed.
Hei whakakororia	To give glory
Te Atua i runga rawa	to God in the highest
Ka mau te rongo	and peace was declared
ki Aotearoa	throughout New Zealand,
Tena ano ra ko ana purapura	and its seeds
I ruiruia ra i roto nga iwi	have been broadcast among the tribes,
Ka tupu ka hua e - Hua nei!	and have grown and borne fruit - bears now.
Whiti rawa atu koe	When you have crossed
Ki a Raukawa	to Raukawa country
Ko Rota Waitoa	it is Rota Waitoa
Hei mataamua,	the very first Maori ever
	to be ordained to the
	sacred ministry.
Kei roto Wanganui	And at Wanganui
Ko Te Tauri	there is Wiremu Te Tauri
Ka tae nga rongo	the first person to introduce
	Christianity there.
Ki Ngati-Ruanui	And the news has also reached
	the Ngati-Ruanui people
Ko Manihera ra	among whom were Manihera
Ko Kereopa hoki	and also Kereopa
I whakamatea nei	the first Christian martyrs

Mo te Whakapono e
– Ka tau!

for the faith in New Zealand.
– Indeed!

Ka rere taku poi
Ki te Tairawhiti
Kei reira e ngaki ana
Ko Taumataakura

My poi now flies
to the Eastern seas
and there strives
Piripi Taumataakura who
introduced Christianity to
the Ngati Porou

Kei Mataatua
Ko Ngakuku ra
Kei Te Arawa
Ko Ihaia
Kei roto Kahungunu
Ko Te Wera ra e...Te Wera!

while in Mataatua country
is Ngakuku
and in Arawa country
is Ihaia
and in Ngati-Kahungunu country
is Te Wera...Yes, Te Wera!

Ka tuhi, ka rarapa, ka uira
Te rangi e tu iho nei, e
Toia te waka
Te utanga o runga
Ko te aroha;
Paiheretia mai
Te rangimarie,
Aue! Hei!

The lightning glows and flashes
well above the heavens
drag the canoe
with its cargo
of love;
bind it
with peace,
Aue! Hei!

3   A Hymn for Sunday

To God our Father, thanks and praise
For this, the first and dawn of days:
The day when thou, creation's spring,
Didst light and life from chaos bring.

The day on which thy well-loved Son
O'er death and hell the triumph won;
The day on which the Spirit came,
Thy gift to us in wind and flame.

All laud to God the Father be,
All praise, eternal Son to thee;
All glory, as is ever meet,
To God the holy Paraclete. Amen.

4 The Lake of Beauty

Edward Carpenter

Let your mind be quiet, realising the beauty of the world,
  and the immense, the boundless treasures that it holds in store.
All that you have within you, all that your heart desires,
  all that your Nature so specially fits you for - that or the
  counterpart of it waits embedded in the great Whole, for you.
It will surely come to you.

Yet equally surely not one moment before its appointed time
  will it come. All your crying and fever and reaching out of
  hands will make no difference.
Therefore do not begin that game at all.
Do not recklessly spill the waters of your mind
  in this direction and in that,
  lest you become like a spring lost and
  dissipated in the desert.

But draw them together into a little compass, and hold them
  still, so still;
And let them become clear, so clear - so limpid, so mirror-like;
at last the mountains and the sky shall glass themselves in
  peaceful beauty,
and the antelope shall descend to drink and to gaze at her
  reflected image, and the lion to quench his thirst,
and Love himself shall come and bend over and catch his
  own likeness in you.

5 Song to the Holy Spirit

James K. Baxter

Lord, Holy Spirit,
You blow like the wind in a thousand paddocks,
Inside and outside the fences,
You blow where you wish to blow.

Lord, Holy Spirit,
You are the sun who shines on the little plant,
You warm him gently, you give him life,
You raise him up to become a tree with many leaves.

Lord, Holy Spirit,
You are as the mother eagle with her young,
Holding them in peace under your feathers.
On the highest mountain you have built your nest,
Above the valley, above the storms of the world,
Where no hunter ever comes.

Lord, Holy Spirit,
You are the bright cloud in whom we hide,
In whom we know already that the battle has been won.
You bring us to our Brother Jesus
To rest our heads upon his shoulder.

Lord, Holy Spirit,
You are the kind fire who does not cease to burn,
Consuming us with flames of love and peace,
Driving us out like sparks to set the world on fire.

Lord, Holy Spirit,
In the love of friends you are building a new house,
Heaven is with us when you are with us.
You are singing your song in the hearts of the poor.
Guide us, wound us, heal us. Bring us to the Father.

6 St Patrick's Breastplate

Verses may be selected

I bind unto myself today
    the strong name of the Trinity.
By invocation of the same,
    the Three in One, and One in Three.

I bind this day to me for ever,
    by power of faith, Christ's incarnation;
His baptism in the Jordan river;
    his death on cross for my salvation.
His bursting from the spicèd tomb;
    his riding up the heavenly way;
His coming at the day of doom:
    I bind unto myself today.

I bind unto myself today
 the virtues of the star-lit heaven,
The glorious sun's lifegiving ray,
 the whiteness of the moon at even,
The flashing of the lightning free,
 the whirling wind's tempestuous shocks,
The stable earth, the deep salt sea
 around the old eternal rocks.

I bind unto myself today
 the power of God to hold and lead,
His eye to watch, his might to stay,
 his ear to hearken to my need;
The wisdom of my God to teach,
 his hand to guide, his shield to ward,
The word of God to give me speech,
 his heavenly host to be my guard.

Christ be with me, Christ within me,
 Christ behind me, Christ before me,
Christ beside me, Christ to win me,
 Christ to comfort and restore me,
Christ beneath me, Christ above me,
 Christ in quiet, Christ in danger,
Christ in hearts of all that love me,
 Christ in mouth of friend and stranger.

I bind unto myself the name,
 the strong name of the Trinity,
By invocation of the same,
 the Three in One, and One in Three,
Of whom all nature hath creation,
 eternal Father, Spirit, Word.
Praise to the Lord of my salvation:
 salvation is of Christ the Lord.

7 Song to the Lord God

James K. Baxter

Lord God, you are above and beyond all things,
Your nature is to love,
You put us in the furnace of the world
To learn to love you and love one another.

Father, we sing to you in the furnace
Like the three Jewish children.
The hope and the doom of the love of friends
Is eating up the marrow of our bones.

Lord Christ, you are the house in whom we live,
The house in which we share the cup of peace,
The house of your body that was broken on the cross,
The house you have built for us beyond the stars.

Lord, Holy Spirit, beyond, within, above,
Beneath all things, you give us life.
Blaze in our hearts, you who are Love himself,
Till we shine like the noonday sun.

Lord God, we are the little children,
The feeble ones of the world.
Carry us for ever in your breast, Lord God,
Give us the power by love to be your holy ones.

8 The Song of the Women

T. S. Eliot

We praise thee, O God, for thy glory displayed in all the
 creatures of the earth,
In the snow, in the rain, in the wind, in the storm; in all of
 thy creatures, both the hunters and the hunted.
For all things exist only as seen by thee, only as known by
 thee, all things exist
Only in thy light, and thy glory is declared even in that
 which denies thee; the darkness declares the glory of light.
Those who deny thee could not deny, if thou didst not
 exist; and their denial is never complete, for if it were so,
 they would not exist.

They affirm thee in living; all things affirm thee in living;
   the bird in the air, both the hawk and the finch; the beast
   on the earth, both the wolf and the lamb.
Therefore we, whom thou hast made to be conscious of
   thee, must consciously praise thee, in thought and in
   word and in deed.

Prayers

Lord have mercy.
   E te Ariki kia aroha mai.
      Kyrie eleison.

Christ have mercy.
   E te Karaiti kia aroha mai.
      Christe eleison.

Lord have mercy.
   E te Ariki kia aroha mai.
      Kyrie eleison.

One of the following three sections is said, ending with the **Collect for Midday**
and **The Lord's Prayer.**

1

O God of many names,
lover of all peoples;
we pray for peace
in our hearts and homes,
in our nations and our world;
the peace of your will,
the peace of our need.

Dear Christ, our friend and our guide,
pioneer through the shadow of death,
passing through darkness to make it light,
be our companion that we may fear no evil,
and bring us to life and to glory.

O God of peace and justice,
of holiness and love;
knit us together in mind and flesh,
in feeling and in spirit,
and make us one,
ready for that great day;
the fulfilment of all our hopes,
and the glory of Jesus Christ.

Keep us in the spirit of joy and simplicity and mercy.
Bless us and those you have entrusted to us,
in and through Jesus Christ our Saviour. Amen.

2

For the hungry and the overfed
May we have enough.

For the mourners and the mockers
May we laugh together.

For the victims and the oppressors
May we share power wisely.

For the peacemakers and the warmongers
May clear truth and stern love lead us to harmony.

For the silenced and the propagandists
May we speak our own words in truth.

For the unemployed and the overworked
May our impress on the earth be kindly and creative.

For the troubled and the sleek
May we live together as wounded healers.

For the homeless and the cosseted
May our homes be simple, warm and welcoming.

For the vibrant and the dying
May we all die to live.

3

Let us be at peace within ourselves.

Silence

Let us accept that we are profoundly loved
and need never be afraid.

Silence

Let us be aware of the source of being
that is common to us all
and to all living creatures.

Silence

Let us be filled with the presence of the great compassion
towards ourselves and towards all living beings.

Silence

Realising that we are all nourished
from the same source of life,
may we so live that others be not deprived
of air, food, water, shelter, or the chance to live.

Silence

Let us pray that we ourselves cease to be
a cause of suffering to one another.

Silence

With humility let us pray for the establishment
of peace in our hearts and on earth.

Silence

May God kindle in us
the fire of love
to bring us alive
and give warmth to the world.

**Lead me from death to life,
from falsehood to truth;
lead me from despair to hope,
from fear to trust;
lead me from hate to love,
from war to peace.
Let peace fill our heart,
our world, our universe.**

COLLECT FOR MIDDAY

Blessed Saviour, at this hour you hung upon the cross, stretching
out your loving arms; grant that all the peoples of the earth may
be drawn to your uplifted love; for your kingdom's sake.
Amen.

THE LORD'S PRAYER

Jesus, remember us in your kingdom and teach us to pray

**Our Father in heaven,
    hallowed be your name,
    your kingdom come,
    your will be done,
        on earth as in heaven.
Give us today our daily bread.
Forgive us our sins
    as we forgive those who sin against us.
Save us from the time of trial
    and deliver us from evil.**

**For the kingdom, the power, and the glory are yours
    now and for ever.   Amen.**

E te Ariki, maharatia mai matou i tou rangatiratanga;
Akona hoki matou ki te inoi

E to matou Matua i te rangi
   Kia tapu tou Ingoa.
   Kia tae mai tou rangatiratanga.
   Kia meatia tau e pai ai
      ki runga ki te whenua,
         kia rite ano ki to te rangi.
Homai ki a matou aianei
   he taro ma matou mo tenei ra.
Murua o matou hara,
      Me matou hoki e muru nei
         i o te hunga e hara ana ki a matou.
Aua hoki matou e kawea kia whakawaia;
   Engari whakaorangia matou i te kino:
Nou hoki te rangatiratanga, te kaha,
   me te kororia,
      Ake ake ake.   Amine.

Blessing

In the following a deacon or layperson says 'us' instead of 'you'.

May the Creator
bless you and keep you;
may the beloved companion face you
and have mercy upon you;
may the eternal Spirit's countenance
be turned to you and give you peace;
may the Three in One bless you.

Or

Kia koa koutou
Kia tino tika,
Kia marie te ngakau,
Kia kotahi te whakaaro,
Kia mau te rongo.
Tera te Atua o te aroha
O te maungarongo,
E noho ki a koutou.
Amine.

Silence

The service concludes

The divine Spirit dwells in us.
Kia noho te Wairua o te Runga Rawa ki a tatou.

Thanks be to God.
Whakamoemititia a Ihowa.

Night Prayer

The offering of prayer late in the evening, by laity, religious orders or clergy, often called Compline, has sometimes been described as the 'goodnight prayer of the Church'. It rounds off the day and prepares us for a quiet night. As the psalmist wrote:

> I lie down in peace and take my rest
> for it is in God alone that I dwell unafraid.

Night Prayer derives its content from the wisdom of the centuries in Scripture and above all in the psalms, but also from contemporary Christian experience of God. It celebrates the awareness that each of us who tries to pray is a part of the human whole. So we are taken over the threshold from daytime, not in a mood of self-centred spirituality, but as representatives of humanity, acknowledging our creaturehood before God.

This service may begin at the **Invocation**.

Approach

The angels of God guard us through the night,
and quieten the powers of darkness.

The Spirit of God be our guide
to lead us to peace and to glory.

It is but lost labour that we haste to rise up early,
and so late take rest, and eat the bread of anxiety.
For those beloved of God are given gifts even while they sleep.

Silence

E te whanau/My brothers and sisters,
our help is in the name of the eternal God,
who is making the heavens and the earth.

Dear God,
thank you for all that is good,
for our creation and our humanity,
for the stewardship you have given us of this planet earth,
for the gifts of life and of one another,
for your love which is unbounded and eternal.

O thou, most holy and belovèd,
my Companion, my Guide upon the way
taku whetu marama i te po / my bright evening star.

We repent the wrongs we have done:

Silence

We have wounded your love.
O God, heal us.

We stumble in the darkness.
Light of the world transfigure us.

We forget that we are your home.
Spirit of God, dwell in us.

Eternal Spirit, living God,
in whom we live and move and have our being,
all that we are, have been, and shall be is known to you,
to the very secret of our hearts
and all that rises to trouble us.
Living flame, burn into us,
cleansing wind, blow through us,
fountain of water, well up within us,
that we may love and praise in deed and in truth.

Invocation

Eternal Spirit,
flow through our being and open our lips,
that our mouths may proclaim your praise.

Let us worship the God of love.
Alleluia, alleluia.

Psalm

One of the following or some other psalm may be said.

Psalm 4

Answer me when I call, O God,
   for you are the God of justice.
 You set me free when I was hard-pressed:
   be gracious to me now and hear my prayers.

Men and women,
   how long will you turn my glory to my shame?
 How long will you love what is worthless and run after lies?

Know that God has shown me such wonderful kindness:
   when I call out in prayer, God hears me.

Tremble, admit defeat, and sin no more.
 Look deep into your heart before you sleep and be still.

Bring your gifts, just as you are, and put your trust in God.
 Many are asking, Who can make us content?

The light of your countenance has gone from us, O God.
 Yet you have given my heart more gladness
   than those whose corn and wine and oil increase.

I lie down in peace and sleep comes at once,
   for in you alone, O God, do I dwell unafraid.

Psalm 16

O God, I give you thanks for the wisdom of your counsel,
   even at night you have instructed my heart.

I have set your face always before me,
   you are at my right hand and I shall not fall.

Therefore my heart is glad and my spirit rejoices,
   my flesh also shall rest secure.

For you will not give me over to the power of death,
   nor let your faithful one see the Pit.

In your presence is the fulness of joy,
   and from your right hand flow delights for evermore.

Psalm 23

Dear God, you sustain me and feed me:
    like a shepherd you guide me.

You lead me to an oasis of green,
    to lie down by restful waters.

You refresh my soul for the journey,
    and guide me along trusted roads.

The God of justice is your name.
    Though I must enter the darkness of death,
        I will fear no evil.

For you are with me,
    your rod and staff comfort me.

You prepare a table before my very eyes,
    in the presence of those who trouble me.

You anoint my head with oil,
    and you fill my cup to the brim.

Your loving kindness and mercy will meet me
      every day of my life,
    and I will dwell in the house of my God for ever.

Psalm 31

O God, I have come to you for shelter:
    let me never be put to shame.

Deliver me in the justice of your ways:
    incline your ear to me and be swift to save me.

Be for me a rock of refuge, a fortress to defend me:
    for you are my rock and my stronghold.

Lead me and guide me for your name's sake:
    deliver me out of the net that they have laid secretly for me,
        for you are my strength.

Into your hands I commit my spirit,
    for you will redeem me, eternal God of truth.

Psalm 65

A Version for New Zealand

Praise is your due O God in the holy city;
   promises made to you shall be fulfilled;
      prayer you always listen to.

You accept all who come to you with shame;
   sin would overwhelm us, but you wash it away.

Blest is anyone you choose to live with you;
   your house is an inspiration, a hallowed place.

You spread your justice, God our Saviour,
   across the world to the farthest oceans.

You have laid down the mountain ranges and set them fast;
   you make the seas calm and the sounds peaceful;
      you reconcile the peoples who dwell here.

So in this corner of the earth we wonder at your deeds;
   at the meeting of east and west we sing your praise.

You water the land and make it flourish,
   from your own bursting river.

To provide our crops, you plough and irrigate the land,
      softening it with rain to make it fruitful;
   a record harvest is achieved, and the stores are overflowing.

The tussock land becomes pasture
      and the brown hills turn green;
   the paddocks are crowded with sheep
      and the plains thick with wheat:
   the world itself a canticle of praise.

Psalm 121

I will lift up my eyes to the mountains,
   but where shall I find help?

From you alone, O God, does my help come,
   creator of the ever changing hills.

You will not let me stumble on the rough pathways,
   you care for me and watch over me without ceasing.

I am sure that the Guardian of my people
    neither slumbers nor sleeps.
  The God of all nations keeps watch,
    like a shadow spread over me.
So the sun will not strike me by day,
  nor the moon by night.
You will defend me in the presence of evil,
  you will guard my life.
You will defend my going out and my coming in,
  this night and always.

Psalm 134

We your servants bless you, O God,
  as we stand by night in your house.
We lift up our hands towards the holy place,
  and give you thanks and praise.
Bless us from all places where you dwell,
  O God, creator of the heavens and the earth.

Reading

One of the following or some other passage of scripture is read.

Silence may follow the reading.

Sunday

God has not given us a spirit of fear, but of power, and of love,
and of a sound mind.
                                          2 Timothy 1:7

Monday

You Lord are in the midst of us, and we are called by your name.
Leave us not.
                                          Jeremiah 14:9

Tuesday

Love your enemies. Do good to those who hate you. Bless those who curse you. Pray for those who abuse you. Do good and lend, expecting nothing in return; for God is kind to the ungrateful and the selfish.

Be merciful as your Father is merciful. Judge not and you will not be judged. Condemn not and you will not be condemned. Forgive and you will be forgiven.

Give, and it will be given to you; for the measure you give will be the measure you receive.

From Luke 6: 27-38

Wednesday

Do not ask anxiously, What are we to eat? What are we to drink? What shall we wear? The whole world runs after such things. Set your heart and mind on God's commonwealth and justice first, and all the rest will come to you as well. So do not be anxious about tomorrow. Today has enough problems of its own; tomorrow can look after itself.

Matthew 6: 31-34

Thursday

There is no fear in love, but perfect love casts out fear. For fear has to do with punishment, and those who are afraid are not perfected in love. We love because God first loved us. If anyone says, I love God, and hates a brother or sister, that person is a liar; for those who do not love their brothers and sisters whom they have seen, cannot love God whom they have not seen.

1 John 4: 18-20

Friday

It is the God who said, Let light shine out of darkness, who has shone in our hearts to give the light of the knowledge of the glory of God in the face of Jesus Christ. But we have this treasure in earthen vessels, to show that the transcendent power belongs to God and not to us. We are afflicted in every way, but not crushed;

perplexed, but not driven to despair; persecuted, but not forsaken; struck down, but not destroyed; always carrying in the body the death of Jesus, so that the life of Jesus may also be manifested in our body.

2 Corinthians 4: 6-10

Saturday

According to the riches of God's glory, may you be strengthened with might through the Holy Spirit in your inner being, and may Christ dwell in your hearts through faith; that you, being rooted and grounded in love, may have power to comprehend, with all the saints, what is the breadth and length and height and depth, and to know the love of Christ which surpasses knowledge; that you may be filled with all the fulness of God.

Ephesians 3: 16-19

Hymn

One of the following or some other hymn may be sung.

1

1 Tama ngakau marie,
Tama a t'Atua,
Tenei tonu matou,
Arohaina mai.

2 Murua ra nga hara:
Wetekina mai
Enei here kino,
Whakararu nei.

3 Takahia ki raro,
Tau e kino ai;
Kei pa kaha tonu
Ko nga mahi he.

4 Homai he aroha
Mou i mate nei.
Tenei ra, e Ihu,
Takina e koe;

5 Tenei arahina
A tutuki noa:
Puta i te pouri,
Whiwhi hari nui.

6 Tama ngakau marie,
Tama a t'Atua,
Tenei tonu matou,
Arohaina mai. Amine.

2

Hail, gladdening Light, of God's pure glory poured,
Who is the immortal Father, heavenly, blest,
Holiest of holies, Jesus Christ our Lord.

Now we are come to the sun's hour of rest,
The lights of evening round us shine,
We hymn the Father, Son, and Holy Spirit divine.

Worthiest art thou at all times to be sung,
With undefilèd tongue,
Son of our God, Giver of life, alone!
Therefore in all the world thy glories, Lord, they own.

3

Glory to you, my God, this night,
For all the blessings of the light,
To you, from whom all good does come,
Our life, our health, our lasting home.

Teach me to live, that I may dread
The grave as little as my bed,
Teach me to die, that so I may
Rise glorious at the aweful day.

O may I now on you repose,
And may kind sleep my eyelids close,
Sleep that may me more vigorous make
To serve my God when I awake.

If I lie restless on my bed,
Your word of healing peace be said,
If powerful dreams rise in the night,
Transform their darkness into light.

All praise to God, sustaining us,
Redeeming and transfiguring us,
Thanksgiving in eternity,
All praise, belovèd Trinity.

4

Before the ending of the day,
Creator of the world we pray,
that you, with love and lasting light,
would guard us through the hours of night.

From all ill dreams defend our eyes,
from nightly fears and fantasies;
redeem through us our evil foe,
that we no lasting harm may know.

O wisest Guide, grant all we ask,
fulfil in us your holy task,
surround us with your love and care,
and lead us on, your life to share.

All praise to God, sustaining us,
redeeming and transforming us,
thanksgiving in eternity,
all praise, belovèd Trinity.

5

Be thou my vision, O Christ of my heart,
Be all else but naught to me save that thou art,
Be thou my best thought in the day and the night,
Both waking and sleeping, thy presence my light.

Riches I heed not, nor folk's empty praise,
Be thou my inheritance now and always,
Be thou and thou only the first in my heart,
O Sovereign of heaven, my treasure thou art.

6

Be still and know that I am God.
Be still and know that I am God.
Be still and know that I am God.

I am the God that healeth thee.
I am the God that healeth thee.
I am the God that healeth thee.

In thee, O God, I put my trust.
In thee, O God, I put my trust.
In thee, O God, I put my trust.

7

Ma te marie a te Atua
Tatou katoa e tiaki;
Mana ano e whakau
O tatou ngakau ki te pai.

Ma te Atua Tamaiti ra,
Ma te Wairua Tapu hoki,
Ratou, Atua kotahi nei.
Tatou katoa e whakapai.   Amine.

8

God that madest earth and heaven,
    Darkness and light;
Who the day for toil hast given,
    For rest the night;
May thine angel guards defend us,
Slumber sweet thy mercy send us,
Holy dreams and hopes attend us,
    This livelong night.

Guard us waking, guard us sleeping,
    And, when we die,
May we in thy mighty keeping
    All peaceful lie:
When the last dread call shall wake us,
Do not thou our God forsake us,
But to reign in glory take us
    With thee on high.

9

God be in my head, and in my understanding;
God be in my eyes, and in my looking;
God be in my mouth, and in my speaking;
God be in my heart, and in my thinking;
God be at my end, and at my departing.

Prayers

Into your hands, O God, I commend my spirit,
    Toku wairua ki ou ringaringa, e te Atua,
for you have redeemed me, O God of truth and love.
    nau nei ahau i hoko, e te Atua o te pono, o te aroha.

Keep me, O God, as the apple of an eye;
    Ko koe hei totara whakamarumaru moku;
hide me under the shadow of your wings.
    huna ahau ki raro i ou parirau.

One of the following antiphons is said together, before the **Nunc Dimittis.**

Alleluia. The Lamb who was slain has conquered. Alleluia.
All who follow the Way will share in the victory. Alleluia,
alleluia.

Preserve us, O God, while waking,
and guard us while sleeping,
that awake we may watch with Christ,
and asleep may rest in your peace.

Song of Simeon

Nunc Dimittis

Praise be to God, I have lived to see this day.
God's promise is fulfilled, and my duty done.

At last you have given me peace,
for I have seen with my own eyes
the salvation you have prepared for all nations -
a light to the world in its darkness,
and the glory of your people Israel.

Glory be to God, sustaining, redeeming, sanctifying,
as in the beginning, so now, and for ever.
Amen.

The antiphon may be repeated.

Lord, have mercy.
    E te Ariki kia aroha mai.
        Kyrie eleison.

Christ, have mercy.
    E te Karaiti kia aroha mai.
        Christe eleison.

Lord, have mercy.
　　　E te Ariki kia aroha mai.
　　　　Kyrie eleison.

The Lord's Prayer *or* **the alternative** *is said.*

Our Father in heaven,
　　hallowed be your name,
　　your kingdom come,
　　your will be done,
　　　on earth as in heaven.
Give us today our daily bread.
Forgive us our sins
　　as we forgive those who sin against us.
Save us from the time of trial
　　and deliver us from evil.

For the kingdom, the power, and the glory are yours
　　now and for ever. Amen.

E to matou Matua i te rangi
　　Kia tapu tou Ingoa.
　　Kia tae mai tou rangatiratanga.
　　Kia meatia tau e pai ai
　　　ki runga ki te whenua,
　　　　kia rite ano ki to te rangi.
Homai ki a matou aianei
　　he taro ma matou mo tenei ra.
Murua o matou hara,
　　Me matou hoki e muru nei
　　　i o te hunga e hara ana ki a matou.
Aua hoki matou e kawea kia whakawaia;
　　Engari whakaorangia matou i te kino:
Nou hoki te rangatiratanga, te kaha,
　　me te kororia,
　　　Ake ake ake. Amine.

Or

Eternal Spirit,
Earth-maker, Pain-bearer, Life-giver,
Source of all that is and that shall be,
Father and Mother of us all,
Loving God, in whom is heaven:

The hallowing of your name echo through the universe!
The way of your justice be followed by the peoples
    of the world!
Your heavenly will be done by all created beings!
Your commonwealth of peace and freedom
    sustain our hope and come on earth.

With the bread we need for today, feed us.
In the hurts we absorb from one another, forgive us.
In times of temptation and test, strengthen us.
From trials too great to endure, spare us.
From the grip of all that is evil, free us.

For you reign in the glory of the power that is love,
    now and for ever. Amen.

The minister and people pray responsively.

I will lie down in peace and take my rest,
    Ka takoto ahau, ka whakata,
for it is in God alone that I dwell unafraid.
    i roto i te Atua e kore ahau e wehi.

Let us bless the Earth-maker, the Pain-bearer, the Life-giver,
    Tatou ka whakapai i te Kai-hanga, i te Kai-whakamarie,
        i te Kai-homai i te ora,
let us praise and exalt God above all for ever.
    tatou ka whakapai, ka whakanui i te Atua mo ake tonu atu.

May God's name be praised beyond the furthest star,
    Whakanuia te ingoa o te Atua ki nga Tuarangi,
glorified and exalted above all for ever.
    whakapaingia, whakamoemititia mo ake tonu atu.

*One or more of the following is said, concluding with the **Sentence of the Day** and **Final Versicle.***

1 A General Thanksgiving

Eternal God, compassionate and merciful,
we your unworthy servants give you humble thanks
for all your goodness and loving kindness
   to us and to all people.
We bless you for our creation, preservation,
   and all the blessings of this life;
but above all for your boundless love
   in the redemption of the world by our Saviour Jesus Christ;
   for the means of grace, and for the hope of glory.
And, we pray, give us that due sense of all your mercies,
that our hearts may be truly thankful,
and that we praise you, not only with our lips but in our lives,
   by giving ourselves to your service
   and by walking before you in holiness and righteousness
   all our days;
through Jesus Christ our Redeemer,
to whom, with you and the Holy Spirit, be all honour and glory,
now and for ever.
Amen.

2

O living God, in Jesus Christ you were laid in the tomb at this evening hour, and so sanctified the grave to be a bed of hope to your people. Give us courage and faith to die daily to our sin and pride, that even as this flesh and blood decays, our lives still may grow in you, that at our last day our dying may be done so well that we live in you for ever.
Amen.

3

Be present, Spirit of God,
within us, your dwelling place and home,
that this house may be one where
all darkness is penetrated by your light,
all troubles calmed by your peace,
all evil redeemed by your love,
all pain transformed in your suffering,
and all dying glorified in your risen life. Amen.

4

God our Creator, our centre, our friend,
we thank you for our good life,
for those who are dear to us,
for our dead, and for all who have helped and influenced us.
We thank you for the measure of freedom we have,
and the extent to which we control our lives;
and most of all we thank you for the faith that is in us,
for our awareness of you and our hope in you.
Keep us, we pray you, thankful and hopeful
and useful until our lives shall end.
Amen.

5

Ma te Atua o te tumanako,
e whakau o koutou ngakau
ki te koa, ki te rangimarie
kia pono ai koutou,
i runga i te ihi, i te mana,
o te Wairua Tapu.
Amine.

6

Lord,
it is night.

The night is for stillness.
    Let us be still in the presence of God.

It is night after a long day.
    What has been done has been done;
    what has not been done has not been done;
    let it be.

The night is dark.
    Let our fears of the darkness of the world and of our own lives
    rest in you.

The night is quiet.
    Let the quietness of your peace enfold us,
        all dear to us,
        and all who have no peace.

The night heralds the dawn.
    Let us look expectantly to a new day,
        new joys,
        new possibilities.

In your name we pray.
Amen.

Sentence of the Day

SUNDAY

O God of love and mercy,
grant us, with all your people, rest and peace.

MONDAY

God bless us and keep us,
God's face shine on us and be gracious to us,
and give us light and peace.

TUESDAY

To God the Creator,
who loved us first and gave this world to be our home,
to God the Redeemer,
who loves us and by dying and rising
pioneered the way of freedom,
to God the Sanctifier,
who spreads the divine love in our hearts,
be praise and glory for time and for eternity.

WEDNESDAY

O God,
strengthen your servants with your heavenly grace,
that we may continue yours for ever,
and daily increase in your Holy Spirit more and more,
until we come to your everlasting kingdom.

Christ be within us to keep us,
   beside us to guard,
   before us to lead,
   behind us to protect,
   beneath us to support,
   above us to bless.

The blessing of God, the eternal goodwill of God, the shalom of God, the wildness and the warmth of God, be among us and between us, now and always.

Blessing, light, and glory surround us
and scatter the darkness of the long and lonely night.

Final Versicle

The service concludes

The divine Spirit dwells in us.
   Kia noho te Wairua o te Runga Rawa ki a tatou.

Thanks be to God.
   Whakamoemititia a Ihowa.

Family Prayer

Praying together as a family is a simple but effective way of bringing God into our home life, and it can be the most unifying activity a family does together.

It is best to make a time when the family is normally together, for example at a regular meal time. We need to be quite informal in taking this service, which only lasts three to five minutes, and prepared to accept the disturbances that sometimes arise. It may be helpful to have various members of the family taking turns in leading parts of the service.

*The Bible Reading may be one of those set down for the preceding Sunday and found in the **Sentences, Prayers and Readings**, pages 549-641, or may follow some other course.*

In the Prayers it is good to mention the activities of each one in the family, and the needs of others as well. Useful prayers may be found among the collects for the various daily services and also among the collects for the Eucharist.

*It may be helpful to use parts of **The Blessing of a Home: The Family Liturgy**, **A Householder's Prayer** and **A Blessing of Peace** (pages 771-773).*

Over the years there will be a need to be flexible in adapting this pattern to changing family circumstances, but it is worth persevering.

Praise

One of the following may be read.

1   In the name of God the Father, and of the Son,
    and of the Holy Spirit.
    Amen.

2   Glory to the Father, and to the Son,
    and to the Holy Spirit:
    as it was in the beginning, is now,
    and shall be for ever.
    Amen.

3   God is love. Since God loves us, we should love one another.

4   Holy, holy, holy Lord, God of power and might,
    heaven and earth are full of your glory.
    Hosanna in the highest.

5   This is the day which the Lord has made.
    Let us rejoice and be glad in it.

6   Amen! Praise and glory and wisdom,
    thanksgiving and honour, power and might,
    be to our God for ever and ever!
    Amen.

Bible Reading

This may be introduced by one of the following.

1   Jesus said, 'Ask, and you will receive; seek, and you will find;
    knock, and the door will be opened.'   *Matthew 7:7*

2   Turn for help to the Lord your strength:
    and constantly seek God's presence.
    Remember the marvellous things the Most High has done:
    the wonders, and the judgments God has given.   *Psalm 105:4-5*

Prayers

One or more of the following may be used.

MORNING PRAYERS

Father, we thank you for bringing us to the beginning of another day. Help us through your Holy Spirit, so that we may not fall into sin, but may do everything that pleases you, through Jesus Christ our Lord.
Amen.

With Young Children
Loving God, thank you for this new day.
Thank you for your love and care for us.
Thank you for making each of us special.
Help us today to be kind to each other.
Amen.

EVENING PRAYERS

We thank you, Lord Jesus, for the day you have given us, and for all the pleasure we have had. Guard us while we sleep, and bless all those we love, this night and for ever.
Amen.

With Young Children
Dear God, thank you for today.
We are sorry if we have been unkind to anyone.
Help us to forgive each other.
Thank you for our family and for our friends.
Please be with us tonight.
Amen.

A PRAYER FOR FORGIVENESS

God of mercy, we are sorry that we have not always done what you wanted us to do. We have not loved you with all our heart, and we have not cared enough for other people. Forgive us, for Jesus' sake.
Amen.

A PRAYER FOR THE FAMILY

Lord Jesus, at Nazareth you shared in the life of your family. Help us to live together in our family with love and respect for each other. Make our home a place of blessing, peace and joy for everyone, to the glory of God the Father.
Amen.

A COLLECT

In darkness and in light,
in trouble and in joy,
help us, heavenly Father,
to trust your love,
to serve your purpose,
and to praise your name,
through Jesus Christ our Lord.
Amen.

A PRAYER FOR GOD'S LIGHT

Eternal God, shed your light on us who watch for you,
that our lips may praise you,
our hearts bless you,
and our lives glorify you,
through Jesus Christ our Saviour.
Amen.

Personal prayers may follow.

The Lord's Prayer

Our Father in heaven,
  hallowed be your name,
  your kingdom come,
  your will be done,
    on earth as in heaven.
Give us today our daily bread.
Forgive us our sins
  as we forgive those who sin against us.
Save us from the time of trial
  and deliver us from evil.

For the kingdom, the power, and the glory are yours
  now and for ever.   Amen.

E to matou Matua i te rangi
  Kia tapu tou Ingoa.
  Kia tae mai tou rangatiratanga.
  Kia meatia tau e pai ai
    ki runga ki te whenua,
      kia rite ano ki to te rangi.
Homai ki a matou aianei
  he taro ma matou mo tenei ra.
Murua o matou hara,
    Me matou hoki e muru nei
      i o te hunga e hara ana ki a matou.
Aua hoki matou e kawea kia whakawaia;
  Engari whakaorangia matou i te kino:
Nou hoki te rangatiratanga, te kaha,
  me te kororia,
    Ake ake ake.   Amine.

The Grace

The grace of our Lord Jesus Christ,
and the love of God,
and the fellowship of the Holy Spirit
be with us all.
Amen.

Psalms for Worship

Concerning Psalms for Worship

A collection of poems and songs that grew out of the life and experience of the people of ancient Israel, the psalms have been treasured as a source of spirituality and devotion since long before the time of Jesus.

Jesus himself knew the psalms, and used them. The Christian Church has continued throughout its history to use them in public worship and private devotions.

The wide appeal of the psalms rests on their ability to give words to some of our deepest feelings in the face of life's experiences. Whether for joy, worship and exaltation, or degradation and rejection, or hope, faith, love, anger, or despair, the psalms contain verses that reflect such moods. In them the various writers expressed to God the thoughts of their heart and spirit. The richness of the psalms still speaks to us and in them we too can find words to match many of our moods and express them before God. In turn God can still address us through these psalms.

The psalms can be used in a number of ways. So valued are they as a spiritual resource that many Christians over the centuries have recited them in a regular pattern as part of their daily worship. Equally we can browse through them in a less formal way. Many phrases and verses have been used to give expression to worship in the services of the Church.

*In order to make the collection of psalms as widely appreciated now as possible, several changes have been made in this version. The text has been checked with modern translations and commentaries, and corrected to ensure accuracy. Attention has been paid to contemporary English to ensure that as far as possible all those using these **Psalms for Worship** may identify with the psalmist's expressions of prayer or praise.*

Some omissions have been made on the grounds that we are not making a new translation of the Book of Psalms, but providing psalms suitable for Christian worship. Some verses of the psalms are not suitable for use in the corporate worship of the Church.

The passages omitted are:

18:38-43;	*21:8-12;*	*28:4,5;*	*35:4-8;*	*54:5,7;*
55:16;	*58 in toto;*	*59:5,11-13;*	*68:21-23;*	*69:24-30;*
79:10,12;	*83 in toto;*	*101:6,9;*	*106:34;*	*109:5-19;*
110:5-7;	*137:7-9;*	*139:19-22;*	*140:9-11;*	*141:7,8;*
143:13;	*149:7-9.*			

The recital of the psalms, whether said or sung, can enhance public worship. There are various ways of saying the psalms corporately:

by minister and congregation saying the psalm together;

by alternate verses (the minister reading a verse, and the congregation responding with the next verse);

antiphonally (when the congregation divides into parts, and each in turn reads every alternate verse);

by use of a repeated refrain after each two or three verses, the refrain being some key verse of the psalm itself (e.g. verses 3 and 5 of Psalm 67, or 7 and 11 of Psalm 46);

or the psalms may be sung.

When the psalms are sung to Anglican chant (as pointed in this version) the following conventions apply:

(a)   Breath is to be taken at the end of lines, except where the sign ⌣ indicates a 'carry-over'.

(b)   The inverted dot (·) is used to indicate how the syllables are to be divided between the notes of the bar when there are more than two syllables between the bar-marks (').

(c)   An obelus (†) indicates that the second half of a double chant is to be sung to the verse.

(d)   A double space between verses, and the division of some psalms into parts indicates sections of psalms that may be used independently, or that a change of chant may be appropriate.

(e)   The final 'ed' should be pronounced as a separate syllable when it is marked with an accent (e.g. blessèd).

The Gloria, in one of the following forms, is usually said or sung at the end of each psalm.

The Gloria

Glory to the Father and ' to the ' Son:
    and ' to the ' Holy ' Spirit;
as it was in the be'ginning · is ' now:
    and shall be for ' ever. ' A'men.

Or

Kia whakakororiatia te Matua, te Tama:
    me te Wairua Tapu;
ko te ritenga ia i te timatanga, a tenei ano inaianei:
    a ka mau tonu iho, a ake ake ake. Amine.

Or

Kororia ki a koe, e te Ariki.

Or

Kororia ki te Matua, ki te Tama,
    ki te Wairua Tapu;
mai i te timatanga, ki tenei wa,
    a, haere ake nei. Amine.

Psalms for Worship

1

1   Blessèd are those⌣
    who do not follow the ' counsel · of the ' wicked:
  or linger in the way of sinners,
    or sit down a'mong ' those who ' mock.

2   But their delight is in the ' law · of the ' Lord:
  and on that law they ' medi·tate ' day and ' night.

3   They are like trees planted be'side a ' watercourse:
  which yield their ' fruit in ' due ' season.

4   Their leaves also ' do not ' wither:
  and look, what'ever · they ' do · it shall ' prosper.

5   As for the wicked, it is not ' so with ' them:
  but they are like the chaff,
    which is ' driven · a'way · by the ' wind.

6   Therefore the wicked shall not be able to stand⌣
    when ' judgment ' comes:
  nor sinners in the as'sembly ' of the ' righteous.

7† For the Lord watches over⌣
    the ' way · of the ' righteous:
  but the ' way · of the ' wicked · is ' doomed.

2

1   Why are the ' nations · in ' turmoil:
  and why are the peoples⌣
    en'gaged in ' futile ' plotting?

2   The kings of the earth arise,
    and the rulers take ' counsel · to'gether:
  against the Lord and against the ' Lord's an'ointed ' king.

3† 'Let us break their ' fetters,' · they ' say:
  'and let us ' cast ' off their ' chains.'

4   The one whose throne is in heaven'⌣
      laughs them · to ' scorn:
     the Lord ' has them ' in de'rision.

5   Then you speak to them ' in your ' wrath:
     and ' terrify · them ' in your ' fury.

6†   'I myself have set ' up my ' king:
     up'on my ' holy ' hill.'

7   I will recite the de'cree · of the ' Lord:
     who has said to me, 'You are my son,
      today have ' I be'come your ' father.

8   'Ask, and I will give you the nations⌣
      for ' your in'heritance:
     and the ends of the ' earth for ' your pos'session.

9   'You shall crush them with a ' rod of ' iron:
     and break them in pieces ' like a ' potter's ' vessel.'

10   Now therefore you ' kings be ' wise:
     be prudent, you ' rulers ' of the ' earth.

11   Serve the ' Lord with ' fear:
     and with trembling bow down be'fore the ' Most ' High,

12   lest the Lord be angry, and you perish,
      for God's anger is ' quickly ' kindled:
     blessèd are all who ' put their ' trust · in the ' Lord.

3

1   Lord, how my ' enemies · have ' multiplied:
     how many there are who ' rise ' up a'gainst me.

2   Many there are who ' say a'bout me:
     that there is no ' help · for me ' in my ' God.

3   But you Lord are a ' shield to ' cover me:
     you are my glory,
      and the ' lifter ' up · of my ' head.

4   I cry aloud to ' you O ' Lord:
     and you answer me ' from your ' holy ' hill.

5   I lie ' down and ' sleep:
        I wake up again ' for the ' Lord sus'tains me.

6   I will not be afraid of ten thousands ' of the ' people:
        who have set themselves a'gainst me · on ' every ' side.

7   Rise up Lord, and help me ' O my ' God:
        for you strike all my enemies across the face,
           and ' break the ' teeth · of the ' wicked.

8   Victory be'longs · to the ' Lord:
        your blessing Lord ' be up'on your ' people.

4

1   Answer me when I call,
        O God, the defender ' of my ' cause:
    You set me free when I was in distress,
        be gracious to me ' now and ' hear my ' prayer.

2   How long, O mortals, will you de'fame my ' honour:
        how long will you love⌣
        what is worthless and ' seek ' after ' lies?

3   Know this, that the Lord has chosen '⌣
        those · who are ' righteous:
        the Lord ' hears me ' when I ' call.

4   Stand in awe, and ' cease from ' sin:
        commune with your own heart⌣
        up'on your ' bed · and be ' still.

5   Offer the sacrifices that ' are ap'pointed:
        and ' put your ' trust · in the ' Lord.

6   There are many who say,
        'O that we might ' see pros'perity:
        lift up the light of your ' face on ' us O ' Lord.'

7   But you have put gladness ' in my ' heart:
        more than they have⌣
        when corn and ' wine ' are in ' plenty.

8   I lie down in peace, and sleep ' comes at ' once:
        for O Lord, it is you only⌣
        who ' make me ' dwell in ' safety.

5

1   Listen to my ' words O ' Lord:
       give heed to the ' sound ' of my ' groaning.

2   Hear my cry for help, my ' king · and my ' God:
       for to ' you · I di'rect my ' prayer.

3   In the morning Lord you ' hear my ' voice:
       early in the morning I make my plea,
         and look ' up to ' you · for an ' answer.

4   For you are not a God who takes '⌣
       pleasure · in ' wickedness:
       no one who is ' evil · can ' be your ' guest.

5   The boastful may not ' stand in · your ' sight:
       you hate all ' those who ' work ' mischief.

6   You destroy all those who ' speak ' lies:
       the bloodthirsty and treacherous O ' Lord ' you ab'hor.

7   But I, through the abundance of your steadfast love,
       will come ' into · your ' house:
       and bow low in reverence to'ward your ' holy ' temple.

8   Lead me O Lord in your righteousness,
       be'cause of · my ' enemies:
       make straight your ' way be'fore my ' face.

9   There is no truth ' in their ' mouth:
       and there is de'struction ' in their ' heart.

10   Their throat is an ' open ' grave:
       they ' flatter ' with their ' tongue.

11   Give judgment against them O God,
       let them perish through their ' own de'vices:
       cast them out because of their many transgressions,
         for ' they have · re'belled a'gainst you.

12   But let all who put their trust in ' you re'joice:
       let them ever give thanks because you defend them,
         those who love your name ' shall be ' joyful · in ' you.

13†   For you Lord will give your blessing ' to the ' righteous:
       and with your favour⌣
         you will de'fend them ' as · with a ' shield.

6

1   Lord, do not rebuke me ' in your ' anger:
     do not ' punish · me ' in your ' wrath.

2   Be merciful to me O Lord, for ' I am ' weak:
     O Lord heal me, for my ' bones are ' racked with ' pain.

3   My soul also is shaken ' with dis'may:
     how ' long O ' Lord · will you ' punish me?

4   Turn O ' Lord · and de'liver me:
     O save me ' for your ' mercy's ' sake.

5   For in death ' no one · re'members you:
     and who will ' give you ' thanks · in the ' grave?

6   I am wearied ' with my ' groaning:
     every night I weep upon my bed,
       and ' drench my ' couch · with my ' tears.

7   My eyes have become dim ' through my ' grief:
     and worn ' out with ' all my ' troubles.

8   Away from me, all ' you that · do ' evil:
     for the Lord has ' heard the ' sound · of my ' weeping.

9   The Lord has ' heard · my en'treaty:
     the ' Lord · will re'ceive my ' prayer.

10   All my enemies shall be confounded‿
     and ' greatly · dis'mayed:
     they shall turn back,
     and be ' put to ' sudden · con'fusion.

7

1   O Lord my God, in you I ' take ' refuge:
     save me from all my pur'suers ' and de'liver me,

2   lest like a lion, they ' tear me · to ' pieces:
     dragging me a'way with ' no one · to ' rescue me.

3   O Lord my God, if I have done ' any · such ' thing:
     if there is any ' wicked·ness ' on my ' hands,

4   if I have done harm to one who ' was my ' friend:
     or plundered my ' enemy · with'out · any ' cause,

5† then let my enemies pur'sue me · and ' take me:
    indeed let them trample my life to the ground,
       and lay my ' soul ' in the ' dust.

6   Arise O Lord in your anger,
    rise up against the fury ' of my ' enemies:
    awake O my God,
       for ' you · have de'manded ' judgment.

7   Let the people be as'sembled · a'round you:
    and take your seat on high above them,
       O ' Lord the ' judge · of the ' nations.

8   Give judgment for me O Lord,
    according ' to my ' righteousness:
    and ac'cording · to my ' soul's in'tegrity.

9   O let the evil of the wicked ' come · to an ' end:
    but up'hold the ' cause · of the ' just.

10† For you O ' God are ' righteous:
    you search the very ' secrets ' of the ' heart.

11 You are my ' shield and · de'fence:
    you preserve ' those · who are ' true of ' heart.

12 You are a ' righteous ' judge:
    one who is moved to indig'nation ' every ' day.

13 If people will not repent, you ' sharpen · your ' sword:
    you bend your ' bow and ' make it ' ready.

14 You have prepared your ' deadly ' weapons:
    and ' tipped your ' arrows · with ' fire.

15 Look at those who are in ' labour · with ' mischief:
    they conceive ' wickedness · and ' bring forth ' lies.

16 They have made a pit and ' dug it ' out:
    but will fall themselves＿
       into the ' trap they ' made for ' others.

17 For their mischief shall recoil up'on them'selves:
    and their violence descend ' on their ' own ' head.

18 I will give thanks to the Lord＿
    for giving ' righteous ' judgment:
    and I will praise the ' name · of the ' Lord most ' high.

8

1   O Lord our God,
       how glorious is your name in ' all the ' earth:
     from the lips of infants and children,
       your praises reach ' up ' to the ' heavens.

2   You have set up a stronghold⌣
       a'gainst your ' adversaries:
     to quell the ' ene·my ' and · the a'venger.

3   When I look up at the heavens,
       the ' work · of your ' fingers:
     the moon and the ⌣
       stars you have ' set ' in their ' places,

4   what are we mortals, that you should be ' mindful · of ' us:
     mere human beings that ' you should ' care for ' us?

5   You have made us little ' less · than di'vine:
     and ' crowned · us with ' glory · and ' honour.

6   You made us rulers over ' all · your cre'ation:
     and put all things in sub'jection ' under · our ' feet,

7   all ' sheep and ' cattle:
     and all the ' creatures ' of the ' wild,

8   the birds of the air and the ' fish · in the ' sea:
     and all that make their ' way ' through the ' waters.

9†   O ' Lord our ' God:
     how glorious is your ' name in ' all the ' earth.

9

Day 2 Morning

PART ONE

1   I will give thanks to you O Lord with ' all my ' heart:
     I will speak of ' all your ' marvel·lous ' deeds.

2   I will be glad and re'joice in ' you:
     my songs I will make to your '⌣
       name O ' God most ' high,

3   for my enemies are ' driven ' back:
        they ' stumble · and ' perish · be'fore you.

4   You have upheld the justice ' of my ' cause:
        seated on your throne
            you have ' given ' righteous ' judgment.

5   You have rebuked the nations‿
        and de'stroyed the ' wicked:
        you have blotted out‿
            their ' name for ' ever · and ' ever.

6   The enemy have perished,
        you have made their cities a ' deso'lation:
    even the ' memory · of ' them has ' vanished.

7   You O Lord sit en'throned for ' ever:
    you have set ' up your ' seat for ' judgment.

8   You will judge the ' world with ' righteousness:
    and mete out true ' justice ' to the ' peoples.

9   The Lord also is a stronghold ' for · the op'pressed:
    a tower of ' strength in ' time of ' trouble.

10   Those who cherish your name‿
         will put their ' trust in ' you:
    for you Lord‿
        have never ' failed ' those who ' seek you.

PART TWO

11   Sing praise to the Lord who dwells ' in Je'rusalem:
    proclaim to the peoples the ' things that ' God has ' done.

12   For the one who avenges ' blood · has re'membered:
    and has not forgotten the ' cry ' of the ' poor.

13   Have pity on me Lord,
        consider the trouble I suffer‿
        from ' those who ' hate me:
    you that lift me up ' from the ' gates of ' death,

14   so that I may recount all your praises‿
        within the ' gates · of the ' city:
    and rejoice ' in your ' saving ' help.

15 The nations have fallen into a pit of their ' own ' making:
    in the net they laid in secret‿
        their own ' feet ' are en'tangled.

16 You have made yourself known O Lord,
        and ' given ' judgment:
    the wicked are trapped‿
        in the ' work · of their ' own ' hands.

17 The wicked go down ' to the ' dead:
    all the nations ' that are ' heedless · of ' God.

18 The needy shall not always ' be for'gotten:
    the hope of the poor shall ' not for ' ever · be ' vain.

19 Rise up Lord, let not mere ' mortals · pre'vail:
    let the ' nations · be ' judged be'fore you.

20 Strike them with ' fear O ' Lord:
    let the nations ' know · that they ' are but ' human.

10

1 Why do you stand so far ' off O ' Lord:
    and hide your face in ' time of ' need and ' trouble?

2 The wicked in their pride hunt ' down the ' poor:
    let them be snared ' by their ' own de'vices.

3 The wicked boast of their ' heart's de'sire:
    the covetous have the Lord in contempt,
        and blaspheme the ' name ' of the ' Lord.

4 In their pride they care ' nothing · for ' God:
    they say in their heart that ' there is ' no ' God.

5 They prosper in ' all their ' ways:
    your judgments Lord are far above out of their sight,
        all their ' enemies · they ' hold · in con'tempt.

6 They say in their heart, 'I shall ' never · be ' shaken:
    there shall ' no harm ' happen · to ' me.'

7 Their mouth is full of cursing, de'ceit and ' fraud:
    under their ' tongue are ' mischief · and ' wrong.

8   They lie in ambush ' in the ' villages:
      · and in secret they murder the innocent,
          stealthily they ' watch ' for the ' helpless.

9   They lie in hiding, as a lion ' lurks · in its ' den:
      they lie ' waiting · to ' seize their ' prey.

10   They ' seize the ' poor:
      and ' drag them ' off · in their ' net.

11   The innocent are crushed,
        and sink ' down be'fore them:
      the weak cannot ' stand a'gainst their ' might.

12   They say in their heart, ' 'God · has for'gotten:
      God has looked away ' and will ' never ' see it.'

13   Arise O Lord God, and lift ' up your ' hand:
      do not forget the ' poor ' in their ' need.

14   Why should the wicked make ' light of ' God:
      and say in their hearts,
        'God will not ' call us ' to ac'count'?

15   Surely you have seen it,
        for you take note of ' trouble · and ' sorrow:
      so that you may take the ' matter ' into · your ' hand.

16   The poor commit them'selves to ' you:
      for you are the ' helper ' of the ' orphaned.

17†   Break the power of the wicked ' and ma'licious:
      search out their wickedness,
        till ' nothing · is ' left · unre'vealed.

18   The Lord shall reign for ' ever · and ' ever:
      the heathen shall ' perish ' out of · the ' land.

19   Lord you have heard the lament ' of the ' poor:
      you will strengthen their heart,
        and ' you · will in'cline your ' ear,

20†   to do justice to the orphaned ' and · the op'pressed:
      so that no one on earth‿
        may ' any · more ' cause them ' terror.

11

1   In the Lord I have ' taken ' refuge:
    how then can you say to me,
      'Flee like a ' bird ' to the ' mountains.

2   'See how the wicked are bending their bow,
    and fitting their arrow ' to the ' string:
    to shoot from ambush ' at the ' true of ' heart.

3   'If the foundations ' are de'stroyed:
    what ' can the ' righteous ' do?'

4   You O Lord are in your ' holy ' temple:
    your ' throne ' is in ' heaven.

5   Your eyes are upon ' human'kind:
    you take our ' measure ' at a ' glance.

6   You put the righteous and the wicked ' to the ' test:
    those who delight in ' violence · your ' soul ab'hors.

7   On the wicked you shall rain⌣
    coals of ' fire and ' brimstone:
    scorching wind shall ' be their ' portion · to ' drink.

8   For you are just O Lord, and you 'love just' dealing:
    the 'upright · shall be'hold your 'face.

12

Day 2 Evening

1   Help Lord, for there is not one godly ' person ' left:
    the faithful have ' vanished ' from a 'mong us.

2   They all speak falsely ' to their ' neighbours:
    they flatter with their lips,
      but dissemble ' in their ' double ' heart.

3   O that the Lord would cut off all ' flatter·ing ' lips:
    and the ' tongue that ' speaks so ' boastfully.

4   They have said, 'With our tongue we ' will pre'vail:
    our lips are our own, ' who is ' Lord · over ' us?'

5   'Because the poor ' are op'pressed:
    and because of the ' groans ' of the ' needy,

6 'I will arise,' ' says the ' Lord:
   'and give them the ' place of ' safety · they ' long for.'

7 The words of the Lord are pure⌣
      as silver refined ' in a ' furnace:
      as gold that is purified ' seven · times ' in the ' fire.

8 Pro'tect us · O ' Lord:
   and guard us from ' this · gener'ation · for ' ever,

9† for the wicked flaunt themselves on ' every ' side:
      and the worthless are ex'alted · a'mong the ' people.

13

1 How long O Lord will you ' utterly · for'get me:
   how long will you ' hide your ' face ' from me?

2 How long must I suffer anguish in my soul,
      and be so grieved in my heart ' day and ' night:
   how long shall my ' ene·my ' triumph ' over me?

3 Look at me, and answer me O ' Lord my ' God:
   give light to my eyes, lest I ' fall a'sleep in ' death,

4 lest my enemies should claim⌣
      to have pre'vailed a'gainst me:
   lest my foes should re'joice ' at my ' downfall.

5 But my trust is ' in your ' mercy:
   let my heart be ' joyful · in ' your sal'vation.

6 I will sing to you O Lord,
      because you have dealt so ' loving·ly ' with me:
   I will praise your ' name O ' Lord most ' high.

14

1 The foolish have spoken ' in their ' heart:
   and said, ' 'There is ' no ' God.'

2 All are corrupt, they do a'bomin·able ' things:
   there is ' no one · who ' does · what is ' good.

3 The Lord looks down from ' heaven · on ' all of us:
    to see if there are any who⁀
        act wisely and ' seek ' after ' God.

4 But they have all gone astray,
    all alike have ' been cor'rupted:
        there is not one that does ' good ' no not ' one.

5 Have they no knowledge, all ' those · who do ' evil?:
    they eat up my people like eating bread,
        and ' do not ' pray · to the ' Lord.

6 See now, they ' tremble · with ' fear:
    for God is on the ' side ' of the ' righteous.

7 Though you mock at the ' hope · of the ' poor:
    yet the ' Lord ' is their ' refuge.

8 O that deliverance for God's people⁀
    would come ' forth · from Je'rusalem:
        when the Lord restores the fortunes of the people,
            then shall Jacob re'joice and ' Israel · be ' glad.

15   *Day 3 Morning*

1 Lord, who may be a ' guest · in your ' house:
    or who may dwell ' on your ' holy ' mountain?

2 One who leads a ' blameless ' life:
    who does what is right,
        and speaks ' truthful·ly ' from the ' heart,

3 whose tongue is free from malice,
    who never ' wrongs a ' friend:
        and utters no re'proach a'gainst a ' neighbour,

4 who does not ' honour · the un'worthy:
    but makes much of ' those who ' fear the ' Lord.

5 Such a one stands by a ' promise ' given:
    though it be at ' person·al ' disad'vantage,

6 and will not take interest ' on a ' loan:
    nor accept a bribe⁀
        to ' testi·fy a'gainst the ' innocent.

7† Whoever ' does all ' this:
    shall ' never · be ' over'thrown.

16

1   Preserve ' me O ' God:
      for in ' you · I have ' taken ' refuge.

2   I have said to the Lord, "You are · my ' God:
      from you alone ' comes all ' my pros'perity.'

3   All my delight is in the faithful‿
      who ' dwell · in the ' land:
      and in ' those · who ex'cel in ' virtue.

4   But as for those who run after ' other ' gods:
      their ' troubles ' shall be ' multiplied.

5   Libations of blood I will not offer to ' those ' gods:
      nor will I take their ' names up'on my ' lips.

6   You Lord are my allotted portion ' and my ' cup:
      you your'self have ' cast my ' lot.

7   My boundaries enclose a ' pleasant ' land:
      indeed I ' have a ' noble ' heritage.

8   I will thank you O Lord for ' giving · me ' counsel:
      at night ' also · you ' teach my ' heart.

9   I keep you ' always · be'fore me:
      you are on my right hand,'
        therefore · I ' shall not ' fall.

10 So my heart is glad, and my ' soul re'joices:
      my body ' also · shall ' rest in ' safety.

11 For you will not give me up to the ' power · of ' death:
      nor suffer your be'lovèd · to ' see · the A'byss.

12 You will show me the path of life,
      in your presence is the ' fulness · of ' joy:
      and from your right hand flow de'lights for ' ever'more.

17

1   Hear my just cause, attend to my ' cry O ' Lord:
      listen to my prayer from ' lips that ' do not ' lie.

2   Let judgment in my favour‿
      come ' forth · from your ' presence:
      and let your ' eyes dis'cern · what is ' right.

3   You have searched my heart,
        and visited ' me by ' night:
        if you test me, you will find no wickedness in me,
        my ' mouth does ' not of'fend.

4   With regard to ' human ' deeds:
        because of the word of your lips,
        I have a'voided · the ' ways · of the ' violent.

5†   My steps have been ' firm in · your ' paths:
        and my ' feet ' have not ' stumbled.

6   I call upon you O God for ' you will ' answer me:
        incline your ear to ' me and ' hear my ' words.

7   Show me the wonders of your ' steadfast ' love:
        for by your right hand
          you save from their adversaries '‿
          those · who take ' refuge · with ' you.

8   Guard me as the ' apple · of your ' eye:
        hide me under the ' shadow ' of your ' wings,

9   from the wicked ' who as'sail me:
        from ' deadly ' foes · who sur'round me.

10   They have closed their ' hearts to ' pity:
        and their ' mouths speak ' arro·gant ' things.

11   They press hard upon me from ' every ' side:
        watching how they may '‿
        strike me ' down · to the ' ground,

12† like a lion that is ' greedy · for ' prey:
        like a young lion '‿
        crouching ' in a ' place of ' ambush.

13   Arise O Lord, stand in their way‿
        and ' bring them ' down:
        let your sword ' rescue · me ' from the ' wicked.

14   Let your hand deliver me from people‿
        whose portion in life is ' of the ' world:
        who have gorged themselves ' with your ' good ' things.

15   They have children at ' their de'sire:
        and leave to heirs ' what re'mains · of their ' wealth.

16   But as for me, I shall see your face
        because my ' plea is ' just:
    when I awake
        and see your ' face I ' shall be ' satisfied.

18

PART ONE

1   I love you O ' Lord my ' strength:
        the Lord is my rock, my ' fortress · and ' my de'liverer;

2   my God, the rock where ' I take ' refuge:
        my shield, my sal'vation ' and my ' stronghold.

3†   I will call upon the Lord,
        who is worthy of ' all ' praise:
        so shall I be ' saved ' from my ' enemies.

4   The waves of death were ' all a'round me:
        the torrents of de'struction ' over'took me.

5   The cords of death ' tightened · up'on me:
        and its snares were ' laid ' in my ' path.

6   In my trouble I ' called · to the ' Lord:
        and cried for ' help ' to my ' God.

7   From your temple you ' heard my ' voice:
        and my ' cry to · you ' reached your ' ears.

8   Then the earth ' heaved and ' quaked:
        the very foundations of the hills were shaken,
        they ' reeled be'cause of · your ' anger.

9   Smoke issued from your nostrils,
        and a consuming fire came ' out of · your ' mouth:
        glowing ' coals flamed ' forth · from your ' presence.

10   You parted the heavens and ' came ' down:
        a ' storm cloud ' under · your ' feet.

11   Mounted on the ' cherubim · you ' flew:
        you swooped on the ' wings ' of the ' wind.

12   You made darkness your ' covering · a'round you:
        thick clouds ' dark with ' rain your ' canopy.

13   Out of the brightness ' of your ' presence:
            there broke through the clouds,'
                hailstones · and ' coals of ' fire.

14   You O Lord most high thundered ' out of ' heaven:
            you uttered your voice,'
                hailstones · and ' coals of ' fire.

15   You sent out your arrows and ' scattered · your ' enemies:
            you flashed forth your '‿
                lightnings · and ' put them · to ' flight.

16†   The bed of the sea was laid bare,
            the foundations of the world ' were un'covered:
        at your rebuke O Lord,
            at the blasting of the ' breath of ' your dis'pleasure.

PART TWO

17   You O Lord reached down from on ' high and ' grasped me:
            you drew me ' out · of the ' great ' waters.

18   You delivered me from my powerful enemy,
            and from ' those who ' hated me:
                be'cause they ' were too ' strong for me.

19   They came upon me in the day of ' my cal'amity:
            but you were ' my up'holder · O ' Lord.

20   You brought me out into a ' place of ' liberty:
            you rescued me be'cause · you de'lighted · in ' me.

21   You rewarded me for my ' righteous ' dealing:
            you recompensed me be'cause my ' hands were ' clean.

22   For I have kept your ' ways O ' Lord:
            and have not ' wickedly · for'saken · my ' God.

23   All your laws are be'fore my ' eyes:
            and your commandments I have not ' put a'way ' from me.

24   I was also ' blameless · be'fore you:
            and I ' kept my'self from ' wickedness.

25†   So you rewarded me for my ' righteous ' dealing:
            because my ' hands were ' clean in · your ' sight.

26 With the faithful you ' show your self ' faithful:
      with the ' upright · you ' show your·self ' upright.

27 With the pure you ' show your·self ' pure:
      but with the ' crafty · ones ' you are ' crafty.

28 For you will deliver a ' humble ' people:
      but you will bring down the '‿
            high looks ' of the ' proud.

29 You light my lamp O ' Lord my ' God:
      you turn my ' darkness ' into ' light.

30† With you I can ' break · through a ' hedge:
      with the help of my God I can ' leap ' over · a ' wall.

PART THREE

31 The way of our God is perfect,
            the word of the ' Lord proves ' true:
      you are the shield of ' all · who take ' refuge · in ' you.

32 For who is ' God · but the ' Lord:
      and who is a ' rock ex'cept our ' God?

33 It is God who ' girds me · with ' strength:
      and makes the ' path be'fore me ' safe.

34 You make my feet like the ' feet · of a ' deer:
      and ' set me · up'on the ' heights.

35 You teach my ' hands to ' fight:
      so that my arms can bend ' even · a ' bow of ' bronze.

36 You have given me the shield of ' your sal'vation:
            your right hand held me up,
            and your loving ' care has ' made me ' great.

37 You have made a broad ' path · for my ' feet:
      and my ' footsteps ' have not ' faltered.

            * * *

44 You delivered me from the ' strife · of the ' peoples:
      and you ' made me · the ' head · of the ' nations.

45 A people whom I ' had not ' known:
      became ' subjects ' under · my ' rule.

46   As soon as they heard of me ' they o'beyed me:
         and foreigners ' humbled · them'selves be'fore me.

47†   The strength of the ' ali·ens ' failed:
         in fear they ' came out ' from their ' strongholds.

48   The Lord lives, and blessèd ' be my ' rock:
         and ' praised · be the ' God who ' saves me.

49   You are the God ' who a'venged me:
         and sub'dued the ' peoples ' under me.

50   You delivered me ' from my ' enemies:
         you set me up above my adversaries,
            and ' saved me ' from the ' violent.

51   Therefore Lord, I will extol you a'mong the ' nations:
         and sing ' praises ' to your ' name.

52†   Great triumphs O Lord you ' give · to your ' king:
         and show unfailing love to your anointed one,
            to David and ' his de'scendants · for ' ever.

19

1   The heavens proclaim the ' glory · of ' God:
         and the vault of the ' sky re'veals God's ' handiwork.

2   One day ' speaks · to an'other:
         and night ' shares its ' knowledge · with ' night,

3   and this without ' speech or ' language:
         their ' voices ' are not ' heard.

4   But their sound goes out into ' all ' lands:
         their ' words · to the ' ends · of the ' earth.

5   In them God has pitched a ' tent · for the ' sun:
         which comes out like a bridegroom,
            like an athlete ' eager · to ' run a ' race.

6   Its rising is at one end of the sky,
         it runs its ' course · to the ' other:
         and there is nothing that is ' hidden ' from its ' heat.

7   The law of the Lord is perfect, re'freshing · the ' soul:
         the instruction of the Lord is sure,
            and gives ' wisdom ' to the ' simple.

8   The precepts of the Lord are right,
      and re'joice the ' heart:
     the commandment of the Lord is‿
      pure and gives ' light ' to the ' eyes.

9   The fear of the Lord is clean, and en'dures for ' ever:
     the judgments of the Lord are true‿
      and ' righteous ' every ' one.

10   They are more to be desired than gold,
      even ' much fine ' gold:
     sweeter also than honey,
      pure ' honey ' from the ' comb.

11   By them is your ' servant ' taught:
     and for keeping them ' there is ' great re'ward.

12   Who can discern un'witting ' sins?:
     O cleanse me ' from my ' secret ' faults.

13   Keep your servant also from presumptuous sins,
      lest they get the ' better ' of me:
     then shall I be clean,
      and ' innocent · of ' great of'fence.

14   Let the words of my mouth‿
      and the ' thoughts · of my ' heart:
     be acceptable in your sight,
      O Lord my ' strength and ' my re'deemer.

20

1   May the Lord answer you in the ' day of ' trouble:
     the name of the ' God of ' Jacob · de'fend you,

2   send you ' help · from the ' sanctuary:
     and give you sup'port · from the ' holy ' mountain.

3   May the Lord remember ' all your ' offerings:
     and ac'cept your ' burnt ' sacrifices,

4   grant you your ' heart's de'sire:
     and give suc'cess to ' all your ' plans,

5†   so that we may rejoice in your victory,
      and triumph in the ' name · of our ' God:
     because the Lord has ' granted ' all · your pe'titions.

6   Now I know O Lord that you help your anointed king,
        and will answer him from your ' holy ' heaven:
    with the victorious ' might of ' your right ' hand.

7   Some put their trust in chariots,
        and ' some in ' horses:
    but we will trust in the '⌣
    name · of the ' Lord our ' God.

8   They will ' totter · and ' fall:
    but we shall ' rise and ' stand ' upright.

9   O Lord ' save the ' king:
    and ' answer · us ' when we ' call.

21

1   The king rejoices in your ' strength O ' Lord:
    how greatly ' he ex'ults · in your ' victory.

2   You have given him his ' heart's de'sire:
    and not de'nied him · the re'quest · of his ' lips.

3   You come to meet him with the ' blessings · of suc'cess:
    and set a crown of pure ' gold up'on his ' head.

4   He asked you for life, and you ' gave it ' to him:
    length of ' days for ' ever · and ' ever.

5   Great is his glory be'cause of · your ' victory:
    splendour and majesty ' you have ' laid up'on him.

6   You have given him ever'lasting · fe'licity:
    and you make him ' glad with ' joy · in your ' presence.

7   For the king puts his ' trust · in the ' Lord:
    and through the steadfast love of God most high,'
    he · will re'main un'shaken.

* * *

13   Arise O Lord ' in your ' strength:
    and we will ' sing and ' praise your ' power.

PART ONE

1   My God my God, why have ′ you for′saken me:
        why are you so far from my help,
            and from my ′ cry ′ of dis′tress?

2   O my God I cry out in the daytime,
        but you ′ do not ′ answer:
        · at night also, ′ but I · get ′ no re′lief.

3   But ′ you · are the ′ Holy One:
        enthroned on the ′ praises ′ of your ′ people.

4   Our ancestors ′ trusted · in ′ you:
        they ′ trusted · and ′ you de′livered them.

5   They called to ′ you · and were ′ rescued:
        they put their trust in you,′
            and were ′ not · disap′pointed.

6   But I am a worm and something ′ less than ′ human:
        an object of scorn and an ′ outcast ′ of the ′ people.

7   All those who see me ′ laugh · me to ′ scorn:
        they curl their lips and ′ toss their ′ heads ′ saying,

8   'You trusted in ′ God · for de′liverance:
        if God ′ cares · for you, ′ let God ′ rescue you.'

9   But you are the one who took me ′ out · of the ′ womb:
        you kept me safe up′on my ′ mother's ′ breast.

10 On you have I been cast ever ′ since · I was ′ born:
        and you are my God ′ even · from my ′ mother's ′ womb.

11 Be not far from me, for trouble is ′ close at ′ hand:
        and ′ there is ′ no one · to ′ help me.

12 Many bulls have ′ come a′round me:
        great bulls of Bashan‿
            close in on ′ me from ′ every ′ side.

13 They open ′ wide their ′ mouths at me:
        like ′ ravening · and ′ roaring ′ lions.

14 I am poured out like water,
        and all my bones are ′ out of ′ joint:
        my heart within my ′ breast has ′ melted · like ′ wax.

15 My mouth is parched as dry clay,
        my tongue ' clings · to my ' jaws:
      and I am ' laid · in the ' dust of ' death.

16 Many dogs have ' come a'round me:
      and the wicked hem me ' in on ' every ' side.

17 They pierce my hands and my feet,
        I can count ' all my ' bones:
      they stand ' staring · and ' gloating ' over me.

18 They share out my ' garments · a'mong them:
      and they cast ' lots ' for my ' clothing.

19 Do not stand far off from ' me O ' Lord:
      you are my helper, come ' quickly ' to my ' rescue.

20 Deliver me ' from the ' sword:
      my precious ' life · from the ' mauling · of ' dogs.

21† Save me from the ' lion's ' mouth:
      my afflicted soul from the ' horns · of the ' wild ' cattle.

PART TWO

22 I will declare your ' name · to my ' people:
      in the midst of the as'sembly ' I will ' praise you.

23 Give praise all you that ' fear the ' Lord:
        proclaim God's greatness, all you children of Jacob,
        stand in awe ' all you ' children · of ' Israel.

24 For you O God have not despised or abhorred⌣
        the poor in ' their af'fliction:
      you have not hidden your face from them,
        but you ' heard them ' when they ' called to you.

25 You are the theme of my praise in the ' full as'sembly:
        my vows I will perform⌣
        in the ' sight of ' those who ' fear you.

26 The poor shall ' eat · and be ' satisfied:
        those who seek you O Lord shall praise you,
        may they ' be in · good ' heart for ' ever.

27 Let all the ends of the earth remember⌣
        and turn to ' you O ' Lord:
      and let all the families⌣
        of the ' nations · bow ' down be'fore you.

28   For yours is the ' kingdom · O ' Lord:
        and you are the ' ruler ' over · the ' nations.

29   As for those who sleep in the grave,
            how shall they ' worship ' you:
        all those who go down into the dust,
            how shall they ' bow be'fore ' you?

30   But I shall live through you,
            and my ' children · shall ' serve you:
        they shall tell of you‿
            to the generations ' that are ' yet to ' come.

31   To a people as yet unborn they shall ' make ' known:
        the ' saving ' deeds · you have ' done.

23

1   The Lord ' is my ' shepherd:
        therefore ' can I ' lack ' nothing.

2   You Lord make me lie down in ' green ' pastures:
        and lead me be'side the ' waters · of ' peace.

3   You re'vive my ' spirit:
        and guide me in right pathways '‿
            for your ' name's ' sake.

4   Though I walk through the valley of the shadow of death,
            I will ' fear no ' evil:
        for you are with me,
            your ' rod · and your ' staff · are my ' comfort.

5   You spread a table for me‿
            in the ' sight · of my ' enemies:
        you have anointed my head with oil,
            and my ' cup is ' over'flowing.

6   Surely your goodness and mercy shall follow me‿
            all the ' days · of my ' life:
        and I will dwell in the ' house · of the ' Lord for ' ever.

1   The earth is the Lord's and ' all · that is ' in it:
        the ' world and ' its in'habitants.

2   For the Lord has founded it up'on the ' seas:
        and planted it firm up'on the ' waters · be'neath.

3   Who may ascend the ' hill · of the ' Lord:
        or who may ' stand · in God's ' holy ' place?

4   Those who have clean hands and a ' pure ' heart:
        who have not set their minds on falsehood,
            or ' sworn · a de'ceitful ' oath.

5   They shall receive blessing ' from the ' Lord:
        and ' recompense · from ' God their ' saviour.

6   So it is with those who ' seek the ' Lord:
        with those who seek ⌣
            the ' face · of the ' God of ' Jacob.

7   Lift up your heads you gates,
        lift yourselves up, you ever'lasting ' doors:
        that the king of ' glory ' may come ' in.

8   'Who is the ' king of ' glory?':
        'It is the Lord strong and mighty,
            the ' Lord · who is ' mighty · in ' battle.'

9   Lift up your heads you gates,
        lift yourselves up, you ever'lasting ' doors:
        that the king of ' glory ' may come ' in.

10 'Who is the ' king of ' glory?':
        'It is the Lord, the Lord of hosts who ' ⌣
            is the ' king of ' glory.'

25

1   To you Lord I lift up my soul,
        my God I have put my ' trust in ' you:
        let me not be disappointed,
            nor let my ' ene·mies ' triumph ' over me.

2   For all those who hope in you shall ' not be · a'shamed:
        but only those who ' wanton·ly ' break ' faith.

3   Make known to me your ' ways O ' Lord:
      and ' teach me ' your ' paths.

4   Lead me in the way of your ' truth and ' teach me:
      you are God my saviour,
        for you have I waited ' all the ' day ' long.

5   Call to remembrance O Lord your ' tender ' care:
      and the unfailing love⌣
        which you have ' shown ' from of ' old.

6   Do not remember the sins and offences ' of my ' youth:
      but according to your mercy,
        remember me ' Lord ' in your ' goodness.

7   You O Lord are ' upright · and ' good:
      therefore you show the path to ' those who ' go a'stray.

8   You guide the humble to do ' what is ' right:
      and those who are ' gentle · you ' teach your ' way.

9   All your ways are ' loving · and ' sure:
      to those who keep your '⌣
        covenant · and ' your com'mandments.

10 For your name's ' sake O ' Lord:
      pardon my guilt, ' which in'deed is ' great.

11 If there are any who ' fear the ' Lord:
      to them the Lord will '⌣
        show the ' path · they should ' choose.

12 They themselves shall ' dwell · in pros'perity:
      and their ' children · shall in'herit · the ' land.

13 Your friendship O Lord is for ' those who ' honour you:
      and to ' them · you re'veal your ' covenant.

14 My eyes are always on ' you O ' Lord:
      for you will re'lease my ' feet · from the ' net.

15 Turn to me Lord ' and have ' mercy:
      for I am ' lonely ' and op'pressed.

16 Relieve the ' sorrows · of my ' heart:
      and bring me ' out of ' my dis'tress.

17 Look at my affliction ' and my ' trouble:
      and for'give me ' all my ' sins.

18 See how many ' are my ' enemies:
    how violent ' is their ' hatred ' for me.

19 Preserve my life ' and de'liver me:
    let me not be disappointed,
        for I have ' put my ' trust in ' you.

20 Let integrity and righteous ' dealing · pre'serve me:
    let me not be disappointed,
        for I have ' put my ' trust in ' you.

21† Redeem your ' people · O ' God:
    and bring them ' out of ' all their · dis'tress.

26

1 Give judgment O Lord in my favour,
    for I have walked the ' way · of in'tegrity:
    and I have put un'waver·ing ' trust · in the ' Lord.

2 Examine me O ' Lord and ' try me:
    put my heart and my ' mind ' to the ' test.

3 For your steadfast love is ever be'fore my ' eyes:
    and I walk in the ' way ' of your ' faithfulness.

4 I do not sit down with people ' who are ' false:
    nor ' do I · con'sort with ' hypocrites.

5 I hate the ' company · of ' wrongdoers:
    and ' will not ' sit · with the ' wicked.

6 I wash my hands in ' innocence · O ' Lord:
    and so will I ' go a'round your ' altar,

7 singing a ' song of ' thanksgiving:
    and pro'claiming ' all your ' wonders.

8 Lord I love the house you have ' made your ' home:
    the ' place · where your ' glory ' dwells.

9 Do not sweep me a'way with ' sinners:
    nor my life with ' those who ' thirst for ' blood,

10 whose fingers are ' active · in ' mischief:
    and whose right ' hand is ' full of ' bribes.

11   But as for me, I will walk the ' way · of in'tegrity:
       deliver me and ' show me ' your ' favour.

12   My foot stands firm on ' level ' ground:
       in the full assembly ' I will ' praise the ' Lord.

27

1   The Lord is my light and my salvation,
       whom then ' shall I ' fear?:
       the Lord is the stronghold of my life,
       of whom then ' shall I ' be a'fraid?

2   When the wicked close in on me ' to de'vour me:
       it is they, my enemies⌣
       and my ' foes who ' stumble · and ' fall.

3   If an army should encamp against me,
       my heart shall ' not · be a'fraid:
       if war should arise against me,
       even then ' I will ' not · be dis'mayed.

4   One thing I have asked of the Lord,'
       which I ' long for:
       that I may dwell in the house of the Lord '⌣
       all the ' days · of my ' life,

5†   to gaze on your ' beauty · O ' Lord:
       and to ' seek you ' in your ' temple.

6   For in the time of trouble you will ' give me ' shelter:
       you will hide me under the cover of your tent,
       and set me ' high up'on a ' rock.

7   And now you have ' raised my ' head:
       above my ' ene·mies ' round a'bout me.

8†   Therefore I will offer in your dwelling⌣
       a sacrifice with ' great ' gladness:
       I will sing and give ' praise to ' you O ' Lord.

9   Hear my voice O Lord ' when I ' call:
       have ' mercy · on ' me and ' answer me.

10   Of you my heart has said, ' 'Seek God's ' face':
       your ' face Lord ' I will ' seek.

11　Do not hide your ' face ' from me:
　　　or re'ject your ' servant · in ' anger.

12　You have ' been my ' helper:
　　　do not cast me off,
　　　　　or for'sake me · O ' God my ' saviour.

13†　Though my father and my ' mother · for'sake me:
　　　the ' Lord will ' take me ' up.

14　Teach me your ' way O ' Lord:
　　　and lead me by a level path,
　　　　　safe from ' those who ' lie in ' wait for me.

15　Do not give me up to the ' will · of my ' enemies:
　　　for liars, and those who breathe out malice,
　　　　　have risen ' up to ' witness · a'gainst me.

16　I believe that I shall see the ' goodness · of the ' Lord:
　　　in the ' land ' of the ' living.

17　Wait for the Lord,
　　　be strong and let your ' heart take ' courage:
　　　yes, ' wait I ' say · for the ' Lord.

28

1　To you I call O Lord my rock,
　　　be not ' deaf · to my ' cry:
　　　lest if you answer with silence,
　　　　　I become like those who go ' down ' to the ' grave.

2　Hear the voice of my pleading when I cry to ' you for ' help:
　　　when I lift up my hands⌣
　　　　　towards the ' shrine · of your ' holy ' temple.

3　Do not cast me off with the wicked and ' those · who do ' evil:
　　　who speak peace to their neighbours,
　　　　　but ' mischief · is ' in their ' hearts.

　　　　　　* * *

6　Because they give no heed to your acts O Lord,
　　　or to the ' work · of your ' hands:
　　　you will break them ' down and ' never · re'build them.

7   Blessèd are' you O' Lord:
       for you have' heard my' plea for' mercy.

8   You are my strength and my shield,
         my heart trusts in you and' I am' helped:
      therefore my heart dances for joy,
         and in my' song' I will' praise you.

9   You Lord are the' strength · of your' people:
       and a sure refuge for' your an'ointed' king.

10   O Lord save your people, and' bless · your in'heritance:
       be a shepherd to them, and' bear them' up for' ever.

29

1   Ascribe to the Lord you' heaven·ly' powers:
       ascribe to the' Lord all' glory · and' might.

2   Ascribe due honour to God's' holy' name:
       worship the Lord' in the' beauty · of' holiness.

3   The voice of the Lord is up'on the' waters:
       it is the glorious God‿
         who makes the thunder up'on the' great' waters.

4   The voice of the' Lord is' power:
       the voice of the' Lord is' full of' majesty.

5   The voice of the Lord' breaks the' cedar-trees:
       the Lord' splinters · the' cedars · of' Lebanon.

6   The Lord makes Lebanon' skip · like a' calf:
       and Sirion' like a' young wild' bull.

7   The voice of the Lord di'vides the' lightning:
       the voice of the Lord shakes the wilderness,
         the Lord' shakes the' wilderness · of' Kadesh.

8   The voice of the Lord makes the oaks to writhe,
         and strips the' forests' bare:
      while in God's' temple' all cry, ' 'Glory'.

9   The Lord sits enthroned a'bove the' waters:
       the Lord sits en'throned as' king for' ever.

10   You Lord will give' strength · to your' people:
       you will give your' people · the' blessing · of' peace.

1   I will extol you O Lord for you have ' lifted · me ' up:
      you have not let my ' ene·mies ' triumph ' over me.

2   O Lord my God I cried to ' you for ' help:
      and ' you · have re'stored my ' health.

3† Lord you have brought me back ' from the ' dead:
      you have saved my life⌣
         from among those going ' down ' to · the A'byss.

4   Let all your servants sing praises to ' you O ' Lord:
      and give ' thanks · to your ' holy ' name.

5   For your anger is but for a moment,
      and in your ' kindness · is ' life:
    tears may linger at nightfall,
      but ' joy comes ' with the ' dawn.

6   In my prosperity I said, 'I shall ' never · be ' shaken:
      your favour O Lord has made me⌣
         as firm as ' any ' strong ' mountain.'

7   You turned your ' face a'way from me:
      and ' I was ' greatly · dis'mayed.

8   I called to ' you O ' God:
      to the ' Lord I ' made · my ap'peal.

9   'What profit is there ' in my ' death:
      in my ' going ' down · to the ' grave?

10 'Will the dust ' give you ' praise:
      or ' will it · pro'claim your ' faithfulness?

11 'Hear O Lord, and be ' gracious ' to me:
      O ' Lord ' be my ' helper.'

12 You have turned my mourning ' into ' dancing:
      you have stripped off my '⌣
         sackcloth · and ' clothed · me with ' joy,

13 so that my heart shall sing your ' praise with·out ' ceasing:
      O Lord my God, I will give ' thanks to ' you for ' ever.

31

PART ONE

1 In you Lord I have ' taken ' refuge:
    let me ' never · be ' put to ' shame,

2 deliver me ' in your ' righteousness:
    incline your ear to me,
        come ' quickly ' to my ' rescue.

3 Be to me a ' rock of ' refuge:
    a ' stronghold · to ' keep me ' safe.

4 You are to me a ' rock · and a ' fortress:
    for your name's sake ' lead me ' and ' guide me.

5 Release me from the net they have ' secret·ly ' laid for me:
    for you O ' Lord ' are my ' strength.

6 Into your hands I com'mend my ' spirit:
    for you have redeemed me, O ' Lord ' God of ' truth.

7 You hate those who pay regard to ' worthless ' idols:
    but I ' put my ' trust · in the ' Lord.

8 I will be glad and re'joice in · your ' mercy:
    for you have seen my affliction,
        and taken ' heed · of my ' soul's dis'tress.

9† You have not given me up to the ' power · of the ' enemy:
    you have set my feet where ' I may ' walk at ' liberty.

PART TWO

10 Have mercy on me Lord, for ' I · am in ' trouble:
    my eyes are wasted from grief,
        my ' soul · and my ' body ' also.

11 My life is worn out with sorrow,
    and my ' years with ' sighing:
    my strength fails me in my misery,
        my ' bones are ' wasted · a'way.

12 I am the ' scorn · of my ' enemies:
    and a ' byword · a'mong my ' neighbours.

13 Those of my acquaintance shudder ' at the ' sight of me:
    when they see me in the ' ⏝
        street they ' shrink a'way from me.

14 I have passed out of mind like ' one · who is ' dead:
    I have be'come · like a ' broken ' vessel.

15 I hear the whispering of many,
        fear is on ' every ' side:
    while they conspire together against me,
        and plot to ' take a'way my ' life.

16 But my trust is in ' you O ' Lord:
    I say, 'You are my God,
        my ' fortunes · are ' in your ' hands.'

17 Deliver me from the ' power · of my ' enemies:
    and from the ' hand of ' those who ' persecute me.

18 Make your face to shine ' on your ' servant:
    and save me ' for your ' mercy's ' sake.

19 Let me not be put to shame when I ' call up'on you:
    let the wicked be shamed,
        and put to ' silence ' in the ' grave.

20† Let the lying lips be ' put to ' silence:
    which speak insolently against⏝
        the ' righteous · with ' pride · and con'tempt.

21 O how great is your goodness,
        which you have laid up for ' those who ' fear you:
    which you have prepared in the sight of all,
        for ' those · who take ' refuge · in ' you.

22 You hide them under the cover of your presence⏝
        from those who con'spire a'gainst them:
    you keep them under your shelter,'
        safe · from the ' strife of ' tongues.

23 Blessèd are ' you O ' Lord:
    for you have wonderfully shown your love to me,
        when I was beset like a ' city ' under ' siege.

24 I said in ' my a'larm:
    'I am cut off from the ' sight ' of your ' eyes.'

25 But you heard the ' voice · of my ' plea:
    when I ' called to ' you for ' help.

26   Love the Lord all you servants ' of the ' Lord:
           for the Lord preserves those who are faithful,
               and fully repays the ' haughty · for ' their pre'sumption.

27†   Be strong, and let your ' heart take ' courage:
           all ' you that ' wait · for the ' Lord.

32

1   Blessèd are those whose offences ' are for'given:
           whose ' sin · has been ' put a'way.

2   Blessèd are those to whom the Lord im'putes no ' guilt:
           and in whose spirit ' there is ' no de'ceit.

3   While I held back from con'fessing · my ' sin:
           my body wasted away‿
               through my ' groaning ' all day ' long.

4   For your hand was heavy upon me ' day and ' night:
           I was dried up and withered,
               as it ' were by ' drought in ' summer.

5   Then I acknowledged my ' sin to ' you:
           my ' guilt I ' did not ' hide.

6   I said, 'I will confess my sins ' to the ' Lord':
           and so you forgave the ' wicked·ness ' of my ' sin.

7   Therefore let all those that are faithful‿
               pray to you in ' time of ' trouble:
           when great flood-water rises,'
               it shall ' not come ' near them.

8   You are a place to hide me in,
               you will pre'serve me · from ' trouble:
           you will surround me with ' shouts ' of de'liverance.

9   'I will teach you,
               and guide you in the ' way · you should ' go:
           I will keep you under my ' eye and ' give you ' counsel.

10   'Be not like horse or mule,
               which have no ' under'standing:
           whose course must be ' checked with ' bit and ' bridle.'

11   Many pains are in store ' for the ' wicked:
        but whoever trusts in the Lord⌣
          is sur'rounded · by ' steadfast ' love.

12   Be glad you righteous, and rejoice ' in the ' Lord:
        shout for joy all ' you · that are ' upright · in ' heart.

33

1   Rejoice in the ' Lord, you ' righteous:
        praise comes ' well · from the ' upright · in ' heart.

2   Give thanks to the Lord ' on the ' harp:
        sing God's praise ' with the ' ten-stringed ' lute.

3   Sing to the Lord a ' new ' song:
        play ' loudly · with ' all your ' skill.

4   For your word O ' Lord is ' true:
        and you are ' faithful · in ' all you ' do.

5   You love what is ' just and ' right:
        the ' earth is ' full of · your ' kindness.

6   By your word were the ' heavens ' made:
        and the stars in their '⌣
          hosts · by the ' breath of · your ' mouth.

7   You gathered up the sea as ' into · a ' water-jar:
        you laid up the ' deep as ' in a ' storehouse.

8   Let all the earth ' fear you · O ' Lord:
        and all the inhabitants of the ' world ' stand in ' awe of you.

9   For you spoke, and the world ' came to ' be:
        you commanded ' and it ' stood ' firm.

10   You Lord bring the counsels of the ' nations · to ' nothing:
        and frus'trate · the de'signs · of the ' peoples.

11   Your counsel shall en'dure for ' ever:
        the purpose of your ' heart to ' all · gener'ations.

12   How blest are the people whose ' God · is the ' Lord:
        the people you ' chose · as your ' own pos'session.

13   You Lord look down from heaven upon ' all ' people:
        from the place where you dwell⌣
          you consider ' all · who in'habit · the ' earth.

14   You fashion the ' hearts · of them ' all:
        and ob'serve ' all their ' deeds.

15   A king is not saved by a ' mighty ' army:
        nor is a warrior de'livered · by ' much ' strength.

16   A horse is a vain thing to ' count on · for ' victory:
        nor will it save anyone ' by its ' great ' strength.

17   But your eye O Lord is on ' those who ' fear you:
        on those who rely ' on your ' steadfast ' love,

18   to de'liver them · from ' death:
        and to ' keep them · a'live in ' famine.

19   We have waited eagerly for ' you O ' Lord:
        for you are our ' help ' and our ' shield.

20   Our heart shall re'joice in ' you:
        because we have ' hoped · in your ' holy ' name.

21†   Let your constant love at'tend us · O ' Lord:
        as we ' put our ' trust in ' you.

34

PART ONE

1   I will give thanks to the Lord at ' all ' times:
        God's praise will ' always · be ' on my ' lips.

2   My soul will glory ' in the ' Lord:
        the humble will ' hear ' and be ' glad.

3   O praise the ' Lord with ' me:
        let us ex'alt God's ' name to'gether.

4   I sought your help O Lord ' and you ' answered me:
        and ' freed me · from ' all my ' fears.

5   Look towards the Most High, and be ' radiant · with ' light:
        and your ' faces · will ' not · be a'shamed.

6   In my affliction I cried out,
           and the ' Lord ' heard me:
        and ' saved me · from ' all my ' troubles.

7   Your angel O Lord‿
           keeps guard around ' those who ' fear you:
        to ' rescue · them in ' time of ' danger.

8   Taste and see ' how gracious · the ' Lord is:
       happy are those who find refuge ' in the ' Most ' High.

9   Fear the Lord, you that are God's ' holy ' people:
       for those who fear the Lord ' are in ' want of ' nothing.

10   Strong lions suffer ' want · and go ' hungry:
       but those who seek the Lord‿
          shall lack ' nothing ' that is ' good.

PART TWO

11   Come my children and ' listen · to ' me:
       I will ' teach you · the ' fear · of the ' Lord.

12   Which of you de'lights in ' life:
       and desires ' many ' days · of pros'perity?

13   Keep your ' tongue from ' evil:
       and your ' lips from ' speaking ' lies.

14   Turn away from evil and ' do ' good:
       seek ' peace and ' steadily · pur'sue it.

15   The eyes of the Lord are ' on the ' righteous:
       God's ears are ' open ' to their ' cry.

16   The Lord opposes ' those · who do ' evil:
       to blot out the re'membrance · of them ' from the ' earth.

17   The righteous cry out, and the ' Lord ' hears them:
       and ' rescues · them from ' all their ' troubles.

18   The Lord is near to those who are ' broken-'hearted:
       the Lord saves ' those · who are ' crushed in ' spirit.

19   The troubles of the ' righteous · are ' many:
       but the Lord ' sets them ' free · from them ' all.

20   The Lord guards every bone in the body ' of the ' righteous:
       and so not ' one of ' them is ' broken.

21   Evil brings ' death · to the ' wicked:
       and those who hate the ' righteous · are ' brought to ' ruin.

22   You O Lord ransom the ' lives of · your ' servants:
       and none who take ' refuge · in ' you shall ' perish.

PART ONE

1   Contend O Lord with those who con'tend with ' me:
      and fight against ' those who ' fight a'gainst me.

2   Take hold upon ' shield and ' buckler:
      rise ' up and ' come · to my ' help.

3†   Draw the spear and the javelin a'gainst · my pur'suers:
      and say to me, ' 'I am ' your sal'vation.'

        * * *

9   Then shall my soul be joyful ' in the ' Lord:
      it shall re'joice in ' God's sal'vation.

10   My very bones shall say, 'Lord who is like you,
        for you save the poor from ' those too ' strong for them:
      the poor and needy from ' those ' who de'spoil them?'

11   Witnesses rise up with malice ' in their ' hearts:
      they question me about things of ' which I ' know ' nothing.

12   They repay me ' evil · for ' good:
      I am like ' one · who is ' deeply · be'reaved.

13   Yet when they were sick I put on sackcloth,
        and afflicted my'self with ' fasting:
      I prayed with my whole heart,
        as though for my ' friend ' or my ' brother.

14   I went about like one mourning ' for a ' mother:
      I was bowed ' down with ' heaviness · of ' heart.

15   But when I stumbled they gathered with glee,
        and came to'gether · a'gainst me:
      creatures unknown to me,
        they tore me a'part · with un'ending ' slander.

16   They mocked profanely ' more and ' more:
      and ' gnashed · at me ' with their ' teeth.

17 Lord how long will you look ' on at ' this?:
    rescue me from the evils they intend for me,
      save my ' precious ' life · from the ' lions.

18 Then I will give you thanks in the ' great as'sembly:
    in the ' mighty ' throng · I will ' praise you.

19 Let not my treacherous enemies ' triumph ' over me:
    let not those gloat over me‿
      who ' hate me · with'out · any ' cause.

20 For their talk is ' not of ' peace:
    but they devise lying words‿
      against those who are ' quiet ' in the ' land.

21 They open wide their mouths a'gainst me · and ' say:
    ' Shame on you, shame on you,
      we have seen it ' with our ' own ' eyes.'

22 You also have ' seen O ' Lord:
    do not be silent then,
      and go not ' far from ' me ' Lord.

23 Awake, and bestir yourself to ' do me ' justice:
    to defend my cause, my ' God ' and my ' Lord.

24 Give me judgment O Lord my God,
    according ' to your ' righteousness:
    and ' let them · not ' triumph ' over me.

25 Let them not say to themselves,
    ' There, we have our ' heart's de'sire ':
    let them not ' say they ' have de'stroyed me.

26 Let all those who rejoice at my misfortune‿
    be put to disgrace ' and con'fusion:
    let those who exult over me‿
      be ' clothed with ' shame · and dis'honour.

27 Let those who favour my righteous cause‿
    shout for ' joy · and be ' glad:
    let them cry out continually, 'Great is the Lord,
      who de'lights · in a ' servant's · pros'perity.'

28 Then shall my tongue ' speak of · your ' justice:
    and ' all the · day ' long · of your ' praise.

36

1 Sin speaks to the wicked ' deep · in their ' heart:
   there is no fear of ' God be'fore their ' eyes.

2 They flatter themselves in their ' own ' sight:
   that their iniquity will ' not be · found ' out and ' hated.

3 The words of their mouth are mischief ' and de'ceit:
   they have ceased to act ' wisely · and ' do ' good.

4 They plot mischief as they ' lie in ' bed:
   they are set on a course that is not good,
     and hold back from ' nothing ' that is ' evil.

5 Your steadfast love, O Lord, ex'tends · to the ' heavens:
   your ' faithful·ness ' up · to the ' clouds.

6 Your righteousness is like the strong mountains,
     your judgments are like the ' great ' deep:
   you Lord ' save both ' people · and ' beasts.

7 How precious is your steadfast ' love O ' God:
   mortals take refuge in the ' shadow ' of your ' wings.

8 They feast on the rich abundance ' of your ' house:
   you give them drink⌣
     from the ' stream of ' your de'lights.

9 For with you is the ' well of ' life:
   and in your ' light ' we see ' light.

10 Continue your loving kindness to ' those who ' know you:
   and your justice ' to the ' true of ' heart.

11 Let not the foot of pride ' come a'gainst me:
   nor the hand of the ' wicked ' drive · me a'way.

12 There are they fallen,'
     those · who do ' evil:
   they are thrown down ' and un'able · to ' rise.

PART ONE

1 Do not fret be'cause · of the ' wicked:
  or ' envy ' those · who do ' evil.

2 For they will soon dry up ' like the ' grass:
  and wither ' like the ' green ' herb.

3 Trust in the Lord and ' do ' good:
  then you shall dwell in the land,
    and ' there find ' safe ' pasture.

4 Find your delight ' in the ' Lord:
  and the Lord will ' give you · your ' heart's de'sire.

5 Commit your life ' to the ' Lord:
  put your trust ' in the ' one · who will ' act for you,

6 so that the justice of your cause‿
    will break ' forth · as the ' light:
    your righteousness ' like the ' sun at ' noon.

7 Be still before the Lord, and ' wait in ' patience:
  do not grieve at the prosperity of‿
    those who ' follow ' evil ' purposes.

8 Refrain from anger, and sup'press your ' rage:
  do not fret yourself, for ' that leads ' only · to ' evil.

9 Those who do ' evil · shall ' perish:
  but those who wait‿
    for the ' Lord · shall pos'sess the ' land.

10 A little while, and the wicked shall ' be no ' more:
  look well, and you will ' find their ' place is ' empty.

11† But the humble shall pos'sess the ' land:
  and en'joy the ' fulness · of ' peace.

12 The wicked have evil designs ' on the ' just:
  and ' grind their ' teeth · at the ' sight of them.

13 But the Lord shall ' laugh · at the ' wicked:
  for the Most High ' sees · that their ' time is ' coming.

14 The wicked have drawn the sword and ' bent the ' bow:
  to strike down the poor and needy,
    and to slay ' those who ' walk ' uprightly.

15   Their sword shall pierce their ' own ' hearts:
       and their bow ' shall be ' broken · in ' pieces.

16   The little that the ' righteous ' have:
       is better than the ' riches ' of the ' wicked.

17   The power of the wicked ' shall be ' broken:
       but the Lord ' will up'hold the ' righteous.

PART TWO

18   The Lord cares for the upright ' all their ' days:
       and their ' heritage · will ' last for ' ever.

19   They will not be dismayed when ' times are ' evil:
       and in days of famine their ' food ' will not ' fail.

20   But the wicked, enemies of the ' Lord, shall ' perish:
       like fuel in the furnace ' they shall ' vanish · in ' smoke.

21   The wicked person borrows but does ' not re'pay:
       but the righteous ' is a ' gener·ous ' giver.

22   Those whom God has blessed shall pos'sess the ' land:
       but those whom God has cursed ' shall be ' rooted ' out.

23   The Lord directs the ' steps · of the ' upright:
       the Lord steadies them,
         and ' keeps them ' safe · in the ' path.

24†   Though they stumble they shall ' not fall ' down:
       for the Lord ' holds them ' each · by the ' hand.

25   I have been young and ' now · I am ' old:
       but never have I seen the righteous forsaken,
         or their ' children ' begging · their ' bread.

26   The righteous are always open'handed · in ' lending:
       and their ' children · are ' destined · for ' blessing.

PART THREE

27   Turn from evil and ' do ' good:
       and ' dwell · in the ' land for ' ever.

28   For the Lord is a ' lover · of ' justice:
       and will ' not for'sake a ' friend.

29   The unrighteous shall be wiped ' out for ' ever:
       and the ' children · of the ' wicked · shall ' perish.

30 The just shall in'herit · the ' land:
    and ' dwell there'in for ' ever.

31 The mouth of the righteous ' utters ' wisdom:
    and their tongue ' speaks of ' that · which is ' right.

32 The law of their God is ' in their ' heart:
    and their ' footsteps ' will not ' falter.

33 The wicked are on the watch ' for the ' righteous:
    and ' seek oc'casion · to ' slay them.

34 But the Lord will not leave them ' in their ' power:
    or let them be condemned ' when · they are ' put on ' trial.

35† Wait for the Lord and keep to the way of holiness,
    and the Lord will raise you up to pos'sess the ' land:
  the wicked shall perish,
    and ' you · shall be ' there to ' see it.

36 I have seen the wicked in ' great pros'perity:
    and towering ' like the ' cedars · of ' Lebanon.

37 I passed by again, and ' they were ' gone:
    I searched for them, but ' nowhere · could ' they be ' found.

38 Mark well the blameless person,
    and take ' note · of the ' upright:
  for those who seek ' peace shall ' have pos'terity.

39 But sinners shall be alto'gether · de'stroyed:
    the descendants ' of the ' wicked · shall ' perish.

40 Deliverance for the righteous ' comes · from the ' Lord:
    the Most High is their ' stronghold · in ' time of ' trouble.

41 God will help them ' and de'liver them:
    and will save them,
      because they take ' refuge ' in the ' Lord.

38

1 Do not rebuke me Lord ' in your ' anger:
    do not ' punish · me ' in your ' wrath.

2 For your arrows stick ' fast · in my ' body:
    and your ' hand lies ' heavy · up'on me.

3   There is no health in my flesh
              because of your ' indig'nation:
        no soundness in my ' bones be'cause of · my ' sin.

4   My sins are like a flood risen ' over · my ' head:
        like a burden too ' heavy · for ' me to ' bear.

5   My wounds are ' foul and ' festering:
        by ' reason ' of my ' foolishness.

6   I am bowed down, and ' utter·ly ' prostrate:
        I go about ' mourning ' all the · day ' long.

7   For my loins are ' filled with ' burning:
        there is no ' soundness · in ' all my ' body.

8   I am numbed and ' utter·ly ' crushed:
        I groan in the ' anguish ' of my ' heart.

9   Lord, all my longing is ' known to ' you:
        and my sighing ' is not ' hidden ' from you.

10 My heart is pounding, my ' strength has ' failed me:
        and the light of my ' eyes has ' gone ' from me.

11 My friends and companions avoid me in ' my af'fliction:
        and my own ' family · keep ' far a'way.

12 Those who seek my ' life lay ' snares for me:
        those who desire my hurt speak mischief,
              and plan treachery ' all the ' day ' long.

13 But I am like the deaf, who ' do not ' hear:
        like one who is dumb ' and un'able · to ' speak.

14 Yes, I am like one who ' does not ' hear:
        and in whose ' mouth · there is ' no re'tort.

15 On you O Lord I ' fix my ' hope:
        you O ' Lord my ' God will ' answer me.

16 For I pray, 'Let not the people ex'ult ' over me:
        who rejoice ' if my ' foot should ' slip.'

17 Indeed I am on the ' point of ' falling:
        and my ' pain is ' with me · con'tinually.

18 I confess that ' I am ' guilty:
        I am dismayed ' at the ' thought · of my ' sin.

19   Those who are my enemies without ' cause are ' strong:
        those who ' hate me ' wrongfully · are ' many.

20   Those who repay evil for good are ' also · a'gainst me:
        because I ' seek to ' do · what is ' right.

21   Do not for'sake me · O ' Lord:
        be not ' far · from me ' O my ' God.

22   Make haste and ' come · to my ' help:
        O Lord ' God of ' my sal'vation.

39

1   I said, 'I will be watchful ' over · my ' ways:
        lest I ' should of'fend · with my ' tongue.

2   'I will ' bridle · my ' mouth:
        so long as the wicked ' are be'fore my ' eyes.'

3   I was dumb and ' kept ' silent:
        I refrained from speaking,
           but my dis'tress be'came more ' painful.

4   My heart grew ' hot with'in me:
        and at the thought of it the fire kindled,
           and my ' tongue broke ' out · into ' speech.

5   'Lord let me know my end, and the number ' of my ' days:
        that I may learn how ' fleeting ' is my ' life.

6   'You have made my days but a hand's breadth,
        and my lifetime is as nothing ' in your ' sight:
        even at our best, each of us is ' only · a ' puff of ' wind.

7   'We go about like phantoms,
        and trouble ourselves ' to no ' purpose:
        we heap up riches,
        and ' cannot · tell ' who will ' gather them.'

8   And now ' what · do I ' hope for?:
        indeed truly my ' hope ' is in ' you.

9   Deliver me from all ' my of'fences:
        and do not ' make me · the ' butt of ' fools.

10   I was dumb, I did not ' open · my ' mouth:
        because ' it was ' your ' doing.

11   Take away your ' scourge ' from me:
       I am crushed by the ' stroke · of your ' heavy ' hand.

12   When you rebuke us, and ' chasten us · for ' sin:
       you consume all we treasure,
         like a moth ' eating · a'way a ' garment.

13†   It is ' so with ' all of us:
       truly each is no more ' than a ' puff of ' wind.

14   Hear my prayer O Lord, and give ' ear · to my ' cry:
       do not be ' silent ' at my ' tears.

15   For I am only a passing guest ' in your ' house:
       a wayfarer as ' all my ' forbears ' were.

16†   Turn your frowning gaze from me, that I may ' smile a'gain:
       before I go from here ' and am ' seen no ' more.

40

1   I waited patiently for ' you O ' Lord:
       and you bent down to ' me and ' heard my ' cry.

2   You lifted me out of the horrible pit, out of the ' miry ' clay:
       and set my feet upon a rock,
         and ' made my ' foothold ' sure.

3   And you put a new ' song · in my ' mouth:
       a song of ' praise ' to our ' God.

4   Many shall see it, and be ' filled with ' awe:
       and so they will ' trust ' in the ' Lord.

5   Blessèd are those who have put their ' trust · in the ' Lord:
       who have not turned to the proud,
         or to those who stray ' after ' false ' gods.

6   O Lord my God,
         great are the wonderful things you have done,
         and the things you ' have in ' mind for us:
       there is none to ' be com'pared with ' you.

7†   I would pro'claim them · and ' speak of them:
       but they are ' more than ' can be ' numbered.

8   Sacrifice and offering you do not desire,
         but you have opened my ' ears to ' hear:
         burnt-offering and sacrifice for sin ' ⌣
             you have ' not re'quired of me.

9   Then I said, ' 'Look, · I have ' come:
         in the scroll of the book it is written ⌣
             that ' I should ' do your ' will.'

10   I delight to do your will ' O my ' God:
         truly your ' law is ' in my ' heart.

11   I have told the glad news of deliverance ⌣
         in the ' great as'sembly:
         I did not restrain my lips, as ' you well ' know O ' Lord.

12   I have not kept your goodness hidden ' in my ' heart:
         I have spoken of your faithfulness ' ⌣
             and your ' saving ' help.

13   I have not concealed your ' steadfast ' love:
         nor your truth ' from the ' great as'sembly.

14   Lord, do not withhold from me your ' tender ' care:
         let your love and ' faithful·ness ' ever · pre'serve me.

15   For innumerable ' troubles · be'set me:
         my sins have overtaken me, ' and I ' cannot ' see.

16   They are more in number than the ' hairs · of my ' head:
         and my ' heart ' utter·ly ' fails me.

17   Be pleased O ' Lord · to de'liver me:
         O ' Lord make ' haste to ' help me.

18   Let those who seek my life be put to ' shame · and con'fusion:
         let those who desire my hurt be ' turned back ' in dis'grace.

19   Let those who mock at my hu'mili'ation:
         be appalled at ' their re'ward of ' shame.

20   Let all who seek you rejoice and be ' glad in ' you:
         may those who love your saving help ⌣
             say ' always · ' The ' Lord is ' great.'

21   As for me, I am ' poor and ' needy:
         but the ' Lord ' will take ' care of me.

22† You are my helper and ' my de'liverer:
         make no long de'lay ' O my ' God.

1   Blessèd are those who consider the ' poor and ' helpless:
the Lord will ' save them · in ' time of ' trouble.

2   The Lord protect them and keep them alive,
so that they are counted happy ' in the ' land:
and never give them up ' to the ' will · of their ' enemies.

3   The Lord comfort them ' on their ' sick-bed:
and turn their ' sickness ' into ' health.

4   I said, 'Lord have ' mercy · up'on me:
heal me, for ' I have ' sinned a'gainst you.'

5   My enemies say to ' me in ' malice:
'When will you ' die · and your ' name ' perish?'

6   If any come to see me, they speak ' insin'cerely:
their heart gathers mischief,
then they go ' out and ' spread it · a'broad.

7   All who hate me whisper to'gether · a'gainst me:
they imagine about me the ' worst ' that can ' happen.

8   They say that a deadly thing has ' fastened · up'on me:
that I will rise up no ' more from ' where I ' lie.

9   Even the friend I trusted, who ate ' bread · at my ' table:
has ' lifted · a ' heel a'gainst me.

10 Lord have ' mercy · up'on me:
raise me up again, ' so that ' I may · re'pay them.

11 By this I shall ' know · that you ' favour me:
in that my enemy ' shall not ' triumph ' over me.

12 Because of my integrity ' you up'hold me:
you have set me ' in your ' presence · for ' ever.

13† Blessèd be the ' Lord our ' God:
from everlasting to everlasting. ' Amen. ' A'men.

42

1 Like a deer that longs for the ' running ' streams:
 so do I ' long for ' you my ' God.

2 My soul is thirsting for you O God,
 thirsting for the ' living ' God:
 when shall I come to ap'pear in ' your ' presence?

3 My tears have been my food ' day and ' night:
 while all day long they ask me,'
  'Where now ' is your ' God?'

4 This I remember as I pour out my ' soul · in dis'tress:
 how I went with the throng,
  and led them ' to the ' house of ' God,

5† amid cries of gladness ' and thanks'giving:
 from people ' keeping · a ' holy ' day.

6 *Why are you cast ' down my ' soul:*
 and why are ' you so ' troubled · with'in me?

7 *Wait in ' hope for ' God:*
 for I will yet praise the one ＿
  who is my ' saviour ' and my ' God.

8 My soul is cast ' down with'in me:
 therefore I remember you from the land of Jordan,
  from Mizar a'mong the ' hills of ' Hermon.

9 Deep calls to deep in the ' roar · of your ' waters:
 all your ' waves · and your ' torrents · pass ' over me.

10 You will grant me loving ' kindness · by ' day:
 and at night I will sing to you,
  and ' pray · to the ' God of · my ' life.

11 I say to God my rock, 'Why have ' you for'gotten me:
 why do I go mourning＿
  be'cause the ' enemy · op'presses me?'

12 I am like one whose bones are ' broken · to ' pieces:
 through the ' taunting ' of my ' enemies,

13 while they say to me ' all day ' long:
 'Tell us, ' where now ' is your ' God?'

14 *Why are you cast ' down my ' soul:*
 and why are ' you so ' troubled · with'in me?

15 *Wait in ' hope for ' God:*
　　for I will yet praise the one ⌣
　　　　who is my ' saviour ' and my ' God.

43

1 Give judgment for me O God,
　　and plead my cause against an un'godly ' people:
　　save me from the de'ceitful ' and the ' wicked.

2 You are my stronghold, why have ' you re'jected me:
　　why do I go mourning op'pressed ' by the ' enemy?

3 O send out your light and your ' truth to ' lead me:
　　and bring me to your holy ' hill and ' to your ' dwelling.

4 Then I will go to the altar of God,
　　the God of my ' joy and ' gladness:
　　and praise you with the ' harp O ' God my ' God.

5 *Why are you cast ' down my ' soul:*
　　and why are ' you so ' troubled · with'in me?

6 *Wait in ' hope for ' God:*
　　for I will yet praise the one ⌣
　　　　who is my ' saviour ' and my ' God.

44

Day 9 Morning

1 We have heard with our ears O God,
　　we have ' learned · from our ' ancestors:
　　the things you did in their ' time in ' days of ' old.

2 With your own hand you uprooted the nations⌣
　　and ' planted · us ' in:
　　you broke up the peoples, and ' caused · us to ' strike ' root.

3 It was not by their own sword⌣
　　that our forbears got pos'session · of the ' land:
　　nor did their ' own arm ' bring them ' victory,

4 but it was your right hand, your arm⌣
　　and the ' light · of your ' face:
　　because you ' looked up·on ' them with ' favour.

5   You are my king ' and my ' God:
        it was ' you · that sent ' help to ' Jacob.

6   Through you we beat ' down our ' foes:
        and in your name we ' trampled ' down · our as'sailants.

7   For I did not ' trust · in my ' bow:
        nor ' was it · my ' sword that ' saved me.

8   But it was you that saved us ' from our ' enemies:
        and put ' those who ' hate us · to ' shame.

9†   In God we made our ' boast con'tinually:
        and gave thanks to your ' name with'out ' ceasing.

10   But now you have re'jected · and ' humbled us:
        you no longer ' go out ' with our ' armies.

11   You make us turn our ' backs · to the ' enemy:
        who ' plunder · us ' now at ' will.

12   You have given us like ' sheep · to the ' slaughter:
        and ' scattered us · a'mong the ' nations.

13   You have sold your ' people · for ' nothing:
        and made no ' profit ' from the ' sale.

14   You have made us the ' taunt · of our ' neighbours:
        derided and scorned by ' those ' round a'bout us.

15   You have made us a byword a'mong the ' nations:
        so that the peoples ' toss their ' heads in ' scorn.

16   All day long my dis'grace · is be'fore me:
        and ' shame has ' covered · my ' face,

17   at the words of those who ' taunt · and re'vile me:
        as the ' ene·my ' takes re'venge.

18   All this has come upon us, yet we do ' not for'get you:
        nor have we been ' false ' to your ' covenant.

19   Our heart has not turned ' back from ' you:
        nor have our feet ' strayed from ' your ' path.

20† Yet you have crushed us in a ' place of ' sorrows:
        and covered us ' with the ' shadow · of ' death.

21   If we had forgotten the ' name · of our ' God:
        and stretched out our ' hands in ' prayer · to an'other,

22   would you not find it ' out O ' God:
         for you know the very ' secrets ' of the ' heart?

23   For your sake we face death ' all the · day ' long:
         and are ' counted · as ' sheep · for the ' slaughter.

24   Rise up Lord, ' why · do you ' sleep?:
         Awake, and do not re'ject ' us for ' ever.

25   Why do you ' hide your ' face:
         and for'get · our op'pression · and ' misery?

26   For we are brought low, down to the ' very ' dust:
         our body lies ' prone ' on the ' ground.

27†   Rise up Lord, and ' come · to our ' help:
         deliver us ' for your ' mercy's ' sake.

45

1   My heart overflows with a ' noble ' theme:
         I utter the song I have made for a king,
             my tongue is like the ' pen · of a ' ready ' writer.

2   You are the fairest of men,
             grace is up'on your ' lips:
         therefore ' God has ' blessed you · for ' ever.

3   Gird your sword upon your ' thigh O ' mighty one:
         in ' splendour ' and in ' state.

4   In your majesty ride on to conquer,
             in the cause of ' truth and ' justice:
         and let your right hand ' teach · by its ' awesome ' deeds.

5   Your arrows will be very sharp,
             in the heart of the ' king's ' enemies:
         and the nations shall ' fall ' at your ' feet.

6   Your throne is as God's throne, it en'dures for ' ever:
         your royal sceptre ' is a ' sceptre · of ' righteousness.

7   You are a lover of right and a ' hater · of ' wrong:
         therefore God your God, has anointed you‿
             with the oil of gladness a'bove ' other ' kings.

8 All your garments are fragrant with⌣
  myrrh ' aloes · and ' cassia:
  music of strings from ivory ' pala·ces ' makes you ' glad.

9† Kings' daughters are among your ' ladies · of ' honour:
  on your right hand is the ' queen in ' gold of ' Ophir.

10 Listen my daughter, hear and ' ponder · my ' words:
  forget your own ' people · and your ' father's ' house.

11 The king de'sires your ' beauty:
  he is your lord, ' therefore · bow ' down be'fore him.

12† The people of Tyre will come ' with their ' gifts:
  the richest in the ' land will ' court your ' favour.

13 The bride is a king's daughter,
  in the palace all ' honour · a'waits her:
  her ' clothes · are em'broidered · with ' gold.

14 In robes of many colours she is brought to ' you O ' king:
  her maiden companions with her⌣
  to ' bring her ' into · your ' presence.

15† With joy and ' gladness · they ' bring her:
  they ' enter · the ' royal ' palace.

16 In place of your fathers ' you shall · have ' sons:
  and you will make them princes ' over ' all the ' earth.

17 And I will cause your name to be remembered⌣
  from one generation ' to an'other:
  therefore the ' peoples · shall ' praise you · for ' ever.

46

1 God is our ' refuge · and ' strength:
  a very ' present ' help in ' trouble.

2 So we will not be afraid though the ' earth should ' quake:
  and mountains fall into the ' depths ' of the ' sea,

3† though the waters of the sea ' rage and ' foam:
  and the mountains ' tremble ' at the ' tumult.

4 There is a river, its streams make glad the ' city · of ' God:
  which the Most High has ' made a ' holy ' dwelling.

5   God is within her, she ' cannot · be ' shaken:
     God will help her ' at the ' break of ' day.

6   Nations are in tumult, ' kingdoms · are ' shaken:
     but God has spoken, and the ' earth ' melts a'way.

7   *The Lord of ' hosts is ' with us:*
     the God of ' Jacob ' is our ' stronghold.

8   Come and see what the ' Lord has ' done:
     the devastation ' brought up'on the ' earth.

9   The Lord makes wars to cease in ' all the ' world:
     the Lord breaks the bow and snaps the spear,
       and ' burns the ' shields · in the ' fire.

10   'Be still then, and know that ' I am ' God:
     high over the nations, ' high a'bove the ' earth.'

11   *The Lord of ' hosts is ' with us:*
     the God of ' Jacob ' is our ' stronghold.

47

1   Clap your hands ' all you ' peoples:
     cry out to ' God with ' shouts of ' joy.

2   For the Lord most high is ' to be ' feared:
     and is the great sovereign ' over ' all the ' earth.

3   The Lord has subdued the ' peoples ' under us:
     and the ' nations ' under · our ' feet.

4   The Lord chose a land to ' be our ' heritage:
     it is the pride of ' Jacob ' whom God ' loves.

5   God has gone up with ' shouts of ' triumph:
     the Lord has gone ' up · with a ' fanfare · of ' trumpets.

6   Sing praises, sing ' praises · to ' God:
     sing praises, sing ' praises ' to our ' king.

7   For God is the king of ' all the ' earth:
     sing praises ' with your ' utmost ' skill.

8   God reigns ' over · the ' nations:
     God is seated ' on a ' holy ' throne.

9   The princes of the ' nations · as'semble:
       with the ' people · of the ' God of ' Abraham.

10   For the mighty ones of the earth⌣
       have become the ' servants · of ' God:
       the Lord is ex'alted ' over ' all.

48

1   Great is the Lord and ' highly · to be ' praised:
       in the ' city ' of our ' God.

2   Fair and lofty is God's ' holy ' mountain:
       it is the ' joy of ' all the ' earth.

3†   On Mount Zion, as in the far north,
       stands the city of the ' Most ' High:
       in her citadels God is well ' known · as a ' sure de'fence.

4   See how the ' rulers · as'sembled:
       they came ' on to'gether · a'gainst her.

5   They were amazed ' when they ' saw her:
       they were dis'mayed and ' ready · to ' flee.

6   Trembling came upon ' them and ' anguish:
       as it ' comes · on a ' woman · in ' child-birth,

7   or as when the ' east wind ' blows:
       and ' breaks up · the ' ships of ' Tarshish.

8   As we have heard, so have we seen⌣
       in the city of the ' Lord of ' hosts:
       the city our ' God up'holds for ' ever.

9   We have called to mind your steadfast ' love O ' God:
       in the ' midst of ' your ' temple.

10   As your name is great O God,
       so is your praise to the ' ends · of the ' earth:
       your right ' hand is ' filled with ' victory.

11   Let God's mountain rejoice,
       and the daughter-cities of ' Judah · be ' glad:
       be'cause of ' your ' judgments.

12   Go in procession around the circuit ' of Je'rusalem:
       count the ' number ' of her ' towers,

13   take note of her ramparts, ex'amine · her ' citadels:
        so that you may ' tell the ' next · gener'ation,

14†   that such is God, our God for ' ever · and ' ever:
        God shall be our ' guide to ' all e'ternity.

49

1   Hear this ' all you ' people:
        give heed, ' all · who in'habit · the ' world,

2   people of both low and ' high es'tate:
        the ' rich · and the ' poor to'gether.

3   My mouth shall speak ' words of ' wisdom:
        the thoughts of my heart are ' full of ' under'standing.

4   I will turn my ' mind · to a ' proverb:
        and with harp and ' song de'clare its ' meaning.

5   Why should I fear in ' evil ' days:
        when the wicked ' dog my ' steps · and be'set me?

6   They are people who ' trust · in their ' wealth:
        and boast of ' their a'bundant ' riches.

7   Truly one cannot ' ransom · one'self:
        or pay to ' God the ' price of · one's ' life,

8   the ransom that would permit life to go ' on for ' ever:
        and never ' come · to the ' pit of ' death.

9†   For that ransom would be ' far too ' costly:
        for ever beyond ' human · a'bility · to ' pay.

10   We see that the wise also die,
        as well as the ' foolish · and ' stupid:
        they perish alike, and ' leave their ' wealth to ' others.

11   Their tomb is their home for ever,
        their dwelling-place from ' age to ' age:
        though once they called estates ' after · their ' own ' names.

12   One who is rich but without ' under'standing:
        is ' like the ' beasts that ' perish.

13   This is the fate of those with a ' foolish · self'confidence:
        the fate too of those who follow them,
        who ap'prove of ' their ' boastings.

14 Like sheep they are driven into Sheol,
      death shall ' be their ' shepherd:
      quickly they de'scend ' to the ' grave.

15 Their bodies shall con'sume a'way:
      the grave shall ' be their ' home for ' ever.

16 But God will ' ransom · my ' life:
      and save me ' from the ' power · of ' death.

17 Do not fear when some be'come ' rich:
      or when the ' wealth · of their ' household · in'creases.

18 For at death they take ' nothing · a'way with them:
      and their ' riches ' will not ' follow them.

19 While they lived they counted them'selves ' happy:
      and others ' praise them ' in their · pros'perity,

20 but they will go to ' join their ' ancestors:
      who will never a'gain ' see the ' light.

21 One who is rich but without ' under'standing:
      is ' like the ' beasts that ' perish.

50

PART ONE

1 The Lord, the most mighty ' God has ' spoken:
      and summoned the world,
         from the rising of the ' sun ' to its ' setting.

2 God shines ' out from ' Zion:
      a ' city ' perfect · in ' beauty.

3 Our God is coming, and will ' not keep ' silence:
      before you O God runs a consuming fire,
      and a mighty ' tempest ' rages · a'bout you.

4 You call on the heavens above, and on the ' earth be'low:
      to witness the ' judgment ' of your ' people.

5 'Gather my ' people · be'fore me:
      the people who made ' covenant · with ' me by ' sacrifice.'

6 The heavens pro'claim your ' justice:
      for ' you your'self are ' judge.

7 'Listen my people, and ' I will ' speak:
   I will testify against you Israel, ' I am ' God your ' God.

8 'I find no fault ' with your ' sacrifices:
   your burnt-'offerings · are ' always · be'fore me.

9 'I need take no young ' bull · from your ' farm:
   nor ' he-goat ' out of · your ' folds.

10 'For all the beasts of the ' forest · are ' mine:
    and so are the cattle ' on a ' thousand ' hills.

11 'I know all the ' birds · of the ' air:
    and all living things in the ' field are ' in my ' care.

12 'If I were hungry I ' would not ' tell you:
    for the world is ' mine and ' all · that is ' in it.

13 'Do you think that I eat the ' flesh of ' bulls:
    or ' drink the ' blood of ' goats?

14 'Offer to God the ' sacrifice · of ' thanksgiving:
    and pay your ' vows · to the ' One Most ' High.

15† 'And call upon me in ' time of ' trouble:
    then I will de'liver you · and ' you shall ' honour me.'

PART TWO

16 But God's word to the ' wicked · is ' this:
    'How can you recite my laws,
       and take my ' covenant · up'on your ' lips?

17 'For you hate to ' be cor'rected:
    and turn your ' back when ' I am ' speaking.

18 'You go along with a thief ' when you ' meet one:
    and you throw ' in your ' lot · with a'dulterers.

19 'You unbridle your mouth to ' speak ' evil:
    and with your tongue ' you con'trive de'ception.

20 'You sit down and ' slander · your ' brother:
    and malign your ' own ' mother's ' son.

21 'All this you have done, and I ' kept ' silence:
    and you thought I was ' one ' like your'self.

22 'But now ' I re'buke you:
    and ' lay the ' charge be'fore you.

23   'Mark this, you that for'get ' God:
        lest I tear you to pieces,
           and ' there will · be ' no one · to ' save you.

24†   'Whoever offers a sacrifice of thanksgiving⌣
        does me ' due ' honour:
        and to those who follow my way⌣
           I will ' show · the sal'vation · of ' God.'

51

1   Have mercy on me O God in your ' great ' kindness:
        in the fulness of your mercy ' blot out ' my of'fences.

2   Wash away ' all my ' guilt:
        and ' cleanse me ' from my ' sin.

3   For I ac'knowledge · my ' faults:
        and my ' sin is ' always · be'fore me.

4   Against you only have I sinned⌣
        and done evil ' in your ' sight:
        so that you are justified in your sentence,
           and ' blameless ' in your ' judging.

5   Evil have I been ' from my ' birth:
        sinner I am from the ' time of ' my con'ception.

6   But you desire truth in our ' inward ' being:
        therefore teach me wisdom ' in my ' secret ' heart.

7   Take hyssop,
        sprinkle me with water and I ' shall be ' clean:
        wash me, and I ' shall be ' whiter · than ' snow.

8   Let me hear the sounds of ' joy and ' gladness:
        that the bones you have ' broken ' may re'joice.

9   Turn away your face ' from my ' sins:
        and ' blot out ' all my · mis'deeds.

10   Create in me a clean ' heart O ' God:
        and re'new a · right ' spirit · with'in me.

11   Do not cast me away ' from your ' presence:
        do not take your ' holy ' spirit ' from me.

12   Give me the joy of your ' help a'gain:
        and strengthen me ' with a ' willing ' spirit.

13†   Then I will teach trans'gressors · your ' ways:
       and sinners will ' turn to ' you a'gain.

14   Rescue me from bloodshed O ' God my ' saviour:
       and my tongue shall ' sing of ' your de'liverance.

15   O Lord ' open · my ' lips:
       and my ' mouth · shall pro'claim your ' praise.

16   You desire no sacrifice, or ' I would ' give it:
       but you take no de'light in ' burnt-'offerings.

17   The sacrifice acceptable to God is a ' broken ' spirit:
       a broken and contrite heart O God ' you will ' not de'spise.

18   Let it be your pleasure to do ' good · to Je'rusalem:
       to re'build the ' walls · of the ' city.

19   Then will you delight in the appointed sacrifices,
       in burnt-offerings ' and ob'lations:
       then will they offer young ' bulls up'on your ' altar.

52

1   Why O mighty one do you ' boast · of your ' wickedness?:
       always bent on harming ' those ' faithful · to ' God.

2   Your tongue is like a ' sharpened ' razor:
       you contriver ' of de'ceit and ' slander.

3   You love evil ' rather · than ' good:
       lying ' rather · than ' speaking · the ' truth.

4   You love all words that ' may do ' hurt:
       O lying ' tongue ' that you ' are.

5   Therefore God will de'stroy you · for ' ever:
       God will pluck you from your tent,
         and uproot you ' from the ' land · of the ' living.

6   The righteous will look ' on with ' awe:
       and ' then · will they ' laugh and ' say,

7†   'Here is one who would not look to ' God for ' strength:
       but trusted in great wealth,
         and ' in · the se'curity · of ' riches.'

8   But I am like a green olive tree in the ' house of ' God:
       I trust in the goodness of ' God for ' ever · and ' ever.

9   I will always give you thanks, for this was ' your ' doing:
       I will proclaim that your name is good,
          in the ' presence ' of the ' faithful.

53

1   The foolish have spoken ' in their ' heart:
       and said, ' 'There is ' no ' God.'

2   All are corrupt, they do a'bomina·ble ' things:
       there is ' no one · who ' does · what is ' good.

3   God looks down from heaven up'on us' all:
       to see if any are ' wise and ' seek · after ' God.

4   But they have all gone astray,
          all alike have ' been cor'rupted:
       there is not one that does ' good, ' no not ' one.

5   Have they no knowledge, all ' those · who do ' evil?:
       they devour my people like so much bread,
          and ' do not ' pray · to the ' Lord.

6   There they are, in great terror;
          terror such as ' never · has ' been:
       for God will scatter the ' bones ' of the · un'godly.

7   They shall be ' put to ' shame:
       because ' God ' has re'jected them.

8   O that deliverance for God's people
          would come forth ' from Je'rusalem:
       when God restores the fortunes of the people,
          then shall Jacob re'joice and ' Israel · be ' glad.

54

1   Save me O God by the ' power · of your ' name:
       and ' vindicate · me ' by your ' might.

2   Hear my ' prayer O ' God:
       and ' listen · to the ' words of · my ' mouth.

3   For insolent people have ' risen · a'gainst me:
       ruthless ones are seeking my life,
          they ' give no ' thought to ' God.

4   But see, ' God · is my ' helper:
       it is the Lord ' who up'holds my ' life.

      * * *

6†   The offering of a willing heart ' I will ' give you:
       and praise your ' name O ' Lord · in your ' faithfulness.

      * * *

55

PART ONE

1   Hear my ' prayer O ' God:
       do not ' hide your· self ' from my ' pleading.

2   Give heed to ' me and ' answer me:
       for I am ' anxious · and ' greatly ' troubled,

3   because my enemies shout,
         and the wicked press ' hard up'on me:
       they bring down trouble upon me,
         and as'sail me ' in their ' fury.

4   My heart is dis'tressed with'in me:
       and the terrors of ' death have ' fallen · up'on me.

5   Fear and ' trembling · come ' over me:
       and ' horror ' over'whelms me.

6   And I said, 'O that I had ' wings · like a ' dove:
       for then I would fly a'way and ' be at ' rest.

7   'I would escape ' far a'way:
       and find a ' refuge ' in the ' wilderness.

8   'I would hasten to ' find a ' shelter:
       from the raging ' wind ' and the ' storm.'

9   Frustrate their counsels O Lord,
         and con'fuse their ' speech:
       for I have seen ' violence · and ' strife · in the ' city.

10   Day and night they patrol a'long its ' walls:
       trouble and ' mischief ' are with'in it.

11† Wickedness is ' at its ' centre:
  oppression and fraud ' never ' leave its ' streets.

PART TWO

12 It was not an open enemy ' who in'sulted me:
  for then I ' could have ' borne the ' taunts.

13 Nor was it a rival who made ' boasts a'gainst me:
  for then I might have ' kept out ' of the ' way.

14 But it was you, one of my ' own ' kind:
  my companion ' and my ' inti·mate ' friend.

15 Pleasantly we con'versed to'gether:
  and walked in the ' house of ' God as ' friends.

  * * *

17 But I will call to ' you O ' God:
  you O ' Lord my ' God will ' save me.

18 Evening, morning, ' and at ' noon:
  I cry out to you in my grief,
    and ' you will ' hear my ' cry.

19 You will deliver me in ' safety · from ' battle:
  for ' those · who be'set me · are ' many.

20 You O God will hear.
    You, the eternal ' judge will ' humble them:
  because they keep no law, and ' have no ' fear of ' you.

21 The treacherous have raised their hand‿
    against those who ' were at ' peace with them:
  they have ' broken · their ' solemn ' covenant.

22 The words of their mouth were softer than butter,
    yet war was ' in their ' heart:
  their words were smoother than oil,
    but ' they · were like ' naked ' swords.

23 Cast your burden on the Lord‿
    and the ' Lord · will sus'tain you:
  the Lord will never al'low the ' righteous · to ' stumble.

24 But as for the treacherous ' and the ' bloodthirsty:
  you O God will cast them ' into · the ' pit · of de'struction.

25† They shall not live out ' half their ' days:
    but I will ' put my ' trust in ' you.

56

1 Be merciful to me O God,
    for my assailants are ' treading · me ' down:
    they harass me ' all the ' day ' long.

2 My enemies tread me down ' all day ' long:
    for many are ' those who ' fight a'gainst me.

3 When I am afraid O ' God most ' high:
    I will ' put my ' trust in ' you.

4 In God whose word I praise,
    in God I trust and will not ' be a'fraid:
    for what can human ' malice ' do to ' me?

5 All day long they dis'tort my ' words:
    all their ' thoughts · are to ' do me ' evil.

6 They gather together and ' lie in ' ambush:
    they track me down, and ' seek to ' take my ' life.

7 Recompense them O God ' for their ' wickedness:
    in your ' anger ' bring · down the ' nations.

8 You have taken account of my wanderings,
    you have stored up my ' tears · in your ' bottle:
    are not these things ' entered ' in your ' book?

9 My enemies shall turn back on the ' day · that I ' call:
    this I know, for ' God is ' on my ' side.

10 In God whose ' word I ' praise:
    in the ' Lord whose ' word I ' praise,

11† in God I trust, I shall ' not · be a'fraid:
    for what can human ' malice ' do to ' me?

12 To you O God I must per'form my ' vows:
    to you I will ' offer ' my thanks'giving.

13 For you have saved me from death,
    and kept my ' feet from ' stumbling:
    so that I may walk‿
    in your presence ' in the ' light · of the ' living.

57

1   Be merciful to me O ' God, be ' merciful:
    for ' I have ' made · you my ' refuge.

2   In the shadow of your wings ' I take ' shelter:
    until the storms of de'struction ' pass ' by.

3   I call to you O ' God most ' high:
    for you ful'fil your ' purpose ' for me.

4   You will send from heaven and save me,
    you will put to shame those⌣
    who would ' trample · me ' down:
    you will send forth your ' steadfast ' love and ' faithfulness.

5   For I lie down amongst lions greedy for ' human ' prey:
    their teeth are spears and arrows,
    and their ' tongues are ' sharpened ' swords.

6   *Be exalted O God a'bove the ' heavens:*
    and let your glory be ' over ' all the ' earth.

7   They set a net for my feet, and ' I · was brought ' low:
    they dug a pit in my path, but ' fell · into ' it them'selves.

8   My heart is steadfast O God, my ' heart is ' steadfast:
    I will ' sing and ' make ' melody.

9   Awake my soul, awake ' lute and ' harp:
    I myself ' will a'waken · the ' dawn.

10 I will give you thanks O Lord a'mong the ' peoples:
    I will sing your ' praise a'mong the ' nations.

11 For the greatness of your mercy reaches ' to the ' heavens:
    and your ' faithful·ness ' up · to the ' clouds.

12 *Be exalted O God a'bove the ' heavens:*
    and let your glory be ' over ' all the ' earth.

59

Day 11 Evening

1   Rescue me from my enemies ' O my ' God:
    pro'tect me · from ' those · who as'sail me.

2   Deliver me from ' those · who do ' evil:
    and ' save me ' from the ' bloodthirsty.

3   See, they lie in ' wait · for my ' life:
        cruel enemies are gathered against me‿
           through no fault of mine,
           nor for ' any ' wrong · I have ' done.

4   They run and take position against me,
        innocent ' though I ' am:
        arise O Lord to help me, and ' see it ' for your'self.

      * * *

6   Each evening they come back ' howling · like ' dogs:
        and ' prowling · a'bout the ' city.

7   They snarl contempt from their mouths,
        and swords come ' out · from their ' lips:
        but they say, ' 'Who is ' there to ' hear us?'

8   But you Lord will treat them ' with de'rision:
        you will laugh ' all the ' nations · to ' scorn.

9   It is to you my strength ' that I ' turn:
        because ' you O ' God · are my ' refuge.

10† In your love you will ' come to ' meet me:
        you will let me look in ' triumph ' on my ' foes.

      * * *

14   Let people know that God ' rules · over ' Jacob:
        and to the ' very ' ends · of the ' earth.

15   Each evening they come back ' howling · like ' dogs:
        and ' prowling · a'bout the ' city.

16   They roam about ' looking · for ' food:
        and growl if they ' do not ' get their ' fill.

17   But I will sing of your power O Lord,
        and each morning ac'claim your ' love:
        for you have been my stronghold,
           and a refuge in the ' day of ' my dis'tress.

18† To you O my strength ' I will ' sing:
        for you are my refuge, and my ' God · of un'failing ' love.

60

1 O God you have re'jected us · and ' broken us:
   you have been angry, re'store · us a'gain · to your ' favour.

2 You have made the earth shudder, and ' torn it ' open:
   heal its wounds, for ' it is ' falling · to ' pieces.

3 You have made your people drink a ' cup of ' bitterness:
   you have given us ' wine that ' makes us ' stagger.

4 You have given a warning to ' those who ' fear you:
   to make their escape ' from the ' power · of the ' bow.

5† Save us by your right ' hand and ' answer us:
   so that your be'lovèd · may ' be de'livered.

6 You have spoken in your ' holy ' place:
   'I will go up and divide Shechem,
      and measure ' out the ' valley · of ' Succoth.

7 'Gilead and Ma'nasseh · are ' mine:
   Ephraim is my helmet, and ' Judah ' is my ' sceptre.

8 'Moab is my wash-basin, to Edom I will ' cast my ' shoe:
   over Philistia ' I will ' shout in ' triumph.'

9 Who will bring me into the ' forti·fied ' city:
   who will ' lead me ' into ' Edom,

10† since you O God ' have re'jected us:
   and no longer go ' out ' with our ' armies?

11 Grant us help a'gainst the ' enemy:
   for vain ' is all ' human ' help.

12 With the help of our God we ' shall do ' valiantly:
   for it is God ' who will ' tread down · our ' foes.

61

1 Hear my ' cry O ' Lord:
   and ' listen ' to my ' prayer.

2 From the ends of the earth I ' call to ' you:
   when my ' heart is ' faint with'in me.

3 Set me on a rock that is too high for ' me to ' reach:
   for you have been my refuge,
      and a strong tower for ' me a'gainst the ' enemy.

4   Let me dwell in your ' tent for ' ever:
      and find shelter under the ' cover·ing ' of your ' wings.

5   For you Lord have ' heard my ' vows:
      and granted the desire of ' those · who re'vere your ' name.

6   Give long life ' to the ' king:
      may his years cover ' many ' gener'ations.

7   May he live in God's ' presence · for ' ever:
      your steadfast love and ' faithfulness · be ' his pro'tection.

8   So will I always sing praise ' to your ' name:
      while I ' daily · per'form my ' vows.

62

1   My soul truly is still, and ' waits for ' God:
      from ' whom comes ' my de'liverance.

2   In truth the Lord is my rock and ' my sal'vation:
      my tower of strength, ' so · that I ' stand un'shaken.

3   How long will all of you set upon ' me and ' batter me:
      as though I were a tottering ' wall · or a ' leaning ' fence?

4   Their purpose is to thrust me down ' from my ' eminence:
      they delight in lies,
         they bless with their lips‿
       but ' curse me ' in their ' hearts.

5   Yet be still my soul, and ' wait for ' God:
      from whom ' comes my ' hope · of de'liverance.

6   God only is my rock and ' my sal'vation:
      my tower of strength, ' so that · I ' stand un'shaken.

7   In God is my deliverance ' and my ' honour:
      the rock of my strength ' and my ' place of ' refuge.

8   Put your trust in God ' always · you ' people:
      pour out your hearts before the ' one who ' is our ' refuge.

9   For we mortals are only a puff of wind,
        the great among us are ' but il'lusion:
      weighed in the balance they rise upward,'
        all · of them ' lighter · than ' air.

10   Put no trust in extortion, set no vain ' hopes on ' plunder:
         if riches increase, do not ' set your ' heart up'on them.

11   Once God has spoken,
         and twice I have ' heard God ' say:
     'Power be'longs to ' God a'lone.'

12   Steadfast love O ' Lord is ' yours:
         and you reward us all ac'cording ' to our ' deeds.

63

1   O God ' you are · my ' God:
         and ' earnest·ly ' will I ' seek you.

2   My soul thirsts for you, my body ' yearns for ' you:
         like a land that is ' dry and ' thirsty · for ' water.

3   With this longing I have come before you ' in the ' sanctuary:
         that I may see your ' power ' and your ' glory.

4   Your steadfast love is better than ' life it'self:
         therefore my ' lips will ' speak your ' praise.

5   As long as I live ' I will ' bless you:
         and lift up my ' hands to ' pray · in your ' name.

6   I shall be satisfied as with a rich and ' sumptu·ous ' feast:
         and my mouth shall ' praise you · with ' joyful ' lips.

7   When I remember you up'on my ' bed:
         and think of you in the ' watches ' of the ' night,

8   how you have ' been my ' helper:
         how I am safe in the ' shadow ' of your ' wings,

9†   then my ' soul ' clings to you:
         and ' your right ' hand up'holds me.

10   But those who seek to de'stroy my ' life:
         shall go down to the ' depths ' of the ' earth.

11   They shall be given over to the ' power · of the ' sword:
         their bodies shall ' be a ' prey for ' jackals.

12† But the king shall rejoice in God,
         and all who swear by God ' shall ex'ult:
     for the mouths of ' liars ' shall be ' stopped.

64

1   Hear my voice O God ' in my ' prayer:
      preserve my ' life from ' fear · of the ' enemy.

2   Hide me from those who con'spire a'gainst me:
      from the ' turbu·lent ' throng · of the ' wicked.

3   They sharpen their ' tongues like ' swords:
      they aim ' bitter ' words like ' arrows,

4   to shoot from ambush at ' one · who is ' blameless:
      sudden the attack ' and by ' foes un'seen.

5   They hold fast to their ' evil ' purpose:
      they conspire to lay their snares,
        and they ' say, ' 'Who will ' see us?'

6   With skill and cunning they con'trive ' mischief:
      for the human heart and ' mind are ' very ' deep.

7   But God will shoot at them with a ' swift ' arrow:
      and ' sudden·ly ' strike them ' down.

8   Their own tongue will be ' their un'doing:
      and all who see their ' fate shall ' flee ' from them.

9   Then all shall fear, and say, ' 'This is ' God's work':
      and they shall ' ponder · what ' God has ' done.

10 The righteous shall rejoice in the Lord,
        and find their refuge in the ' Most ' High:
      and all who are ' true of ' heart · shall be ' glad.

65

1   You O God are to be ' praised · in Je'rusalem:
      to ' you shall ' vows · be per'formed.

2   You give ' heed to ' prayer:
      to you all mortals shall come ' to con'fess their ' sins.

3† The burden of our ' sins · is too ' great for us:
      but ' you will ' purge · them a'way.

4   Blessèd are the people you choose,
        and bring to ' dwell · in your ' courts:
      we shall be filled with the blessings␣
        of your ' house your ' holy ' temple.

5   With awesome deeds you answer⌣
      our prayers for deliverance, O ' God our ' saviour:
    you that are the hope of all the ends of the earth,'
      and · of the ' far-off ' seas.

6   By your strength you made ' fast the ' mountains:
    and ' gird your·self ' round with ' power.

7   You still the raging of the seas,
      and the ' roar · of their ' waves:
    and the ' tumult ' of the ' peoples.

8†   The dwellers at the ends of the earth⌣
      are awed ' by your ' wonders:
    you make the lands of sunrise and sunset⌣
      re'sound with ' shouts of ' joy.

9   You visit the ' earth and ' water it:
    you ' make it ' very ' fruitful.

10   The waters of heaven brim ' over · their ' channel:
    providing us with grain,
      for so you ' have pre'pared the ' land,

11   drenching its furrows, ' levelling · its ' ridges:
    softening it with ' showers · and ' blessing · its ' growth.

12   You crown the year ' with your ' goodness:
    and your paths ' over'flow with ' plenty.

13   The pastures of the wilderness a'bound with ' grass:
    and the ' hills are ' girded · with ' joy.

14   The fields are ' clothed with ' sheep:
    the valleys are decked with wheat,
      so that they ' shout for ' joy and ' sing.

66

1   Cry out with joy all ' people · on ' earth:
    sing to the honour of God's name,
      make the ' praise · of the ' Lord ' glorious.

2   Say to the Almighty, 'How awesome ' are your ' deeds:
    seeing your great power,
      your ' ene·mies ' cringe be'fore you.

3 'For all the ' world shall ' worship you:
    sing to ' you and ' praise your ' name.'

4 O come and see what the ' Lord has ' done:
    what God has wrought in ' terror · a'mong all ' people.

5 The Lord turned the sea into dry land,
    and they crossed the ' river · on ' foot:
    therefore in ' God let ' us re'joice,

6 who rules with power for ever,
    whose eyes keep ' watch · on the ' nations:
    let not the re'bellious · lift ' up their ' heads.

7 Praise our ' God all ' peoples:
    and let the ' sound of ' praise be ' heard.

8 The Lord has preserved us a'mong the ' living:
    and ' kept our ' feet from ' stumbling.

9 For you O ' God have ' tested us:
    and refined us as ' silver ' is re'fined.

10 You led us ' into · the ' snare:
    you laid a burden of ' trouble · up'on our ' backs.

11† You let enemies ride over our heads,
    we went through ' fire and ' water:
    but you have brought us out ' into · a ' place of ' liberty.

12 I will come into your house with ' burnt-'offerings:
    and I will ' pay you ' my ' vows,

13 the vows which I made ' with my ' lips:
    and swore with my mouth ' when I ' was in ' trouble.

14 I will offer fat beasts in sacrifice,
    with the smoke of ' burning ' rams:
    I will prepare you an ' offering · of ' bulls and ' goats.

15 Come then and listen, all you that ' fear the ' Lord:
    and I will ' tell you · what ' God has ' done for me.

16 I cried a'loud to ' God:
    high praise was ' ready ' on my ' tongue.

17 If I had cherished evil ' in my ' heart:
    the ' Lord would ' not have ' heard me.

18 But truly ' God has ' heard me:
    and has ' given ' heed · to my ' prayer.

19   Blessèd are you O God,
        for you have not re'jected · my ' prayer:
        nor withdrawn from ' me your ' steadfast ' love.

67

1   Be gracious to us O ' God and ' bless us:
        and make the light of your ' face to ' shine up'on us,

2   that your ways may be ' known up·on ' earth:
        your saving ' power · a'mong all ' nations.

3   Let the peoples ' praise you · O ' God:
        let ' all the ' peoples ' praise you.

4   Let the nations be glad, and ' sing for ' joy:
        for you judge the peoples righteously,
        and ' guide the ' nations · on ' earth.

5   Let the peoples ' praise you · O ' God:
        let ' all the ' peoples ' praise you.

6   The earth has ' yielded · its ' harvest:
        and ' you our ' God will ' bless us.

7†   Your blessing O God ' be up'on us:
        and let all the ' ends · of the ' world re'vere you.

68

Day 13 Morning

PART ONE

1   Arise O God and let your ' enemies · be ' scattered:
        let those who ' hate you ' flee be'fore you.

2   As smoke vanishes before the wind,
        and as wax ' melts · in the ' fire:
        so let the wicked ' perish · at the ' presence · of ' God.

3   But let the righteous be glad and ex'ult be·fore ' God:
        let them re'joice · with ex'ceeding ' joy.

4   Sing praises to God's ' holy ' name:
        make a highway for the one who rides on the clouds,
        whose name is the Lord, ' in whose ' presence · ex'ult.

5   Guardian of orphans and pro'tector · of ' widows:
       such are you O God ' in your ' holy ' dwelling-place.

6   You give the lonely a home to live in,
           and lead out the prisoners ' into · pros'perity:
       but the re'bellious · must ' live · in the ' wasteland.

7   O God when you went out at the ' head · of your ' people:
       when you ' marched a'cross the ' wilderness,

8   the earth quaked, the heavens ' poured down ' rain:
       before God the Lord of Sinai,
           before ' God the ' Lord most ' high.

9   You sent down a generous ' rain O ' God:
       to refresh the wilting ' land of ' your pos'session.

10 There your people ' found a ' home:
       which in your goodness you pro'vided ' for the ' poor.

11 The Lord ' gave the ' word:
       and great was the company⁀
           of ' those who ' carried · the ' news,

12 'Kings with their armies are in ' headlong ' flight:
       the women at home ' are di'viding · the ' spoil.

13 'You lingered a'mong the ' sheepfolds:
       but Israel is like a dove, its wings covered with silver,
           and its ' feathers ' shining · with ' gold.'

14 When the Almighty ' scattered ' kings:
       it was like snowflakes ' falling · up'on Mount ' Zalmon.

15 A mighty mountain is the ' mountain · of ' Bashan:
       the mountain of Bashan is a ' mountain · of ' many ' peaks.

16 O mountain of many peaks,
           why do you look with envy⁀
               at the mountain where God has ' chosen · to ' dwell:
       and where the ' Lord will ' live for ' ever?

17 The chariots of God are twenty thousand,
           indeed ' thousands up·on ' thousands:
       you O Lord have come from Sinai ' into · your ' holy ' place.

18 You have gone up on high, leading ' captives ' with you:
       and receiving tribute, even from among the rebellious,
           that ' you might ' dwell a'mong them.

PART TWO

19 Blessèd are you O Lord,
   for you bear us daily ' as your ' burden:
   you are the ' God of ' our de'liverance.

20 Our God is a ' God · of sal'vation:
   God is the Lord through whom ' we es'cape from ' death.

* * *

24 Your procession O God has ' come · into ' view:
   the procession of my God and king '⌣
   as it ' enters · the ' sanctuary.

25 The singers walk in front, the ' minstrels ' follow:
   with them the maidens '⌣
   playing · the ' timbrels · and ' singing,

26 'Give thanks to the Lord in the ' great · congre'gation:
   bless the Lord,
   all you that ' spring · from the ' fountain · of ' Israel.'

27 There in the lead is the little tribe of Benjamin,
   there the company of the ' princes · of ' Judah:
   the princes of Zebulun ' and the ' princes · of ' Naphtali.

28 Summon your ' strength O ' God:
   the strength in which⌣
   you performed for ' us your ' mighty ' deeds.

29 For your temple's sake ' at Je'rusalem:
   summon ' kings to ' bring you ' gifts.

30 Rebuke the wild ' beast · of the ' reeds:
   that ' herd of ' bulls · with their ' calves.

31 Trample under foot those who are ' greedy · for ' silver:
   and scatter the people ' whose de'light · is in ' war.

32† Let tribute be brought ' out from ' Egypt:
   and Ethiopia stretch ' out her ' hands to ' God.

33 Sing to God you ' kingdoms · of the ' earth:
   sing ' praises ' to the ' Lord,

34 who rides on the heavens, the ' ancient ' heavens:
   who speaks aloud ' with a ' mighty ' voice.

35 Ascribe power to God, whose majesty is ' over · our ' people:
   and whose ' strength is ' in the ' skies.

36   Terrible are you O God, as you come from your ' holy ' place:
            you give power and strength to your people. '
                Blessèd ' be ' God.

69

PART ONE

1   Save ' me O ' God:
            for the waters have ' risen ' up · to my ' neck.

2   I am sinking into miry depths and ' have no ' foothold:
            I have come into deep waters,'
                and the ' flood en'gulfs me.

3   I am wearied with crying out, my ' throat is ' parched:
            my eyes grow dim with ' watching · so ' long · for my ' God.

4   Those who hate me without reason⌣
            are more in number than the ' hairs · of my ' head:
            mighty are those who ' seek · to de'stroy me · with ' lies.

5   They bid me give back things that I ' never ' took:
            God you know how foolish I am,
                and my faults ' are not ' hidden · from ' you.

6   Let not those who hope in you⌣
            be put to shame through ' me O ' God:
            let not those who seek you⌣
                be dismayed at ' me, Lord ' God of ' hosts.

7   It is for you I have ' suffered · re'proach:
            and ' shame has ' covered · my ' face.

8   I have become a stranger ' to my ' family:
            an alien ' to my ' mother's ' children.

9   Zeal for your house ' has con'sumed me:
            and insults aimed at ' you have ' fallen · on ' me.

10   When I afflicted my'self with ' fasting:
            that was turned ' as a · re'proach a'gainst me.

11   I put on ' sackcloth ' also:
            and I be'came a ' by-word · a'mong them.

12   I am the talk of those who ' sit · at the ' gate:
            and the ' drunkards · make ' songs a'bout me.

13   But Lord I make my ' prayer · to ' you:
       accept me ' now in ' your great ' love.

14   Answer ' me O ' God:
       with ' your un'failing ' help.

15   Rescue me from the mire, do not ' let me ' sink:
       let me be delivered ' from the ' muddy ' depths.

16   Do not let the flood engulf me,
          or the deep ' swallow · me ' up:
       or the Abyss of death ' close its ' mouth up'on me.

17   Answer me Lord, for your ' love is ' good:
       turn to me ' in your ' great com'passion.

18   Do not hide your face ' from your ' servant:
       be swift to answer me, for ' I am ' in dis'tress.

19   Come near to me ' and re'deem me:
       O ' ransom me · be'cause of · my ' enemies.

20   You know my reproach, my shame and hu'mili'ation:
       my enemies are ' all ' in your ' sight.

21   Reproach has ' broken · my ' heart:
       and my ' sickness · is ' past all ' healing.

22   I looked for compassion, ' but I · re'ceived none:
       for someone to console me, ' but I ' found ' no one.

23†   They gave me ' poison · for ' food:
       and in my thirst they ' gave me ' vinegar · to ' drink.

        * * *

PART THREE

31   As for me, I am afflicted ' and in ' pain:
       O God, lift me up ' by your ' saving ' power.

32   I will praise your name ' with a ' song:
       and ' glori· fy ' you with ' thanksgiving.

33   And that will please you⏜
          more than the offering ' of an ' ox:
       more than a ' bull with ' horns and ' hoofs.

34   Consider this, you that are humble, ' and be ' glad:
       let your heart rejoice, ' you that ' seek · after ' God.

35   For you O God ' listen · to the ' poor:
        and do not despise your ' servants ' in cap'tivity.

36   Let the heavens and the ' earth ' praise you:
        the ' seas and ' all that ' moves in them.

37   For you will deliver Jerusalem,
        and rebuild the ' cities · of ' Judah:
        and your people shall ' dwell there ' and pos'sess it.

38   Your servants' children ' shall in'herit it:
        and those who ' love your ' name shall ' dwell in it.

70

1   O God be ' pleased · to de'liver me:
        make ' haste O ' Lord to ' help me.

2   Let those who seek my life⌣
        be put to ' shame · and con'fusion:
        let those who desire my hurt⌣
        be turned ' back and ' brought · to dis'honour.

3   Let those who mock at my hu'mili'ation:
        be ap'palled · at their ' own dis'grace.

4   Let all who seek you rejoice and be ' glad in ' you:
        and let those who long for your saving help⌣
        say ' always, ' 'God is ' great.'

5   As for me I am ' poor and ' needy:
        come ' quickly·O ' God · to my 'aid.

6   You are my helper and ' my de'liverer:
        O ' Lord make ' no de'lay.

71

Day 14 Morning

1   In you O Lord I have ' taken ' refuge:
        let me ' never · be ' put to ' shame.

2   In your righteousness de'liver me · and ' rescue me:
        incline your ' ear to ' me and ' save me.

3   Be to me a rock of refuge,
        a fortress where I may ' find ' safety:
        for you are my ' rock ' and my ' stronghold.

4 Rescue me O my God, from the ' hand · of the ' wicked:
   from the ' grasp of · the un'righteous · and ' cruel.

5 For you O Lord ' are my ' hope:
   my trust has been in you ' from the ' time · of my ' youth.

6 On you have I leaned since ' I was ' born:
   it is you that brought me out of my mother's womb,
      you are the ' theme · of my ' constant ' praise.

7 I have become a warning ' sign to ' many:
   but you are my ' strength ' and my ' refuge.

8 My mouth shall be ' filled · with your ' praises:
   I will sing of your ' glory ' all the · day ' long.

9 Do not cast me off in the time of ' old ' age:
   or forsake me ' when my ' strength is ' failing,

10 when my enemies ' speak a'gainst me:
   and those who lie in wait for me‿
      con'spire to'gether · a'gainst me.

11† They are sure that ' you · have for'saken me:
   that they may pursue me and seize me,
      for ' there is ' no one · to ' save me.

12 O God, do not ' stand off ' from me:
   my ' God make ' haste to ' help me.

13 Let my accusers be put to ' shame · and con'fusion:
   let those who seek my hurt‿
      be ' covered · with ' scorn · and dis'grace.

14 But as for me, I will wait in ' hope con'tinually:
   and I will ' praise you ' more and ' more.

15 My mouth shall speak of your righteousness‿
      and of your saving acts ' all the · day ' long:
   for their ' number · is be'yond my ' telling.

16 I will begin with your mighty acts O ' Lord my ' God:
   and speak of your ' righteous·ness, ' yours a'lone.

17 O God you have taught me ' from my ' childhood:
   and to this day I pro'claim your ' wondrous ' deeds.

18   Do not forsake me now that I am old and ' grey'headed:
         till I have made known the strength of your arm⌣
            to the generations ' that are ' yet to ' come.

19   Your righteousness O God reaches ' to the ' heavens:
         great are the things you have done, '
            who O ' God is ' like you?

20   Many bitter troubles you have laid upon me,
         yet you will ' turn · and re'vive me:
         and raise me up again ' from the ' depths · of the ' earth.

21   Restore me to more than my ' former ' greatness:
         O ' turn to me · a'gain and ' comfort me.

22   Then will I praise you on the lute⌣
         for your faithfulness ' O my ' God:
         I will sing to you with the ' harp, O ' Lord most ' high.

23   My lips will shout for ' joy · when I ' sing to you:
         and my soul also ' which you ' have de'livered.

24†   My tongue shall speak of your righteousness '⌣
         all the · day ' long:
         for those who sought to harm me⌣
            shall be ' put to ' shame · and dis'grace.

72

1   Give the king your ' justice · O ' God:
         and your righteousness ' to a ' king's ' son,

2   that he may judge your ' people ' rightly:
         and up'hold the ' poor with ' justice.

3   Let the mountains bring forth peace ' for the ' people:
         and the ' hills pros'perity · with ' justice.

4   May the king defend the cause of the poor⌣
         a'mong the ' people:
         save the children of the '⌣
            needy · and ' crush · the op'pressor.

5   May he live as long as the ' sun en'dures:
         as long as the ' moon from ' age to ' age.

6   May he come down like rain up'on the ' grass:
    like ' showers · that ' water · the ' earth.

7   In his days may ' righteous·ness ' flourish:
    and abundance of peace ' till the ' moon · is no ' more.

8   May his rule extend from ' sea to ' sea:
    and from the ' River · to the ' ends · of the ' earth.

9   May the tribes of the desert bow ' down be'fore him:
    and his ' ene·mies ' lick the ' dust.

10 May the kings of Tarshish and of the ' isles pay ' tribute:
    the kings of Sheba and ' Seba ' bring their ' gifts.

11† May all kings fall ' prostrate · be'fore him:
    and all ' nations ' render · him ' service.

12 He shall deliver the needy ' when they ' cry:
    and the ' poor who ' have no ' helper.

13 He shall have pity on the ' weak · and the ' needy:
    and ' save the ' lives · of the ' poor.

14† He shall rescue them from op'pression · and ' violence:
    and their blood shall be ' precious ' in his ' sight.

15 Long may the king live,
        and receive gifts of ' gold from ' Sheba:
    may prayer be made for him continually,
        and may people ' bless him ' every ' day.

16 Let there be abundance of wheat in the land,
        growing thick ' up · to the ' hill-tops:
    may its crops flourish like those of Lebanon,
        and the sheaves be ' numberless · as ' blades of ' grass.

17 May the king ' live for ' ever:
    and his name en'dure as ' long · as the ' sun.

18 May all nations pray to be ' blessed as ' he is:
    and all ' peoples ' call him ' blessèd.

19 Blessèd are you O ' Lord our ' God:
    for you a'lone do ' marvel·lous ' things.

20 Blessèd be your glorious ' name for ' ever:
        let the whole earth be filled with your glory. '
        Amen. ' A'men.

PART ONE

1 Truly God is ' good · to the ' upright:
    to ' those · who are ' pure in ' heart.

2 Nevertheless my feet had ' almost ' stumbled:
    my ' steps had ' well-nigh ' slipped.

3 For the boasting of the wicked ' roused me · to ' envy:
    when I ' saw how ' greatly · they ' prosper.

4 They ' suffer · no ' pain:
    their ' bodies · are ' sound and ' sleek.

5 They come to no misfortune as ' others ' do:
    nor are they af'flicted · like ' other ' people.

6 So they wear their pride ' like a ' necklace:
    and cover themselves with ' vio·lence ' as · with a ' cloak.

7 Iniquity comes ' forth · from with'in them:
    and folly ' over'flows · from their ' hearts.

8 They scoff, they ' speak ma'liciously:
    indeed they speak of oppression ' by the ' Most ' High.

9 Their slanders reach ' up to ' heaven:
    while their tongues ply ' to and ' fro on ' earth.

10 So the people ' turn and ' follow them:
    and ' find in ' them no ' fault.

11† They say, ' 'How can · God ' know:
    is there ' knowledge ' in the · Most ' High?'

12 So the ' wicked ' talk:
    yet they prosper, and ' still their ' riches ' grow.

13 So it was all in vain that I kept my ' heart ' clean:
    and ' washed my ' hands in ' innocence.

14 All the day long have ' I been ' buffeted:
    and ' punished · a'new · every ' morning.

15 If I had said, 'I will go on ' speaking · like ' this':
    then I should have be'trayed the ' children · of ' God.

16 So I kept thinking how to ' under·stand ' this:
    but I ' found it · too ' hard for ' me,

17   till I went into the ' sanctuary · of ' God:
         and then I perceived ' what be'comes · of the ' wicked.

18   Surely it is on slippery ground ' that you ' set them:
         and make them ' fall ' headlong · to ' ruin.

19   How suddenly they ' come · to de'struction:
         they are swept away, and ' come · to a ' fearful ' end.

20† Like a dream when ' one a'wakens:
         so Lord you a'rise · to dis'miss them · as ' phantoms.

PART TWO

21   When therefore I ' was em'bittered:
         and ' envy ' goaded · my ' heart,

22   stupid was ' I and ' ignorant:
         no ' better · than a ' beast in · your ' sight.

23   Yet I am ' always ' with you:
         for you hold me ' by my ' right ' hand.

24   You guide me ' with your ' counsel:
         and afterwards ' will re'ceive me · with ' glory.

25   Whom have I in ' heaven · but ' you?:
         and having you, I desire ' nothing ' else up·on ' earth.

26   My flesh and my ' heart may ' fail:
         but God is the strength of my heart‿
             and ' my pos'session · for ' ever.

27   Those who go far from you ' Lord shall ' perish:
         and all who are ' faithless ' you will · de'stroy.

28   But for me it is good to draw ' near to ' God:
         I have made you Lord God my refuge,
             and I will ' speak of ' all · you have ' done.

74

1   O God, why have you cast us ' off for ' ever:
    why is your anger so hot‿
      a'gainst the ' sheep of · your ' pasture?

2   Remember the assembly ' of your ' people:
    whom you long ago ' chose ' for your ' own.

3   Remember the tribe you redeemed‿
    to be your ' own pos'session:
    and the hill ' where you ' made your ' dwelling.

4   Draw near, and see how ' all · is in ' ruins:
    how the enemy have '‿
      utterly · laid ' waste your ' sanctuary.

5   Your adversaries have made uproar in your ' holy ' place:
    and set up their ' standards · in ' token · of ' victory.

6   Like timber cutters hacking at a ' thicket · of ' trees:
    they broke the carved ' ‿
      woodwork · with ' axes · and ' hammers.

7   They set ' fire · to your ' sanctuary:
    defiled your dwelling-place, and ' razed it ' to the ' ground.

8   They said in their hearts, ' 'Let us · de'stroy them':
    and they burned every ' shrine of ' God · in the ' land.

9   We see no signs, we have no ' prophet ' now:
    no one knows how ' long these ' things · shall con'tinue.

10   How long O God shall the ' adver·sary ' scoff:
    will the enemy blas'pheme your ' name for ' ever?

11†   Why do you hold ' back your ' hand:
    why do you keep your ' right hand ' in your ' bosom?

12   Yet God ' reigns · from of ' old:
    achieving ' victory · up'on the ' earth.

13   It was you that split the sea in two ' by your ' power:
    and smashed the heads of the ' monsters ' in the ' waters.

14   It was you that crushed the ' heads · of Le'viathan:
    and gave him for food to the ' creatures ' of the ' deep.

15 It was you that opened channels for ' springs and ' torrents:
    and ' dried up · per'enni·al ' rivers.

16 Yours is the day, and yours ' also · the ' night:
    you ap'pointed · the ' moon · and the ' sun.

17 It was you that fixed the ' bounds · of the ' earth:
    and ' you made ' summer · and ' winter.

18 Remember O Lord the ' taunts · of the ' enemy:
    see how an ungodly ' people · re'viles your ' name.

19 Do not hand over to wild beasts_
    the ' soul · that con'fesses you:
    do not forget your af'flicted ' people · for ' ever.

20 Look upon the ' world · you have ' made:
    see how full it is of darkness,
    and how ' violence · in'habits · the ' earth.

21 Let not the oppressed be turned away ' disap'pointed:
    but let the poor and ' needy ' praise your ' name.

22 Arise O God, and defend your ' own ' cause:
    remember how the ungodly '_
    taunt you ' all the · day ' long.

23 Do not ignore the clamour ' of your ' foes:
    or the uproar of your adversaries,
    which ' rises ' up con'tinually.

75

1 To you O God ' we give ' thanks:
    yes, to you O ' Lord ' we give ' thanks.

2 We ' call on · your ' name:
    and tell of ' all your ' marvel·lous ' deeds.

3 'At the time of ' my ap'pointing:
    I will ' judge the ' world with ' justice.

4 'The earth may shake, with ' all who ' dwell in it:
    but it is ' I · who keep ' steady · its ' pillars.

5 'To the boastful I say, ' "Boast no ' longer":
    and to the wicked, ' "Do not ' toss your ' horns.

6 ' "Do not toss your ' horns so ' high:
    or ' speak with ' stiff-necked ' pride." '

7   For help comes neither from the east nor ' from the ' west:
      neither from the ' desert · nor ' yet · from the ' mountains.

8   But it is ' God · who is ' judge:
      the Lord puts down one, and ' raises ' up an'other.

9   In the Lord's hand is a cup of wine ' foaming · and ' spiced:
      the Lord gives it to ' each of ' them to ' drink.

10   All the wicked of the ' earth shall ' drink from it:
      they shall ' drain it ' to the ' dregs.

11   But I will re'joice for ' ever:
      I will sing ' praises · to the ' God of ' Jacob.

12   'All the horns of the wicked ' I will ' break:
      but the horns of the righteous ' shall be ' lifted ' high.'

76

1   In Judah you are ' known O ' God:
      your ' name is ' great in ' Israel.

2   Your tent is ' pitched in ' Salem:
      and your dwelling is ' on your ' holy ' hill.

3   There you broke the ' flashing ' arrows:
      the shield, the ' sword · and the ' weapons · of ' battle.

4   Glorious are ' you O ' Lord:
      more majestic than the ' ever'lasting ' mountains.

5   The mighty ones have been despoiled,
        they sleep their ' last ' sleep:
      the strongest ' cannot ' lift a ' hand.

6   At your rebuke O ' God of ' Jacob:
      both ' horse and ' rider · fell ' stunned.

7   Terrible are ' you O ' Lord:
      who can stand in your ' presence · when ' you are ' angry?

8   You gave ' sentence · from ' heaven:
      the ' earth in ' terror · was ' still,

9   when God a'rose to · give ' judgment:
      to save all that are op'pressed up'on ' earth.

10 The fierceness of Edom shall ' turn · to your ' praise:
      and the remnant of ' Hamath · shall ' keep your ' festival.

11 Make your vows to the Lord your ' God, and ' keep them:
      let all the surrounding nations bring gifts to the Lord,
        as to the ' one who ' is · to be ' feared,

12 who curbs the ' spirit · of ' princes:
      and is the terror of the ' rulers ' of the ' earth.

77

PART ONE

1 I cry a'loud to ' God:
     I cry aloud ' to the ' one · who will ' hear me.

2 In the day of my distress I ' sought the ' Lord:
     by night my hands were⌣
       spread out in prayer without ceasing,
         my ' soul re'fused all ' comfort.

3 I remembered my God, ' and I ' groaned:
     in my ' thinking · my ' spirit ' fainted.

4 You kept my ' eyelids · from ' closing:
     I was ' dazed · and I ' could not ' speak.

5 I thought of the ' days of ' old:
     I re'membered · the ' years long ' past.

6 At night I communed ' with my ' heart:
     I pondered, ' and I ' questioned · my ' spirit,

7 'Will you O Lord re'ject us · for ' ever:
     and ' never · more ' show us · your ' favour?

8 'Has your unfailing love now ' failed us · for ' ever:
     is your promise made ' void for ' all · gener'ations?

9 'Have you for'gotten · to be ' gracious:
     and in ' anger · with'held · your com'passion?'

10 And I said, 'This thought ' causes · me ' grief:
      that the right hand of the Most '⌣
        High has ' lost its ' strength.'

11 But then I remember what the ' Lord has ' done:
and call to ' mind your ' wonders · of ' old.

12 I meditate on ' all your ' works:
and ' ponder · the ' things · you have ' done.

13 Your way O ' God is ' holy:
what god is so ' great as ' our ' God?

14 You are the God ' who does ' wonders:
you have shown your ' power · a'mong the ' nations.

15 With your strong arm you de'livered · your ' people:
the ' offspring · of ' Jacob · and ' Joseph.

16 The waters saw you O God,
the waters saw you and ' were a'fraid:
they ' trembled ' in their ' depths.

17 The clouds poured out water, the ' heavens ' thundered:
and your ' arrows ' flashed a'broad.

18 The voice of your thunder was ' heard · in the ' whirlwind:
the ' earth was ' shaken · and ' trembling.

19 Your path was in the sea,
and your way was through the ' great ' waters:
and your ' footprints ' were not ' seen.

20 You led your ' people · like ' sheep:
by the ' hand of ' Moses · and ' Aaron.

78

PART ONE

1 Give heed to my teaching ' O my ' people:
turn your ' ears · to the ' words of · my ' mouth.

2 I will open my ' mouth · in a ' parable:
I will reveal the hidden '‿
meanings · of ' things · in the ' past,

3 things we have ' heard and ' known:
and ' such · as our ' forbears · have ' told us.

4   We will not hide them from their children,
         but declare to the ' next · gener'ation:
      your glories O Lord and your might,
         and the ' wonders · that ' you have ' done,

5   the testimony that you gave to Jacob,
         and the law you ap'pointed · in ' Israel:
      which you com'manded · them to ' teach their ' children,

6   that their posterity might know it, the children ' yet un'born:
         and these in turn should a'rise and ' tell their ' children,

7   that they should put their ' trust in ' you:
         and not forget your great acts,
            but ' keep all ' your com'mandments,

8   and not be like their ancestors,
         a stubborn and re'belli·ous ' race:
      a generation fickle of heart,
            whose spirit ' was not ' faithful · to ' you.

9   The sons of Ephraim ' armed · with the ' bow:
         turned ' back · on the ' day of ' battle.

10   They did not ' keep your ' covenant:
         and they would not live ac'cording ' to your ' law.

11   They forgot what ' you had ' done:
         and the ' wonder·ful ' things · you had ' shown them.

12   Marvellous things you did in the ' sight · of our ' ancestors:
         in the land of Egypt, ' in the ' plain of ' Zoan.

13   You divided the sea and ' let them · go ' through:
         and made the waters ' stand up ' like a ' wall.

14   In the daytime you led them ' with a ' cloud:
         and all the night ' long · with a ' beacon · of ' fire.

15   You split ' rocks · in the ' wilderness:
         and gave them drink in plenty, as ' from the ' great ' deep.

16   You brought streams ' out · of the ' cliff:
         and made ' water · run ' down like ' rivers.

PART TWO

17 But for all this they sinned yet ' more a'gainst you:
     and provoked the Most ' High ' in the ' desert.

18 They tried your ' patience ' wilfully:
     demanding ' food to ' satisfy · their ' craving.

19 They spoke a'gainst you · and ' said:
     'Can God prepare a ' table ' in the ' wilderness?

20 'God struck the rock indeed,
       so that water gushed out and streams ' over'flowed:
     but can God also give bread,
       or provide ' meat · for the ' people · to ' eat?'

21 When you heard this O Lord, ' you were ' angry:
     a fire was kindled against Jacob,
       your ' fury ' rose a·gainst ' Israel,

22 because they had no ' faith in ' you:
     and would ' not re'ly · on your ' help.

23 Yet you commanded the ' clouds a'bove:
     and ' opened · the ' doors of ' heaven.

24 You rained down manna for ' them to ' eat:
     and ' gave them · the ' grain of ' heaven.

25 So mortals ate the ' bread of ' angels:
     you ' sent them ' food · in a'bundance.

26 You made the east wind ' blow from ' heaven:
     and brought in the ' south wind ' through your ' power.

27 You rained food upon them as ' thick as ' dust:
     winged ' birds · like the ' sand · of the ' sea.

28 You let it fall in the ' midst · of the ' camp:
     all a'round the ' tents · where they ' dwelt.

29 So the people ate, and ' had their ' fill:
     for you had ' given · them ' what they ' craved.

30 But they had not satisfied their craving,
       and the food was ' still · in their ' mouths:
     when your ' anger · rose ' up a'gainst them.

31† You laid low the ' strongest · a'mong them:
     and struck down the ' flower of ' Israel's ' youth.

PART THREE

32   But for all this they ' went on ' sinning:
    and despite your wonders ' they did ' not be'lieve.

33   So you made their days vanish ' like a ' breath:
    and ' ended · their ' years · in ca'lamity.

34   When you struck them down, ' they would ' seek you:
    they would re'pent and ' earnest·ly ' look for you.

35   They would remember that ' you · were their ' rock:
    and that God most ' high was ' their re'deemer.

36   But such words on their lips ' were but ' flattery:
    and their ' tongues were ' speaking ' lies.

37   For their heart was not ' steadfast · to'wards you:
    nor were they ' faithful ' to your ' covenant.

38   But in your mercy you for'gave · their mis'deeds:
    and ' did not ' utterly · de'stroy them.

39   Many a time you turned your ' wrath a'way:
    and did not let your anger ' rise · to its ' full ' height.

40†   For you remembered that they ' were but ' mortal:
    like a wind that ' passes · and ' never · re'turns.

PART FOUR

41   How often they rebelled against you ' in the ' wilderness:
    and ' grieved you ' in the ' desert.

42   Again and again they ' put you · to the ' test:
    and pro'voked the ' Lord most ' high.

43   They did not keep in ' mind your ' power:
    or the day when you ' saved them ' from the ' enemy,

44   how you worked your ' miracles · in ' Egypt:
    and your ' wonders · in the ' plain of ' Zoan.

45   You turned their rivers ' into ' blood:
    so that they ' could not ' drink · from their ' streams.

46   You sent flies in swarms ' to de'vour them:
    and ' frogs · to make ' devas'tation.

47   You gave their ' crops · to the ' locust:
    and the fruit of their ' labour ' to the ' grasshopper.

48   You destroyed their ' vines with ' hail:
       and their ' syca·more ' trees with ' frost.

49   You gave up their ' cattle · to the ' plague:
       and their ' flocks · to a ' burning ' fever.

50   You loosed upon them the fierceness of your anger,
       wrath, indig'nation · and ' havoc:
       these were the messengers ' sent for ' their de'struction.

51   You gave free course to your anger,
       and did not ' spare them · from ' death:
       but gave up their ' lives ' to the ' plague,

52   and struck down the ' first-born · of ' Egypt:
       the first-fruits of their ⌣
       strength ' in the ' dwellings · of ' Ham.

53   But your own people you led ' out like ' sheep:
       and guided them in the ' wilder·ness ' like a ' flock.

54   You brought them out safely,
       and they were ' not a'fraid:
       but the sea ' over'whelmed their ' enemies.

55   So you brought them to your ' holy ' land:
       to the mountain you had ' ⌣
       won · by your ' own right ' hand.

56   You drove out the ' nations · be'fore them:
       you allotted their lands to Israel for a heritage,
       and ' settled · your ' tribes · in their ' tents.

PART FIVE

57   Still they tried your patience O God,
       and rebelled against the ' Most ' High:
       for they ' did not ' keep · your com'mandments.

58   They turned away, faithless ' like their ' forbears:
       they started back,
       like a ' bow · when its ' string is ' loosed.

59   They grieved you ' with their ' hill-altars:
       and provoked you to ' anger ' with their ' idols.

60   When you heard this you were ' filled with ' fury:
       and ' utterly · re'jected ' Israel,

61   so that you forsook your ' dwelling-place · at ' Shiloh:
        the tent ' where you ' lived a'mong them.

62   You gave the ark of your power ' into · cap'tivity:
        your glory ' into · the ' hands · of the ' enemy.

63   You delivered your ' people · to the ' sword:
        and vented your ' wrath on ' your in'heritance.

64   The fire of war consumed their ' young ' men:
        and for their ' maidens · there ' was no ' marriage song.

65†   Their priests ' fell · by the ' sword:
        and their ' widows · made ' no · lamen'tation.

66   Then you awoke O Lord, as ' one from ' sleep:
        as one who is strong ' throws · off the ' stupor · of ' wine.

67   You struck down your enemies and ' drove them ' back:
        and ' put them · to per'petu·al ' shame.

68   You rejected the ' tent of ' Joseph:
        you did not ' choose the ' tribe of ' Ephraim.

69   But you chose the ' tribe of ' Judah:
        and the ' mountain ' which you ' loved.

70   There you built your temple, like the ' heights of ' heaven:
        like the ' earth · you had ' founded · for ' ever.

71   You chose ' David · your ' servant:
        and ' took him · a'way · from the ' sheepfolds.

72   From following the ' sheep, you ' brought him:
        to be shepherd of Jacob your people,
           and ' Israel ' your in'heritance.

73   He tended them with ' upright ' heart:
        and ' guided them · with ' skilful ' hands.

79   *Day 16 Morning*

1   O God the heathen have come ' into · your ' land:
        your holy temple they have defiled,
           and made Je'rusalem · a ' heap of ' stones.

2   They have given the dead bodies of your servants⌣
        to be food for the ' birds · of the ' air:
        and the flesh of your ' people · to the ' beasts of · the ' land.

3   Their blood has been spilled like water all ' round Je'rusalem:
          and ' there is ' no one · to ' bury them.

4   We have become the ' taunt · of our ' neighbours:
          the scorn and de'rision · of ' those a'round us.

5   How long O Lord?
              Will you be ' angry · for ' ever:
          will your jealous ' wrath ' burn like ' fire?

6   Pour out your rage on the nations that ' do not ' know you:
          and on the kingdoms that ' do not ' call · on your ' name.

7   For they have de'voured ' Jacob:
          and ' laid ' waste his ' homeland.

8   Do not remember against us the sins of our forbears,
              let your compassion come ' swiftly · to ' meet us:
          for we are ' brought ' very ' low.

9   Help us O God our saviour,
              for the ' glory · of your ' name:
          deliver us,
              and wipe out our ' sins · for your ' name's ' sake.

          *   *   *

11   Let the groans of the prisoners ' come be'fore you:
          and by your strong arm‿
              set free ' those con'demned to ' die.

          *   *   *

13†   So we your people, and the sheep of your pasture,
              will give you ' thanks for ' ever:
          we will recount your ' praise to ' all · gener'ations.

80

1   Hear O Shepherd of Israel,
              you that led Joseph ' like a ' flock:
          shine forth from your ' throne up'on the ' cherubim.

2   Before Ephraim, Benjamin ' and Man'asseh:
          stir up your ' strength and ' come · to our ' rescue.

3†   *Restore us a'gain O ' God:*
          show us the light of your ' face and ' we · shall be ' saved.

4   O Lord ' God of ' hosts:
      how long will you set your face⏝
        a'gainst your ' people's ' prayer?

5   You have fed them with the ' bread of ' tears:
      and given them ' tears in ' plenty · to ' drink.

6   You make a mockery of us ' to our ' neighbours:
      and our ' ene·mies ' laugh us · to ' scorn.

7   *Restore us again O ' God of ' hosts:*
      show us the light of your ' face and ' we · shall be ' saved.

8   You brought a vine ' out of ' Egypt:
      you drove out the ' nations · and ' planted · it ' in.

9   You ' cleared the ' ground for it:
      and when it had taken ' root it ' filled the ' land.

10   The mountains were covered ' with the ' shade of it:
      and its boughs were like ' those of ' mighty ' cedars.

11   It stretched out its branches as ' far · as the ' Sea:
      and its ' shoots as ' far · as the ' River.

12   Why then have you broken ' down its ' fences:
      so that all who go ' by pluck ' off its ' grapes?

13   The boar out of the forest ' roots it ' up:
      and the ' beasts · of the ' field de'vour it.

14   Turn to us again O ' God of ' hosts:
      look ' down from ' heaven · and ' see.

15   Bestow your care up'on this ' vine:
      upon its stock which ' your right ' hand has ' planted.

16   As for those who burn it with fire, and ' cut it ' down:
      let them perish ' at the ' frown · of your ' face.

17   Let your hand rest upon the one at your ' right ' hand:
      the one you have ' made so ' strong · for your ' service.

18   Then we will ' never · for'sake you:
      O give us life, and we will ' call up'on your ' name.

19   *Restore us again Lord ' God of ' hosts:*
      show us the light of your ' face and ' we · shall be ' saved.

81

1   Sing out with joy to ' God our ' strength:
       shout in ' triumph · to the ' God of ' Jacob.

2   Raise a song and ' sound the ' hand-drum:
       the ' tuneful ' harp · with the ' lute.

3   Blow the trumpet in the ' new ' moon:
       and at the ' full moon ' on our ' festival.

4   For this was made a ' statute · for ' Israel:
       and a ' law · of the ' God of ' Jacob,

5†   which was imposed as a ' duty · on ' Joseph:
       when he came ' out · of the ' land of ' Egypt.

6   'I eased your shoulders ' from the ' burden:
       and your ' hands were ' freed · from the ' load.

7   'You called to me in trouble ' and I ' saved you:
       I answered you in the thunder-cloud,
          but put you to the test ' at the ' waters · of ' Meribah.

8   'Hear O my people, and ' I · will ad'monish you:
       O Israel, if ' only ' you would ' listen.

9   'There shall be no strange ' god a'mong you:
       nor shall you ' worship · an ' ali·en ' god.

10† 'I am the Lord your God,
       who brought you out of the ' land of ' Egypt:
       open wide your ' mouth and ' I shall ' fill it.

11   'But my people would not ' hear my ' voice:
       and ' Israel · would ' not o'bey me.

12   'So I left them in their ' stubbornness · of ' heart:
       to ' follow · their ' own de'vices.

13   'O that my ' people · would ' listen to me:
       and that ' Israel · would ' walk · in my ' ways.

14   'I would soon put ' down their ' enemies:
       and turn my ' hand a'gainst their ' adversaries.

15   'Those who hate me would ' cringe be'fore me:
       and their ' fate · would be ' sealed for ' ever.

16   'But Israel I would feed with the ' finest ' wheat-flour:
       and satisfy them with ' honey ' from the ' rock.'

1   God stands in the ' council · of ' heaven:
     in the midst of the ' gods the ' Lord gives ' judgment.

2   'How long will you ' judge un'justly:
     and favour the ' cause ' of the ' wicked?

3   'Defend the ' weak · and the ' orphaned:
     maintain the ' cause of · the af'flicted · and ' destitute.

4   'Rescue the ' weak · and the ' needy:
     and save them ' from the ' hands · of the ' wicked.

5   'You neither know nor understand,
     but go a'bout in ' darkness:
     all the found'ations · of the ' earth are ' shaken.

6   'I say then to you, ' "Gods you ' may be:
     and all of you ' offspring ' of the · Most ' High,

7   ' "but you shall ' die like ' mortals:
     and fall like ' any ' of the ' princes.' "

8   Arise O God and ' judge the ' earth:
     for you shall take all ' nations · as ' your pos'session.

84

1   How lovely ' is your ' dwelling-place:
     Lord ' God of ' power and ' might.

2   My soul has a desire and longing⌣
     to enter the ' courts · of the ' Lord:
     my heart and my flesh re'joice · in the ' living ' God.

3   The sparrow finds for her'self a ' house:
     and the swallow a nest⌣
     where ' she may ' lay her ' young.

4   Even so have the singers a ' home · at your ' altars:
     they stand always praising you my ' king ' and my ' God.

5   O Lord ' God of ' hosts:
     blessèd are ' those who ' dwell in · your ' house.

6   Blessèd are those whose ' strength · is in ' you:
     who have ' set their ' hearts on ' pilgrimage.

7 Going through the arid valley,
    they find a spring from ' which to ' drink:
    the early rain ' covers it · with ' pools of ' water.

8 They go from ' strength to ' strength:
    and appear every one before ' God ' in Je'rusalem.

9 O Lord God of hosts, ' hear my ' prayer:
    give ' ear O ' God of ' Jacob.

10 Show favour O God to the ' king · our de'fender:
    and look upon the face of ' your an'ointed ' prince.

11 Truly one day ' in your ' courts:
    is better ' than a ' thousand ' elsewhere.

12 I would rather stand at the threshold‿
    of the ' house · of my ' God:
    than ' live · in the ' homes of · the ' wicked.

13 For the Lord God is a defence and shield,
    the Lord will give ' grace and ' honour:
    and no good thing will be withheld‿
    from those who ' live a ' blameless ' life.

14 O Lord ' God of ' hosts:
    blessèd are those who ' put their ' trust in ' you.

85

1 Lord you were once gracious ' to your ' land:
    you re'stored the ' fortunes · of ' Jacob.

2 You forgave the of'fence · of your ' people:
    and ' covered ' all their ' sin.

3 You put away ' all · your dis'pleasure:
    and ' turned · from your ' bitter ' wrath.

4 Restore us again O ' God our ' saviour:
    and ' let your ' anger ' cease from us.

5 Will you be displeased at ' us for ' ever:
    will you prolong your wrath‿
      from one gener'ation ' to an'other?

6 Will you not re'vive us · a'gain:
    so that your ' people ' may re'joice in you?

7† Show us your ' mercy · O ' Lord:
    and ' give us · your ' saving ' help.

8 Let me hear what you will ' say O ' Lord:
    for you will speak peace to your people,
        to your servants whose ' hearts are ' turned to ' you.

9 For deliverance is at hand for ' those who ' fear you:
    so that your ' glory · may ' dwell · in our ' land.

10 Mercy and faithfulness have ' met to'gether:
    justice and ' peace · have em'braced each ' other.

11 Faithfulness will spring up ' from the ' ground:
    and righteousness will ' look ' down from ' heaven.

12 You Lord will ' give pros'perity:
    and our ' land shall ' yield its ' harvest.

13 Justice shall ' go be'fore you:
    and the path for your ' feet ' shall be ' peace.

86

Day 17 Morning

1 Turn your ear to me O ' Lord and ' answer me:
    for I am ' poor ' and in ' misery.

2 Preserve my life for ' I am ' faithful:
    my God save your servant for I ' put my ' trust in ' you.

3 Be merciful to ' me O ' Lord:
    for I call to you ' all the ' day ' long.

4 Gladden the ' heart · of your ' servant:
    for to you Lord I ' lift ' up my ' soul.

5 For you Lord are ' good · and for'giving:
    and of great mercy to ' all who ' call up'on you.

6 Give heed O Lord ' to my ' prayer:
    and listen to my ' cry of ' suppli'cation.

7† In the day of my distress ' I will ' call:
    and ' surely ' you will ' answer me.

8   Among the gods there is none like ' you O ' Lord:
      nor can the deeds of ' any · be com'pared with ' yours.

9   All the nations you have made‿
      shall come and bow ' down be'fore you:
      and they shall ' glori'fy your ' name.

10   For you are great, and do ' marvel·lous ' things:
      truly ' you a'lone are ' God.

11   Show me your way O Lord,
      that I may ' walk in · your ' truth:
      let my heart rejoice in ' rever·ence ' for your ' name.

12   I will praise you O Lord my God with ' all my ' heart:
      and ' glorify · your ' name for ' ever.

13   For great is your steadfast ' love for ' me:
      you have delivered my ' life · from the ' pit of ' death.

14   O God the proud have ' risen · a'gainst me:
      the ruthless seek my life, and ' pay no ' heed to ' you.

15   But you are a God of com'passion · and ' mercy:
      slow to anger, a'bounding · in ' love and ' faithfulness.

16   Turn to me then and have mercy,
      give your ' strength · to your ' servant:
      and ' save the ' son of · your ' handmaid.

17   Give me a sign of your favour,
      that those who hate me may see it,
      and be ' put to ' shame:
      because you Lord have ' been my ' help · and my ' comfort.

87

1   The Lord loves the city that is founded on the ' holy ' hill:
      its gates are dearer to God‿
      than ' all the ' dwellings · of ' Jacob.

2   Glorious things are ' spoken · of ' you:
      Zion, ' city ' of our ' God.

3   'I the Lord will count ' Egypt · and ' Babylon:
      as among ' those who ' are my ' friends.

4   'The people of Philistia, Tyre and ' Ethi'opia:
      each ' one was ' born in ' her.

5   'All shall call Je'rusa·lem, ' "Mother":
        for each one of ' them was ' born in ' her.'

6   The Most High will ' keep her · se'cure:
        when the roll of the peoples is written up,
            the Lord shall record, ' 'Each · one was ' born in ' her.'

7†   Singers and dancers a'like · shall pro'claim:
        'In ' you all ' find their ' home.'

88

1   O Lord my God, I call for ' help by ' day:
        and I cry ' out to ' you by ' night.

2   Let my prayer enter ' into · your ' presence:
        and ' turn your ' ear · to my ' cry.

3   For my soul is ' full of ' trouble:
        and my life is ' on the ' brink · of the ' grave.

4   I am counted among those who go‿
            down to the ' pit of ' death:
        I am a ' person · quite ' drained of ' strength,

5   like one forsaken among the dead,
            like the slain in battle who ' lie · in the ' grave:
        whom you remember no more,
            cut off as they ' are from ' your ' care.

6   You have put me in the ' lowest · a'byss:
        in a place of ' darkness ' in the ' depths.

7   Your wrath lies ' heavy · up'on me:
        you over'whelm me · with ' all your ' waves.

8   You have taken away my friends,
            and made me loathsome ' in their ' sight:
        I am im'prisoned · and ' cannot · es'cape.

9   My eyes grow ' dim with ' sorrow:
        Lord I have called to you every day,
            and stretched ' out my ' hands in ' prayer.

10   Do you work wonders ' for the ' dead:
        will the ' shades rise ' up to ' praise you?

11 Do they speak of your ' love · in the ' grave:
     or of your faithfulness ' in the ' place · of de'struction?

12 Will your wonders be known ' in the ' darkness:
     or your saving help ' in the ' land · of ob'livion?

13 Yet Lord I ' cry to ' you:
     in the morning my ' prayer ' comes be'fore you.

14 Lord why do you ' cast me ' off:
     why do you ' hide your ' face ' from me?

15 From childhood I have suffered,
          and come ' near to ' death:
     helpless ' I have ' borne your ' terrors.

16 Your fury has swept ' down up'on me:
     and your dread as'saults have ' utter·ly ' crushed me.

17 They surround me like a flood ' all the · day ' long:
     they close in on ' me from ' every ' side.

18 Friend and acquaintance you have ' taken · a'way from me:
     and my ' one com'panion · is ' darkness.

89

PART ONE

1 I will sing of your steadfast love for ' ever · O ' Lord:
     my mouth will proclaim your faithfulness ⌣
          from one gener'ation ' to an'other.

2 For your love is such as to en'dure for ' ever:
     your faithfulness is e'stablished · as ' firm · as the ' heavens.

3 You have said, 'I have made a covenant ' with my ' chosen:
     I have ' sworn to ' David · my ' servant,

4 'I will establish your pos'terity · for ' ever:
     and uphold your ' throne for ' all · gener'ations.'

5 O Lord the heavens pro'claim your ' wonders:
     and the council of the ⌣
          holy ones ' praises ' your ' faithfulness.

6 For who is there in the skies to com'pare · with the ' Lord:
     or who is like the Lord a'mong the ' heaven·ly ' beings?

7   A God to be feared in the council ' of the ' holy ones:
      great and terrible above ' all · that are ' round a'bout.

8   O Lord God of hosts,
         who is a mighty ' one like ' you?:
      your ' faithfulness · is ' all a'round you.

9   You rule the sea in its ' swelling ' pride:
      and ' check the ' surge · of its ' waves.

10 You crushed the monster of the deep with a ' mortal ' blow:
      you scattered your foes ' with your ' mighty ' arm.

11 The heavens are yours, the earth ' also · is ' yours:
      you founded the ' world and ' all · that is ' in it.

12 You made the ' north · and the ' south:
      Tabor and ' Hermon · re'joice · in your ' name.

13 Yours is a ' mighty ' arm:
      strong is your hand, your ' right hand ' lifted ' high.

14 Righteousness and justice
         are the foundation ' of your ' throne:
      love and ' faithfulness · at'tend your ' presence.

15 Blessèd are the people
         who know the shout ' that ac'claims you:
      the people who walk ' in the ' light · of your ' presence.

16 They rejoice in your name ' all the · day ' long:
      and because of your ' righteousness · they ' are ex'alted.

17 For you are their glory ' and their ' strength:
      and through your favour our ' heads are ' lifted ' high.

18 Truly the ' Lord · is our ' shield:
      the ' Holy · One ' is our ' sovereign.

PART TWO

19 Once in a vision to your ' servant · you ' said:
      'I have set the crown upon one who is mighty,
         I have exalted one ' chosen ' from the ' people.

20 'I have found ' David · my ' servant:
      and with my holy ' oil I ' have an'ointed him.

21 'My hand shall ' always · be ' with him:
      and my ' arm shall ' give him ' strength.

22   'The enemy shall ' never · out'wit him:
        nor the ' wicked ' bring him ' low.

23   'I will beat down his ' foes be'fore him:
        and ' vanquish ' those who ' hate him.

24   'My faithfulness and constant love ' shall be ' with him:
        and through my name his ' head · shall be ' lifted ' high.

25   'I will stretch out his ' hand · to the ' Sea:
        and his ' right · hand as ' far · as the ' River.

26   'He will say to me, ' "You · are my ' father:
        my God and the ' rock of ' my sal'vation."

27   'And I will ' name him · my ' first-born:
        the highest among the ' rulers ' of the ' earth.

28   'My steadfast love for him I will main'tain for ' ever:
        and my covenant with ' him shall ' stand ' firm.

29†   'I will maintain his pos'terity · for ' ever:
        and make his throne en'dure as ' long · as the ' heavens.

30   'But if his children for'sake my ' law:
        and cease to ' live · as I ' have de'creed,

31   'if they break my statutes,
           and do not ' keep · my com'mandments:
        I will punish their offences with the rod,'
           and their ' sin with ' lashes.

32   'But I will not take back my ' love ' from him:
        nor ' let my ' promise ' fail.

33   'My covenant I ' will not ' break:
        nor go ' back · on the ' word · I have ' spoken.

34†   'Once and for all I have ' sworn · by my ' holiness:
        that I ' will not ' lie to ' David.

35   'His posterity shall en'dure for ' ever:
        and his throne as ' long · as the ' sun be'fore me.

36   'It shall stand fast for ever ' like the ' moon:
        for as ' long · as the ' heavens · en'dure.'

37 But now you have cast off and rejected your an'ointed ' king:
    and poured ' out your ' wrath up'on him.

38 You have renounced your covenant ' with your ' servant:
    you have de'filed his ' crown · in the ' dust.

39 You have broken down ' all his ' walls:
    and re'duced his ' strongholds · to ' ruins.

40 All those who pass ' by de'spoil him:
    and he has be'come the ' scorn · of his ' neighbours.

41 You have increased the power ' of his ' adversaries:
    and given ' joy to ' all his ' foes.

42 You have blunted the ' edge · of his ' sword:
    and ' failed · to sup'port him · in ' battle.

43 You have removed the sceptre ' from his ' hand:
    and ' cast his ' throne · to the ' ground.

44 You have cut short the ' days · of his ' youth:
    and ' covered ' him with ' shame.

45 Lord how ' long · will you ' hide yourself:
    how long will your ' wrath ' burn like ' fire?

46 Remember how ' short my ' life is:
    have you created ' human'kind for ' nothing?

47 Who is there alive that shall ' not see ' death:
    or who can escape ' from the ' power · of the ' grave?

48 Where O Lord are your former acts of ' loving ' kindness:
    and your faithful ' promis·es ' made to ' David?

49 Remember Lord how your ' servant · is ' taunted:
    how I bear in my heart the ' insults ' of the ' peoples.

50 Remember O Lord how your ' ene·mies ' mock:
    how they fling back their taunts at ' your an'ointed ' king.

51† Blessèd be the ' Lord for ' ever:
     A'men and ' A'men.

PART ONE

1 Lord you have ' been our ' refuge:
      from one gener'ation ' to an'other.

2 Before the mountains were brought forth,
         or the earth and the ' world were ' made:
      you are God, from ' age to ' age · ever'lasting.

3 You turn humanity ' back · into ' dust:
      saying, 'Return to ' dust you ' children · of ' mortals.'

4 For a thousand years in your sight are ' only · as ' yesterday:
      as it ' were · but a ' day · that is ' past.

5 As a night-watch that comes‿
         quickly to an ' end you ' scatter them:
      they ' fade · like a ' dream at ' daybreak.

6 They are like the grass which in the ' morning · is ' green:
      but in the ' evening · is ' dried up · and ' withered.

7 For we consume away ' in your ' anger:
      and are ' terri·fied ' by your ' wrath.

8 You set our mis'deeds be'fore you:
      our secret ' sins · in the ' light of · your ' face.

9 All our days pass away ' under · your ' anger:
      we bring our years to an end ' as it ' were a ' sigh.

10 The span of our life is seventy years,
         though the strong may ' come to ' eighty:
      yet all the years bring is labour and sorrow,
         so soon they ' pass and ' we are ' gone.

11 But who understands the ' power · of your ' wrath:
      or who considers the ' fierceness ' of your ' anger?

12 Teach us to know how ' few · are our ' days:
      that we may ap'ply our ' hearts to ' wisdom.

PART TWO

13 Turn from your wrath O Lord,
how long be'fore · you re'lent?:
have ' pity ' Lord · on your ' servants.

14 Satisfy us in the morning with your ' constant ' love:
so that we may rejoice⁔
and be glad ' all the ' days · of our ' life.

15 Make us glad for as many days as you ' have af'flicted us:
for as many years as ' we have ' suffered · ad'versity.

16 Show your ' servants · your ' work:
and let their ' children ' see your ' glory.

17† May your favour O Lord our God ' be up'on us:
and prosper the work of our hands,
O ' prosper · the ' work · of our ' hands.

91

1 Whoever dwells in the shelter of the ' Most ' High:
and passes the night⁔
under the ' shadow ' of the · Al'mighty,

2 will say to the Lord,
'You are my refuge ' and my ' stronghold:
my ' God in ' whom I ' trust.'

3 The Lord will free you from the ' snare · of the ' hunter:
and ' from · the de'stroying ' pestilence.

4 The wings of the Most High will cover you,
and you will be safe ⁔
under the feathers ' of · the Al'mighty:
the faithfulness of the Lord will '⁔
be your ' shield · and de'fence.

5 You will not be afraid of any ' terror · by ' night:
nor of the ' arrow · that ' flies by ' day,

6 of the pestilence that ' stalks in ' darkness:
nor of the ' plague · that lays ' waste at ' noon.

7 A thousand may fall beside you,
ten thousand at your ' right ' hand:
but ' you · will re'main un'scathed.

8   You have only to ' look · with your ' eyes:
       to see the re'ward ' of the ' wicked.

9   Because you have said, 'The ' Lord · is my ' refuge':
       and ' made the · Most ' High your ' stronghold,

10   there shall no ' evil · be'fall you:
       no ' plague · shall come ' near your ' dwelling.

11   For the angels of God ' have been ' charged:
       to ' keep you · in ' all your ' ways.

12   They shall bear you up ' in their ' hands:
       lest you should strike your ' foot a'gainst a ' stone.

13   You shall tread on the ' asp · and the ' adder:
       the viper and the serpent you shall ' trample ' under'foot.

14   'Because they have set their love upon me‿
         I ' will de'liver them:
       I will uphold them be'cause they ' know my ' name.

15   'When they call to me ' I will ' answer:
       I will be with them in trouble,
         I will ' rescue them · and ' bring them · to ' honour.

16   'With long life ' I will ' satisfy them:
       and ' show · them my ' saving ' power.'

92

1   It is good to give ' thanks · to the ' Lord:
       to sing praise to your ' name ' O Most ' High,

2   to tell of your love ' in the ' morning:
       and of your ' faithful·ness ' during · the ' night,

3†   on the ten-stringed ' lyre · and the ' lute:
       with the ' tuneful ' sound · of the ' harp.

4   For you Lord have made me glad ' by your ' deeds:
       I shout for joy at the ' works ' of your ' hands.

5   O Lord, what great things ' you have ' done:
       your ' thoughts are ' very ' deep.

6   The dull of heart ' do not · per 'ceive this:
       the foolish ' do not ' under'stand,

7   how the wicked may ' sprout like ' grass:
       and ' evil'doers · may ' flourish,

8   yet they shall be destroyed for ' all ' time:
            while you Lord are en'throned on ' high for ' ever.

9   See Lord how your ' ene·mies ' perish:
            and all ' evil'doers · are ' scattered.

10   But you have lifted up my head͜
            like the ' wild bull's ' horns:
            you have an'ointed me · with ' fresh ' oil.

11   My eyes have looked down in triumph ' on my ' enemies:
            and my ears were '͜
            gladdened · with ' news · of their ' downfall.

12   The just shall flourish ' like a ' palm tree:
            and grow ' like a ' cedar · in ' Lebanon.

13   Planted in the ' house · of the ' Lord:
            they flourish in the ' courts of ' our ' God.

14   Still bearing fruit in their ' old ' age:
            they are still ' green and ' full of ' sap,

15   to show that the ' Lord is ' just:
            the Lord my rock, in ' whom is ' no un'righteousness.

93

1   You O Lord are king, you are ' clothed in ' majesty:
            you have robed yourself,
              and put ' on the ' girdle · of ' strength.

2   You have made the ' world so ' firm:
            that it can ' never ' be ' moved.

3   Your throne O Lord has stood firm ' from of ' old:
            from all e'terni·ty ' you are ' God.

4   The waters have lifted up O Lord,
            the waters have lifted ' up their ' voice:
            the waters lift ' up their ' pounding ' waves.

5   Mightier than the noise of great waters,
            mightier than the ' waves · of the ' sea:
            so the ' Lord on ' high is ' mighty.

6   Truly your ' law stands ' firm:
            holiness O Lord a'dorns your ' house for ' ever.

94

1   O Lord God to whom ' vengeance · be'longs:
     God to whom vengeance belongs,'
       shine out ' in your ' glory.

2   Rise up O ' judge · of the ' earth:
     and give the ' proud what ' they de'serve.

3   How long shall the ' wicked · O ' Lord:
     how ' long · shall the ' wicked · ex'ult?

4   How long shall evildoers pour out ' arro·gant ' words:
     and ' flaunt themselves · with ' much ' boasting?

5   They crush your ' people · O ' Lord:
     and af'flict your ' chosen ' nation.

6   They murder the widow ' and the ' alien:
     and ' put the ' orphan · to ' death.

7† And they say, 'The ' Lord · does not ' see:
     the God of ' Jacob ' gives no ' heed to it.'

8   Consider this, you most ' stupid · of the ' people:
     fools, when ' will you ' under'stand?

9   Does the one who planted the ' ear not ' hear:
     does the one who ' formed the ' eye not ' see?

10 Shall the one who instructs the ' nations · not ' punish:
     is the one who teaches ' all of us · with'out ' knowledge?

11 The Lord knows our ' human ' thoughts:
     the Lord knows that they are ' no more ' than a ' breath.

12 Blessèd are those you in'struct O ' Lord:
     to whom you give ' teaching ' out of · your ' law,

13 so that they may have respite from ' days · of ad'versity:
     until a ' pit is ' dug · for the ' wicked.

14 For you O Lord will not a'bandon · your ' people:
     you will ' never · for'sake your ' own.

15 But justice shall return to the ' place of ' judgment:
     all the ' true of ' heart · shall up'hold it.

16   Who is on my side a'gainst the ' wicked:
        who will stand up for me against ' those who ' do ' evil?

17   If the Lord ' had not ' helped me:
        I would soon have gone to ' dwell · in the ' land of ' silence.

18   But when I said, 'I have ' lost my ' foothold':
        your love O ' Lord ' held me ' up.

19   When the cares of my ' heart are ' many:
        your consolations give ' joy ' to my ' soul.

20   You are no friend of un'righteous ' judges:
        who frame mischief ' under ' cover · of ' law.

21   They band together against the ' life · of the ' righteous:
        and con'demn the ' innocent · to ' death.

22   But the ' Lord · is my ' stronghold:
        my God ' is the ' rock · of my ' refuge.

23   The Lord shall recompense them for their wickedness,
        and destroy them for their ' evil ' deeds:
        truly the ' Lord our ' God · shall de'stroy them.

95

1   O come let us ' sing · to the ' Lord:
        let us shout with joy to the ' rock of ' our sal'vation.

2   Let us come into God's ' presence · with ' thanksgiving:
        and sing to the ' Lord with ' psalms of ' triumph.

3   For you Lord are a ' great ' God:
        and a great ' king a·bove ' all ' gods.

4   In your hand are the ' depths · of the ' earth:
        so also are the ' heights ' of the ' mountains.

5† The sea is yours ' and you ' made it:
        the dry land also ' which your ' hands have ' fashioned.

6   O come let us bow ' down and ' worship:
        let us kneel be'fore the ' Lord our ' maker.

7   For the Lord ' is our ' God:
        we are the Lord's people,
            the ' flock that ' God ' shepherds.

8　O that today you would listen to ' God's ' voice:
　　　'Do not harden your hearts as at Meribah,
　　　　　as on that day at ' Massah ' in the ' wilderness,

9　'when your forbears tried me, and ' put me · to the ' test:
　　　although ' they had ' seen my ' works.

10　'Forty years long I had a loathing for⏜
　　　　　this gener'ation · and ' said:
　　　"They are a people whose hearts are perverse,
　　　　　for they ' give no ' heed · to my ' ways."

11　'Then I vowed ' in my ' anger:
　　　"They shall ' never ' enter · my ' rest."'

96

1　O sing to the Lord a ' new ' song:
　　　sing to the ' Lord ' all the ' earth.

2　Sing, and give praise to ' God's ' name:
　　　tell the glad news of sal'vation · from ' day to ' day.

3　Proclaim God's glory ' to the ' nations:
　　　God's marvellous ' deeds to ' all the ' peoples.

4　For you O Lord are great and highly ' to be ' praised:
　　　more to be ' feared than ' all the ' gods.

5　The gods of the nations are no ' more than ' idols:
　　　but you O Lord are the ' one who ' made the ' heavens.

6　Glory and ' majesty · at'tend you:
　　　strength and ' beauty · are ' in your ' sanctuary.

7　Ascribe to the Lord, you families ' of the ' nations:
　　　ascribe to the ' Lord ' honour · and ' might.

8　Ascribe due honour to God's ' holy ' name:
　　　bring offerings, and ' enter · the ' courts · of the ' Lord.

9　Worship the Lord in the ' beauty · of ' holiness:
　　　let the ' whole earth ' stand in ' awe.

10　Proclaim to the nations, 'The ' Lord is ' king:
　　　the Lord has made the world so firm it cannot be moved,
　　　　and will ' judge the ' peoples · with ' justice.'

11   Let the heavens rejoice, and the ' earth be ' glad:
        let the sea roar and ' all the ' creatures ' in it.

12   Let the fields be joyful and ' all · that is ' in them:
        then all the trees of the forest‿
           will shout with ' joy be'fore the ' Lord.

13†   For you O Lord are coming to ' judge the ' earth:
        with righteousness you will judge the world,
           and the ' peoples ' with your ' truth.

97

1   You are king O Lord, let the ' earth be ' glad:
        let the many ' islets · and ' coastlands · re'joice.

2   Clouds and darkness are ' round a'bout you:
        righteousness and justice are‿
           the found'ation ' of your ' throne.

3   Fire ' goes be'fore you:
        and burns up your ' enemies · on ' every ' side.

4   The world is lit up ' by your ' lightnings:
        and earth ' trembles ' at the ' sight.

5   The mountains melt like ' wax be'fore you:
        before the ' Lord of ' all the ' earth.

6   The heavens pro'claim your ' righteousness:
        and all the ' peoples ' see your ' glory.

7   Shame on all who worship images,
        and glory in their ' worthless ' idols:
        bow down before the ' Lord ' all you ' gods.

8   Jerusalem hears ' and is ' glad:
        the cities of Judah rejoice O ' Lord ' at your ' judgments.

9   For you Lord are most high over ' all the ' earth:
        you are exalted ' far a·bove ' all the ' gods.

10   You love those who ' hate ' evil:
        you preserve the lives of your servants,
           and deliver them ' from the ' hand · of the ' wicked.

11   Light has dawned ' for the ' righteous:
        and ' joy · for the ' upright · in ' heart.

12 Rejoice in the ' Lord you ' righteous:
    and give ' thanks · to God's ' holy ' name.

98

1 Sing to the Lord a ' new ' song:
   for the Lord has ' done ' marvel·lous ' things.

2 With your own right hand O Lord, and with your ' holy ' arm:
   you have ' gained · for your'self the ' victory.

3 You have made ' known your ' victory:
   you have displayed your saving '⌣
       power · to ' all the ' nations.

4 You have remembered your faithfulness,
       and your love for the ' house of ' Israel:
   and all the ends of the ' earth have ' seen your ' victory.

5 Shout with joy to the Lord ' all the ' earth:
   sing and rejoice ' with the ' sound of ' melody.

6 Sing to the Lord ' with the ' harp:
   with the harp ' and the ' voice of ' song.

7 With trumpets ' also · and ' horns:
   shout with joy be'fore the ' Lord our ' king.

8 Let the sea roar and ' all · that is ' in it:
   the world and ' those ' who in'habit it.

9 Let the rivers ' clap their ' hands:
   and let the hills rejoice to'gether · be'fore the ' Lord.

10 For you O Lord are coming to ' judge the ' earth:
    with righteousness you will judge the world,
        and the ' peoples ' with ' equity.

99

1 You are king O Lord, and the ' people ' tremble:
   you sit enthroned upon the cherubim, '
       and the ' earth is ' quaking.

2 You O Lord are great upon your ' holy ' mountain:
   you are exalted ' over ' all the ' nations.

3   Let them praise your great and ' terri·ble ' name:
    holy are you and mighty,
        a ' king · who de'lights in ' justice.

4   You have e'stablished ' equity:
    you have dealt ' justice · and ' righteousness · in ' Jacob.

5† *We proclaim your greatness O ' Lord our ' God:*
    we bow down before your '␣
        footstool · for ' you are ' holy.

6   Moses and Aaron among your priests,
    and Samuel among those who ' called · on your ' name:
    these called to you O ' Lord ' and you ' answered.

7   You spoke to them out of the ' pillar · of ' cloud:
    they kept your teachings␣
    and the ' law ' that you ' gave them.

8   You answered them O ' Lord our ' God:
    to them you were a God who forgives,
        though you ' punished ' their of'fences.

9   *We proclaim your greatness O ' Lord our ' God:*
    we bow down towards your holy hill,
        for you O ' Lord our ' God are ' holy.

100

1   Cry out with joy to the Lord ' all the ' earth:
    worship with gladness,
        and enter the Lord's ' presence · with ' songs of ' joy.

2   Know that the Lord is God,
    our maker, whose ' people · we ' are:
    the flock which the ' Lord our ' God ' shepherds.

3   Enter the gates of the temple with thanksgiving,
    and go into its ' courts with ' praise:
    give thanks, and ' bless God's ' holy ' name.

4   For the Lord is a gracious God,
    whose mercy is ' ever'lasting:
    and whose faithfulness endures␣
        from gener'ation · to ' gener'ation.

101

1   My song is of ' mercy · and ' justice:
        to ' you O ' Lord · I will ' sing.

2   I will give heed to the ' way · that is ' blameless:
        O Lord ' when ' will you ' come to me?

3   I will walk with'in my ' house:
        in ' puri'ty of ' heart.

4   No base aim will I set be'fore my ' eyes:
        I hate the ways of disloyalty,
            and I will ' have no ' part with ' them.

5†   Perversity of heart shall be ' far from ' me:
        I will ' have no ' dealings · with ' evil.

       * * *

7   I will look with favour on the faithful in the land,
        that they may ' dwell with ' me:
        whoever leads a blameless ' life shall ' be my ' servant.

8   No treacherous person shall ' live · in my ' house:
        the liar shall be ' banished ' from my ' presence.

       * * *

102

PART ONE

1   Hear my ' prayer O ' Lord:
        and let my ' cry ' come be'fore you.

2   Do not hide your face from me in my ' time of ' trouble:
        incline your ear to me,
            and be swift to ' answer · me ' when I ' call.

3   For my days pass a'way like ' smoke:
        and my bones are burnt ' up as ' in a ' furnace.

4   I am beaten down and ' withered · like ' grass:
        I waste away, be'cause I ' cannot ' eat.

5   I ' groan ' loudly:
        I am ' nothing · but ' skin and ' bones.

6   I am like a vulture ' in the ' wilderness:
        like an ' owl in ' desol·ate ' places.

7   I lie a'wake ' moaning:
        I am like a sparrow a'lone up'on a ' housetop.

8   My enemies taunt me ' all the · day ' long:
        and those who deride me ' use my ' name in ' cursing.

9   The bread I eat ' is like ' ashes:
        and tears are ' mingled ' with my ' drink,

10   because of your ' anger · and ' fury:
        for you have picked me ' up and ' flung · me a'way.

11†   My days decline as the ' shadows ' lengthen:
        and I ' wither · a'way like ' grass.

PART TWO

12   But you O Lord shall ' reign for ' ever:
        and your name shall be remembered⌣
            through'out all ' gener'ations.

13   You will arise and have mercy ' on Je'rusalem:
        for the ' time has ' come to ' pity her.

14   Even her tumbled stones are ' dear · to your ' servants:
        it moves them with pity to ' see her ' in the ' dust.

15   The nations shall fear your ' name O ' Lord:
        and all the ' kings · of the ' earth your ' majesty,

16   when you build up Je'rusalem · a'gain:
        and ' show your·self ' in your ' glory,

17   when you turn to the ' prayer · of the ' destitute:
        and do ' not re'ject · their ap'peal.

18   Let this be written for ' those who · come ' after:
        and a people yet to be ' born shall ' praise the ' Lord,

19   'The Lord looked down from the holy ' place on ' high:
        out of heaven the ' Lord ' looked · at the ' earth,

20   'to hear the groaning of ' those held ' prisoner:
        and give freedom to those ' under ' sentence · of ' death,

21   'so that the Lord's name may be pro'claimed · in Je'rusalem:
        and God's praises ' in the ' holy ' city,

22†   'when peoples are' gathered · to'gether:
     and' kingdoms · to' serve the' Lord.'

23   God has broken my strength be'fore my' time:
     and shortened the' number' of my' days.

24   O my God, do not take me away in the' midst · of my' life:
     for your life en'dures through' all · gener'ations.

25   You Lord in the beginning laid the' earth's found'ations:
     and the' heavens · are the' work of · your' hands.

26   They shall perish, but' you · shall en'dure:
     like clothes they shall all wear out,
        you will cast them off‿
     like a' cloak and' they shall' vanish.

27   But you remain the' same for' ever:
     and your' years shall' have no' end.

28   The children of your servants shall' dwell se'cure:
     and their posterity' shall stand' fast · in your' sight.

103

PART ONE

1   Praise the Lord' O my' soul:
     and all that is within me' praise God's' holy' name.

2   Praise the Lord' O my' soul:
     and forget not' all that' God has' done for you.

3   The Lord forgives you' all your' sin:
     and heals you of' all' your in'firmities.

4   The Lord saves your' life · from the' grave:
     and' crowns you · with' love and' mercy.

5†   The Lord fills your life with' good' things:
     so that your' youth · is re'newed · like the' eagle's.

6   You Lord are righteous' in your' acts:
     and bring justice to' all that' are op'pressed.

7   You showed your' ways to' Moses:
     your' deeds · to the' children · of' Israel.

8 You are full of com'passion · and ' mercy:
    slow to ' anger · and ' rich in ' kindness.

9 You will not ' always · be ' chiding:
    nor do you ' keep your ' anger · for ' ever.

10 You have not dealt with us ac'cording · to our ' sins:
    nor punished us ac'cording ' to our ' wickedness.

11 For as the heavens are high a'bove the ' earth:
    so great is your ' mercy · over ' those who ' fear you.

12 As far as the east is ' from the ' west:
    so far have you put a'way our ' sins ' from us.

13 As parents have compassion ' on their ' children:
    so do you Lord‿
        have com'passion · on ' those who ' fear you.

14† For you know what ' we are ' made of:
    you re'member · that we ' are but ' dust.

PART TWO

15 Our days are ' like the ' grass:
    we flourish ' like a ' flower · of the ' field.

16 But as soon as the wind goes over it, ' it is ' gone:
    and its ' place shall ' know it · no ' more.

17 But your merciful goodness O Lord‿
        extends for ever toward ' those who ' fear you:
    and your ' righteousness · to ' children's ' children,

18 when they are true ' to your ' covenant:
    and re'member · to ' keep · your com'mandments.

19 You O Lord have established your ' throne in ' heaven:
    and you rule as ' sovereign ' over ' all.

20 O praise the Lord all you angels,
        you mighty ones who ' do God's ' bidding:
    and heed the com'mand · of the ' Most ' High.

21 Praise the Lord all you ' heaven·ly ' hosts:
    you ' servants · who ' do God's ' will.

22 Praise the Lord all things created,
        in all places ' under · God's ' rule:
    praise the ' Lord ' O my ' soul.

104

PART ONE

1 Praise the Lord ' O my ' soul:
>   O Lord my God you are great indeed,
>>   you are ' clothed in ' majesty · and ' splendour.

2 You cover yourself with light as it were ' with a ' garment:
>   you have spread out the ' heavens ' like a ' tent.

3 You laid out the beams of your dwelling⌣
>>   on the ' waters · a'bove:
>   you make the clouds your chariot,
>>   and ride up'on the ' wings · of the ' wind.

4 You make the ' winds your ' messengers:
>   and ' flames of ' fire your ' servants.

5 You fixed the earth on ' its found'ations:
>   so that ' it can ' never · be ' shaken.

6 You wrapped it with the ocean ' as · with a ' cloak:
>   the ' waters ' covered · the ' mountains.

7 The waters fled at ' your re'buke:
>   at the voice of your ' thunder · they ' rushed a'way.

8 They flowed over the mountains,
>>   and down ' into · the ' valleys:
>   to the place ' you · had ap'pointed ' for them.

9 You set the limits which they ' may not ' pass:
>   lest they should re'turn to ' cover · the ' earth.

10 You cause springs to gush ' forth · in the ' valleys:
>   their waters ' flow be'tween the ' hills.

11 They give drink to the ' beasts · of the ' field:
>   and the wild ' asses ' quench their ' thirst.

12 The birds make their nests⌣
>>   in the trees a'long their ' banks:
>   and ' sing a'mong the ' branches.

13 From your dwelling on high you ' water · the ' hills:
>   the earth is filled with the ' fruits ' of your ' bounty.

14 You cause the grass to ' grow · for the ' cattle:
>   and ' plants for ' us to ' cultivate,

15   that we may bring out ' food · from the ' earth:
       and ' wine to ' gladden · our ' heart,

16   oil to give us a ' shining ' face:
       and ' bread to ' give us ' strength.

17   The trees of the Lord are ' watered · a'bundantly:
       the cedars of Lebanon ' which the ' Lord has ' planted.

18   There the birds ' make their ' nests:
       and the stork has its ' home ' in their ' tops.

19   The high hills are a refuge for the ' wild ' goats:
       and the boulders are a ' shelter ' for the ' rabbits.

20   You created the moon to ' mark the ' seasons:
       and the sun ' knows the ' time · for its ' setting.

21   You make darkness that it ' may be ' night:
       when all the ' beasts · of the ' forest · creep ' out.

22   The young lions ' roar · for their ' prey:
       and ' seek their ' food from ' God.

23   When the sun rises they ' slink a'way:
       and ' go to ' rest · in their ' dens.

24   The labourer goes ' out to ' work:
       and will ' toil un'til the ' evening.

PART TWO

25   O Lord how manifold ' are your ' works:
       in wisdom you have made them all,
          the ' earth is ' full of · your ' creatures.

26   There is the great and ' mighty ' sea:
       which teems with living ' things both ' great and ' small.

27   Upon it ' sail the ' ships:
       and there is Leviathan,
          the ' monster · you ' made to ' sport in it.

28   All these ' look to ' you:
       to give them their ' food in ' due ' season.

29   What you give them they ' gather ' up:
       when you open your hand,
          they are ' filled with ' good ' things.

30   But when you hide your face ' they · are dis'mayed:
          when you take away their breath they die,
              and re'turn · to the ' dust they ' came from.

31   When you send out your spirit they ' are cre'ated:
          and you re'new the ' face · of the ' earth.

32   May your glory O Lord en'dure for ' ever:
          may you re'joice O ' Lord · in your ' works.

33   When you look at the ' earth it ' trembles:
          when you ' touch the ' mountains · they ' smoke.

34   I will sing to the Lord as ' long · as I ' live:
          I will praise my God ' while I ' have my ' being.

35   May my meditation ' please the ' Lord:
          as I ' show my ' joy in ' God.

36   Let sinners vanish from the earth,
              and the wicked ' come · to an ' end:
          bless the Lord O my soul.
              Whaka'moemi'titia · a ' Ihowa. / O ' praise ' - the ' Lord.

105

PART ONE

1   Give thanks and call upon the ' name · of the ' Lord:
          make known to the ' nations · what ' God has ' done.

2   Sing to God, O ' sing God's ' praise:
          tell of all the wonderful ' deeds · of the ' Most ' High.

3   Exult in God's ' holy ' name:
          let the heart of those who ' seek the ' Lord re'joice.

4   Turn for help to the ' Lord your ' strength:
          and ' constant·ly ' seek God's ' presence.

5   Remember the marvellous things the Most ' High has ' done:
          the wonders, and the ' judgments ' God has ' given,

6   O children of Abraham the ' servant · of ' God:
          O offspring of Jacob the ' chosen ' of the ' Lord.

7   You are the ' Lord our ' God:
       and your judgments ' are in ' all the ' earth.

8   You are mindful of your ' coven·ant ' always:
       and of the promise you made‿
         to a ' thousand ' gener'ations,

9   the covenant that you ' made with ' Abraham:
       and the ' oath · that you ' gave to ' Isaac,

10   which you confirmed to ' Jacob · as ' binding:
       as your ever'lasting ' covenant · with ' Israel,

11   saying, 'To you I will give the ' land of ' Canaan:
       as ' your ap'pointed · in'heritance.'

12   They were as yet ' few in ' number:
       and ' ali·ens ' in that ' land,

13   wandering from ' country · to ' country:
       and from one ' kingdom ' to an'other.

14   But you let ' no one · op'press them:
       and re'buked · even ' kings for · their ' sake,

15†   saying, 'Do not touch my an'ointed ' servants:
       and ' do my ' prophets · no ' harm.'

16   You called down famine ' on the ' land:
       and cut ' off · the sup'ply of ' bread.

17   But you had sent a ' man be'fore them:
       Joseph ' who was ' sold · as a ' slave,

18   whose feet they ' bound with ' fetters:
       and a collar of ' iron · was ' round his ' neck.

19   Until his pre'dictions · came ' true:
       he was ' tested ' by · your com'mand.

20   The king ' sent · and re'leased him:
       the ruler of ' nations ' let him · go ' free.

21   He made him ' lord · of his ' household:
       and ruler ' over ' all · his pos'sessions,

22†   to correct his ' officers · at ' will:
       and to ' teach his ' counsel·lors ' wisdom.

23   Then Israel ' came · into ' Egypt:
       Jacob settled ' in the ' land of ' Ham.

24   There Lord you made your ' people ' fruitful:
       and they became ' stronger ' than their ' enemies,

25   whose hearts you turned to hatred ' of your ' people:
       and to deceitful ' dealing ' with your ' servants.

26   Then you sent ' Moses · your ' servant:
       and ' Aaron · whom ' you had ' chosen.

27   They performed your ' signs a'mong them:
       and your wonders ' in the ' land of ' Ham.

28   You sent darkness, and all ' was ' dark:
       but they would ' not o'bey your ' word.

29   You turned their waters ' into ' blood:
       and ' caused their ' fish to ' die.

30   Their land ' swarmed with ' frogs:
       yes, even ' in the ' rooms · of the ' palace.

31   You commanded, and there rose up ' clouds of ' flies:
       and ' gnats · throughout ' all their ' country.

32   You gave them ' hail for ' rain:
       and ' lightning · flashed ' over · their ' land.

33   You struck their ' vines · and their ' fig-trees:
       and shattered the ' trees with'in their ' borders.

34   You gave the word,
          and grasshoppers came, and ' locusts · in'numerable:
       they ate up everything green in the land,
          and devoured all ' produce ' of the ' soil.

35†   You struck down all the first-born ' in the ' land:
       the ' first-fruits · of ' their vir'ility.

36   You led Israel out, with spoil of ' silver · and ' gold:
       among the tribes not one ' person ' fell be'hind.

37   The Egyptians were glad ' when they ' went:
       for dread of ' Israel · had ' fallen · up'on them.

38   You O Lord spread out a cloud ' as a ' screen:
       and ' fire · to give ' light at ' night.

39   The people asked, and you ' sent them ' quails:
        and you ' filled · them with ' bread from ' heaven.

40   You opened a rock and ' water · gushed ' out:
        it flowed like a river ' through the ' arid ' land.

41   For you remembered your ' sacred ' promise:
        which you had made to ' Abra'ham your ' servant.

42   So you led out your ' people · re'joicing:
        your ' chosen ones · with ' songs of ' gladness.

43   You gave them the ' lands · of the ' heathen:
        and they took pos'session · where ' others · had ' toiled,

44†   so that they might keep your statutes and o'bey your ' laws:
        Whaka'moemi'titia · a ' Ihowa. / O ' praise ' - the ' Lord.

106 *Day 21 Evening*

PART ONE

1   Whakamoemititia a Ihowa. / Praise the Lord.
           O give thanks, for the ' Lord is ' good:
        God's ' love en'dures for ' ever.

2   Who can recount your mighty ' acts O ' Lord:
        or ' tell of ' all your ' praise?

3   Blessèd are those who ' act ' justly:
        and ' always · do ' what is ' right.

4   Remember me Lord,
           when you show favour ' to your ' people:
        and come to me ' with your ' saving ' help.

5†   So that I may see the prosperity ' of your ' chosen:
           rejoice with the nation's gladness,
               and exult with the people '⌣
           you have ' made your ' own.

6   We have sinned ' like our ' ancestors:
        we have erred, and ' we have ' acted ' wickedly.

7   They made light of your wonders in Egypt,
           they did not recall your many great ' acts of ' kindness:
        but showed themselves re'bellious · at the ' Red ' Sea.

8   Yet you saved them for your ' name's ' sake:
        so that they might make ' known your ' mighty ' power.

9   At your rebuke the Red Sea ' dried ' up:
        and you led them through the deep as ' over ' dry ' land.

10   Thus you saved them ' from their ' adversary:
        and delivered them ' out · of the ' ene·my's ' hand.

11   As for their oppressors, the waters ' over'whelmed them:
        not ' one of them · was ' left a'live.

12† Then they be'lieved your ' words:
        then too they ' sang ' your ' praises.

13   But they soon forgot all the ' Lord had ' done:
        they would not ' wait to ' hear God's ' counsel.

14   Greed came upon them ' in the ' wilderness:
        and they tried God's ' patience ' in the ' desert.

15   So the Lord gave them ' what they ' asked for:
        but sent a ' wasting ' sickness · a'mong them.

16   Some in the camp grew ' envious · of ' Moses:
        and of Aaron the ' Lord's ' holy ' servant.

17   So the earth opened and ' swallowed · up ' Dathan:
        and closed over the ' compa·ny ' of A'biram.

18   Fire broke ' out a'mong them:
        and the ' flames burnt ' up · the un'godly.

19   They made a young ' bull in ' Horeb:
        and ' worshipped · that ' molten ' image.

20   So they exchanged the ' glory · of ' God:
        for the image of a ' creature · that ' feeds on ' grass.

21   They forgot that you were the ' God · who had ' saved them:
        by your ' mighty ' acts in ' Egypt,

22   wonderful things in the ' land of ' Ham:
        and awesome things ' at the ' Red ' Sea.

23† So you would have destroyed them⌣
            but for ' Moses · your ' chosen one:
        who stood before you in the breech,
            to turn back your ' wrath from ' their de'struction.

PART TWO

24 They thought ill of the ' pleasant ' land:
  because they did ' not be'lieve God's ' promise.

25 They complained in'side their ' tents:
  and would not ' listen · to the ' voice of · the ' Lord.

26 So you lifted your ' hand and ' vowed:
  that you would ' strike them ' down · in the ' wilderness,

27 and scatter their descendants a'mong the ' nations:
  and dis'perse them · through'out the ' world.

28 They joined in the worship of ' Baal of ' Peor:
  in the feasts of ' gods that ' have no ' life.

29 Their wanton deeds provoked the ' Lord to ' anger:
  and ' plague broke ' out a'mong them.

30 Then Phinehas stood up and ' inter'ceded:
  and ' so the ' plague was ' checked,

31 and this was counted ' in his ' favour:
  throughout ' all · gener'ations · for ' ever.

32 Then they angered the Lord at the ' waters · of ' Meribah:
  and Moses ' suffered · on ' their ac'count.

33 For they em'bittered · his ' spirit:
  and he uttered ' ill-con'sidered ' words.

PART THREE

        * * *

35 They intermarried ' with the ' heathen:
  and ' learned to ' follow · their ' ways.

36 They worshipped foreign idols,
        which be'came a ' snare to them:
  they sacrificed their '⌣
        sons · and their ' daughters · to ' demons.

37 They shed innocent blood,
        the blood of those ' sons and ' daughters:
  and the ' land · was de'filed with ' blood.

38 Thus they polluted themselves ' by their ' deeds:
  and wantonly broke ' faith ' with their ' Lord.

39   Therefore your wrath was ' kindled · a'gainst them:
       and you loathed the '‿
         people · you had ' made your ' own.

40   You gave them into the ' hands · of the ' nations:
       and people who ' hated them · be'came their ' rulers.

41   Their ' enemies · op'pressed them:
       and made them ' subject ' to their ' power.

42   Many a ' time you ' rescued them:
       but they were bent on rebellion,
         and were brought ' low ' by their ' wickedness.

43   Yet you gave heed to ' their dis'tress:
       when'ever · you ' heard their ' cry.

44   You remembered your covenant with them,
       and in your boundless love ' you re'lented:
       causing even their ' captors · to ' pity ' them.

45   Deliver us O Lord our God,
       and gather us from a'mong the ' nations:
       that we may give thanks to your holy name,
       and ' make it · our ' glory · to ' praise you.

46   Blessèd be the Lord our God‿
       from age to ' age for ' ever:
       and let all the people say, 'Amen.'
       Whaka'moemi'titia · a ' Ihowa. / O ' praise '- the ' Lord.

107

PART ONE

1   'O give thanks, for the ' Lord is ' gracious:
       God's steadfast ' love en'dures for ' ever.'

2   So let the people say whom the ' Lord · has re'deemed:
       whom the Lord has redeemed‿
         from the ' hand ' of the ' enemy,

3†   and gathered out of the lands,
       from the east and ' from the ' west:
       from the ' north and ' from the ' south.

4   Some went astray in the ' desert ' wastes:
        and found no way to a ' city ' where · they could ' dwell.

5   They were ' hungry · and ' thirsty:
        and their ' soul was ' fainting · with'in them.

6   Then they cried to you O Lord ' in their ' trouble:
        and you rescued ' them from ' their dis'tress.

7   You led them by a ' straight ' path:
        until they came to a ' city ' where · they could ' live.

8   *Let them thank you O Lord for your ' steadfast ' love:*
        for the ' wonders ' that you ' do for us.

9   *For you ' satisfy · the ' thirsty:*
        and fill the ' hungry · with ' good ' things.

10   Some lay in ' darkness · and ' gloom:
        prisoners fast ' bound in ' fetters · of ' iron,

11   because they had defied the ' words · of the ' Lord:
        and spurned the ' counsel · of ' God most ' high.

12   So their hearts were subdued by ' hard ' labour:
        they ' stumbled · with ' no one · to ' help them.

13   Then they cried to you O Lord ' in their ' trouble:
        and you ' rescued them · from ' their dis'tress.

14†   You brought them out of ' darkness · and ' gloom:
        and ' broke their ' fetters · in ' pieces.

15   *Let them thank you O Lord for your ' steadfast ' love:*
        for the ' wonders ' that you ' do for us.

16   *For you break open ' doors of ' bronze:*
        and ' smash the ' bars of ' iron.

PART TWO

17   Some were sick be'cause of · their ' sins:
        afflicted ' on ac'count · of their ' wrongdoing.

18   They loathed every ' kind of ' food:
        and drew ' near · to the ' gates of ' death.

19   Then they cried to you O Lord ' in their ' trouble:
        and you ' rescued them · from ' their dis'tress.

20 You sent forth your ' word and ' healed them:
    and ' saved their ' life · from the ' grave.

21 *Let them thank you O Lord for your ' steadfast ' love:*
    for the ' wonders ' that you ' do for us.

22 *Let them offer the ' sacrifice · of ' thanksgiving:*
    and tell of your ' deeds with ' shouts of ' joy.

23 Those who go down to the ' sea in ' ships:
    and ply their ' trade on ' great ' waters,

24 they have seen your ' works O ' Lord:
    and the ' wonders · you ' do · in the ' deep.

25 At your command the stormy ' wind a'rose:
    and ' lifted ' up the ' waves.

26 They were carried up to the sky,
        and down again ' to the ' depths:
    their courage ' melted · a'way · in their ' peril.

27 They reeled to and fro, and staggered ' as if ' drunken:
    their seafaring skill was ' utterly · with'out a'vail.

28 Then they cried to you O Lord ' in their ' trouble:
    and you ' rescued them · from ' their dis'tress.

29 You made the ' storm be ' still:
    and the ' roaring ' waves were ' hushed.

30 Then they were glad be'cause it · was ' calm:
    and so you brought them to the harbour⌣
        where ' they had ' longed to ' be.

31 *Let them thank you O Lord for your ' steadfast ' love:*
    for the ' wonders ' that you ' do for us.

32 *Let them extol you in the as'sembly · of the ' people:*
    and praise you ' in the ' council · of ' elders.

PART THREE

33 The Lord turns rivers ' into ' desert:
    and springs of water ' into ' thirsty ' ground.

34 A fruitful land you make a ' salty ' waste:
    because of the ' wickedness · of ' those who ' live in it.

35   You turn desert into ' standing ' pools:
        and dry land ' into ' springs of '· water.

36   There you ' settle · the ' hungry:
        and they ' build there · a ' city · to ' live in.

37   They sow fields and ' plant ' vineyards:
        which ' yield them · a ' bounti·ful ' harvest.

38   You bless them, and their ' numbers · in'crease:
        and you permit ' no de'crease · of their ' herds.

39   When they are weakened and ' brought ' low:
        through stress of mis'fortune ' and ' sorrow,

40   you pour contempt on their ' princely · op'pressors:
        whom you send a'stray · in the ' trackless ' desert.

41   But the poor you ' lift · out of ' misery:
        and increase their ' families · like ' flocks of ' sheep.

42   The upright see it, ' and are ' glad:
        but the ' wicked · are ' put to ' silence.

43†   Let·those who are wise ' ponder · these ' things:
        and consider the ' Lord's un'failing ' love.

108

Day 22 Evening

1   My heart is steadfast O God, my ' heart is ' steadfast:
        I will ' sing and ' make ' melody.

2   Awake my soul, awake ' lute and ' harp:
        I my'self · will a'waken · the ' dawn.

3   I will give thanks to you Lord a'mong the ' peoples:
        I will ' praise you · a'mong the ' nations.

4   For the greatness of your love ' reaches · to the ' heavens:
        and your ' faithful·ness ' up · to the ' clouds.

5   Show yourself O God a'bove the ' heavens:
        let your glory shine ' over ' all the ' earth,

6   so that your belovèd may ' be de'livered:
        O save us by ' your right ' hand and ' answer us.

7   You have spoken in your ' holy ' place:
        'I will go up and divide Shechem,
           and measure ' out the ' valley · of ' Succoth.

8 'Gilead and Man'asseh · are ' mine:
   Ephraim is my helmet, ' Judah ' is my ' sceptre,

9† 'Moab is my wash-basin, to Edom I will ' throw my ' shoe:
   and over Philistia ' I will ' shout in ' triumph.'

10 Who will bring me to the ' forti·fied ' city:
   who will ' lead me ' into ' Edom,

11 since you O ' God · have re'jected us:
   and no ' longer · go ' out · with our ' armies?

12 Grant us help a'gainst the ' enemy:
   for vain is ' any ' human ' help.

13 With the help of our God we ' shall do ' valiantly:
   for it is God who will ' tread ' down our ' enemies.

109

1 Be silent no longer O ' God · of my ' praise:
   for the mouth of the wicked and⏝
       de'ceitful · is ' opened · a'gainst me.

2 They speak against me with ' lying ' tongues:
   they beset me with words of hatred,
       and at'tack me · with'out · any ' cause.

3 In return for my love ' they ac'cuse me:
   though I con'tinue · to ' pray for ' them.

4 Thus have they repaid me ' evil · for ' good:
   and ' hatred · for ' my good'will.

       * * *

20 O Lord my God, deal with me as be'fits your ' name:
   in the goodness of your ' steadfast ' love de'liver me.

21 For I am ' poor and ' needy:
   and my ' heart is ' wounded · with'in me.

22 I fade like a ' shadow · at ' evening:
   I am ' shaken ' off · like a ' locust.

23 My knees are ' weak from ' fasting:
   my body is ' gaunt from ' meagre ' nourishment.

24† I have become the scorn of ' my ac'cusers:
>   when they see me, they ' toss their ' heads · in de'rision.

25 Help me O ' Lord my ' God:
>   save me ' in your ' steadfast ' love,

26 that all may know this is ' your ' doing:
>   and that you a'lone O ' Lord have ' done it.

27 They may curse, but ' you will ' bless:
>   my assailants will be put to shame,
>   and your ' servant ' will re'joice.

28 Let my accusers be ' clothed · with dis'honour:
>   let them be covered in ' shame as ' with a ' cloak.

29 As for me, loud thanks to the Lord are ' on my ' lips:
>   I will praise the Lord ' in the ' midst · of the ' throng.

30 For the Lord stands at the right ' hand · of the ' poor:
>   to save from death ' those un'justly · con'demned.

110
Day 23 Morning

1 The Lord ' said to ' my lord:
>   'Sit at my right hand,
>   until I ' make your ' enemies · your ' footstool.'

2 From the holy mountain ⌣
>   the Lord hands you the ' sceptre · of ' power:
>   saying, ' 'Rule · in the ' midst · of your ' enemies.'

3 On the day of your power your people ⌣
>   shall willingly ' offer · them'selves:
>   in holy array they will come to you ⌣
>   like ' dew · at the ' birth of · the ' morning.

4 The Lord has sworn an oath that will never ' be re'tracted:
>   'You are a priest for ever ' ⌣
>   in the ' line · of Mel'chizedek.'

* * *

111

1 Whakamoemititia a Ihowa. / Praise the Lord.
  I will thank you O Lord with ' all my ' heart:
  in the company of the ' upright · in ' their as'sembly.

2 Great are your ' works O ' Lord:
  and to be ' studied · by ' all · who de'light in them.

3 Your deeds are full of ' majesty · and ' splendour:
  and your ' righteousness · en'dures for ' ever.

4 You have caused your marvellous acts to ' be re'membered:
  you Lord are ' gracious · and ' full of · com'passion.

5 You give food to ' those who ' fear you:
  you keep your ' cove·nant ' always · in ' mind.

6 You have shown your people your ' power in ' action:
  by giving them the ' lands of ' other ' nations.

7 The works of your hands are ' faithful · and ' just:
  and ' all your ' precepts · are ' trustworthy.

8 They stand fast for ' ever · and ' ever:
  they are ' grounded · in ' truth and ' justice.

9 You sent redemption to your people,
  you decreed your e'ternal ' covenant:
  holy and ' awesome ' is your ' name.

10 The fear of you O Lord is the beginning of wisdom,
  those who revere you have ' good · under'standing:
  your ' praise · shall en'dure for ' ever.

112

1 Whakamoemititia a Ihowa. / Praise the Lord.
  Blessèd are those who ' fear the ' Lord:
  and greatly de'light in ' God's com'mandments.

2 Their descendants will be ' mighty · in the ' land:
  the children of the ' upright ' will be ' blessed.

3 Riches and plenty shall ' fill their ' houses:
  righteousness ' shall be ' theirs for ' ever.

4 They are a light in the darkness ' for the ' upright:
  being ' gracious · com'passionate · and ' just.

5   It goes well with those who are ' generous · in ' lending:
      who con'duct · their af'fairs with ' justice.

6   For the righteous will ' never · be ' shaken:
      they will be ' kept · in re'membrance · for ' ever.

7   They will not live in fear of ' bad ' news:
      because with steadfast ' heart they ' trust · in the ' Lord.

8   Their heart is steady, they ' will not ' fear:
      in the end they shall ' see their ' ene·mies' ' downfall.

9   They give freely ' to the ' poor:
      their righteousness stands for ever,
        and they will hold ' up their ' head with ' honour.

10   The wicked will be vexed ' when they ' see it:
      they will grind their teeth and slink away,
        for the hopes of the ' wicked · shall ' come to ' nothing.

113

1   Whakamoemititia a Ihowa. / Praise the Lord.
      O praise the Lord, you servants ' of the ' Lord:
      O ' praise the ' name · of the ' Lord.

2   Blessèd be the ' name · of the ' Lord:
      both ' now · and for ' ever'more.

3   The Lord's ' name be ' praised:
      from the ' rising · of the ' sun · to its ' setting.

4   The Lord is high a'bove the ' nations:
      and the glory of the ' Lord a'bove the ' heavens.

5   Who can be likened to the Lord our God,
      who sits en'throned on ' high:
        yet deigns to look ' down from ' heaven · to ' earth?

6   The Lord lifts the weak ' out · of the ' dust:
      and raises the ' poor ' from the ' dung-heap,

7   to make them ' sit with ' princes:
      with the ' princes ' of God's ' people.

8   The Lord gives the barren ' woman · a ' home:
      and makes her the joyful mother of children.
        Whaka'moemi'titia · a ' Ihowa. / O ' praise ' - the ' Lord.

114

1 When Israel came ' out of ' Egypt:
    the house of Jacob⌣
        from among a ' people · of an ' ali·en ' tongue,

2 Judah became the ' Lord's ' temple:
    and ' Israel · be'came God's ' kingdom.

3 The sea fled ' at the ' sight of it:
    and ' Jordan · turned ' back · in its ' course.

4 The mountains ' skipped like ' rams:
    and the ' hills like ' yearling ' sheep.

5 Why was it that you ' fled O ' sea:
    and you Jordan ' that you ' turned ' back,

6 you mountains that you ' skipped like ' rams:
    and you ' hills like ' yearling ' sheep?

7 Tremble O earth at the ' presence · of the ' Lord:
    at the ' presence · of the ' God of ' Jacob,

8 who turned the hard rock into a ' pool of ' water:
    and the flint-stone ' into · a ' gushing ' spring.

115

1 Not to us O Lord not to us,
    but to your name ' give the ' glory:
    because of your ' love ' and your ' faithfulness,

2 lest the ' nations · should ' ask:
    'And ' where then ' is their ' God?'

3 You O God ' are in ' heaven:
    you ' do what'ever · you ' will.

4 As for their idols, they are ' silver · and ' gold:
    the ' work of ' human ' hands.

5 They have mouths that ' cannot ' speak:
    and ' eyes that ' cannot ' see.

6 They have ears that ' cannot ' hear:
    and ' noses · that ' cannot ' smell.

7   With their hands they cannot feel,
         with their feet they ' cannot ' walk:
         and no ' sound comes ' from their ' throat.

8   Those who make idols ' grow · to be ' like them:
         and so do all who ' put their ' trust in ' them.

9   But you O Israel, put your ' trust · in the ' Lord:
         God is your ' help ' and your ' shield.

10   O house of Aaron, put your ' trust · in the ' Lord:
         God is your ' help ' and your ' shield.

11   You that fear the Lord, put your ' trust · in the ' Lord:
         God is your ' help ' and your ' shield.

12   The Lord has remembered us, ' and will ' bless us:
         the Lord will bless the house of Israel,
            the Lord will ' bless the ' house of ' Aaron.

13†   You Lord will bless ' those who ' fear you:
         the ' little · no ' less · than the ' great.

14   May the Lord increase you ' more and ' more:
         both ' you · and your ' children ' after you.

15   May you be ' blessed · by the ' Lord:
         the Lord who ' made ' heaven · and ' earth.

16   The heavens be'long · to the ' Lord:
         but the earth has been ' given · to ' human'kind.

17   It is not the dead who ' praise the ' Lord:
         nor do those who ' go down ' into ' silence.

18†   But we the living ' bless the ' Lord:
         now and for ever.
            Whaka'moemi'titia · a ' Ihowa. / O ' praise ' - the ' Lord.

116

PART ONE

1   I love you O Lord because you ' heard my ' voice:
     when I ' made my ' suppli'cation,

2   because you turned your ' ear to ' me:
     when I ' called up'on your ' name.

3   The cords of death entangled me,
     and the grip of ' Sheol · laid ' hold on me:
     distress and ' anguish · de'scended · up'on me.

4   Then I called upon the ' name · of the ' Lord:
     'Deliver me O ' Lord ' I be'seech you.'

5   Gracious is the ' Lord and ' righteous:
     truly our God ' is a ' God · of com'passion.

6   The Lord preserves the ' simple-'hearted:
     when I was brought ' low the ' Lord ' saved me.

7   Be at rest once more ' O my ' soul:
     for the ' Lord has ' treated · you ' kindly.

8   The Lord has ' saved me · from ' death:
     and kept my eyes from '‿
       tears · and my ' feet from ' stumbling,

9† so that I may walk in the presence ' of the ' Lord:
     in the ' land ' of the ' living.

PART TWO

10 I kept my faith,
     even when I said, 'I am in ' sore dis'tress':
     in my haste I said, ' 'No one ' can be ' trusted.'

11 How can I re'pay you · O ' Lord:
     for all the good things ' you have ' done to ' me?

12 I will take up the ' cup · of sal'vation:
     and call on the ' name ' of the ' Lord.

13 I will pay my ' vows · to the ' Lord:
     in the ' presence · of ' all God's ' people.

14 Grievous in the ' sight · of the ' Lord:
   is the ' death · of a ' faithful ' servant.

15 Lord I am your servant, the ' child · of your ' maidservant:
   you have ' freed me ' from my ' bonds.

16 I will offer a ' sacrifice · of ' thanksgiving:
   and call on the ' name ' of the ' Lord.

17 I will pay my ' vows · to the ' Lord:
   in the ' presence · of ' all God's ' people,

18† in the courts of the ' Lord's ' house:
    in your midst O Jerusalem.
        Whaka'moemi'titia · a ' Ihowa. / O ' praise ' - the ' Lord.

117

1 Praise the Lord ' all you ' nations:
   acclaim the Most ' High ' all you ' peoples.

2 For great is God's ' love for ' us:
   and the faithfulness of the Lord endures for ever.
        Whaka'moemi'titia · a ' Ihowa. / O ' praise ' - the ' Lord.

118

PART ONE

1 We give thanks to you O Lord for ' you are ' gracious:
   and your ' love en'dures for ' ever.

2 Let the house of ' Israel ' say:
   'God's ' love en'dures for ' ever.'

3 Let the house of ' Aaron ' say:
   'God's ' love en'dures for ' ever.'

4 Let those who fear the ' Lord ' say:
   'God's ' love en'dures for ' ever.'

5 I called to you O Lord in ' my dis'tress:
   and your ' answer · was to ' set me ' free.

6 The Lord is on my side, I ' will not ' fear:
   for what can human ' power ' do to ' me?

7   The Lord is on my ' side to ' help me:
        I will ' triumph ' over · my ' enemies.

8   It is better to take refuge ' in the ' Lord:
        than to ' put · any ' trust in ' people.

9†   It is better to take refuge ' in the ' Lord:
        than to ' put · any ' trust in ' princes.

10   The nations ' all sur'rounded me:
        but in the name of the ' Lord I ' drove them ' back.

11   They hemmed me in,
            they hemmed me in on ' every ' side:
        but in the name of the ' Lord I ' drove them ' back.

12   They swarmed around me like bees,
            they blazed like fire a'mong the ' thorns:
        but in the name of the ' Lord I ' drove them ' back.

13   They pressed hard upon me, so that I ' almost ' fell:
        but the ' Lord ' came · to my ' help.

14† The Lord is my strength and ' my de'fence:
        and has be'come ' my de'liverer.

15   There are shouts of joy and deliverance⌣
            in the ' tents · of the ' righteous:
        the right hand of the ' Lord does ' mighty ' things.

16   The right hand of the Lord ' raises ' up:
        the right hand of the ' Lord does ' mighty ' things.

17   I shall not ' die but ' live:
        and pro'claim · what the ' Lord has ' done.

18   The Lord in'deed has ' punished me:
        but did not ' give me ' over · to ' death.

PART TWO

19   Open to me the ' gates · of the ' temple:
        that I may enter and give ' thanks ' to the ' Lord.

20   This is the ' gate · of the ' Lord:
        through ' which the ' righteous · shall ' enter.

21   I will thank you because ' you have ' answered me:
        and you have be'come ' my de'liverer.

22 The stone which the ' builders · re'jected:
    has be'come the ' head · of the ' corner.

23 This is the ' Lord's ' doing:
    and it is ' marvel·lous ' in our ' eyes.

24 This is the day which the ' Lord has ' made:
    let us re'joice ' and be ' glad in it.

25 Save us O ' Lord we ' pray:
    Lord we ' pray · you to ' give us · suc'cess.

26 Blessèd is the one who comes in the ' name · of the ' Lord:
    we bless you ' from the ' house · of the ' Lord.

27 The Lord is God, and has ' given · us ' light:
    with branches in your hands,
        go forward in procession up to the ' horns ' of the ' altar.

28 You are my God and ' I will ' thank you:
    you are my ' God and ' I · will ex'tol you.

29† We give thanks to you O Lord for ' you are ' gracious:
    and your ' love en'dures for ' ever.

119

A

1 Blessèd are those who live a ' blameless ' life:
    who ' follow · your ' law O ' Lord.

2 Blessèd are those who o'bey · your in'struction:
    and ' seek you · with ' all their ' heart.

3 They also ' do no ' wrong:
    but ' always ' walk · in your ' ways.

4 You laid ' down your ' precepts:
    for ' us to ' keep them ' diligently.

5 O that my ways ' might be ' steadfast:
    in the ' keeping ' of your ' statutes.

6 Then I would not be ' put to ' shame:
    when I give ' heed to ' all · your com'mandments.

7 I will truly thank you ' from the ' heart:
    when I ' learn your ' just de'crees.

8   I will ' keep your ' statutes:
         O ' do not ' utterly · for'sake me.

B

9   How shall the young keep themselves ' unde'filed:
         surely by ' obeying ' your ' word.

10   With my whole ' heart I ' seek you:
         let me not ' stray from ' your com'mandments.

11   I treasure your word ' in my ' heart:
         for fear ' I should ' sin a'gainst you.

12   Blessèd are ' you O ' Lord:
         O ' teach me ' your ' statutes.

13   With my lips have ' I been ' telling:
         of all the ' judgments ' you have ' uttered.

14   I have found more joy‿
         in the way of ' your com'mandments:
         than in ' all ' manner · of ' riches.

15   I will meditate ' on your ' precepts:
         and I will give ' heed ' to your ' ways.

16   I will delight ' in your ' statutes:
         and I will ' not for'get your ' word.

C

17   Deal kindly with your servant that ' I may ' live:
         and living ' I shall ' keep your ' word.

18   Take the veil away ' from my ' eyes:
         that I may see the ' wonder·ful ' things · of your ' law.

19   I am but a ' stranger · on ' earth:
         do not ' hide · your com'mandments ' from me.

20   My soul is con'sumed · with the ' longing:
         it has at ' all times ' for your ' judgments.

21   You have re'buked the ' insolent:
         and cursed are those ‿
             who ' stray from ' your com'mandments.

22   Turn from me their re'proach and ' scorn:
         for ' I have ' kept your ' testimonies.

23 Rulers sit ' plotting · a'gainst me:
    but your servant will give ' thought ' to your ' statutes.

24 For your testimonies are ' my de'light:
    and ' they ' are my ' counsellors.

D

25 I lie ' prone · in the ' dust:
    revive me ac'cording ' to your ' word.

26 I acknowledged my ways, ' and you ' answered me:
    in'struct me ' in your ' statutes.

27 Help me to understand the ' way of · your ' precepts:
    and I will ' medi·tate ' on your ' wonders.

28 My soul melts a'way through ' sorrow:
    strengthen me ac'cording ' to your ' word.

29 Keep me from the ' way of ' falsehood:
    and in your ' goodness ' teach me · your ' law.

30 I have chosen the ' way of ' faithfulness:
    and ' set your ' judgments · be'fore me.

31 I hold fast to your de'crees O ' Lord:
    let me ' never · be ' put · to con'fusion.

32 I will run the way of ' your com'mandments:
    when you en'large my ' under'standing.

E

33 Teach me Lord the ' way · of your ' statutes:
    and in keeping them ' I shall ' have · my re'ward.

34 Give me understanding, and I shall ' keep your ' law:
    I shall ' keep it · with ' all my ' heart.

35 Make me walk in the path of ' your com'mandments:
    for ' that is ' my de'sire.

36 Incline my heart to ' your in'struction:
    and a'way from ' covetous · de'sires.

37 Turn away my eyes from what is ' empty · and ' false:
    and ' give me ' life · in your ' way.

38 Fulfil your promise ' to your ' servant:
    your ' promise · to ' those who ' fear you.

39   Turn away from me the scorn ' that I ' dread:
       for your ' judgments · are ' very ' good.

40   How I ' long · for your ' precepts:
       in your ' righteous·ness ' give me ' life.

F

41   Let your steadfast love come to ' me O ' Lord:
       your saving help ac'cording ' to your ' promise.

42   Then shall I have my answer for ' those who ' taunt me:
       for my ' trust is ' in your ' word.

43   Let my mouth never fail to ' speak the ' truth:
       for my ' hope is ' in your ' judgments.

44   I shall always ' keep your ' law:
       I shall ' keep it · for ' ever · and ' ever.

45   I shall walk in the ' path of ' freedom:
       be'cause I ' study · your ' precepts.

46   I will speak of your de'crees be·fore ' kings:
       and I will ' not · be a'bashed in · their ' presence.

47   I find delight in ' your com'mandments:
       which ' I have ' greatly ' loved.

48   I will revere your com'mandments · and ' love them:
       and I will ' medi·tate ' on your ' statutes.

G

49   Remember your ' word · to your ' servant:
       by ' which · you have ' given · me ' hope.

50   This is my ' comfort · in ' trouble:
       for your ' promise · has ' given · me ' life.

51   The arrogant may ' utterly · de'ride me:
       but I ' do not ' swerve · from your ' law.

52   I remember your ' judgments · of ' old:
       and ' then O ' Lord · I take ' comfort.

53   I am seized with ' hot · indig'nation:
       because of the wicked ' who for'sake your ' law.

54 But your statutes are the ' theme · of my ' song:
in the ' house ' of my ' pilgrimage.

55 I remember your name O Lord ' in the ' night:
and ' dwell up'on your ' law.

56 This is ' true of ' me:
be'cause · I have ' kept your ' precepts.

H

57 You Lord are ' all · that I ' have:
I have ' promised · to ' keep your ' word.

58 I have sought your favour with ' all my ' heart:
be gracious to me ac'cording ' to your ' promise.

59 I have given thought ' to my ' ways:
and always turned ' back to ' your in'struction.

60 I made ' no de'lay:
but hastened to ' keep ' your com'mandments.

61 Though the nets of the ' wicked · en'snared me:
I did ' not for'get your ' law.

62 At midnight I rise to ' give you ' thanks:
for the ' justice · of ' your de'crees.

63 I keep company with ' those who ' fear you:
with ' those who ' keep · your com'mandments.

64 The earth is full of your un'failing ' love:
O Lord in'struct me ' in your ' statutes.

I

65 Lord you have been ' good · to your ' servant:
ac'cording ' to your ' word.

66 Teach me good ' judgment · and ' knowledge:
for I ' trust in ' your com'mandments.

67 Before I was afflicted I ' went a'stray:
but ' now I ' keep your ' word.

68 You are good, and your ' deeds are ' good:
in'struct me ' in your ' statutes.

69   The proud have ' smeared me · with ' lies:
        but I will keep your ' precepts · with ' all my ' heart.

70   Their heart is ' gross like ' fat:
        but my de'light is ' in your ' law.

71   It is good for me that ' I · was af'flicted:
        so that ' I might ' learn your ' statutes.

72   The law from your mouth is to ' me more ' precious:
        than a ' fortune · in ' gold and ' silver.

J *Day 25 Evening*

73   Your hands have ' made me · and ' shaped me:
        give me understanding‿
           that ' I may ' learn · your com'mandments.

74   Let those who fear you be glad ' when they ' see me:
        be'cause I ' trust · in your ' word.

75   Lord I know that your de'crees are ' just:
        and that in your very faithfulness‿
           you have ' caused · me to ' be af'flicted.

76   Let your unfailing love ' be my ' comfort:
        according to your ' promise ' to your ' servant.

77   Let your compassion come to me, that ' I may ' live:
        for your ' law is ' my de'light.

78   Let the arrogant be put to shame,
        for with their lies ' they have ' wronged me:
        but I will ' medi·tate ' on your ' precepts.

79   Let those who fear you ' turn to ' me:
        that ' they may ' know your ' testimonies.

80   Let my heart be sound ' in your ' statutes:
        so that I may ' never · be ' put to ' shame.

K

81   I yearn for your ' saving ' help:
        hoping for the ful'filment ' of your ' word.

82   My eyes are strained with ' watching · for your ' promise:
        and I say, ' 'When O ' Lord · will you ' comfort me?'

83   I am shrivelled like a wineskin ' in the ' smoke:
        yet I do ' not for'get your ' statutes.

84   How long must your ' servant ' wait:
        for you to give ' judgment ' on my ' persecutors?

85   The arrogant have dug ' pitfalls · to ' trap me:
        and ' thus they ' flout your ' law.

86   All your com'mandments · are ' true:
        help me, for ' they pur'sue me · with ' lies.

87   They had almost made an end of ' me on ' earth:
        but I did ' not for'sake your ' precepts.

88   Give me life, because of your ' steadfast ' love:
        so that I may keep the ' testi·monies ' of your ' mouth.

L

89   Your word O Lord is ' ever'lasting:
        it is ' firmly ' fixed · in the ' heavens.

90   Your faithfulness endures throughout ' all · gener'ations:
        stable as the earth you created and ' made to ' stand ' firm.

91   Your ordinances stand fast ' to this ' day:
        for ' all things ' are your ' servants.

92   If my delight had not ' been · in your ' law:
        I should have ' perished · in ' my af'fliction.

93   I will never for'get your ' precepts:
        for by them ' you have ' given · me ' life.

94   I am ' yours O ' save me:
        for ' I have ' studied · your ' precepts.

95   Though the wicked lie in wait ' to de'stroy me:
        I will apply my ' mind to ' your in'struction.

96   I see that all things ' reach a ' limit:
        but your com'mandment ' has no ' bounds.

M

97   Lord how I ' love your ' law:
     all the day long ' it is ' in my ' mind.

98   Your commandment has made me wiser ' than my ' enemies:
     for ' it is ' always ' with me.

99   I have more understanding than ' all my ' teachers:
     for your in'struction ' is my ' study.

100 I am wiser ' than the ' agèd:
     be'cause I ' keep · your com'mandments.

101 I have held back my feet from every ' evil ' way:
     in ' order · to ' keep your ' word.

102 I have not swerved ' from your ' judgments:
     because ' you your'self have ' taught me.

103 How sweet are your ' words · to my ' taste:
     sweeter than ' honey ' in my ' mouth.

104 Through your commandments I get ' under'standing:
     therefore I hate ' all the ' ways of ' falsehood.

N   *Day 26 Morning*

105 Your word is a lamp ' for my ' feet:
     and a ' light up'on my ' path.

106 I have sworn an oath, ' and con'firmed it:
     to ' keep your ' righteous ' judgments.

107 I am in ' deep dis'tress:
     revive me O Lord, ac'cording ' to your ' word.

108 Accept O Lord the willing tribute ' of my ' lips:
     and ' teach me ' your de'crees.

109 I take my life in my ' hands con'tinually:
     yet I ' never · for'get your ' law.

110 The wicked have ' laid a ' snare for me:
     but I ' have not ' strayed · from your ' precepts.

111 Your testimonies are my ' heritage · for ' ever:
     they are the ' very ' joy · of my ' heart.

112 I have applied my heart to ful'fil your ' statutes:
     for ' ever · and ' to the ' end.

O

113   I detest those who are not ' single-'minded:
        but my ' love is ' for your ' law.

114   You are my shelter ' and my ' shield:
        my ' hope is ' in your ' word.

115   Away from me, ' you · that do ' evil:
        I will keep the com'mandments ' of my ' God.

116   Support me Lord according to your promise,
        so that ' I may ' live:
        and let me not be disap'pointed ' in my ' hope.

117   Hold me up and I ' shall be ' safe:
        and I shall be occupied ' with your ' statutes · con'tinually.

118   You spurn all those who ' swerve · from your ' statutes:
        their ' cunning · is ' all in ' vain.

119   All the wicked of the earth are to you as ' so much ' dross:
        therefore I ' love ' your in'struction.

120   My flesh trembles with ' dread of ' you:
        I ' stand in ' awe · of your ' judgments.

P

121   I have done what is ' just and ' right:
        do not a'bandon me · to ' my op'pressors.

122   Stand surety for your ' servant's ' welfare:
        let ' not the ' arrogant · op'press me.

123   My eyes grow dim from watching for your ' saving ' help:
        for the fulfilment ' of your ' righteous ' promise.

124   Deal with your servant according to your ' loving ' mercy:
        and ' teach me ' your de'crees.

125   I am your servant, O give me ' under'standing:
        that ' I may ' know your ' testimonies.

126   It is time for you O ' Lord to ' act:
        for people have ' flouted ' your ' law.

127   I love your commandments ' more than ' gold:
        yes, ' more · than the ' finest ' gold.

128   Therefore I direct my steps by ' all your ' precepts:
        and I hate ' all the ' ways of ' falsehood.

Q

129 Your in'struction · is ' wonderful:
    therefore I ' keep it · with ' all my ' heart.

130 The unfolding of your ' word gives ' light:
    and those who are untaught re'ceive ' under'standing.

131 I open my ' mouth and ' sigh:
    with ' longing · for ' your com'mandments.

132 Turn to me and be ' merci·ful ' to me:
    as is your ' way with ' those who ' love you.

133 Keep steady my footsteps, according ' to your ' promise:
    and let no evil get ' master·y ' over ' me.

134 Rescue me from ' human · op'pression:
    so that ' I may ' keep your ' precepts.

135 Let your face ' shine · on your ' servant:
    and ' teach me ' your de'crees.

136 Tears stream ' from my ' eyes:
    because people ' do not ' heed your ' law.

R

137 Lord you are ' just in'deed:
    and ' upright ' are your ' judgments.

138 The decrees that ' you have ' made:
    are ex'ceeding·ly ' righteous · and ' true.

139 My indig'nation · con'sumes me:
    because my enemies ' have for'gotten · your ' words.

140 Your promise has been tested ' to the ' uttermost:
    and ' therefore · your ' servant ' loves it.

141 I am small and of ' little · ac'count:
    but I do ' not for'get · your com'mandments.

142 Your justice is an ever'lasting ' justice:
    and your ' law ' is the ' truth.

143 Trouble and anguish have ' fallen · up'on me:
    yet my de'light · is in ' your com'mandments.

144 The righteousness of your decrees is ' ever'lasting:
    O give me under'standing · that ' I may ' live.

145 I call with my ' whole ' heart:
      answer me Lord, ' I will ' keep your ' statutes.

146 I cry out to ' you to ' save me:
      that ' I may ' keep your ' testimonies.

147 I rise before dawn and ' call to ' you:
      for my ' hope is ' in your ' word.

148 I wake before the ' hour · of my ' night-watch:
      so that I may ' medi·tate ' on your ' words.

149 Hear me in your un'failing ' kindness:
      and give me ' life by ' your de'crees.

150 Those who pursue me with ' malice · draw ' near:
      and they are ' far ' from your ' law.

151 But you O Lord are ' near at ' hand:
      and ' all · your com'mandments · are ' true.

152 I have long known from ' your de'crees:
      that you have ' given them · e'ternal · found'ations.

T

153 Consider my affliction ' and de'liver me:
      for I do ' not for'get your ' law.

154 Plead my cause and ' win · my re'lease:
      true to your ' promise ' give me ' life.

155 Salvation is ' far · from the ' wicked:
      for they ' give no ' heed · to your ' statutes.

156 Great is your com'passion · O ' Lord:
      give me ' life by ' your de'crees.

157 Many are those who persecute ' me and ' trouble me:
      yet I do not ' swerve from ' your in'struction.

158 I looked at the ' faithless · with ' loathing:
      because they ' do not ' keep · your com'mandments.

159 Consider O Lord how I ' love your ' precepts:
      and in your steadfast ' love pre'serve my ' life.

160 The sum of your ' words is ' truth:
      and all your just de'crees en'dure for ' ever.

U

161 Princes oppress me without ' any ' cause:
　　but my heart ' stands in ' awe · of your ' word.

162 I rejoice ' at your ' promise:
　　as ' one who ' finds great ' spoil.

163 Lies I ' hate · and de'test:
　　but your ' law · is the ' thing · that I ' love.

164 Seven times a ' day I ' praise you:
　　for the ' justice · of ' your de'crees.

165 Great is the peace of those who ' love your ' law:
　　and ' nothing · shall ' make them ' stumble.

166 Lord I have waited for your ' saving ' help:
　　and I have ful'filled ' your com'mandments.

167 From my heart I have o'beyed · your in'struction:
　　and ' I have ' loved it ' deeply.

168 I have kept your precepts ' and com'mands:
　　for all my ' ways are ' open · be'fore you.

V

169 Let my cry come be'fore you · O ' Lord:
　　give me understanding ac'cording ' to your ' word.

170 Let my supplication ' come be'fore you:
　　save me ac'cording ' to your ' word.

171 My lips shall pour ' forth your ' praise:
　　because ' you have ' taught me · your ' statutes.

172 My tongue shall ' sing · of your ' word:
　　for ' all · your com'mandments · are ' just.

173 Let your hand be ' ready · to ' help me:
　　for ' I have ' chosen · your ' precepts.

174 Lord I long for your ' saving ' help:
　　and your ' law is ' my de'light.

175 Let me live, that ' I may ' praise you:
　　and let your ' judgments · be ' my sup'port.

176 I have gone astray like a ' sheep · that is ' lost:
　　O seek your servant,
　　　　for I do ' not for'get · your com'mandments.

120

1   In my distress I called to ' you O ' Lord:
     I ' called · to you ' and you ' answered me.

2   'Deliver me from lying ' lips,' I ' cried:
     'and ' from a ' treacher·ous ' tongue.'

3   What shall be ' given · to ' you:
     what more shall God do to ' you O ' treacher·ous ' tongue?

4   It will be a warrior's ' sharp ' arrows:
     tempered with ' hot ' glowing ' charcoal.

5   Alas, I live like an ' exile · in ' Meshech:
     or like one who dwells a'mong the ' tents of ' Kedar.

6   Too long have I ' had my ' dwelling:
     among ' those · who are ' enemies · to ' peace.

7† I am for peace, but ' when I ' speak of it:
     they ' make them·selves ' ready · for ' war.

121

1   I lift up my ' eyes · to the ' hills:
     but ' where · shall I ' look for ' help?

2   My help ' comes · from the ' Lord:
     who has ' made ' heaven · and ' earth.

3   The Lord will not let your ' foot ' stumble:
     the one who ' guards you ' will not ' sleep.

4   The one who keeps watch ' over · this ' people:
     shall ' neither ' doze nor ' sleep.

5   The Lord is the one ' who will ' guard you:
     the Lord at your right ' hand will ' be · your de'fence,

6   so that the sun shall not ' strike you · by ' day:
     nor ' yet the ' moon by ' night.

7   The Lord shall preserve you from ' all ' evil:
     yes it is the ' Lord · who will ' keep you ' safe.

8   The Lord shall take care of your⌣
     going out, and your ' coming ' in:
     from this time ' forth ' and for ' ever.

122

1   I was glad when they ' said to ' me:
       'Let us ' go · to the ' house · of the ' Lord.'

2   And now our ' feet are ' standing:
       with'in your ' gates · O Je'rusalem,

3   Jerusalem that is ' built · as a ' city:
       where people ' come to'gether · in ' unity.

4   There the tribes go up, the ' tribes · of the ' Lord:
       as was decreed for Israel,
          to give ' thanks · to the ' name · of the ' Lord.

5† There are set ' thrones of ' judgment:
       the ' thrones · of the ' house of ' David.

6   Pray for the ' peace · of Je'rusalem:
       may ' those who ' love you ' prosper.

7   Peace be with'in your ' walls:
       and pros'perity · with'in your ' palaces.

8   For the sake of my kinsfolk ' and com'panions:
       I will ' pray that ' peace · may be ' with you.

9   Because of the house of the ' Lord our ' God:
       I will ' pray ' for your ' good.

123

1   To you I lift ' up my ' eyes:
       to you that are en'throned ' in the ' heavens.

2   As the eyes of servants are on the ' hand · of their ' masters:
       and the eyes of a ' maid · on the ' hand of · her ' mistress,

3† so our eyes are on you O ' Lord our ' God:
       as we wait ' till you ' show us · your ' favour.

4   Have mercy on us O ' Lord, have ' mercy:
       for we have had ' more · than e'nough of · con'tempt.

5   Too long have we suffered the ' scorn · of the ' wealthy:
       and the con'tempt ' of the ' arrogant.

124

1   'If the Lord had not been on our side,'
        now may ' Israel ' say:
      'If the Lord had not been on our side⌣
        when our ' enemies · rose ' up a'gainst us,

2   'then they would have ' swallowed us · a'live:
      when their ' fury · was ' roused a'gainst us.

3   'Then the flood would have ' swept us · a'way:
      and the ' torrent ' would have ' covered us.

4   'Then the ' raging ' waters:
      would have ' gone right ' over · our ' heads.

5   'But praised ' be the ' Lord:
      who has not given us as a ' prey ' to their ' teeth.

6   'We have escaped like a bird from the ' fowler's ' snare:
      the snare is ' broken · and ' we are ' free.

7†   'Our help is in the ' name · of the ' Lord:
      who has ' made ' heaven · and ' earth.'

125

1   Those who trust in the Lord are ' like Mount ' Zion:
      which cannot be ' shaken · but ' stands for ' ever.

2   As the hills en'fold Je'rusalem:
      so you enfold your people O Lord, ' now ' and for ' ever.

3   The sceptre of the wicked shall not hold sway⌣
        over the land as'signed · to the ' just:
      lest the just should put out their ' hand to ' do ' evil.

4   Do good O Lord to ' those · who are ' good:
      to ' those · who are ' upright · in ' heart.

5†   As for those who turn aside into crooked ways,
        the Lord shall lead them away with ' evil-'doers:
      but upon ' Israel ' there shall · be ' peace.

126

1   When the Lord restored the fortunes ' of this ' people:
    it ' seemed · to us ' like a ' dream.

2   Then our mouth was ' filled with ' laughter:
    and our tongues ' uttered ' shouts of ' joy .

3   Then they said a'mong the ' nations:
    'The Lord has ' done great ' things for ' them.'

4   Great things indeed the Lord has ' done for ' us:
    and ' therefore ' we are ' glad.

5   Restore again our ' fortunes · O ' Lord:
    as when streams re'fresh the ' southern ' dry-lands.

6   Those who ' sow in ' tears:
    shall ' reap with ' shouts of ' joy.

7† Those who go out weeping with ' seed for ' sowing:
    shall come back in gladness '‿
        bringing · their ' sheaves ' with them.

127

1   Unless the Lord ' builds the ' house:
    its builders ' will have ' laboured · in ' vain.

2   Unless the Lord watches ' over · the ' city:
    those who keep watch will ' stay a'wake in ' vain.

3   In vain you rise up early and go late to rest,
        eating the bread of ' anxious ' toil:
    for those whom the Lord ' loves are ' given ' sleep.

4   Truly children are a gift ' from the ' Lord:
    and offspring a re'ward from ' God's ' hand.

5   Like arrows in a ' warri·or's ' hand:
    so indeed are the ' children ' of one's ' youth.

6   Happy are those who have their ' quiver ' full of them:
        they will not be put to shame
        when they meet their ' adver·saries ' at the ' gate.

128

1   Blessèd are all those who ' fear the ' Lord:
        those who ' walk in ' God's ' ways.

2   You shall eat the ' fruit · of your ' labours:
        and ' you · shall be ' happy · and ' prosper.

3   Your wife shall be like a ' fruitful ' vine:
        with'in the ' walls of · your ' house;

4   your children like ' slips of ' olive:
        planted ' round a'bout your ' table.

5†   Thus shall all ' those be ' blessed:
        who fear the ' Lord ' in their ' heart.

6   May the Lord bless you from the ' holy ' city:
        may you see the prosperity of Jerusalem '⁔
          all the ' days of · your ' life.

7   May you live to see your ' children's ' children:
        and upon ' Israel ' let there · be ' peace.

129

1   'Much have they afflicted me from the ' time · of my ' youth':
        may God's ' people ' now ' say,

2   'Much have they afflicted me ' from my ' youth:
        but they have ' not pre'vailed a'gainst me.

3   'They scored my back as ' with a ' ploughshare:
        making ' long their ' furrows · up'on it.'

4   But the ' Lord is ' righteous:
        and has cut me ' free · from the ' yoke · of the ' wicked.

5   Let them be put to confusion and ' driven ' back:
        all those who are ' enemies · of ' God's ' people.

6   Let them be like grass that ' grows · on the ' roof:
        which withers be'fore · it is ' full ' grown,

7   which never fills a ' reaper's ' hand:
        nor ' yields a ' sheaf · for the ' harvester,

8   so that passers-by will never say to them,
        ' The blessing of the ' Lord · be up'on you:
        we ' bless you · in the ' name · of the ' Lord.'

130

1   Out of the depths have I called to ' you O ' Lord:
      give ' heed O ' Lord · to my ' cry.

2   Let your ears con'sider ' well:
      the ' plea I ' make for ' mercy.

3   If you should keep account of what is ' done a'miss:
      who ' then O ' Lord could ' stand?

4   But there is for'giveness · with ' you:
      therefore ' you shall ' be re'vered.

5   I wait for you Lord with ' all my ' soul:
      and in your ' word ' is my ' hope.

6   My soul waits for ' you O ' Lord:
      more than those who watch by night＿
         long for the morning,
      more I say than those who watch by night '＿
         long ' for the ' morning.

7   Wait in hope for the Lord,
         for with the Lord there is ' love un'failing:
      and with the Lord ' there is ' ample · re'demption.

8   The Lord ' will re'deem you:
      from ' all your ' many ' sins.

131

1   O Lord my ' heart is · not ' proud:
      my ' eyes · are not ' raised too ' high.

2   I do not occupy myself with ' matters · too ' great for me:
      or with ' marvels · that ' are be'yond me.

3   But I have stilled and made quiet my soul,
         like a weaned child nestling ' to its ' mother:
      so like a child, my ' soul is ' quieted · with'in me.

4   O ' trust · in the ' Lord:
      from ' this time ' forth · and for ' ever.

1   O Lord re'member ' David:
    and all the ' hardships ' he en'dured.

2   How he swore an ' oath · to the ' Lord:
    and made a vow to the ' Mighty ' One of ' Jacob,

3   'I will not enter the house ' where I ' live:
    nor will I climb ' into · the ' bed · where I ' rest,

4   'I will not give ' sleep · to my ' eyes:
    or per'mit my ' eyelids · to ' droop,

5†   'until I find a place ' for the ' Lord:
    a dwelling for the ' Mighty ' One of ' Jacob.'

6   At Ephrathah we heard of the ' ark of ' God:
    and we ' found it · in the ' region · of ' Jearim.

7   And we said, 'Let us go into⌣
    the dwelling-place of the ' Most ' High:
    and kneel in ' worship ' at God's ' footstool.'

8   Arise O Lord and ' enter · your ' resting-place:
    you and the ' ark ' of your ' strength.

9   Let your priests be ' clothed with ' righteousness:
    and let your faithful ' people · cry ' out for ' joy.

10† For your servant ' David's ' sake:
    do not re'ject · your an'ointed ' king.

11   The Lord made a sure ' promise · to ' David:
    a promise that will ' never ' be re'voked,

12   'A son, the ' fruit · of your ' body:
    I will ' set up'on your ' throne.

13   'If your sons keep my covenant,
    and obey the teaching ' that I ' give them:
    their descendants too shall sit on your⌣
    throne ' in suc'cession · for ' ever.'

14   For the Lord has ' chosen · Je'rusalem:
    the Lord desired it ' for a ' home and ' said,

15† 'This is my ' resting-place · for ' ever:
    here I will dwell, for I ' have · a de'light in ' her.

16 'I will abundantly ' bless · her pro'visions:
   and ' satisfy · her ' poor with ' bread.

17 'I will clothe her ' priests · with sal'vation:
   and her faithful ' people · shall re'joice and ' sing.

18 'There I will make a branch to spring⌣
       from the ' stem of ' David:
   and I have prepared a lamp for ' my an'ointed ' king.

19 'His enemies I will ' cover · with ' shame:
   but on him the crown he ' wears will ' shed its ' lustre.'

133

1 How good and pleasant a ' thing it ' is:
   when God's people ' live to'gether · in ' unity.

2 It is like the precious oil on Aaron's head,
       which ran down ' on to · his ' beard:
   and over the ' collar ' of his ' vestment.

3 It is like the ' dew of ' Hermon:
   falling up'on the ' hill of ' Zion.

4 For there the Lord ' promised · the ' blessing:
   which is ' life for ' ever'more.

134

1 Come praise the Lord, all you ' servants · of the ' Lord:
   you that stand by ' night · in the ' house of · the ' Lord.

2 Lift up your hands toward the ' holy ' place:
   and ' bless the ' Lord your ' God.

3 The Lord who made ' heaven · and ' earth:
   give you ' blessing ' out of ' Zion.

135

1 Whakamoemititia a Ihowa. / Praise the Lord.
       O praise the ' name · of the ' Lord:
   give praise O you ' servants ' of the ' Lord,

2   you that stand in the ' house · of the ' Lord:
      in the ' temple ' courts · of our ' God.

3   O praise the Lord, for the ' Lord is ' good:
      sing praises to the name of the '‿
        Lord · for the ' Lord is ' gracious.

4   For you O God have chosen Jacob to ' be your ' own:
      and Israel ' as your ' special ' treasure.

5   For I know that you O ' Lord are ' great:
      and that ' you · are a'bove all ' gods.

6   You do whatever you will in ' heaven · and on ' earth:
      in the sea ' and in ' all the ' depths.

7   You bring up the clouds from the ' ends · of the ' earth:
      you send lightning with the rain,
        and bring out the ' wind ' from your ' storehouse.

8   You struck down the ' first-born · of ' Egypt:
      both of ' man and ' also · of ' beast.

9   You worked signs and ' wonders · in ' Egypt:
      against ' Pharaoh · and ' all his ' servants.

10   You struck down ' great ' nations:
      and put to ' death ' mighty ' kings,

11   Sihon king of the Amorites,
        and Og the ' king of ' Bashan:
      and ' all · who were ' rulers · in ' Canaan,

12   and gave their ' lands · as a ' heritage:
      a ' heritage · for ' Israel · your ' people.

13   Your name O Lord en'dures for ' ever:
      the remembrance of you through'out all ' gener'ations.

14   You Lord will give your ' people ' justice:
      and have com'passion ' on your ' servants.

15   The gods of the heathen‿
        are mere idols of ' silver · and ' gold:
      which are ' made by ' human ' hands.

16   They have mouths, but they ' cannot ' speak:
      they have ' eyes · but they ' cannot ' see.

17   They have ears, but they ' cannot ' hear:
       and there is no ' breath ' in their ' nostrils.

18   Those who make them ' grow · to be ' like them:
       and so do all who ' put their ' trust in ' them.

19   Praise the Lord O ' house of ' Israel:
       praise the ' Lord O ' house of ' Aaron.

20   Praise the Lord O ' house of ' Levi:
       you that stand in ' awe ' praise the ' Lord.

21†   Praised be the Lord from the ' holy ' city:
       the Lord who dwells in Jerusalem.
          Whaka'moemi'titia · a ' Ihowa. / O ' praise ' - the ' Lord.

136

1   O give thanks to the Lord, ' who is ' gracious:
       he mau tonu hoki ' tana ' mahi ' tohu.
         God's ' love en'dures for ' ever.

2   Give thanks to the ' God of ' gods:
       he mau tonu hoki ' tana ' mahi ' tohu.
         God's ' love en'dures for ' ever.

3†   Give thanks to the ' Lord of ' lords:
       he mau tonu hoki ' tana ' mahi ' tohu.
         God's ' love en'dures for ' ever.

4   The Lord alone ' does great ' wonders:
       he mau tonu hoki ' tana ' mahi ' tohu.
         God's ' love en'dures for ' ever.

5   The Lord by wisdom ' made the ' heavens:
       he mau tonu hoki ' tana ' mahi ' tohu.
         God's ' love en'dures for ' ever.

6   The Lord spread out the earth a'bove the ' waters:
       he mau tonu hoki ' tana ' mahi ' tohu.
         God's ' love en'dures for ' ever.

7   The Lord made the ' great ' lights:
       he mau tonu hoki ' tana ' mahi ' tohu.
         God's ' love en'dures for ' ever.

8   the sun to rule ' over · the ' day:
        he mau tonu hoki ' tana ' mahi ' tohu.
          God's ' love en'dures for ' ever.

9   the moon and the stars to ' govern · the ' night:
        he mau tonu hoki ' tana ' mahi ' tohu.
          God's ' love en'dures for ' ever.

[10   The Lord struck down the ' first-born · of ' Egypt:
        he mau tonu hoki ' tana ' mahi ' tohu.
          God's ' love en'dures for ' ever.

11   and brought Israel ' out · from a'mong them:
        he mau tonu hoki ' tana ' mahi ' tohu.
          God's ' love en'dures for ' ever.

12   with a mighty hand and ' outstretched ' arm:
        he mau tonu hoki ' tana ' mahi ' tohu.
          God's ' love en'dures for ' ever.

13   The Lord divided the Red ' Sea in ' two:
        he mau tonu hoki ' tana ' mahi ' tohu.
          God's ' love en'dures for ' ever.

14   and made Israel go ' through the ' midst of it:
        he mau tonu hoki ' tana ' mahi ' tohu.
          God's ' love en'dures for ' ever.

15   But as for Pharaoh and his host,
        the Lord flung them ' into · the ' sea:
        he mau tonu hoki ' tana ' mahi ' tohu.
          God's ' love en'dures for ' ever.

16   The Lord led the people ' through the ' desert:
        he mau tonu hoki ' tana ' mahi ' tohu.
          God's ' love en'dures for ' ever.

17   The Lord overthrew ' mighty ' kingdoms:
        he mau tonu hoki ' tana ' mahi ' tohu.
          God's ' love en'dures for ' ever.

18   and struck down ' famous ' kings:
        he mau tonu hoki ' tana ' mahi ' tohu.
          God's ' love en'dures for ' ever.

19   Sihon ' king · of the ' Amorites:
        he mau tonu hoki ' tana ' mahi ' tohu.
          God's ' love en'dures for ' ever.

20   and Og the ' king of ' Bashan:
        he mau tonu hoki ' tana ' mahi ' tohu.
          God's ' love en'dures for ' ever.

21   and gave their ' land · as a ' heritage:
        he mau tonu hoki ' tana ' mahi ' tohu.
          God's ' love en'dures for ' ever.

22   a heritage to Israel ' God's ' servant:
        he mau tonu hoki ' tana ' mahi ' tohu.
          God's ' love en'dures for ' ever.

23   The Lord remembered us when we ' were in ' trouble:
        he mau tonu hoki ' tana ' mahi ' tohu.
          God's ' love en'dures for ' ever.

24†   and rescued us ' from our ' foes:
        he mau tonu hoki ' tana ' mahi ' tohu.
          God's ' love en'dures for ' ever.]

25   The Lord gives food to ' all things · that ' live:
        he mau tonu hoki ' tana ' mahi ' tohu.
          God's ' love en'dures for ' ever.

26   Give thanks to the ' God of ' heaven:
        he mau tonu hoki ' tana ' mahi ' tohu.
          God's ' love en'dures for ' ever.

137

1   By the waters of Babylon we sat ' down and ' wept:
        when we re'membered · the ' holy ' city.

2   As for our harps, we ' hung them ' up:
        on the ' trees that ' grew near'by.

3   Those who led us away captive‿
          demanded of ' us a ' song:
        our despoilers asked us for mirth,
          ' Sing us,' they said, ' 'one · of the ' songs · of Je'rusalem.'

4   How can we sing the ' Lord's ' song:
        here ' in an ' ali·en ' land?

5   If I forget you ' O Je'rusalem:
        let my ' right hand ' wither · a'way.

6   Let my tongue cling to the roof of my mouth,
          if I do ' not re'member you:
          if I do not set Jerusalem a'bove my ' highest ' joy.

      *   *   *

138

1   I will give thanks to you O Lord with ' all my ' heart:
        before the gods ' I will ' sing your ' praises.

2   I will bow down toward your holy temple,
          and give thanks because of your ' ⌣
        love and ' faithfulness:
        for you have exalted⌣
          your name and your ' word a'bove ' all things.

3   On the day that I ' called, you ' answered me:
        and ' put new ' strength with'in me.

4   All the kings of the earth shall ' praise you · O ' Lord:
        when they ' hear the ' words · of your ' mouth.

5   They shall sing of the ' ways · of the ' Lord:
        that the ' glory · of the ' Lord is ' great.

6   For though Lord you are high,
          yet you ' care · for the ' lowly:
        as for the proud,
          you ' humble · them ' from a'far.

7   Though I walk in the midst of trouble you ' keep me ' safe:
        you stretch out your hand against my enemies' rage,
        and ' your right ' hand will ' save me.

8   You will fulfil your purpose for me,
          your love O Lord is ' ever'lasting:
        do not leave un'finished · the ' work · of your ' hands.

1   Lord you have searched me ' out and ' known me:
  you know when I sit down and when I stand up,
   you dis'cern my ' thoughts · from a'far.

2   You mark my path, and the places ' where I ' rest:
  you are ac'quainted · with ' all my ' ways.

3   Even before there is a ' word · on my ' tongue :
  you Lord ' know it ' alto'gether.

4   You guard me from be'hind · and be'fore:
  and ' cover · me ' with your ' hand.

5† Such knowledge is too ' wonder·ful ' for me:
  so ' high · that I ' cannot · at'tain to it.

6   Where shall I ' go · from your ' spirit:
  or where shall I ' flee ' from your ' presence?

7   If I climb up to heaven ' you are ' there:
  if I make my bed in the grave ' you are ' there ' also.

8   If I take the ' wings · of the ' dawn:
  and alight at the ' utter·most ' parts · of the ' sea,

9   even there your ' hand will ' lead me:
  and your right ' hand will ' hold me ' fast.

10 If I say, 'Let the ' darkness ' cover me:
  and my ' day be ' turned to ' night,'

11 the darkness is no darkness with you,
  but the night is as ' clear · as the ' day:
   for darkness and light to ' you are ' both a'like.

12 It was you that created my ' inward ' parts:
  and pieced me together ' in my ' mother's ' womb.

13 I will praise you, for you are ' awesome · and ' wonderful:
  marvellous are your works,
   and you ' know me ' through and ' through.

14 My body was not ' hidden ' from you:
  when I was being fashioned in secret,
   and woven together ' in the ' depths · of the ' earth.

15 Your eyes ' looked · at my ' body:
  while it was as ' yet im'perfect·ly ' formed.

16   In your book all the days of my ' life were ' written:
        while as ' yet there ' was not ' one of them.

17   How deep are your ' thoughts O ' God:
        and how ' great ' is the ' sum of them.

18†   If I should count them,
        they are more in number ' than the ' sand:
        to finish the count,
        my life-span must ' needs be ' equal · to ' yours.

       * * *

23   Examine me O God and ' know my ' heart:
        test me, ' and dis'cover · my ' thoughts.

24   Watch closely, lest I follow a ' path of ' error:
        and lead me in the ' way ' ever'lasting.

140

1   Deliver me O Lord ' from the ' wicked:
        and pre'serve me ' from the ' violent,

2   who devise evil ' in their ' hearts:
        and ' stir up ' strife con'tinually.

3   They have sharpened their tongues ' like a ' serpent's:
        adder's ' poison · is ' under · their ' lips.

4   Keep me O Lord from the ' hands · of the ' wicked:
        from the violent, who ' plan to ' trip up · my ' feet.

5   The proud have laid a snare for me,
        and spread out a ' net of ' cords:
        they have set ' traps a'long my ' path.

6   I said to the Lord, ' 'You are · my ' God':
        hear O ' Lord my ' prayer for ' mercy.

7   O Lord God, my ' fortress · of ' safety:
        you have shielded my ' head · in the ' day of ' battle.

8   Do not grant the wicked their de'sire O ' Lord:
        or permit their ' evil · de'signs to ' prosper.

       * * *

12   I am sure the Lord will maintain the ' cause · of the ' poor:
        and up'hold the ' rights · of the ' destitute.

13   The righteous will give ' praise · to your ' name:
        and the ' upright · will ' live · in your ' presence.

141

1   Lord I call to you, come quickly ' to my ' help:
        give heed to me ' when I ' cry to ' you.

2   Let my prayer be be'fore you · as ' incense:
        and the lifting up of my '⌣
           hands · as the ' evening ' sacrifice.

3   Set a guard O Lord ' over · my ' mouth:
        and keep watch ' at the ' door of · my ' lips.

4   Keep my heart from any sinful inclination,
        from joining the ill-disposed ' in their ' wickedness:
        and let me ' never ' eat · at their ' table.

5   Rather let the ' righteous ' strike me:
        and ' give me ' friendly · re'buke,

6   than that the oil of the wicked should an'oint my ' head:
        for I pray con'tinually · a'gainst their ' wickedness.

        * * *

9   But my eyes are fixed on ' you Lord ' God:
        in you I take refuge, ' do not ' cast me ' off.

10   Keep me from the snare ' they have ' laid for me:
        and from the traps ' evil'doers · have ' set.

11†   Let the wicked fall together into their ' own ' nets:
        while ' I pass ' by un'harmed.

142

Day 29 Evening

1   I cry aloud to ' you O ' Lord:
        I ' loudly ' plead · for your ' help.

2   I pour out my ' trouble · be'fore you:
        and make ' known to · you ' my dis'tress.

3   When my spirit is faint within me, you ' know my ' way:
              in the path where I walk ' ⌣
              they have ' hidden · a ' snare for me.

4   I look to my ' right ' hand:
              and see ' there is ' no one · who ' heeds me.

5   There is no ' way · of es'cape:
              and ' no one ' gives me · a ' thought.

6   I cry to the Lord and say, ' 'You are · my ' refuge:
              you are all that I have ' in the ' land · of the ' living.'

7   Give heed to my cry for I am brought ' very ' low:
              deliver me from those who pursue me,'
                for they ' are too ' strong for me.

8   Bring me ' out · of my ' prison:
              so that I may give ' thanks ' to your ' name.

9†   When you show me your ' loving ' kindness:
              the ' righteous · will ' gather · a'round me.

143

1   Hear my ' prayer O ' Lord:
              in your faithfulness give heed to my pleading,
              and ' answer · me ' in your ' righteousness.

2   Do not put your ' servant · on ' trial:
              for in your sight ' no one ' living · is ' innocent.

3   For my enemies have hunted me down,
              and beaten me ' to the ' ground:
              they have made me inhabit darkness,
              like ' those · who have ' long been ' dead.

4   Therefore my spirit ' faints with'in me:
              and my ' heart is ' numb with ' grief.

5   Yet I remember times past,
              I think about ' all · you have ' done:
              I meditate on the ' works of ' your ' hands.

6   I stretch out my ' hands to ' you:
              I thirst for you as a ' parched land ' thirsts for ' rain.

7   Make haste to answer me Lord, for my ' spirit · is ' failing:
       do not hide your face from me,
          or I shall be like ' those who · go ' down · to the ' dead.

8   Let me hear of your steadfast love ' in the ' morning:
       for in ' you · I have ' put my ' trust.

9   Show me the way ' I should ' walk in:
       for to ' you · I lift ' up my ' soul.

10   Deliver me Lord ' from my ' enemies:
       for I have ' fled to ' you for ' refuge.

11   Teach me to do your will, for ' you · are my ' God:
       let your good spirit ' lead me · on an ' even ' path.

12   Keep me safe O Lord for your ' name's ' sake:
       and for your righteousness' sake '‿
          bring me ' out of ' trouble.

* * *

144

1   Blessèd be the ' Lord my ' rock:
       who trains my hand for war ' and my ' fingers · for ' battle,

2   my strength and my fortress, my stronghold and my refuge,
       my shield in ' whom I ' trust:
       who brings ' people ' under · my ' rule.

3   Lord, what are we mortals that you should ' care a'bout us:
       mere human beings that '‿
          you should ' give us · a ' thought?

4   Each of us is like a ' puff of ' wind:
       our days are ' like a ' passing ' shadow.

5   Lower your heavens O Lord and ' come ' down:
       touch the ' mountains · and ' they shall ' smoke.

6   Send out your lightnings, and ' scatter · the ' enemy:
       shoot out your ' arrows · and ' put them · to ' flight.

7   Reach down your hand from on ' high and ' rescue me:
       snatch me out of the deep waters,
          from the ' hands of ' ali·en ' foes,

8   whose mouths utter things ' that are ' false:
       and whose right ' hand is ' raised in ' perjury.

9   I will sing you a new ' song O ' God:
       I will sing your praises ' on a ' ten-stringed ' lute.

10   You give ' victory · to ' kings:
       and de'liverance · to ' David · your ' servant.

11   Save me from the ' cruel ' sword:
       deliver me ' from the ' hands of ' aliens,

12   whose mouths utter ' things · that are ' false:
       and whose right ' hand is ' raised in ' perjury.

13   May our sons in their youth be like ' well-grown ' saplings:
       and our daughters like⏝
         sculptured ' pillars · at the ' corners · of ' palaces.

14   May our barns be full to overflowing⏝
       with every ' kind · of pro'vision:
       our sheep bear young⏝
         in thousands upon ' thousands ' in our ' fields.

15   May our cattle be fat and strong,
       suffering no miscarriage or un'timely ' birth:
       and may there be no ' cries · of dis'tress · in our ' streets.

16   Happy are the people to whom such ' blessings ' fall:
       happy the people whose ' God ' is the ' Lord.

145

1   I will extol you O ' God my ' king:
       I will bless your ' name for ' ever · and ' ever.

2   Every day will I give ' thanks to ' you:
       and praise your ' name for ' ever · and ' ever.

3   You are great O Lord, and worthy of ' all ' praise:
       there are no ' bounds ' to your ' greatness.

4   One generation shall praise your ' works · to an'other:
       and pro'claim your ' mighty ' acts.

5   I will speak of the glorious splendour ' of your ' majesty:
       and of ' all your ' marvel·lous ' works.

6 People shall speak of the might of your ' awesome ' deeds:
   and I ' too · will pro'claim your ' greatness.

7† They shall pour out the story of your a'bundant ' kindness:
   and joyfully ' sing ' of your ' righteousness.

8 The Lord is gracious and ' full · of com'passion:
   slow to anger ' and a'bounding · in ' love.

9 You Lord are ' good to ' all of us:
   and your mercy ' rests up·on ' all your ' creatures.

10 All your creation shall ' praise you · O ' Lord:
   and your ' servants · will ' bless your ' name.

11 They shall speak of the glory ' of your ' kingdom:
   and their ' talk shall ' be of · your ' power,

12 so that all may know of your ' mighty ' deeds:
   and the glorious ' splendour ' of your ' kingdom.

13 Your kingdom is an ever'lasting ' kingdom:
   and your dominion en'dures from ' age to ' age.

14 The Lord upholds ' those who ' stumble:
   and ' raises · up ' those · who are ' down.

15 The eyes of all look to ' you O ' Lord:
   and you give them their ' food in ' due ' season.

16 You open ' wide your ' hand:
   and give what they de'sire to ' all things ' living.

17 You Lord are righteous in ' all your ' ways:
   and ' loving · in ' all your ' deeds.

18 You Lord are near to ' all who ' call to you:
   who call to ' you in ' singleness · of ' heart.

19 You fulfil the desire of ' those · who re'vere you:
   you hear their ' cry ' and you ' save them.

20 You protect ' all who ' love you:
   but the ' wicked · you ' will de'stroy.

21 My mouth shall speak the ' praise · of the ' Lord:
   let everyone bless God's holy ' name for ' ever · and ' ever.

146

1   Whakamoemititia a Ihowa. / Praise the Lord.
        Praise the Lord ' O my ' soul:
        as long as I ' live · I will ' praise the ' Lord.

2   Yes, as long as ' I have ' life:
        I will sing ' praises ' to my ' God.

3   Put no trust in princes, nor in any ' human ' power:
        for in ' them there ' is no ' help.

4   When they breathe their last, they re'turn to ' dust:
        then all their ' plans ' come to ' nothing.

5   Happy are those whose helper is the ' God of ' Jacob:
        whose hope is ' in the ' Lord their ' God,

6   who made heaven and earth,
        the sea and ' all · that is ' in them:
        who ' keeps a ' promise · for ' ever,

7   who defends the ' cause of · the op'pressed:
        and gives ' food ' to the ' hungry.

8   The Lord sets free the prisoner,
        and gives ' sight · to the ' blind:
        the Lord raises up those bowed down,
        and ' loves ' those · who are ' just.

9   The Lord cares for the stranger in the land,
        and sustains the ' widows · and ' orphans:
        but turns the ' way · of the ' wicked · to ' ruin.

10   The Lord shall ' reign for ' ever:
        your God O Jerusalem shall reign for all generations.
        Whaka'moemi'titia · a ' Ihowa. / O ' praise ' - the ' Lord.

147

Day 30 Evening

1   Whakamoemititia a Ihowa, / Praise the Lord,
        for it is good to sing praises ' to our ' God:
        how pleasant and seemly it is to ' praise the ' Most ' High.

2   You Lord are re'building · Je'rusalem:
        and gathering the ' scattered ' exiles · of ' Israel.

3   You are healing the ' broken-'hearted:
        and ' binding ' up their ' wounds.

4   You count the ' number · of the ' stars:
        and ' call them ' all · by their ' names.

5   Great are you O Lord, and ' mighty · your ' power:
        yes, ' and your ' wisdom · is ' infinite.

6   You raise ' up the ' lowly:
        and bring down the ' wicked ' to the ' dust.

7   Sing to the ' Lord in ' thanksgiving:
        make music on the ' harp ' to our ' God,

8   who covers the sky with clouds,
            and prepares ' rain · for the ' earth:
        making the hills green with grass⌣
            and with ' plants for ' human ' use.

9   You O Lord give the ' cattle · their ' food:
        and the young ravens ' when they ' call to ' you.

10 You set no store by the ' power · of a ' horse:
        nor by the ' strength · of a ' warri·or's ' thighs.

11 But your delight is in ' those · who re'vere you:
        in ' those · who re'ly on · your ' mercy.

12 Praise the Lord ' O Je'rusalem:
        O holy ' city ' praise your ' God.

13 For the Lord has strengthened the ' bars · of your ' gates:
        and ' blessed your ' children · with'in you.

14 The Lord has established peace with'in your ' borders:
        and fed you amply ' with the ' finest ' wheat.

15 You O Lord send your ' word · to the ' earth:
        and your com'mand runs ' very ' swiftly.

16 You give ' snow like ' wool:
        and ' sprinkle ' hoar-frost · like ' ashes.

17 You scatter ' hailstones · like ' breadcrumbs:
        you send the cold, ' and the ' waters · stand ' frozen.

18 You utter your word and the ' ice is ' melted:
        you blow with your wind ' and the ' waters ' flow.

19 You make known your ' word to ' Jacob:
    your ' statutes · and de'crees to ' Israel.

20 You have not done this for any ' other ' nation:
    nor have you taught them your laws.
        Whaka'moemi'titia · a ' Ihowa. / O ' praise ' - the ' Lord.

148

1   Whakamoemititia a Ihowa. / Praise the Lord.
        Praise the Lord ' from the ' heavens:
        O praise God ' in the ' heights a'bove.

2   Praise the Lord ' all you ' angels:
        O praise God ' all you ' heaven·ly ' host.

3   Praise the Lord ' sun and ' moon:
        praise God ' all you ' shining ' stars.

4   Praise the Lord you ' highest ' heavens:
        and you ' waters · a'bove the ' heavens.

5   Let them praise the ' name · of the ' Lord:
        who commanded, ' and they ' were cre'ated.

6   The Lord fixed them in their ' places · for ' ever:
        by a law ' which shall ' never · be ' broken.

7   Praise the Lord ' from the ' earth:
        you sea-'monsters · and ' ocean ' depths,

8   fire and hail, ' snow and ' ice:
        stormy ' wind o'beying · God's ' word,

9   all ' mountains · and ' hills:
        all ' fruit·bearing ' trees and ' cedars,

10 wild ' beasts and ' cattle:
        reptiles and ' birds ' on the ' wing,

11 kings of the earth and ' all ' peoples:
        princes and all ' rulers ' of the ' world,

12 young ' men and ' maidens:
        old ' people · and ' children · to'gether.

13   Let them praise your ' name O ' Lord:
        for your name alone is exalted,
           and your glory is a'bove ' heaven · and ' earth.

14   You have lifted up your people's head,
        with praise from ' all your ' servants:
        from the people close to your heart.
        Whaka'moemi'titia · a ' Ihowa. / O ' praise ' - the ' Lord.

149

1   Whakamoemititia a Ihowa. / Praise the Lord.
        O sing to the Lord a ' new ' song:
        give praise in the as'sembly ' of the ' faithful.

2   Let the people of God rejoice ' in their ' maker:
        and let the servants of the Most High ex'ult ' in their ' king.

3   Let them praise God's ' name · in the ' dance:
        let them sing God's ' praise with ' timbrel · and ' harp.

4   For you O Lord take de'light · in your ' people:
        and crown your ' humble ' folk with ' victory.

5   Let the faithful exult ' in their ' triumph:
        let them ' shout for ' joy · as they ' feast.

6   Let the praises of God be ' on their ' lips:
        and a two-edged sword in their hand.
        Whaka'moemi'titia · a ' Ihowa. / O ' praise ' - the ' Lord.

      * * *

150

1   Whakamoemititia a Ihowa. / Praise the Lord.
        O praise God in the ' holy ' place:
        praise our God ' in the ' mighty ' heavens.

2   Praise the Lord for many ' acts of ' power:
        praise our God for ' greatness · be'yond ' measure.

3   Praise the Lord with the ′ sound · of the ′ trumpet:
        praise our God up′on the ′ lute and ′ harp.

4   Praise the Lord with ′ timbrels · and ′ dancing:
        praise our God up′on the ′ strings and ′ pipe.

5   Praise the Lord with ′ clash of ′ cymbals:
        praise our God up′on re′sounding ′ cymbals.

6   Let everything that has breath ′ praise the ′ Lord:
        whaka′moemi′titia · a ′ Ihowa. / O ′ praise ′ - the ′ Lord.

The Liturgy of Baptism
and
The Laying on of Hands for Confirmation and Renewal

Concerning this Service

When someone is baptised, that person is brought to Jesus Christ, and made a member of Christ's Church. It is a new start to life in which the baptised person is accepted and sealed by God with the Holy Spirit to represent Christ to the world.

As a response to the baptism which God gives us, we and the candidates declare our faith and intention to serve Christ, and ask for God's continuing grace to support us in the task to which we are called.

When a baptism is of a baby or a child, the baptised receives the love and shared faith of the family to grow up into Christ.

Through prayer and fellowship within the body of Christ God strengthens and nourishes us.

You are here today to help with your presence, your prayers and your love.

> *Jesus Christ came that we might have life,*
> *and have it in all its fulness.*

Introduction

It is widely agreed that these essential elements are to be found in any comprehensive baptismal liturgy:

The proclamation of the Scriptures referring to baptism
Invocation of the Holy Spirit
Renunciation of evil
Profession of faith in Christ and the Holy Trinity
The use of water in baptism
A declaration that those baptised have acquired a new identity
    as sons and daughters of God
A declaration of membership of the Church
The 'call' of the baptised to be witnesses of the gospel.

These elements are incorporated in the Liturgy of Baptism that follows. In common with many churches there is here also provided a service in which baptised Christians respond to their baptism and receive the laying on of hands for confirmation. These two services can be used either together or separately.

*It is the Church's teaching that baptism cannot be repeated in a person's life, because it is the action of God which declares our relationship 'in Christ'. The services of **The Liturgy of Baptism** and **The Laying on of Hands for Confirmation and Renewal** provide for a process of response to the baptismal action by a profession of faith and commitment to Christian service, as well as promises by parents and godparents to nurture the faith of a child baptised.*

Either at the same time as baptism, or at a later stage in the person's life, those making a profession of faith for the first time are confirmed by the bishop through the laying on of hands.

Those seeking to renew such promises also receive the laying on of hands with a suitable prayer.

*It may be appropriate for some candidates to give personal witness to their faith at **The Affirmation**.*

In both services all members of the congregation have an opportunity to renew their faith in Jesus as Lord and in the Creed profess the faith of their baptism.

The Minister of the Services

A bishop presides where there is the laying on of hands for confirmation and renewal, and a bishop or priest presides over a baptism. If the priest is absent it is permissible for a deacon to baptise.

In the case of emergency a lay person may baptise, pouring water on the candidate and saying

> [Name] I baptise you in the name of the Father, and of the Son, and of the Holy Spirit.

These words may be added

> God receives you by baptism into the Church.

When appropriate such emergency baptism is followed by a welcome and acknowledgement by the congregation, at which the priest should make the sign of the cross on the baptised and receive **The Affirmations** from the candidate or from the parent(s) and godparents.

Conditional Baptism

If there is doubt that a person has been baptised, then conditional baptism should take place, the priest preceding the words at baptism with the following

> 'If you are not already baptised... '

The Use of Oil

The sign of the cross after baptism may be made with oil set apart for this purpose either by the bishop or by a priest. It is appropriate for the bishop to do this on Maundy Thursday.

The following form is suggested.

The bishop or priest may say

> God of all creation, at baptism your Son was anointed by the Holy Spirit; in Christ's name we set apart this oil. Grant that those who are signed at their baptism with the cross of their Saviour in this holy oil, may be sealed by your Spirit as yours for ever, and share in the royal priesthood of your Church, for you live and reign one God for ever.
> **Amen.**

Baptismal Discipline

The General Synod has from time to time set out Guidelines for Christian Initiation which govern baptismal discipline. Those celebrating these services are expected to be familiar with such Guidelines and any others adopted in each episcopal jurisdiction of this Church.

Within the fellowship of the Church, and with its help, it is the responsibility of parents and godparents of children baptised to teach the child

> the Lord's Prayer and how to pray
> the Creeds and the Faith of the Church
> the Commandments and how to obey the teaching of Christ
> and how to read the Scriptures to discover the Word of God.

They are also to encourage their child to take her/his place in the eucharistic community, to make a commitment to the Lord, and in Confirmation to receive, in the laying on of hands, the strengthening power of the Holy Spirit for witness and service.

Additional Directions *are to be found on pages 396-399.*

The Liturgy of Baptism
and
The Laying on of Hands for
Confirmation and Renewal

The liturgy takes place when the Church meets for the Eucharist or another service of worship.

*It follows the **New Testament Lesson** or **The Gospel** or **The Sermon**.*

In special circumstances the bishop or priest shall provide a suitable introduction to this liturgy.

God's Call

The bishop or priest says

E te whanau a te Karaiti / Dear friends in Christ,
God is love, God gives us life.
We love because God first loves us.
In baptism God declares that love;
in Christ God calls us to respond.

*If there are no candidates for baptism,
the service continues at **The Presentation for the Laying on of Hands
for Confirmation and Renewal** (page 387)*

The Presentation for Baptism

*Each candidate for baptism is presented individually by a sponsor or,
in the case of a child, by a parent or godparent, who says*

I present N *(my child)* to be baptised
and made a member of the Body of Christ, the Church.

The bishop or priest says

From the beginning the Church has received believers by baptism.
Believers' children have also been baptised so that with help and
encouragement they should grow up in Christ and by the grace of
God serve Christ all the days of their life.

On the day when the apostles first preached the Gospel of Christ's
resurrection, Peter urged his hearers

'Repent and be baptised, every one of you,
in the name of Jesus the Christ
for the forgiveness of your sins,
and you will receive the gift of the Holy Spirit.
For the promise is to you and to your children,
and to all who are far away, everyone whom
the Lord our God may call.'

(Names)   How do you respond to this promise?

Each candidate for baptism replies	*The parents and godparents of each child reply*
I hear God's call and come for baptism.	We hear God's call and ask for baptism.

*The bishop or priest says to the candidates, and (for children),
to the parents and godparents*

Do you renounce all evil influences and powers
that rebel against God?

The candidates and parents and godparents reply

I renounce all evil.

Do you trust in Christ's victory which brings forgiveness, freedom and life?

The candidates reply   *The parents and godparents reply*

In faith I turn to Christ   In faith I turn to Christ,
my way, my truth, my life.   my way, my truth, my life,
                                                        as I care for this child.

People **May God keep you in the way you have chosen.**

The Baptism

The bishop or priest stands by the water for baptism, and says

> Praise God who made heaven and earth,

People **whose promise endures for ever.**

The bishop or priest prays

> We thank you God for your love in all creation,
> especially for your gift of water
> to sustain, refresh and cleanse all life.
>
> We thank you for your covenant
> with your people Israel;
> through the Red Sea waters
> you led them to freedom in the promised land.
> In the waters of the Jordan
> your Son was baptised by John
> and anointed with the Holy Spirit.
>
> Through the deep waters of death
> Jesus fulfilled his baptism.
> He died to set us free
> and was raised to be exalted Lord of all.
> It is Christ who baptises with the Holy Spirit
> and with fire.
>
> **Amen. Come Holy Spirit.**

We thank you that through the waters of baptism
you cleanse us,
renew us by your Spirit
and raise us to new life.

In the new covenant
we are made members of your Church
and share in your eternal kingdom.

Through your Holy Spirit,
fulfil once more your promises
in this water of rebirth,
set apart in the name of our Lord Jesus Christ.

**Amen! Praise and glory and wisdom,
thanksgiving and honour,
power and might,
be to our God for ever and ever.
Amen!**

*The bishop or priest baptises each candidate for baptism, either by immersion
in the water, or by pouring water on the candidate, saying*

[Name], I baptise you in the name of the Father, and of the Son, and of the Holy Spirit.	*[Ingoa],* he iri-iri tenei naku i a koe, i runga i te ingoa o te Matua, te Tama, me te Wairua Tapu.
Amen. **God receives you by baptism** **into the Church.** **Child of God,** **blessed in the Spirit,** **welcome** **to the family of Christ.**	**Amine.** **Kua tohia koe e te Atua,** **ki roto i tana kahui** **hei tamaiti mana,** **i roto i te Wairua.** **Nau mai, haere mai,** **ki te whanau a te Ariki.**

The bishop or priest makes the sign of the cross on each of the baptised, saying

We sign you with the cross, the sign of Christ.	Ka tohia koe ki te ripeka a te Karaiti.

Walk in the faith of Christ	Takahia te ara, i roto i te whakapono o te Karaiti
crucified and risen.	i ripekatia nei, i ara ake i te mate.
Shine with the light of Christ.	Tiaho i roto i te maramatanga o te Karaiti.

**If there are no candidates for the laying on of hands,
The Liturgy of Baptism *continues at* The Affirmation.**

The Presentation
for the Laying on of Hands
for Confirmation and Renewal

The bishop stands before the congregation.

The baptised who come to profess (or to re-affirm) their faith and receive the laying on of hands by the bishop, are brought forward and presented to the bishop with these words

Bishop *N*, I present *N* to profess their faith.
[Bishop *N*, I present *N* to re-affirm their faith].

The bishop shall then say

N, we welcome you as you come to profess
[and/or re-affirm] your faith.
At your baptism you were made a disciple of Christ,
and we signed you with the cross.
Come now to receive the laying on of hands with prayer,
to strengthen you for the work of God's kingdom.

The Affirmation

The congregation, the newly baptised, and any candidates for laying on of hands, stand to respond in these affirmations.

Praise to God who has given us life.
Whakamoemititia te Atua, te Kai-homai i te ora.
Blessed be God for the gift of love.
Kia whakapaingia te Atua, mo tana oha o te aroha.

Praise to God who forgives our sin.
>Whakamoemititia te Atua, e muru nei i o tatou hara.

Blessed be God who sets us free.
>**Kia whakapaingia te Atua, e whakawatea nei i a tatou.**

Praise to God who kindles our faith.
>Whakamoemititia te Atua, te ahi ka o te whakapono.

Blessed be God, our strength, our hope.
>**Kia whakapaingia te Atua, to matou kaha,**
>**to matou tumanako.**

The bishop or priest says to all those present who are baptised Christians

Let us, the baptised,
affirm that we renounce evil
and commit our lives to
Christ.

Tatou kua tohia nei,
me whakarere te kino
tahuri pumau ki a te Karaiti.

All respond

Blessed be God,
JESUS IS LORD!

Whakapaingia te Atua,
KO IHU TE ARIKI!

The bishop or priest then says to the candidates for laying on of hands, and the newly baptised, and/or in the case of children, their parents and godparents

What is your faith?

He aha to whakapono?

They respond

I believe and trust in
God the Father,
maker and sustainer
of all things;
and in God the Son,
my Saviour Jesus Christ;
and in God the Holy Spirit,
giver of life and truth.
This is my faith.

E whakapono ana ahau
ki te Atua, te Matua,
te Kai-hanga
o nga mea katoa;
ki te Atua, te Tama,
taku Kai-hoko, a Ihu Karaiti;
ki te Atua, te Wairua Tapu,
te Kai-homai i te ora me te tika.
Ko tenei taku whakapono.

How then will you care for this child?

The parent(s) and godparents reply together

I will love this child and share my faith with *her/him*.

The bishop or priest says to the congregation

As the community of faith we rejoice at this baptism and will share with *N* what we ourselves have received: a delight in prayer, a love for the word of God, a desire to follow the way of Christ, and food for the journey.

The bishop or priest then says to the child

N, you are now a pilgrim with us.
As a member of Christ's body, the Church,
you will be challenged to affirm your faith in God
and receive the laying on of hands in confirmation.
May you grow in the Holy Spirit,
fulfil your ministry
and follow Christ your whole life long.

The bishop or priest then blesses the family

God bless you with wisdom and love;
may this child find in you, your homes and families,
Christ's love and understanding.
Amen.

The bishop or priest, with the people, prays

God of love,
**we thank you for our calling
to be disciples of Christ.
Help us to nurture *this child*
in the faith we share.
May *s/he* grow to love, worship and serve you,
and bring life to the world.   Amen.**

The parent(s) and godparents return to their places with their children.

If there is not to be a laying on of hands, the service shall continue at
The Celebration of Faith, on page 394.

Commitment to Christian Service

The people being seated, all the candidates for the laying on of hands stand
before the bishop, who says

Either

Those who are baptised are called to worship and serve God. From
the beginning, believers have continued in the apostles' teaching
and fellowship, in the breaking of bread, and in the prayers.

	Will you commit yourself to this life?
Candidate	I will, with God's help.
Bishop	Will you forgive others as you are forgiven?
Candidate	I will, with God's help.
Bishop	Will you seek to love your neighbour as yourself, and strive for peace and justice?
Candidate	I will, with God's help.
Bishop	Will you accept the cost of following Jesus Christ in your daily life and work?
Candidate	I will, with God's help.
Bishop	With the whole Church will you proclaim by word and action the Good News of God in Christ?
Candidate	I will, with God's help.

Or

Those who are baptised are called to worship and serve God. From the beginning, believers have continued in the apostles' teaching and fellowship, in the breaking of bread, and in the prayers.

> Will you commit yourself to this life?

Candidate   I will, with God's help.
Through God's grace I will forgive others
as I am forgiven;
I will seek to love my neighbour as myself,
and strive for peace and justice;
I will accept the cost of following Jesus Christ
in my daily life and work;
with the whole Church
I will proclaim by word and action
the Good News of God in Christ.

The Laying on of Hands

The candidates being conveniently placed, the bishop continues

Let us pray for *these* who *have* declared *their* commitment to Christ's service.

Silence

The bishop and people say responsively

Our help is in the name of the eternal God,
> Ko te Ingoa o te Atua ora tonu, to tatou oranga,

who is making the heavens and the earth.
> **Te Kai-hanga i te rangi, i te whenua.**

Come Holy Spirit
> Haere mai, e te Wairua Tapu

bearing your gifts of grace.
> **uhia mai tou aroha noa.**

God of mercy and love,
new birth by water and the Spirit is your gift,
a gift none can take away;
grant that your servants may grow
into the fulness of the stature of Christ.
Fill them with the joy of your presence.
Increase in them the fruit of your Spirit:
the spirit of wisdom and understanding,
the spirit of love, patience and gentleness,
the spirit of wonder and true holiness.

> E te Atua o te aroha noa,
> nau i whakarite te wai hei tohu whanau hou,
> e kore nei e taea te wewete.
> Tukua kia tipu au pononga ki te tino kaumatuatanga
> e tutuki ai i to te Karaiti,
> kia hari tonu ai ki roto i a koe.
> Kia hira ake ai ki roto i a ratou
> nga hua o te Wairua:
> ara te wairua matau, marama hoki,
> te wairua aroha, humarie, ngawari,
> he wairua hari me te tapu pono.

The bishop lays hand(s) on each candidate in silence and then prays.

FOR CONFIRMATION

Creator Spirit,
strengthen *N*
with your gifts of grace,
to love and serve
as a disciple of Christ.

Guide, protect,
uphold *her/him*
that *s/he* may continue
yours for ever.
Amen.

E te Wairua Kai-hanga,
whakakahangia a *Ingoa*
ki nga manaakitanga
o tau aroha noa,
kia pumau ai te mahi, te aroha,
i nga ara a te Karaiti.

Arahina, tautokona,
tiakina ia
kia u tonu ai ki a koe,
ake tonu atu.
Kororia ki te Atua.

FOR RENEWAL

Creator Spirit,
rekindle in *N* your gifts of grace,
renew *her/his* life in Christ
and bring to completion
all that your calling has begun.
Amen.

*At the conclusion of the laying on of hands for all the candidates,
the bishop prays*

Living God,
empower your disciples
to bring life to the world.

Te Atua ora tonu,
tukua mai tou mana
ki au pononga
hei mau i te ora ki te ao.

The people respond

Amen!
May we and they together
be found in Christ
and Christ in us.

Amine!
Ko tatou katoa ka kitea
i roto i te Karaiti
me ia hoki i roto i a tatou.

The Celebration of Faith

All standing, the bishop or priest says to the congregation

Let us rejoice with those who have committed themselves to Christ and celebrate the faith of our baptism.

Bishop
or
Priest   Do you believe in God the Father?

All   **I believe in God the Father almighty,**
     creator of heaven and earth.

Priest   Do you believe in Jesus Christ, the Son of God?

All   **I believe in Jesus Christ, God's only Son, our Lord,**
     who was conceived by the Holy Spirit,
     born of the Virgin Mary,
     suffered under Pontius Pilate,
     was crucified, died, and was buried;
     he descended to the dead.
     On the third day he rose again;
     he ascended into heaven,
     is seated at the right hand of the Father,
     and will come again to judge the living and the dead.

Priest   Do you believe in God the Holy Spirit?

All   **I believe in the Holy Spirit,**
     the holy catholic Church,
     the communion of saints,
     the forgiveness of sins,
     the resurrection of the body,
     and the life everlasting.   Amen.

*The service may continue at **The Peace** in a Eucharistic Liturgy.*
*During **The Peace** the newly confirmed may be greeted by the congregation.*

Or

*The service may continue with **The Sermon** or **The Prayers of the People**, but*
***The Creed** is not said again.*

Or

*The service may continue with **The Lord's Prayer** in one of the following forms*

As Christ teaches us we pray

Our Father in heaven,
  hallowed be your name,
  your kingdom come,
  your will be done,
    on earth as in heaven.
Give us today our daily bread.
Forgive us our sins
  as we forgive those who sin against us.
Save us from the time of trial
  and deliver us from evil.

For the kingdom, the power, and the glory are yours
  now and for ever.   Amen.

Kua akona nei tatou e to tatou Ariki,
ka inoi tatou

E to matou Matua i te rangi
  Kia tapu tou Ingoa.
  Kia tae mai tou rangatiratanga.
  Kia meatia tau e pai ai
    ki runga ki te whenua,
      kia rite ano ki to te rangi.
Homai ki a matou aianei
  he taro ma matou mo tenei ra.
Murua o matou hara,
  Me matou hoki e muru nei
    i o te hunga e hara ana ki a matou.
Aua hoki matou e kawea kia whakawaia;
  Engari whakaorangia matou i te kino:
Nou hoki te rangatiratanga, te kaha, me te kororia,
  Ake ake ake.   Amine.

Other prayers may follow, concluding with a blessing.

Additional Directions

Arrangement of services

A The Liturgy of Baptism and The Laying on of Hands

These sections are used following the New Testament lesson or Gospel or Sermon

God's Call
The Baptism
The Presentation for the Laying on of Hands (all candidates)
The Affirmation
Commitment to Christian Service
The Laying on of Hands
The Celebration of Faith
The Continuation of the Liturgy of the Eucharist, or Prayers

B The Liturgy of Baptism only

These sections are used following the New Testament lesson or Gospel or Sermon

God's Call
The Presentation for Baptism
The Baptism
The Affirmation (including, in the case of infants, the final section for parent(s) and godparents)
The Celebration of Faith
The Continuation of the Liturgy of the Eucharist, or other service of worship

C The Laying on of Hands for Confirmation (and Renewal) without Baptism

These sections are used following the New Testament lesson or Gospel or Sermon

God's Call
The Presentation for the Laying on of Hands
The Affirmation (omitting final section for parent(s) and
    godparents of children)
Commitment to Christian Service
The Laying on of Hands
The Celebration of Faith
The Continuation of the Liturgy of the Eucharist, or Prayers

Baptisms normally take place in the context of the Eucharist or Morning or Evening Worship. On other occasions, the priest shall choose a suitable introduction for worship, which shall include a New Testament lesson, and the service shall conclude with prayers, including the Lord's Prayer and a blessing.

Sentence, Prayer and Readings for the Baptismal Liturgy

SENTENCE

I will give you a new heart and put a new spirit within you; I will remove from you your heart of stone and give you a heart of flesh.

Ezekiel 36:26

Or

St Paul said: I implore you by God's mercy to offer your very selves as a living sacrifice dedicated and fit for God's acceptance, the worship offered by heart and mind.

Romans 12:1

God of grace, by the power of the Holy Spirit you have given us
new life in the waters of baptism; strengthen us to live in
righteousness and true holiness, that we may grow into the
likeness of your Son, Jesus Christ.
Amen.

Or any of the Collects for Pentecost 10 may be said.

READINGS

Old Testament

Baptism

Exodus 14:21-29	God saves by water
Isaiah 44:1-5	Water on the thirsty land
Ezekiel 36:22-28	A new heart and a new spirit

Baptism of adults, and/or confirmation, and/or renewal

Exodus 3:1-12	The call to Moses
Joshua 24:14-24	Choosing to serve God
Jeremiah 1:4-8	The prophet's call
Jeremiah 31:31-34	The new covenant

New Testament or Epistle

For all occasions

Acts 2:14-47	The first Christians

Some verses may be omitted

Romans 6:3-11	New life in Christ
Romans 8:11-17	The spirit of adoption
Romans 12:1-13	Renewed service
1 Corinthians 12:3-13	Baptised by one spirit into one body
Galatians 3:23-29	Baptised into union with Christ
Ephesians 4:1-6	Baptism and unity
Ephesians 6:10-20	The armour of Christ
1 Peter 2:4-10	A chosen people
1 Peter 3:13-22	Baptism and Christian living

Gospel

Baptism

Mark 1:1-11	The baptism of Jesus
Mark 10:13-16	Jesus blesses the children
John 3:1-8	Born of water and spirit

Baptism of adults, and/or confirmation, and/or renewal

Mark 1:14-20	Christ's invitation: our response
Mark 10:35-45	The cost of discipleship
John 13:3-17	Christian service
John 14:15-21	The Spirit who lives in us

The priest or bishop may use **The Readings** *appointed for the day in place of some or all of the above.*

Records

Records of the Baptisms and Laying on of Hands in Confirmation shall be kept by the Church and a copy handed to the candidates.

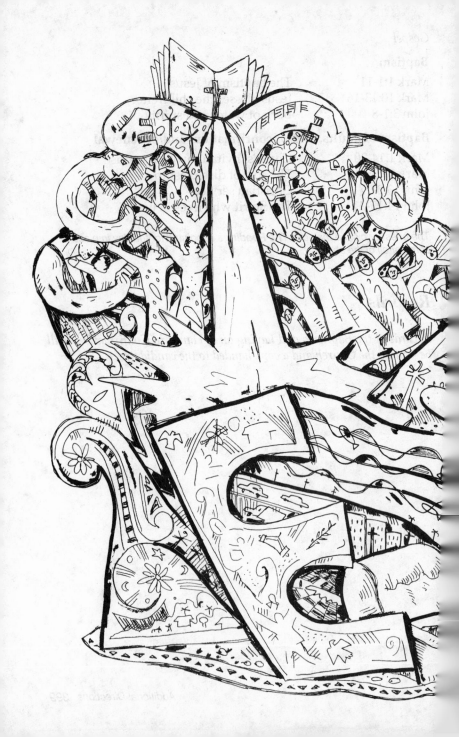

Liturgies of the Eucharist

Nga Hakari Tapu

Concerning these Services

Christ comes to us bringing good news of God's grace and generosity. Christ has inaugurated for us a sacred meal, and summoned us to have communion with him. We give thanks to the Father, remember Christ, call upon the Holy Spirit, unite ourselves with all the faithful, and share God's food and hospitality. Jesus said that the children were to come to him. Children, too, have an important part to play in the eucharistic community.

> 'In the celebration of the Eucharist Christ gathers, teaches and nourishes the Church. It is Christ who invites to the meal and who presides at it.'

The Eucharist is central to Christian spiritual life. For us, Christ is the shepherd who leads us, the prophet who announces God's word to us, and the priest who celebrates God's presence with us.

Sunday, the Lord's day, is the resurrection festival, the special day for the Eucharist. As we take part, as we break the bread and share the cup, our forgiveness is renewed and we are cleansed. As we worship, our hope and conviction that life is stronger than death and that love is the key to life is reinforced. This is food for the baptised; it is food we need week by week and year by year. It is a meal to which we need to come with open and honest hearts.

In the Eucharist we put our belief about God, about our life together and about ourselves into words and actions. We come to touch the hem of Christ's garment.

Christ is the bread of life.

You will find several forms of the Eucharist which are deliberately quite different from each other. This is to provide richness in our worship and to cater for the variety in the church community. There are two forms in Maori, one of which is in English as well as in Maori. It is important to understand that the Maori liturgy expresses the theology and understanding of Maori people. In the parallel service the Maori is not the precise equivalent of the English.

You will also find a section containing the people's part of the Thanksgiving of the People of God in some of the languages of the Diocese of Polynesia.

Eucharistic Liturgy
Thanksgiving of the People of God

The Ministry of Word and Prayer

The Gathering of the Community

The people may be greeted informally.

The theme may be introduced and subjects of special concern or thanksgiving suggested.

Then all standing, the presiding priest or minister continues, using any of the following greetings.

Grace and peace to you from God.
> Kia tau ki a koutou, te atawhai me te rangimarie o te Atua.

God fill you with truth and joy.
> **Ma te Atua koe e whakau, ki te pono me te hari.**

The Lord be with you.
> Kia noho a Ihowa ki a koutou.

The Lord bless you.
> **Ma Ihowa koe e manaaki.**

This is the day which the Lord has made.
> Ko te ra tenei i hanga e Ihowa.

Let us rejoice and be glad in it.
> **Kia hari, kia koa tatou.**

The Sentence of the Day may be read.

The following may be said.

Almighty God,
to whom all hearts are open,
all desires known,
and from whom no secrets are hidden;
cleanse the thoughts of our hearts
by the inspiration of your Holy Spirit,
so that we may truly love you
and worthily praise your holy name;
through our Saviour, Jesus Christ.
Amen.

*The following or **Kororia ki te Atua** (page 494) may be said or sung here,
or after **The Absolution**.*

Glory to God in the highest,
   and peace to God's people on earth.

Lord God, heavenly King,
almighty God and Father,
   we worship you, we give you thanks,
   we praise you for your glory.

Lord Jesus Christ, only Son of the Father,
Lord God, Lamb of God,
you take away the sin of the world:
   have mercy on us;
you are seated at the right hand of the Father:
   receive our prayer.

For you alone are the Holy One,
you alone are the Lord,
you alone are the Most High,
   Jesus Christ,
   with the Holy Spirit,
   in the glory of God the Father. Amen.

The congregation kneels.

The Summary of the Law, or *A New Commandment*,
or *The Ten Commandments* (page 521) may be said.

THE SUMMARY OF THE LAW

Hear the teaching of Christ:
you shall love the Lord your God
with all your heart
and with all your soul
and with all your mind
and with all your strength.
This is the first commandment.
And a second is this:
You shall love your neighbour as yourself.

Spirit of God, search our hearts.
    E te Wairua o te Atua,
        whakamaramatia o matou ngakau.

A NEW COMMANDMENT

Hear the teaching of Christ:
a new commandment I give to you,
that you love one another as I have loved you.

Spirit of God, search our hearts.
    E te Wairua o te Atua,
        whakamaramatia o matou ngakau.

The Kyries may also be used.

Lord, have mercy.
Christ, have mercy.
Lord, have mercy.

E te Ariki, kia aroha mai.
E te Karaiti, kia aroha mai.
E te Ariki, kia aroha mai.

Kyrie eleison.
Christe eleison.
Kyrie eleison.

Hear God's word to all who turn to Christ:

> God so loved the world that he gave his only Son,
> that whoever believes in him should not perish
> but have eternal life.
>
> *John 3:16*

> If we confess our sins,
> God is faithful and just, and will forgive our sins
> and cleanse us
> from every kind of wrong.

Jesus said:

> There is joy among the angels of God
> over one sinner who repents.

> Come to me all who labour and are heavy laden
> and I will give you rest.

The presiding priest or minister says

God has promised forgiveness
to all who truly repent,
turn to Christ in faith
and are themselves forgiving.

In silence we call to mind our sins.

Silence

Let us confess our sins.

**Merciful God,
we have sinned
in what we have thought and said,
in the wrong we have done
and in the good we have not done.
We have sinned in ignorance:
we have sinned in weakness:
we have sinned through our own deliberate fault.
We are truly sorry.
We repent and turn to you.
Forgive us, for our Saviour Christ's sake,
and renew our lives to the glory of your name. Amen.**

The Absolution *is declared by the presiding priest.*

Through the cross of Christ,
God have mercy on you,
pardon you
and set you free.
Know that you are forgiven
and be at peace.
God strengthen you in all goodness
and keep you in life eternal.
Amen.

       I runga i te mana o Ihu Karaiti,
       ka murua e te Atua o koutou hara,
       ka wetekina nga mekameka e here nei i a koutou,
       ka unuhia nga mauiuitanga e pehi nei i a koutou.
       E mea ana te Karaiti,
       Haere mai, haere, i runga i te rangimarie.
       Amine.

Glory to God in the highest *may be said or sung here, all standing.*

The following may be said.

The peace of Christ rule in our hearts.
    Kia mau te rongo o te Karaiti ki o tatou ngakau.
The word of Christ dwell in us richly.
    Kia hira ake te noho o tana kupu ki a tatou.

The Sentence of the Day *may be read.*

A **Collect of the Day** *shall be said here, or before or after the* **Sermon.**

The congregation sits.

The Proclamation

The Readings

The appointed readings follow, the reader first saying

A reading from ... (chapter ... beginning at ...)

Silence may follow each reading.

The reader may say

Hear what the Spirit is saying to the Church.
   Whakarongo ki te kupu a te Wairua ki te Haahi.
Thanks be to God.
   Kia mau tonu tana kupu ki a tatou.

A psalm, hymn or anthem may follow each reading.

*Then, all standing, the reader of the **Gospel** says*

The Holy Gospel according to ... (chapter ... beginning at ...)
   Te Rongopai Tapu ki te ritenga a ...
      (te ... upoko, ka timata ...)
Praise and glory to God.
   Te whakamoemiti, te kororia ki te Atua.

After the Gospel, silence may be kept.

The reader says

This is the Gospel of Christ.
   Te Rongopai tenei a te Karaiti.
Praise to Christ, the Word.
   Whakamoemititia Ia, te Kupu Mana.

The Sermon

The Sermon *is preached here or after* **The Affirmation of Faith.**

The Affirmation of Faith

The Apostles' Creed (page 461), *A Liturgical Affirmation* (page 481), or *The Nicene Creed* as follows, or *Te Whakapono o Naihia* (page 494) may be said or sung, all standing.

We believe in one God,
   the Father, the Almighty,
   maker of heaven and earth,
   of all that is,
   seen and unseen.

We believe in one Lord, Jesus Christ,
   the only Son of God,
   eternally begotten of the Father,
   God from God, Light from Light,
   true God from true God,
   begotten, not made,
   of one being with the Father;
   through him all things were made.
For us and for our salvation
      he came down from heaven,
      was incarnate of the Holy Spirit and the Virgin Mary
      and became fully human.
   For our sake he was crucified under Pontius Pilate;
   he suffered death and was buried.
   On the third day he rose again
   in accordance with the Scriptures;
   he ascended into heaven
      and is seated at the right hand of the Father.
   He will come again in glory to judge
         the living and the dead,
      and his kingdom will have no end.

We believe in the Holy Spirit,
   the Lord, the giver of life,
who proceeds from the Father and the Son,
who in unity with the Father and the Son
   is worshipped and glorified,
   and has spoken through the prophets.

We believe in one holy catholic and apostolic Church.
We acknowledge one baptism for the forgiveness of sins.
We look for the resurrection of the dead,
    and the life of the world to come.   Amen.

The presiding priest or minister says

Let us pray for the Church and for the world, giving thanks for
God's goodness.

The Prayers of the People

Prayer is offered with thanksgiving and intercession for

> *the universal Church and the local Church*
> *the world and our nation*
> *the local community and the community of heaven*
> *those in need, and our ministries.*

*Forms of intercession and thanksgiving are provided below, or intercessions
and thanksgivings may be offered by a minister or members of the congregation
in their own words.*

*After each particular intercession or thanksgiving any one of the following may
be used.*

After thanksgiving

For your love and goodness
we give you thanks,
O God.

Let us bless the Lord.
Thanks be to God.

Give thanks to our God
who is gracious
whose mercy endures
for ever.

Mo nga whakawhetai

Mo tou aroha me au hanga pai
Kia whakapaingia koe,
e te Atua.

Kia whakanuia te Ariki.
Kia whakapaingia te Atua.

Kia whakapaingia to tatou
Atua atawhai
Pumau tonu nei ana mahi
tohu.

	Mo nga inoi
God of love **grant our prayer.**	E te Atua arona **Whakarongo mai ki ta matou inoi.**
God of grace **you hear our prayer.**	E te Atua atawhai **Whakarongo mai ki ta matou inoi.**
Lord, in your mercy **hear our prayer.**	I roto i au mahi tohu **Whakarongo mai ki ta matou inoi.**
Lord, hear our prayer **and let our cry come to you.**	E te Ariki, whakarongo mai ki ta matou inoi **Kia tae atu a matou tangi ki a koe.**

Periods of silence may be kept.

The Prayers of the People *may conclude with an appropriate collect such as appears on pages 417, 464 and 483.*

Intercession and Thanksgiving

Alternative forms of thanksgiving and intercession are found on pages 462-466 and 482-484, or one of the forms below is used.

FIRST FORM

*or **Etahi atu Inoi** (page 496).*

Periods of silence may be kept.

Heavenly Father,
you have promised to hear when we pray
in the name of your Son.
Therefore in confidence and trust
we pray for the Church:
(Particular intercessions/thanksgivings may be offered.)

Father, enliven the Church for its mission
that we may be salt of the earth and light to the world.

Breathe fresh life into your people.
Give us power to reveal Christ in word and action.

We pray for the world:
(Particular intercessions/thanksgivings may be offered.)

Creator of all,
lead us and every people into ways of justice and peace.
That we may respect one another in freedom and truth.

Awaken in us a sense of wonder for the earth and all that is in it.
Teach us to care creatively for its resources.

We pray for the community:
(Particular intercessions/thanksgivings may be offered.)

God of truth, inspire with your wisdom
those whose decisions affect the lives of others
that all may act with integrity and courage.

Give grace to all whose lives are linked with ours.
May we serve Christ in one another, and love as he loves us.

We pray for those in need:

(Particular intercessions/thanksgivings may be offered.)

God of hope, comfort and restore
all who suffer in body, mind or spirit.
May they know the power of your healing love.

Make us willing agents of your compassion.
Strengthen us as we share in making people whole.

We remember those who have died and those who mourn:

(Particular intercessions/thanksgivings may be offered.)

We remember with thanksgiving those who have died in the faith
of Christ, and those whose faith is known to you alone.
Father, into your hands we commend them.

Give comfort to those who mourn.
Bring them peace in their time of loss.

We praise you for (*N* and) all your saints
who have entered your eternal glory.
May their example inspire and encourage us.

We pray for ourselves and our ministries:

*(Particular intercessions/thanksgivings may be offered and the prayers
conclude with one of the following.)*

Lord, you have called us to serve you.
Grant that we may walk in your presence:
your love in our hearts,
your truth in our minds,
your strength in our wills;
until, at the end of our journey,
we know the joy of our homecoming
and the welcome of your embrace,
through Jesus Christ our Lord. Amen.

E te Ariki, nau nei matou i karanga ki au mahi,
Meatia kia hikoi matou i mua i tou aroaro,
whakaungia mai tou aroha ki o matou ngakau,
tou pono ki o matou hinengaro,
tou marohirohi ki o matou whakaaro,
mo te taenga ki te tino tauranga,
ka mohio pu ki te hari, kua tau ki te haukainga,
ki te taanga manawa i roto i a koe,
i roto hoki i to matou Ariki, i a Ihu Karaiti. Amine.

Or

Your word is a lamp for our feet.
In darkness and in light,
in trouble and in joy,
help us, heavenly Father,
to trust your love,
to serve your purpose,
and to praise your name,
through Jesus Christ our Lord. Amen.

He rama tau kupu ki oku wae.
I nga wa o te pouri, o te marama,
o te raru, o te hari,
awhinatia mai matou, e te Matua i te rangi,
kia manako ki tou aroha,
kia mahi i au mahi,
kia whakapai i tou ingoa,
i roto i a Ihu Karaiti, te Ariki. Amine.

SECOND FORM

Periods of silence may be kept.

Each section of this form may include particular intercessions and thanksgivings concluding with a versicle and response or it may be used as a continuous prayer.

God of heaven and earth, through Jesus Christ you promise to hear us when we pray to you in faith with thanksgiving.

We pray for one another, for our families and friends, through whom we learn to love and to be loved. Thank you for all who care for us. Give us grace to serve Christ by serving our neighbours and our community, loving others as he loves us.

Silence

We thank you for the unfailing love you hold out to everyone in Jesus Christ. Comfort and heal those in sorrow, need, sickness or any other trouble. Give them courage and hope in their distress, and bless those who minister to them.

Silence

We remember with gratitude your many gifts to us in creation and the rich heritage of these islands. Help us and people everywhere to share with justice and peace the resources of the earth. Give wisdom to those in authority among us and to all leaders of the nations.

Silence

We pray for your Church throughout the world, thanking you for all who serve Christ and his kingdom. By your Spirit strengthen your people for their work and witness in the world. Unite us in your truth and love, that we who confess your name may also reflect your glory.

Silence

We remember with thanksgiving all who have died in Christ, and we rejoice at the faithful witness of your saints in every age, praying that we may enter with them into the unending joy of your heavenly kingdom.

Silence

Merciful God, you look with compassion on all who turn to you. Hear the prayers of your people.
Grant that what we have asked in faith
we may by your grace receive;
through Jesus Christ our Lord. Amen.

The Prayers of the People *may conclude with one of the following or another appropriate collect.*

1 God of mercy,
  you have given us grace to pray with one heart and one voice;
  and have promised to hear the prayers
  of two or three who agree in your name;
  fulfil now, we pray,
  the prayers and longings of your people
  as may be best for us and for your kingdom.
  Grant us in this world to know your truth,
  and in the world to come to see your glory.
  Amen.

2 Those things, good Lord,
  that your servants have prayed for,
  give us grace to work for;
  and in the purpose of your love
  answer our prayers and fulfil our hopes
  for Jesus' sake.
  Amen.

3 Now to God who is able to do immeasurably more
  than all we can ask or conceive,
  by the power which is at work among us,
  be glory in the Church and in Christ Jesus
  throughout all ages.
  Amen.

The Lord's Prayer *(which is to be used at least once in the service) may be said here, introduced by these or similar words.*

As Christ teaches us we pray

Our Father in heaven,
    hallowed be your name,
    your kingdom come,
    your will be done,
        on earth as in heaven.
Give us today our daily bread.
Forgive us our sins
    as we forgive those who sin against us.
Save us from the time of trial
    and deliver us from evil.

For the kingdom, the power, and the glory are yours
    now and for ever.   Amen.

Kua akona nei tatou e to tatou Ariki,
ka inoi tatou

E to matou Matua i te rangi
    Kia tapu tou Ingoa.
    Kia tae mai tou rangatiratanga.
    Kia meatia tau e pai ai
        ki runga ki te whenua,
            kia rite ano ki to te rangi.
Homai ki a matou aianei
    he taro ma matou mo tenei ra.
Murua o matou hara,
    Me matou hoki e muru nei
        i o te hunga e hara ana ki a matou.
Aua hoki matou e kawea kia whakawaia;
    Engari whakaorangia matou i te kino:
Nou hoki te rangatiratanga, te kaha,
    me te kororia,
        Ake ake ake.   Amine.

The Ministry of the Sacrament

The Peace

All standing, the presiding priest says to the people

The peace of Christ be always with you.
> Kia tau tonu te rangimarie o te Ariki ki a koutou.

And also with you.
> A ki a koe ano hoki.

The people and presiding priest may exchange a sign of peace according to local custom.

The priest then continues

E te whanau, we are the body of Christ.
> Brothers and sisters, ko tatou te tinana o te Karaiti.

By one Spirit we were baptised into one body.
> **Na te Wairua kotahi tatou i iriiri hei tinana kotahi.**

Keep the unity of the Spirit in the bond of peace.
> Kia mau te kotahitanga o te Wairua
> he mea paihere na te rangimarie.

Amen. We are bound by the love of Christ.
> **Amine. Kua paiheretia tatou ki te aroha o te Karaiti.**

The Preparation of the Gifts

A hymn or anthem may be sung.

The holy table is prepared. The presiding priest takes sufficient bread and wine which may be brought forward by representatives of the congregation.

The offerings of the people are presented.

The presiding priest may say

To you, Lord, belongs the greatness,
and the power, and the glory,
and the victory and the majesty.
All that is in the heavens and the earth is yours,
and of your own we give you.

Nou, e te Ariki, te nui,
te mana, te kororia,
te wikitoria, me te honore.
Nau te katoa i te rangi i te whenua,
nau ano hoki enei ka tapaea atu nei e matou.

Or the priest may offer praise for God's gifts in the following or other
appropriate words.

Blessed are you, God of all creation;
through your goodness we have these gifts to share.
Accept and use our offerings for your glory
and for the service of your kingdom.
Blessed be God for ever.

Ka whakapai ki a koe, e te Atua, te Kai-hanga;
na tou pai enei taonga mo te katoa.
Tapaea atu enei ohaoha hei whakakororia i a koe
a, hei whakanui hoki i tou rangatiratanga.
Ki te Atua te whakamoemiti mo ake tonu atu.

*An alternative **Great Thanksgiving** is provided on page 436.*

*Variations and additions to **The Great Thanksgiving** may be found*
on pages 430-435.

The Great Thanksgiving

It is recommended that the people stand or kneel throughout the following
prayer.

The presiding priest says or sings

The Lord is here.
Kei konei te Ariki.

God's Spirit is with us.
> **Kei a matou te Wairua o te Atua.**

Lift up your hearts.
> Kia ara o koutou ngakau.

We lift them to the Lord.
> **Ka ara nei ki te Ariki.**

Let us give thanks to the Lord our God.
> Kia whakapai tatou ki to tatou Ariki ki te Atua.

It is right to offer thanks and praise.
> **He mea tika ki te whakapai ki a ia.**

It is right indeed, it is our joy and our salvation, holy Lord,
almighty Father, everlasting God, at all times and in all places
to give you thanks and praise through Christ your only Son.

You are the source of all life and goodness;
through your eternal Word
you have created all things from the beginning
and formed us in your own image;
male and female you created us.

Variations to the following section are found on pages 430-433.

> When we sinned and turned away
> you called us back to yourself
> and gave your Son to share our human nature.
> By his death on the cross,
> he made the one perfect sacrifice for the sin of the world
> and freed us from the bondage of sin.
> You raised him to life triumphant over death;
> you exalted him in glory.
> In him you have made us a holy people
> by sending upon us your holy and lifegiving Spirit.

Additions from pages 434-435 may follow here.

Therefore with the faithful who rest in him,
with angels and archangels and all the company of heaven,
we proclaim your great and glorious name,
for ever praising you and saying:

**Holy, holy, holy Lord, God of power and might,
heaven and earth are full of your glory.
Hosanna in the highest.**

> **Tapu, tapu, he tapu te Ariki
> Te Atua o te mana me te kaha,
> ki tonu te rangi me te whenua i tou kororia.
> Ohana i runga rawa.**

And these words may be added

> **Blessed is he who comes in the name of the Lord.
> Hosanna in the highest.**

> **Whakapaingia a ia e haere mai nei i runga i
> te Ingoa o te Ariki.
> Ohana i runga rawa.**

All glory and thanksgiving to you, holy Father;
on the night before he died
your Son, Jesus Christ, took bread;
when he had given you thanks,
he broke it, gave it to his disciples, and said:
Take, eat, this is my body
which is given for you;
do this to remember me.

After supper he took the cup;
when he had given you thanks,
he gave it to them and said:
Drink this, all of you,
for this is my blood of the new covenant
which is shed for you and for many
for the forgiveness of sins;
do this as often as you drink it,
to remember me.

Glory to you, Lord Christ;
your death we show forth;
your resurrection we proclaim;
your coming we await;
Amen! Come Lord Jesus.

> Kororia ki a koe, e te Ariki, e te Karaiti:
> ko tou matenga ka whakaatu matou:
> ko tou aranga ka panui matou:
> ko tou haerenga mai ka taria e matou:
> Amine: haere mai e Ihu te Ariki.

Therefore loving God,
recalling your great goodness to us in Christ,
his suffering and death,
his resurrection and ascension,
and looking for his coming in glory,
we celebrate our redemption with this bread of life
and this cup of salvation.
Accept our sacrifice of praise and thanksgiving
which we offer through Christ our great high priest.

Send your Holy Spirit
that these gifts of bread and wine which we receive
may be to us the body and blood of Christ,
and that we, filled with the Spirit's grace and power,
may be renewed for the service of your kingdom.

United in Christ with all who stand before you
in earth and heaven,
we worship you, O God,
in songs of everlasting praise.

**Blessing, honour and glory be yours,
here and everywhere,
now and for ever. Amen.**

> Te whakapai, te honore, te kororia ki a koe,
> i konei, i nga wahi katoa,
> inaianei, a, ake tonu atu. Amine.

Silence may be kept.

The Communion

*The Lord's Prayer (which is to be used at least once in the service)
may be said here, introduced by these or similar words.*

As Christ teaches us we pray

Our Father in heaven,
    hallowed be your name,
    your kingdom come,
    your will be done,
        on earth as in heaven.
Give us today our daily bread.
Forgive us our sins
    as we forgive those who sin against us.
Save us from the time of trial
    and deliver us from evil.

For the kingdom, the power, and the glory are yours
    now and for ever.   **Amen.**

Kua akona nei tatou e to tatou Ariki,
ka inoi tatou

E to matou Matua i te rangi
    Kia tapu tou Ingoa.
    Kia tae mai tou rangatiratanga.
    Kia meatia tau e pai ai
        ki runga ki te whenua,
            kia rite ano ki to te rangi.
Homai ki a matou aianei
    he taro ma matou mo tenei ra.
Murua o matou hara,
    Me matou hoki e muru nei
        i o te hunga e hara ana ki a matou.
Aua hoki matou e kawea kia whakawaia;
    Engari whakaorangia matou i te kino:
Nou hoki te rangatiratanga, te kaha,
    me te kororia,
        Ake ake ake.   **Amine.**

The priest breaks the bread.

Silence may be kept.

We break this bread
to share in the body of Christ.

**We who are many are one body,
for we all share the one bread.**

Ka whatiia e tatou tenei taro,
hei whainga wahi i roto i te tinana o te Karaiti.

**Ko tatou tokomaha nei he tinana kotahi,
e kai ana hoki tatou katoa i te taro kotahi.**

Any of these **Additional Prayers at Communion** *may be used before
or during Communion, or as private devotions.*

Most merciful Lord,
your love compels us to come in.
Our hands were unclean,
our hearts were unprepared;
we were not fit
even to eat the crumbs from under your table.
But you, Lord, are the God of our salvation,
and share your bread with sinners.
So cleanse and feed us
with the precious body and blood of your Son,
that he may live in us and we in him;
and that we, with the whole company of Christ,
may sit and eat in your kingdom.
Amen.

Or

We do not presume
to come to your holy table,
merciful Lord,
trusting in our own righteousness,
but in your great mercy.

We are not worthy
even to gather the crumbs from under your table.
But you are the same Lord
whose nature is always to have mercy.
Grant us therefore, gracious Lord,
so to eat the body of your dear Son, Jesus Christ,
and to drink his blood,
that we may evermore dwell in him
and he in us.
Amen.

E te Ariki tohu, ehara i te mea he whakapakari ki a
matou mahi tika i haere mai ai matou ki tau tepu tapu,
engari he whakaaro ki te nui o au mahi tohu.

Kahore matou e tau hei kohikohi i nga kongakonga i
raro i tau tepu. Otira ko taua Ariki nei ano koe, he
mahi tuturu hoki nau te atawhai.

E te Ariki atawhai, meinga kia tika ta matou kai i te
tinana o tau Tama aroha, o Ihu Karaiti, kia tika ta
matou inu i ona toto, kia noho tonu ai matou ki a ia,
me ia hoki ki roto ki a matou.

Amine.

Lamb of God, you take away the sin of the world,
    have mercy on us.
Lamb of God, you take away the sin of the world,
    have mercy on us.
Lamb of God, you take away the sin of the world,
    grant us your peace.

E te Reme a te Atua, e waha atu nei i te hara o te ao,
    tohungia matou.
E te Reme a te Atua, e waha atu nei i te hara o te ao,
    tohungia matou
E te Reme a te Atua, e waha atu nei i te hara o te ao,
    tukua mai tou rangimarie ki a matou.

Or

Jesus, Lamb of God, have mercy on us.
Jesus, bearer of our sins, have mercy on us.
Jesus, redeemer of the world, give us your peace.

E Ihu, te Reme a te Atua: tohungia matou.
E Ihu, te Kai-waha o o matou hara: tohungia matou.
E Ihu, te Kai-hoko i te ao: tukua mai tou rangimarie.

The Invitation

The priest invites the people saying

Draw near and receive the body and blood of our Saviour
Jesus Christ in remembrance that he died for us.
Let us feed on him in our hearts by faith with thanksgiving.

Whakatata mai tangohia te tinana
me nga toto o to tatou Ariki,
o Ihu Karaiti, hei whakamahara i mate ia mo tatou.
Kia kainga whakaponotia ia i roto i o tatou ngakau me te
whakawhetai.

The presiding priest and people receive communion.

*The minister says the following words (or any of those provided in the other
Eucharistic Liturgies) to each person.*

The body of our Lord Jesus Christ which was given for you.
Ko te tinana o to tatou Ariki, i tukua nei mou.

The blood of our Lord Jesus Christ which was shed for you.
Ko nga toto o to tatou Ariki, i whakahekea nei mou.

The communicant may respond each time

Amen. *or* **Amine.**

If there is insufficient bread and/or wine for the number of communicants, the presiding priest is to return to the holy table and say

> Almighty God,
> obeying the command of your Son, Jesus Christ,
> who took *bread /the cup* and said:
> This is my *body/blood*,
> we also take this *bread/wine*,
> and pray that through your Word and Spirit
> it may be for us the sacrament
> of *the body/the blood* of Christ.
> **Amen.**

Prayer After Communion

The Sentence of the Day *(page 550) or some other appropriate sentence of Scripture may be said.*

Silence may be kept.

The Lord's Prayer *(if it has not been used before) shall be said.*

A seasonal prayer of thanksgiving (pages 525-545) may be used, with or without one of the following, which may be said by the presiding priest, or by the presiding priest and people together.

Father of all,
we give you thanks and praise,
that when we were still far off
you met us in your Son and brought us home.
Dying and living,
he declared your love,
gave us grace
and opened the gate of glory.
May we who share Christ's body
live his risen life;
we who drink his cup
bring life to others;
we whom the Spirit lights
give light to the world.

Keep us firm in the hope you have set before us,
so we and all your children shall be free,
and the whole earth live to praise your name.

Or

Almighty God, giver of all good things,
we thank you for feeding us with the spiritual food
of the precious body and blood of our Saviour, Jesus Christ.
We thank you for your love and care
in assuring us of your gift of eternal life
and uniting us with the blessed company
of all faithful people.

**Therefore, everliving God,
keep us steadfast in your holy fellowship.
And now we offer ourselves, all that we have and are,
to serve you faithfully in the world,
through Jesus Christ our Redeemer,
to whom with you and the Holy Spirit
be all honour and glory, now and for ever. Amen.**

The Dismissal of the Community

*The presiding priest, or the bishop when present, may give the blessing
to the congregation.*

The congregation is sent out with these words.

Go now to love and serve the Lord. Go in peace.
> Haere i runga i te rangimarie i runga i te aroha me te
> ngakau hihiko ki te mahi ki te Ariki.

Amen. We go in the name of Christ.
> **Amine. Ka haere matou i runga i te ingoa o te Karaiti.**

Variations to the Great Thanksgiving for the Seasons of

Advent   Christmas   Epiphany

Lent   Passiontide   Transfiguration

*These variations are made in the indented section of **The Great Thanksgiving** on page 421.*

Any of the passages in brackets may be omitted.

… male and female you created us.

> When we sinned and turned away
> you called us back to yourself
> and gave your Son to share our human nature.

> *The appropriate variation from the page opposite is said.*

> (By his death on the cross,
> he made the one perfect sacrifice for the sin of the world
> and freed us from the bondage of sin.)

> (You raised him to life triumphant over death;
> you exalted him in glory.)

> In him you have made us a holy people
> by sending upon us your holy and lifegiving Spirit.

***The Great Thanksgiving** continues on page 422.*

Therefore with the faithful …

A ADVENT

In his coming among us
the day of our deliverance has dawned,
and through him you will make all things new
when he comes in power and majesty to judge the world.

B CHRISTMAS

In him the light which shines for all
has come into the world,
and he has become one with us
that we may become one with you.

C EPIPHANY

In him we see you, the eternal God,
revealing your glory in our flesh,
for he is the light of the nations
who illuminates our darkness.

D LENT

Who though tempted in every way as we are,
yet did not sin;
through him therefore we may triumph over sin
and grow in grace.

E PASSIONTIDE

Out of love for us he accepted death and,
lifted high upon the cross,
he drew the whole world to himself;
the tree of shame became the tree of glory.
Where life was lost, there life has been restored.

J TRANSFIGURATION

Before his passion you revealed the glory
of Christ to his disciples,
and your voice from heaven
declared him your beloved Son.

Variations for

Easter Ascension Pentecost Trinity Holy Eucharist

... male and female you created us.

> When we sinned and turned away
> you called us back to yourself
> and gave your Son to share our human nature.
> (By his death on the cross,
> he made the one perfect sacrifice for the sin of the world
> and freed us from the bondage of sin.)

The appropriate variation below is said.

The Great Thanksgiving continues on page 422.

Therefore with the faithful ...

F EASTER

> You raised him to life triumphant over death;
> you exalted him in glory.
> By his victory over death,
> the reign of sin is ended,
> a new age has dawned,
> a broken world is restored
> and we are made whole once more.
>
> In him you have made us a holy people
> by sending upon us your holy and lifegiving Spirit.

G ASCENSION

> You raised him to life triumphant over death;
> you exalted him in glory,
> and gave him the name which is above every name:
> at the name of Jesus every knee shall bow
> and every tongue confess that he is Lord.
>
> In him you have made us a holy people
> by sending upon us your holy and lifegiving Spirit.

H PENTECOST

(You raised him to life triumphant over death;
you exalted him in glory.)

In him you have made us a holy people
by sending upon us your holy and lifegiving Spirit,
who came with signs from heaven
to lead your Church into all truth.
In the power of the Spirit,
and made ready with his gifts,
we take the joy of the gospel into all the world.

I TRINITY

You raised him to life triumphant over death;
you exalted him in glory.

In him you have made us a holy people
by sending upon us your holy and lifegiving Spirit.

In the mystery of your Godhead
you have revealed to us
the fulness of your divine glory.
We praise you, Father, with the Son and the Spirit,
three persons,
equal in majesty,
undivided in splendour,
yet one Lord, one God,
ever to be worshipped and adored.

K HOLY EUCHARIST

On the night before he suffered
our Saviour gave us this holy feast,
in which we receive the benefits of his passion
and are filled with the power of his resurrection.

(You raised him to life triumphant over death;
you exalted him in glory.)

In him you have made us a holy people
by sending upon us your holy and lifegiving Spirit.

Additions to the Great Thanksgiving for

Saints Church Baptism Marriage The Departed

These additions are made at the end of the indented section of
The Great Thanksgiving *on page 421.*

Any of the passages in brackets may be omitted.

… male and female you created us.

> When we sinned and turned away
> you called us back to yourself
> and gave your Son to share our human nature.
>
> (By his death on the cross,
> he made the one perfect sacrifice for the sin of the world
> and freed us from the bondage of sin.)
>
> (You raised him to life triumphant over death;
> you exalted him in glory.)
>
> In him you have made us a holy people
> by sending upon us your holy and lifegiving Spirit.

The appropriate addition below is said.

The Great Thanksgiving *continues on page 422.*

Therefore with the faithful …

L FEAST OF THE BLESSED VIRGIN MARY	We give you thanks for the ready obedience of the blessed Virgin Mary, enabling her to answer your call to be the mother of your Son. With all generations we call her blessed, and with her we rejoice and proclaim the greatness of your holy name.
M FEASTS OF APOSTLES	We give you thanks because Jesus, the great shepherd of your flock, after his resurrection sent his apostles to make disciples of all the nations, and promised to be with them always, to the end of time.

N FEASTS OF SAINTS	We give you thanks for the example and encouragement of your saints (especially *N*), for their witness to the truth of your gospel, and for the hope of glory which we share with them in Jesus Christ.
O DEDICATION OF A CHURCH	We give you thanks for your blessing on this house of prayer, where through your grace we offer you the sacrifice of praise, and are built by your Spirit into a temple made without hands, even the body of your Son, Jesus Christ.
P HOLY BAPTISM	Through the waters of baptism, in which we die to sin and rise to new life, you have made us members of Christ, the children of God, and inheritors of the kingdom of heaven.
Q MARRIAGE	You blessed us and called us to share in your work of creation. You join men and women to each other and the two become one flesh to be a sign of your steadfast love. Before you stand *N* and *N*. Raise them in new life as you raised our Saviour.
R THE DEPARTED	We give you thanks that even in death we are safe in Christ's victory over death. Though under judgment we rest in our Saviour's hand; sorrowful, yet we rejoice; for he is the hope of everlasting life to all who put their trust in him.
S THE ANGLICAN CHURCH IN AOTEAROA, NEW ZEALAND AND POLYNESIA	We give you thanks that you have proclaimed your good news to the people of this land; and we give you praise for those whom you have led to be your witnesses here, that we may, with them, set forth your glory.

The following is an alternative to **The Great Thanksgiving** on page 420.

An Alternative Great Thanksgiving

Celebrating the Grace of God

Seasonal additions as provided on pages 440-441 may be inserted where indicated.

It is recommended that the people stand or kneel throughout the following prayer.

The presiding priest says or sings

The Lord is here.
God's Spirit is with us.

Lift up your hearts.
We lift them to the Lord.

Let us give thanks to the Lord our God.
It is right to offer thanks and praise.

Honour and worship are indeed your due,
our Lord and our God, through Jesus Christ,
for you created all things;
by your will they were created,
and for your glory they have their being.

Trinity

In your loving purpose you chose us
before the foundation of the world
to be your people;
you gave your promises to Abraham and Sarah
and bestowed your favour on the Virgin Mary.

Saints

Above all we give you thanks and praise
for your grace in sending Jesus Christ,
not for any merit of our own
but when we had turned away from you.

Christmas, Epiphany

We were bound in sin,
but in your compassion you redeemed us,
reconciling us to yourself with the precious blood of Christ.

Passiontide

In your Son you suffered with us and for us,
offering us the healing riches of salvation
and calling us to freedom and holiness.

Advent, Lent,
Easter, Ascension, Pentecost

Therefore with people of every nation, tribe and language,
with the whole Church on earth and in heaven,
joyfully we give you thanks and say:

Holy, holy, holy Lord, God of power and might,
heaven and earth are full of your glory.
Hosanna in the highest.

All glory and honour to you, God of grace,
for you gave your only Son Jesus Christ
once for all on the cross
to be the one perfect sacrifice for the sin of the world,
that all who believe in him might have eternal life.
The night before he died,
he took bread,
and when he had given you thanks,
he broke it, gave it to his disciples, and said:
Take, eat, this is my body
which is given for you;
do this to remember me.

After supper he took the cup,
and when he had given you thanks,
he gave it to them and said:
Drink this, all of you,
for this is my blood of the new covenant
which is shed for you and for many
for the forgiveness of sins;
do this as often as you drink it,
to remember me.

Therefore heavenly Father,
in this sacrament of the suffering and death of your Son,
we now celebrate the wonder of your grace
and proclaim the mystery of our faith.

Christ has died,
Christ is risen,
Christ will come in glory.

Redeemer God, rich in mercy, infinite in goodness,
we were far off until you brought us near
and our hands are empty until you fill them.
As we eat this bread and drink this wine,
through the power of your Holy Spirit
feed us with your heavenly food,
renew us in your service,
unite us in Christ,
and bring us to your everlasting kingdom.
O the depths and riches of your wisdom, O God;
how unsearchable are your judgments
and untraceable your ways.

From you, and through you, and for you are all things.
To you be the glory for ever. Amen.

Silence may be kept.

The Lord's Prayer *(if it has not been used before) may be said here.*

The priest breaks the bread.

Silence may be kept.

We break this bread
to share in the body of Christ.

We who are many are one body,
for we all share the one bread.

Additional Prayers at Communion *as provided on pages 425-427*
may follow here.

The Invitation

The priest invites the people saying

Draw near and receive the body and blood of our Saviour
Jesus Christ in remembrance that he died for us.
Let us feed on him in our hearts by faith with thanksgiving.

The presiding priest and people receive Communion.

Prayer After Communion

*The service continues with the **Prayer after Communion** on page 428.*

Additions to
the Alternative Great Thanksgiving

These additions are used as directed on page 421.

A ADVENT

In his coming among us,
the day of our deliverance has dawned,
and through him you will make all things new
when he comes in power and majesty to judge the world.

B CHRISTMAS

In him the light which shines for all
has come into the world,
and he has become one with us
that we may become one with you.

C EPIPHANY

In him we see you, the eternal God,
revealing your glory in our flesh,
for he is the light of the nations
who illuminates our darkness.

D LENT

Though tempted in every way as we are,
yet he did not sin;
through him therefore we may triumph over sin
and grow in grace.

E PASSIONTIDE

Lifted high upon the cross,
he drew the whole world to himself;
the tree of shame became the tree of glory.
Where life was lost, there life has been restored.

F EASTER

You raised him to life triumphant over death;
you exalted him in glory.
By his victory over death,
the reign of sin is ended,
a new age has dawned,
a broken world is restored
and we are made whole once more.

G ASCENSION

You raised him to life triumphant over death;
you exalted him in glory;
at the name of Jesus every knee shall bow
and every tongue confess that he is Lord.

H PENTECOST

In him you have made us a holy people
by sending upon us your holy and lifegiving Spirit,
who came with signs from heaven
to lead your Church into all truth.
In the power of the Spirit,
and made ready with his gifts,
we take the joy of the gospel into all the world.

I TRINITY

In the mystery of your Godhead
you have revealed to us
the fulness of your divine glory.
We praise you, Father, with the Son and the Spirit,
three persons,
equal in majesty,
undivided in splendour,
yet one Lord, one God,
ever to be worshipped and adored.

N SAINTS

We give you thanks for the example
and encouragement of your saints (especially *N*),
for their witness to the truth of your gospel,
and for the hope of glory which we share with them.

From the Eucharistic Liturgy
Thanksgiving of the People of God

*Sections translated into Fijian and Tongan
for use within the Anglican Church in Aotearoa,
New Zealand and Polynesia*

In Fijian

Greetings

Grace and peace
  to you from God.
**God fill you
  with truth and joy.**

The Lord be with you.
The Lord bless you.

This is the day which the
  Lord has made.
**Let us rejoice
  and be glad in it.**

The Kyries

Lord, have mercy.
Christ, have mercy.
Lord, have mercy.

Veikidavaki

Me sa nomuni na loloma kei na
vakacegu mai vua na Kalou.
**Me vakasinaiti kemuni na Kalou
ena dina kei na reki.**

Me tiko kei kemuni na Turaga.
**Me vakalougatataki kemuni na
  Turaga.**

Oqo na siga ka a bulia na Turaga.

Meda reki ka marau kina.

Na Kerei ni Loloma ni Turaga

Turaga, ni lomani keimami mai.
Karisito, ni lomani keimami mai.
Turaga, ni lomani keimami mai.

The Absolution

Through the cross
of Christ
God have mercy on you,
pardon you
and set you free.
Know that you
are forgiven
and be at peace.

God strengthen you
in all goodness
and keep you
in life eternal.
Amen.

At the Prayers of the People

During the prayers any of the following may be used.

AFTER THANKSGIVING

For your love
and goodness
**we give you thanks,
O God.**

Let us bless the Lord.
Thanks be to God.

Give thanks to our God
who is gracious
**whose mercy endures
for ever.**

Na Veivaka Bokoci ni Valavala ca

Ena vuku ni kauveilatai
i Karisito
me sa lomani kemuni Vosoti kemuni
ka sereki kemuni
na Kalou.
Moni vakacegu ni koni sa Vosoti.

Me vakaukauwataki kemuni,
na Kalou ena veika vinaka taucoko,
Ka maroroi kemuni ena bula tawa
yalani.
Emeni.

Na Veimasulaki

*Ena gauna ni veimasulaki E dua vei
rau oqo e rawa ni vakayagataki.*

OTI NA YAKAVINAVINAKA

Ena levu ni nomuni
loloma kei na vinaka
**Keimami sa vakavinavinaka kina
vei kemuni na Kalou.**

Meda vakacaucautaka na Turaga.
Me vakavinavinakataki na Kalou.

Me vakavinavinakataki na Kalou
dau lololoma.
**O koya sa tawa mudu na nona
loloma.**

AFTER INTERCESSION	**OTI NA VEIMASULAKI**
God of love **grant our prayer.**	Kalou dau loloma **Ni vakadonuya na neimami masu.**
God of grace **you hear our prayer.**	Kalou na dau veivakacegui **Ko ni dau rogoca na neimami masu.**
Lord, in your mercy **hear our prayer.**	Turaga ena nomuni yalololoma. **Ni rogoca na neimami masu.**
Lord, hear our prayer **and let our cry come to you.**	Turaga, ni rogoca na neimami masu. **Ni laiva na neimani tagi me yacovi keimuni yani.**

## The Peace	## Na Vakacegu
All standing, the presiding priest says to the people	*Me da tucake kece me qai kaya na Bete.*
The peace of Christ be always with you. **And also with you.**	Me tiko vata ga kei kemuni na veivakacegu i Karisito. **Vei kemuni talega.**
The people and presiding priest may exchange a sign of peace according to local custom.	*Me kidavaki ira nai vavakoso na bete ena kena ivakarau.*
Brothers and sisters, we are the body of Christ. **By one Spirit we were baptised into one body.**	Ra veitacini, ko i keda na yago i Karisito. **Eda a papitaisotaki e na dua ga na yalo ki na dua ga na yago.**
Keep the unity of the Spirit in the bond of peace.	Maroroya na duavata sa solia vei kemuni na Yalotabu ena vakacegu koni sa vauci vata tiko kina.
Amen. We are bound by the love of Christ.	**Emeni. Keimami sa vauci vata ena loloma i Karisito.**

At the Preparation of the Gifts

The presiding priest may say

To you, Lord, belongs the greatness, and the power, and the glory, and the victory and the majesty.

All that is in the heavens and the earth is yours, and of your own we give you.

At the Great Thanksgiving

The Lord is here.
God's Spirit is with us.

Lift up your hearts.
We lift them to the Lord.

Let us give thanks
to the Lord our God.
**It is right to offer
thanks and praise.**

Holy, holy, holy Lord,
God of power and might,
heaven and earth
are full of your glory.
Hosanna in the highest.

The following may be used.

**Blessed is he who comes
in the name of the Lord.
Hosanna in the highest.**

Na Vakarautaki ni Solisoli

Me qai kaya na Bete veiliutaki tiko

Sa nomuni na Turaga, na veika cecere, kei na kaukauwa kei na lagilagi, kei na qaqa kei na veika vakaiukuuku.

Sa nomuni na veika kece e tu mai lomalagi kei vuravura ka keimami sa mai vakacabora vei kemuni na veika ga ko ni taukena.

Na Cabori ni Vakavinavinaka

Sa tiko eke na Turaga
Sa tiko vata kei keda na yalo ni Kalou.

Ni vagolea cake na yalomuni.
**Keimami sa vagolea cake vua
na Turaga.**

Meda sa vakavinavinaka vua
na Turaga na noda Kalou.
**Sa dodonu me cabo vua na
vakavinavinaka kei na vei
vakacaucautaki.**

**Donu, donu, donu Turaga,
na Kalou ni qaqa kei na kaukauwa,
sa vakasinaiti ko lomalagi kei
vuravura ena kemuni serau,
Osana ki cake sara.**

Se me vakayagataki oqo.

**Sa kalougata ko koya sa lako mai
ena yaca ni Turaga,
Osana ki cake sara.**

Glory to you,
   Lord Christ;
your death
   we show forth;
your resurrection
   we proclaim;
your coming
   we await;
Amen!
Come Lord Jesus.

Blessing, honour
and glory be yours,
here and everywhere,
now and for ever. Amen.

Lagilagi ko i kemuni
   Turaga na Karisito
na nomuni mate keimami
   vakaraitaka
na nomuni tucake tale keimami
   kacivaka
na nomuni lesu mai keimami
   namaka;
Emeni!
Ni kusa rawa mai Turaga Jisu.

Na vakarokoroko, na dokai kei na
lagilagi me sa nomuni, eke kei na
vei vanua kece sara edaidai ka tawa
mudu. Emeni.

At the Communion

As Christ teaches us,
we pray

Our Father in heaven,
hallowed be your name,
your kingdom come,
your will be done,
on earth as in heaven.
Give us today
   our daily bread.
Forgive us our sins
as we forgive those
who sin against us.
Save us
from the time of trial
and deliver us from evil.

For the kingdom,
the power,
and the glory are yours
now and for ever. Amen.

Na Veivotai kei na Turaga

NA MASU NI TURAGA
Me vaka e a vakavulici keda kina na
Karisito, me da masu.

Tamai keimami mai lomalagi, me
vakarokoroko taki na yacamuni, me
yaco mai na nomuni matanitu, me
yaco na lomamuni e vuravura me
vaka sa yaco tiko mai lomalagi, ni
solia mai vei keimami e daidai na
kakana e rauti keimami, ni vosata
na neimami caka-cala me vaka ni
keimami sa vosoti ira ka caka-cala
ki vei keimami, ni vakabulai
keimami ena gauna ni vei
vakatovolei, ka vagalalataki
keimami mai na ca.

Ni sa nomuni
na matanitu, na kaukauwa,
kei na lagilagi e daidai
ka tawa mudu. Emeni.

The priest breaks the bread.
Silence may be kept.

Vakanomodi ni dovia tiko na madrai
na Bete.

We break this bread to share in the body of Christ.

Eda dovia na madrai oqo ni'da vota vata na yago i Karisito.

We who are many are one body, for we all share the one bread.

Ko i keda na lewe vuqa, eda sa dua bau ga, Ni'da sa vota e dua ga na madrai.

Lamb of God, you take away the sin of the world, have mercy on us.
Lamb of God, you take away the sin of the world, have mercy on us.
Lamb of God, you take away the sin of the world, grant us your peace.

Kemuni na Lami ni Kalou,
koni a kauta tani na ca ni vuravura,
ni lomani keimami mai.
Kemuni na Lami ni Kalou,
koni a kauta tani na ca ni vuravura,
ni lomani keimami mai.
Kemuni na Lami ni Kalou,
koni a kauta tani na ca ni vuravura,
ni solia mai vei keimami na nomuni
    veivakacegui.

The Invitation

Na Veisureti

The priest may say

Me qai kaya na Bete

Draw near and receive the body and blood of our Saviour Jesus Christ in remembrance that he died for us.
Let us feed on him in our hearts by faith with thanksgiving.

Ni toro voleka mai, moni mai vakayagataka na yago kei na dra ni nodai vakabula ko Jisu Karisito, mei vakananumi, ni nona a mate ena vukada.
Me da mai kana kivua ena yaloda ni vakabauta kei na vakavinavinaka.

The body of Christ given for you.

Na yago i Karisito ka a soli ena
    vukumu.

The blood of Christ shed for you.

Na dra i Karisito ka a dave ena
    vukumu.

Or

Se

The body of our Lord Jesus Christ which was given for you.

Na yago ni noda Turaga ko Jisu Karisito ka a soli ena vukumu.

The blood of our Lord Jesus Christ which was shed for you.

Na dra ni noda Turaga ko Jisu Karisito ka a dave ena vukumu.

Or

Se

The body of Christ keep you in eternal life.

Na yago i Karisito ka na maroroi iko kina bula tawa mudu.

The blood of Christ keep you in eternal life.

Na dra i Karisito ka na maroroi iko kina bula tawa mudu.

The communicant may respond each time

Mera na qai sauma ko ira na tauri kakana tabu

Amen.

Emeni.

At the Dismissal

Na Veivakasukai

The congregation is sent out with these words

Mera na vakasukai nai vavakoso ena vosa oqo:

Go now to love and serve the Lord. Go in peace.

Moni lako ena vakacegu kei na veilomani ka qarava na Turaga.

Amen.
We go in the name of Christ.

Emeni.
Keimami na lako ena yaca i Karisito.

A Blessing in Fijian

Na Masu ni Veivaka lougatataki

Na Veivakacegui ni Kalou sa uasivia na ka kecega e kilai rawa, me vakataudeitaka na yalomuni e na vuku i Karisito Jisu, ka me tiko kei kemuni ka sega ni mudu, na loloma ni Kalou Kaukauwa Duadua Ga, na Tamada, kei, na Luvena kei na Yalotabu, ena gauna oqo kei na veigauna sa vo ka sega ni mudu.
Emeni.

In Tongan

Greetings

Grace and peace
   to you from God.
**God fill you
   with truth and joy.**

Ke 'iate kimoutolu 'a e melino mo e
kelesi 'a e 'Otua
**Ke fakafonu kimoutolu 'e he 'Otua
i he mo'oni mo e fiefia.**

The Lord be with you.
The Lord bless you.

Ke 'iate kimoutolu 'a e 'Eiki.
Pea ke 'afio foki 'iate koe.

This is the day which the
Lord has made.
**Let us rejoice
   and be glad in it.**

Ko e 'aho 'eni na'e ngaahi 'e he 'Eiki.

Ke tau fiefia mo nekeneka ai.

The Kyries

Lord, have mercy.
Christ, have mercy.
Lord, have mercy.

'Eiki 'alo'ofa mai.
Kalaisi 'alo'ofa mai.
'Eiki 'alo 'ofa mai.

The Absolution

Through the cross
   of Christ,
God have mercy on you,
pardon you
and set you free.
Know that you
   are forgiven
and be at peace.
God strengthen you
in all goodness
and keep you
   in life eternal.
Amen.

'Ihe kolosi 'o Kalaisi ko Hotau
Fakamo 'ui. Ke fakamolemole'i ai 'e
he 'Otua kimoutolu, pea mo
fakatau'ataina, pea ke mou 'ilo kuo
fakamolemole'i kimoutolu, pe ke
'iate kimoutolu 'a e melino. Ke
fakamalohi kotoa kimoutolu 'e he
'Otua 'aki 'a e angalelei kotoa pe, pea
ke tauhi kimoutolu ki he mo'ui
ta'engata.
'Ameni.

At the Prayers of the People

*During the prayers any of the
following may be used.*

*Lolotonga 'oku fai
e ngaahi lotu ke fai.*

AFTER THANKSGIVING

For your love
  and goodness
**we give you thanks,
O God.**

Let us bless the Lord.
Thanks be to God.

Give thanks to our God
  who is gracious
**whose mercy endures
  for ever.**

AFTER INTERCESSION

God of love
grant our prayer.

God of grace
you hear our prayer.

Lord, in your mercy
hear our prayer.

Lord, hear our prayer
**and let our cry
  come to you.**

HILI MOE LOTU FAKAFETA'I

Koe'uhi ko ho'o 'ofa mo ho' angalelei.

**'Oku mau fakafeta'i ki ho'o 'afio
  'e 'Otua.**

Ke tau fakahikihiki'i 'a e 'Eiki.
Fakefeta'i kiate koe 'e 'Otua.

Ke tau fakafeta'i ki he 'Eiki angalelei.

Ko 'ene 'alo'ofa 'oku ta'engata.

HILI 'A E LOTU HUFAKI

'Eiki 'alo'ofa e
Tali 'emau lotu.

'Eiki e fanongo mai.
**'Eiki e fanongo mai ki he'emau
  lotu.**

'Eiki e 'i ho'o 'ofa.
Fanongo mai ki he'emau lotu.

Eiki e fanongo mai ki he'emau lotu.
**Pea tuku ke a'u 'emau tangi
  kiate Koe.**

The Peace

Ko e Melino

All standing, the presiding priest says to the people

Tu'u katoa, pea 'e fakaafe'i leva O''e he Taula'eiki 'a e kakai ke nau fe'iloaki 'i he melino 'i he anga maheni fakafonua'o nautolu mo lea pehe.

The peace of Christ
  be always with you.
And also with you.

Ke 'iate koe ma'u pe 'a e melino 'a
  Kalaisi.
Pea ke afio foki 'iate koe.

The people and presiding priest may exchange a sign of peace according to local custom.

Pea koe fetongi pe ia 'e he Taula'eiki mo e kakai 'a e faka'ilonga 'o e melino.

Brothers and sisters
we are the body of Christ.

Fanga tokoua mo e tuofafine.
Ko kitautolu ko e sino ia 'o Kalaisi.

By one Spirit we were baptised into one body.

I he Laumalie pe taha na'e papitaiso ai kitautolu ki he Sino pe taha ko ia.

Keep the unity of the Spirit
in the bond of peace.

Tauhi e Laumalie ko ia pe taha 'i he no'o 'o e melino.

**Amen. We are bound
  by the love of Christ.**

'Ameni. 'Oku tau no'o taha pe 'i he'ofa 'a Kalaisi.

At the Preparation of the Gifts

The presiding priest may say

Pea 'e lea pehe 'e he Taula'eiki

To you, Lord, belongs the greatness, and the power, and the glory, and the victory and the majesty.

'E 'Eiki 'oku 'o'ou 'a e malohi, mo e ivi, mo e naunau, mo e ikuna, pea mo e pule.

All that is in the heavens and the earth is yours, and of your own we give you.

Ko e ngaahi me'a kotoa pe 'i hevani pea mo mamani, 'oku 'a'au ia, pea 'oku mau 'atu pe kiate koe 'a e ngaahi me'a 'oku 'a'au.

At the Great Thanksgiving

The Lord is here.
God's Spirit is with us.

'Oku 'afio 'ae Eiki 'i heni.
Ko e Laumalie 'oe 'Otua 'oku 'iate kitautolu.

Lift up your hearts.
We lift them to the Lord.

Hiki hake ho mou loto ki Hevani.
'A ia oku 'i ai 'ae kololia mo e pule 'a Kalaisi.

Let us give thanks
to the Lord our God.
**It is right to offer
thanks and praise.**

Ke tau fakafeta'i ki he 'Eiki ko
hotau 'Otua.
**'Oku tau mo totonu aupito ke tau
fakamalo mo fakahikihiki.**

**Holy, holy, holy Lord,
God of power and might,
heaven and earth
are full of your glory.
Hosanna in the highest.**

**Ma'oni'oni, Ma'oni'oni, 'oku
Ma'oni'oni 'a e 'Eiki 'o e ngaahi
kau tau,
'oku fonu 'a hevani mo mamani 'i
ho naunau.
Hosana ki 'olunga.**

The following may be used.

**Blessed is he who comes
in the name of the Lord.
Hosanna in the highest.**

'Oku monu'ia la 'oku haele mai
i'he huafa 'oe Eiki.
Hosana 'i 'olunga.

**Glory to you,
Lord Christ;
your death
we show forth;
your resurrection
we proclaim;
your coming
we await;
Amen!
Come Lord Jesus.**

Kololia kiate koe 'e Kalaisi

ko ho'o pekia 'oku mau fakaha atu

ko ho'o Toefu'u
'Oku mau fakamafola'i;
ko ho'o ha'ele mai 'oku mau Teu'i
Ameni! Ha'ele mai Eiki Sisu.

**Blessing, honour
and glory be yours,
here and everywhere,
now and for ever. Amen.**

Ko e Kelesi, naunau mo e Kololia
'Oku a'au ia 'i heni pea,
Ta'efakangata ngata mei he taimi 'ni
pea ta'e ngata, Ameni.

At the Communion

'Ihe Taimi Feohianga Ma'oni'oni

As Christ teaches us,
we pray

Our Father in heaven,
hallowed be your name,
your kingdom come,
your will be done,
on earth as in heaven.
Give us today
    our daily bread.
Forgive us our sins
as we forgive those
who sin against us.
Save us
from the time of trial
and deliver us from evil.

For the kingdom,
the power,
and the glory are yours
now and for ever. Amen.

The priest breaks the bread.

Silence may be kept.

We break this bread to
share in the body of Christ.

**We who are many are one
body, for we all share the
one bread.**

Na'e ako'i kitautolu 'e he 'Eiki ke tau
    ka lo tu pea tau pehe

Ko'emau Tamai 'oku 'i hevani
Ke tapuha ho Huafa,
Ke hoko mai ho pule'anga,
Ke fai ho fingalo 'i mamani,
'O hange ko ia 'i Hevani.
Pea foaki mai kiate kimautolu he
    'aho
ni ha'a mau me'akai.
Pea fakamolemole 'emau ngaahi
angahala, 'O hange ko 'emau
fakamolemole 'a kinautolu 'oku fai
angahala mai kiate kimautolu. 'Oua
na'ake tuku 'a kimautolu ki he
'ahi'ahi, ka ke fakahaofi 'a
kimautolu mei he kovi. He 'oku
'O'ou 'a e pule'anga, pea mo e
malohi, mo e Kololia, 'o ta'engata
pea ta'engata. 'Ameni.

E pakipaki 'ae ma 'ehe Taula'eiki.

Fakalongolongo.

Ko e ma 'oku tau pakipaki ni, 'ikai
koa ko ia ia 'oku tau ma'u 'inasi ai 'i
he Sino 'o Kalaisi.

**Neongo 'oku tau tokolahi, ka 'oku
tau ma'u 'inasi ko toa pe ai.**

Lamb of God, you take
away the sin of the world,
have mercy on us.
Lamb of God, you take
away the sin of the world,
have mercy on us.
Lamb of God, you take
away the sin of the world,
grant us your peace.

'E Lami 'a e 'Otua 'a ia 'oku ne 'ave
'a e angahala 'a mamani,
'alo'ofa mai kiate kimautolu.
'E Lami 'a e 'Otua 'a ia 'oku ne 'ave
'a e angahala 'a mamani,
'alo'ofa mai kiate kimautolu.
'E Lami 'a e 'Otua 'a ia 'oku ne 'ave
'a e angahala 'a mamani,
tuku kiate kimautolu 'a ho 'o melino.

The Invitation

The priest may say

Pea lea pehe 'a e Taula'eiki

Draw near and receive the
body and blood of our
Saviour Jesus Christ in
remembrance that he died
for us.
Let us feed on him in our
hearts by faith with
thanksgiving.

Mou 'unu'unu mai 'o ma'u e Sino mo
e Ta'ata 'a Hotau 'Eiki ko Sisu Kalaisi
pea mou manatu'i na'e pekia 'a
Kalaisi ma'a moutolu. To'o 'eni 'o kai
mo ma'u ia 'i hotau laumalie 'i he tui
moe fakafeta'i.

The body of Christ
given for you.

Ko e Sino eni 'o Kalaisi kuo foaki atu
ma 'au.

The blood of Christ
shed for you.

Ko e Ta'ata'a eni 'o Kalaisi kuo lilingi
atu ma'au.

Or

Pe Pehe

The body of our Lord
Jesus Christ which was
given for you.

Ko e Sino eni 'o hotau 'Eiki ko Sisu
Kalaisi kuo foaki atu ma'au.

The blood of our Lord
Jesus Christ which was
shed for you.

Ko e Ta'ata'a eni 'o hotau 'Eiki ko Sisu
Kalaisi kuo lilingi atu ma'au.

Or	Pe Pehe

The body of Christ
keep you in eternal life.

Ko e Sino eni 'o Kalaisi kene tauhi koe
he mo'ui ta'engata.

The blood of Christ
keep you in eternal life.

Ko e Ta'ata'a eni 'o Kalaisi kene tauhi
koe ki he mo'ui ta'engata.

*The communicant may respond
each time*

*Koia 'oku ne ma'u ke ne tali 'Ameni
ma'u pe.*

Amen.

At the Dismissal

Tapuaki

*The congregation is sent out
with these words*

Ke fakatutuku atu e Kainga lotu 'o pehe

Go now to love and serve
the Lord. Go in peace.

Mou 'alu atu 'i he melino, pea 'ofa mo
tauhi ki he 'eiki.

Amen.

'Ameni.

**We go in the name
of Christ.**

Te mau 'alu 'i he huafa 'o Kalaisi.

A Blessing in Tongan

Ko e melino 'ae 'Otua
'a ia 'oku lahi hake i he ilo kotoa pe tu'u ke ma'u homou loto'
mo homou laumalie, 'ia Kalaisi Sisu ko hotau 'Eiki,
pea ko e tapuaki 'ae 'Otua Mafimafi,
ko e Tamai, mo e Alo, pea mo e Laumalie Ma'oni'oni,
ke 'iate Kimoutolu he taimi ni
pea ta'engata.
'Ameni.

Eucharistic Liturgy

Thanksgiving for Creation and Redemption

The Ministry of Word and Prayer

The Gathering of the People

The people may be greeted informally.

The theme may be introduced and subjects of special concern or thanksgiving suggested.

All standing, the presiding priest or minister continues

In the name of God: Creator, Redeemer and Giver of life.
Amen.

The Sentence of the Day *may be said.*

The minister continues

Grace to you and peace
from God our Creator,
the love at our beginning
and without end,
in our midst and with us.

**God is with us,
here we find new life.**

The people and presiding priest or minister may exchange a sign of peace here or at **The Peace.**

Let us give thanks
for the coming of God's reign of justice and love.

Jesus Christ is good news for the poor,
release for the captives,
recovery of sight for the blind
and liberty for those who are oppressed.

A psalm, canticle, waiata or the following may be used.

Benedicite Aotearoa*

1   O give thanks to our God who is good:
    whose love endures for ever.

2   You sun and moon, you stars of the southern sky:
    give to our God your thanks and praise.

3   Sunrise and sunset, night and day:
    give to our God your thanks and praise.

4   All mountains and valleys, grassland and scree,
    glacier, avalanche, mist and snow:
    give to our God your thanks and praise.

5   You kauri and pine, rata and kowhai, mosses and ferns:
    give to our God your thanks and praise.

6   Dolphins and kahawai, sealion and crab,
    coral, anemone, pipi and shrimp:
    give to our God your thanks and praise.

7   Rabbits and cattle, moths and dogs,
    kiwi and sparrow and tui and hawk:
    give to our God your thanks and praise.

8   You Maori and Pakeha, women and men,
    all who inhabit the long white cloud:
    give to our God your thanks and praise.

9   All you saints and martyrs of the South Pacific:
    give to our God your thanks and praise.

* A pointed version of Benedicite Aotearoa can be found on page 63.

The congregation then kneels.

One of the following penitential forms is used.

1

Happy are those whose sins are forgiven,
whose wrongs are pardoned.
I will confess my sins to the Lord,
I will not conceal my wrongdoings.

Silence

God forgives and heals us.
We need your healing, merciful God:
give us true repentance.
Some sins are plain to us;
some escape us,
some we cannot face.
Forgive us;
set us free to hear your word to us;
set us free to serve you.

The presiding priest says

God forgives you.
Forgive others;
forgive yourself.

Silence

Through Christ, God has put away your sin:
approach your God in peace.

2

Either

Creator, we disfigure your world.
Lord, have mercy.
Lord, have mercy.

Redeemer, we reject your redemption and crucify you daily.
Christ, have mercy.
Christ, have mercy.

Giver of life, we too often choose death.
Lord, have mercy.
Lord, have mercy.

Or

Jesus, our deliverer, we take your freedom from others.
Lord, have mercy.
Lord, have mercy.

Jesus, our hope, we deprive others of hope.
Christ, have mercy.
Christ, have mercy.

Jesus, God's shalom, we distort your peace.
Lord, have mercy.
Lord, have mercy.

In silence before God,
we confess our sins.

Silence

The presiding priest says

God forgives you.
Be at peace.

Or

God the Creator brings you new life,
forgives and redeems you.
Take hold of this forgiveness
and live your life
in the Spirit of Jesus.
Amen.

Silence may be kept.

The Sentence of the Day *may be read.*

A Collect of the Day *shall be said here, or before or after* **the Sermon**.

The congregation sits.

The Proclamation

The Readings

One or two appointed readings follow, the reader first saying

A reading from ... (chapter ... beginning at ...)

Silence may follow each reading.

The reader may say

Hear what the Spirit is saying to the Church.
Thanks be to God.

A psalm, hymn or anthem may follow each reading.

The Holy Gospel according to ... (chapter ... beginning at ...)
Praise and glory to God.

After the Gospel, silence may be kept.

The reader says

This is the Gospel of Christ.
Praise to Christ the Word.

The Sermon

The Sermon *is preached here or after* **The Affirmation of Faith.**

The Affirmation of Faith

The Nicene Creed *(page 410), or* **A Liturgical Affirmation** *(page 481), or* **The Apostles' Creed** *as follows, or* **Te Whakapono a nga Apotoro** *(page 496) may be said here.*

I believe in God, the Father almighty,
    creator of heaven and earth.

I believe in Jesus Christ, God's only Son, our Lord,
    who was conceived by the Holy Spirit,
    born of the Virgin Mary,
    suffered under Pontius Pilate,
    was crucified, died, and was buried;
    he descended to the dead.
    On the third day he rose again;
    he ascended into heaven,
    is seated at the right hand of the Father,
    and will come again to judge the living and the dead.

I believe in the Holy Spirit,
    the holy catholic Church,
    the communion of saints,
    the forgiveness of sins,
    the resurrection of the body,
    and the life everlasting.   Amen.

Let us pray for the Church and for the world, giving thanks for God's goodness.

The Prayers of the People

Prayer is offered with thanksgiving and intercession for

> the universal Church and the local Church
> the world and our nation
> the local community and the community of heaven
> those in need, and our ministries.

A form of intercession and thanksgiving is provided below, or intercessions and thanksgivings may be offered by a minister or members of the congregation in their own words.

After each particular intercession or thanksgiving any one of the following may be used.

AFTER THANKSGIVING

For your love and goodness
we give you thanks, O God.

Let us bless the Lord.
Thanks be to God.

Give thanks to our God
who is gracious
whose mercy endures for ever.

AFTER INTERCESSION

God of love
grant our prayer.

God of grace
you hear our prayer.

Lord, in your mercy
hear our prayer.

Lord, hear our prayer
and let our cry come to you.

Periods of silence may be kept.

The Prayers of the People *may conclude with an appropriate collect such as appear on pages 417, 464 and 483.*

Alternative forms of thanksgiving and intercession are found on pages 413-418, 482-484.

Intercession and Thanksgiving

The minister and people pray responsively.

Particular intercessions and thanksgivings may be offered before any section.

Periods of silence may be kept.

Caring God,
we thank you for your gifts in creation:

for our world,
the heavens tell of your glory;

for our land, its beauty and its resources,
for the rich heritage we enjoy.

We pray:

for those who make decisions about the resources of the earth,
that we may use your gifts responsibly;

for those who work on the land and sea, in city and in industry,
**that all may enjoy the fruits of their labours
and marvel at your creation;**

for artists, scientists and visionaries,
that through their work we may see creation afresh.

Silence

We thank you for giving us life;
for all who enrich our experience.

We pray:

for all who through their own or others' actions
are deprived of fulness of life,
for prisoners, refugees, the handicapped, and all who are sick;

for those in politics, medical science, social and relief work,
and for your Church,
for all who seek to bring life to others.

Silence

We thank you that you have called us to celebrate your creation.
Give us reverence for life in your world.

We thank you for your redeeming love;
**may your word and sacrament
strengthen us to love as you love us.**

Silence

God, Creator, bring us new life.
Jesus, Redeemer, renew us.
Holy Spirit, strengthen and guide us.

The Prayers of the People *may conclude with an appropriate collect or one of
the following*

1 God of peace,
   let us your people know,
   that at the heart of turbulence
   there is an inner calm that comes
   from faith in you.
   Keep us from being content with things as they are,
   that from this central peace
   there may come a creative compassion,
   a thirst for justice,
   and a willingness to give of ourselves
   in the spirit of Christ.
   Amen.

2 God, you shape our dreams.
   As we put our trust in you
   may your hopes and desires
   be ours,
   and we your expectant people.
   Amen.

3 Blessed are you,
    God of growth and discovery;
    yours is the inspiration
    that has altered and changed our lives;
    yours is the power that has brought us
    to new dangers and opportunities.
    Set us, your new creation,
    to walk through this new world,
    watching and learning,
    loving and trusting,
    until your kingdom comes.
    Amen.

The Lord's Prayer (which is to be used at least once in the service) may be said here, introduced by these, or similar words.

As Christ teaches us we pray

Our Father in heaven,
    hallowed be your name,
    your kingdom come,
    your will be done,
        on earth as in heaven.
Give us today our daily bread.
Forgive us our sins
    as we forgive those who sin against us.
Save us from the time of trial
    and deliver us from evil.

For the kingdom, the power, and the glory are yours
    now and for ever.   Amen.

Kua akona nei tatou e to tatou Ariki,
ka inoi tatou

E to matou Matua i te rangi
   Kia tapu tou Ingoa.
   Kia tae mai tou rangatiratanga.
   Kia meatia tau e pai ai
      ki runga ki te whenua,
         kia rite ano ki to te rangi.
Homai ki a matou aianei
     he taro ma matou mo tenei ra.
Murua o matou hara,
     Me matou hoki e muru nei
        i o te hunga e hara ana ki a matou.
Aua hoki matou e kawea kia whakawaia;
    Engari whakaorangia matou i te kino:
Nou hoki te rangatiratanga, te kaha,
    me te kororia,
       Ake ake ake.   Amine.

The Ministry of the Sacrament

The Peace

All standing, the presiding priest says to the people

The peace of God be with you all.
In God's justice is our peace.

E te whanau /Brothers and sisters,
Christ calls us to live in unity.
We seek to live in the Spirit of Christ.

The presiding priest may invite the people to exchange a sign of peace according to local custom.

The Preparation of the Gifts

The offerings of the people are presented. Bread and wine for communion are placed on the table.

The presiding priest says

God of all creation, you bring forth
bread from the earth
and fruit from the vine.
By your Holy Spirit this bread and wine
will be for us
the body and blood of Christ.

All you have made is good.
Your love endures for ever.

***Variations** as provided on pages 474-475 may be used in*
The Great Thanksgiving.

The Great Thanksgiving

It is recommended that the people stand or kneel throughout the following prayer.

The presiding priest says or sings

The Spirit of God be with you.
And also with you.

Lift your hearts to heaven
where Christ in glory reigns.

Let us give thanks to God.
It is right to offer thanks and praise.

It is right indeed to give you thanks most loving God,
through Jesus Christ, our Redeemer,
the first born from the dead,
the pioneer of our salvation,
who is with us always,
one of us, yet from the heart of God.

For with your whole created universe,
we praise you for your unfailing gift of life.
We thank you that you make us human
and stay with us
even when we turn from you to sin.
God's love is shown to us:
while we were yet sinners,
Christ died for us.

In that love, dear God,
righteous and strong to save,
you came among us in Jesus Christ,
our crucified and living Lord.
You make all things new.
In Christ's suffering and cross
you reveal your glory
and reconcile all peoples to yourself,
their true and living God.

A Variation may follow as on pages 474-475.

The priest continues

In your mercy you are now our God.
Through Christ you gather us,
new-born in your Spirit,
a people after your own heart.
We entrust ourselves to you,
for you alone do justice
to all people, living and departed.

Now is the acceptable time,
now is the day of salvation.

Therefore with saints and martyrs,
apostles and prophets,
with all the redeemed,
joyfully we praise you and say:

Holy, holy, holy :
God of mercy, giver of life;
earth and sea and sky
and all that lives,
declare your presence and your glory.

All glory to you, Giver of life
sufficient and full for all creation.
Accept our praises,
living God, for Jesus Christ,
the one perfect offering for the world,
who in the night that he was betrayed,
took bread,
and when he had given thanks,
broke it, gave it to his disciples, and said:
Take, eat, this is my body
which is given for you;
do this to remember me.

After supper he took the cup;
and when he had given thanks,
he gave it to them and said:
Drink this, all of you.
This is my blood of the new covenant
which is shed for you, and for many,
to forgive sin.
Do this as often as you drink it
to remember me.

Therefore, God of all creation,
in the suffering and death
of Jesus our redeemer,
we meet you in your glory.
We lift up the cup of salvation
and call upon your name.
Here and now, with this bread and wine,
we celebrate your great acts of liberation,
ever present and living in Jesus Christ,
crucified and risen,
who was and is and is to come.

Amen! Come Lord Jesus.

May Christ ascended in majesty
be our new and living way,
our access to you, Father,
and source of all new life.
In Christ we offer ourselves
to do your will.

Empower our celebration with your Holy Spirit,
feed us with your life,
fire us with your love,
confront us with your justice,
and make us one in the body of Christ
with all who share your gifts of love.

**Through Christ,
in the power of the Holy Spirit,
with all who stand before you
in earth and heaven,
we worship you, Creator God. Amen.**

Silence may be kept.

The Communion

The Lord's Prayer *(which is to be used at least once in the service)
may be said here, introduced by these or similar words.*

As Christ teaches us we pray

**Our Father in heaven,
     hallowed be your name,
     your kingdom come,
     your will be done,
          on earth as in heaven.
Give us today our daily bread.
Forgive us our sins
     as we forgive those who sin against us.
Save us from the time of trial
     and deliver us from evil.**

**For the kingdom, the power, and the glory are yours
     now and for ever.   Amen.**

Kua akona nei tatou e to tatou Ariki,
ka inoi tatou

E to matou Matua i te rangi
  Kia tapu tou Ingoa.
  Kia tae mai tou rangatiratanga.
  Kia meatia tau e pai ai
    ki runga ki te whenua,
      kia rite ano ki to te rangi.
Homai ki a matou aianei
  he taro ma matou mo tenei ra.
Murua o matou hara,
    Me matou hoki e muru nei
      i o te hunga e hara ana ki a matou.
Aua hoki matou e kawea kia whakawaia;
  Engari whakaorangia matou i te kino:
Nou hoki te rangatiratanga, te kaha,
  me te kororia,
      Ake ake ake.   Amine.

The priest breaks the bread in silence and then says

The bread we break
is a sharing in the body of Christ.

We who are many are one body,
for we all share the one bread.

The priest may lift the cup.

The priest says

The cup of blessing
for which we give thanks
is a sharing in the blood of Christ.

The Invitation

Lifting the bread and cup, the priest invites the people, saying

Bread and wine; the gifts of God
for the people of God.

**May we who share these gifts
be found in Christ
and Christ in us.**

The presiding priest and people receive communion.

The minister says the following words (or any of those provided in the other Eucharistic Liturgies) to each person.

The body of Christ, given for you.
Ko te tinana o to tatou Ariki, i tukua nei mou.

The blood of Christ, shed for you.
Ko nga toto o to tatou Ariki, i whakahekea nei mou.

The communicant may respond each time

Amen. *or* **Amine.**

If there is insufficient bread and wine for the number of communicants the presiding priest prepares more, using the words on page 428.

Prayer After Communion

The Sentence of the Day *or some other appropriate sentence of Scripture may be said.*

The Lord's Prayer *(if it has not been used before) shall be said here.*

A seasonal prayer of thanksgiving (pages 525-545) may be used.

The priest says

Most loving God, creator and redeemer,
we give you thanks
for this foretaste of your glory.

Through Christ, and with all your saints,
we offer ourselves
and our lives to your service.
Send us out in the power of your Spirit,
to stand with you in your world.
We ask this through Jesus Christ, the servant,
our friend and brother. Amen.

Silence may be kept.

The Dismissal of the Community

A blessing may be given.

The congregation is sent out with these words.

Grace be with you.
Thanks be to God.

Go in peace.
Amen. We go in the name of Christ.

Variations to the Great Thanksgiving

These variations are used as directed on page 468.

Each variation follows the words

> ...and reconcile all peoples to yourself,
> their true and living God.

The text of the Great Thanksgiving resumes at the words

> In your mercy you are now our God.
> Through Christ you gather us,
> new-born in your Spirit...

A   **ADVENT**

> We give you thanks
> because Christ the Sun of Righteousness
> has dawned as our deliverance,
> and as your power to renew the world in love and justice.

BC   **CHRISTMAS AND EPIPHANY**

> In Christ you fully shared our life.
> Light of the world, joy of every human heart,
> Jesus accepted our estranged and broken state
> and gave us back our life, our world-
> renewed, whole, healed - your gift!

DE   **LENT AND PASSIONTIDE**

> By Christ's journey into darkness
> are we all brought home;
> by his agony and bloody sweat
> are we come finally to life;
> the tree of shame is now the tree of glory.

FG   EASTER AND ASCENSION

In the power of endless life
Christ is risen from the grave.
His death has broken death
and opened for us the new and living way.
Christ is now our peace,
our freedom and our joy.

H   PENTECOST AND MINISTRY

You pour out your Spirit on all.
You empower us to know your truth
and fearlessly to proclaim your gospel among the nations.
Your love fires our hearts;
and in your Spirit
we hunger and thirst for justice in the world.

Q   MARRIAGE

We give you thanks
because you draw together men and women
in a sacramental union
sharing your love with N and N.

N   SAINTS

We give you thanks for all your saints (especially N)
who heard your call to holiness
and obeyed the heavenly vision.
We rejoice in their fellowship
with us in our pilgrimage.

Te Hakari Tapu

Te Whakawhetai me te Whakamoemiti

The Maori and the English are parallels.

Te Minitatanga
O Te Kupu Me Nga Inoi

Te Whakatikatika

Nga Mihi

Te kaupapa o te ra. Nga take pa manawa me nga whakawhetai.

E tu.

Ka mea te pirihi whakahaere, te minita ranei

E te whanau a te Karaiti,
ko tatou nei tona tinana, e mahi nei i te ao,
naumai, haere mai, ki tona ahurewa tapu.
E mihi ana ki a koutou kua karangatia nei
hei tote, hei maramatanga mo te ao,
i roto i to koutou tohinga.
Kia koa, kia hari.
Whakamoemititia te Atua, te Kai-homai o te tumanako,
te Kai-hohou i te rongo.

Amine.
Kia hari tahi tatou.
Ko Ihu Karaiti te maramatanga,
te matapuna o te ora.

Eucharistic Liturgy
Thanksgiving and Praise

The Ministry of Word and Prayer

The Gathering of the Community

The people may be greeted informally.

The theme may be introduced and subjects of special concern or thanksgiving suggested.

Then all standing, the presiding priest or minister continues

E te whanau a te Karaiti,
welcome to this holy table;
welcome to you,
for we are Christ's body,
Christ's work in the world.
Welcome to you whose baptism makes you
salt of the earth and light to the world.
Rejoice and be glad.
Praise God who gives us forgiveness and hope.

Amen.
Christ is our light,
the joy of our salvation.

Ki a ia te whakamoemiti, te kororia,
i tonoa mai nei, e te Matua,
hei whakahou i te ao,
hei huri i te wai hei waina,
hei whakatahuri i te ngakau
kia tu-tapu ai ki tona aroaro.

**Tapaea atu o tatou ngakau ki a te Karaiti,
nana nei i whakatinana te kupu
hei toko i te ora.
Kororia ki a koe, e te Karaiti,
whakatapua mai matou.**

He Waiata Whakamoemiti

*E ahei ana te whakahaere i te waiata, i te himene ranei, i te Kororia (wharangi
494) ko tetahi ranei o enei e whai ake nei.*

Ko Tenei

Ko te Karaiti te Waiora,
E horoi nei, e whakahou nei i nga mea katoa.
Ko Ia te Taro-o-te-Ora,
Hei Kai ma te hunga Matekai,
Hei Kaha mo te Manene, mo nga Kai-mahi.

**No reira matou ka tapae ki a koe
I a matou whakamoemiti.
Mo Ranginui i runga nei, mo Papa-Tuanuku e takoto nei.
Mo nga Maunga whakahii, mo nga Puke-korero
Mo nga Tai-mihi-tangata, mo nga Moana e hora nei.**

No runga nga homaitanga papai katoa
Tukua mai - kia aio nga rangi i runga
Kia tuku te puehu o Papa-Tuanuku e takoto nei.
Kia whakapapa pounamu te moana
Kia hora te marino ki Aotearoa-whanui.

Praise and glory to Christ,
God's new beginning for humanity
making ritual water gospel wine,
cleansing all our worship.

Love and loyalty to Christ,
who gives us the gospel.
Praise to Christ who calls us to holiness.

Song of Praise

A psalm, canticle or hymn may be used, or the following.

Either

Christ is the living water
    cleansing, refreshing, making all things new.
Christ is the living bread;
    food for the hungry,
    strength for the pilgrim and the labourer.

So now we offer our thanks
    for the beauty of these islands;
    for the wild places and the bush,
    for the mountains, the coast and the sea.

We offer thanks and praise to God for this good land;
    for its trees and pastures,
    for its plentiful crops
    and the skills we have learned to grow them.

Our thanks for marae and the cities we have built;
    for science and discoveries,
    for our life together,
    for Aotearoa, New Zealand.

Kia whakapaingia a te Karaiti,
Mo nga tupuna, matua, mo te hunga tapu.
Nga totara Whakamarumaru, nga Toka Tumoana,
Nga Kaka Wahanui, nga Puna Roimata.
Kia tiaho te maramatanga ki a ratou,
Kia au ta ratou moe.
Kororia ki te Atua.

Ko Tenei Ranei

Ko te Karaiti te hepara pai,
e mohio ana, e atawhai ana i nga hipi katoa o ia kahui.
I roto i a te Karaiti,
kahore he tangata whenua, kahore he tauiwi,
Kahore ano hoki he tau-arai.
I roto i a te Karaiti,
ka tohungia te rawakore,
ka hunaia te pono i te hunga kawe mohio,
ka whakaaturia ki te hunga ngakau papaku.

Areruia!
Kororia ki te Atua o te tika, o te aroha,
Nau i toha nga mahi ma matou,
I rumakina ai matou ki te mamaetanga,
puea ake ana ki nga hua o te aranga.
Pupu ake i a koe te mana atawhai,
kia ai ta matou atawhai i etahi atu,
kia mau ai te rongo ki te hunga katoa
e manawa pa ana, ki tau nei ao.

Te Hohou-i-te-rongo

Tuturi

Ka mea te minita

E te whanau a te Karaiti, i te mea kua hara tatou,
whakatata mai ki te hohou i te rongo.

Nohopuku

And/Or

Christ is the good shepherd
who knows and cares for every one of the sheep
in different folds.
In Christ there is neither Jew nor Gentile;
in Christ there is no discrimination
of gender, class or race.
In Christ the poor are blessed,
the simple receive truth hidden from the wise.

Alleluia!
God of justice and compassion,
you give us a work to do
and a baptism of suffering and resurrection.
From you comes power to give to others
the care we have ourselves received
so that we, and all who love your world,
may live in harmony and trust.

Forgiveness

The congregation kneels.

The minister then says

We come seeking forgiveness
for all we have failed to be and do
as members of Christ's body.

Silence

He aroha to tatou Atua.

**E te Atua aroha e mohio nei ki nga mea katoa,
whakaarahia matou i roto i o matou ngoikoretanga.
Aroha mai i o matou takanga ki te he;
i o matou whakaaro, i a matou mahi,
tohungia matou.**

Ka mea te pirihi whakahaere

Ma te Atua e muru o koutou hara; kia mau te rongo.

Nohopuku

Kia koa, kia hari,
ko te Karaiti te aranga, te taroi o te riri.

Ka mea te minita me te whakaminenga

**Ko te Karaiti te pou herenga waka,
Whakapaingia te Atua to tatou Kai-hanga,
Whakapaingia te Atua to tatou Kai-taurima,
Whakapaingia te Atua to tatou Kai-unga ki te ao whanui.**

*Hei konei te inoi o te ra, e ahei ana mo konei te rarangi o te ra, mo mua, mo
muri ranei i te kauwhau.*

E noho.

In God there is forgiveness.

**Loving and all-seeing God,
forgive us where we have failed to support one another
and to be what we claim to be.
Forgive us where we have failed to serve you;
and where our thoughts and actions have been
contrary to yours we ask your pardon.**

The presiding priest says

God forgives us; be at peace.

Silence

Rejoice and be glad,
for Christ is resurrection,
reconciliation for all the human race.

The minister and people say

**We shall all be one in Christ,
one in our life together.
Praise to God who has created us,
praise to God who has accepted us,
praise to God who sends us into the world.**

The Sentence of the Day may be read.

A Collect of the Day *shall be said here, or before or after* **the Sermon**.

The congregation sits.

Nga Whaikorero

Nga Karaipiture

Nga panui karaipiture, ka mea te kai-panui

Te panui kei te … (te …o nga upoko, ka timata…)

I muri i ia panui ka ahei te nohopuku.

Ka ahei te kai-panui, ki te mea

Whakarongo ki te kupu a te Wairua ki te Haahi.
Whakapaingia te Atua.

Ka ahei he waiata, he himene i muri iho i ia panui.

E tu te katoa, ka mea te kai-panui Rongopai

Te Rongopai tapu ki te ritenga a …
(te … o nga upoko, ka timata…)
Whakamoemititia, whakakororiatia te Atua.

I muri iho i te Rongopai ka ahei te nohopuku.

Ka mea te kai-panui

Te Rongopai tenei a te Karaiti
Whakamoemititia Ia, te Kupu Mana.

Te Kauwhau

Mo konei te Kauwhau mo muri ranei te Whakapono.

The Proclamation

The Readings

The appointed readings follow, the reader first saying

A reading from ... (chapter ... beginning at ...)

Silence may follow each reading.

The reader may say

Hear what the Spirit is saying to the Church.
Thanks be to God.

A psalm, hymn or anthem may follow each reading.

*Then, all standing, the reader of the **Gospel** says*

The Holy Gospel according to ... (chapter ... beginning at ...)
Praise and glory to God.

After the Gospel, silence may be kept.

The reader says

This is the Gospel of Christ.
Praise to Christ, the Word.

The Sermon

The Sermon *is preached here or after the **Affirmation of Faith**.*

He Tikanga Whakapono

Te Whakapono a nga Apotoro *(wharangi 496),* ***Te Whakapono o Naihia***
(wharangi 494), me tenei ranei e whai ake nei.

Ko koe, e te Atua tapu, te tino Atua,
Nou te mana, te ihi, te wehi.
Nou te ao, te mauri, te ora.
Nau te katoa, i te rangi, i te whenua.
Ko koe tonu te Atua.

Ko koe te maramatanga o te ao,
I tiaho ra koe i roto i te pouri,
Kia puta ake tau Tama ko Ihu Karaiti
Hei pou tokomanawa mo te ao.
Ko koe tonu te Atua.

Ko koe te Wairua Tapu,
Ko koe taku rakau,
Ko koe taku tokotoko,
Ko koe taku oranga ngakau e,

Ko koe tonu ra te Atua. Kororia ki a koe.

Ka mea te pirihi whakahaere, te minita ranei

Kia inoi tatou mo te Haahi, mo te ao, me te tuku whakawhetai ki
te Atua mo ana hanga pai.

Nga Inoi a Te Iwi

Ka haere nga inoi me nga whakawhetai

> *mo te Haahi puta noa i te ao; mo te ao*
> *mo tenei motu, me ona hua, me ona rangatira*
> *mo nga whanau takiwa*
> *mo te hunga e pehia ana e nga whakawai o te wa.*

E ahei ana te minita, (t)etahi o te whakaminenga ranei, ki te whakahaere i nga
inoi me nga whakawhetai e whai ake nei, ki tana ranei e pai ai.

The Affirmation of Faith

*The Apostles' Creed (page 461), The Nicene Creed (page 410), or
A Liturgical Affirmation as follows may be said or sung, all standing.*

You, O God, are supreme and holy.
You create our world and give us life.
Your purpose overarches everything we do.
You have always been with us.
You are God.

You, O God, are infinitely generous,
good beyond all measure.
You came to us before we came to you.
You have revealed and proved
your love for us in Jesus Christ,
who lived and died and rose again.
You are with us now.
You are God.

You, O God, are Holy Spirit.
You empower us to be your gospel in the world.
You reconcile and heal; you overcome death.

You are our God. We worship you.

The presiding priest or minister says

Let us pray for the Church and for the world,
giving thanks for God's goodness.

The Prayers of the People

Prayer is offered with thanksgiving and intercession for

> the universal Church and the local Church
> the world and our nation
> the local community and the community of heaven
> those in need, and our ministries.

*A form of intercession and thanksgiving is provided below, or intercessions and
thanksgivings may be offered by a minister or members of the congregation in
their own words.*

I muri iho i ia inoi, i ia whakawhetai e ahei ana tetahi o enei e whai ake nei.

MO MURI I NGA WHAKAWHETAI

Mo tou aroha me au hanga pai
**Kia whakapaingia koe,
e te Atua.**

Kia whakanui te Ariki.
Kia whakapaingia te Atua.

Kia whakapaingia to tatou
Atua atawhai
**Pumau tonu nei ana mahi
tohu.**

MO MURI I NGA INOI

E te Atua aroha
**Whakarongo mai ki ta matou
inoi.**

E te Atua atawhai
**Whakarongo mai ki ta matou
inoi.**

I roto i au mahi tohu
**Whakarongo mai ki ta matou
inoi.**

E te Ariki, whakarongo mai ki
ta matou inoi.
**Kia tae atu a matou tangi
ki a koe.**

Ka ahei te nohopuku mo etahi wa.

*Kei te wharangi 483 nga inoi e rite ana hei whakarapopoto i enei inoi
takawaenga.*

Kei te wharangi 496 etahi atu o nga inoi me nga whakawhetai.

Nga Inoi Takawaenga Me Nga Whakawhetai

He inoi whakautuutu enei i waenga i te minita me te whakaminenga.

E ahei ana te tapiri atu i etahi inoi, whakawhetai ranei, i muri i ia wahanga.

E ahei hoki te nohopuku i nga wa e rite ana.

Kia whakapaingia koe e te Atua ora tonu,
Ki a koe te whakamoemiti, te kororia mo ake tonu atu.

E te Matua i te rangi, whakarongo ki a matou inoi,
kia whakakotahitia tau Haahi
Meinga matou kia kotahi kia whakapono ai te ao.

After each particular intercession or thanksgiving any one of the following may be used.

AFTER THANKSGIVING

For your love and goodness
we give you thanks, O God.

Let us bless the Lord.
Thanks be to God.

Give thanks to our God
who is gracious
whose mercy endures for ever.

AFTER INTERCESSION

God of love
grant our prayer.

God of grace
you hear our prayer.

Lord, in your mercy
hear our prayer.

Lord, hear our prayer
and let our cry come to you.

Periods of silence may be kept.

The Prayers of the People *may conclude with an appropriate collect such as appear on pages 417, 464 and 483.*

Alternative forms of thanksgiving and intercession are found on pages 413-418 and 462-466.

Intercession and Thanksgiving

The minister and people pray responsively.

Particular intercessions and thanksgivings may be offered before any section.

Periods of silence may be kept.

Blessed are you eternal God,
to be praised and glorified for ever.

Heavenly Father, hear us as we pray for the unity of the Church.
May we all be one that the world may believe.

Meinga nga tangata katoa o te Haahi kia mahi ki a koe i runga i
te ngakau pono i te ngakau iti.
Kia tiaho ai te ahua o te Karaiti i roto i a matou.

E maumahara ana matou ki te hunga kua mate.
E te Matua, ka tukua atu ratou e matou ki ou ringa.

(He maumahara ana mo *Ingoa*)
E whakapai ana matou ki a koe mo au hunga tapu katoa kua
uru atu nei ki tou kororia mutungakore.
Meinga matou kia whai wahi ki tou rangatiratanga i te rangi.

Titiro atawhai mai ki te hunga e pehia ana e te mauiui, e te
pouri, e te raruraru ranei.
I raro i tou maru, whakakahangia ratou.

Titiro atawhai mai ki o matou kainga, whanau hoki.
Meinga kia puawai tou aroha i roto i o matou ngakau.

Meinga matou kia aro ki nga mea e matea ana e o matou hoa
tata.
**Awhinatia mai matou kia kotahi ai i roto i nga hari, i nga
mauiui o te iwi.**

Tohaina mai tou Wairua, a arahina hoki te hunga kawe tikanga i
roto i nga iwi o te ao.
**Arahina matou, nga iwi katoa hoki i nga huarahi o te tika, o te
rangimarie.**

Whakakahangia te katoa e minita ana i runga i te ingoa o te
Karaiti.
Meinga matou kia hihiko ki te kauwhau i tau Rongopai.

Tatou ka inoi puku mo nga mea e matea ana e tena, e tena....

*Nga inoi a te whakaminenga, me whakamutu ki te inoi e tika ana, ko tetahi ranei
o enei e whai ake nei.*

1   Te whakamoemiti ki a koe, e te Ariki,
    te Kai-homai i nga mea katoa,
    Nau te ki, 'Inoia, a ka hoatu; Rapua, a ka kitea;
    Patukia, a ka uakina ki a koutou.'
    Kororia ki a koe.

Grant that every member of the Church
may truly and humbly serve you,
that the life of Christ may be revealed in us.

We remember those who have died.
Father, into your hands we commend them.

(Remembering N)
We praise you for all your saints
who have entered your eternal glory.
May we also come to share your heavenly kingdom.

Have compassion on those who suffer from sickness,
grief or trouble.
In your presence may they find strength.

Look with your kindness on our homes and families.
Grant that your love may grow in our hearts.

Make us alive to the needs of our community.
Help us to share one another's joys and burdens.

Inspire and lead those who hold authority
in the nations of the world.
Guide us and all people in the way of justice and peace.

Strengthen all who minister in Christ's name.
Give us courage to proclaim your Gospel.

We pray in silence for our own needs...

The Prayers of the People may conclude with one of the following or another appropriate collect.

1 Praise to you, abundant God,
    for when we ask, you give;
    when we seek, you show the way.
    When we knock, you answer.
    Praise to you for your unfailing grace.
    Make us now your faithful people.
    Amen.

2 E te Atua o te tumanako, ma tau manaaki e u ai a matou
    whakamoemiti,
  inoi hoki, ka whakapono matou ko koe te Atua ora,
  koi wawata, koi tutuki, koi mahi, koi taea, ka u tonu.
  Kororia ki a koe.

3 E te Atua, te whakawhetai, te whakapai, te whakamoemiti, ki
    a koe;
  i aro mai koe ki a matou e tahuri atu nei.
  Meatia kia puawai to aroha ina inoi matou ki a koe.
  Kororia ki a koe.

Te Inoi a te Ariki *(kia kotahi te wa e inoi ai i te karakia) ka ahei te inoi ki konei,
ko enei kupu e whai ake nei hei timata, ko etahi atu ranei e tika ana.*

Kua akona nei tatou e to tatou Ariki,
ka inoi tatou

E to matou Matua i te rangi
  Kia tapu tou Ingoa.
  Kia tae mai tou rangatiratanga.
  Kia meatia tau e pai ai
    ki runga ki te whenua,
      kia rite ano ki to te rangi.
Homai ki a matou aianei
  he taro ma matou mo tenei ra.
Murua o matou hara,
    Me matou hoki e muru nei
      i o te hunga e hara ana ki a matou.
Aua hoki matou e kawea kia whakawaia;
    Engari whakaorangia matou i te kino:
Nou hoki te rangatiratanga, te kaha,
  me te kororia,
    Ake ake ake.   Amine.

2 God our hope,
   may your blessing empower
   our thanksgivings and our prayer;
   for we put our trust in you the living God,
   risking disappointment, risking failure,
   working and waiting expectantly.
   Amen.

3 Thanksgiving, blessing and praise be yours,
   God of the incarnation;
   because you care for us and for our prayer.
   May our love for you and our likeness to you
   be strengthened every time we pray.
   Amen.

The Lord's Prayer (which is to be used at least once in the service) may be said here, introduced by these or similar words.

As Christ teaches us we pray

Our Father in heaven,
   hallowed be your name,
   your kingdom come,
   your will be done,
      on earth as in heaven.
Give us today our daily bread.
Forgive us our sins
   as we forgive those who sin against us.
Save us from the time of trial
   and deliver us from evil.

For the kingdom, the power, and the glory are yours
   now and for ever.   Amen.

Te Minitatanga O Te Hakarameta

Te Maungarongo

Ka tu te katoa, ka mea te pirihi whakahaere

Kia whakapaingia a te Karaiti, te Ariki o te rongomau.
E turaki nei i nga tau-arai o te wehe.

Kia tau te rangimarie o te Atua ki a koutou.
**Kia whakapaingia te Karaiti e tuitui nei i a tatou i roto i te
rongomau.**

*Ki te whakahaua e te pirihi whakahaere, mo konei te hohou rongo a tetahi ki
tetahi, kia rite ki nga kaupapa a tena iwi, a tena iwi.*

Te Whakatikatika I Te Ohaoha

*Ko konei tapaea ai nga ohaoha a te iwi. Ka mauria mai te taro me te waina mo
te hakari ki te tepu.*

Kei nga wharangi 491-493 etahi atu tikanga mo te Whakawhetai Nui.

Te Whakawhetai Nui

Me tu me tuturi ranei te iwi i te roanga ake o te inoi e whai ake nei.

Ka mea, ka waiata ranei te pirihi whakahaere

Kua ara a te Karaiti!
He pono tonu, kua ara a Ia.

Whakareia o koutou ngakau ki te rangi
kei reira nei te Karaiti kei tona ahurewa tapu.

Kia whakapaingia te Atua.
He mea tika kia tapaea te whakapai, te whakamoemiti.

Ko te hari mo to matou whakaoranga,
e te Atua o Tua-whakarere,
ki te tuku whakawhetai ki a koe
i roto i a Ihu Karaiti.

The Ministry of the Sacrament

The Peace

All standing, the presiding priest says to the people

Blessed be Christ the Prince of Peace
who breaks down the walls that divide.

The peace of God be always with you.
Praise to Christ who unites us in peace.

The presiding priest may invite the people to exchange a sign of peace according to local custom.

The Preparation of the Gifts

The offerings of the people are presented. Bread and wine for communion are placed on the table.

Variations *as provided on page 491-493 may be used in* **The Great Thanksgiving***.*

The Great Thanksgiving

It is recommended that the people stand or kneel throughout the following prayer.

The presiding priest says or sings

Christ is risen!
He is risen indeed.

Lift your hearts to heaven
where Christ in glory reigns.

Let us give thanks to God.
It is right to offer thanks and praise.

It is the joy of our salvation,
God of the universe,
to give you thanks
through Jesus Christ.

Paoho ana tau kupu, 'Kia tiaho te marama';
na, ka marama.
E tiaho tonu nei tou maramatanga i roto i to matou pouri.
Nau i pou te mauri-ora mo nga mea katoa.
Nau hoki matou i waihanga,
ki te whakarongo ki tau kupu,
ki te mahi i tau i pai ai,
kia eke ai ki te taumata o tou aroha.
He mea tika kia whakapaingia koe.

Nau i tono mai tau Tama
hei ara whainga ma matou,
hei pono e manakohia ana e matou.

Mo konei nga whakaritenga mo nga ra o te Haerenga Mai, o te Whanautanga,
o te Whakaaturanga, mo te Ra Tapu Nikau ara Parekawakawa.

Ka whakahoki ano te pirihi whakahaere

I tukua mai e koe tau Tama
kia whakamatea hei toha i te ora,
hei wewete i o matou hara.
Kua unuhia o matou he e tona ripeka.

Mo konei nga whakaritenga mo Reneti, mo nga ra o tona Tukinotanga, mo te
Aranga, mo te Kakenga, mo te Petekoha, mo te Marena, mo nga Hunga Tapu.

Ka whakahoki ano te pirihi whakahaere

I tonoa mai tou Wairua Tapu
hei whakakaha, hei arataki,
hei whakatupato, hei whakahou i tau Haahi.
Waihoki, i tenei roopu whakaatu
e karapoti nei i a matou,
ko tona rite ki nga whetu, te taea te tatau,
ka whakamoemiti matou i runga i te ngakau aroha, i te ngakau
    hari,
mou i waihanga, i karanga i a matou,

You said, 'Let there be light';
there was light.
Your light shines on in our darkness.
For you the earth has brought forth life
in all its forms.

You have created us
to hear your Word,
to do your will
and to be fulfilled in your love.
It is right to thank you.

You sent your Son to be for us
the way we need to follow
and the truth we need to know.

*The **Variation** for Advent, Christmas, Epiphany or Palm Sunday
may follow here.*

The presiding priest continues

You sent your Son to give his life
to release us from our sin.
His cross has taken our guilt away.

*The **Variation** for Lent, Passiontide, Easter, Ascensiontide, Pentecost,
Marriage or a Saint may follow here.*

The presiding priest continues

You send your Holy Spirit
to strengthen and to guide,
to warn and to revive your Church.
Therefore, with all your witnesses
who surround us on every side,
countless as heaven's stars,
we praise you for our creation
and our calling,
with loving and with joyful hearts:

E te Atua tapu rawa, mahi tohu,
tino tapu, tino tika,
nou te kororia, nou te purotu.
Kororia ki a koe, e te Atua,
te Runga rawa,
te Atua mahaki.

E te tino Tapu, ka whakapaingia koe, i roto i tau Tama
i tuohu nei ki te horoi i nga wae o ana akonga,
te tohu o te Kai-mahi tuturu.

I te po i mua i tona matenga
ka tango ia i te taro ka tuku whakawhetai ki a koe.
Ka whawhati, ka hoatu ki ana akonga, a ka mea:
Tangohia, kainga, ko toku tinana tenei ka hoatu nei mo koutou
meinga tenei hei whakamahara ki ahau.

Ka mutu te hapa, ka mau ia i te kapu,
ka tuku whakawhetai ki a koe,
ka hoatu ki a ratou, a, ka mea:
Inumia tenei, ko oku toto o te Kawenata hou
i whakahekea mou, mo te katoa,
hei murunga hara,
meinga tenei hei whakamahara ki ahau.

No reira ma tenei taro me tenei waina ka maumahara matou
ki au painga ki a matou.

Te Atua o nga wa katoa,
e maumahara ana matou ki tau Tama.
Ka whakawhetai matou,
mo tona ripekatanga, me tona aranga mai.
Ka whakamanamana matou mo tona whakareanga.
Ka tumanako ki tona haerenga mai i runga i te kororia,
I roto i a ia, ka mau tonu matou ki a koe.

Whakahangia iho tou Wairua Tapu,
Meatia tenei taro, ko te tinana tonu,
tenei waina, ko nga toto tonu o te Karaiti.
Kia tuhono ki tona tinana,
Kia u ai matou ki roto i te aka pono.

**Holy God, holy and merciful, holy and just,
glory and goodness come from you.
Glory to you most high and gracious God.**

Blessed are you, most holy, in your Son,
who washed his disciples' feet.
'I am among you,' he said, 'as one who serves.'

On that night before he died
he took bread and gave you thanks.
He broke it, gave it to his disciples, and said:
Take, eat, this is my body
which is given for you;
do this to remember me.

After supper, he took the cup,
and gave you thanks.
He gave it to them and said:
Drink this. It is my blood of the new covenant,
shed for you, shed for all,
to forgive sin;
do this to remember me.

Therefore with this bread and wine
we recall your goodness to us.

**God of the past and present,
we your people remember your Son.
We thank you for his cross and rising again,
we take courage from his ascension;
we look for his coming in glory
and in him we give ourselves to you.**

Send your Holy Spirit,
that we who receive Christ's body
may indeed be the body of Christ,
and we who share his cup
draw strength from the one true vine.

Ka aru matou i a te Karaiti,
Tui, tui, tuituia matou.
Tuia ki te mamae.
Tuia ki te tumanako,
Tui, tui, tuia ki te ora.

Kei a koe, e te tapu o te rangi,
te orokohanga ra ano o te ao,
te timatanga, te otinga,
te arepa me te omeka.

Kei a koe, te whakapai, te kororia, te aroha,
I tenei ra, i tena ra,
Mai i a matou, mai i te katoa,
I konei, i nga wahi katoa. Amine.

Ka ahei ki te nohopuku.

Hakari Tapu

Te Inoi a te Ariki *(kia kotahi te wa e inoi ai i te karakia) ka ahei te inoi ki konei, ko enei kupu e whai ake nei hei timata, ko etahi atu ranei e tika ana.*

Kua akona nei tatou e to tatou Ariki,
ka inoi tatou

E to matou Matua i te rangi
 Kia tapu tou Ingoa.
 Kia tae mai tou rangatiratanga.
 Kia meatia tau e pai ai
  ki runga ki te whenua,
   kia rite ano ki to te rangi.
Homai ki a matou aianei
 he taro ma matou mo tenei ra.
Murua o matou hara,
 Me matou hoki e muru nei
  i o te hunga e hara ana ki a matou.
Aua hoki matou e kawea kia whakawaia;
 Engari whakaorangia matou i te kino:
Nou hoki te rangatiratanga, te kaha,
 me te kororia,
  Ake ake ake. Amine.

Called to follow Christ,
help us to reconcile and unite.
Called to suffer,
give us hope in our calling.

For you, the heavenly one, make all things new;
you are the beginning and the end, the last and the first.

Praise, glory and love be yours,
this and every day,
from us and all people,
here and everywhere. Amen.

Silence may be kept.

The Communion

The Lord's Prayer (which is to be used at least once in the service)
may be said here, introduced by these or similar words.

As Christ teaches us we pray

Our Father in heaven,
   hallowed be your name,
   your kingdom come,
   your will be done,
      on earth as in heaven.
Give us today our daily bread.
Forgive us our sins
   as we forgive those who sin against us.
Save us from the time of trial
   and deliver us from evil.

For the kingdom, the power, and the glory are yours
   now and for ever.   Amen.

Ka nohopuku te pirihi, ka whawhati i te taro, me te ki

Te tinana o te Karaiti i whatiia mo tatou.
Ko Ia te taro o te ora.

Ka ahei te pirihi ki te whakarewa i te kapu.

Ka mea te pirihi

I maringi ona toto hei murunga hara.
Kua ara mai te Karaiti i te mate.

Te Powhiri

Ka whakarewa te pirihi i te taro me te kapu, ka karanga ki te whakaminenga

Haere mai e te kahui a te Atua,
tangohia enei kai rangatira a te Karaiti.

Ka tango te pirihi whakahaere me te whakaminenga i te taro, i te waina.

Ka mea te minita i nga kupu e whai ake nei (me era ranei i roto i etahi atu whakahaere) ki ia tangata.

Ko te tinana o to tatou Ariki, i tukua nei mou.

Ko nga toto o to tatou Ariki, i whakahekea nei mou.

Ko Tenei Ranei

Te taro o te ora, i whatiia nei mou.

Te kapu o te ora, i whakahekea nei mou.

Ka ahei te ki

Amine

Ki te kore e kapi te taro me te waina mo te hunga tango hapa ma te pirihi whakahaere e whakatapu ano, tirohia te wharangi 516.

The priest breaks the bread in silence and then says

Christ's body was broken for us on the cross.
Christ is the bread of life.

The priest may lift the cup.

The priest says

His blood was shed for our forgiveness.
Christ is risen from the dead.

The Invitation

Lifting the bread and cup, the priest invites the people saying

Come God's people,
come to receive Christ's heavenly food.

The presiding priest and people receive communion.

The minister says the following words (or any of those provided in the other Eucharistic Liturgies) to each person.

The body of Christ keep you in eternal life.

The blood of Christ keep you in eternal life.

Or

The bread of life, broken for you.

The cup of blessing, poured out for you.

The communicant may respond each time

Amen.

If there is insufficient bread or wine for the number of communicants the presiding priest prepares more, using the words on page 516.

Nga Inoi mo Muri I te Hapa

Ka ahei te nohopuku.

Te Inoi a te Ariki *(mehemea kahore noa i panuitia) me panui i konei.*

Ka mea te pirihi

Whakapaingia te Atua e whakamine nei i a tatou.
Whakamoemititia te Atua kua kotahi nei tatou.

Whakapaingia te Atua e hohou nei i te rongo.
Whakamoemititia te Atua ko Ia te tumanako te herekore.

Whakapaingia Ia kua hora nei tana kupu.
Whakamoemititia Ia, koia nei te aroha.

Whakapaingia Ia nana nei tatou i karanga.
**Waihangatia matou,
kia rite ki tou ake te ahua.**

Manakohia e te Atua a matou whakahere, whakamoemiti.
Ko tau rourou, ko taku rourou, ka makona matou.

Te Haerenga Atu

Hei konei te manaakitanga e rite ana.

Ka ahei te pirihi whakahaere ki te whakaatu tetahi rarangi o te Rongopai.

Whakahau ki te whakaminenga

Haere i runga i te aroha. Haere i runga i te rangimarie.
**Amine. Ka haere matou i runga i te ingoa o te Karaiti.
Kororia ki te Atua.**

Prayer After Communion

Silence may be kept.

The Lord's Prayer *(if it has not been used before) shall be said here.*

The presiding priest may use an appropriate collect.

The priest says

Blessed be God who calls us together.
Praise to God who makes us one people.

Blessed be God who has forgiven our sin.
Praise to God who gives hope and freedom.

Blessed be God whose Word is proclaimed.
Praise to God who is revealed as love.

Blessed be God who alone has called us.
**Therefore we offer all that we are
and all that we shall become.**

Accept, O God, our sacrifice of praise.
**Amen. Accept our thanks for all you have done.
Our hands were empty, and you filled them.**

The Dismissal of the Community

A general blessing or one appropriate to the theme may be given.

The presiding priest or the bishop may use one of the Gospel sayings of Jesus.

The congregation is sent out with these words

(Go now to love and serve the Lord.) Go in peace.
Amen. We go in the name of Christ.

Hei Whakauru ki te Whakawhetai nui

Mo nga wa e rite ana (wharangi 486).

A TE HAERENGA MAI

Tenei Ia te haere mai nei hei taroi i te riri,
hei hohou i te rongo.
Ko te Karaiti te puaotanga o te ata.

B TE RA WHANAU

Kua whanau a te Karaiti ki Peterehema,
te whakatinanatanga o te Atua,
te Tamaiti i te whare kararehe,
te manene i te huarahi ki Ihipa.

C TE WHAKAATURANGA

Tiaho ana tona whetu hei karanga i a tatou
kia tuohu ki te Karaiti kua whanau nei.
Kua tata mai te Atua ki a tatou;
kua whakatinanatia ki te ao;
Tapae atu nga whakamoemiti me nga koha.

D RENETI

Ko tona ripeka to tatou kaha,
E ahei ai te tomo i te tatau kuiti
i nga ara o te ora,
kia uru atu ai ki ona paweratanga
i nga ra o Reneti.

Variations to the Great Thanksgiving

*These **Variations** are used as directed on page 486.*

A ADVENT

> He is coming to reconcile
> and forgive.
> Christ is the new beginning.

B CHRISTMAS

> For Christ is born in Bethlehem,
> God revealed in human form;
> the baby in a manger,
> the refugee on the Egypt road.

C EPIPHANY

> His star, mysterious and inviting,
> calls us to worship the Christ who is born.
> For he is Emmanuel, God revealed in human form
> for all the human race;
> to him we offer our homage and our gifts.

D LENT

> His cross has given us strength
> and freedom to enter by the narrow gate,
> to choose the path of life,
> and in these forty days to share his trials.

E TE WHAKAMAMAETANGA

Tona ripeka te taroi o te riri.
Ko te Karaiti te maungarongo a te Atua
ki te ao.

Ko Tenei Ranei

Ana, te tino tangata,
te Kai-whakaora e kore nei
e whakaora i a ia ano;
Ara te Kai-hanga i rukea e te ao.

RATAPU NIKAU

Kia whakanuia te Tama a Rawiri!
Te kingi whakaiti i runga i tana kaihe.
E whakapakari nei te mana o te hoariri,
O te tao.

F TE ARANGA

Kua ara te Karaiti i te mate.
Kua horahia te aroha:
koia te Ariki o te wa,
te Ariki o te Atea.

G TE KAKENGA

Ko te Karaiti te Kingi o nga kingi,
e whakaora nei i ana pononga
hei hoa pumau mona.
Ko ia tonu te Ariki.

E PASSIONTIDE

Behold the Man,
the Saviour who will not save himself;
Creator, whom the world disowns.
His cross is the reconciliation;
Christ is peace between God and the world,
peace between the world and God.

PALM SUNDAY

Hosanna to the Son of David!
He challenges the power and the sword;
the gentle rider on a humble beast,
the Servant King.

F EASTER

Christ is risen from the dead.
Love is come again:
Christ is sovereign over space and time.

G ASCENSION

Christ is the universal King
who calls his servants friends.
He is the Lord.

H PETEKOHA

E karanga ana tou Wairua Tapu,
i nga hunga, i nga iwi, i nga reo,
kia manako ki nga mea miharo i poua e koe.
Na tou Wairua Tapu,
i tiri te rongopai ki Aotearoa.
(E karanga ana koe i tenei ra, i tenei ra,
kia kotahi nga iwi i raro i tou maru,
kia whangaia te hunga matekai,
kia whakaorangia nga turoro,
kia tukua nga whakarau kia haere noa,
kia mataara te tatari atu
ki tou rangatiratanga).

Q MO TE MARENA

Kua tuhonotia tatou e te Karaiti,
ki to tatou Atua, tetahi hoki ki tetahi.
E hono ana te Karaiti,
i te tane, i te wahine
i runga i te ngakau kotahi.
Tenei te taonga a te Karaiti
ki a *Ingoa* raua ko *Ingoa*

N TE HUNGA TAPU

I tumanako, i whakapakari
te hunga tapu ki tou ripeka.
Tenei ta ratou whakamanamana,
to ratou kororia,
te maramatanga i tiaho i roto i a ratou
i a *Ingoa* hoki.
Koia ka whakamoemiti ki a koe.

H PENTECOST

Through the Holy Spirit
nations, races, and languages are called
to welcome the great things you have done.
Through the Holy Spirit
you have brought the good news to our land.
(Day by day you call us to be one people,
to be your people.
Day by day you call us to feed the hungry,
heal the sick, deliver the oppressed,
and to wait and watch for your kingdom.)

Q MARRIAGE

Christ has restored our intimacy
with God and with each other;
Christ brings men and women together for a perfect unity.
This gift is offered now to N and N.

N SAINTS

And in the cross your saints have hoped and dared.
It is their boast and glory,
the light within them
and of N for whom we praise you.

He Tikanga Ano

Kororia ki te Atua

Mo te wharangi 477.

Kororia ki te Atua i runga rawa,
    he maungarongo ki tona iwi i runga i te whenua,

E te Ariki e te Atua, e te Kingi o te rangi,
    e te Atua Kaha rawa e te Matua,
        ka koropiko matou ki a koe, ka whakawhetai,
        ka whakamoemiti ki a koe mo tou kororia.

E te Ariki e Ihu Karaiti, te Tama kotahi a te Matua,
e te Ariki e te Atua, e te Reme a te Atua,
e waha atu nei i nga hara o te ao:
        tohungia matou,
e noho mai na koe i te ringa matau o te Matua:
        whakarongo mai ki ta matou inoi.

Ko koe anake te Tapu,
ko koe anake te Ariki,
ko koe anake te Runga Rawa,
    e Ihu Karaiti,
    me te Wairua Tapu,
    i roto i te kororia o te Atua Matua.   Amine.

Te Whakapono o Naihia

Mo nga wharangi 481 ko tenei ranei 503.

E whakapono ana matou ki te Atua kotahi,
    ki te Matua, te Mana tino nui,
    ki te Kai-hanga o te rangi me te whenua,
    o nga mea katoa e kitea ana,
    o nga mea hoki e kore e kitea.

E whakapono ana matou ki te Ariki kotahi, ki a Ihu Karaiti,
   ki te Tama kotahi a te Atua,
  no tuawhakarere i puta mai ai i te Matua,
  He Atua no te Atua,
  he Maramatanga no te Maramatanga,
  he tino Atua no te tino Atua.
  i whakawhanautia, kahore i hanga,
  kotahi ano ia me te Matua.
  Nana nei nga mea katoa i hanga.
  Mo tatou mo te tangata,
    mo to tatou oranga hoki, i heke iho ai ia i te rangi:
    na te mana o te Wairua Tapu,
    i whanau mai ai ia i te Puhi i a Meri, a i whakatangatatia.
    I ripekatia ia mo tatou i te wa i a Ponotio Pirato:
    i whakamamaetia, i mate, a i tanumia.
    I ara ake ano hoki ia i te toru o nga ra,
    ki te whakatutuki i ta nga Karaipiture:
    i kake atu ia ki te rangi,
    a e noho mai nei i te ringa matau o te Matua.
    Ka hoki mai ano ia i runga i te kororia,
    ki te whakawa i te hunga ora i te hunga mate,
    kahore hoki he mutunga o tona rangatiratanga.

E whakapono ana matou ki te Wairua Tapu,
    ki te Ariki, ki te Kai-homai i te ora.
  E ahu mai nei i te Matua i te Tama.
  E koropikoria nei
    e whakakororia tahitia nei me te Matua me te Tama.
  Kua whakapuakina ana korero e nga poropiti.
  E whakapono ana matou kotahi ano Haahi tapu
  ko to nga Apotoro, a, puta noa i te ao.
  E whakaae ana matou kotahi ano iriiri hei murunga hara.
  E tumanako atu ana matou ki te aranga mai o te
    hunga mate,
    ki te oranga hoki ki tera ao atu. Amine.

Te Whakapono a nga Apotoro

Mo nga wharangi 481 ko tenei ranei 503.

E whakapono ana ahau ki te Atua, ki te Matua Kaha rawa,
  Ko ia te Kai-hanga o te rangi, o te whenua;

Ki tana Tama Kotahi ano hoki, ki to tatou Ariki, ki a Ihu
    Karaiti;
  I whakatangatatia nei e te Wairua Tapu,
  I whanau i te Puhi, i a Meri,
  I whakamamaetia i te wa i a Ponotio Pirato,
  I ripekatia, i mate, i tanumia
  I heke atu ki te reinga;
  No te toru o nga ra i ara ake ai ia i te mate,
  A kake atu ana ki te rangi;
  E noho mai nei i te ringaringa matau o te Atua,
  o te Matua Kaha rawa;
  Ka hoki mai ano ia i reira ki te whakarite whakawa mo nga
    tangata ora, mo nga tangata mate.

E whakapono ana ahau ki te Wairua Tapu;
  Ki te Haahi tapu puta noa i te ao;
  Ki te Kotahitanga o te Hunga tapu;
  Ki te Murunga hara;
  Ki te Aranga mai o te tinana,
  Me te ora tonu.   Amine.

Etahi atu Inoi

Mo nga wharangi 482, 503.

E te Matua i te rangi, tenei matou te inoi atu nei mo tau Haahi,
i runga i te ingoa o tau Tama, o Ihu Karaiti, te upoko o te Haahi.

(ko enei karakia / whakamoemiti ranei)

E te Matua, meinga kia mataara tau Haahi mo taua mahi i te ao.
Kia meinga ai matou, hei tote mo te ao, hei maramatanga hoki.

Whakahangia mai tou mauri ki te iwi.
**Whakamana mai a matou kupu, a matou mahi,
  hei whakanui i a te Karaiti.**

Tatou ka inoi mo te ao

(ko enei karakia / whakamoemiti ranei)

E te Kai-hanga, aratakina nga iwi katoa ki te whai i te tika, i te
    rongomau.
Kia aro ai matou, tetahi ki tetahi, i runga i te mahaki, i te pono.

Whakapuawaitia i roto i a matou, te miharo mo te whenua me
    ona mea katoa
Tohutohungia mai ki au tikanga rahui.

Tatou ka inoi mo te wa-kainga

(ko enei karakia / whakamoemiti ranei)

E te Atua pono, homai tou maramatanga ki te hunga
    whakatakoto tikanga.
Kia mahi ai ratou i runga i te pono, i te tika.

Tukua mai au manaakitanga ki o matou whanaunga, hoa hoki.
**Kia mahi ai ki taua Karaiti kei roto nei i a matou katoa, kia
    taurite ai, to matou aroha ki te aroha o te Karaiti mo ratou.**

Tatou ka inoi mo nga whakarau:

(ko enei karakia / whakamoemiti ranei)

E te Atua e tumanakohia nei, atawhaitia, whakaorangia te
    hunga mauiui ana nga tinana, nga hinengaro, nga wairua.
Kia piki tou ora ki a ratou.

Meinga matou hei kai-hapai i au mahi tohu.
Whakakahangia a matou mahi whakaora katoa.

Kia maumahara tatou ki te hunga kua mate, ki te hunga e pouri
    ana:

(ko enei karakia / whakamoemiti ranei)

E whakapai ana matou mo te hunga kua hinga i roto i te
    whakapono o te Karaiti, me ratou hoki e mohiotia nei e koe.
E te Matua, e tukua atu ana ratou ki ou ringa.

Atawhaitia te hunga e mamae ana.
Tauawhitia mai te hunga e noho pani ana.

E whakapai ana matou mo (...,mo) te kahui tapu kua uru atu
nei ki tou oranga mutungakore.
Ma tenei tauira matou e mea kia hihiko, kia mataara.

Tatou ka inoi mo tatou ake, me a tatou mahi.

(ko enei karakia / whakamoemiti ranei)

E te Ariki, nau nei matou i karanga ki au mahi,
Meatia kia hikoi matou i mua i tou aroaro,
whakaungia mai tou aroha ki o matou ngakau,
tou pono ki o matou hinengaro,
tou marohirohi ki o matou whakaaro,
mo te taenga ki te tino tauranga,
ka mohio pu ki te hari, kua tau ki te haukainga,
ki te taanga manawa i roto i a koe,
i roto hoki i to matou Ariki, i a Ihu Karaiti. Amine.

Ko Tenei Ranei

He rama tau kupu ki oku wae
I nga wa o te pouri, o te marama,
o te raru, o te hari,
awhinatia mai matou e te Matua i te rangi,
kia manako ki tou aroha,
kia mahi i au mahi,
kia whakapai i tou ingoa,
i roto i a Ihu Karaiti, te Ariki. Amine.

Te Hakari Tapu
Na te Whanau a te Karaiti

Himene

Te Whakaoho

Ka hui te iwi, ka karangatia.

Minita   Tihei, Mauriora:
Ki te wheiao, ki te ao marama.

Maranga, whakatiaho,
kua tae mai tou maramatanga.
Kua maiangi te kororia o te Atua ki a koe:
Kua hui mai nga iwi ki tou maramatanga.
Kia mataara, tirohia atu,
kei te hui mai te nuinga,
kei te whakaeke.
E Ihowa, ko wai e tomo ki tou whare tapu?
Ko wai hoki e piki ki tou maunga tapu? *Waiata 15:2*

Minenga   **Ko ia e tapatahi ana te haere, he tika te mahi, e korero
pono ana i roto i tona ngakau.
Uakina mai nga tatau o te tika, kia tomo atu ahau,
kia whakamoemiti ki a Ihowa.** *Waiata 115:19*

Ko Tenei Ranei

Minita   Kia whakapaingia te tangata e haere mai ana i runga i
te ingoa o Ihowa. Ka whakapaingia koutou e matou i
roto i te whare o Ihowa. Nau mai, haere mai, i runga
i te ingoa o Ihowa. *Waiata 118:26*

Minenga	Tukua mai tou pono me tou marama, hei arahi, hei kawe i ahau ki tou maunga tapu, ki tou whare.

Waiata 43:3

Minita	Tomokia ona tatau i runga i te whakawhetai: ona marae i runga i te whakamoemiti.

Waiata 100:3

Te Whakawatea

Pirihi anake	E te Atua Kaha Rawa

E te Atua Kaha Rawa
e tuwhera ana nga ngakau katoa ki a koe,
e mohiotia ana nga hiahia katoa,
e kore hoki e ngaro i a koe te mea huna:
whakahangia iho tou Wairua Tapu,
hei whakama i nga whakaaro o matou ngakau,
kia tino aroha ai matou ki a koe,
kia tika ai te whakanui i tou ingoa tapu:
ko Ihu Karaiti nei to matou Ariki.
Amine.

Whakarapopoto i nga Ture. Te Ture Hou ranei.

Nga Kupu whakamarie.

Te Whakinga Hara

Minenga	**E te Matua Kaha Rawa, he hira ake nei tou aroha noa i tou riri, tenei tau whanau te tuohu nei i mua i tou aroaro, te whakaae nei kua he matou ki a koe, kua takatakahi i au ture tapu i te poka ke o nga whakaaro, i te horihori o nga kupu, i te rere ke o nga mahi. Kua hara matou ki a koe i runga i te ngoikore, i te kuare, i te maro o nga kaki. Kia aroha mai ki a matou, murua atu o matou hara, wetekia nga mekameka e here nei i a matou. Meinga matou kia tapu, kia tu watea i mua i tou aroaro, hei mea kia whakanuia ai tou ingoa tapu: ko Ihu Karaiti hoki to matou Kai-whakaora. Amine.**

Te Wetekanga Hara

Pirihi anake He Aroha te Atua, e pumau ana aana mahi tohu ki te hunga e tahuri pono ana ki a ia, e whaki ana i o ratou hara. Kua tukua mai e ia te mana unu i te hara ki ana minita i runga i te kaupapa i poua e tana Tama e Ihu Karaiti. I runga i tona ingoa, ka wetekia o koutou hara, ka unuhia nga mauiui, nga taimahatanga i runga i a koutou. Mana koutou e whakatapu, e whakahou. Mana koutou e whakakaha i roto i nga mahi pai katoa, e whakau kei taea te whakakorikori: e arahi hoki ki te Ora Tonu; ko Ihu Karaiti hoki to tatou Kai-wawao.
Amine.

Te Mihi

Minita Kia noho a Ihowa ki a koutou.

Minenga **Ki a koe ano hoki.**

Minita Tena koutou e te whanau kua tatu mai nei i runga i te reo powhiri a to tatou Ariki: Haere mai ki ahau e koutou katoa e mauiui ana e taimaha ana, a, maku koutou e whakaokioki. Tenei te mihi atu nei ki a koutou ki te Haahi a te Atua kua whakatapua nei i roto i a Karaiti Ihu, kua karangatia hei hunga whiriwhiri mana, ara, koutou e whakahua nei i tona ingoa tapu.

Waha mai nga mate kei runga i a koutou kia mihia, kia tangihia, kia maharatia, e tatou e te Haahi.

Kua tuhono ratou te Hunga Tapu ki a ratou, kua watea i nga raru o tenei ao. Tatou ka whakawhetai ki to tatou Atua. Ka hari te hunga mate e mate ana i roto i te Ariki.

Ae ra, e ai ta te Wairua, kua okioki ratou i a ratou mahi. Kia inoi tatou.

Minenga	E te Ariki tohu, meinga nga wairua o te hunga pono kua mawehe atu ki a koe, kia okioki i runga i te rangimarie. Kia tiaho mai ano tou maramatanga ki a ratou. Meinga matou kia uru tahi atu me ratou ki tou haringa mutunga kore. Amine.
Minita	Kua mihia nga mate, kua mihia koutou, kua whakawateatia.

Tatou ka huri ki te whakamoemiti ki a Ihowa, ki tana Tama ki to tatou Kai-whakaora; ki te Wairua Tapu ki to tatou Kai-whakamarie; i runga i te waiata e kiia nei ko te Kororia...

Te Kororia

Kororia ki te Atua i runga rawa,
   he maungarongo ki tona iwi i runga i te whenua,

E te Ariki e te Atua, e te Kingi o te rangi,
   e te Atua Kaha rawa e te Matua,
      ka koropiko matou ki a koe, ka whakawhetai,
      ka whakamoemiti ki a koe mo tou kororia.

E te Ariki e Ihu Karaiti, te Tama kotahi a te Matua,
   e Ihowa e te Atua, e te Reme a te Atua,
e waha atu nei i nga hara o te ao:
   tohungia matou,
e noho mai na koe i te ringa matau o te Matua:
   whakarongo mai ki ta matou inoi.

Ko koe anake te Tapu,
ko koe anake te Ariki,
ko koe anake te Runga Rawa,
   e Ihu Karaiti,
   me te Wairua Tapu,
   i roto i te kororia o te Atua Matua.   Amine.

Kawa mo te Kupu

Minita	Kia noho a Ihowa ki a koutou.
Minenga	**Ki a koe ano hoki.**

Te Kaupapa o te Ra

Te Rarangi o te Ra

Te Inoi o te Ra

Kawenata Tawhito

Tuhituhi

*Ka mutu to korero i te Kawenata Tawhito, i teTuhituhi hoki,
ka mea te kai-panui i tenei.*

Kai-panui	**Ko te Kupu tenei a te Ariki.**
Minenga	**Kia whakapaingia te Atua.**

Himene

Rongopai

*Ka panuitia te timatanga o te **Rongopai** ka mea te minenga*

Kia whakapaingia koe e te Ariki.

Ka mutu me mea

Kia whakamoemititia koe e te Karaiti.

Kauwhau

Te Whakapono *Kupu tautoko a te whakaminenga*
kei nga wharangi 494, 496.

Te Inoi Takawaenga *kei nga wharangi 496-498.*

Me waiho te inoi mo te hunga mate ki waho. Kua inoia nga inoi mo ratou i te timatanga.

Te Kawa mo te Hakari

Pirihi	E te whanau, ko tatou te tinana o te Karaiti.
Minenga	**Na te Wairua kotahi tatou i iriiri hei tinana kotahi.**

Pirihi	Kia u ki te kotahitanga o te Wairua, he mea paihere na te rangimarie.
Minenga	**Amine.**

Pirihi   Kua oti te tuhituhi, 'Ki te mauria e koe tau koha ki te ahurewa, a, ka maumahara kua he koe ki tou hoa, waiho tau koha i reira. Maatua houhia te rongo, ka tapae ai i tau koha'.

Minenga   **E te whanau, e nga hoa aroha; mehemea kua he ahau ki tetahi, unuhia taku he me ahau hoki e unu nei i te he o tetahi ki ahau i mua i to koutou aroaro, i te aroaro ano hoki o te Ariki, o te Rangi.**

Pirihi   Ka koa te hunga hohou rongo, ka kiia ratou he tamariki na te Atua. Kia tau te rangimarie o te Atua ki a koutou.

Minenga   **Ki a koe ano hoki.**

Himene

Mo konei te ohaoha, te hohou rongo.

Te Tapae Tuatahi

Pirihi	Nou e Ihowa te wehi, te mana, te ihi, te tapu.
Minenga	**Nau nga mea katoa o te rangi, o te whenua, enei koha ka tapaea atu nei.**

Pirihi   Whakapaoho iho e te Wairua Tapu, e te Atua Ora: Manakohia mai matou me enei koha ka tapaea atu nei.

Te Whakawhetai Nui

Pirihi	Kia ara o koutou ngakau.
Minenga	**Ka ara nei ki te Ariki.**
Pirihi	Kia whakapai tatou ki to tatou Atua.
Minenga	**Ko te mea tika ano tena.**
Pirihi	He mea tika, he mahi whakahari te whakapai atu ki a koe i nga wa katoa, i nga wahi katoa, e Ihowa, e te Matua Kaha Rawa, Ora Tonu: i runga i te ingoa o tau Tama o Ihu Karaiti, o to matou Kai-whakaora.

Ra roto mai i a Ia, waihangatia ana e koe nga mea katoa, me te tangata ano hoki kia rite ki tou te ahua.

Nau matou i whakawatea i te hara i tau tukunga mai i tau Tama, kia whanau mai hei tangata, kia whakamatea i runga i te Ripeka, kia whakaarahia.

Nana matou i meinga ai e koe kia tapu, i tau tukunga mai i tou Wairua Tapu, wairua whakaora.

Koia matou ko te hunga Tapu e okioki nei i roto i a Ia, me te ope whakahirahira o te rangi, ka whakamoemiti ai ki a koe, ka mea.

Minenga   **Tapu, Tapu, Tapu Rawa a Ihowa te Atua o te Mana o te Kaha:**

Kii tonu te rangi me te whenua i tou kororia. Kia hira ake tou nui i runga rawa.

Kia whakapaingia a Ia e haere mai nei i runga i te ingoa o te Ariki:

Kia hira ake tou nui i runga rawa.

Te Inoi Whakatapu Me tuturi

Pirihi anake Kia hira ake te kororia te whakawhetai ki a koe e te Matua Tapu, mou i homai i tau Tama i a Ihu Karaiti hei tino patunga tapu mo te hara o te ao, kia whiwhi ai ki te ora tonu te hunga e manako ana ki a Ia, Nana hoki te whakahau kia maharatia tona matenga a kia hoki mai ra ano Ia. Koia matou e whakarite nei i te kupu tapu a tau Tama a Ihu Karaiti i tana pounga i tenei Hakarameta Tapu:

Waihoki, no te po i mua i tona ripekatanga, ka tango Ia i te Taro, a, ka mutu te whakawhetai ka whawhati, ka hoatu ki ana akonga, a, ka mea: Tangohia, kainga: Ko toku tinana tenei ka tukua nei mo koutou: meinga tenei hei whakamahara ki ahau.

Ka mutu te hapa, ka mau Ia ki te Kapu, a, ka mutu te whakawhetai ka hoatu ki a ratou, ka mea: Inumia tenei e koutou katoa. Ko oku toto enei ka whakahekea mo koutou, mo te tokomaha, hei murunga hara. Meinga tenei i nga inumanga katoatanga, hei whakamahara ki ahau.

No reira e te Matua Tapu, mona i whakaae kia whakamatea Ia ki runga i te ripeka, ka whakareia e koe ki runga rawa, hoatu ana ki a Ia he ingoa kei runga ake i nga ingoa katoa e taea te whakahua i te rangi, i te whenua, i raro i te whenua;
Koia hoki matou ka tuohu ai, ka whakaae ai Ko Ihu Karaiti te Ariki, hei whakakororia i a koe e te Matua Tapu.

Minenga **Kia whakakororiatia koe e Ihu e te Ariki.**
Ka whakaatu matou i tou matenga.
Ka panui i tou whakaaranga,
Ka tatari atu i tou hokinga mai.
Ae ra: Nau mai e Ihu e te Ariki.

Tapae Tuarua

Pirihi

Waihoki e te Matua Aroha, i a matou e tatari atu nei
ki te taenga mai o tou rangatiratanga, tenei matou te
whakarite nei i te ohaki a tau Tama, kia maumahara
ki to matou hokonga ki tenei Taro o te Ora; ki tenei
Kapu o te Whakaoranga. Ahakoa kahore matou e tau,
manakohia mai ra matou, me enei whakamoemiti,
whakawhetai hoki, ka tapaea atu nei.
Whakakiia matou ki tou Wairua Tapu:
Ma tona aroha noa me tona mana e mea matou kia
kotahi kua whakawhiwhia nei ki enei mea tapu, kia
uru atu hoki ki te tinana o Ihu Karaiti.

Minenga

**Ki a koe e te Matua Kaha Rawa,
Te kororia me te honore, te whakanui,
te whakapai,
i konei, i nga wahi katoa;
Inaianei, a, mo ake tonu atu, Amine.**

Inoi a te Ariki

Kua akona nei tatou e to tatou Ariki,
ka inoi tatou

E to matou Matua i te rangi
  Kia tapu tou Ingoa.
  Kia tae mai tou rangatiratanga.
  Kia meatia tau e pai ai
    ki runga ki te whenua,
      kia rite ano ki to te rangi.
Homai ki a matou aianei
  he taro ma matou mo tenei ra.
Murua o matou hara,
  Me matou hoki e muru nei
    i o te hunga e hara ana ki a matou.
Aua hoki matou e kawea kia whakawaia;
  Engari whakaorangia matou i te kino:
Nou hoki te rangatiratanga, te kaha,
  me te kororia,
    Ake ake ake.   **Amine.**

Te Whatiwhatinga i te Taro

Pirihi   Ko te taro e whatiwhatiia nei e tatou,
           he tohanga no te tinana o te Karaiti.

Minenga   **Ko tatou tokomaha he tinana kotahi:**
           no te mea e kai tahi ana tatou i te tinana
           kotahi.

Inoi Whakapapaku

E te Ariki tohu, ehara i te mea he whakapakari
ki a matou mahi tika i haere mai ai matou ki tau tepu
e tu nei, engari he whakaaro ki te nui o au mahi tohu.
Kahore matou e tau hei kohikohi i nga kongakonga
i raro i tau tepu; otira, ko taua Ihowa nei ano koe,

he mahi tuturu nau te atawhai.
Meinga kia tika ta matou kai
i te tinana o tau Tama aroha, o Ihu Karaiti,
kia tika ta matou inu i ona toto,
kia noho tonu ai matou ki roto ki a Ia,
me Ia hoki ki roto i a matou.   Amine.

Te Reme a Te Atua *ko tenei ranei*

E te Reme a te Atua, e waha atu nei i te
hara o te ao, tohungia matou.
E te Reme a te Atua, e waha atu nei i te
hara o te ao, tohungia matou.
E te Reme a te Atua e waha atu nei i te
hara o te ao, whakarongo ki ta matou inoi.

Te Karanga

Pirihi Haere mai koutou, tangohia te tinana me nga toto o to
tatou Ariki o Ihu Karaiti, hei whakamahara i mate Ia
mo koutou. Kainga whakaponotia i roto i o koutou
ngakau, me te whakawhetai ano.

Nga Kupu Toha

Minita Te tinana o to tatou Ariki i tukua mou.
Nga toto o to tatou Ariki i whakahekea mou.

Poroporoaki

Minenga E te Matua aroha, kua manakohia nei matou, kua
whangaia ki enei kai tapu, ara, ki te tinana, ki nga toto
o to matou Kai-whakaora, o Ihu Karaiti hei manaaki,
hei whakakaha i a matou i ona huanga, hei tuitui hoki
i a matou ki a Ia, tetahi hoki ki tetahi. Tenei matou te
whakawhetai nei ki a koe i a matou ka haere atu ki nga
mahi i karangatia e koe.

Tukua matou kia haere i runga i te rangimarie, i a
matou ka whiwhi nei ki tau whakaoranga.

Te Manaakitanga

Pirihi Haeremai, haere,
ki te ao whanui i runga i te rangimarie.
Kia maia, kia kaha.
Kia u ki te mea tika.
Kaua e utua te kino ki te kino
engari manaakitia,
nga hunga e tukino ana i a koe.
Kua riro mai nei i a koutou te marama,
tohaina ki te ao.
Amine.

Ko Tenei Ranei

Kia u ki to koutou Ariki;
mahi atu ki a Ia i runga i te hari
i runga hoki i te mana
o te Wairua Tapu.
Amine.

Ko Tenei Ranei

Kia tau mai ano ki a koutou,
nga manaakitanga a te Atua Kaha Rawa,
a te Matua, a te Tama, a te Wairua Tapu.
Amine.

A Form for Ordering the Eucharist

This rite requires careful preparation by the presiding priest and participants.

It is intended for particular occasions and not for the regular Sunday Celebration of the Eucharist.

The people and presiding priest

Gather in the Lord's Name

Proclaim and respond to the Word of God

The proclamation and response may include readings, music, dance and other art forms, comment, discussion and silence.

A reading from the Gospel is always included.

Pray for the world and the church

Exchange the Peace

Prepare the table and set bread and wine on it

Make Eucharist

The presiding priest gives thanks in the name of the assembly.

The presiding priest uses one of The Great Thanksgivings provided (pages 420, 436, 467, 485), or the following

The Great Thanksgiving

*The following **Great Thanksgiving** may be used either as a framework within which insertions may be made or as a continuous whole.*

The presiding priest says or sings

The Lord is here.
God's Spirit is with us.

Lift up your hearts.
We lift them to the Lord.

Let us give thanks to the Lord our God.
It is right to offer thanks and praise.

The presiding priest gives thanks to God for the work of creation and God's self revelation.

The particular occasion being celebrated may also be recalled.

The following or any other suitable words are used.

It is indeed right, always and everywhere,
to give thanks to you, the true and living God,
through Jesus Christ.
You are the source of life for all creation
and you made us in your own image.

The presiding priest now gives thanks for the salvation of the world through Christ.

The following or any other suitable words are used.

In your love for us
you sent your Son to be our Saviour.
In the fulness of time he became incarnate,
and suffered death on the cross.
You raised him in triumph,
and exalted him in glory.
Through him you send your Holy Spirit
upon your church
and make us your people.

And so, we proclaim your glory, as we say

Holy, holy, holy Lord, God of power and might:
heaven and earth are full of your glory.
Hosanna in the highest.

Then follows

To you indeed be glory, almighty God,
because on the night before he died,
your Son, Jesus Christ, took bread;
when he had given you thanks,
he broke it, gave it to his disciples, and said:
Take, eat, this is my body
which is given for you;
do this to remember me.

After supper he took the cup;
when he had given you thanks,
he gave it to them and said:
This cup is the new covenant in my blood
poured out for you;
do this as often as you drink it
to remember me.

The people may say this or some other acclamation.

Christ has died,
Christ is risen,
Christ will come in glory.

Then follows

Therefore, loving God,
recalling now Christ's death and resurrection,
we ask you to accept
this our sacrifice of praise.
Send your Holy Spirit upon us
and our celebration,
that we may be fed with the body and blood of your Son
and be filled with your life and goodness.

Strengthen us to do your work,
and to be your body in the world.
Unite us in Christ
and give us your peace.

*The presiding priest may add further prayer that all may receive the
benefits of Christ's work and renewal in the Spirit.*

The prayer ends with these or similar words.

All this we ask through your Son
Jesus Christ our Lord,
to whom with you and the Holy Spirit
be all honour and glory,
now and for ever.
Amen.

The people and presiding priest

Break the bread

Share the gifts of God

The bread and wine of the Eucharist are shared reverently.

When all have received, any of the sacrament remaining is then consumed.

Give thanks

Depart in the name of the Lord

Additional Directions
for the Liturgies of the Eucharist

The celebration of the Eucharist is the work of the whole People of God.

*For the community to celebrate as a unity there needs to be a person who focuses and coordinates the community's action. This normally is a priest or bishop, but for **The Ministry of Word and Prayer** may be a deacon or duly authorised lay person.*

*Lay members of the community may be appointed to lead the worship, including reading the Scriptures, leading **The Prayers of the People**, and where authorised administering the communion. However it is the priest's task to pronounce **The Absolution**, lead **The Great Thanksgiving**, and pronounce **The Blessing**.*

In the absence of a priest, a deacon or a lay person in using the form of Absolution or Blessing says 'us' for 'you' and makes any consequential changes.

The presiding priest at the Eucharist should wear a cassock and surplice with stole or scarf, or an alb with the customary vestments.

It is appropriate that the holy table or altar be covered with a clean white cloth during the celebration.

*The bread for the Eucharist should be a good quality bread (either loaf or wafer) and the wine for the Eucharist should be a good quality wine. At **The Preparation of the Gifts** water may be added to the wine.*

The Scriptures may be read in any of the languages used within the Anglican Church in Aotearoa, New Zealand and Polynesia.

*With the **Sentences, Prayers and Readings for the Church's Year**, the readings for Year 1 begin on the First Sunday in Advent in odd-numbered years; in the Three Year Series, the readings for Year A begin on that Sunday in years whose number is divisible by three.*

*It is appropriate that **The Peace** be shared liturgically at the beginning of **The Ministry of the Sacrament** for it constitutes and gathers the eucharistic community for the liturgical action of **The Great Thanksgiving**.*

Care should be taken to ensure that sufficient bread and wine is placed on the holy table for the administration of communion to the people.

If the consecrated bread and/or wine is insufficient for the number of communicants, the presiding priest consecrates more of either or both, saying

Almighty God,
obeying the command of your Son, Jesus Christ,
who took *bread/the cup* and said:
This is my *body/blood*,
we also take this *bread/wine*,
and pray that through your Word and Spirit
it may be for us the sacrament
of the *body/blood* of Christ.
Amen.

Or

E te Atua kaha rawa,
he whakarite i te whakahau a tau Tama, a Ihu Karaiti,
i tango ia i *te taro/te kapu*, a, ka mea:
Ko *toku tinana tenei/oku toto enei*,
Ka tango ano matou *i tenei taro/ tenei waina*,
ka inoi matou i runga i tau Kupu, i tou Wairua,
kia ahei ai *tenei/enei* ki a matou ko te hakarameta
o *te tinana/nga toto* o te Karaiti.
Amine.

Any remaining consecrated bread and wine, unless required for the communion of persons not present, is consumed at the end of the distribution, or immediately after **The Dismissal of the Community**.

When kneeling, sitting, or standing is a particularly appropriate posture, it is indicated within the service.

The Great Thanksgiving is a unity, and either standing or kneeling throughout may be chosen by local custom.

Either standing or kneeling is an appropriate posture when receiving communion in church.

The priest or duly authorised minister gives the bread and the cup into the hands of the people with the appropriate words.

Communion may be received by intinction.

In accordance with Anglican tradition there shall be no celebration of the Eucharist unless at least one other person is present to receive communion with the presiding priest.

The choices of variant material either by addition or by omission shall normally be made by the presiding priest.

On an occasion when there is a small group, the presiding priest or minister and congregation may agree that it is appropriate for the communicants to administer the sacrament to one another.

On Principal Feasts and Holy Days it is appropriate to include **The Gloria in excelsis** and **The Nicene Creed** at weekday celebrations.

Wherever there is a celebration of the Eucharist on a Sunday, the preaching of the Word is an integral part of **The Ministry of the Word**.

A Service of the Word
with Holy Communion

The bishop may authorise a deacon or a lay person to distribute Holy Communion to a congregation from the Sacrament consecrated elsewhere.

Under such circumstances the duly authorised minister, having placed the consecrated bread and wine on the holy table, shall use the following form.

The Ministry of the Word and Prayer

from any of the Eucharistic Liturgies beginning on pages 404, 456 or 476, up to and including **The Affirmation of Faith***.*

Then follow **The Prayers of the People***, not including* **The Lord's Prayer***.*

This prayer follows

Let us give glory to God, our Creator, Redeemer and Sanctifier.
Glory to God in the highest.
Glory to God in the highest.

God our Creator, we thank you for the world you have made;
we thank you for your loving care watching over all creation;
we thank you for entrusting part of your world to us to tend,
to care for and to develop.
Glory to God in the highest.

You have made us, women and men in your image,
so that in each other we can trace your likeness
and serve you by serving our brothers and sisters.
Glory to God in the highest.

You made us to know you and to be near you,
our hearts are restless until we come to you.
To bring us nearer to you when we were still far off,
you sent your prophets and teachers
to show us the glory of your steadfast love.
Glory to God in the highest.

The wonder of your redeeming love was fully shown
in Jesus the Christ, who walked among us as one of us,
meeting us face to face,
person to person, God in human form.
Glory to God in the highest.

Yet we did not value him and sent him to death,
a death he freely accepted,
stretching out his arms on the cross
to embrace the whole human race
and to bear our sin in himself.

By his death and resurrection,
death is destroyed and we are delivered from sin
to share his risen life.
Glory to God in the highest.

You sent your Holy Spirit upon your Church
so that, in Jesus, we are united to you, Father,
with all the redeemed.
Glory to God in the highest.

We thank you that we can worship you
with prayer and praise as one with all your people.
Above all we thank you for this sacrament
of the body and blood of Christ.
Glory to God in the highest.

The minister then invites the people to share the peace, saying

Let us give one another a sign of peace.

The minister continues

E te whanau, we are the body of Christ.
By one Spirit we were baptised into one body.

God, creator of time and space,
may the love and faith which makes
    this bread the body of Christ
    this wine his blood
enfold us now.
Make us one with (the people of ...* and)
the whole body of Christ.
May Christ's Holy Spirit
bring to us in the sacrament
the strength we need,
and an abiding trust
in your gift of eternal life.
Amen.

* The minister refers to the congregation with whom the celebration of the Eucharist took place.

The minister says

Come God's people,
come to receive Christ's heavenly food.

The bread and cup are given to each person in the customary manner with the appropriate words.

The service concludes with the section **Prayer After Communion** *from any* **Liturgy of the Eucharist**, *including* **The Lord's Prayer**, *but omitting the* **Blessing**.

Any consecrated bread or wine remaining shall be reverently consumed by the minister, and the vessels cleansed, either immediately after the administration of communion, or after **The Dismissal of the Community**.

The Ten Commandments

Hear the commandments which God's people
were given through Moses.

You shall have no other gods but me.

You shall not make yourself idols;
you shall not worship them or serve them.

You shall not take the name of the Lord your God in vain.

Remember the sabbath day and keep it holy.

Spirit of God, search our hearts.

Honour your father and your mother.

You shall not murder.

You shall not commit adultery.

You shall not steal.

You shall not bear false witness.

You shall not covet anything which belongs to your neighbour.

Spirit of God, search our hearts.

The response may be used after each commandment.

Nga Ture Kotahi Tekau

Whakarongo ki nga ture na te Atua nei i homai ki te whanau a
Iharaira e tana pononga e Mohi.

*I muri mai i ia ture, i muri mai ranei i te Tuawha i te Tekau, me whakahoki te
Whakaminenga:*

Wairua o te Atua, whakamaramatia o matou ngakau.

Kaua etahi atua ke atu mou i ko atu i ahau.

Kei hanga koe i etahi whakapakoko mou;
    Kei koropiko koe kei mahi ranei ki ena mea.

Kei whakahuatia noatia e koe te ingoa o Ihowa o tou Atua.

Kia mahara ki te ra hapati kia whakatapua.

Whakahonoretia tou papa me tou whaea.

Kaua koe e kohuru.

Kaua koe e puremu.

Kaua koe e tahae.

Kaua koe e whakapae teka.

Kaua koe e hiahia apo ki tetahi mea a tou hoa tata.

Themes for the Church's Year

The Coming of Christ

Advent 1	The coming of the Lord
Advent 2	The hope of Israel
Advent 3	The forerunner
Advent 4	A God near at hand
Christmas	God with us
Christmas 1	A new creation
Christmas 2	The children of God

The Revelation of Christ

Epiphany	Revelation to the gentiles
Epiphany 1	Revelation at baptism
Epiphany 2	Revelation in the childhood of Christ
Epiphany 3	Revelation in Galilee
Epiphany 4	Revelation in transfiguration
Epiphany 5	Revelation in Jerusalem
Epiphany 6	The final revelation

Our Human Condition

Epiphany 7 (Septuagesima)	Creation
Epiphany 8 (Sexagesima)	Human frailty
Epiphany 9 (Quinquagesima)	The promise of redemption
Ash Wednesday	Self denial
Lent 1	Temptation
Lent 2	Repentance
Lent 3	Forgiveness
Lent 4	Refreshment

Passiontide and Holy Week

Lent 5	The Cross - Passion Sunday
Lent 6	The Cross - Palm Sunday
Monday in Holy Week	Cleansing of the temple
Tuesday in Holy Week	Teaching in the temple
Wednesday in Holy Week	Anointing at Bethany
Maundy Thursday	The last supper
Good Friday	The crucifixion
Easter Even	The grave

New Life

Easter Day	Christ is risen
Monday in Easter Week	
Tuesday in Easter Week	
Easter 1	Christ our victory
Easter 2	Christ our shepherd
Easter 3	Christ our light
Easter 4	Christ our prophet
Easter 5	Christ our high priest
Ascension Day	Christ, risen, ascended, glorified
Sunday after Ascension	Christ, sovereign over all
Pentecost	The Spirit poured out
Trinity Sunday(Pentecost 1)	The holy Trinity

The Being of God

Pentecost 2	God's love for us
Pentecost 3	God our strength and support
Pentecost 4	God's righteousness
Pentecost 5	God's call to us
Pentecost 6	God's purpose
Pentecost 7	God's work

Church – The Work of the Holy Spirit

Pentecost 8	The Church, the body of Christ
Pentecost 9	The holy Bible
Pentecost 10	Holy baptism
Pentecost 11	Holy communion
Pentecost 12	Ministry

The Gifts of the Holy Spirit

Pentecost 13	The gift of faith
Pentecost 14	The gift of hope
Pentecost 15	The gift of love
Pentecost 16	The gift of wisdom
Pentecost 17	The fulfilment of life
Pentecost 18	Fear of the Lord
Pentecost 19	Joy in the Lord
Pentecost 20	Prayer in the Lord

Our Life – Our Response to the Holy Spirit

Pentecost 21	Our lives
Pentecost 22	Our homes
Pentecost 23	Our neighbours
Pentecost 24	Our country
Pentecost 25	Our world

Christ and the World

Pentecost 26	Things of eternal worth
Pentecost 27	The two ways
Sunday before Advent	Preparedness

Seasonal Sentences, Prayers, and Blessings for use after Communion

Season of Advent

Sentences

Watch at all times, praying for the strength to stand with confidence before the Son of man.

Luke 21:36

Look up and raise your heads, because your redemption is drawing near.

Luke 21:28

In the wilderness prepare the way of the Lord, make straight in the desert a highway for our God.

Isaiah 40:3

The glory of the Lord shall be revealed, and all the world shall see it together.

Isaiah 40:5

Prepare the way of the Lord, make the paths straight, and all the world shall see the salvation of God.

Luke 3: 4,6

Restore us again O God: show us the light of your face and we shall be saved.

Psalm 80:3

Prayers

Creator God,
We praise you for your love in coming to us,
unworthy though we are.
Give us grace to accept the Christ who comes in your name,
and the courage to be Christ for others.

We praise and thank you, Creator God,
for you have not left us alone.
Each year you come to us, Emmanuel,
God with us in a manger.
Each time you come to us
in the broken bread and the cup we share.
In time or out of time you will be revealed
and we shall see you face to face.

Give us courage, God our strength,
to see your Christ in all who suffer,
to be hands to the helpless,
food for the hungry,
and rescue for the oppressed.

Blessings

One of the following or some other appropriate introduction to the blessing is said.

May Christ, as he comes, deliver you from your guilt, anxiety and resentment...

May Christ be our new beginning, the hope and salvation of the world...

Christ the sun of righteousness shine upon you and scatter the darkness from before your path...

Followed by

...and the blessing of God almighty, Father, Son and Holy Spirit, be with you and remain with you for ever.
Amen.

Or

...and the blessing of God our Creator, Redeemer and Giver of life be with you always.
Amen.

Season of Christmas

Sentences

The Word became flesh, and dwelt among us, and we have seen his glory.

John 1:14

The bread of God is the one who comes down from heaven and gives life to the world.

John 6:33

Be not afraid; for behold, I bring you good news of a great joy which will come to all people; for to you is born this day in the city of David a Saviour, who is Christ the Lord.

Luke 2:10,11

Put on the new nature, created after the likeness of God in true righteousness and holiness.

Ephesians 4:24

How great is the love that the Father has shown to us! We were called God's children, and such we are.

1 John 3:1

Prayers

Son of Mary, Son of God,
may we, for whom the heavens have opened
never lose that heavenly vision.
May we, who like the shepherds,
have seen in your birth a new kind of love,
witness to that love in our lives.

Welcome, welcome, Jesus Christ our infant saviour,
baby who makes every birth holy.
May we, who like the shepherds
have witnessed in the stable a new kind of love
return to our work with joy.
May we, for whom the heavens have opened
to proclaim that God is with us,
we who have fed on living bread
and drunk the wine of heaven,
go out to be instruments of your peace, day by day.

Father of all,
the child born for us is the Saviour of the world.
May he who made us your children
welcome us into your kingdom,
where he is alive and reigns with you now and for ever.

Blessings

One of the following or some other appropriate introduction to the blessing is said.

May Christ our infant saviour give you the joy of the Bethlehem shepherds, the awe of the worshipping sages and the humility and love of the holy family. May you become as little children...

Christ, who by his incarnation, gathered into one all things earthly and heavenly, fill you with joy and peace...

Christ the Son of God, born of Mary, fill you with grace to trust his promises and obey his will...

May Christ the Prince of Peace give you his peace...

Followed by

...and the blessing of God almighty, Father, Son and Holy Spirit, be with you and remain with you for ever.
Amen.

Or

...and the blessing of God our Creator, Redeemer and Giver of life be with you always.
Amen.

Season of Epiphany

Sentences

Arise, shine; for your light has come, and the glory of the Lord has risen upon you.

Isaiah 60:1

A voice came from heaven, saying, 'This is my beloved Son with whom I am well pleased.'

Matthew 3:17

O Lord my God you are great indeed, you are clothed in majesty and splendour. You cover yourself with light as it were with a garment.

Psalm 104:1,2

I have seen it myself, and bear witness, that this is the chosen one of God.

John 1:34

Jesus said, 'I am the light of the world; those who follow me will not walk in darkness, but will have the light of life.'

John 8:12

Prayers

Praise to you, Jesus Christ,
God in human form.
You show us the fulness of life;
help us to find this life for ourselves
and for others.

Thanksgiving and love and praise to you Jesus Christ.
You are God revealed in human form;
you are the baby visited by the shepherds,
the boy in the temple learning the law;
the man baptised in water and the Spirit
driven to the desert to face the devil.
You are Christ the teacher, Christ the healer.
You went to Jerusalem to give your life
as a ransom for us all.

May we who have been your guests
at this communion
reveal your life to all the world.
May we be no longer your servants,
but know your will,
and be your friends.
You give us your life, may we be worthy of it;
you give us yourself, may we embody you.

Gracious God, lover of all,
by this sacrament
you make us one family in Christ your Son,
one in the sharing of his body and blood,
one in the communion of his Spirit.
Help us to grow in love for one another
and come to the full maturity of the body of Christ.
We ask this in his name.

God of glory,
you nourish us with bread from heaven.
Fill us with your Holy Spirit,
that through us your light may shine in all the world.
We ask this in the name of Jesus Christ.

Blessings

One of the following or some other appropriate introduction to the blessing is said.

May Christ's star in heaven bring you to humility and worship, bring you to look upon God at work...

May Christ's bright star enlighten your mind and heart as you strive for equality, justice and kindness in the world...

Christ the Son be manifest to you, that your lives may be a light to the world...

...and the blessing of God almighty, Father, Son and Holy Spirit, be with you and remain with you for ever.
Amen.

Or

...and the blessing of God our Creator, Redeemer and Giver of life be with you always.
Amen.

Season of Lent

Sentences

The sacrifice acceptable to God is a broken spirit: a broken and contrite heart O God you will not despise.   *Psalm 51:17*

Create in me a clean heart O God: and renew a right spirit within me.   *Psalm 51:10*

Be kind to one another, tenderhearted, forgiving one another, as God in Christ forgave you.   *Ephesians 4:32*

Jesus said: 'I am the living bread which came down from heaven; whoever eats of this bread, will live for ever; and the bread which I shall give for the life of the world is my flesh.'   *John 6:51*

We do not live on bread alone, but on every word that comes from the mouth of God.   *Matthew 4:4*

Unless a grain of wheat falls on the ground and dies, it remains a single grain; but, if it dies, it yields a rich harvest.   *John 12:24*

Far be it from me to glory except in the cross of our Lord Jesus
Christ, through which the world has been crucified to me and I to
the world.

Galatians 6:14

If we claim to be sinless, we are self-deceived, and strangers to the
truth. If we confess our sins God is just, and may be trusted to
forgive our sins, and cleanse us from every kind of wrong.

1 John 1:8,9

Prayers

Jesus our only Saviour,
you renounced the way of ease
for the way of truth and life.
Draw us to seek God's kingdom
whatever the cost,
for the sake of the true treasure in heaven.

Praise and glory to you, Jesus Christ our Saviour,
for you do not call the righteous
but us sinners to repentance.
You draw us away from the easy road
that would lead to our destruction.
You call us instead to seek God's kingdom,
to strive for what is right,
and to lay up our treasure in heaven.

Faithful God,
in this communion
you increase our faith and hope and love.
Lead us in the path of Christ
who is your Word of life.

God of our pilgrimage,
we have found the living water.
Refresh and sustain us
as we go forth on our journey,
in the name of Jesus Christ.

Blessings

One of the following or some other appropriate introduction to the blessing is said.

May Christ who calls you to take up your cross, give you strength to bear your own and one another's burdens...

Christ give you grace to grow in holiness, to deny yourself, and to take up your cross and follow him...

followed by

...and the blessing of God almighty, Father, Son and Holy Spirit, be with you and remain with you for ever.
Amen.

Or

...and the blessing of God our Creator, Redeemer and Giver of life be with you always.
Amen.

Holy Week

Sentences

Christ became obedient unto death, even death on a cross.

Philippians 2:8

All of us like sheep have gone astray, and we have turned to our own way; but the Lord has caused the iniquity of us all to fall on him.

Isaiah 53:6

Jesus our Lord was given up to death for our misdeeds, and raised to life to justify us.

Romans 4:25

The Son of man came not to be served but to serve, and to give his life as a ransom for many.
Matthew 20:28

Whoever serves me, must follow me; and where I am, there shall my servant be also; the Father will honour anyone who serves me.
John 12:26

Christ our passover lamb has been sacrificed.
1 Corinthians 5:7

For as often as we eat this bread and drink this cup we proclaim the death of the Lord until he comes.
1 Corinthians 11:26

Out of love for the world God gave the only Son, that whoever believes in him should not perish but have eternal life.
John 3:16 (adapted)

If while we were God's enemies we were reconciled by the death of God's Son, much more, now that we are reconciled, shall we be saved by his life.
Romans 5:10

As Moses lifted up the serpent in the wilderness, so must the Son of man be lifted up, that whoever believes in him may have eternal life.
John 3:14

Prayers

Jesus, you suffered on the cross for our redemption;
help us, if we are called to suffer,
to be like you:
to forgive and to trust
in the power of the Holy Spirit.

Jesus, Son of God, our true and only Saviour:
you died on the cross, a criminal under a curse;
you are God who forgives.
You died helpless, a failure and in pain.
You are God with whom there is hope;
you showed us the greatest love there is;
for you died for us with the passover lambs.

Help us to forgive as you have forgiven us.
Help us to trust you, even when hope is failing.
Help us, if we are called to suffer,
to take up our cross
and to follow you in your redeeming work.

God of our salvation,
in this eucharist
you have renewed us in your covenant.
Help us to follow in the path of him
who came to open the eyes of the blind
and bring prisoners out of darkness.

Almighty and eternal God,
you have restored us to life
by the triumphant death
and resurrection of Christ.
Continue this healing work within us.
May we who partake of this mystery
never cease to give you dedicated service.

Blessings

One of the following or some other appropriate introduction to the blessing is said.

May Christ the crucified convince you that God loves you and has forgiven you...

May the cross carry you through whatever pain and suffering assails you. May you go forward with courage in the faith of Christ...

Christ crucified draw you to himself...

May you find in the cross a sure ground for faith, a firm support for hope, and the assurance of sins forgiven...

Followed by

...and the blessing of God almighty, Father, Son and Holy Spirit, be with you and remain with you for ever.
Amen.

Or

...and the blessing of God our Creator, Redeemer and Giver of life be with you always.
Amen.

The Season of Easter

Sentences

Christ our passover lamb has been sacrificed for us; therefore let us keep the feast with the unleavened bread of sincerity and truth. Alleluia.
1 Corinthians 5: 7,8

Jesus said to his disciples, 'Come and eat'; and he took bread, and gave it to them. Alleluia.
John 21:12,13

The disciples knew the Lord Jesus in the breaking of the bread. Alleluia.
Luke 24:35 (adapted)

Thanks be to God who gives us the victory through our Lord Jesus Christ.
1 Corinthians 15:57

All you who have been baptised have been clothed with Christ. Alleluia.
Galatians 3:27

Set your minds on things that are above, and not on things that are on the earth. For you have died, and your life is hidden with Christ in God. Alleluia.

Colossians 3:2,3

Prayers

Christ, you are risen from the dead.
We are risen with you.
May our life never deny
this eternal life,
this peace and hope and joy.
Praise and glory to the God of life
who is stronger than all kinds of death. Alleluia.

Christ, you are risen with the sun;
you are light in our darkness,
warmth in our cold.
You are peace and hope and joy,
for you went willingly to death.
You turned defeat and failure to victory for all.
You live eternally, and with you live the millions,
living and dead, who trust in you.

May we who in baptism die to sin,
rise again to new life
and find our true place in your living body.
May the new covenant sealed in your blood
through us bring healing and reconciliation
to this wounded world.
Alleluia. You are risen. We are risen with you.
Praise and glory to the living God.

Father,
we have seen with our eyes
and touched with our hands
the bread of life.
Strengthen our faith
that we may grow in love for you and for each other;
through Jesus Christ the risen Lord.

Blessings

One of the following or some other appropriate introduction to the blessing is said.

May Christ who out of defeat brings new hope and new alternatives, bring you new life...

May you be a new creation, Christ for those to whom Christ shall send you...

May Christ, who by death has destroyed death, give you all courage and joy in believing...

The God of peace,
who by the blood of the eternal covenant
brought again from the dead our Lord Jesus Christ,
that great shepherd of the sheep,
make you perfect in every good work;
working in you that which is pleasing and good...

The God of peace who brought again from the dead our Lord Jesus, that great shepherd of the sheep, make you perfect in every good work to do his will...

God the Father, by whose glory Christ was raised from the dead, strengthen you to walk with him in his risen life...

God, who through the resurrection of our Lord Jesus Christ has given us the victory, give you joy and peace in your faith...

Followed by

...and the blessing of God almighty, Father, Son and Holy Spirit, be with you and remain with you for ever.
Amen.

Or

...and the blessing of God our Creator, Redeemer and Giver of life be with you always.
Amen.

Ascension

Sentences

Jesus said, 'I am with you always, to the end of the world.'

Matthew 28:20

We have a great high priest who has passed into the heavens, Jesus
the Son of God.

Hebrews 4:14

The disciples worshipped Jesus and went back to Jerusalem full of
joy; and were continually in the temple, praising God.

Luke 24: 52,53

Sing praises to God's holy name: make a highway for the one who
rides on the clouds, whose name is the Lord, in whose presence
exult.

Psalm 68:4

Prayers

King of kings, Lord of lords,
you have ascended your royal throne
carrying the crossbar for your crucifixion.
Now you are lifted high,
exalted to draw us all to your love.
You are the captive saviour,
who has led us in triumph
from the sin, the anxiety, and the doom
which held us captive.
May we whom you have redeemed
and called to be guests at your table
receive and put to use the gifts you offer us.
Praise and glory to you, God of space and time,
humble saviour, king of love.

Give praise to God,
for the risen Christ is with us now
in power and majesty,
in grace and peace.
May we live in him as he lives in the glory
of the eternal Trinity.

Eternal Giver of love and power,
your Son Jesus Christ has sent us into all the world
to preach the gospel of his kingdom.
Confirm us in this mission,
and help us to live the good news we proclaim.

Blessings

One of the following or some other appropriate introduction to the blessing is said.

May Christ, who is human and divine, who is of heaven and also of earth, lift up your hearts, lift up your lives to God...

Christ make you faithful and strong to do his will that you may reign with him in glory...

Followed by

...and the blessing of God almighty, Father, Son and Holy Spirit, be with you and remain with you for ever.
Amen.

Or

...and the blessing of God our Creator, Redeemer and Giver of life be with you always.
Amen.

The Day of Pentecost   Whitsunday

Sentences

The disciples were all filled with the Holy Spirit, and spoke of the great things God had done.

Acts 2: 4,11

God's love has been poured into our hearts through the Holy Spirit which has been given to us.

Romans 5:5

The wind blows where it wills and you hear its sound, but do not know where it comes from or where it is going; so it is with everyone born of the Spirit.

John 3:8

Prayers

God of power,
may the boldness of your Spirit transform us,
may the gentleness of your Spirit lead us,
may the gifts of your Spirit
be our goal and our strength
now and always.

Praise and glory to you creator Spirit of God;
you make our bread Christ's body
to heal and reconcile
and to make us the body of Christ.
You make our wine Christ's living sacrificial blood
to redeem the world.
You are truth.
You come like the wind of heaven, unseen, unbidden.
Like the dawn
you illuminate the world around us;
you grant us a new beginning every day.
You warm and comfort us.
You give us courage and fire
and strength beyond our every day resources.
Be with us Holy Spirit in all we say or think,
in all we do this and every day.

Father,
may we who have received this sacrament
live in the unity of your Holy Spirit,
that we may show forth your gifts to all the world.
We ask this in the name of Jesus Christ.

Blessings

One of the following or some other appropriate introduction to the blessing is said.

May Christ's holy, healing, enabling Spirit be with you every step of the way, and be your guide as your road changes and turns…

The Spirit of truth lead you into all truth, give you grace to confess that Jesus Christ is Lord, and to proclaim the word and works of God…

Followed by

…and the blessing of God almighty, Father, Son and Holy Spirit, be with you and remain with you for ever.
Amen.

Or

…and the blessing of God our Creator, Redeemer and Giver of life be with you always.
Amen.

Sentences for the Sundays after Pentecost

We are children of God, so God has sent the Spirit into our hearts.

Galatians 4:6

We are the body of Christ and individually members of it.

1 Corinthians 12:27

Jesus said, 'The bread of life is that which comes down from heaven, and gives life to the world.' *John 6:33*

Through faith we are all children of God in union with Christ Jesus. *Galatians 3:26*

God has given us eternal life, and this life is in Jesus the Son. Anyone who has the Son has life. *1 John 5:12*

We look not to the things that are seen but to the things that are unseen; for the things that are seen are transient, but the things that are unseen are eternal. *2 Corinthians 4:18*

Additional Blessings

One of the following or some other appropriate introduction to the blessing is said.

Trinity Sunday

God the Holy Trinity, make you strong in faith and love, defend you, and guide you in truth and peace...

Saints

God give you grace to follow the saints in faith and hope and love...

God give you grace to follow the saints in faith and truth and gentleness...

May the saints inspire and encourage you...

All Saints

May Christ who makes saints of sinners, who has transformed those whom we remember today, raise and strengthen you that you may transform the world...

General

The God of all grace who called you to eternal glory in Christ Jesus, restore establish and strengthen you in the faith...

The peace of God which passes all understanding keep your hearts and minds in Christ Jesus...

The peace of God which passes all understanding keep your hearts and minds in the knowledge and love of God, and of his Son Jesus Christ our Lord...

Christ who has nourished us with himself, the living bread, make you one in praise and love, and raise you up at the last day…

The God of hope fill you with all joy and peace in believing…

Followed by

…and the blessing of God almighty, Father, Son and Holy Spirit, be with you and remain with you for ever.
Amen.

Or

…and the blessing of God our Creator, Redeemer and Giver of life be with you always.
Amen.

Alternative Blessings

Ma te marie a te Atua e kore nei e taea te whakaaro e tiaki o koutou ngakau o koutou hinengaro i roto i a Karaiti Ihu; a kia mau kia u hoki ki a koutou te manaaki a te Atua Kaha Rawa, a te Matua, a te Tama, a te Wairua Tapu aianei a ake tonu atu.
Amine.

May God whom Jesus called Abba embrace you in love for ever;
may God the Servant bear your burdens with you;
may God the Paraclete grant you life in one another:
so may the blessing of God,
Abba, Servant, Paraclete,
be with you always.
Amen.

Alternative Dismissal of the Community

When more appropriate this Dismissal may be used in any liturgy.

Grace and peace remain with you,
and keep you in the love of Christ.
Amen.

Easter

the Sundays afte

Sentences, Prayers and Readings for the Church's Year

advent
christmas
Epiphany
Lent
Holy week
Pentecost

Concerning Sentences, Prayers and Readings for the Church's Year

The minister chooses one or more of the Collects set down for the Day for use in the service, and selects the Sentence, Psalms, and Set Readings either from pages 550-690 or according to the Three Year Series on pages 691-723.

At the end of a Collect, when needed, the minister may add

Hear this prayer for your love's sake. **Amen.**

Or Praise to you our God; you answer prayer. **Amen.**

Or *when the prayer is addressed to God*

This we ask through Christ our Mediator/ Saviour/ Redeemer/ Lord. **Amen.**

Or *when the prayer is addressed to God and ends with words referring to Jesus Christ*

Who lives and reigns with you and the Holy Spirit, one God for ever. **Amen.**

Seasons and Sundays

The Season of Advent

The First Sunday in Advent

The coming of the Lord

Sentence

To you Lord I lift up my soul; my God I have put my trust in you;
you are God my Saviour; for you have I waited all the day long.

Psalm 25:1,4

Collects

God of hope,
when Christ your Son appears
may he not find us asleep or idle,
but active in his service and ready.

Come, O come Emmanuel,
you are the way, the truth and the life;
you are the true vine and the bread of life.
Come, living Saviour,
come to your world which waits for you.

Almighty God,
give us grace to cast off the works of darkness
and put on the armour of light,
now in the time of this mortal life,
in which your Son Jesus Christ came to us in great humility;
so that when he shall come again in his glorious majesty
we may rise to the life immortal;
through him who lives and reigns with you
and the Holy Spirit,
one God now and for ever.

Psalms   96;   50

Readings

1 Isaiah 40:1-8   The way of the Lord
  Romans 13:11-14   The night is far spent
  Matthew 25:31-45   The Lord comes as judge

2 Amos 5:18-24   The day of the Lord
  Revelation 1:4-8   Behold he is coming
  Matthew 24:1-14   Signs of the end

The Second Sunday in Advent

The hope of Israel

Sentence

You are the Holy One enthroned on the praises of your people.
Our ancestors trusted in you and you delivered them; they put
their trust in you and were not disappointed.   *Psalm 22:3-5*

Collects

Praise and honour to you, living God;
you chose the Hebrew people
and brought them step by step
to look for a redeemer, and hope for the Christ.
Give us grace to see our need
and recognise salvation when it comes.

God of Israel old and new,
write in our hearts the lessons of your law;
prepare our minds to receive the gospel
made visible in your Son Jesus Christ.

Living God, you called your people out of Egypt
and gave them the covenant;
prepare our hearts to hear your call,
so that we may receive with joy the gospel of your Son
and be your faithful people,
now and for ever.

Psalms   40:1-11;   63

Readings

1 Isaiah 11:1-10   The messianic king
    1 Peter 1:10-16   The hope of the prophets
    Luke 4:14-30   Fulfilment of the prophecy

2 Isaiah 2:2-5   The coming reign of peace
    Romans 9:30-10:4   The Law brought to an end
    John 5:33-47   Moses wrote of me

The Third Sunday in Advent

The forerunner

Sentence

In the wilderness prepare the way of the Lord, make straight in
the desert a highway for our God.   *Isaiah 40:3*

Collects

God for whom we wait and watch,
you sent John the Baptist
to prepare for the coming of your Son;
give us courage to speak the truth
even to the point of suffering.

Almighty God,
you sent your servant John the Baptist
to prepare the way for the coming of your Son;
grant that those who proclaim your word
may so guide our feet into the way of peace,
that we may stand with confidence before him
when he comes in his glorious kingdom;
through Jesus Christ our Judge and our Redeemer.

Praise and honour to you living God for John the Baptist,
and for all those voices crying in the wilderness
who prepare your way.
May we listen when a prophet speaks your word, and obey.

Psalms   75;   119:41-48

Readings

1 Malachi 3:1-5   The messenger of the covenant
   1 Corinthians 4:1-5   Ministers and stewards
   Matthew 11:2-19   More than a prophet

2 Malachi 4   I will send you Elijah
   Acts 13:13-25   After me one is coming
   John 3:22-30   Sent before him

The Fourth Sunday in Advent

A God near at hand

Sentence

You heavens above rain down righteousness; let the clouds
shower it down. Let the earth open wide, let salvation spring up.

Isaiah 45:8

Collects

God of all hope and joy,
open our hearts in welcome,
that your Son Jesus Christ at his coming
may find in us a dwelling prepared for himself;
who lives and reigns with you and the Holy Spirit,
one God now and for ever.

Praise and honour to you living God;
your coming will be like a thief in the night,
like lightning flashing across the sky.
Grant that we may be ready,
and our hearts answer, Come Lord Jesus.

God faithful and true,
make us eager with expectation,
as we look for the fulfilment of your promise
in Jesus Christ our Saviour.

Psalms   89:1-36;   94

Readings

1 Zechariah 2:10-13   Lo, I come
   2 Peter 3:8-13   The coming day of God
   Matthew 25:1-13   Prepared or unprepared

2 Isaiah 51:1-6   God's coming victory
   1 Thessalonians 5:12-24   Blameless at Christ's coming
   Matthew 3:1-12   Wheat and chaff

The Season of Christmas

The Birth of our Lord Jesus Christ
Christmas

God with us

Sentence

The Word became flesh and dwelt among us, full of grace and truth; we have seen his glory, glory as of the only Son from the Father.

John 1:14

Collects

AT MIDNIGHT
Son of God, light that shines in the dark,
child of joy and peace,
help us to come to you
and be born anew this holy night.

Almighty God,
you make us glad with the yearly festival
of the birth of your Son, Jesus Christ,
the light of the world;
grant that we,
who have known the revelation of that light on earth,
may see the radiance of your heavenly glory;
through Jesus Christ our Lord,
who lives and reigns with you and the Holy Spirit,
one God now and for ever.

Welcome Jesus, our humble gentle Saviour,
welcome to Bethlehem,
where we have loved and fought
and longed for the peace
the world can never give.
We ask for your peace, your love, your gentleness,
and the courage to live that way.

Almighty God,
you gave your only-begotten Son
to take our nature upon him,
and be born of the Virgin Mary;
grant that we, who have been born again
and made your children by adoption and grace,
may daily be renewed by your Holy Spirit;
through our Saviour Jesus Christ,
who lives and reigns with you and the Holy Spirit,
one God now and for ever.

Son of God, Child of Mary,
born in the stable at Bethlehem,
be born again in us this day
that through us the world may know
the wonder of your love.

Psalms   19;   85

Readings

AT MIDNIGHT

Micah 5:2-4   A ruler from Bethlehem
Titus 2:11-14   Grace for salvation
Luke 2:1- 16   The birth of the Saviour

IN THE DAY

Isaiah 7:10-14   His name Emmanuel
Hebrews 1:1-9   God has spoken to us
John 1:1-14   The Word made flesh

Isaiah 9:1-2,6-7   To us a child is born
Colossians 1:11-20   The image of the invisible God
Matthew 1:18-25   The birth of the Saviour

The First Sunday after Christmas

A new creation

Sentence

I will cause a righteous branch to spring forth for David; and he
shall execute justice and righteousness in the land.   Then Judah
will be saved and Jerusalem will dwell securely.   *Jeremiah 33:15,16*

Collects

God in Trinity,
Creator, Saviour, Giver of life and truth,
reveal the possibilities within us,
that we may attain to the fulness of our humanity.

As we are glad, Creator God,
when the dawn reveals the world to us,
innocent and fresh,
so may we discover the infant in the manger,
and in delight be ready to start anew.

O God,
you wonderfully created
and yet more wonderfully restored
the dignity of human nature;
grant that we may share the divine life
of your Son Jesus Christ,
who lives and reigns with you
in the unity of the Holy Spirit,
one God now and for ever.

Psalms   8;   45

Readings

1 Jeremiah 31:31-34   A new covenant
    Galatians 4:1-7   Adoption as children of God
    Or
    Ephesians 4:17-24   Created in God's likeness
    Luke 13:10-17   Christ brings freedom

2 Ezekiel 11:17-20   A new spirit
    2 Corinthians 5:17-21   A new creation
    Mark 2:18-22   New wineskins for new wine

The Second Sunday after Christmas

The children of God

Sentence

Jesus went down with his parents and came to Nazareth, and was
obedient to them; and his mother kept all these things in her heart.
And Jesus increased in wisdom and stature, and in favour with
God and the people.   *Luke 2:51,52*

Collects

Eternal God, giver of love and peace,
you call your children to live together as one family;
give us grace to learn your ways
and to do your will,
that we may bring justice and peace to all people,
in the name of Jesus Christ,
who lives and reigns with you and the Holy Spirit
one God now and for ever.

Heavenly Father, tender and compassionate,
create in us, your family, love so true and deep
that in this broken world
we may be a sign of unity.

Look on your family our God,
and teach us to care for one another,
for you are child and parent,
you alone are love's source and secret.

Psalms   128;   133

Readings

1	Isaiah 43:1-7	The return of the family
	1 John 3:1-3	Children of God
	Mark 3:31-35	The members of Christ's family
2	Jeremiah 31:7-9	Restoration of the family
	Romans 8:27-39	First born among many children
	Matthew 2:19-23	Return from Egypt

The Season of the Epiphany

The Epiphany of our Lord Jesus Christ

Revelation to the Gentiles

Sentence

The Lord whom you seek will suddenly come to his temple; the messenger of the covenant in whom you delight is coming, says the Lord of hosts.   *Malachi 3:1b*

Collects

Jesus, as we travel far and fast,
lead our minds back to the wise men following your star,
and forward to the day
when all will see your shining light.

Jesus, light of the world,
let your bright star stand over the place
where the poor have to live;
lead our sages to wisdom and our rulers to reverence.

O God, by the leading of a star
you revealed your Son Jesus Christ to the gentiles;
grant that your Church may be a light to the nations,
so that the whole world may come to see
the splendour of your glory;
through Jesus Christ our Lord.

Psalms   72;   96

Readings

1 Isaiah 60:1-6   Nations shall come to
                                                your light
   Romans 15:5-13   The hope of the gentiles
   Matthew 2:1-12   Wise men from the east

2 Isaiah 49:5-7   Kings shall see and arise
   Ephesians 3:1-12   To preach to the gentiles
   Luke 13:22-30   From east and west

The Baptism of the Lord
The First Sunday after the Epiphany

Revelation at baptism

Sentence

My people, I took you from the ends of the earth, from its farthest
corners I called you. I said, 'You are my servant, I have chosen you
and not rejected you.'
Isaiah 41:8,9

Collects

Almighty God,
you anointed Jesus at his baptism
with the Holy Spirit,
and revealed him as your beloved Son;
grant that we who are baptised into his name
may give up our lives to your service,
and be found worthy of our calling;
through Jesus Christ our Lord.

Open the heavens, Holy Spirit,
for us to see Jesus interceding for us;
may we be strengthened to share his baptism,
strengthened to share his cup,
and ready to serve him forever.

Holy Spirit,
as you drove Jesus into the wilderness,
when John baptised him and the heavens opened,
drive us to wrestle and reflect
so that we may fulfil our baptism,
and live your life of victory.

Psalms   2;   36

Readings

1 Isaiah 42:1-7   God's chosen one
  Galatians 3:23-29   Baptised into Christ
  Mark 1:1-15   The baptism of Jesus

2 Isaiah 61:1-4   Anointed by the Spirit
  Acts 8:26-40   Philip baptises
  John 1:26-42   The baptism of Jesus

The Second Sunday after the Epiphany*

Revelation in the childhood of Christ

Sentence

We call to mind your steadfast love, O God, in the midst of your
temple. As your name is great O God, so is your praise to the ends
of the earth.   *Psalm 48:9,10*

Collects

Jesus, your ways are not our ways.
You are the Jewish boy,
you are the questioning child the parents lost.
Make us willing to listen
and humble in what we believe is right.

Holy and eternal God,
your Son Jesus Christ has taught us
to learn from the simple trust of children;
give us pure hearts and steadfast faith
to worship you in spirit and in truth;
through Jesus Christ our Lord.

Jesus,
you saw the world through the eyes of a child.
Save us from the pride
that would refuse your command to live like you
in simplicity and joy.

Psalms   119:1-8;   131

Readings

1 Exodus 2:1-10   The birth of Moses
   1 Corinthians 1:18-25   Strength and wisdom of God
                                         in Christ
   Luke 2:41-52   The child in the temple

2 1 Samuel 3:1-18   God's word to a child
   1 Corinthians 1:25-31   God chose what is weak
   Matthew 18:1-14   The greatest in the kingdom

---

* When there are fewer than 9 Sundays after the Epiphany, the 6th, 5th, 4th, 3rd and 2nd are omitted as far as necessary.

The Third Sunday after the Epiphany

Revelation in Galilee

Sentence

With awesome deeds you answer our prayers for deliverance,
O God our Saviour; you that are the hope of all the ends of the
earth, and of the far off seas. *Psalm 65:5,6*

Collects

God of all mercy,
your Son brought good news to the despairing,
freedom to the oppressed
and joy to the sad;
fill us with your Spirit,
that the people of our day may see in us his likeness
and glorify your name.

Jesus, our Redeemer,
give us your power to reveal and proclaim the good news,
so that wherever we may go
the sick may be healed, lepers embraced,
and the dead and dying given new life.

Almighty God,
your Son revealed in signs and wonders
the greatness of your saving love;
renew your people with your heavenly grace,
and in all our weakness
sustain us by your mighty power;
through Jesus Christ our Lord.

Psalms   65;   111

Readings

1 Isaiah 52:7-10   Good tidings
   Acts 10:34-43   Beginning from Galilee
   John 2:1-11   The sign at Cana of Galilee

2 2 Kings 5:1-14   Sign of a prophet
   Acts 3:1-10   Jesus Christ of Nazareth
   John 4:46-54   The second sign in Galilee

The Fourth Sunday after the Epiphany

Revelation in transfiguration

Sentence

One thing I have asked of the Lord, which I long for, that I may
dwell in the house of the Lord all the days of my life, to gaze on
your beauty O Lord and to seek you in your temple.   *Psalm 27:4,5*

Collects

Jesus, your justice goes beyond the ancient law,
your wisdom embodies all prophetic insight;
make us glad to be yours,
and able to follow you to Jerusalem.

God of life and glory,
your Son was revealed in splendour
before he suffered death upon the cross;
grant that we, beholding his majesty,
may be strengthened to follow him
and be changed into his likeness from glory to glory;
for he lives and reigns with you and the Holy Spirit,
one God now and for ever.

God of glory,
you gave the vision of your Son
to those who watched on the mountain;
grant that by our glimpses of him
we may be changed into his glorious likeness.

Psalms   27;   97

Readings

1 Exodus 24:12-18   Moses on the mountain
   2 Peter 1:16-21   Eyewitnesses of
                               Christ's majesty
   Luke 9:28-36   The transfiguration

2 Exodus 34:29-35   Moses' face shone
   2 Corinthians 3:7-18   Beholding the glory
                               of the Lord
   Mark 9:2-13   The transfiguration

The Fifth Sunday after the Epiphany

Revelation in Jerusalem

Sentence

You Lord will surely comfort your people. You will make their
deserts like Eden, their wastelands like a garden. Joy and gladness
will be found among them, thanksgiving and the sound of singing.

Isaiah 51:3 (adapted)

Collects

Merciful God,
in Christ you make all things new;
transform the poverty of our nature
by the riches of your grace,
and in the renewal of our lives
make known your heavenly glory;
through Jesus Christ our Redeemer.

Jesus our Lord,
you have taught us that judgment begins at the house of God;
save us from our self-satisfaction, rigidity and corruption,
so that we may stand ready to do your will.

Jesus, when you call us to challenge authority,
help us to follow closely your example,
that we may be ready to suffer for the truth,
and to give whatever glory there may be to God.

Psalms 48; 119:73-80

Readings

1 Jeremiah 4:11-18   A warning to Jerusalem
   Hebrews 11:13-16   The city God has prepared
   John 2:13-22   Jesus cleanses the temple

2 Jeremiah 26:1-16   A prophecy against Jerusalem
   Romans 11:25-36   A hardening of Israel
   John 11:45-57   The plot against Jesus

The Sixth Sunday after the Epiphany

The final revelation

Sentence

The earth shall be full of the knowledge of the glory of the Lord,
as the waters cover the sea.   *Habakkuk 2:14*

Collects

Lord Jesus Christ,
before whose judgment seat we shall appear;
enable us to see ourselves as you see us,
to repent and to change,
and to be found worthy to bear your name.

Jesus, Saviour in storm,
when the waters of the deep are broken up,
when the landmarks are washed away or drowned,
come to us across the water.

Everloving God,
your Son was revealed that he might overcome evil
and make us heirs of eternal life;
grant that we who have this hope in us
may purify ourselves as he is pure,
that when he appears in power and great glory,
we may be made like him,
to the honour of your name;
for he lives and reigns with you and the Holy Spirit,
one God now and for ever.

Psalms   50;   98

Readings

1 Hosea 2:16-23   The crown of love
  Hebrews 4:9-16 The sabbath rest
  Matthew 24:23-28 Christ revealed to all

2 Isaiah 41:8-14   Called from the ends
            of the earth

  Hebrews 2:9-18 Brought to glory
  Mark 13:28-37   Alert for his coming

The Seventh Sunday after the Epiphany
Septuagesima

Creation

Sentence

O Lord how manifold are your works; in wisdom you have made
them all; the earth is full of your creatures.   *Psalm 104:25*

Collects

God, you have made our world and seen that it is good;
grant to us, created to complete your work,
the bright, delightful vision that makes us care for what we do.

God of unchangeable power,
when you fashioned the world
the morning stars sang together
and the host of heaven shouted for joy;
open our eyes to the wonders of creation
and teach us to use all things for good,
to the honour of your glorious name;
through Jesus Christ our Lord.

You made us Lord, and we are yours;
grant that we may so use your gifts
that all your creatures may enjoy the harmony you planned.

Psalms 8; 147

Readings

1	Genesis 8:15-22	The covenant with Noah
	1 Timothy 4:1-6	Everything created by God is good
	John 5:1-19	My Father is working still
2	Genesis 1:26-31	We are made in God's image
	Revelation 21: 1-7	All things made new
	Mark 7:31-37	He has done everything well

The Eighth Sunday after the Epiphany
Sexagesima

Human frailty

Sentence

Be merciful to me O Lord, for I call to you all the day long; for you Lord are good and forgiving, and of great mercy to all who call upon you.   *Psalm 86:3,5*

Collects

Have pity Father, on us your estranged and wilful children;
grant that we may know the things we ought to do
and have grace to do them;
through Jesus Christ, your Son.

Christ, you are the second Adam,
the first in a reborn humanity;
take from us our inborn greed and pride
and make us whole.

God of grace and goodness,
you know that by reason of our frailty we cannot but fail;
keep us always under your protection
and lead us to all things profitable to our salvation;
through Jesus Christ our Lord.

Psalms   53;   51

Readings

1 Genesis 3:1-8   Human disobedience
   Romans 5:12-21   The first Adam and the second
   Mark 7:14-23   Defilement from within

2 Genesis 3:8-19   The curse upon disobedience
   Romans 8:1-8   Set free in Christ
   John 8:31-47   A slave to sin

The Ninth Sunday after the Epiphany
Quinquagesima

The promise of redemption

Sentence

The ransomed of the Lord will return; everlasting joy will crown
their heads; gladness and joy will overtake them, and sorrow and
sighing will flee away.

Isaiah 51:11

Collects

Christ our Redeemer,
you have crushed the serpent's head;
you have freed us from our sin;
rescue all your suffering world from the evil
that attracts us still.

God of compassion,
deepen and increase our love for you
so that we may leave behind the sins
from which you have redeemed us,
and serve you in perfect freedom.

Almighty God,
the Redeemer of all who trust in you;
give heed to the cry of your people,
deliver us from the bondage of sin
that we may serve you in perfect freedom
and rejoice in your unfailing love;
through Jesus Christ our Saviour.

Psalms   115;   20

Readings

1	Zechariah 8:1-8	A promise of deliverance
	Titus 3:1-7	He saved us
	Luke 19:1-10	Salvation to the house of Zacchaeus

2	Jeremiah 32:36-41	I will bring them back
	Romans 6:9-23	From death to life
	Matthew 12:22-28	Satan's power overthrown

The Season of Lent

Ash Wednesday
The First Day of Lent

Sentence

Examine me O God and know my heart, test me and discover my
thoughts, and lead me in the way everlasting.   *Psalm 139:23,24*

Collects

Jesus, holy and strong,
by your fasting and temptation teach us self-denial;
control and discipline us,
that we may learn to obey.

Almighty and merciful God,
you hate nothing that you have made
and forgive the sins of all who are penitent;
create in us new and contrite hearts,
so that when we turn to you and confess our sins
we may receive your full and perfect forgiveness;
through Jesus Christ our Redeemer.

God of the desert, as we follow Jesus into the unknown,
may we recognise the tempter when he comes;
let it be your bread we eat,
your world we serve and you alone we worship.

Psalms   51;   6

Readings

The First Sunday in Lent

Temptation

Sentence

Lord be gracious to us; we long for you. Be our strength every
morning; our salvation in time of distress.   *Isaiah 33:2*

Collects

Hear us, Jesus Christ, when we ask
for help to recognise temptation,
for honesty to face it,
for strength to resist it and the humility to give God the glory.

Almighty God,
your Son Jesus Christ fasted forty days in the wilderness;
give us grace to direct our lives in obedience to your Spirit;
and as you know our weakness
so may we know your power to save;
through Jesus Christ our Redeemer.

God, you know better than we
the temptations that will bring us down.
Grant that our love for you may protect us
from all foolish and corrupting desire.

Psalms   36;   39

Readings

1 Ecclesiasticus 2:1-11   All subject to temptation
   Or
   Job 1:6-22   Job resists temptation
   James 1:2-15   Enduring trial
   Or
   Galatians 6:1-10   Bear each other's burdens
   Matthew 26:36-46   A safeguard against temptation

2 Job 2:1-10   Job put to the test
   Romans 7:15-25   The struggle against sin
   Luke 4:1-15   The temptation of Jesus

The Second Sunday in Lent

Repentance

Sentence

Rend your hearts and not your garments; turn back to the Lord
your God who is gracious and compassionate, long-suffering and
abounding in love.
                                                    Joel 2 :13

Collects

Almighty God,
give your people grace to withstand
the temptations of the world, the flesh and the devil,
and with pure hearts and minds to follow you,
the only true God;
through Jesus Christ our Saviour.

God of the unexpected,
when we come to our senses like the prodigal son,
give us grace to repent and turn to you again;
for where else can we go?

Gentle Father,
show us our sins as they really are
so that we may truly renounce them
and know the depth and richness of your mercy.

Psalms   32;   141

Readings

1 Ezekiel 18:20-24   If the wicked turn
     1 John 1:5 - 2:2   Self-deceit in sin
     Luke 15:11-32   The prodigal son

2 Job 42:1-6   The repentance of Job
     Or
     Isaiah 59:9-16   We long for God to save us
     Acts 2:36-42   Preaching repentance
     Matthew 21:23-32   A disobedient son repents

The Third Sunday in Lent

Forgiveness

Sentence

We have rebelled against the Lord our God who still shows mercy
and forgiveness.   *Daniel 9:9*

Collects

God of infinite mercy,
grant that we who know your pity
may rejoice in your forgiveness
and gladly forgive others
for the sake of Jesus Christ our Saviour.

God our light,
make your Church like a rainbow
shining and proclaiming to all the world
that the storm is at an end,
there is peace for those who seek it
and love for the forgiving.

Merciful God,
grant to your faithful people pardon and peace;
that we may be cleansed from all our sins
and serve you with a quiet mind;
through Jesus Christ our Redeemer.

Psalms   15;   103

Readings

1 Genesis 50:15-21   Joseph forgives his brothers
   Colossians 3:12-17   Forgive each other
   Matthew 18:21-35   The unmerciful servant

2 Hosea 14:1-7   The healing of Israel
   Colossians 2:6-15   Cancelling the bond
   Or
   1 Timothy 1:12-17   Christ Jesus came
                                to save sinners
   Luke 6:27-38   The forgiving spirit

The Fourth Sunday in Lent

Refreshment

Sentence

They will neither hunger nor thirst, nor will the desert heat or the
sun beat upon them, for the One who loves them will lead them
and guide them beside the springs of water.   *Isaiah 49:10 (adapted)*

Collects

Heavenly Father,
you see how your children hunger for food,
and fellowship, and faith.
Help us to meet one another's needs of body, mind and spirit,
in the love of Christ our Saviour.

O God, giver of life and health,
your Son Jesus Christ has called us
to hunger and thirst to see right prevail;
refresh us with your grace
that we may not be weary of well-doing;
for the sake of him who meets all our needs,
our Saviour Jesus Christ.

God of the the hungry,
make us hunger and thirst for the right,
till our thirst for justice has been satisfied
and hunger has gone from the earth.

Psalms   23;   4

Readings

1 1 Kings 17:1-16   Food from God
   Acts 11:19-30   Relief of the hungry
   John 6:1-15   Feeding the multitude

2 Isaiah 55:1-7   Buy and eat without money
   2 Corinthians 9:6-15   God loves a cheerful giver
   John 6:24-35   Bread from heaven

The Fifth Sunday in Lent
Passion Sunday

Sentence

Is it nothing to you, all you who pass by? Look and see if there is
any sorrow like my sorrow.   *Lamentations 1:12*

Collects

Most merciful God,
by the passion of your Son Jesus Christ
you delivered us from the power of darkness;
grant that through faith in him who suffered on the cross
we may be found acceptable in your sight,
through our Saviour Jesus Christ.

Jesus crucified, despised and suffering,
you made yourself one with us.
Help us to follow you and bear the shame.

Jesus, they hung you on a cross
because you love sinners.
Save us from our self-righteousness
and from our contempt for those who differ from us.

Psalms   130;   51

Readings

1 Numbers 21:5-9   The healing serpent
   Or
   Genesis 32:22-32   Jacob wrestles with God
   Ephesians 2:11-18   Brought near through the
                                  blood of Christ

   John 3:11-21   The Son of man lifted up

2   Lamentations 3:19-33   Suffering in hope
    Hebrews 13:7-16   Jesus also suffered
    Luke 18:18-34   Going up to Jerusalem

The Sixth Sunday in Lent
Palm Sunday

The Cross

Sentence

Hosanna to the Son of David! Blessed is he who comes in the name
of the Lord! Hosanna in the highest!   *Matthew 21:9*

Collects

Jesus, when you rode into Jerusalem
the people waved palms
with shouts of acclamation.
Grant that when the shouting dies
we may still walk beside you even to a cross.

Almighty and everliving God,
in your tender love towards us
you sent your Son to take our nature upon him,
and to suffer death upon the cross;
grant that we may follow the example
of his great humility
and share in his glorious resurrection;
through him who lives and reigns
with you and the Holy Spirit,
one God now and for ever.

Lord Jesus,
acclaimed as king,
crucified as a criminal,
teach us to accept our sufferings and triumphs
for your glory alone.

The following may also be used every day during Holy Week.

Assist us mercifully, Lord God of our salvation,
to contemplate those mighty acts
by which you have given us life and immortality;
through Jesus Christ our Lord.

Psalms   118:19-26;   22

Readings

1 Zechariah 9:9-10   Your King comes
   Philippians 2:3-11   He emptied himself
   Mark 11:1-11   The triumphal entry
   Or
   Luke 19:28-46

Or one of the accounts of the passion of Christ
Mark 15:1-39; Luke 23:1-49

2 Isaiah 62:6-7, 10-12   Your salvation comes
   Romans 5:1-11   Christ died for us
   Matthew 21:1-13   Blessed is he who comes
   Or
   John 12:12-19

Or one of the accounts of the passion of Christ
Matthew 27:11-54; John 18:28 - 19:37

Holy Week
Monday in Holy Week

Cleansing of the temple

Sentence

My soul is thirsting for you O God, thirsting for the living God;
when shall I come to appear in your presence?   *Psalm 42:2*

Collects

Teach us, Jesus,
how to live and worship
without being worldly or greedy.
Drive from our lives what spoils them
and make us temples of the Spirit.

Jesus, you spoke with passion,
you acted without fear, and we remember.
Help us when we have to speak out,
to speak the truth
and without malice to speak.

Gracious and merciful God,
for our sake your Son became incarnate
and suffered death upon the cross;
purify our hearts and grant us zeal in your service;
through Jesus Christ our Redeemer.

Psalms   54;   26

Readings

Isaiah 56:6-8   A house of prayer for
                                                 all nations
1 Corinthians 3:10-17   You are God's temple
Mark 11:15-18   The temple cleansed

Tuesday in Holy Week

Sentence

Listen to me, my people, and give ear to me, my nation; for a law
shall go forth from me; and my justice for a light to the peoples.

Isaiah 51:4

Collects

When all we are and everything we do
are called into question,
grant us dignity and direction,
grant us patience;
Jesus, be there then.

Gracious and merciful God,
for our sake your Son became incarnate
and suffered death upon the cross;
have mercy on all who have not known you
or who deny the faith of Christ crucified,
and take from us all hardness of heart
and contempt of your word;
for the sake of our Saviour Jesus Christ.

God,
you have made known your love
through Jesus' life and words.
Help us to receive his teaching,
to find the fulness of that love
and bring its fragrance to others.

Psalms   31;   88

Readings

Ezekiel 3:4-11   Rebellious house
Ephesians 4:25 - 5:2   He gave himself up for us
Luke 22:47-53   Daily in the temple

Wednesday in Holy Week

Anointing at Bethany

Sentence

Hear me, you that know what is right, the people in whose heart
is my law; fear not those who reproach you, and be not dismayed
at their insults.   *Isaiah 51:7*

Collects

Gracious and merciful God,
for our sake your Son became incarnate
and suffered death upon the cross;
give us grace to choose him as master and king
who for us was crowned with thorns
and died in shame,
and now lives and reigns with you
and the Holy Spirit,
one God for ever and ever.

Jesus the anointed,
teach us to honour those who need our help,
and we shall give without condescension,
and receive with humility.

Jesus,
receive our love and worship.
Show us how to give you what we have,
for nothing is too big or small
for us to offer, or for you to use.

Psalms   43;   23

Readings

    Isaiah 50:4-9   A sufferer unafraid
    2 Corinthians 2:14-17   Fragrance of Christ
    Matthew 26:1-15   Anointing for burial

Maundy Thursday

The Last Supper

Sentence

We are to glory in the cross of our Lord Jesus Christ, through which
the world has been crucified to us, and we to the world.

Galatians 6:14 (adapted)

Collects

Gracious God,
we praise you for this sacrament,
the gift of your Son to his Church.
As we share this supper together
may we know his strength
and enter the fulness of his life and love.

Infinite, intimate God;
this night you kneel before your friends
and wash our feet.
Bound together in your love,
trembling, we drink your cup
and watch.

Gracious and merciful God,
in a wonderful sacrament you have given us
a memorial of the passion of your Son
Jesus Christ;
grant that we who receive these sacred mysteries
may grow up into him in all things
until we come to your eternal joy;
through our Saviour Jesus Christ.

Everlasting God,
your Son Jesus Christ girded himself with a towel
and washed his disciples' feet;
grant us the will to be the servant of others
as he was servant of all,
who gave up his life and died for us,
yet lives and reigns with you
and the Holy Spirit,
one God now and for ever.

Psalms 56; 27

Readings

	Exodus 12:1-14	The passover meal
	1 Corinthians 11:23-29	The new covenant in my blood
1	Mark 14:12-31	The account of the last supper
	Or	
	Luke 22:7-23	
2	John 13:1-35	The account of the last supper
	Or	
	Matthew 26:17-35	

Good Friday

The Crucifixion

Sentence

O my people, what have I done to you? In what have I wearied
you? Answer me! For I redeemed you from the house of bondage,
that you may know the saving acts of the Lord.   Micah 6:3-5

Collects

Gracious and eternal God,
look with mercy on this your family
for which our Lord Jesus Christ was willing
to be betrayed into the hands of his adversaries
and to suffer death upon the cross;
and grant us to rejoice
in the benefits of his passion;
through him who lives and reigns
with you and the Holy Spirit,
one God now and for ever.

Lord Jesus Christ,
as we kneel at the foot of your cross,
help us to see and know your love for us,
so that we may place at your feet
all that we have and are.

Lord Jesus Christ,
crucified for us,
we kneel at the foot of your cross to watch with you.
Help us to see the cost of our forgiveness
so that we may be made new through your love.

Almighty and everlasting God,
by your Spirit the whole body of the Church
is governed and sanctified;
hear the prayers we offer
for all your faithful people,
that in the particular ministry
to which you have called us,
we may serve you in holiness and truth;
through Jesus Christ our Saviour.

Crucified saviour, naked God,
you hang disgraced and powerless.
Grieving, we dare to hope,
as we wait at the cross
with your mother and your friend.

God of all the world
whose Son was born a Jew,
have mercy on your ancient people;
on all who have not known you
or deny the faith of Christ crucified.
Fetch us home to your fold
so that we become one flock
under one shepherd,
Jesus Christ our Lord.

Merciful God,
creator of all the peoples of the earth
and lover of every soul;
have compassion on all who do not know you,
let your gospel be preached with grace and power
to those who have not heard it,
turn the hearts of those who oppose it,
and bring home to your fold
all who have gone astray;
through Jesus Christ our Lord.

Psalms   22;   40

Readings

1 Isaiah 52:13 - 53:12   Wounded for our
                                                         transgressions

   Hebrews 10:4-18   The true sacrifice
   Mark 15:6-41   The crucifixion
   Or
   Luke 23:13-49

   Or the complete account of the passion may be read
   Mark 14: 32 - 15:41
   Or
   Luke 22:24 - 23:49

2 Genesis 22:1-18   The offering of Isaac
   Hebrews 9:11-15,24-28   Redeemed by his blood
   John 19:1-37   The crucifixion
   Or
   Matthew 27:15-56

   Or the complete account of the passion may be read
   John 18:1 - 19:37
   Or
   Matthew 26:36 - 27:56

Holy Saturday
Easter Eve

The grave

Sentence

When we were baptised into Christ Jesus, we were baptised into
his death; so that as Christ was raised from the dead by the glory
of the Father, we too might walk in newness of life.   *Romans 6:3,4*

Collects

We remember, O God,
the grief of the disciples when Jesus died.
Lead us beyond our fear of death
to the joyful knowledge of eternal life
in him who lives for ever.

Eternal God, give us a sure and certain trust
for those who are with Christ.
When our loved ones come to die,
beyond our sorrow,
grant us confidence and hope.

Grant O God,
that we who are baptised into the death
of your Son Jesus Christ,
may continually die to sin
and be buried with him,
that through the grave and gate of death
we may pass to our joyful resurrection;
for his sake, who died and was buried
and rose again for us,
your Son our Saviour Jesus Christ.

Psalms   30;   142

Readings

	Job 19:23-27a	Vindication after death
	1 Peter 3:18-22	The spirits in prison
1	Mark 15:42-47	The burial of Jesus
	Or	
	Luke 23:50-56	
2	John 19:38-42	The burial of Jesus
	Or	
	Matthew 27:57-66	

The Season of Easter

Easter Eve

Collects

Lord of the passover,
you have lit this night with the radiance of Christ;
renew in us our baptism,
and bring us through the Red Sea waters
to the promised land.

Lord God,
you have made this night bright with the radiance of the risen
    Christ;
may we who have been raised with him in baptism
reflect the light of his glory,
and live with him for ever.

Easter Day

Sentence

Alleluia! The Lord is risen indeed. To him be glory and dominion
for ever and ever. Alleluia!   *Luke 24:34; Revelation 1:6*

Collects

Glorious Lord of Life,
we praise you,
that by the mighty resurrection of your Son,
you have delivered us from sin and death
and made your whole creation new;
grant that we who celebrate with joy
Christ's rising from the dead,
may be raised from the death of sin
to the life of righteousness;
through him who lives and reigns
with you and the Holy Spirit,
one God now and for ever.

Jesus Christ our Saviour,
you have delivered us
from death and sin.
You have brought with the dawn
a new beginning and an empty tomb;
grant us strength and humility
to enter into life.

Living Christ, you are risen from the dead!
Love reigns!
You are life stronger than death;
raise our eyes to see you
as the new day dawns.

Almighty God,
through your Son Jesus Christ
you overcame death and opened to us
the gate of everlasting life;
grant us so to die daily to sin,
that we may evermore live with him
in the joy of his resurrection;
who lives and reigns with you
and the Holy Spirit,
one God now and for ever.

Psalms   16;   113

Readings

1 Exodus 12:21-32   The Passover
   Colossians 3:1-10   Risen with Christ
   Mark 16:1-8   He is risen
   Or
   Luke 24:1-12

2 Exodus 14:21-31   Saved from the Egyptians
   1 Corinthians 15:12-26   In Christ all made alive
   John 20:1-18   He is risen
   Or
   Matthew 28:1-10

Monday in Easter Week

Sentence

Did not the Christ have to suffer these things and then enter his
glory? Alleluia!
                                                    Luke 24:26

Collects

of Easter Day

Psalms   16:8-12;   118:19-24

Readings

Deuteronomy 4:32-40   The Lord has done all this
Acts 3:11-16   God raised Jesus from death
John 21:1-14   It is the Lord

Tuesday in Easter Week

Sentence

Jesus showed himself to his disciples and gave many convincing
proofs that he was alive. Alleluia!   *Acts 1:3*

Collects

of Easter Day

Psalms   33:13-21;   105:1-8

Readings

Isaiah 42:8-13   The power of the Lord
                                            revealed

Revelation 1:10-18   Alive for evermore
Mark 16:9-15,20   The risen Lord

The First Sunday after Easter

Sentence

Let us give thanks to the Father who has qualified us to share in
the inheritance of the saints in light. Alleluia!

Colossians 1:12 (adapted)

Collects

Eternal Father,
through the resurrection of your Son,
help us to face the future
with courage and assurance,
knowing that nothing in death or life
can ever part us from your love.

Jesus, we believe you; all we heard is true.
You break the bread; we recognise you,
you are the fire that burns within us;
use us to light the world.

Almighty God,
by the glorious resurrection of your Son Jesus Christ
you have broken the power of death
and brought life and immortality to light;
grant that we who have been raised with him
may triumph over all temptation
and rejoice in the hope of eternal glory;
through him who lives and reigns with you
and the Holy Spirit,
one God now and for ever.

Psalms   93;   57

Readings

1 Zephaniah 3:14-20   Bringing Israel home in victory
   1 John 5:1-12   The world overcome
   Luke 24:13-35   Journey to Emmaus

2 Isaiah 25:1-8   God will swallow up death
   1 Corinthians 15:42-58   God gives us the victory
   John 20:19-31   The risen Lord

The Second Sunday after Easter

Christ our shepherd

Sentence

In your constant love, O Lord, you have led the people whom you
ransomed; you have guided them by your strength to your holy
dwelling-place.   *Exodus 15:13*

Collects

Good Shepherd of the sheep,
by whom the lost are sought
and guided into the fold;
feed us and we shall be satisfied,
heal us and we shall be whole,
and lead us that we may be with you,
with the Father and the Holy Spirit.

God of mercy, we are as Peter;
we lose our nerve
and deny you in the time of trial.
Calm our anxiety, heal our cowardice,
take away our shame, and make us free.

God of peace,
by the blood of the eternal covenant
you brought again from the dead our Lord Jesus,
that great shepherd of the sheep;
make us perfect in every good work,
and work in us that which is pleasing and good;
through Jesus Christ to whom be glory for ever and ever.

Psalms   23;   100

Readings

1 Ezekiel 34:11-16   God the shepherd
   1 Peter 2:18-25   Our shepherd and guardian
   John 10:11-18   The good shepherd

2 Isaiah 40:9-11   He will feed his flock
   Hebrews 13:16-21   Pastoral leadership
   John 10:1-10   He calls his own sheep by
                             name

The Third Sunday after Easter

Christ our light

Sentence

Shine forth from your throne upon the cherubim; restore us O God;
show us the light of your face and we shall be saved.

Psalm 80:1,3

Collects

God, you are the first light
cutting through the void.
You are the final light
which we shall enjoy forever.
Help us to welcome the light and walk in it always.

We praise you, God,
that the light of Christ shines in our darkness
and is never overcome;
show us the way we must go to eternal day;
through Jesus Christ our Lord.

Almighty God,
you show to those who are in error
the light of your truth
that they may return into the way of righteousness;
may we and all who have been admitted
into the fellowship of Christ's religion
reject those things which are contrary
to our profession
and follow all that is agreeable to it;
through Jesus Christ our Lord.

Psalms   27;   80

Readings

1   Isaiah 60:18-20   The Lord our light
    2 Corinthians 4:1-11   The light of Christ
    John 9:1-11   The light of the world

2   Exodus 13:17-18, 21-22   A pillar of fire
    Ephesians 5:1-16   Christ shall give you light
    John 8:12-20   The testimony of the light

The Fourth Sunday after Easter

Christ our prophet

Sentence

Jesus said, If you dwell within the revelation I have brought, you
are indeed my disciples; you shall know the truth, and the truth
shall make you free.   *John 8:31,32*

Collects

Eternal God,
your Son Jesus Christ
is the way, the truth and the life for all creation;
grant us grace to walk in his way,
to rejoice in his truth,
and to share his risen life;
who lives and reigns with you and the Holy Spirit,
one God now and for ever.

Word of God,
sharper than a two-edged sword,
penetrate our lives to expose our secrets
and the world's secret sins;
open us to cleansing and to cure.

Living God,
for whom no door is closed,
no heart is locked,
draw us beyond our doubts,
till we see your Christ
and touch his wounds
where they bleed in others.

Psalms   119:9-16;   87

Readings

1 Deuteronomy 18:15-19   A second Moses
   Acts 3:17-26   A prophet like Moses
   John 9:13-33   He is a prophet

2 Ezekiel 37:1-14   Life out of death
   1 John 1:1-7   The life made manifest
   Luke 7:11-17   A great prophet has arisen

The Fifth Sunday after Easter

Christ our high priest

Sentence

Without having seen Christ you love him; though you do not now
see him you believe in him and rejoice with unutterable and
exalted joy.

1 Peter 1:8

Collects

Holy God, you feed us
with earthly and with spiritual food.
Deathless, unalterable, you have chosen us,
sinful as we are,
to hear your word and to proclaim your truth.
Alleluia! Make us salt of the earth;
make us yeast in the loaf.

Almighty God,
your Son our Saviour Jesus Christ
ever lives to make intercession for us;
have pity on our weakness,
and in your mercy give us those good things
which we are not worthy to ask,
except through his merits,
who lives and reigns with you
and the Holy Spirit,
one God for ever and ever.

Christ our great high priest,
you understand our weakness;
you pray for us while we are sinners.
Help us, through you,
to find a new and living way to God.

Psalms   110;   99

Readings

1   Genesis 14:14-16, 18-20   A priestly king
    Hebrews 4:14 - 5:10   A great high priest
    John 17:1-19   Christ's prayer for his disciples

2   Exodus 29:38-46   Sacrifice and priesthood
    Hebrews 10:11-25   We have a great priest
    John 14:1-14   The way, the truth, and the life

Ascension Day

Christ risen, ascended, glorified

Sentence

Lift up your heads you gates! Lift yourselves up you everlasting
doors! that the King of Glory may come in.   *Psalm 24:7*

Collects

The heavens are open wide
since Jesus our brother, our Redeemer,
has entered through the veil.
We thank you for his new and living way,
by which we join the unnumbered millions
who are with you forever.

Eternal God,
by raising Jesus from the dead
you proclaimed his victory,
and by his ascension
you declared him king.
Lift up our hearts to heaven
that we may live and reign with him.

Eternal and gracious God,
we believe your Son our Saviour Jesus Christ
to have ascended with triumph
into your kingdom in heaven;
may we also in heart and mind
ascend to where he is,
and with him continually dwell;
who lives and reigns with you and the Holy Spirit,
one God now and forever.

Psalms   47;   24

Readings

1 Daniel 7:13-14   Dominion and glory and
                                                    a kingdom
     Ephesians 1:15-23   Seated at God's right hand
     Luke 24:44-53   He parted from them

2 2 Kings 2:1-12a   Elijah taken up into heaven
     Acts 1:1-11   The ascension
     Matthew 28:16-20   Authority in heaven
                                                    and earth

The Sunday after Ascension Day

Christ, sovereign over all

Sentence

Blessing and honour, glory and might, to the one who is seated on
the throne and to the lamb for ever and ever!   *Revelation 5:13*

Collects

Eternal God, the king of glory,
you have exalted your only Son
with great triumph to be Lord of all;
leave us not comfortless
but send your Holy Spirit to strengthen us
that we may labour for the coming of your kingdom;
through Jesus Christ our Lord,
who lives and reigns with you
and the Spirit,
one God now and for ever.

Jesus Christ, you left your disciples,
only that you might send the Holy Spirit
to be our advocate.
Grant us the Spirit of truth
to convince the world
that you are risen from the dead.

Eternal God,
you have given your Son authority
in heaven and in earth;
grant that we may never lose
the vision of his kingdom
but serve him with hope and joy.

Psalms   67;   72

Readings

1 Ezekiel 43:1-5   The glory of the Lord
   Revelation 5   Worthy is the Lamb
   Matthew 28:16-20   All authority in heaven
                                         and earth

2 Jeremiah 23:5-8   He shall reign as king
   Acts 7:52-60   Stephen's vision
   John 17:20-26   To see God's glory

The Day of Pentecost
Whitsunday

Sentence

The love of God has been poured into our hearts through the Holy
Spirit who has been given to us.   *Romans 5:5*

Collects

Father,
you have filled your people with the Spirit
who rested first on your Son
and united us in your Church;
open the channels for your Spirit
that we may freely work together,
and your kingdom and your rule increase.

Almighty God,
you kindled this day the light of your Spirit
in the hearts of your faithful people;
may we by the same Spirit
have a right judgment in all things,
and evermore rejoice in your love and power;
through Jesus Christ our Saviour,
who lives and reigns with you
and the Holy Spirit,
one God now and for ever.

Living God, eternal Holy Spirit,
let your bright intoxicating energy
which fired those first disciples
fall on us
to turn the world again.

Almighty God,
at the feast of Pentecost
you sent your Holy Spirit to the disciples,
filling them with joy and boldness
to preach the gospel;
send us out in the power of the same Spirit
to witness to your redeeming love
and draw all people to you;
through Jesus Christ our Lord,
who lives and reigns with you
and the Holy Spirit,
one God now and for ever.

Psalms   29;   48

Readings

1 Joel 2:23-29   The promise
    Acts 2:1-12   Pentecost
    John 14:15-29   The Paraclete

2 Ezekiel 36:23-28   I will put my Spirit within you
    Galatians 5:16-26   The fruit of the Spirit
    John 15:26 - 16:11   The Spirit of truth

The Season after Pentecost

Trinity Sunday
The First Sunday after Pentecost

The holy Trinity

Sentence

You O Lord reign for ever; your throne endures from generation
to generation.   *Lamentations 5:19*

Collects

God of unchangeable power,
you have revealed yourself
to us as Father, Son and Holy Spirit;
keep us firm in this faith
that we may praise and bless your holy name;
for you are one God now and for ever.

Trinity of love,
maker of man and woman in your image,
help us to accept ourselves as we are,
and to know our need for each other.

Father,
you sent your Son to bring us truth
and your Spirit to make us holy;
open our hearts to exalt you,
open our lives to reveal you,
our one true God,
Father, Son and Holy Spirit.

Eternal and glorious God,
you dwell in a high and holy place,
yet draw us near in your beloved Son;
we humble ourselves before you
and pray that we may know your loving presence,
Creator, Redeemer, and Life-giver
our one true God for ever.

Psalms   97;   86

Readings

1 Isaiah 6:1-8   A vision of God
   Revelation 4   The throne in heaven
   John 16:12-15   Jesus speaks of his Father
                                              and the Spirit

2 Deuteronomy 10:17 - 11:1   God of gods and Lord of lords
   1 Thessalonians 1:1-10   Servants of the living God
   John 4:5-26   Worship the Father in spirit
                                              and in truth

The Second Sunday after Pentecost

God's love for us

Sentence

You, O Lord, are our Father. We are the clay, you are the potter;
we are all the work of your hand.   *Isaiah 64:8*

Collects

Abba God, we call you Father,
and your care for us
is motherly as well.
Protect our power to love and be loved,
and make us glad to be called your children,
one whanau in Christ.

Loving God,
in Jesus you gather us into your family;
confidently we call you Father;
may your Spirit bring us to share
the glorious liberty of your children.

Almighty God,
you have sent the Spirit of your Son into our hearts
and set us free from bondage to sin;
give us grace to dedicate our freedom to your service,
that we and all people may be brought
to the glorious liberty of the children of God;
through Jesus Christ our Lord.

Psalms   113;   92

Readings

1 Jeremiah 31:1-6   God's constant love
  Romans 8:9-17   Abba! Father
  Matthew 7:7-14   Giver of all good things

2 Isaiah 45:9-12   The Creator likened to father
                    and mother
  2 Corinthians 1:3-7   The Father of mercies
  Matthew 11:25-30   My yoke is easy

The Third Sunday after Pentecost

God our strength and support

Sentence

There is none like the God of the upright, who rides on the heavens
to help you and on the clouds in majesty. The eternal God is your
refuge, and underneath are the everlasting arms.

Deuteronomy 33:26,27 (adapted)

Collects

God our friend, you never change,
you are always here.
When we are lonely or helpless
you watch over us.
Hear us,
be with us, as you were with your Son,
alone on his cross.

Mighty God,
strong, loving and wise,
help us to depend upon your goodness
and to place our trust in your Son.

God of unchangeable power,
our strength at all times;
guard us from all dangers
and support us in all difficulties
that we may live victoriously now and forever;
through Jesus Christ our Saviour.

Psalms   121;   18:1-20

Readings

1 Isaiah 26:1-4, 7-9   An everlasting rock
2 Thessalonians 2:13 - 3:5   The Lord is faithful
Matthew 6:25-34   Do not be anxious

2 Deuteronomy 8:11-18   Preservation in the wilderness
1 Peter 5:6-11   Cast all your anxieties on God
Matthew 14:22-36   Where is your faith?

The Fourth Sunday after Pentecost

God's righteousness

Sentence

Give due honour to God's holy name, bring offerings and enter the
courts of the Lord; for you O Lord are coming to judge the earth;
with righteousness you will judge the world and the peoples with
your truth.   *Psalm 96:8,13*

Collects

God of all power and might,
the author and giver of all good things,
graft in our hearts the love of your name,
increase in us true religion,
nourish in us all goodness,
and of your great mercy
keep us in the same;
through Jesus Christ our Lord.

Holy God,
before your face all sin must stand condemned;
help us to know our sins and to repent of them;
so may we find salvation in the cross
and mercy on the day of judgment.

Almighty God, you alone are our true judge,
for you know what we are,
you know what we should be,
and with you there is mercy.
Give us feeling for what is right;
set us on fire to see that right is done.

Psalms   76;   19

Readings

1 Isaiah 32:14-20   Righteousness and justice
      Romans 10:1-10   The message of faith
      Luke 18:9-14   True righteousness

2 Isaiah 51:4-8   God's victory will be final
      Romans 3:21-26   God's righteousness shown
      John 5:19-29   The judgment of the Son

The Fifth Sunday after Pentecost

God's call to us

Sentence

In Christ we have been given our share in the heritage, as was
decreed in God's design, whose purpose is everywhere at work.

Ephesians 1:11

Collects

Lord of the Church,
you have called us to witness in every nation.
May we do your work and bear your cross,
await your time and see your glory.

Call us to you, Jesus,
like Martha from her kitchen,
like Zacchaeus from the tree,
to hear and to do your will.

Almighty God,
you have called us to serve you,
yet without your grace
we are not able to please you;
mercifully grant that your Holy Spirit
may in all things direct and rule our hearts;
through Jesus Christ our Lord.

Psalms   50:1-15;   27

Readings

1 Jeremiah 1:4-10   The prophet's call
    1 Corinthians 1:26 - 2:5   God's choice
    Mark 1:14-22   Calling the apostles

2 Exodus 3:1-12   The call of Moses
    2 Timothy 1:8-14   Called with a holy calling
    Luke 5:27-35   Calling sinners to repentance

The Sixth Sunday after Pentecost

God's purpose

Sentence

O Lord my strength and my fortress, my refuge in time of distress;
to you the nations will come from the ends of the earth, and they
will know that your name is the Lord.   *Jeremiah 16:19-21 (adapted)*

Collects

Almighty and eternal God,
it is your will to bring the whole creation
into unity in Christ;
grant that your Church may faithfully proclaim
the good news
until all people are saved
and the earth is full of your glory;
through Jesus Christ our Lord.

Almighty God,
in your Son Jesus Christ
you have created a people for yourself;
make us willing to obey you,
till your purpose is accomplished
and the earth is full of your glory.

Praise to you, God, for all your work among us.
Yours is the vigour in creation,
yours is the impulse in our new discoveries.
Make us adventurous, yet reverent and hopeful
in all we do.

Psalms   67;   119:137-144

Readings

1 Deuteronomy 7:6-11   Holy to the Lord
   Ephesians 1:3-14   God's purpose in Christ
   Matthew 5:13-20   The salt of the earth

2 Exodus 20:1-17   The ten commandments
   Romans 13:8-10   Love fulfilling the Law
   Luke 4:31-43   Sent for this purpose

The Seventh Sunday after Pentecost

Sentence

As the new heavens and the new earth which I am making shall
endure in my sight, so shall your race and your name endure; all
people shall come to bow down before me, says the Lord.

Isaiah 66:22,23

Collects

Make us glad, we pray you, gentle God,
to give each other your loving care;
make us happy to receive it.
May there daily grow within us
a generous, trusting spirit.

Merciful God,
you gave your only Son
to be both a sacrifice for sin
and an example of godly life;
help us gladly to receive
all that he has done for us
and follow in his footsteps;
through Jesus Christ our Saviour.

God, you are working still,
breaking down and building up;
open our eyes to discern your hands
so that we may take our place
as labourers together with you.

Psalms   117;   62

Readings

1 Isaiah 49:1-6   You are my servant
1 Corinthians 15:1-11   Paul's work
Matthew 20:1-16   Workers in the vineyard

2 Ezekiel 2:1-7   A prophet's task
2 Corinthians 11:21b-29   Labours of an apostle
John 4:27-42   Accomplishing God's work

The Eighth Sunday after Pentecost

The Church, the body of Christ

Sentence

Do not fear, for I am with you; do not be dismayed, for I am your
God. I will strengthen you and help you. I will uphold you with
my saving right hand.
Isaiah 41:10

Collects

Creator God,
you have made us
not in one mould, but in many:
so deepen our unity in Christ
that we may rejoice in our diversity.

Almighty and everlasting God,
by your Spirit the whole body of the Church
is governed and sanctified;
hear the prayers we offer
for all your faithful people,
that in the ministry to which you have called us
we may serve you in holiness and truth;
through our Lord and Saviour Jesus Christ.

Christ of the new covenant,
give us the happiness to share,
with full measure, pressed down,
shaken together and running over,
all that you give us.

Psalms   87;   122

Readings

1 Exodus 19:1-6   A kingdom of priests
   Romans 12:1-8   One body in Christ
   John 15:1-11   The vine and the branches

2 Joshua 24:16-24   The people choose the Lord
   1 Peter 2:1-9   A spiritual house
   Matthew 16:13-19   I will build my Church

The Ninth Sunday after Pentecost

The Holy Bible

Sentence

God chose to give us birth through the word of truth, that we might
be a kind of first fruits of all creation.   *James 1:18*

Collects

Almighty God,
your word is a lamp for our feet
and a light upon our path;
grant that by patient study of the Scriptures
we may follow more closely the way
that you set before us;

through Jesus Christ
who lives and reigns with you and the Holy Spirit,
one God now and for ever.

Lord Jesus,
as we search the Scriptures
patiently and reverently,
may we be led to you
the Word made flesh;
for you have the words of eternal life.

God of the living word,
give us the faith to receive your message,
the wisdom to know what it means,
and the courage to put it into practice.

Psalms   119:105-112;   119:89-96

Readings

1 Joshua 1:6-9   Heeding the book
   2 Timothy 3:14 - 4:5   All Scripture inspired by God
   Luke 20:27-40   Jesus' use of Scripture

2 2 Kings 22:3-13   The book of the Law
                                              rediscovered
   Romans 15:1-6   Hope from Scripture
   Luke 4:16-30   Jesus' use of Scripture

The Tenth Sunday after Pentecost

Holy Baptism

Sentence

I will give you a new heart and put a new spirit within you; I will
remove from you your heart of stone and give you a heart of flesh.

Ezekiel 36:26

Collects

Almighty Father,
grant that we your children
may never be ashamed
to confess the faith of Christ crucified,
but continue his faithful servants
to our lives' end.

Come Holy Spirit, to all baptised in your name,
that we may turn to good
whatever lies ahead.
Give us passion, give us fire;
make us transform the world from what it is,
to what you have created it to be.

Eternal God,
you have given us one baptism
for the remission of sins;
grant that we who are born of water and the Spirit
and made members of Christ,
may be one in inward faith and outward service;
through Jesus Christ our Lord.

Psalms   23;   85

Readings

1	Ezekiel 47:1,2,6-12	Living water
	Romans 6:3-14	New life in Christ
	John 3:1-13	Born of water and the Spirit
2	Isaiah 44:1-5	Water on the thirsty land
	1 Corinthians 12:1-13	Baptised by one Spirit into one body
	Matthew 3:13-17	The baptism of Jesus

The Eleventh Sunday after Pentecost

Sentence

I would feed you with the finest wheat-flour; and satisfy you with honey from the rock. *Psalm 81:16 (adapted)*

Collects

Living host, call us together,
call us to eat and drink with you.
Grant that by your body and your blood
we may be drawn to each other
and to you.

Everloving God,
your Son Jesus Christ
gave himself as living bread
for the life of the world;
give us such a knowledge of his presence
that we may be strengthened
and sustained by his risen life
to serve you continually;
through Jesus Christ our Lord.

Father,
your Son gave his disciples a sign
by which to remember him
until he comes again;
as bread is broken and wine poured out
may our eyes be opened to know him,
Jesus our Lord.

Psalms   105:1-5, 38-44;   116

Readings

1   Exodus 16:11-18   Bread from heaven
      1 Corinthians 10:1-17   Communion in and with Christ
      John 6:35-51   The bread of life

2   Exodus 24:3-11   The blood of the covenant
      1 Corinthians 11:23-29   The institution of the
                                       Holy Communion
      John 6:51-59   The flesh and blood of Christ

The Twelfth Sunday after Pentecost

Ministry

Sentence

To him who loves us and freed us from our sins with his life's blood, who made of us a royal house to serve as the priests of his God and Father – to him be glory and dominion for ever and ever. Amen.   *Revelation 1:6*

Collects

Almighty God,
by your grace alone
we are accepted and called to your service;
strengthen us by your Holy Spirit
and empower our calling;
through Jesus Christ our Lord.

Servant God, grant us opportunity,
give us willingness
to serve you day by day;
that what we do
and how we bear each other's burdens,
may be our sacrifice to you.

Jesus, you took a towel
but Peter would have refused you;
make us eager to honour the ministry of others
and after your example to exercise our own.

Psalms   99;   132

Readings

1 Ezekiel 33:1-6   The watcher
   Ephesians 4:1-13   Gifts of ministry
   John 21:15-19   Feed my sheep

2 Numbers 11:24-29   Moses' ministry shared
   1 Corinthians 12:14-31a One body, many parts
   Luke 10:1-9   Harvest plentiful,
                              labourers few

The Thirteenth Sunday after Pentecost

The gift of faith

Sentence

Blessed are those who trust in the Lord. They will be like trees
planted by the waterside that do not fear when heat comes, and
are not anxious in the year of drought.   *Jeremiah 17:7,8*

Collects

Jesus, you turned death into life,
turned defeat into victory.
Grant that with your help
we may raise our expectations
and achieve what is yet impossible.

God, the strength of all who believe in you,
increase our faith and trust
in your Son Jesus Christ,
that in him we may live victoriously.

God of our forbears,
as your chosen servant Abraham
was given faith to obey your call
and go out into the unknown,
so may your Church be granted such faith
that we may follow you courageously
now and forever;
through Jesus Christ our Lord.

Psalms   91;   3

Readings

1 Genesis 12:1-9   Abraham's faith
   Ephesians 2:1-10   Saved by grace though faith
   Luke 7:1-10   The centurion's servant

2 Isaiah 40:25-31   Trust renews strength
   Hebrews 11:32 - 12:2   People of faith
   Mark 9:14-29   Healing the epileptic child

The Fourteenth Sunday after Pentecost

The gift of hope

Sentence

We have waited eagerly for you O Lord; for you are our help and
our shield; our hearts shall rejoice in you, because we have hoped
in your holy name.
                                              Psalm 33:19,20

Collects

Eternal Father,
your Son Jesus Christ,
now exalted as Lord of all,
pours out his gifts on the Church;
grant us that unity which your Spirit gives,
keep us in the bond of peace,
and bring all creation to worship
before your throne;
for you live and reign
one God for ever and ever.

Almighty God,
give us such a vision of your purpose
and such an assurance of your love and power,
that we may ever hold fast the hope
which is in Jesus Christ our Lord.

Give us courage to hope, and to risk disappointment.
Teach us to pray expectantly,
and when our prayers seem to fail,
bring us to pray again and again;
for you are our God,
who acts and will act again.

Psalms   72;   46

Readings

1	Job 19:21-27a	Job's hope in God
	1 Peter 1:3-9	A living hope
	John 11:17-27	Hope even in death
2	Jeremiah 31:15-20	Hope shall be rewarded
	Romans 8:14-27	The hope of the creation
	Luke 12:22-34	Fear not, little flock

The Fifteenth Sunday after Pentecost

The gift of love

Sentence

I shall live through you O Lord and my children shall serve you;
to a people as yet unborn they shall make known the saving deeds
you have done.   *Psalm 22:30,31*

Collects

Give us, we pray you, gentle God,
a mind forgetful of past injury,
a will to seek the good of others
and a heart of love.

Grant us, Jesus, that tender, indestructible love
which asks forgiveness for its executioners
and gives hope to the thief on the cross.
Keep us compassionate when the way is hard,
and gentle with those who oppose us.

Lord God,
you have taught us
that anything we do without love is worth nothing,
for whoever lives without love
is counted dead before you;
send your Holy Spirit,
and pour into our hearts
that most excellent gift of love,
the true bond of peace and of all virtues;
grant this for the sake of your Son Jesus Christ.

Psalms   116;   103

Readings

1 Deuteronomy 6:4-9   Love the Lord your God
   1 John 4:7-21   God is love
   Luke 7:36-50   The woman who was a sinner

2 2 Samuel 23:13-17   A precious gift
   1 John 3:11-24   The way of love
   John 15:9-17   Abiding in love

The Sixteenth Sunday after Pentecost

The gift of wisdom

Sentence

Satisfy us in the morning O Lord with your constant love. Teach us to know how few are our days, that we may apply our hearts to wisdom.
Psalm 90:14, 12

Collects

Almighty God,
fount of all wisdom, crown of all knowledge;
give us eyes to see
and minds to understand your marvellous works,
that we may know you through your handiwork
and use your creations to your glory;
through Jesus Christ our Lord.

God of mercy,
you have blessed us beyond our dreams;
you have set before us promises and perils
beyond our understanding;
help us to struggle and pray
that the perils may be averted
and your promises fulfilled.

Save us, Lord,
from the worship of power or science.
Save us from making you in our image,
and keep us humble.

Psalms   111;   18:1-30

Readings

1 Proverbs 3:13-23   The blessings of wisdom
James 3:13-18   The two wisdoms
Matthew 7:21-29   The wise and the foolish
                                     builder

2 Wisdom 9:1-12   A king's prayer for wisdom
Or
1 Kings 3:4-15a
Colossians 1:24 - 2:7   The riches of assured
                                     understanding
Matthew 25:14-30   The parable of the talents

The Seventeenth Sunday after Pentecost

The fulfilment of life

Sentence

Happy are those whose helper is the God of Jacob; whose hope is
in the Lord their God, who made heaven and earth, the sea and all
that is in them, who keeps a promise for ever.   *Psalm 146:5,6*

Collects

Eternal God,
light of the minds that know you,
joy of the hearts that love you,
strength of the wills that serve you;
grant us so to know you that we may truly love you,
and so to love you that we may gladly serve you,
now and always.

We pray you, Jesus, take the old water,
our busy, conscientious lives,
and turn them into gospel wine,
that everyone may see your life
and thirst.

Merciful God,
you have prepared for those who love you
such good things as pass our understanding;
pour into our hearts such love towards you
that, loving you above all else,
we may obtain your promises,
which exceed all that we can desire;
through Jesus Christ our Lord.

Psalms   84;   20

Readings

1 Isaiah 65:17-25   New heavens and new earth
   1 Thessalonians 3:6-13   Perfected at his coming
   Matthew 5:1-12   The truly blessed

2 Isaiah 62:1-7   Jerusalem to be transformed
   Revelation 21:22 - 22:5   The heavenly city
   Mark 10:17-31   One thing necessary

The Eighteenth Sunday after Pentecost

Fear of the Lord

Sentence

You O Lord are in your holy temple; let all the earth keep silence
before you. *Habakkuk 2:20 (adapted)*

Collects

Father,
imprint upon our hearts
that because we belong to you
no one can pluck us from your hand,
and because we fear you
we need fear no other.

Holy God, grant us the beginning of wisdom
and love to cast out every fear:
that we may grow more brave,
more ready to hear,
more ready to obey.

Holy God, holy and strong, holy and immortal,
keep us under the protection of your good providence,
and help us continually
to revere and love your holy name;
through Jesus Christ our Lord.

Psalms   65;   96

Readings

1 Genesis 28:10-17   An awesome place
   Hebrews 12:18-29   Worship with reverence
                                              and awe

   Mark 4:35-41   They were filled with awe

2 Job 28:20-28   The fear of the Lord is wisdom
1 Peter 1:13-21   Conduct yourselves with fear
Luke 5:1-11   He was astonished

The Nineteenth Sunday after Pentecost

Joy in the Lord

Sentence

You O Lord are my strength and my shield; my heart trusts in you
and I am helped; therefore my heart dances for joy, and in my song
I will praise you.

Psalm 28:8

Collects

God of all delight, grant us that joy
which none can take from us,
of having a work to do,
a life to live;
that joy in believing
which will carry us through temptation,
anxiety and grief.

Father,
let us not serve you grudgingly like slaves,
but with the gladness of children
who delight in you
and rejoice in your work.

Almighty God,
for the joy that was set before him
your Son endured the cross,
and by his resurrection turned our sorrow into joy;
help us to rejoice in his power
that we may walk in his way with glad obedience;
through our Saviour Jesus Christ.

Psalms   100;   126

Readings

1 Isaiah 12   Joy in salvation
    Hebrews 12:1-11   Joy set before him
    John 16:16-24   Sorrow turned into joy

2 Isaiah 61:10-11   I will greatly rejoice
    Philippians 4:1-9   Joy and peace
    Luke 15:1-10   Joy in heaven

The Twentieth Sunday after Pentecost

Prayer in the Lord

Sentence

Through the abundance of your steadfast love, I will come into
your house, and bow low in reverence toward your holy temple.

Psalm 5:7

Collects

Almighty and merciful God,
more ready to hear than we to pray,
giving more than either we desire or deserve;
pour down upon us the abundance of your mercy,
forgive us those things
of which our conscience is afraid,
and give us those good things
which we are not worthy to ask,
except through your Son our Saviour
Jesus Christ.

Come, Holy Spirit, with the new fire;
when our prayer seems to fail,
when we hear no voice nor any answer,
rouse us and light our way.

All-seeing God,
teach us to be open with you about our needs,
to seek your support in our trials,
to admit before you our sins,
and to thank you for all your goodness.

Psalms   42;   121

Readings

1 1 Kings 18:30-39   A prayer of Elijah
    Philippians 1:3-11   A prayer of Paul
    Luke 11:1-13   Jesus on prayer

2 1 Kings 8:27-30   Solomon's prayer
    Colossians 1:1-14   A prayer of Paul
    Matthew 6:5-15   Jesus on prayer

The Twenty-first Sunday after Pentecost

Our lives

Sentence

Taste and see how gracious the Lord is; happy are those who find
refuge in the Most High.   *Psalm 34:8*

Collects

Holy and eternal God,
give us such trust in your sure purpose,
that we measure our lives
not by what we have done or failed to do,
but by our faithfulness to you.

Almighty God,
you have made us for yourself,
and our hearts are restless
till they find their rest in you;
so lead us by your Spirit
that in this life we may live to your glory
and in the life to come enjoy you for ever;
through Jesus Christ our Lord.

Your cross, Jesus, remains like a tree on a hill.
You show me where I am,
you take away my fear,
and set me on my course again;
help me to watch for you night and day.

Psalms   139:1-18;   81

Readings

1 Job 29:7-17   A model life
   Philippians 3:3-14   Put no confidence in the flesh
   Mark 10:35-45   You must be perfect

2 Genesis 13:1-12   A generous offer
   Philippians 2:1-13   Do nothing from selfishness
   Matthew 5:38-48   True greatness

The Twenty-second Sunday after Pentecost

Our homes

Sentence

How good and pleasant a thing it is when God's people live together in unity.

Psalm 133:1

Collects

Gentle God,
grant that at home
where we are most truly ourselves,
where we are known at our best and worst,
we may learn to forgive and be forgiven.

God, the mother and father of us all,
you have created families and love of every kind.
Give us courage to listen to each other and to learn,
and grant us the gentle blessing
which a home can give.

Almighty and everloving God,
your Son Jesus Christ shared at Nazareth
the life of an earthly home;
grant that we and all your children
may live together in peace and joy,
until we come to that eternal home
which you have prepared for those that love you;
through Jesus Christ our Lord.

Psalms   127;   128

Readings

1 Genesis 45:1-15   Family affection
    Titus 2:1-10   An early Christian household
    Mark 10:1-16   Marriage and children
    Or
    Luke 8:40-42,49b-56   Jesus' compassion for a family

2 Deuteronomy 11:18-21   Family teaching
    Ephesians 3:14-21   From the Father every family
                           is named
    Luke 10:38-42   The home of Martha and Mary

The Twenty-third Sunday after Pentecost

Our neighbours

Sentence

Arise O Lord God and lift up your hand; do not forget the poor in
their need; the poor commit themselves to you; for you are the
helper of the orphaned.   *Psalm 10:13, 16*

Collects

Almighty God,
you teach us in your word
that love is the fulfilling of the law:
grant that we may love you with all our heart
and our neighbours as ourselves;
through Jesus Christ our Lord.

Save us, Jesus, from hurrying away,
because we do not wish to help,
because we know not how to help,
because we dare not.
Inspire us to use our lives
serving one another.

Jesus Christ, you have taught us
that what we do to each other, we do to you;
make us quick to help and slow to hurt,
knowing that in our neighbour it is you
who receive our love or our neglect.

Psalms   15;   41

Readings

1 Leviticus 19:9-18   Love of neighbour
      1 Corinthians 13   A hymn to love
      Luke 10:25-37   Who is my neighbour?

2 Deuteronomy 22:1-4   Neighbourly conduct
      1 John 2:1-11   Obedience and love
      Luke 14:1-14   Expecting no return
      Or
      Luke 16:19-31   The rich man and Lazarus

The Twenty-fourth Sunday
after Pentecost*

Our country

Sentence

The Lord who dwells on high is exalted, and will be the sure
foundation for your times, a rich store of salvation and wisdom
and knowledge.   *Isaiah 33:5,6*

Collects

God of nations, help us to reflect and share
the goodness that surrounds us.
Help us to win justice for poor and rich alike,
and bring trust and friendship
to all our different races.

God of all the earth,
you have given us the heritage
of this good and fertile land;
grant that we may so respect and use it
that others may thank us
for what we leave to them.

God of nations,
you have given us a good land for our heritage;
inspire in the people of our country
a love of peace and a zeal for justice,
that we may use our liberty
in accordance with your will;
through Jesus Christ our Lord.

Psalms   72:1-14;   149

Readings

1 Deuteronomy 8:6-10   A good land
   1 Peter 2:11-17   Respect for authority
   Mark 12:13-17   The things of Caesar

2 Isaiah 5:1-7   God's land is judged
   Romans 13:1-7   Authority in the state
   Mark 12:1-12   A treacherous nation

* The 24th to 27th Sunday after Pentecost are used each year as required.

The Twenty-fifth Sunday after Pentecost

Our world

Sentence

From the rising of the sun to its setting my name is great among
the nations, and in every place incense is offered to my name, and
a pure offering; for my name is great among the nations, says the
Lord of hosts.

Malachi 1:11

Collects

Almighty God,
govern the hearts and minds of those in authority
and mercifully grant that the peoples of the world,
divided and torn apart by sin,
may be brought together
under the gentle rule of Christ.

Almighty and eternal God,
you have made of one blood all the nations of the earth
and will that they live together
in peace and harmony;
so order the course of this world
that all peoples may be brought together
under Christ's most gentle rule;
through Jesus Christ our Lord.

Universal and unchanging God,
we are one, unalterably one,
with all the human race.
Grant that we who share Christ's blood
may, through your unifying Spirit,
break down the walls that divide us.

Psalms   82;   16

Readings

1 Zechariah 8:20-23   Many nations seek God
   Romans 10:9-17   Salvation for all who believe
   John 12:20(27)-36   I will draw everyone to myself

2 Isaiah 19:21-25   Egypt and Assyria one
                                with Israel
   Acts 17:22-31   From one,
                                God made every nation
   Matthew 8:5-13   Many will come

The Twenty-sixth Sunday after Pentecost

Things of eternal worth

Sentence

Your throne O Lord has stood firm from of old; from all eternity
you are God. Mightier than the noise of great waters; mightier
than the waves of the sea; so the Lord on high is mighty.

Psalm 93:3, 5

Collects

God, you have given us a lodging in this world
but not an abiding city.
Help us, as a pilgrim people, to endure hardness,
knowing that at the end of our journey
Christ has prepared a place for us.

Eternal God,
protector of all who put their trust in you,
without whom nothing is strong, nothing is holy;
fill us with your mercy and your grace
that with you to rule and guide
we may so use the good things of this present life
that we do not neglect things of eternal worth;
through Jesus Christ our Lord.

Lord,
help us to see:
to see what is eternally good and true,
and having seen, to go on searching
until we come to the joys of heaven.

Psalms   9:1-10;   71

Readings

1 2 Kings 6:8-17   Armies visible and invisible
       2 Corinthians 4:16 - 5:10   Things seen and unseen
       Luke 16:1-13   No one can serve two masters

2 Isaiah 55:6-11   God's ways and ours
       Philippians 3:13b-21   Citizenship in heaven
       John 15:18-25   Jesus and the world

The Twenty-seventh Sunday
after Pentecost

The two ways

Sentence

What does the Lord who has showed you what is good require of
you? To act justly and to love mercy and to walk humbly with
your God.
                                                        Micah 6:8

Collects

Jesus our guide, we journey in faith to resurrection,
through failure, through success,
through whatever lies ahead;
for you are the way, and life.

Almighty God, you alone can bring order
to our unruly wills and affections;
give us grace to love what you command
and desire what you promise,
that in all the changes and chances
of this uncertain world,
our hearts may surely there be fixed
where true joys are to be found;
through Jesus Christ our Lord.

God our ruler and guide,
when we come to the place where the road divides,
keep us true to the way of Christ,
alive to present opportunities,
and confident of eternal life.

Psalms   1;   112

Readings

1 Deuteronomy 30:11-20   Life or death
   Philippians 2:12-18   Lights in a dark world
   Luke 9:18-27   The way of the cross

2 Proverbs 4:10-19   The way of wisdom
   Ephesians 5:15-20   Look carefully how you walk
   Matthew 7:13-23   The easy way and the hard

Sunday before Advent

Sentence

But as for me, I keep watch for the Lord; I wait in hope for God my
Saviour; my God will hear me.   *Micah 7:7 (adapted)*

Collects

Keep your Church alert, Holy Spirit,
ready to hear when you are calling,
and when you challenge us.
Keep us hopeful, Holy Spirit,
knowing that Christ will come again.

Rouse our spirits, Lord Jesus,
that whenever you come to the door and knock
you may find us awake,
ready to admit and serve you.

Stir up, O Lord,
the wills of your faithful people
that, richly bearing the fruit of good works,
they may by you be richly rewarded;
through Jesus Christ our Lord.

Psalms   98;   70

Readings

1	Malachi 3:13-18	The Day is coming
	1 Thessalonians 5:1-11	The coming of the Lord
	Luke 12:35-40	Waiting for the master
2	Isaiah 30:8-14	A people unprepared
	1 Peter 4:7-19	The end at hand
	Matthew 24:32-44	Watch, therefore

Other Feasts and Holy Days

The Naming of Jesus

1 January

Sentence

There is salvation in no one else, for there is no other name under
heaven given among us by which we must be saved.   *Acts 4:12*

Collects

We thank you, Lord God, for the gift of your Son
whom you commanded to be called Jesus;
grant that we may so honour his name on earth,
that others may be led to him who alone is Lord and Saviour.

Praise to you, Christ our Redeemer
for you were circumcised this day
and given Jesus as your name.
Praise to you, Jesus, well are you named
for you save us from our sins.

NEW YEARS DAY
Eternal God,
to whom a thousand years are no more than a moment;
renew us in your Holy Spirit,
so that we may serve you with courage
while we have life and breath;
through the grace of Jesus your Son.

God of time and eternity,
as we enter this new year
day by day
open us to your new age.

Psalms   25:1-11;   98

Readings

Post Communion Sentence

You shall call his name Jesus, for he will save his people from their sins.

Matthew 1:21

The Conversion of Saint Paul

25 January

Sentence

I am not ashamed, for I know whom I have believed, and I am sure that he is able to guard until that day what he has entrusted to me.

2 Timothy 1:12

Collects

Almighty God,
you have caused the light of the gospel
to shine throughout the world
through the preaching of your servant Paul;
grant that we who remember his wonderful conversion
may follow him in bearing witness to your truth;
through Jesus Christ our Lord.

Convert us,
Jesus the persecuted,
as you converted Paul
and sent him as apostle to the world.
May our love, our prayers, our suffering
carry your gospel at whatever cost
to all who wait to hear it.

Psalms   67;   87

Readings

TWO YEAR SERIES

Jeremiah 1:4-10	A prophet's appointment
Acts 9:1-20	The conversion of Paul
Matthew 19:23-30	Loss and gain

THREE YEAR SERIES

Psalm 117	Acts 22:3-16 *Or* 9:1-22
	Galatians 1:11-24
	Mark 16:15-18

Post Communion Sentence

I live by faith in the Son of God, who loved me and gave himself
up for me.   *Galatians 2:20*

The Presentation of Jesus in the Temple

2 February

Sentence

Be renewed in the spirit of your minds, and put on the new nature,
created after the likeness of God in righteousness and true
holiness.   *Ephesians 4:23-24*

Collects

Everliving God,
your Son Jesus Christ was presented as a child in the temple
to be the hope of your people;
grant us pure hearts and minds
that we may be transformed into his likeness,
who lives and reigns with you and the Holy Spirit,
one God for ever.

Holy God,
they brought the little Christ to his Father's house,
with peasant gifts, to consecrate him;
grant to us, little or great,
that consecration.

Psalms   118:19-26;   122

Readings

TWO YEAR SERIES

1 Samuel 1:20-28	A child lent to the Lord
Romans 12:1-8	Presentation and transformation
Luke 2:22-40	The presentation of the child Jesus

THREE YEAR SERIES

Psalm 24

Malachi 3:1-4
Hebrews 2:14-18
Luke 2:22-40

Post Communion Sentence

We have called to mind your steadfast love O God in the midst of
your temple. As your name is great O God, so is your praise to the
ends of the earth; your right hand is filled with victory.

Psalm 48:9,10

Holy Innocents

16 February (alternative date)

See 28 December

Saint Matthias the Apostle

24 February

Sentence

You have not chosen me, I have chosen you, says the Lord.
Go and bear fruit that will last.   *John 15:16*

Collects

Almighty God,
your faithful apostle Matthias
was chosen in place of Judas;
grant that your Church may be saved from false teachers
and guided by faithful and true pastors,
to the glory of your holy name.

Holy Spirit, grant to us who serve your Church
to mend what is spoiled,
to strengthen what is sound,
and to follow you
wherever and however you may lead.

Psalms   119:33-40;   61

Readings

TWO YEAR SERIES

Isaiah 22:15-22	An unworthy steward replaced
Acts 1:15-26	The choice of Matthias
Matthew 7:15-20	Beware of false prophets

Psalm 113

Acts 1:15-17, 20-26
Philippians 3:13-21
John 15:9-17

Post Communion Sentence

One of them must become with us a witness of the resurrection of
Jesus.

Acts 1:22

The Annunciation of our Saviour to the Blessed Virgin Mary

25 March

Sentence

Mary said, 'Behold I am the handmaid of the Lord; let it be to me
according to your word.'

Luke 1:38

Collects

God of grace,
grant that Mary's obedience may inspire us
to obey your will
and receive Jesus Christ in our hearts as Lord;
who lives and reigns with you and the Holy Spirit,
one God for ever.

Father of love,
through your most Holy Spirit,
Mary the Jewish girl conceived your Son;
may his beauty, his humanity,
his all-transforming grace be born in us,
and may we never despise the strange and stirring gentleness
of your almighty power.

Psalms   89:1-18;   45

Readings

Post Communion Sentence

And Mary said, 'From this day all generations will call me blessed; for you O Most Mighty have done great things for me, and holy is your name.'   *Luke 1:48,49 (adapted)*

Saint Mark the Evangelist

25 April

Sentence

Go out into all the world and preach the gospel to all creation.
                                              Mark 16:15

Collects

Almighty God,
by your grace John Mark rose above failure,
and proved useful in your service;
grant that we may steadfastly abide in Christ,
and be fruitful in good works,
to the honour of your name.

When new fashions, new ideas, new fears,
burst on us, unchanging God,
grant us then to know with Mark the evangelist,
that Christ is risen
and the gospel stands.

Psalms   119:1-8;   62

Readings

TWO YEAR SERIES

Isaiah 52:7-10	Messengers of salvation
Ephesians 6:10-20	Stand fast
Or	
Acts 15:36-40	Mark and Barnabas
Mark 13:9-13	Enduring to the end

THREE YEAR SERIES

Psalm 89:1-9

Isaiah 62:6-12
Ephesians 4:7-16
Or
1 Peter 5:5b-14
Mark 16:15-20

Post Communion Sentence

Jesus is going before you to Galilee; there you will see him as he
told you.
Mark 16:7

Saint Philip and Saint James, Apostles

1 May

Sentence

Jesus said, 'Whatever you ask in my name, I will do it, that the
Father may be glorified in the Son.'   *John 14:13*

Collects

Merciful God,
whom truly to know is eternal life;
teach us to know your Son Jesus Christ
as the way, the truth and the life
that, following in the steps of your apostles Philip and James,
we may walk in the way that leads to eternal life;
through our Saviour Jesus Christ.

God,
whose work is never done,
look on us with Philip, James,
and all the countless millions
who have served you, and who serve you still.

Psalms   119:9-16;   33

Readings

TWO YEAR SERIES

Isaiah 30:18-21	Walk in the way
Acts 2:36-43	The apostles' teaching and fellowship
John 14:1-12	Lord, show us the Father

THREE YEAR SERIES

Psalm 19:1-6	Isaiah 30:18-21
	1 Corinthians 15:1-8
	John 14:6-14

Post Communion Sentence

O Lord the heavens proclaim your wonders; and the council of
the holy ones praises your faithfulness. *Psalm 89:5*

Saint John the Evangelist

6 May (alternative date)

See 27 December

Saint Barnabas the Apostle

11 June

Sentence

When Barnabas came and saw the grace of God, he was glad; and
he exhorted them all to remain faithful to the Lord with steadfast
purpose. *Acts 11:23*

Collects

Almighty God,
we remember today your servant Barnabas,
whose great joy was to proclaim your love;
grant us also the gift of your Holy Spirit,
to bring others to know your goodness,
to encourage the faint hearted
and to minister to those in need;
in the name of Jesus Christ our Lord.

Holy and humble Spirit,
we thank you for Barnabas
who went to seek for Saul;
grant us the integrity and perception
to recognise the one you choose.

Psalms   34;   119:153-160

Readings

TWO YEAR SERIES

Job 29:7-16	The compassion of Job
Acts 11:19-30	The mission of Barnabas
John 15:12-17	Love one another

THREE YEAR SERIES

Psalm 98   Job 29:11-16
                            Acts 11:19-26
                            Or
                            21b-26;13:1-3
                            Matthew 10:7-13

Post Communion Sentence

Barnabas was a good man, full of the Holy Spirit and of faith.

Acts 11:24

Saint John the Baptist

24 June

Sentence

There was a man sent from God, whose name was John. He came
to bear witness to the light.   *John 1:6,7*

Collects

God our strength and our hope,
grant us the courage of John the Baptist,
constantly to speak the truth,
boldly to rebuke vice
and patiently to suffer for the truth's sake;
in the name of Jesus Christ our Lord.

Terror and doom, and wrath to come,
John your herald preached
to bring us to repentance;
open our eyes, almighty God,
show us our sin,
and grant us forgiveness.

Psalms   75;   119:41-48

Readings

TWO YEAR SERIES

Malachi 4	Elijah, the prophet to come
Acts 19:1-6	John's baptism
Luke 1:57-80	The birth of John the Baptist
Or	
Matthew 11:2-19	John and Jesus

THREE YEAR SERIES

Psalm 139:1-11

Isaiah 49:1-6
Acts 13:(16-)22-26
Luke 1:57-66,80

Post Communion Sentence

You will go before the Lord to prepare the way, to give God's
people knowledge of salvation.   *Luke 1:76,77*

Saint Peter and Saint Paul, Apostles, Martyrs

Sentence

His gifts were that some should be apostles, some prophets, some evangelists, some pastors and teachers, for the equipment of the saints, for the work of ministry, for building up the body of Christ.

Ephesians 4:11,12

Collects

Almighty God,
we thank you for your servants Peter and Paul,
leaders of your Church and martyrs for your name;
fill us like them with your Spirit
that we may follow in the way of Jesus Christ
who endured the cross,
despising the shame,
and is at your right hand,
now and for ever.

God of the new and the old,
we praise you for Peter and Paul,
for the Church their leadership has established,
and for all we have received from them;
grant that we, like them,
may recognise our moment when it comes
and choose for you.

God of grace,
your Church is built on Peter's faith;
grant that we, like him, forgiven and restored,
may overcome our weakness
and serve you without wavering,
now and for ever.

Psalms   18:1-7;   61

Readings

Post Communion Sentence

By God's power Paul was made an apostle to the gentiles, just as
Peter was made an apostle to the Jews.   *Galatians 2:8 (adapted)*

The Visitation of Mary to Elizabeth

2 July

Sentence

The Lord has lifted up the lowly and has filled the hungry with
good things.   *Luke 1:52,53*

Collects

Everloving God,
by your grace Elizabeth rejoiced with Mary
and hailed her as the mother of the Lord.
Fill us with your grace,
that we may acclaim her Son as our Saviour
and rejoice in our fellowship with him;
through Jesus Christ our Lord.

God of the humble and expectant,
you bless those who believe when you promise;
help us, like Mary and Elizabeth,
simply to delight
in the good things you prepare for us,
to say, 'Yes'.

Psalms   113;   121

Readings

Zechariah 2:10-13	The Lord will live among you
Romans 12:9-16	Love one another
Luke 1:39-56	Mary and Elizabeth

Post Communion Sentence

Blessèd is she who believed that the Lord's promise would be
fulfilled.

Luke 1:45

Saint Thomas, Apostle, Martyr

3 July (alternative date)

See 21 December

Saint Mary Magdalene

Sentence

Jesus said to Mary, 'Go to my friends and say to them, "I am
ascending to my Father and your Father, to my God and your
God."'
John 20:17

Collects

Merciful God,
your Son restored Mary Magdalene to health
of body and mind
and called her to be a witness
of his resurrection;
heal us and make us whole
that we may serve you
in the power of his risen life;
through Jesus Christ our Lord.

Sweet is your friendship, Saviour Christ;
Mary you accepted,
Mary you drew to the foot of the cross,
Mary you met in the garden;
grant us a like redemption.

Psalms   116;   124

Readings

TWO YEAR SERIES

Isaiah 65:17-19	An end to weeping
2 Corinthians 5:14-19	A new creation
John 20:11-18	Revelation to Mary

Psalm 63

Song of Songs 3:1-4a
2 Corinthians 5:14-17(-21)
John 20:1-18
Or
1-2,11-18

Post Communion Sentence

Jesus said to her, 'Mary'. She turned and said to him in Hebrew, 'Rabboni!' (which means Teacher).
John 20:16

Saint James and Saint John, Apostles

25 July

Sentence

Jesus said, 'In the world you have tribulation; but be of good cheer, I have overcome the world.'
John 16:33b

Collects

Grant to us, merciful God,
that as James and John left their father
and all that they had
to follow your Son Jesus Christ,
so may we be ready to follow,
even unto death,
to the glory of your name.

Grant us, Christ our life,
the courage of James and John, your friends,
to undergo your baptism,
to drink the cup you drank,
to follow you, even to the place of death.

These collects may be used omitting the references to John.

Psalms   16;   129

Readings

Post Communion Sentence

Jesus said to them, 'You will drink my cup, but to sit at my right hand and at my left is not mine to grant, but it is for those for whom it has been prepared by my Father.'   *Matthew 20:23*

Saint Stephen, the first Christian Martyr

3 August (alternative date)

See 26 December

The Transfiguration of the Beloved Son

6 August

TWO YEAR SERIES

Sentence, Prayers and Readings for the Fourth Sunday after Epiphany, page 565.

Psalm 97

Daniel 7:9-14
Or
9-10,13-14
2 Peter 1:16-19(-21)

A	B	C
Matthew 17:1-9	Mark 9:2-10	Luke 9:28b-36

COLLECT OF
Epiphany 4

Saint Mary, the Mother of Jesus

15 August

Sentence

The Angel Gabriel came to her and said, 'Hail, O favoured one!'

Luke 1:28a

Collect

God of love,
you chose the blessèd virgin Mary
to be the mother of your only Son;
grant that we who have been redeemed by his blood,
may share with her the glory of your eternal kingdom;
through the same Jesus Christ our Lord.

Jesus, your birth is wonderful
and your mother is the most beloved woman of all time.
Help all of us who believe in you
to honour each other equally,
whatever our gender,
whatever our ability,
whatever our social state may be.

Psalms   34:1-4;   46

Readings

Post Communion Sentence

Hail, O favoured one, the Lord is with you! The Holy Spirit will
come upon you.   *Luke 1:28,35*

Saint Bartholomew (Nathanael), Apostle

24 August

Sentence

What we preach is not ourselves, but Jesus Christ as Lord, with
ourselves as your servants for Jesus' sake.   *2 Corinthians 4:5*

Collects

Almighty God,
grant that as the apostle Bartholomew truly believed
and preached the word of life,
so now your Church may continually hear and proclaim
the gospel of Jesus Christ,
to the glory of your name.

Bestow upon us, Lord,
the grace of the honest and open heart
which you gave to Bartholomew,
so that we may rightly discern the truth
and willingly believe in your Son Jesus Christ.

Psalms   112;   116

Readings

TWO YEAR SERIES

Genesis 28:10-17   Jacob's vision
2 Corinthians 4:1-10   The apostolic preaching
John 1: 45-51   The call of Nathanael

THREE YEAR SERIES

Psalm 145:10-18   Deuteronomy 18:15-18
                         Revelation 21:9b-14
                         John 1:45-51

Post Communion Sentence

When Jesus saw Nathanael he said, 'Here is a true Israelite, in
whom there is nothing false!'   *John 1:47*

Builders of the Anglican Church in Aotearoa, New Zealand and Polynesia

Sentence

Call to remembrance O Lord your tender care and the unfailing
love which you have shown from of old.   *Psalm 25:5*

Collects

Everlasting God,
your messengers have carried the good news of Christ
to the ends of the earth;
grant that we who commemorate
the builders of your Church in these islands
may know the truth of the gospel in our hearts
and build well on the foundations they have laid;
through Jesus Christ our Lord.

God of every generation
that has been and is yet to be,
we praise and thank you
for those who have served and shaped
your Church beneath the Southern Cross;
in our day
raise up prophets and visionaries
to bring us new insights, new challenges
and renewed confidence in you
and the gospel of your Son.

Psalms   126;   145

Readings

Ecclesiasticus 44:1-15	Famous people of the past
Or	
Proverbs 8:1-13	Wisdom for the people
1 Corinthians 3:11-17	Christ the true foundation
Matthew 5:1-12	The beatitudes

Post Communion Sentence

Come to him, our living stone; come and let yourselves be built as
living stones into a spiritual temple.   *1 Peter 2:4-6 (adapted)*

Saint Matthew, Apostle, Evangelist

21 September

Sentence

Go and make disciples of all nations, baptizing them, and teaching
them to observe all that I have commanded you.   *Matthew 28:19-20*

Collects

Gracious and eternal God,
through your Son Jesus Christ
you called Matthew from his place of business
to be an apostle and evangelist;
free us from all greed and selfish love of money
that we may follow in the steps
of Jesus Christ our Redeemer.

Jesus, Word of God, may we hear your call
to lay aside sharp practices and ruthlessness;
and still, like Matthew, to love
all those with whom we live and work.

Psalms   146;   119:121-128

Readings

TWO YEAR SERIES

Proverbs 3:13-23	The true riches
1 Timothy 6:6-19	Right use of wealth
Matthew 9:9-13	The call of Matthew

THREE YEAR SERIES

Psalm 19:1-6   Proverbs 3:1-6
                                 Ephesians 4:1-14
                                 Or
                                 1-7,11-13
                                 Matthew 9:9-13

Post Communion Sentence

For it is the God who said, 'Let light shine out of darkness,' who
has shone in our hearts to give the light of the knowledge of the
glory of God in the face of Christ.   *2 Corinthians 4:6*

Saint Michael and All Angels

29 September

Sentence

I looked, and heard around the throne and the living creatures and
the elders the voice of many angels, numbering myriads of
myriads and thousands of thousands.   *Revelation 5:11*

Collects

Almighty and everlasting God,
whom we adore with all the angelic host,
may we always rejoice in your heavenly protection
and serve you faithfully in this present life;
through Jesus Christ our Lord.

Make us your messengers, Jesus,
make us the guardians of your faith,
and grant us also that great and ancient vision
Michael,
numberless angels
the dazzling host of heaven
to accompany and inspire us for all time.

Psalms   103:15-22;   91

Readings

Post Communion Sentence

O praise the Lord all you angels, you mighty ones who do God's bidding; and heed the command of the Most High.   *Psalm 103:20*

Saint Luke the Evangelist

18 October

Sentence

How beautiful on the mountains are the feet of those who bring good tidings of salvation.   *Isaiah 52:7*

Collects

Almighty God,
you inspired Luke the physician to proclaim
the love and healing power of your Son;
give your Church grace through his teaching
to strengthen the afflicted,
heal the desolate
and bind up the broken-hearted;
through Jesus Christ our Lord.

Jesus, the crucified,
let not our feet take us from suffering
to the other side of the road;
keep us, with Luke,
helpers, healers and bearers of hope.

Psalms 78:1-7; 62

Readings

TWO YEAR SERIES

Ecclesiasticus 38:1-14	Honour a physician
Or	
Jeremiah 30:10-17	The healing of the nation
2 Timothy 4:5-18	Paul and his companions
Luke 1:1-4	Luke's preface of dedication
Or	
Luke 10:1-9	The seventy

THREE YEAR SERIES

Psalm 145:10-18	Jeremiah 8:22 - 9:3
	2 Timothy 4:9-17a
	Luke 10:1-9

Post Communion Sentence

Jesus said, 'Those who are well have no need of a physician, but those who are sick; I have not come to call the righteous, but sinners to repentance.'

Luke 5:31

Saint James of Jerusalem, Brother of our Lord

Sentence

How good and pleasant a thing it is when God's people live together in unity.

Psalm 133:1

Collects

Grant, O God,
that following the example of your servant James,
the brother of our Lord,
your Church may give itself continually
to prayer and to the reconciliation
of all who are at variance and enmity;
through Jesus Christ our Lord.

God of revelation and reform,
we thank you for James
and his change from unbelief
to knowing Jesus, his brother, as Saviour,
and dying for his faith.
Grant that when we are wrong
we may trust you enough to change.

Psalms   1;   119:65-72

Readings

Genesis 33:1-11   Jacob and Esau reconciled
Acts 15:12-22a   The Council of Jerusalem
Matthew 13:53-58   James the brother of Jesus

Post Communion Sentence

The risen Christ appeared to James, then to all the apostles.

1 Corinthians 15:7

Saint Simon and Saint Jude, Apostles

28 October

Sentence

You are a chosen race, a royal priesthood, a holy nation, God's own people, that you may declare the wonderful deeds of the one who called you out of darkness into God's marvellous light.

1 Peter 2:9

Collects

Almighty God,
your Church is built on the foundation
of the apostles and prophets
with Christ our Lord as the cornerstone;
grant that, united with them in faith and love,
we may be part of that living temple
which is being built to your glory,
now and for ever.

Your Church, Christ Jesus,
is home for the Judes and Simons,
recognition for the unregarded,
hope for the hopeless,
fulfilment for the obscure.
Make us proud of those whom you call friend.

Psalms   134;   99

Readings

TWO YEAR SERIES

Isaiah 28:14-18   A sure foundation
Ephesians 2:11-22   You are God's temple
Luke 6:12-19   The choice of the twelve

Psalm 19:1-6

Deuteronomy 32:1-4
Ephesians 2:(11-) 19-22
Luke 6:12-16

Post Communion Sentence

But you, my friends, must build yourselves up on the foundation
of your most holy faith, praying in the Holy Spirit.   *Jude 20*

All Saints' Day

1 November

Sentence

Know what is the hope to which God has called you, what are the
riches of the glorious inheritance in the saints, and what is the
immeasurable greatness of God's power in us who believe.

Ephesians 1:18,19

Collects

Almighty God,
your saints are one with you
in the mystical body of Christ;
give us grace to follow them
in all virtue and holiness
until we come to those inexpressible joys
which you have prepared for those
who truly love you;
through Jesus Christ our Lord.

Eternal God,
you have always taken men and women
of every nation, age and colour
and made them saints;
like them, transformed,
like them, baptised in Jesus' name,
take us to share your glory.

Psalms   1;   145

Readings

TWO YEAR SERIES

Daniel 12:1-3	The rule of the saints
Revelation 7:1-4, 9-17	The triumph of the saints
Matthew 5:1-12	The character of the saints

THREE YEAR SERIES

Psalm 24:1-6

Revelation 7:2-14 or 2-4, 9-14
1 John 3:10-13
Matthew 5:1-12a

Post Communion Sentence

These are they who have put off mortal clothing and have put on
the immortal, and have confessed the name of God; now they are
being crowned, and receive palms.   *2 Esdras 2:45*

Prayer after Communion

God,
we give you praise and glory
for all your saints,
who have followed the way of Christ
in the power of the Holy Spirit.
May we learn from their example and rejoice in your call to us
to bring your kingdom to all.

We praise and thank you Holy Spirit of God,
for the men and women you have called to be saints;
from your first fallible, frightened friends
who followed you to Jerusalem,
through the centuries of discovery and growth,
people of every class and temperament
down to the present day.

We praise you, Holy Spirit, for calling us
to serve you now,
for baptising us to represent you
in this broken world.

Help us to be Christ's united body to heal and reconcile;
help us to share Christ's life with everyone.

Lord of hosts,
we praise your glory reflected in your saints;
may we who share at this table
be filled with the joy of your eternal kingdom,
where Jesus is Lord
now and for ever.

Saint Andrew, Apostle, Martyr

30 November

Sentence

Andrew said, 'Here are five barley loaves and two small fish,
but what are they among so many?' *John 6:9*

Collects

Everliving God,
your apostle Andrew obeyed the call of your Son
and followed him without delay;
grant that we like him may give ourselves readily
to do what you command;
through our Saviour Jesus Christ.

Jesus, when you call
may we like Andrew leave our nets,
our home, our everything, to follow you.

Psalms   67;   107:23-32

Readings

TWO YEAR SERIES

Jonah 3:1-10   Response from the gentiles
Romans 10:12-18   Good news for all
Matthew 4:17-22   The call of Andrew
Or
John 1:35-42a

THREE YEAR SERIES

Psalm 19:1-6

Deuteronomy 30:11-14
Romans 10:8-18
Matthew 4:18-22

Post Communion Sentence

Andrew first found his brother Simon, and said to him, 'We
have found the Messiah', and he brought him to Jesus.

John 1:41,42

Saint Thomas, the Apostle

21 December or 3 July

Sentence

Jesus said to Thomas, 'Have you believed because you have seen
me? Blessed are those who have not seen and yet believe'.

John 20:29

Collects

Almighty and everliving God,
your Son's resurrection was doubted
by the apostle Thomas;
grant that though we cannot see Jesus,
we may learn to put our whole trust in him,
our Lord and our God.

Christ our light,
like Thomas we need to see,
need to touch,
need to be sure before we believe.
When we don't know, help us to trust;
when we can't see, help us to keep on walking.

Psalms   27;   66

Readings

TWO YEAR SERIES

Job 42:1-6	Now my eyes see
1 Peter 1:3-9	Believing without seeing
John 20:24-31	Thomas sees and believes

THREE YEAR SERIES

Psalm 117   Habakkuk 2:1-4
                         Ephesians 2:19-22
                         John 20:24-29

Post Communion Sentence

Jesus said to Thomas, 'Put your finger here, and see my hands; and put out your hand, and place it in my side; do not be faithless, but believing'.   *John 20:27*

Saint Stephen, the first Christian Martyr

26 December or 3 August

Sentence

Stephen said, 'I can see heaven open, and the Son of man standing at the right hand of God'.

Acts 7:56

Collects

Merciful God,
give us grace in all our sufferings for the truth
to follow the example
of your martyr Stephen,
that we also may look to him who was crucified
and pray for those who persecute us;
through Jesus Christ our Redeemer.

Jesus,
your glory is not in power alone
but even more in suffering and death;
may Stephen's vision
crown our resolution and keep us true.

Psalms   73:24-28;   119:9-16

Readings

TWO YEAR SERIES

2 Chronicles 24:17-22	The blood of Zechariah
Acts 7:54-60	The stoning of Stephen
Matthew 23:34-38	Rejection of the prophets

THREE YEAR SERIES

Psalm 31;1-8

2 Chronicles 24:17-22
Acts 6:8-10; 7:54-60
Matthew 10:17-22

Post Communion Sentence

Stephen, full of grace and power, did great wonders and signs among the people.

Acts 6:8

Saint John, the Evangelist

27 December or 6 May

Sentence

The life was made visible, we have seen it, and bear our testimony; we here declare to you the eternal life which dwelt with the Father and was made visible to us.

1 John 1:2

Collects

God our Father,
we praise you for John, your evangelist,
whose gospel reveals the mystery of the Word made flesh;
grant that, enlightened by his teaching,
we may walk in the way of your truth,
and finally come to the light of eternal life;
through Jesus Christ our Lord.

Jesus,
new beginning, heavenly bread, living water,
we hear the word of life,
we see and grasp the truth;
help us to proclaim it.

Psalms   27;   71

Readings

Post Communion Sentence

One of his disciples, whom Jesus loved, was lying close to the breast of Jesus.

John 13:23

The Holy Innocents

28 December or 16 February

Sentence

I will turn their mourning into joy; I will comfort them and give them gladness for sorrow.

Jeremiah 31:13

Collects

Holy Father,
your Son was saved from the slaughter of infants
at the hand of Herod;
grant that we may never be indifferent
to the sufferings of your children,
but may bring them help and compassion in your unfailing love,
now and for ever.

Loving Jesus, let the tears of Rachel express our desolation,
let her weep for battered babies and clinical deformity,
weep for human cruelty and ignorance and arrogance.
Loving Jesus, may we weep with her,
may we see what we are doing,
what is happening to us;
help us repair it soon.

Psalms   131;   8

Readings

TWO YEAR SERIES

Jeremiah 31:15 - 17	Hope in sorrow
1 Corinthians 1:25-29	The weakness of God
Matthew 2:13-18	The murder of the innocents

THREE YEAR SERIES

Psalm 124

Jeremiah 31:15-20
1 John 1:5 - 2:2
Matthew 2:13-18

Post Communion Sentence

It is these who follow the Lamb wherever he goes; these have been
redeemed from humanity as first fruits for God and the Lamb.

Revelation 14:4

Saints' Days and Other Special Days

Regional Commemorations *(see page 9)*

Sentence

Praise the Lord all you nations, acclaim the Most High all you peoples; for great is God's love for us, and the faithfulness of the Lord endures for ever.
Psalm 117:1,2

Collects

Almighty God,
you call witnesses from every nation
and reveal your glory in their lives;
make us thankful for their example,
and strengthen us by their fellowship
that like them we may be faithful
in the service of your kingdom;
through Jesus Christ our Lord.

God of earth and heaven,
on your Church the sun is always rising;
we commend to you our sisters and brothers in ....
Be with them in the work they do,
as you are with us.

Psalms   67;   87

Readings

Isaiah 52:7-10	Ecclesiasticus 2:10-18	Ecclesiasticus 44:1-15
2 Corinthians 4:5-12	Hebrews 11:32 - 12:2	Hebrews 13:7,8,15,16
John 12:20-26	John 15:16-27	John 17:18-23

Post Communion Sentence

You Lord have made known your victory; you have displayed
your saving power to all the nations. *Psalm 98:3 (adapted)*

For a Martyr

Sentence

Those who want to save their life will lose it; but those who lose
their life for the sake of Christ and the gospel will save it.

Mark 8:35

Collects

Everloving God,
by your grace and power
your holy martyr N triumphed over suffering
and was faithful even to death;
strengthen us with your grace
that we may faithfully witness
to Jesus Christ our Saviour.

Jesus our Redeemer,
you gave your life to ransom us;
you have called us to drink your cup
and undergo your baptism.
Thank you for N's witness;
may we have faith and resolution too.

Almighty God,
you gave your servant N
courage to confess Jesus Christ
and to die for this faith;
may we always be ready
to give a reason for the hope that is in us
and to suffer gladly for Christ's sake.

Psalms   3;   116

Readings

2 Chronicles 24:17-21   Isaiah 43:1-7   Wisdom 3:1-9
Hebrews 11:32-40   1 Peter 4:12-19   Revelation 12:10-12
Matthew 10:16-22   Luke 12:2-12   John 15:18-21

Post Communion Sentence

Blessed are those who have suffered for the cause of right, for the
kingdom of heaven is theirs.   *Matthew 5:10*

For a Bishop or Pastor

Sentence

How beautiful on the mountains are the feet of those who bring
good tidings, who publish salvation.   *Isaiah 52:7*

Collects

Good and gracious God,
the light of the faithful and shepherd of souls,
you set your servant N
to be a bishop/priest in your Church
to feed your sheep with your word
and to guide them by *her/his* example;
give us grace to keep the faith *s/he* taught
and to follow in *her/his* footsteps.

Good Shepherd, king of love,
accept our thanks and praise
for all the love and care we have received;
and for your servant, N.
May our care for each other grow constantly
more reverent and more discerning.

Psalms 15; 99

Readings

Jeremiah 1:4-10	Ezekiel 3:16-21	Ezekiel 34:11-16
Acts 20:28-35	2 Corinthians 4:1-10	1 Peter 5:1-4
Matthew 24:42-47	John 10:11-16	John 21:15-19

Post Communion Sentence

Jesus said to Peter, 'Feed my sheep.'

John 21:15

For a Missionary

Sentence

Proclaim God's glory to the nations, God's marvellous deeds to all the peoples. For the Lord is great and highly to be praised.

Psalm 96:3,4

Collect

Everlasting God,
you have sent your messengers
to carry the good news of Christ
into the world;
grant that we who commemorate N
may know the hope of the gospel
in our hearts
and show forth its light in all our ways;
through Jesus Christ our Lord.

Jesus, incarnate God,
good news for all who have ears to hear;
thank you for N,
and for all who bring the gospel to ....
Hasten the time, we pray,
when the earth is filled with your glory
as the waters cover the sea.

Almighty God,
we thank you for N,
whom you called to preach the gospel
to the people of ....
Raise up in this and every land
heralds and evangelists of your kingdom,
that your Church may make known
the immeasurable riches of our Saviour Christ,
who lives and reigns with you and the Holy Spirit,
one God now and for ever.

Psalms   67;   96

Readings

Isaiah 49:1-6	Isaiah 52:7-10	Isaiah 61:1-3
Acts 16:6-10	Acts 17:22-31	Romans 15:17-21
Matthew 9:35-38	Matthew 28:16-20	Luke 10:1-9

Post Communion Sentence

To all to whom I send you you shall go, and whatever I command
you you shall speak.

Jeremiah 1:7b

For a Teacher or Confessor of the Faith

Sentence

Jesus said, 'Whoever serves me must follow me; and where I am, my servant will also be. My Father will honour the one who serves me.'

Collects

Almighty God,
you have enlightened your Church
by the teaching of your servant *N*;
enrich it evermore with your heavenly grace,
and raise up faithful witnesses,
who by their life and teaching
may proclaim to all people
the truth of your salvation;
through Jesus Christ our Lord.

Jesus Christ, invincible light of the world,
thank you for *N*,
and for all whose vision has enlightened us
and brought us near to you.
Keep us imaginative, expectant
and willing to learn,
so that we may come even closer to the light.

Psalms   34:11-17;   119:97-104

Readings

Nehemiah 8:1-10	Proverbs 4:1-9	Ecclesiasticus 39:1-10
1 Corinthians 2:6-16	1 Corinthians 3:5-11	1 Timothy 4:1-8
Matthew 5:13-19	Matthew 13:52-58	John 16:12-15

Post Communion Sentence

If you continue in my word, you are truly my disciples, and you
will know the truth, and the truth will set you free. *John 8:31,32*

For a Monastic or Other Religious

Sentence

You Lord are all that I have; I have promised to keep your Word.
I have sought your favour with all my heart; be gracious to me
according to your promise. *Psalm 119:57,58*

Collects

Gracious and eternal God,
by your grace N,
kindled with the fire of your love,
became a burning and a shining light in your Church;
inflame us with the same spirit of discipline and love
that we may always walk before you as children of light;
through Jesus Christ our Lord.

Jesus, Son of God,
thank you for N, and for all
who strive for holiness;
grant us also a readiness to strive
and an obedience to suffer,
for the joy of being one with you.

Psalms   27:1-8;   119:161-168

Readings

1 Kings 19:9-18	1 Kings 19:15-16,19-21	Jeremiah 17:7-10
2 Corinthians 6:1-10	Philippians 3:7-14	3 John 2-8
Matthew 6:24-33	Matthew 19:23-30	Luke 12:32-37

Post Communion Sentence

Jesus said, 'Anyone who has left brothers or sisters, father, mother, or children, land or houses for the sake of my name will be repaid many times over, and given eternal life.'

Matthew 19:29

For Any Saint

Sentence

Those who have clean hands and a pure heart, who have not set their minds on falsehood, or sworn a deceitful oath, shall receive blessing from the Lord and recompense from God their saviour.

Psalm 24:4,5

Collects

Almighty God,
you have built up your Church
through the love and devotion of your saints;
we give you thanks for your servant *N*
whom we commemorate today.
Inspire us to follow *her/his* example
that like *her/him* we may in our day rejoice
in the vision of your glory;
through Jesus Christ our Lord.

Jesus, founder and member
of the reconciled society,
thank you for *N*,
whom you called to a forgiving and forgiven life,
and for the success
with which you crowned *her/his* work.
May we too reflect the glory
we receive from you.

Almighty God,
by your grace
you surround us with so great a cloud of witnesses;
may we, encouraged by the example of your servant *N*,
persevere and run the race you set before us,
until at last, through your mercy,
we with *her/him* attain to your eternal joy;
through Jesus Christ our Lord.

Psalms 34; 119:1-8

Readings

Proverbs 8:1-11	Micah 6:6-8	Ecclesiasticus 2:1-11
2 Corinthians 4:11-18	Ephesians 6:11-18	Philippians 4:4-9
Matthew 19:16-21	Matthew 25:31-46	Luke 6:17-23

Post Communion Sentence

Walk in love, as Christ loved us and gave himself up for us.

Ephesians 5:2a

Holy Cross Day

14 September

Sentence

We should glory in the cross of our Lord Jesus Christ, through which the world is crucified to us and we to the world.

Galatians 6:14

Collects

Almighty God,
in the passion of your blessed Son
you made an instrument of shameful death
to be for us the means of life;
grant us so to glory in the cross of Christ
that we may gladly suffer for his sake,
who lives and reigns with you and the Holy Spirit,
one God now and for ever.

Jesus, crucified and risen,
you have turned a criminal's cross
into release and reconciliation.
Let us who are marked with the cross
be not ashamed to witness to you.

Psalms   2;   98

Readings

Isaiah 45:20-25
Philippians 2:5-11
John 12:31-36a

Post Communion Sentence

Jesus said, 'When I am lifted up from the earth, I will draw all people to myself.'

John 12:32

All Souls

Sentence

We believe that Jesus died and rose again, and so we believe that
God will bring with Jesus those who have fallen asleep in him.

1 Thessalonians 4:14

Collects

Merciful God,
your Son is the resurrection and the life
of all the faithful;
raise us from the death of sin
to the life of righteousness,
that at the last,
with all your faithful servants,
we may come to your eternal joy;
through our Saviour Jesus Christ.

Jesus Christ, Lord of the living and dead;
with each generation
your body of believers grows and grows.
Thank you for all who have gone before us,
for what they achieved and what they learned.
Give us strength to do your will,
to be your body now.

Psalms   16;   116

Readings

Isaiah 25:6-9
1 Peter 1:3-9
John 11:21-27

Post Communion Sentence

Jesus said, 'I am the resurrection and the life; whoever lives and
believes in me will never die.'

John 11:25,26

Mothering Sunday

Sentence

'As a mother comforts her child, so will I comfort you, and you shall be comforted in Jerusalem,' says the Lord. *Isaiah 66:13*

Collect

Everloving God,
your care for us is greater
even than a mother's love for her child;
teach us to value a mother's love
and see in it an expression of your grace,
that we may ever feel more deeply your love for us
in Christ Jesus our Saviour.

Blessed are you, God of strength and patience;
yours is the love our mothers showed us,
yours the care we need;
as we learn to care for one another
and to share your love,
may it be with our mother we share it
first of all.

Psalms   84;   122

Readings

Isaiah 49:13-16	A mother's love
Ephesians 3:14-21	Christ lives in our hearts
Luke 2:40-52	The Holy Family

Post Communion Sentence

Jerusalem above is free, and she is our mother. *Galatians 4:26*

The Readings for Holy Communion
Three Year Series

The following are the readings of the three year series for the Seasons and Ordinary Sundays of the Church's year.

On the Sundays after the Epiphany, the Ordinary Sunday readings are used, in order, on the dates shown until the Sunday before Lent.

After Pentecost the series is resumed on the second Sunday with readings appropriate to the date.

Suitable collects from the two year series have been suggested, but other collects appropriate to the theme may be selected from any source. Where only one reference to the two year series is given, the same collect is appropriate for all three years.

The psalm verse numbers in the Tables below have been amended to conform with **Psalms for Worship** *(pages 198-374).*

The Season of Advent

The First Sunday in Advent

A	**B**	**C**
Psalm 122	Psalm 80:1-7	Psalm 25:1-8
Isaiah 2:1-5	Isaiah 63:15 - 64:12 *Or* 63:16b-17; 64:1,3b-8	Jeremiah 33:14-16
Romans 13:11-14	1 Corinthians 1:3-9	1 Thessalonians 3:12 - 4:2
Matthew 24:37-44	Mark 13:33-37	Luke 21:25-36 *Or* 25-28, 34-36

COLLECT OF
Advent 1

The Second Sunday in Advent

A	**B**	**C**
Psalm 72:12-21	Psalm 85:8-13	Psalm 126
Isaiah 11:1-10	Isaiah 40:1-11 *Or* 1-5,9-11	Baruch 5:1-9 *Or* Isaiah 40:1-11
Romans 15:4-13 *Or* 4-9	2 Peter 3:8-14	Philippians 1:3-11 *Or* 3-6, 8-11
Matthew 3:1-12	Mark 1:1-8	Luke 3:1-6

COLLECT OF
Pentecost 9
Or
St John the Baptist

The Third Sunday in Advent

A	**B**	**C**
Psalm 146:5-10	*For the Psalm*	*For the Psalm*
	The Magnificat	Isaiah 12:2-6
		Or
		Benedictus
Isaiah 35:1-10	Isaiah 61:1-7	Zephaniah 3:14-18a
Or	*Or*	
1-6a,10	1-2a, 10-11	Philippians 4:4-7
James 5:7-10	1 Thessalonians 5:16-24	
Matthew 11:2-11	John 1:6-8,19-28	Luke 3:10-18

COLLECT OF
Advent 3

The Fourth Sunday in Advent

A	**B**	**C**
Psalm 24	Psalm 89:19-29	Psalm 80:8-19
Isaiah 7:10-14	2 Samuel 7:1-12	Micah 5:2-5a
	Or	
	1-5, 8b-12, 14a, 16	
Romans 1:1-7	Romans 16:25-27	Hebrews 10:5-10
Matthew 1:18-25	Luke 1:26-38	Luke 1:39-45

COLLECT OF
Advent 4 | Advent 4 | Advent 4 |
| | *Or* | |
| | The Annunciation | |

The Season of Christmas

Christmas Day at Midnight

Psalm 96:7-13

Isaiah 9:2-7 or 2-4,6-7
Titus 2:11-14
Luke 2:1-14

Christmas Day during the day

FIRST SERVICE
Psalm 97

Isaiah 62:11-12
Titus 3:4-7
Luke 2:15-20

SECOND SERVICE
Psalm 98

Isaiah 52:7-10
Hebrews 1:1-6
John 1:1-18 or 1-5,9-14

COLLECT OF
Christmas

The Sunday after Christmas

Psalm 128

Sirach 3:2-14
Or
2-6,12-14
Or
Genesis 1:26-31
Colossians 3:12-21

A

Matthew 2:13-23
Or
13-15,19-23

B

Luke 2:22-40

C

Luke 2:41-52

COLLECT OF
Epiphany 2

The Second Sunday after Christmas

Psalm 147:12-20

Proverbs 8:22-31
Or
Sirach 24:1-12
Or
1-2,8-12
Ephesians 1:3-6,15-18
John 1:1-18

COLLECT OF
Christmas 1

The Season of the Epiphany

The Epiphany of our Lord

Psalm 72:1-11

Isaiah 60:1-6
Ephesians 3:1-6
Or
2-3a,5-6
Matthew 2:1-12

COLLECT OF
The Epiphany of our Lord Jesus Christ

Note:
The readings for the Ordinary Sundays on pages 707-711 are used between the Epiphany of our Lord Jesus Christ and Ash Wednesday.

The Season of Lent

Ash Wednesday
The First Day of Lent

Psalm 51:1-13

Joel 2:12-18
2 Corinthians 5:16 - 6:2
Or
5:20 - 6:2
Matthew 6:1-21
Or
1-6,16-18

COLLECT OF
Ash Wednesday

The First Sunday in Lent

A	**B**	**C**
Psalm 51:1-13	Psalm 25:1-8	Psalm 91:1-12
Genesis 2:7-9; 3:1-7	Genesis 9:8-15	Deuteronomy 26:(1-)4-10
Romans 5:12-19	1 Peter 3:18-22	Romans 10:5-13
Or		*Or*
17-19		8-13
Matthew 4:1-11	Mark 1:12-15	Luke 4:1-13

COLLECT OF
Lent 1

The Second Sunday in Lent

A	**B**	**C**
Psalm 33:13-21	Psalm 116:11-16	Psalm 27:9-17
Genesis 12:1-4a	Genesis 22:1-18	Genesis 15:5-18
	Or	*Or*
	1-2,9a,10-13,15-18	5-12,17-18
2 Timothy 1:8b-10	Romans 8:31b-34	Philippians 3:17 - 4:1
		Or
		3:20 - 4:1
Matthew 17:1-9	Mark 9:2-10	Luke 9:28b-36

COLLECT OF
Epiphany 4

The Third Sunday in Lent

The readings for Year A may be used every year

A	**B**	**C**
Psalm 95	Psalm 19:7-14	Psalm 103:8-18
Exodus 17:3-7	Exodus 20:1-17	Exodus 3:1-15
	Or	*Or*
	1-3,7-8,12-17	1-8a,13,15
Romans 5:1-8	1 Corinthians 1:22-25	1 Corinthians 10:1-13
Or		*Or*
1-2,5-8		1-6,10-12
John 4:5-42	John 2:13-25	Luke 13:1-9
Or		
4:4-15,19b-26,39a, 40-42		

COLLECT OF

Pentecost 14	Pentecost 26	Epiphany 8

The Fourth Sunday in Lent

The readings for Year A may be used every year

A	B	C
Psalm 23	Psalm 137:1-6	Psalm 34:1-10
1 Samuel 16:1-13	2 Chronicles 36:15-21	Joshua 5:2-12
Or	Or	Or
1,6-7,10-13a	14-16,19-23	9a,10-12
Ephesians 5:8-14	Ephesians 2:4-10	2 Corinthians 5:14-21
		Or
		17-21
John 9:1-41	John 3:14-21	Luke 15:1-3,11-32
Or		Or
1,6-9,13-17,34-38		11-32

COLLECT OF

Epiphany 7	Epiphany 5	Easter 3

The Fifth Sunday in Lent

The readings for Year A may be used every year

A	B	C
Psalm 130	Psalm 51:1-10	Psalm 126
Ezekiel 37:12-14	Jeremiah 31:31-34	Isaiah 43:16-21
Romans 8:1-11	Hebrews 5:7-9	Philippians 3:2-14
Or		Or
8-11		8-14
John 11:1-45	John 12:20-33	John 8:1-11
Or		
3-7,17,20-27,33b-45		

COLLECT OF

Epiphany 9	Lent 5	Epiphany 6

The Sunday before Easter
Palm Sunday

Psalm 22:6-21

Isaiah 50:4-7
Philippians 2:5-11

A	**B**	**C**
Matthew 26:14 - 27:66	Mark 14:1 - 15:47	Luke 22:14 - 23:56
Or	*Or*	*Or*
27:11-54	15:1-39	23:1-49

COLLECT OF
Lent 6

Holy Week

Monday Before Easter

Psalm 27:1-7
Isaiah 42:1-7
John 12:1-11

COLLECT OF
Wednesday in Holy Week

Tuesday Before Easter

Psalm 71:1-8
Isaiah 49:1-6
John 13:21-38
Or
21-33 (36-38)

COLLECT OF
Tuesday in Holy Week

Wednesday Before Easter

Psalm 69:17-22

Isaiah 50:4-9a
Matthew 26:14-25

COLLECT OF
Lent 5

Thursday Before Easter
Maundy Thursday

Psalm 116:11-16

Exodus 12:1-14 or 1-8,11-14
1 Corinthians 11:23-26
John 13:1-15

COLLECT OF
Maundy Thursday

Good Friday

Psalm 31:12-18

Isaiah 52:13 - 53:12
Hebrews 4:14 - 5:10
Or
4:14-16 and 5:7-9
John 18:1 - 19:42

COLLECT OF
Good Friday

The Season of Easter

Easter Day

AT MIDNIGHT
Psalm 18:26-30
Or
Exodus 15:1b-3,4-8,9-10,11-12,13-18
Exodus 14:15 - 15:1a
Romans 6:1-11
Or
3-11
Psalm 118:14-24

A	**B**	**C**
Matthew 28:1-10	Mark 16:1-8	Luke 24:1-12

DURING THE DAY
Psalm 118:19-29

Acts 10:34-43
Or
34a,37-43
Colossians 3:1-4
Or
1 Corinthians 5:6b-8
John 20:1-9
Or
The appropriate Gospel from Easter Day at Midnight
Or
Luke 24:13-35

COLLECT OF
Easter Day

The Sunday after Easter

A	**B**	**C**
Psalm 118:19-29	Psalm 118:19-29	Psalm 118:19-29
Acts 2:42-47	Acts 4:32-35	Acts 5:12-16
1 Peter 1:3-9	1 John 5:1-6	Revelation 1:9-19
		Or
		9-13,17-19
John 20:19-31	John 20:19-31	John 20:19-31

COLLECT OF
Easter 1

The Second Sunday after Easter

A	**B**	**C**
Psalm 16	Psalm 4	Psalm 30
Acts 2:(14,)22-28	Acts 3:13-19	Acts 5:27b-41
	Or	*Or*
	13-15,17-19	27b-32,40-41
1 Peter 1:17-21	1 John 2:1-6	Revelation 5:11-14
Luke 24:13-35	Luke 24:35-48	John 21:1-19 or 1-14

COLLECT OF

Pentecost 13	Pentecost 26	Pentecost 11

The Third Sunday after Easter

A

Psalm 23

Acts 2:(14,)36-41
1 Peter 2:20b-25
John 10:1-10

COLLECT OF
Easter 2

B

Psalm 118:1-9

Acts 4:8-12
1 John 3:1-2
John 10:11-18

C

Psalm 100

Acts 13:(14,)43-52
Revelation 7:9,13-17
John 10:27-30

The Fourth Sunday after Easter

A

Psalm 33:1-5
Or
1-12

Acts 6:1-7
1 Peter 2:4-9(-10)
John 14:1-12

COLLECT OF
Easter 4

B

Psalm 22:22-31

Acts 9:26-31
1 John 3:18-24
John 15:1-8

C

Psalm 145:8-21

Acts 14:21b-27
Revelation 21:1-5
John 13:31-35

The Fifth Sunday after Easter

A	**B**	**C**
Psalm 66:1-8	Psalm 98	Psalm 67
Acts 8:5-17	Acts 10:25-48	Acts 15:1-2,22-29
Or	*Or*	
5-8,14-17	25-26,34-35,44-48	
1 Peter 3:15-22	1 John 4:7-10	Revelation 21:10-23
Or		*Or*
15-18		10-14,22-23
John 14:15-21	John 15:9-17	John 14:23-29

COLLECT OF
Sunday before Advent

Ascension Day

Psalm 47
Acts 1:1-11
Ephesians 1:15-23 or 17-23

A	**B**	**C**
Matthew 28:16-20	Mark 16:15-20	Luke 24:46-53
	Or	
	Luke 24:46-53	

COLLECT OF
Ascension Day

The Sunday after the Ascension

A	**B**	**C**
Psalm 27:1-8	Psalm 103:19-22	Psalm 97
Acts 1:12-14	Acts 1:15-26 *Or* 15-17,20-26	Acts 7:55-60
1 Peter 4:13-16	1 John 4:11-16	Revelation 22:12-20 *Or* 12-14,17-20
John 17:1-11	John 17:11b-19	John 17:20-26

COLLECT OF
Easter 5

Whitsunday (Pentecost)

Psalm 104:25-31

Acts 2:1-11
1 Corinthians 12:1-13
Or
3-7,12-13
John 20:19-23

COLLECT OF
The Day of Pentecost

Trinity Sunday

A

For the Psalm
Song of the Three
Young Men 29-34

Exodus 34:4-9
Or
4-6,8-9
2 Corinthians
   13:11-14
John 3:16-18

COLLECT OF
Pentecost 1

B

Psalm 33:13-21

Deuteronomy 4:32-40
Or
32-34,39-40
Romans 8:14-17

Matthew 28:16-20

C

Psalm 8

Proverbs 8:22-31

Romans 5:1-5

John 16:12-15

Ordinary Sundays

The Baptism of the Lord
The First Ordinary Sunday

Sunday between 7 and 13 January

Psalm 29

Isaiah 42:1-7 or 1-4,6-7
Acts 10:34-38

A	B	C
Matthew 3:13-17	Mark 1:7-11	Luke 3:15-22 *Or* 15-16, 21-22

COLLECT OF
Epiphany 1

The Second Ordinary Sunday

Sunday between 14 and 20 January

A	B	C
Psalm 40:8-13	Psalm 40:8-13	Psalm 96:7-13
Isaiah 49:3-6 *Or* 3,5-6 1 Corinthians 1:1-3	1 Samuel 3:2-19 *Or* 3-10,19 1 Corinthians 6:12-20 *Or* 13-15,17-20	Isaiah 62:1-5 1 Corinthians12:4-11
John 1:29-34	John 1:35-42	John 2:1-12
COLLECT OF		
Pentecost 14	Pentecost 6	Pentecost 17

The Third Ordinary Sunday

Sunday between 21 and 27 January

A	B	C
Psalm 27:9-17	Psalm 25:1-8	Psalm 19:7-14
Isaiah 9:1b-4(-7)	Jonah 3:1-10 Or 1-5,10	Nehemiah 8:2-10 Or 2-4a,5-6,8-10
1 Corinthians 1:10-17 Or 10-13,17	1 Corinthians 7:29-31	1 Corinthians12:12-30 Or 12-14,27
Matthew 4:12-23 Or 12-17	Mark 1:14-20	Luke 1:1-4; 4:14-21

COLLECT OF
Epiphany 3

The Fourth Ordinary Sunday

Sunday between 28 January and 3 February

A	B	C
Psalm 146	Psalm 95	Psalm 71:1-13
Zephaniah 3:11-13 Or 2:3; 3:12-13	Deuteronomy 18:15-20	Jeremiah 1:4-5,17-19
1 Corinthians 1:26-31	1 Corinthians 7:32-35	1 Corinthians 12:31–13:13 Or 13:4-13
Matthew 5:1-12	Mark 1:21-28	Luke 4:21-30

COLLECT OF
Monday in Holy Week

The Fifth Ordinary Sunday

Sunday between 4 and 10 February

A	B	C
Psalm 112	Psalm 146	Psalm 138:1-6
Isaiah 58:7-10	Job 7:1-7	Isaiah 6:1-8(-13)
	Or	
	1-4, 6-7	
1 Corinthians 2:1-5	1 Corinthians 9:16-23	1 Corinthians 15:1-11
	Or	Or
	16-19,22-23	3-8,11
Matthew 5:13-16	Mark 1:29-39	Luke 5:1-11

COLLECT OF

Easter 3	Pentecost 5	Pentecost 6 (or 5)

The Sixth Ordinary Sunday

Sunday between 11 and 17 February

A	B	C
Psalm 119:1-8	Psalm 32:1-8	Psalm 1
Deuteronomy 10:12-22	Leviticus 13:1-2,45-46	Jeremiah 17:5-8
Or		
Sirach 15:15-20		
1 Corinthians 2:6-10	1 Corinthians 10:31 - 11:1	1 Corinthians 15:12-20
		Or
		12,16-20
Matthew 5:17-37	Mark 1:40-45	Luke 6:17-26
Or		Or
20-22,27-28,33-34,37		17,20-26

COLLECT OF

Advent 2	Pentecost 3	Lent 4

The Seventh Ordinary Sunday

Sunday between 18 and 24 February

A	B	C
Psalm 103:1-5	Psalm 41:1,2(3-10), 11-13	Psalm 103:1-5
Leviticus 19:1-2,17-18	Isaiah 43:18-25	1 Samuel 26:2-23
	Or	*Or*
	18-19,21-22,24-25	2,7-9,12-13,22-23
1 Corinthians 3:16-23	2 Corinthians 1:18-22	1 Corinthians 15:42-50
		Or
		45-49
Matthew 5:38-48	Mark 2:1-12	Luke 6:27-38
COLLECT OF		
Pentecost 15	Lent 3	Pentecost 15

The Eighth Ordinary Sunday

Sunday between 25 February and 3 March or 24 and 28 May

A	B	C
Psalm 62:1-8	Psalm 103:6-18	Psalm 92:5-15
Isaiah 49:14-18	Hosea 2:16-22	Ecclesiastes 10:12-14
Or	*Or*	*Or*
14-15	16-17,21-22	Sirach 27:4-7
1 Corinthians 4:1-5	2 Corinthians 3:1-6	1 Corinthians 15:54-58
Matthew 6:24-34	Mark 2:18-22	Luke 6:39-45
COLLECT OF		
Pentecost 2	Pentecost 17	Epiphany 8

The Ninth Ordinary Sunday

Sunday between 4 and 7 March or 29 May and 4 June

A	B	C
Psalm 31:1-9	Psalm 81:1-7	Psalm 117
Deuteronomy 11:18-28 *Or* 18,26-28	Deuteronomy 5:12-15	1 Kings 8:41-43
Romans 3:21-31 *Or* 21-25(,28)	2 Corinthians 4:6-11 (-12)	Galatians 1:1-10 *Or* 1-2,6-10
Matthew 7:21-27	Mark 2:23 - 3:6 *Or* 2:23-28	Luke 7:1-10

COLLECT OF

Pentecost 27	Epiphany 7	Pentecost 14

The Tenth Ordinary Sunday

Sunday between 5 and 11 June

A	B	C
Psalm 50:7-15	Psalm 130	Psalm 30:4-13
Hosea 6:3-6 Romans 4:18-25	Genesis 3:8-15 2 Corinthians 4:13 - 5:5 *Or* 4:13 - 5:1	1 Kings 17:17-24 Galatians 1:11-19
Matthew 9:9-13	Mark 3:20-35	Luke 7:11-17

COLLECT OF

Pentecost 5	Epiphany 9	Pentecost 13

The Eleventh Ordinary Sunday

Sunday between 12 and 18 June

A	B	C
Psalm 100	Psalm 92:1-5	Psalm 32:1-8
Exodus 19:2-6	Ezekiel 17:22-24	2 Samuel 12:7-13 *Or* 7-10,13
Romans 5:6-11	2 Corinthians 5:6-10	Galatians 2:16-21 *Or* 16,19-21
Matthew 9:36 - 10:8	Mark 4:26-34	Luke 7:36 - 8:3 *Or* 7:36-50

COLLECT OF

Pentecost 12	Pentecost 14	Lent 3

The Twelfth Ordinary Sunday

Sunday between 19 and 25 June

A	B	C
Psalm 69:7-13	Psalm 107:23-32	Psalm 63:1-9
Jeremiah 20:10-13	Job 38:1-11 *Or* 1,8-11	Zechariah 12:10-11
Romans 5:12-17 *Or* 12-15	2 Corinthians 5:14-21 *Or* 14-17	Galatians 3:26-29
Matthew 10:26-33	Mark 4:35-41	Luke 9:18-24

COLLECT OF

Pentecost 18	Epiphany 6	Pentecost 21

The Thirteenth Ordinary Sunday

Sunday between 26 June and 2 July

A	B	C
Psalm 89:1-9	Psalm 30:4-13	Psalm 16
2 Kings 4:8-16 *Or* 8-11,14-16	Genesis 3:8-19 *Or* Wisdom 1:13-15; 2:23-24	1 Kings 19:15-21 *Or* 16b,19-21
Romans 6:3-11 *Or* 3-4,8-11	2 Corinthians 8:7-15 *Or* 7,9,13-15	Galatians 5:(1,)13-18
Matthew 10:37-42	Mark 5:21-43 *Or* 21-24,35-43	Luke 9:51-62

COLLECT OF

Pentecost 10	Pentecost 16	Lent 5

The Fourteenth Ordinary Sunday

Sunday between 3 and 9 July

A	B	C
Psalm 145:1-7	Psalm 123	Psalm 66:1-8
Zechariah 9:9-10 Romans 8:9-13 *Or* 9,11-13	Ezekiel 2:2-5 2 Corinthians 12:7-10	Isaiah 66:10-14 Galatians 6:14-18
Matthew 11:25-30	Mark 6:1-6	Luke 10:1-20 *Or* 1-12,17-20 *Or* 1-9

COLLECT OF

Pentecost 21	Pentecost 8	Pentecost 7

The Fifteenth Ordinary Sunday

Sunday between 10 and 16 July

A	B	C
Psalm 65:9-14	Psalm 85:8-13	Psalm 69:31-38
Isaiah 55:6-11 *Or* 10-11	Amos 7:12-15	Deuteronomy 30:10-14
Romans 8:18-23(-25)	Ephesians 1:3-14 *Or* 3-10	Colossians 1:15-20
Matthew 13:1-23 *Or* 1-9	Mark 6:7-13	Luke 10:25-37

COLLECT OF

Pentecost 6	Pentecost 12	Pentecost 23

The Sixteenth Ordinary Sunday

Sunday between 17 and 23 July

A	B	C
Psalm 86:4-13	Psalm 23	Psalm 15
Deuteronomy 32:36-41 *Or* Wisdom 12:13-19 *Or* 13,16-19	Jeremiah 23:1-6	Genesis 18:1-10a
Romans 8:26-30 *Or* 26-27	Ephesians 2:13-18	Colossians 1:24-28
Matthew 13:24-43 *Or* 24-30	Mark 6:30-34	Luke 10:38-42

COLLECT OF

Pentecost 4	Pentecost 18	Pentecost 19

The Seventeenth Ordinary Sunday

Sunday between 24 and 30 July

A	B	C
Psalm 119:57-64	Psalm 145:8-21	Psalm 138
1 Kings 3:5-12	2 Kings 4:42-44	Genesis 18:20-32
Or		
5,7-12		
Romans 8:28-30	Ephesians 4:1-6	Colossians 2:11-14
Matthew 13:44-52	John 6:1-15	Luke 11:1-13

COLLECT OF

Pentecost 16	Pentecost 20	Pentecost 20

The Eighteenth Ordinary Sunday

Sunday between 31 July and 6 August

A	B	C
Psalm 145:14-21	Psalm 78:17-31	Psalm 95
Isaiah 55:1-3	Exodus 16:2-15	Ecclesiastes 2:18-23
	Or	Or
	2-4,12-15	1:2; 2:20-23
Romans 8:35-39	Ephesians 4:17-24	Colossians 3:1-11
Or	Or	Or
35,37-39	17,20-24	1-5,9-11
Matthew 14:13-21	John 6:24-35	Luke 12:13-21

COLLECT OF

Lent 4	Lent 4	Pentecost 24

The Nineteenth Ordinary Sunday

Sunday between 7 and 13 August

A	B	C
Psalm 85:8-13	Psalm 34:1-10	Psalm 33:13-21
1 Kings 19:9-13	1 Kings 19:4-8	Isaiah 63:7-9
Or		Or
9,11-13		Wisdom 18:5-9
Romans 9:1-5	Ephesians 4:30 - 5:2	Hebrews 11:1-19
		Or
		1-2,8-19
		Or
		1-2,8-12
Matthew 14:22-33	John 6:41-51	Luke 12:32-48
		Or
		35-40

COLLECT OF

Epiphany 6	Pentecost 7	Pentecost 8

The Twentieth Ordinary Sunday

Sunday between 14 and 20 August

A	B	C
Psalm 67	Psalm 34:11-18	Psalm 40:1-7
Isaiah 56:1-7	Proverbs 9:1-6	Jeremiah 38:2-10
Or		Or
1,6-7		4-6,8-10
Romans 11:13-32	Ephesians 5:15-20	Hebrews 12:1-4
Or		
13-15,29-32		
Matthew 15:21-28	John 6:51-58	Luke 12:49-53

COLLECT OF

Pentecost 20	Pentecost 11	Pentecost 10

The Twenty-First Ordinary Sunday

Sunday between 21 and 27 August

A	B	C
Psalm 138	Psalm 34:11-18	Psalm 117
Isaiah 22:19-23	Joshua 24:1-18 *Or* 1-2,15-18	Isaiah 66:18b-21
Romans 11:33-36	Ephesians 5:21-32(-33)	Hebrews 12:5-13 *Or* 5-7,11-13
Matthew 16:13-20	John 6:60-69	Luke 13:22-30

COLLECT OF

A	B	C
Pentecost 8	Advent 2	Pentecost 25

The Twenty-Second Ordinary Sunday

Sunday between 28 August and 3 September

A	B	C
Psalm 63	Psalm 15	Psalm 68:1-8
Jeremiah 20:7-9	Deuteronomy 4:1-8 *Or* 1-2,6-8	Proverbs 2:1-15 *Or* Sirach 3:17-29 *Or* 17-18,20,28-29
Romans 12:1-12 *Or* 1-8	James 1:17-27 *Or* 17-18,21-22	Hebrews 12:18-24 *Or* 18-19,22-24a
Matthew 16:21-27	Mark 7:1-23 *Or* 1-8,14-15,21-23	Luke 14:7-14

COLLECT OF

A	B	C
Pentecost 3	Lent 2	Pentecost 26

The Twenty-Third Ordinary Sunday

Sunday between 4 and 10 September

A	B	C
Psalm 95	Psalm 146	Psalm 90:1-12
Ezekiel 33:7-9	Isaiah 35:(3-)4-7	Exodus 15:1-12
		Or
		Wisdom 9:13-18
Romans 13:8-14	James 2:1-5	Philemon
Or		*Or*
8-10		Philemon 9-10,12-17
Matthew 18:15-20	Mark 7:31-37	Luke 14:25-33
COLLECT OF		
Epiphany 8	Pentecost 13	Pentecost 12

The Twenty-Fourth Ordinary Sunday

Sunday between 11 and 17 September

A	B	C
Psalm 103:6-14	Psalm 116:1-9	Psalm 51:10-19
Exodus 34:5-9	Isaiah 50:4-9	Exodus 32:7-14
Or		*Or*
Sirach 27:30 - 28:7		7-11,13-14
Romans 14:7-12	James 2:14-26	1 Timothy 1:12-17
Or	*Or*	
7-9	14-18	
Matthew 18:21-35	Mark 8:27-35	Luke 15:1-32 or 1-10
COLLECT OF		
Lent 3	Pentecost 21	Lent 2

The Twenty-Fifth Ordinary Sunday

Sunday between 18 and 24 September

A	B	C
Psalm 145:14-21	Psalm 54	Psalm 113
Isaiah 55:6-9	Hosea 4:1-6 Or Wisdom 2:12-20 Or 12,17-20	Amos 8:4-7(-10)
Philippians 1:19-26 Or 20-24,27	James 3:16 - 4:3 Or 3:13-18	1 Timothy 2:1-8
Matthew 20:1-16	Mark 9:30-37	Luke 16:1-13 Or Luke 16:10-13

COLLECT OF

Pentecost 26	Pentecost 15	Pentecost 16

The Twenty-Sixth Ordinary Sunday

Sunday between 25 September and 1 October

A	B	C
Psalm 25:1-8	Psalm 19:7-14	Psalm 146
Ezekiel 18:25-28(-32)	Numbers 11:25-29	Amos 6:1-7 Or 1a,4-7
Philippians 2:1-11	James 5:1-6	1 Timothy 6:11-16
Matthew 21:28-32	Mark 9:38-48 Or 38-43,45,47-48	Luke 16:19-31

COLLECT OF

Pentecost 7	Epiphany 8	Pentecost 4

The Twenty-Seventh Ordinary Sunday

Sunday between 2 and 8 October

A	B	C
Psalm 80:8-19	Psalm 128	Psalm 95:1-9
Isaiah 5:1-7	Genesis 2:18-24	Habakkuk 1:2-3; 2:2-4 *Or* 2:1-4
Philippians 4:(4-)6-9	Hebrews 2:9-11	2 Timothy 1:6-14 *Or* 6-8,13-14
Matthew 21:33-43	Mark 10:2-16 *Or* 2-12	Luke 17:5-10

COLLECT OF

Epiphany 5	Pentecost 22	Pentecost 18

The Twenty-Eighth Ordinary Sunday

Sunday between 9 and 15 October

A	B	C
Psalm 23	Psalm 90:11-17	Psalm 98
Isaiah 25:6-9	1 Kings 3:3-14 *Or* Wisdom 7:7-11	2 Kings 5:(10-)14-17
Philippians 4:12-20 *Or* 12-14,19-20	Hebrews 4:12-13	2 Timothy 2:8-13
Matthew 22:1-14 *Or* 1-10	Mark 10:17-30 *Or* 17-27	Luke 17:11-19

COLLECT OF

Pentecost 11	Pentecost 4	Epiphany 9

The Twenty-Ninth Ordinary Sunday

Sunday between 16 and 22 October

A	B	C
Psalm 96	Psalm 33:13-21	Psalm 121
Isaiah 45:1-6	Isaiah 53:7-12	Exodus 17:8-13
Or	*Or*	
1,4-6	10-11	
1 Thessalonians 1:1-5	Hebrews 4:14-16	2 Timothy 3:14 - 4:2
Matthew 22:15-21	Mark 10:35-45	Luke 18:1-8
	Or	
	42-45	

COLLECT OF

A	B	C
Pentecost 24	Pentecost 10	Pentecost 3

The Thirtieth Ordinary Sunday

Sunday between 23 and 29 October

A	B	C
Psalm 18:48-52	Psalm 126	Psalm 34:11-22
Exodus 22:21-27	Jeremiah 31:7-9	Exodus 12:12-22
		Or
		Sirach 35:12b-18a
		Or
		12b-14,16-18a
1 Thessalonians 1:5b-10	Hebrews 5:1-6(-10)	2 Timothy 4:6-18
		Or
		6-9,16-18
Matthew 22:34-40	Mark 10:46-52	Luke 18:9-14

COLLECT OF

A	B	C
Pentecost 23	Easter 3	Epiphany 5

The Thirty-First Ordinary Sunday

Sunday between October 30 and 5 November

A	B	C
Psalm 131	Psalm 18:48-52	Psalm 145
Malachi 1:14 - 2:10 Or 1:14 - 2:2,8-10	Deuteronomy 6:1-6	Hosea 14:1-7 Or Wisdom 11:22 - 12:2

1 Thessalonians
  2:7-13
Or
7-9,13
	Hebrews 7:23-28	2 Thessalonians
		  1:11 - 2:2

Matthew 23:1-12	Mark 12:28-34	Luke 19:1-10

COLLECT OF

A	B	C
Lent 2	Pentecost 23	Pentecost 5

The Thirty-Second Ordinary Sunday

Sunday between 6 and 12 November

A	B	C
Psalm 63:1-9	Psalm 146	Psalm 17:6-12
Proverbs 3:21-26 Or Wisdom 6:12-16	1 Kings 17:10-16	Malachi 3:16-18 Or 2 Maccabees 7:1-14 Or 1-2,9-14

1 Thessalonians
  4:13-18
Or
13-14
	Hebrews 9:24-28	2 Thessalonians
		  2:16 – 3:5

Matthew 25:1-13	Mark 12:38-44 Or 41-44	Luke 20:27-38 Or 34-38

COLLECT OF

A	B	C
Pentecost 19	Pentecost 19	Pentecost 2

The Thirty-Third Ordinary Sunday

Sunday between 13 and 19 November

A	B	C
Psalm 128	Psalm 16	Psalm 98
Proverbs 31:10-31 *Or* 10-13,19-20,30-31	Daniel 12:1-3	Malachi 4:1-2a
1Thessalonians 5:1-6(-11)	Hebrews 10:11-18 *Or* 11-14,18	2 Thessalonians 3:6-13
Matthew 25:14-30 *Or* 14-15,19-20	Mark 13:24-32	Luke 21:5-19

COLLECT OF

Pentecost 17	Pentecost 27	Pentecost 27

The Thirty-Fourth Ordinary Sunday

Sunday Before Advent

A	B	C
Psalm 23	Psalm 93	Psalm 122
Ezekiel 34:11-16 *Or* 11-12,15-17	Daniel 7:13-14	2 Samuel 5:1-3
1 Corinthians 15:20-28 *Or* 20-26,28	Revelation 1:4-8	Colossians 1:11-20 *Or* 15-20
Matthew 25:31-46	John 18:33-37	Luke 23:35-43

COLLECT OF

Epiphany 9

Pastoral
Liturgies

Concerning these Services

In our lives there are many times of special need when we look for a deep experience of God's love and power. In his ministry, Jesus showed particular concern for the healing of the sick. The Church continues that ministry now. Each of these services provides resources for a particular pastoral occasion.

A Service of Holy Communion

This brief service takes into consideration the needs of sick and frail people unable to concentrate for more than a limited time.

For larger groups (for example, with collected groups of people in a hospital) it may be expanded, and suitable hymns may be added.

For a very sick person, the service may be abbreviated even further by using only the following sections

> Scripture
> Confession and Absolution
> Prayer
> Great Thanksgiving Prayer, or prayer when the Sacrament has been consecrated elsewhere
> Communion
> Lord's Prayer.

Ministry of Healing

The directions on page 746 show how **Ministry of Healing** may be incorporated within a Eucharist.

Ministry of Healing includes two actions. Those ministering may use the laying on of hands, either with or without anointing. It may be used as a service on its own, or be incorporated with any other service where this ministry is appropriate.

The Reconciliation of a Penitent

The priest and penitent may meet in Church for this order. The penitent may kneel at the communion rail, with the priest seated alongside.

It may be used in any other convenient place where the penitent may open his or her heart without fear of being overheard.

Thanksgiving for the Gift of a Child

The coming of a child, at birth or adoption, is a time to celebrate God's gift of life, to thank God for the goodness of creation, and to ask a blessing on the new person, who is part of it, and part of us.

This service offers an opportunity to do so.

The Blessing of a Home

This may be used when people wish to have a blessing in the place where they live, and to dedicate their life in their home to God.

A Service of Holy Communion

For use with individuals or small groups to meet special pastoral needs

It is the joy, right and responsibility of all who have been admitted to the Holy Communion to receive the sacrament regularly.

When members of the Christian community are prevented by frailty or sickness from taking part in the common worship of the Church, they should be able to continue to receive the sacrament.

Under such circumstances, it is the responsibility of the priest either to attend personally, or to ensure that such faithful receive Communion from another duly authorised person.

A Service of Holy Communion *makes provision for the above, either by a celebration of the Eucharist in the place where the person or persons are able to be present, or by use of the sacrament which has been consecrated elsewhere.*

*When a person is prevented from receiving the Holy Communion by reason of very serious illness, the order for **Ministry of Healing** may be used.*

When people who desire to receive the Holy Communion are unable to do so for any other reason, their desire and such prayers as they are able to offer ensure that they do spiritually receive the body and blood of Christ.

The Preparation and Readings

The minister may say

Grace and peace to you from God.
>Kia tau ki a koutou, te atawhai me te rangimarie a te Atua.

God fill you with truth and joy.
>**Ma te Atua koe e whakau, ki te pono me te hari.**

The following may be said.

Almighty God,
to whom all hearts are open,
all desires known,
and from whom no secrets are hidden;
cleanse the thoughts of our hearts
by the inspiration of your Holy Spirit,
so that we may truly love you
and worthily praise your holy name:
through our Saviour Jesus Christ.
Amen.

A collect may follow.

The Gospel for the day or other Scripture may be read here
or after the Confession.

The minister says

Happy are those whose sins are forgiven,
whose wrongs are pardoned.
I will confess my sins to the Lord,
I will not conceal my wrongdoings.

Silence

God forgives and heals us.
We need your healing, merciful God:
give us true repentance.
Some sins are plain to us;
some escape us,
some we cannot face.

Forgive us;
set us free to hear your word to us;
set us free to serve you.

The presiding priest says

God forgives you.
Forgive others;
forgive yourself.

Silence

Through Christ, God has put away your sin:
approach your God in peace.

If a priest is not present the following shall be said.

Hear the word of God to all.
God shows love for us
in that while we were yet sinners Christ died for us.
Amen.

The Gospel for the day or other Scripture may be read here.

The Prayers

A collect may be said here, followed by biddings for intercession
and thanksgiving.

A period of silence may be kept.

During **The Prayers** *the following may be used.*

AFTER THANKSGIVING
Give thanks to our God who is gracious
whose mercy endures for ever.

AFTER INTERCESSION
God of love
grant our prayer.

Lord, in your mercy
hear our prayer.

God of mercy,
you have given us grace to pray with one heart and one voice;
and have promised to hear the prayers
of two or three who agree in your name;
fulfil now, we pray,
the prayers and longings of your people
as may be best for us and for your kingdom.
Grant us in this world to know your truth,
and in the world to come to see your glory.
Amen.

The bread and wine for communion are prepared.

The Great Thanksgiving *is NOT said when using the sacrament consecrated elsewhere.*

In **The Great Thanksgiving***, the marked passages may be omitted.*

The Great Thanksgiving

The priest says

The Lord is here.
God's Spirit is with us.

Lift up your hearts.
We lift them to the Lord.

Let us give thanks to the Lord our God.
It is right to offer thanks and praise.

It is right indeed, everliving God,
to give you thanks and praise through Christ your only Son.

You are the source of all life and goodness;
through your eternal Word
you have created all things from the beginning.

When we sinned and turned away
you called us back to yourself
and gave your Son to share our human nature.
He made the one perfect sacrifice for the sin of the world.

Therefore we proclaim your great and glorious name,
saying,
Holy, holy, holy Lord, God of power and might;
heaven and earth are full of your glory.
Hosanna in the highest.

On the night before he died, he took bread;
when he had given you thanks,
he broke it, gave it to his disciples, and said:
Take, eat, this is my body
which is given for you;
do this to remember me.

After supper he took the cup;
when he had given you thanks,
he gave it to them and said:
Drink this, all of you,
for this is my blood of the new covenant
which is shed for you and for many
for the forgiveness of sins;
do this as often as you drink it,
to remember me.

Therefore loving God,
recalling your great goodness to us in Christ,
we celebrate our redemption with this bread of life
and this cup of salvation.

Send your Holy Spirit
that these gifts of bread and wine which we receive
may be to us the body and blood of Christ,
and that we, filled with the Spirit's grace and power,
may be renewed for the service of your kingdom.

United in Christ with all who stand before you
in earth and heaven,
we worship you, O God,
in songs of everlasting praise.
Blessing, honour and glory be yours,
here and everywhere
now and forever.

Amen.

The Communion

*After **The Great Thanksgiving**,*
the priest breaks the bread
and says

When the sacrament has been
consecrated elsewhere the minister
says

We break this bread
to share
in the body of Christ.

**We who are many
are one body,
for we all share
the one bread.**

God, creator of time and space
may the love and faith
which makes
this bread the body of Christ
this wine his blood
enfold us now.
Make us one
with (the people of ...* and)
the whole body of Christ.
May Christ's Holy Spirit
bring to us in the sacrament
the strength
and peace we need
and an abiding trust
in your gift of eternal life.
Amen.

* The name of the congregation may be inserted here.

One of the following may be said

Jesus, Lamb of God, have mercy on us.
Jesus, bearer of our sins, have mercy on us.
Jesus, redeemer of the world, give us your peace.

Or

Lamb of God, you take away the sin of the world,
    have mercy on us.
Lamb of God, you take away the sin of the world,
    have mercy on us.
Lamb of God, you take away the sin of the world,
    grant us your peace.

*The following may be used as a preparation to receive **Communion** and is especially appropriate when the sacrament has been consecrated elsewhere.*

We do not presume
to come to your holy table, merciful Lord,
trusting in our own righteousness,
but in your great mercy.
We are not worthy
even to gather the crumbs from under your table.
But you are the same Lord
whose nature is always to have mercy.
Grant us therefore, gracious Lord,
so to eat the body of your dear Son, Jesus Christ,
and to drink his blood,
that we may evermore dwell in him and he in us.
Amen.

The Bread and the Cup are given to each person with the following or other authorised words.

The body of Christ given for you.
     Ko te tinana o to tatou Ariki, i tukua nei mou.

The blood of Christ shed for you.
     Ko nga toto o to tatou Ariki, i whakahekea nei mou.

Or

The body and blood of Christ given for you.
     Ko te tinana me nga toto o to tatou Ariki i tukua nei mou.

The communicant may respond each time

Amen. *or* Amine.

As Christ teaches us, we pray

Our Father in heaven,
   hallowed be your name,
   your kingdom come,
   your will be done,
      on earth as in heaven.
Give us today our daily bread.
Forgive us our sins
   as we forgive those who sin against us.
Save us from the time of trial
   and deliver us from evil.

For the kingdom, the power, and the glory are yours
   now and for ever.   Amen.

Kua akona nei tatou e to tatou Ariki,
   ka inoi tatou

E to matou Matua i te rangi
   Kia tapu tou Ingoa.
   Kia tae mai tou rangatiratanga.
   Kia meatia tau e pai ai
      ki runga ki te whenua,
         kia rite ano ki to te rangi.
Homai ki a matou aianei
   he taro ma matou mo tenei ra.
Murua o matou hara,
   Me matou hoki e muru nei
      i o te hunga e hara ana ki a matou.
Aua hoki matou e kawea kia whakawaia;
   Engari whakaorangia matou i te kino:
Nou hoki te rangatiratanga, te kaha,
   me te kororia,
      Ake ake ake.   Amine.

Further prayer and thanksgiving may follow.

The Blessing

The minister may say

Our Lord Jesus Christ be with you to defend you,
within you to keep you,
before you to lead you,
beside you to guard you,
and above you to bless you.
Amen.

A priest may give a blessing using one of the following, or some other form

God be your comfort, your strength;
God be your hope and support;
God be your light and your way;
and the blessing of God,
Creator, Redeemer and Giver of life,
remain with you now and for ever.
Amen.

Or

Ma te Atua koe e manaaki
e tiaki i nga wa katoa
e noho i roto i te aroha o te Atua:
ko te aroha hoki te mea nui.
Amine.

The Ministry of Healing

This service makes provision for the Church's ministry of healing through the laying on of hands and/or anointing. When required each ministry may be carried out separately by omitting the other section.

They may be used privately, by small groups, in the Eucharist, or other appropriate public worship.

They may be conducted by a priest, or other person duly authorised by the bishop.

Laying on of Hands

From ancient times the laying on of hands has been a symbol for the conveying of God's power.

Among the gifts received from God by this means is that of healing. In Scripture we see this practice commonly used and the healings which ensued.

Anointing

Anointing provides a vivid, sacramental expression of God's love in time of sickness. It is helpful at the onset of an illness, as well as in times of crisis.

The New Testament makes it clear that the anointing of the sick accompanied by prayer was used for healing.

A later practice was to restrict it to the moment of death. While still being available for the dying, its purpose is to convey healing in all sickness.

Preparation: The priest, minister and those seeking healing should prepare beforehand through prayer and instruction.

Additional Directions and **Prayers for Critical Situations** are to be found on pages 746-748.

The Ministry of the Word

The minister greets the person(s) present and then may say

May God bless you.
Receive God's healing grace
to comfort and support you.
Amen.

*One or more of the following or some other appropriate passages of Scripture,
is read.*

Psalm 91
Romans 8: 35-end
2 Corinthians 1: 3-5

Luke 13: 10-13
Luke 9: 1-2,6
Luke 4: 40
Luke 17: 11-19

The following are particularly suitable when the service includes anointing.

James 5: 13-15
Mark 6: 7,12-13

*The **Readings** may be followed by silence for reflection.*

The minister may speak to those present.

The Confession

*If the sick person wishes, **The Reconciliation of a Penitent** on pages 750-753 is used.*

Or

The minister says

Hear God's word to all.
God shows love for us
in that while we were yet sinners Christ died for us.
Amen.

If we confess our sins,
God is just, and may be trusted to forgive our sins
and cleanse us from every kind of wrong.

In silence we call to mind our sins.

Silence

Let us confess our sins.

**God of grace,
we confess that we have sinned,
in what we have thought, and said, and done.
Forgive us for the sake of Jesus Christ. Amen.**

***The Absolution** is declared by the priest saying*

N, God forgives your sins.
Know that God pardons you
and sets you free.
Amen.

Or

Through the cross of Christ,
God have mercy on you,
pardon you
and set you free.
Know that you are forgiven
and be at peace.
God strengthen you in all goodness
and keep you in life eternal.
Amen.

If a priest is not present, the minister shall say

Almighty God,
who pardons all who truly repent,
forgive us our sins,
strengthen us by the Holy Spirit,
and keep us in life eternal;
through Jesus Christ our Saviour.
Amen.

The Invocation

The minister says

Like the first disciples
before the coming of God's power at Pentecost,
we wait in faith, and pray.

Silence

Be with us, Holy Spirit;
nothing can separate us from your love.

Be with us as of old,
fill us with your power,
direct all our thoughts to your goodness.

Be present, Holy Spirit;
bring faith and healing and peace.

Silence

The minister says

The Lord is here.
God's Spirit is with us.

The following sections may be conducted by a priest or by a duly authorised layperson.

The Laying on of Hands

The minister, with any others invited, in silence lays hands on the person(s); then, using the name if desired, may say these or other words.

In the name of God most high
we lay our hands upon you.
Receive Christ's healing touch to make you whole
in body, mind and spirit.
The power of God strengthen you,
the love of God dwell in you
and give you peace.
Amen.

When the laying on of hands is completed, or after the anointing, the minister prays

God our healer,
keep us aware of your presence,
support us with your power,
comfort us with your protection,
give us strength
and establish us in your peace.

The Anointing

The oil for the anointing of the sick is to be oil previously consecrated by a priest or bishop.

The minister dips a thumb in the holy oil and makes the sign of the cross on the person's forehead, saying

N, I anoint you with this holy oil.
Receive Christ's forgiveness and healing.
The power of the Saviour who suffered for you
flow through your mind and body,
lifting you to peace and inward strength.
Amen.

If the person wishes, other parts of the body may also be anointed.

When the anointing is completed, the minister continues

God our healer,
keep us aware of your presence,
support us with your power,
comfort us with your protection,
give us strength
and establish us in your peace.

The Lord's Prayer

The minister or priest continues with one of the following forms.

N, joining with those who pray for you,
and with the whole Church, we pray

Our Father in heaven,
   hallowed be your name,
   your kingdom come,
   your will be done,
     on earth as in heaven.
Give us today our daily bread.
Forgive us our sins
   as we forgive those who sin against us.
Save us from the time of trial
   and deliver us from evil.

For the kingdom, the power, and the glory are yours
   now and for ever. Amen.

Hei whakakotahi i a tatou inoi, me nga inoi o te Haahi katoa
mou, ka inoi tatou

E to matou Matua i te rangi
   Kia tapu tou Ingoa.
   Kia tae mai tou rangatiratanga.
   Kia meatia tau e pai ai
     ki runga ki te whenua,
       kia rite ano ki to te rangi.
Homai ki a matou aianei
   he taro ma matou mo tenei ra.
Murua o matou hara,
   Me matou hoki e muru nei
     i o te hunga e hara ana ki a matou.
Aua hoki matou e kawea kia whakawaia;
   Engari whakaorangia matou i te kino:
Nou hoki te rangatiratanga, te kaha,
   me te kororia,
     Ake ake ake. Amine.

The Blessing of the Sick

When a priest is not present a minister may say

Our Lord Jesus Christ be with you to defend you,
within you to keep you,
before you to lead you,
beside you to guard you,
and above you to bless you.
Amen.

A priest may give a blessing using one of the following, or some other form.

God be your comfort, your strength;
God be your hope and support;
God be your light and your way;
and the blessing of God,
Creator, Redeemer and Giver of life,
remain with you now and for ever.
Amen.

Or

Ma te Atua koe e manaaki
e tiaki i nga wa katoa
e noho i roto i te aroha o te Atua:
ko te aroha hoki te mea nui.
Amine.

Additional Directions

1 For use with a Sunday Eucharist

The Invocation, *The Laying on of Hands* and/or *The Anointing* follow after *The Prayers of the People* or *The Communion* and the service concludes with *The Blessing of the Sick*.

2 For use with A Service of Holy Communion

This service up to and including *The Blessing of the Sick* is followed by *A Service of Holy Communion*, beginning either at *The Prayers* or at *The Great Thanksgiving* or, when the sacrament has been consecrated elsewhere, at *The Communion*.

3 Use of Oil

It is customary to use oil consecrated on Maundy Thursday by the bishop.

If the oil to be used has not been consecrated, this form may be used.

The oil may be consecrated only by a bishop or a priest.

> God of healing and hope,
> your Son our Saviour sent his disciples
> to anoint the sick with oil;
> fulfil your promise through this oil
> which we set apart in his name
> to be used as a sign of forgiveness,
> healing and salvation.

Prayers for use in Critical Situations

FOR PEOPLE AGEING

God of the unknown,
as age draws in on us, irresistible as the tide,
make our life's last quarter the best that there has been.
As our strength ebbs, release our inner vitality,
all you have taught us over the years;
as our energy diminishes
increase our compassion, and educate our prayer.
You have made us human to share your divine life;
grant us the first-fruits;
make our life's last quarter the best that there has been.

**FOR PEOPLE FACING THE LOSS OF A LIMB
OR SERIOUS IMPAIRMENT**

God of this uncertain world,
you sent Jesus to bring
comfort and good news to the troubled and the suffering:
Reveal yourself to N, who *(the trouble is described)*.
Help *her/him* to come to terms with this misfortune,
and still to hope,
still to search out what there remains to do.
Help *her/him* to be reconciled.

FOR PEOPLE CRITICALLY ILL, OR FACING GREAT UNCERTAINTY

God of the present moment,
God who in Jesus stills the storm
and soothes the frantic heart;
bring hope and courage to N
as *s/he/they*
wait/s in uncertainty.
Bring hope that you will make *her/him/them* the equal
of whatever lies ahead.
Bring *her/him/them* courage to endure what cannot be avoided,
for your will is health and wholeness;
you are God, and we need you.

FOR PEOPLE WATCHING AT A DEATH

God of the dark night,
you were with Jesus praying in the garden,
you were with Jesus all the way to the cross
and through to the resurrection.
Help us to recognise you now, as we watch with *N*,
and wait for what must happen;
help us through any bitterness and despair,
help us accept our distress,
help us to remember that you care for us
and that in your will is our peace.

FOR PEOPLE IN SEVERE PAIN

Jesus, you knew pain,
you knew the loneliness, the weakness
and the degradation it brings;
you knew the agony.
Jesus, your suffering is the only hope,
the only reconciliation for those who suffer.
Be with *N* as *s/he* grapples with the pain *s/he* suffers now.
Be a promise to *him/her*
that this present suffering will cease;
be the hand that *s/he* can hold;
be present, Saviour, for we need you now.

FOR PEOPLE DYING

God our creator and our end,
give us grace to bear bravely
the changes we must undergo,
the pain we may have to face
to come to our home with you.
Give us the courage to welcome
that unimaginable moment awaiting us;
give us trust and confidence;
and at the last give us peace.

Reconciliation of a Penitent

Scripture makes it clear that whenever a sinner turns to God in penitence, forgiveness follows. In addition, to reassure the consciences of those who continue to remain troubled, and to provide a discipline which many find beneficial, the Church offers this ministry of reconciliation.

In it the priest, on behalf of the Christian community, listens to the penitent's confession of sins and declares God's forgiveness.

The penitent is thus enabled to express the source of guilt, and the priest then offers counsel and the assurance of reconciliation.

The priest exercises this ministry in complete confidentiality. The penitent is therefore able to confess in the assurance that the priest will not refer to the matter again, except at the penitent's request, and under no circumstances will ever repeat to any other person what has been divulged.

A Form of Private Confession

This order may be used in church or elsewhere.
It may be varied as appropriate.

Preparation

The priest and penitent prepare in silence.

Then the priest says

> Your Saviour welcomes you.
> Christ came to call sinners.
> Have confidence in him.

Penitent   I put my trust in the mercy of God.

Have mercy on me O God in your great kindness:
  in the fulness of your mercy blot out my offences.
Wash away all my guilt:
  and cleanse me from my sin.
Do not cast me away from your presence:
  do not take your Holy Spirit from me.
Give me the joy of your help again:
  and strengthen me with a willing spirit.
Then I will teach transgressors your ways:
  and sinners will turn to you again.
You desire no sacrifice, or I would give it:
  but you take no delight in burnt offerings.
The sacrifice acceptable to God is a broken spirit:
  a broken and contrite heart O God you will not despise.

Psalm 51:1-2, 11-13, 16-17

The priest may say

Hear God's word:
If we claim to be sinless,
we are self-deceived and strangers to the truth.
If we confess our sins,
God is just, and may be trusted to forgive our sins
and cleanse us from every kind of wrong.

1 John 1: 8,9

Other suitable Scripture passages may be read by the priest or the penitent.

The Confession

The priest says

God be in your heart and on your lips,
that you may truly and humbly confess your sins.

*The penitent may use the following form or make confession in
her/his own words.*

Merciful God,
I confess that I have sinned against you and against others.
I have sinned through my own fault by thought, word and deed
in things done and left undone.
Especially I confess that I have......*
I repent;
for these and all my sins I am truly sorry,
and pray for forgiveness.
I firmly intend to make amends and seek for help.
I ask for strength to serve you in newness of life.

*   *Or*   Especially I confess that since my last confession I have...

The priest may give counsel to the penitent.

The Absolution

When absolution is given, the priest says

All things have been reconciled to God the creator
through the life, death and resurrection
of God's only Son Jesus Christ,
and the Holy Spirit has been sent among us
for the forgiveness of sins.

By the authority of Christ given to the Church
I absolve you from your sins*
in the name of God, Father, Son and Holy Spirit.
May God give you peace.
Amen.

** At this point the priest may extend a hand, make the sign of the cross,
or lay hands on the penitent.*

Prayer of Thanksgiving

The priest may say

Most loving God,
we thank you for your pardon and forgiveness.
By the power of your Spirit within,
enable us to overcome temptation and evil,
keep us securely in the fellowship of your Church,
and as we live daily in your presence,
grant victory, peace, and joy,
through the merits of your Son, our Saviour, Jesus Christ.
Amen.

The priest may give this or another blessing.

May God the Father bless you,
may the Holy Spirit strengthen you in all goodness,
and the love of Christ our Saviour give you peace of mind.
Amen.

The priest may add

> The Lord has set you free.

Penitent   Thanks be to God.

Priest   Go in peace.
Pray for me a sinner.

The penitent may make private prayers of thanksgiving and commitment.

Thanksgiving for the Gift of a Child

This service provides an opportunity for parents and families to give thanks for the birth or adoption of a child and to offer prayer for family life. It may take place in the home, the hospital, in church, or some other suitable setting as soon as convenient after the birth or adoption of a child.

This service has no connection with Baptism, which is the sacrament of initiation into the Church, the body of Christ.

A priest, deacon or duly authorised lay person may lead the service with the family.

Welcome

The minister greets the family and friends informally, and then says

In the name of God,
the giver of life,
who creates and loves us all.

The minister continues in these or similar words.

E te whanau a te Karaiti / Dear friends in Christ,
we have come to celebrate the gift of this child,
born into the world;
given to us
to love, to nurture and to enjoy.

A hymn or song may be sung.

The minister may say to the parent(s)

N *(and N)*, what name have you given this child?

The family, holding the child, responds

We have named you *(name or names).*

*The family may wish to explain the choice of name
and may give a gift or token to the child.*

A Gospel may be presented with the words

Receive this book.
In it is the good news of God's love.

The Ministry of the Word

One of the following or some other suitable psalm may be read.

Psalm 121, Psalm 127 or Psalm 128

One of the following or some other suitable scripture passage may follow.

1 Samuel 2:1-10   Mark 10:13-16
Luke 1:46-55   Luke 2: 21-32

The minister may speak to those present.

A hymn or song may be included here.

The Thanksgiving

The parents of the child may say together

God our Creator,
thank you for the waiting and the joy,
thank you for new life and for parenthood,
thank you for the gift of N,
entrusted to our care.
May we be patient and understanding,
ready to guide and forgive,
that in our love N may know your love.
May *s/he* learn to love your world
and the whole family of your children;
through Christ our life.
Amen.

Or

If only one parent of a child is present the above form may be used or the parent may say

God our Creator,
thank you for the waiting and the joy,
thank you for new life and for parenthood,
thank you for the gift of N,
entrusted to my care.
May I be patient and understanding,
ready to guide and forgive,
that in my love N may know your love.
May *s/he* learn to love your world
and the whole family of your children;
through Christ our life.
Amen.

Or

The parent(s) may use this thanksgiving for a child born handicapped.

God the creator of us all,
we give you thanks for the life of *this child*.
Grant us accepting and understanding hearts,
and the gifts of courage and patience to face the challenge
of caring for *her/him*.
Let your love for us be seen in our lives,
that we may create an atmosphere
in which *s/he* will live a life of dignity and worth.
We ask this in the name of Jesus, the compassionate.
Amen.

The minister may say one of the above thanksgivings with, or on behalf of, the parents.

The Prayers

The mother may pray

Creator Spirit,
I thank you for the experience of giving birth;
for the preparation and expectancy,
and for my part in creation.
I thank you for sustaining me through the pain of labour,
and for the birth of *our/my son/daughter N.*
Amen.

The father may pray

Living God,
I thank you for the gift of *N,*
this new member of our family,
and for the promise of *her/his* personality.
Guard *her/him* from all that may harm *her/him,*
and make *her/him* happy in receiving and giving love.
Amen.

Adoptive parents may pray

O God,
you have warmly accepted us into your family;
we thank you for this child,
whom we now receive into our family with love.
May *s/he* be nourished with all that is good,
and grow day by day into a complete faith in you,
through Jesus Christ our Saviour.
Amen.

The grandparents and wider family may pray

We thank you, Father, that you have set us in family groups,
with relatives and friends of all ages.
Help us to respect and care for one another, and for this child,
so that in our family *s/he* may see and enjoy
many loving relationships;
through Jesus, our Saviour, who loves us.
Amen.

Or the minister may pray

FOR THE MOTHER AFTER THE DELIVERY OF HER CHILD

Holy Spirit of God, creator and sustainer of human life,
we praise you that you have called N
to share in your creative acts by the great mystery of childbirth.
We give you thanks that she has been brought safely
through the time of pregnancy and labour,
bringing new life into this world which you love;
in the name of him who was born of a woman,
Jesus Christ our Redeemer.
Amen.

FOR THE NATURAL PARENTS OF AN ADOPTED CHILD

God,
whose nature is always to have mercy,
look down with love on N's natural* father and mother;
keep them in your good care,
and give them peace in their hearts,
through Jesus Christ our Lord.
Amen.

* The word 'natural' refers to the child's 'birth' parents

The minister may add one or more of the following prayers.

God of the humble and hopeful,
you bless those who believe when you promise.
Help us, like Mary and Elizabeth,
simply to delight in the good things
you prepare for us,
to say 'yes',
and to trust that your strength and your love
will provide the wisdom needed by those
who care for N.
Amen.

We thank you God for this new person,
child of your creation.
May the knowledge of you dawn on *her/him*,
may the love of you grow in *her/him*,
and may the grace of your Spirit draw *her/him* to you.
Amen.

THE FAMILY AND HOME

Eternal Spirit, Earth-maker, Pain-bearer, Life-giver,
Source of all that is and shall be,
Father and Mother of us all,
Loving God, in whom is heaven,
enfold this family with your grace.
May their home be a place of your presence,
your forgiveness and your freedom.
May your will be done in them and through them
this day and for ever.
Amen.

The minister concludes the prayers, saying one of the introductions to
The Lord's Prayer.

Gathering our prayers and praises into one,
let us pray as our Saviour teaches us

Or

As God's children and heirs with Christ
we cry in the Spirit, 'Abba!'

Our Father in heaven,
   hallowed be your name,
   your kingdom come,
   your will be done,
      on earth as in heaven.
Give us today our daily bread.
Forgive us our sins
   as we forgive those who sin against us.
Save us from the time of trial
   and deliver us from evil.

For the kingdom, the power, and the glory are yours
   now and for ever.   Amen.

Kua akona nei tatou e to tatou Ariki,
ka inoi tatou

E to matou Matua i te rangi
   Kia tapu tou Ingoa.
   Kia tae mai tou rangatiratanga.
   Kia meatia tau e pai ai
      ki runga ki te whenua,
         kia rite ano ki to te rangi.
Homai ki a matou aianei
   he taro ma matou mo tenei ra.
Murua o matou hara,
   Me matou hoki e muru nei
      i o te hunga e hara ana ki a matou.
Aua hoki matou e kawea kia whakawaia;
   Engari whakaorangia matou i te kino:
Nou hoki te rangatiratanga, te kaha,
   me te kororia,
      Ake ake ake.   Amine.

Final Prayer or Blessing

When a priest is present, the child and family are blessed,
using either of these forms or another blessing.

The blessing of the God of Sarah and of Abraham,
the blessing of the Son, born of Mary,
the blessing of the Spirit, who broods over us
as a mother over her children,
be with you now and for ever.
Amen.

Ma te Atua koe e manaaki,
e tiaki i nga wa katoa,
e noho i roto i te aroha o te Atua;
ko te aroha hoki te mea nui.
Amine.

The priest or minister concludes with this prayer.

Our Lord Jesus Christ be with you to defend you,
within you to keep you,
before you to lead you,
beside you to guard you,
and above you to bless you.
Amen.

The family responds

All embracing God
the hope of every generation,
complete our joy by your presence;
give us quiet strength and patient wisdom
as we nurture *N*
in all that is good, and true, and just,
through Jesus Christ our friend and brother. Amen.

The Blessing of a Home

It is in the home that the first experience of love occurs; it is there that love is nurtured and grows to maturity. The Christian home is also the ground for much of people's spiritual growth.

The ministry of Jesus occurs in many different homes. Therefore to hallow the home as an environment for nurture and renewal, is a deeply felt need by many Christian households.

The blessing of a home encourages Christians to dedicate their life at home to God and to others.

*The service may be used in a variety of ways and contexts. A scheme for this is provided in the **Additional Directions** (page 775).*

A minister may take this service in place of a priest, but may not celebrate the Eucharist or use a formal blessing.

Approach

A table may be prepared for a celebration of the Eucharist inside the house.

AT THE GATEWAY

The family or householder(s), any friends and the priest gather outside the gateway.

The priest greets the people and says

E te whanau/Dear friends in Christ
we enter this gateway in the name of God
creating, redeeming, sanctifying.

The Lord is here.
God's Spirit is with us.

A priest may sign the lintel or post with the sign of the cross and use some symbol of blessing, saying

Enter the gates with thanksgiving in your heart.
Come into God's presence with praise.

ONTO THE LAND

The group moves onto the land on which the house or building stands.

The priest says

The earth is God's, and all that is in it, the world and all those who dwell there.

The Lord your God cares for the land.
God watches over it season by season.

A priest may use a symbol of blessing, saying

O God of earth and sky, you visit the land and bless it, you greatly enrich it, you water it abundantly and bless its growth with your goodness.

You formed us from the dust of the ground.
You breathed into us the breath of life.

OUTSIDE THE HOUSE

The group moves around the outside of the house or building.

The priest says

Except the Lord build the house,
their labour is but lost that build it.

Encircle this dwelling place with your protection, O God;
may your holy angels encompass these walls,
and peace be within them.

A priest may use a symbol of blessing, saying

Open the windows and doors of this house that the light and love of your Holy Spirit may shine within,
a light in the world for warmth and welcome.

Entry

The group moves to immediately outside the front door.

The priest says

In the name of God,
peace to this *house/place*.
God make it a haven for all who live here.

The priest stands at the door.

'Behold I stand at the door and knock,' says the Lord *(the priest may knock at the door)*. 'If you hear my voice and open the door, I will come in and eat with you and you with me.' *Revelation 3:20*

The householder(s) then say

Welcome to *this/our* home.

Blessed be God who dwells in love.
Blessed be God who gives peace and shelter.
Amen.

A priest may use a symbol of blessing saying

God of hearth and home, maker of love and laughter,
make this a place for reflection and restoration,
rest and renewal,
a place where the life of N *(and N)* may find its strength.

The priest faces the householder(s) and says

The Lord watch over your going out and your coming in
from this time forward for evermore.

Blessing in the Home

AT THE LIVING ROOM

The group moves into the living room.

The householder says

Indwelling God, you are ever welcome in this house.
May we hear and share your Word.

A member of the group may read the following.

Be compassionate as your Father is compassionate. Do not judge
and you will not be judged yourselves: do not condemn, and you
will not be condemned yourselves; grant pardon, and you will be
pardoned. Give, and there will be gifts for you: a full measure,
pressed down, shaken together and running over, will be poured
into your lap, because the amount you measure out is the amount
you will be given back.   *Luke 6:36-38*

*One of the following or some other suitable Scripture may be read in place of or
in addition to the above.*

John 14:21-23
Luke 24:13-32   *(suitable if the Eucharist is to be celebrated)*
1 Corinthians 13

The priest says

O how good and pleasant it is, when God's people live together in
unity.

Above everything, love one another fervently,
for love covers many sins.

A priest may use a symbol of blessing, saying

God in Trinity,
you have made us to need each other
and to grow best with companions;
bless those who shall sit or talk or work together here.
May they share your care and understanding.

If there are dependents, the priest may speak to the parent(s)

N (and N), will you be true to this family?
Will you support and care for each other
so that together you may care
for those whom God has given you?

The parent(s) respond

Yes, we will.
May God give us joy in what we do
and patience when our work seems hard.

The priest addresses the family and friends.

Will you, their family (and friends)
give them your support?

The family (and friends) respond

Yes we will. May God be with you.

The following may be added.

May you grow on and grow old in the love of God.
May this place be for you a place where
    relationships mature,
    quarrels are made up,
    failures forgiven and strength renewed.

The priest says

Blessed be Christ the prince of peace
who breaks down the walls that divide.

The peace of God be always with you.
Praise to Christ who unites us in peace.

*The group greet each other and share **a sign of peace**.*

AT A BEDROOM

The group moves to each bedroom in turn.

The priest says

Guide us waking, O God,
and guard us sleeping,
that awake we may watch with Christ,
and asleep we may rest in your peace.

I lie down in peace and take my rest
for it is in God alone that I dwell unafraid.

The priest may use a symbol of blessing, saying

God of the night,
may this be a holy and blessèd place
for *N (and N)* and all who may sleep here.
Here may *they* know your loving presence,
find rest for *their* fatigue,
and peace for *their* anxiety.

May your holy angels guard *them*,
and your continual blessing strengthen *them*.

AT THE BATHROOM

The priest says

'I will sprinkle you with clean water, and you will be cleansed.'

Let us hold fast the confession of our hope without wavering,
having our bodies washed with pure water.

A priest may use a symbol of blessing, saying

Blessed are you, our Saviour Jesus Christ,
fountain of living water springing up to eternal life;
in you is our baptism, in you is our faith.

Blessed are you God of the rain, the rivers, and the lakes,

you give water for life and health
to refresh and cleanse all creatures.

FOR A STUDY

The priest says

Teach us, O God, where wisdom is to be found, and show us the place of understanding.

Seek your God and you will be found.

**Search for God with all your heart
and with all your mind.**

Silence may be kept.

A priest may use a symbol of blessing, saying

O God, the source of all wisdom,
may this be a place of reflection and awareness,
of knowledge and understanding.

**Show yourself for us,
lest we go about in ignorance;
reveal yourself to us,
for in you we know the incarnate word.**

FOR A WORKSHOP

The priest says

Many there are who rely upon their hands
and are skilful in their own creativity and work.

Prosper, O God, the work of our hands.
Prosper our handiwork.

The priest may use a symbol of blessing, saying

O God,
your blessed son worked with his hands
in the carpenter's shop at Nazareth:
be present we pray with those who work in this place.

Give them work till their life ends,
and life till their work is done,

**that labouring together with you
they may share the joy of your creation.**

FOR A TERRACE OR GARDEN

The priest says

As the earth brings forth its blossom,
or bushes in a garden burst into flower,
so shall the Lord God make righteousness and praise
blossom before all the people.

The earth brought forth vegetation,
plants yielding seed,
and fruit trees bearing fruit in which is their seed,
each according to its kind.
And God saw that it was good.

Silence may be kept.

The priest may use a symbol of blessing, saying

Jesus, our good companion,
often you withdrew with your friends
for quiet and refreshment;
be present with your servants in this place.
Make it a place of serenity and peace.

AT THE KITCHEN

The group moves to the kitchen.

The priest says

You shall eat in plenty and be satisfied,
and praise the name of the Lord your God,
who has dealt so wondrously with you.

The eyes of all wait upon you O God
and you give them their food in due season.

The priest may use a symbol of blessing, saying

God of garden, farm and factory
may what is prepared here bring strength and health.
Bless the hands that work in this place,
nourish us with all goodness
and give us grateful hearts for daily bread.

**May Christ our constant guest
make our humblest meal a welcome offering.**

Or

Creator, Sustainer and Life-giver
food shared between mother and child is your first gift,
is the first taste we know of love.
May the food we prepare,
the work of love done in this room,
be a sign that you dwell for ever with us
in the everyday things of your world.

**May Christ our constant guest
make our humblest meal a welcome offering.**

AT THE DINING AREA

The group moves to the dining room or area.

The priest says

The living God gave you from heaven
rain and fruitful seasons
satisfying your hearts with food and gladness.

**God brings forth food from the earth
and wine to gladden the heart.**

A priest may use a symbol of blessing, saying

Blessed are you, Sovereign of the universe,
for gifts from your bounty which we receive.
May our hearts be thankful;
may we always have room for a guest.

**Make us grateful for all your mercies,
and mindful of the needs of others.**

It may be appropriate to return to the living room.

*If there is to be a celebration of the Eucharist, the guidelines on page 774
should be observed.*

*If there is not to be a celebration of the Eucharist the service may continue with
either **The Family Liturgy** and/or **A Householder's Prayer** and **A Blessing of
Peace**.*

The Family Liturgy

*The following may be said by a member or members of the family or household,
with others lighting the candles. This liturgy may be shared at the table before a
meal, with three unlighted candles (and flowers) in the centre of the table.*

*If **The Family Liturgy** is not used the service continues with **A Householder's
Prayer**.*

The first candle is lit.

Loving God,
(Father and Mother of us all),
in the family life you have given to us,
you have offered us yourself.

The second candle is lit.

Your Son lived with us
in all the uncertainty and darkness of life
so that we might walk in your light.

The third candle is lit.

And your Spirit is given to us,
as a light to guide our steps
and as a brightness of heart to signal welcome
to those who have found other doors closed.

Three candles shed one light;
(two of your children become one flesh);
many foods eaten build one body.
Within each one, Abba, you have planted a seed,
the seed of Christ that grows no matter how deeply buried;
the seed that becomes a tree in whose branches
all your children may come and rest.

Teach us to share, Abba, as your Son shared.
Teach us to be both Mary and Martha.
Teach us to know that we are your home.
Amen.

The priest says

Never forget to show kindness
and to share what you have with others
for these are the gifts that please God.

*This prayer follows or is used in the Eucharist at the **Prayer after Communion**.*

A Householder's Prayer

Jesus of the wedding feast,
of breakfast by the lake,
(bless this food we have prepared for you and all our friends).

Be with us now and at all our meals
give us appetite and joy in eating together.

Blessed be God for daily bread.

It may be appropriate to share a meal here.

A Blessing of Peace

*The priest offers this blessing either at the end of the Eucharist or at the conclusion of **The Family Liturgy**.*

The priest may lay hands on each member of the household, saying to each

N, God bless you and keep you secure in this place.
May your *family/companion(s)* find
in you Christ's love and understanding.

The priest says to all present

Hear God's word of benediction:
the fruit of righteousness will be peace
and the result of righteousness,
tranquillity and trust for ever,
my people will abide
in secure dwellings
and in quiet resting places.

And now the eternal Spirit,
enfold this home with love;
indwell this home with joy;
and build this home in peace
evermore and evermore.
Amen.

Additional Directions

At a Eucharist

If the service includes a celebration of the Eucharist, a table is prepared with bread and wine, before the service begins.

*Either at the conclusion of **Blessing in the Home** (pages 765-771) or after **The Family Liturgy** (page 771), the priest continues with **The Preparation of the Gifts** from any of the **Liturgies of the Eucharist**, but using the following form*

> Jesus is the bread of life:
> Jesus is the food of life eternal.
> Let us eat and drink at his table.

> **God our creator, our companion, our life,**
> **we celebrate your presence in humble thankfulness,**
> **you who call us to sit and eat, and drink with you.**

*The service then continues from **The Great Thanksgiving** of any of the **Liturgies of the Eucharist**.*

*A **Householder's Prayer** and A **Blessing of Peace** are included in the Eucharistic section **Prayer after Communion** at some appropriate point.*

Shared Meal

*A shared meal for those present may be held at any point of the service after the **Blessing in the Home** is concluded (pages 765-771), but it is appropriate that A **Blessing of Peace** is the conclusion of the whole occasion.*

For Various Circumstances

The variety of situations in which this service may be used means that it may take a number of different forms according to circumstances.

It may not be possible to begin the service at the gate or to move on to the land or to go round the house, in which case **The Approach** *is altered accordingly, or the service may begin at the* **Entry.**

It may on occasion be necessary for some of the group to remain in the living area while the service proceeds.

In special circumstances it may be appropriate for the priest alone to read the service.

Some Possible Forms of the Service

(Approach)
Entry
Blessing in the Home
Eucharist
A Householder's Prayer
Shared Meal
A Blessing of Peace

(Approach)
Entry
Blessing in the Home
The Family Liturgy
A Householder's Prayer
Shared Meal
A Blessing of Peace

(Approach)
Entry
Blessing in the Home
A Householder's Prayer
A Blessing of Peace

(Approach)
Blessing in the Home
The Family Liturgy
Eucharist
A Householder's Prayer
A Blessing of Peace

(Approach)
Blessing in the Home
The Family Liturgy
A Householder's Prayer
A Blessing of Peace

For Various Translations

The quality of translation in a blessing service may be judged mostly from the smoothness with which several scenes unfold, so certain changes.

If you want to focus more on the joyous celebration, you may wish to omit the blessing, provided the scene unfolds true. The lines may, after all, be done lightly, moving and completely in the home.

If you would rather be relaxed with the normal blessing happening in the blessing, you may use other elements.

In general the service may adapt to a style appropriate to the local community, other than formal.

Some Possible Points of the Service

(Approach)
Entry
Blessing in the Home
Gathering
Of Those who I meet
Shared Meal
A Blessing of Peace

(Approach)
Entry
Blessing in the Home
Gathering
Of Those who I meet
Shared Meal
A Blessing of Peace

(Approach)
Entry
Blessing in the Home
The Family Liturgy
Eucharist
A Remembrance of Peace
A Blessing of Peace

(Approach)
Entry
Blessing in the Home
Traditional Liturgy
A Blessing of Peace
A Blessing of Peace

Marriage
Liturgies

The congregation is invited to read this before the service begins.

A wedding is one of life's great moments, a time for good wishes, feasting and joy. St John tells us how Jesus shared in such an occasion, and gave there a sign of new beginnings.

Marriage is intended by God to be a creative relationship – God's blessing enables husband and wife to love and support each other in good times and bad. For Christians, marriage is also an invitation to share life together in the spirit of Jesus Christ. It is based upon a solemn, public and life-long covenant between a man and a woman, made and celebrated in the presence of God and before a priest and congregation.

The couple has prepared the service of their choice, assisted by the priest. On this their wedding day they face each other, make their promises with clear understanding, and receive the Church's blessing.

You, the congregation, are witnesses of the marriage, and express your support by your presence and your prayers. Your part is written in **bold type**.

'Love is patient and kind. Love never comes to an end.'

The marriage may be set within any of the **Liturgies of the Eucharist**.
Guidance for this may be found among the **Additional Directions** on page 807.

Marriage Liturgy
First Form

Welcome and Introduction

The priest may greet the people.

The priest says to the congregation

We have come together in the presence of God to witness and celebrate the marriage of N and N, and to pray God's blessing upon them now and in the years ahead.

Marriage is a gift of God our Creator, whose intention is that husband and wife should be united in heart, body and mind.
In their union they fulfil their love for each other.

Marriage is given to provide the stability necessary for family life, so that children may be cared for lovingly and grow to full maturity.

Marriage is a way of life to be upheld and honoured. No one should enter into it lightly. It involves a serious and life-long commitment to each other's good in a union of strength, sympathy and delight.

The priest says to the couple

N and N, we rejoice with you;
we are glad to join with you
in the celebration of your marriage,
to witness your vows,
to pray with you
and to wish you joy in your life together.

The priest prays

God our Creator,
be with us now
as we celebrate the marriage of N and N.

Give them your blessing.
Grant them happiness and long life together
and help us to support them with our love.
Amen.

The Ministry of the Word

A suitable reading (or readings) follows either here or before **The Marriage**,
or before **The Prayers**.

After the reading a minister may speak to the people.

The Declarations

The priest asks the bridegroom

N, of your own free choice will you take N to be your wife?

The bridegroom answers I will.

Will you love her, comfort her, honour and keep her,
in sickness and in health, and forsaking all others
be faithful to her as long as you both shall live?

The bridegroom answers I will.

The priest asks the bride

N, of your own free choice will you take N to be your husband?

The bride answers I will.

Will you love him, comfort him, honour and keep him,
in sickness and in health, and forsaking all others
be faithful to him as long as you both shall live?

The bride answers I will.

The priest may ask the parents

As *N* and *N* enter a new life together, will you, their parents, give them your blessing?

The parents say to the couple

May God bless you both.

The priest may ask the whole congregation

You, as friends and family,
have come to witness this exchange of vows.
Will you do all in your power to support this marriage now
and in the years ahead?

The people reply **We will.**

The priest prays

Eternal God, creator and sustainer of us all, give your grace to *N* and *N*. Grant that in the years ahead they may be faithful to the vows they make this day, and that in the strength of the Holy Spirit they may grow together in the love, joy and peace of our Saviour Jesus Christ.
Amen.

The Ministry of the Word *may follow here.*

The Marriage

The bride and bridegroom face each other.

The bridegroom takes the bride's hand(s) in his and says

I, *N*, take you, *N*, to be my wife,
to have and to hold
from this day forward,
for better, for worse,
for richer, for poorer,
in sickness and in health,
to love and to cherish
until we are parted by death.
This is my solemn vow.

They loose hands.

The bride takes the bridegroom's hand(s) in hers, and says

I, *N*, take you, *N*, to be my husband,
to have and to hold
from this day forward,
for better, for worse,
for richer, for poorer,
in sickness and in health,
to love and to cherish
until we are parted by death.
This is my solemn vow.

They loose hands.

The priest receives the ring(s) and may say

Most holy God, bless these rings *(this ring).*
Grant that they who wear them
(he who gives it and she who wears it)
may be faithful to each other and continue
bound together in love to their lives' end,
through Jesus Christ, our Lord.
Amen.

The giver places the ring on the other's finger, holds it there and says

N, I give you this ring
as a symbol of our marriage.
With my body I honour you,
and all I have I share with you.

If only one ring is used, before they loose hands, the bride may say

N, I receive this ring
as a symbol of our marriage.
With my body I honour you,
and all I have I share with you.

The priest joins the couple's right hands and declares

N and N have given themselves to each other with solemn vows
and have declared their marriage
by joining hands
and the giving and receiving of rings *(of a ring)*;
they are now husband and wife.

Let no one come between those whom God has joined together.

The priest says

The power of God keep you,
the love of God be in your life and work together,
the grace of God strengthen your love that it may endure
forever.
Amen.

The register may be signed here in the presence of the congregation.

The Ministry of the Word *may follow here.*

The Prayers

*The service continues on page 796 with **The Prayers** and concludes with **The Blessing** on page 804.*

*When the marriage is part of a **Liturgy of the Eucharist**, directions are to be found on page 807.*

Marriage Liturgy
Second Form

The priest may greet the people

Welcome to you all.

Introduction and Declarations

The priest then says to the people

We have come together
to ask God's blessing on *N* and *N*,
to witness their marriage
and to bring them our love and support.

I ask you now to pray for them;
and not just to pray today
or only in this place
but to pray in your hearts continually
and over the years.

It is praying, their praying and ours,
which will fulfil God's purposes for *N* and *N*.
Praying is an outlook, a sustained energy,
which creates a marriage
and makes love and forgiveness life-long.

Eternal love never fails;
our love needs to forgive and be forgiven.
As we pray and forgive we minister reconciliation.
Those who marry
are God's ministers to each other
of reconciliation and change.
As they grow together,
wife and husband foster one another's strengths,
they provide each other with the reassurance and love
needed to overcome their weaknesses.

From this beginning
God draws them now to a completely new life.
They become awake to each other,
aware of each other,
sensitive to each other's needs.

The priest says to the couple

N and N, you are welcome.
Pray that God will uphold and cheer your life together,
that your promises be honoured,
your words true,
now and in time to come.

For our part we ask you to make your public declaration.

The bridegroom says

I love N,
and I want to marry her.

The bride says

I love N,
and I want to marry him.

The priest may say to the parents

N N, will you accept and support this marriage?

The parents respond

We will. May God bless you both.

The priest may say to any children of the bride or groom

N, will you help N and N in their marriage?

Children   Yes, I will.

The priest may say

May God's grace surround you
and keep you all,
and so we pray

**The peace of God
which is beyond our understanding
keep guard over your thoughts and hearts.**

God keep you friends with one another,
forgiving one another in kindness.

**May you follow Jesus in happiness or suffering.
May hope keep you joyful.
Stand firm in trouble.
Be strong in prayer.**

May God make you compassionate and brave.

**Above all,
may there always be love
to bind and keep you whole.**

The Ministry of the Word

*A suitable reading (or readings) follows here or before **The Prayers**.*

After the reading a minister may speak to the people.

The Marriage

The priest may pray

Jesus,
do for N and N
as you did in Cana of Galilee.
Take the old water, their busy individual lives,
and turn them into gospel wine.

The bride and bridegroom face each other and join hands.

The bridegroom says

N, I take you to be my wife.
All that I have I offer you;
what you have to give I gladly receive;
wherever you go I will go.
You are my love.
God keep me true to you always
and you to me.

The bride says

N, I take you to be my husband.
All that I have I offer you;
what you have to give I gladly receive;
wherever you go I will go.
You are my love.
God keep me true to you always
and you to me.

The priest receives the ring(s) and prays

Christ our light,
encircle *these rings* with your blessing,
(a) ring(s) to show the love of *N* and *N*.
Bind them together
and keep them in your love eternally.

The giver places the ring on the other's finger and says

N, this ring I give to you,
with my body I honour you.
God make me your true *husband/wife*
in the spirit of Jesus Christ.

The priest joins their right hands together and says

God so join you together that nothing shall ever part you.

Blessed are you, heavenly Father,
you give joy to bridegroom and bride.

Blessed are you, Jesus our Redeemer,
you have brought new life to us all.

Blessed are you, Holy Spirit of God,
you bring us together in love.

Blessed are you Creator, Saviour and Giver of life,
one God to be praised for ever. Amen.

The priest continues

N and *N*
may Christ's love purify your love for each other,
Christ's humanity keep you sensitive and practical.

May the Light of the world illuminate your way ahead,
the Bread of heaven nourish you,
the true Vine enliven you.

May Christ be the beginning
of a new, fulfilled and blessed life,
and Christ the end.

The register may be signed here in the presence of the congregation.

The Ministry of the Word *may follow here.*

The Prayers

*The service continues on page 796 with **The Prayers** and concludes with **The Blessing** on page 804.*

*When the marriage is part of a **Liturgy of the Eucharist**, directions are to be found on page 807.*

Marriage Liturgy
Third Form

In this service the couple, in consultation with the priest, make a choice for each section from the options provided in the two columns.

Introduction

The priest may greet the people.

The priest says to the congregation

We have gathered to celebrate the marriage of *N* and *N*. Marriage is the promise of hope between a man and a woman who love each other, who trust that love, and who wish to share the future together.

It enables two separate people to share their desires, longings, dreams and memories, and to help each other through their uncertainties. It provides the encouragement to risk more and thus to gain more. In marriage, husband and wife belong together, providing mutual support and a stability in which their children may grow.

Here in the presence of God we recognise and affirm their relationship as they begin their married life in the community.

We have come together to witness the promises of *N* and *N* in marriage; to share with them in their happiness and in their hopes for the future.

Marriage involves caring and giving. It involves learning to share one's life with another person, forgiving as Christ forgives; enjoying the love and meaning which can be found together. It involves facing together whatever adversity may arise.

Here before God, *N* and *N* wish to pledge their love for each other and their desire to spend their lives together.

Welcome

The priest says to the couple

N and N , we welcome you.
We are glad to join with you
in the celebration of your marriage,
to witness your vows, to pray with you,
and to wish you joy in your life together.

The priest says

Father, touch us with an awareness of your presence in all the world around us. Awaken in us a sense of wonder that you have created us in love. As we celebrate the marriage of N and N, deepen our love for those close to us, and for those who, although strangers, need our concern. Help N and N as they commit themselves to each other, and grant us all a heightened sense of joy in life, because we share this moment with them.
Amen.

The priest and people say together

**God of love,
we thank you
for the gift of marriage
and for the joys it brings.
Bless us as we share
in this wedding.
We thank you for the love
which has brought N and N
to each other
and for their desire
to share that love
for the rest of their lives.
Amen.**

The Ministry of the Word

*A suitable reading (or readings) follows either here or before **The Marriage** or before **The Prayers**.*

After the reading a minister may speak to the people.

The Declarations

The priest asks the bridegroom

N, do you love and trust N and want to be her husband ?

The bridegroom answers

Yes, I do.

The priest asks the bridegroom

Will you stand by her no matter what happens, respecting her as a person, understanding her needs and enjoying her love until death parts you?

The bridegroom answers

Yes, I will.

The priest asks the bride

N, do you love and trust N and want to be his wife?

The bride answers

Yes, I do.

The priest asks the bride

N, will you take N to be your husband? Will you share his joys and ease his burdens? Will you be honest with him, and be faithful to him always, as long as you both live?

The bride answers

I will, with the help of God.

The priest asks the bridegroom

N, will you take N to be your wife? Will you share her joys and ease her burdens? Will you be honest with her, and be faithful to her always, as long as you both live?

The bridegroom answers

I will, with the help of God.

Will you stand by him no matter what happens, respecting him as a person, understanding his needs and enjoying his love until death parts you?

The bride answers

Yes, I will.

Affirmation

The priest may ask the parents

In your new relationship with *N* and *N*, do you, as their parents, pledge your loving support?

Are you willing to strengthen this marriage by upholding both *N* and *N* with your love and concern?

The parents reply

We do.

The parents reply

We are.

They may say to the couple

May you find a rich and full life together.

May you find a rich and full life together.

The priest may ask the whole congregation

Will you, their friends and family, do all in your power to support this couple now, and in the years ahead?

The people reply   **We will.**

The Ministry of the Word *may follow here.*

The Marriage

The bride and bridegroom face each other.

The Vows

The bridegroom takes the bride's hand(s) in his and says

N, I take you to be my wife,
to be with you
whatever happens to us.
In prosperity and in hardship,
in health and in sickness,
in sorrow and in joy,
I will love, protect and serve you
as long as we live.
This I vow before God.

They loose hands.

N, today I take you
to be my wife.
Whatever life may bring,
I will love and care for you
always.

The bride takes the bridegroom's hand(s) in hers and says

N, I take you to be my husband,
to be with you
whatever happens to us.
In prosperity and in hardship,
in health and in sickness,
in sorrow and in joy,
I will love, protect and serve you
as long as we live.
This I vow before God.

They loose hands.

N, today I take you
to be my husband.
Whatever life may bring
I will love and care for you
always.

The Ring

The priest receives the ring or rings, and may say

Eternal God, bless *these rings* as *symbols* of the love and trust between N and N.

Let *these rings* say to all that your commitment is deep and life-long.

This ring is a token
of my faithfulness and love,
and a symbol
that all I have I share with you.

Let this ring symbolise
our one life together.

If only one ring is used, before they loose hands the bride may say

I accept this ring as a symbol
of our one life together.

I accept this ring as a symbol
of our one life together.

The Pronouncement

The priest says to the couple

N and *N*, you have declared the love you have for each other and your hopes for the future. You have made promises to each other, and have symbolised them by joining hands and giving *(a) ring(s)*. You are now husband and wife.

The priest says to the congregation

We have witnessed the promises made by *N* and *N*, and now recognise them as husband and wife.

God's Guidance

The priest says to the couple

May God give you
light to guide you
and love to unite you,
so that you may be faithful
to the vows
you have made this day,
and live together
in joy and peace
till your lives end.
Amen.

N and *N*,
you have committed yourselves
to one another in love,
joy and tenderness.
Become one.
Fulfil your promises.
And may God's grace
be with you for ever.
Amen.

The register may be signed here in the presence of the congregation.

The Ministry of the Word *may follow here.*

The Prayers

*The service continues as below with **The Prayers** and concludes with **The Blessing** on page 804.*

*When the marriage is part of a **Liturgy of the Eucharist,** directions are to be found on page 807.*

The Prayers

The priest may say to the couple

N and N, we welcome you now as husband and wife.
Pray, and we will pray with you.
May God enrich the life you have chosen,
and fulfil your hopes.

Unless it has already been used in the second form of the marriage liturgy the priest and congregation may say the following.

Blessed are you, heavenly Father,
you give joy to bridegroom and bride.

Blessed are you, Jesus our Redeemer,
you have brought new life to us all.

Blessed are you, Holy Spirit of God,
you bring us together in love.

Blessed are you Creator, Saviour and Giver of life,
one God to be praised for ever.   Amen.

As Christ teaches us, we pray

Our Father in heaven,
 hallowed be your name,
 your kingdom come,
 your will be done,
  on earth as in heaven.
Give us today our daily bread.
Forgive us our sins
 as we forgive those who sin against us.
Save us from the time of trial
 and deliver us from evil.

For the kingdom, the power, and the glory are yours
 now and for ever. Amen.

Kua akona nei tatou e to tatou Ariki,
ka inoi tatou

E to matou Matua i te rangi
 Kia tapu tou Ingoa.
 Kia tae mai tou rangatiratanga.
 Kia meatia tau e pai ai
  ki runga ki te whenua,
   kia rite ano ki to te rangi.
Homai ki a matou aianei
 he taro ma matou mo tenei ra.
Murua o matou hara,
 Me matou hoki e muru nei
  i o te hunga e hara ana ki a matou.
Aua hoki matou e kawea kia whakawaia;
 Engari whakaorangia matou i te kino:
Nou hoki te rangatiratanga, te kaha,
 me te kororia,
  Ake ake ake.   Amine.

*One of the following **Forms of Prayer** is used.*

1

Some or all of the following petitions may be used.

The minister and people pray responsively.

Gracious God we pray for N and N and give thanks that you have brought them together in marriage.
Spirit of God bless this marriage.

We thank you for the love and care which, through their parents, has guided N and N to maturity, and prepared them for this commitment.
Spirit of God bless this marriage.

Help them *(to be wise and loving parents and)* to grow together in faithfulness and honesty, in mutual support and patience.
Spirit of God bless this marriage.

Make their life together a sign of your love in this broken world; may forgiveness heal injury and joy triumph over sorrow.
Spirit of God bless this marriage.

Be with them in their work and renew them in their leisure.
Spirit of God bless this marriage.

May they welcome into their home both friends and strangers and so reflect Christ's love for all people.
Spirit of God bless this marriage.

In all their future together may they enjoy each other's lives and grow through the love they share.
Amen.

Other prayers may be offered.

*Then follows **The Marriage Blessing** and **The Dismissal** as on pages 804-805.*

2

All or part of the following prayer may be used.

There may be silence between sections.

Eternal God, creator of us all,
we praise you for all the ways
in which your love comes into our lives,
and for all the joys
that can come to men and women through marriage.

Today we especially pray for N and N
as they begin their married life.
With them we thank you for the love and care of their parents,
which has guided them to maturity
and prepared them for this commitment.

Give them strength
to keep the vows they have made,
to be loyal and faithful to each other,
and to support each other throughout their life,
that they may bear each other's burdens
and share each other's joys.
Help them to be honest and patient with each other,
(to be wise and loving parents)
and to welcome both friends and strangers into their home.

In all their future together
may they enjoy each other
and grow through the love they share,
until, at the end of this life,
you receive us all into your eternal kingdom,
through Jesus Christ our Redeemer.
Amen.

Other prayers may be offered.

Then follows **The Marriage Blessing** *and* **The Dismissal** *as on pages 804-805.*

3

Holy creator Spirit,
you made us and you change us.
Let your loving wisdom work with N and N,
deepening and developing their desire,
moulding and freeing their generosity.
May they achieve stability
and sweetness in their daily lives until their lives shall end.
May they train, support and inspire the children
with whom you entrust them
to enjoy your blessing and to serve your world.

Holy Spirit of God,
you know our strength
and for our frailty you have compassion.
Be with N and N
in all they undertake.
And grant that we their friends,
with all who become their friends,
may sense and understand their needs
and help as opportunity demands.

Other prayers may be offered.

Then follows **The Marriage Blessing** *and* **The Dismissal** *as on pages 804-805.*

4

Loving Spirit,
grant to *N* and *N*,
that in giving and forgiving
they may receive from each other lasting joy.
Bind them together with cords that cannot be broken.
Bind them together with love.

Grant that they may always take delight in each other,
and each remain the other's heart's desire.
Bind them together with cords that cannot be broken.
Bind them together with love.

May they reach such trust and confidence in each other
as shall keep them from unnecessary distress.
May they find courage to meet
the heartaches, disappointments and agonies life can bring.
Be their rock, their fortress,
for they put their trust in you.

Help them to look beyond their own family
and their own concerns
to see the world, suffering and struggling,
the world you have given us to share with one another.
Open their eyes and their hearts.

Give them grace to accept that they are mortal,
to face the possibility of death
and the separation it must bring.
Jesus, you are resurrection, you are life.

Other prayers may be offered.

Then follows **The Marriage Blessing** *and* **The Dismissal** *as on pages 804-805.*

Additional Prayers

Creating and redeeming God,
it is your love which in marriage makes two persons fully one.
As *N* and *N* love each other, may they also grow in love for you.
Walking together with Christ as their companion on the way,
may they come to those inexpressible joys
which you have prepared for all who love you.
Amen.

God of peace,
your love is generous,
and reaches out to hold us all in your embrace.
Fill our hearts with tenderness
for those to whom we are linked today.
Give us sympathy with each other's trials;
give us patience with each other's faults;
that we may grow in the likeness of Jesus
and share in the joy of your kingdom.
Amen.

Father of all,
we thank you for this new family,
and for everything these parents
and their children have to share;
by your Spirit of peace draw them together
and help them be true friends to one another.
Let your love surround them and your care protect them,
through Jesus Christ our Lord.
Amen.

Dear God,
you are merciful and forgiving.
Grant that *N* and *N*,
their family and all who care for them,
may accept your generous love.
Heal their memories, comfort them,
and send them all from here
renewed and hopeful.
Amen.

Creator Spirit,
we thank you for your gift of sexual love,
by which husband and wife
may express their delight in each other,
find refreshment,
and share with you the joy of creating new life.
By your grace may N and N remain lovers,
rejoicing in your goodness.
Amen.

God, the source of love,
we pray now for all who are committed to each other in love.
Through their love may they know your love
and so be renewed for your service in the world.
Amen.

God, the author of love,
we pray for all who are married.
Through their love for each other
may they know the reality of your love
for the whole world;
through Jesus Christ our Lord.
Amen.

This prayer may be said by the couple.

God of tenderness and strength,
you have brought our paths together
and led us to this day;
go with us now as we travel through good times,
through trouble, or through change.
Bless our home, our partings and our meetings.
Make us worthy of each other's best,
and tender with each other's dreams,
trusting in your love in Jesus Christ.
Amen.

The Blessing

The Marriage Blessing

The priest shall pronounce the marriage blessing, using one of the following.

All praise and glory to you most gracious God,
for in the beginning you created us men and women.
Grant your blessing then, we pray, to N and N,
so that in marriage they may be a source of blessing
to each other and to all,
and live together in holy love until their lives' end.
Amen.

Or

Ma te Atua Matua, ma te Atua Tama, ma te Atua Wairua Tapu,
korua e manaaki, e tiaki;
ma te Ariki tohu e titiro atawhai ki a korua,
e whakakii o korua ngakau
ki nga mea pai katoa o te wairua;
kia pai ai to korua noho tahi i tenei ao,
kia whiwhi ai hoki korua ki te ora tonu i tera ao atu.
Amine.

Or

All praise and blessing to you, God of love,
creator of the universe, maker of man and woman in your
    likeness,
source of blessing for married life.
All praise to you for you have created courtship and marriage,
joy and gladness, feasting and laughter, pleasure and delight.
May your blessing come in full upon N and N.
May they know your presence in their joys and in their sorrows.
May they reach old age in the company of friends
and come at last to your eternal kingdom.
Amen.

Or

Ma te Atua Kaha rawa,
nana nei o tatou tupuna,
i hanga i te timatanga i whakatapu,
i hono hoki i runga i te marena;
Mana e riringi ki runga ki a korua tona kaha nui,
mana korua e whakatapu, e manaaki,
kia paingia ai e ia o korua tinana, o korua wairua,
kia noho tahi tonu ai korua i runga i te aroha hara-kore,
a mate noa.
Amine.

The Dismissal

The priest says to the couple

N and *N*, go now in peace and love.

and to the whole congregation

And the blessing of God,
Creator, Saviour and Giver of life,
be with you all, now and for ever.
Amen.

Or

And the blessing of God almighty,
Father, Son, and Holy Spirit,
be with you and remain with you for ever.
Amen.

The register may be signed here.

The priest may say to the congregation

Go now to love and serve the Lord. Go in peace.
Amen.   We go in the name of Christ.

Additional Directions

Some Suggested Readings

Genesis 1:26-29a, 31a	Man and woman in God's image
Ruth 1:16-18	Faithfulness
Psalm 23	Our shepherd
Psalm 67	The Lord's goodness
Psalm 121	The Lord's blessing
Psalm 128	The gift of a family
Song of Songs 2:8-14	The lovers
Matthew 7:21, 24-27	Hearing and doing
Mark 10:6-9	The two are one
John 2:1-11	Jesus at a wedding
John 15:9-12	Dwelling in Christ's love
Romans 12:9-21	Love in practice
1 Corinthians 12:31 - 13:13	The greatest gift
or selected verses	
Ephesians 3:14-21	Grounded in love
Ephesians 5:21-31	Husband and wife in Christian marriage
Colossians 3:12-17	The love and peace of Christ
1 John 4:7-16	God's love and ours
Revelation 19:6-9	The Lamb's marriage supper

Some Suggested Hymns and Songs

A new commandment
Arahina, e Ihowa
Be thou my vision
Bind us together
Brother, sister, let me serve you
E te Atua, kua ruia nei
Father, hear the prayer we offer
Gracious Spirit, Holy Ghost
Jesus, Lord, we pray

Lord of all hopefulness, Lord of all joy
Lead us, heavenly Father, lead us
Lord Jesus Christ, invited guest
Lord of love, we ask thy blessing
Love divine, all loves excelling
Ma te marie a te Atua
Make me a channel of your peace
May the grace of Christ our Saviour
Nga wahi ra e mine ai
Now thank we all our God
O Holy Spirit, Lord of grace
O perfect love, all human thought transcending
Praise and thanksgiving, Father, we offer
Praise, my soul, the king of heaven
Praise to the Lord, the Almighty
Tama ngakau marie
The Lord's my shepherd

Marriage and the Eucharist

The Marriage Liturgy may be combined with a Eucharist, in either of the following orders:

a) **The Marriage Liturgy**, *omitting the final general blessing and dismissal.*
   This is followed by the Eucharist, beginning at **The Peace** *and ending with* **The Marriage Blessing** *and* **The Dismissal**.

b) **The Preparation** *section and* **The Readings** *from the Eucharist with sentences, prayers and readings appropriate to a marriage.*
   This is followed by **The Marriage,** *without Readings.*
   This is followed by the Eucharist, beginning at **The Peace** *and ending with* **The Marriage Blessing** *and* **The Dismissal.**

In both orders, one of the **Marriage Blessings** *on pages 804-805 is used, and may come before the* **Prayer after Communion**, *or replace it.*

The couple may exchange a greeting of peace with each other, with their parents, and with other members of the congregation.

The couple remain before the Lord's Table and receive Holy Communion before any other members of the congregation do so.

In each of the **Eucharistic Liturgies** an addition to **The Great Thanksgiving** appropriate for marriage is provided on pages 435, 475 and 493.

General

A priest or bishop presides at the celebration of a marriage.

The selection of the service, and the various alternatives within any service, should be made by the couple in consultation with the priest.

In the Third form of the Marriage Liturgy, selections are made for each section of the service from either column.

Family or friends of the bride and bridegroom may read, speak to the people, or conduct the prayers.

Non-scriptural lessons approved by the priest may be read provided there is at least one New Testament reading.

Hymns, psalms, anthems, or instrumental music may be used at appropriate points in the service. The following are noted as possible places:
   at the entry of the bride, or of the bride and groom,
   in association with **The Ministry of the Word**,
   before **The Prayers**,
   as the wedding party leaves the church.

The bride and bridegroom may learn the vows by heart, or they may repeat them phrase by phrase after the priest, or they may read them from cards held by attendants.

When the marriage register is signed in the presence of the congregation, it is signed either after **The Marriage** or at the conclusion of the service.

Funeral Liturgies
and
Services in the
Time of Death

Concerning these Services

Of all human events, death concerns us the most deeply. When death approaches, whether it be our own or that of someone close to us, it immediately becomes our principal and overriding concern. When people die, their family and friends suffer loss, shock and grief. Grief is like a wound which requires time and care if it is to heal. Nevertheless, God's love continues through our loss and in our grieving. These services aim to strengthen our assurance of this.

On the one hand, Christians know that Christ has triumphed over death, and that therefore we need no longer fear it. The last event in our lives leads on to something richer. On the other hand, when we have loved deeply and received love, especially when this love has been lasting, the grief and pain suffered is extreme. The loved person will not be encountered again in this life. The future seems uncertain and forbidding. It can be almost impossible for the sufferer to accept the loss.

As death approaches, the person and immediate family require regular, loving support. At the time of and immediately after death the need for care is critical. People need to be strengthened by prayers at the time of death and their grieving before the funeral, whether prayer is offered at home, in church, or on the marae.

In these funeral services there is comfort for the mourners, the commendation to God of the person who has died, and the committal of the body for burial or cremation. After the funeral, there is provision in the home for beginning a new life; committal of ashes after a cremation; and prayers at the anniversary or the unveiling of a memorial.

The services in this book contain many options. There are also additional prayers, sentences and readings. The circumstances in which death occurs vary greatly, and material selected should reflect the particular needs. It is imperative therefore that the minister shall always prepare carefully, and use selections appropriate to the occasion.

> *Jesus said,*
> *'Blessed are those who mourn for they shall be comforted.'*

Prayer at Time of Death

Where possible the minister ensures that the dying person is prepared beforehand.

The person should be helped to be aware of the nature of her/his condition, and that the time of death is approaching.

If the sick person wishes, **The Reconciliation of a Penitent** *is used.*

Prior to this service the person may receive Holy Communion and/or receive anointing.

It is appropriate that those who are gathered (the dying person's family and friends) may receive the Holy Communion together with the dying person.

Though I walk through the valley of the shadow of death,
I will fear no evil:
for you are with me,
your rod and your staff are my comfort.

Psalm 23:4

If we live, we live for the Lord;
and if we die, we die for the Lord.
Whether therefore we live or die,
we belong to the Lord.

Romans 14:8

Blessèd be the God and Father of our Lord Jesus Christ,
by whose great mercy
we have been born anew to a living hope
by the resurrection of Jesus Christ from the dead.

1 Peter 1:3

The Song of Simeon *Nunc Dimittis*

Lord now you let your servant go in peace:
   your word has been fulfilled.
My own eyes have seen the salvation:
   which you have prepared in the sight of every people,
a light to reveal you to the nations:
   and the glory of your people Israel.

Glory to the Father, and to the Son,
   and to the Holy Spirit:
as it was in the beginning, is now,
   and shall be for ever. Amen.

*One of the psalms, found on pages 817- 821, or some other suitable psalm, ·
may be read.*

The Lord's Prayer is said in one of the following forms, or in the form on page 817.

As Jesus teaches us, we pray

Our Father in heaven,
 hallowed be your name,
 your kingdom come,
 your will be done,
  on earth as in heaven.
Give us today our daily bread.
Forgive us our sins
 as we forgive those who sin against us.
Save us from the time of trial
 and deliver us from evil.

For the kingdom, the power, and the glory are yours
 now and for ever.   Amen.

Kua akona nei tatou e to tatou Ariki,
ka inoi tatou

E to matou Matua i te rangi
 Kia tapu tou Ingoa.
 Kia tae mai tou rangatiratanga.
 Kia meatia tau e pai ai
  ki runga ki te whenua,
   kia rite ano ki to te rangi.
Homai ki a matou aianei
 he taro ma matou mo tenei ra.
Murua o matou hara,
  Me matou hoki e muru nei
   i o te hunga e hara ana ki a matou.
Aua hoki matou e kawea kia whakawaia;
 Engari whakaorangia matou i te kino:
Nou hoki te rangatiratanga, te kaha,
 me te kororia,
  Ake ake ake.   Amine.

The Commendation

The minister continues

Let us pray.

Gracious God,
nothing in death or life,
in the world as it is or the world as it shall be,
nothing in all creation can separate us from your love.

We commend *N* into your loving care.
Enfold *her/him* in the arms of your mercy.
Bless *her/him* in *her/his* dying and in *her/his* rising again in you.
Bless those whose hearts are filled with sadness,
that they too may know the hope of resurrection;
for the sake of our Saviour Jesus Christ.
Amen.

The minister may say

Go forth *N (Christian soul)*, on your journey from this world,
in the love of God the Father who created you,
in the mercy of Jesus the Redeemer who suffered for you,
in the power of the Holy Spirit who keeps you in life eternal.
May you dwell this day in peace,
and rest in the presence of God. Amen.

Then may follow this prayer for family and friends.

God of all consolation,
grant to those who sorrow
the spirit of faith and courage,
that they may have the strength to meet the days to come
with steadfastness and patience;
not sorrowing without hope,
but trusting in your goodness;
through him who is the resurrection and the life,
Jesus Christ our Saviour.
Amen.

Other prayers may follow.

The Blessing

The minister may say

Our Lord Jesus Christ be with you to defend you,
within you to keep you,
before you to lead you,
beside you to guard you,
and above you to bless you.
Amen.

A priest may give a blessing using one of the following, or some other form.

God be your comfort, your strength;
God be your hope and support;
God be your light and your way;
and the blessing of God,
Creator, Redeemer and Giver of life,
remain with you now and for ever.
Amen.

Or

Ma te Atua koe e manaaki
e tiaki i nga wa katoa
e noho i roto i te aroha o te Atua:
ko te aroha hoki te mea nui.
Amine.

Additional Material

*The following form of **The Lord's Prayer** may be said.*

The Lord's Prayer

Our Father, which art in heaven,
   hallowed be thy Name,
   thy kingdom come,
   thy will be done,
      in earth as it is in heaven.
Give us this day our daily bread.
And forgive us our trespasses,
   as we forgive them
      that trespass against us.
And lead us not into temptation,
   but deliver us from evil.

For thine is the kingdom, the power, and the glory
   for ever and ever.   Amen.

Psalms

At the end of each psalm the Gloria is said.

Glory to the Father, and to the Son,
   and to the Holy Spirit:
as it was in the beginning, is now,
   and shall be for ever. Amen.

Psalm 23

1   The Lord is my shepherd:
      therefore can I lack nothing.

2   You Lord make me lie down in green pastures:
      and lead me beside the waters of peace.

3   You revive my spirit:
        and guide me in right pathways
            for your name's sake.

4   Though I walk through the valley of the shadow of death,
            I will fear no evil:
        for you are with me,
            your rod and your staff are my comfort.

5   You spread a table for me
            in the sight of my enemies:
        you have anointed my head with oil,
            and my cup is overflowing.

6   Surely your goodness and mercy shall follow me
            all the days of my life:
        and I will dwell in the house of the Lord for ever.

Psalm 25

1   To you Lord I lift up my soul,
            my God I have put my trust in you:
        let me not be disappointed,
            nor let my enemies triumph over me.

2   For all those who hope in you shall not be ashamed:
        but only those who wantonly break faith.

3   Make known to me your ways O Lord:
        and teach me your paths.

4   Lead me in the way of your truth and teach me:
        you are God my saviour,
            for you have I waited all the day long.

5   Call to remembrance O Lord your tender care:
        and the unfailing love
            which you have shown from of old.

6   Do not remember the sins and offences of my youth:
        but according to your mercy,
            remember me Lord in your goodness.

7   You O Lord are upright and good:
        therefore you show the path to those who go astray.

8   You guide the humble to do what is right:
        and those who are gentle you teach your way.

9   All your ways are loving and sure:
        to those who keep your covenant
            and your commandments.

10 For your name's sake O Lord:
        pardon my guilt, which indeed is great.

11 If there are any who fear the Lord:
        to them the Lord will show the path they should choose.

12 They themselves shall dwell in prosperity:
        and their children shall inherit the land.

13 Your friendship O Lord is for those who honour you:
        and to them you reveal your covenant.

14 My eyes are always on you O Lord:
        for you will release my feet from the net.

15 Turn to me Lord and have mercy:
        for I am lonely and oppressed.

16 Relieve the sorrows of my heart:
        and bring me out of my distress.

17 Look at my affliction and my trouble:
        and forgive me all my sins.

18 See how many are my enemies:
        how violent is their hatred for me.

19 Preserve my life and deliver me:
        let me not be disappointed,
            for I have put my trust in you.

20 Let integrity and righteous dealing preserve me:
        let me not be disappointed,
            for I have put my trust in you.

21 Redeem your people O God:
        and bring them out of all their distress.

Psalm 91

1   Whoever dwells in the shelter of the Most High:
     and passes the night under the shadow of the Almighty,

2   will say to the Lord,
     'You are my refuge and my stronghold:
     my God in whom I trust.'

3   The Lord will free you from the snare of the hunter:
     and from the destroying pestilence.

4   The wings of the Most High will cover you,
     and you will be safe under the feathers of the Almighty:
     the faithfulness of the Lord
     will be your shield and defence.

5   You will not be afraid of any terror by night:
     nor of the arrow that flies by day,

6   of the pestilence that stalks in darkness:
     nor of the plague that lays waste at noon.

7   A thousand may fall beside you,
     ten thousand at your right hand:
     but you will remain unscathed.

8   You have only to look with your eyes:
     to see the reward of the wicked.

9   Because you have said, 'The Lord is my refuge':
     and made the Most High your stronghold,

10   there shall no evil befall you:
     no plague shall come near your dwelling.

11   For the angels of God have been charged:
     to keep you in all your ways.

12   They shall bear you up in their hands:
     lest you should strike your foot against a stone.

13   You shall tread on the asp and the adder:
     the viper and the serpent you shall trample underfoot.

14   'Because they have set their love upon me I will deliver them:
     I will uphold them because they know my name.

15   'When they call to me I will answer:
          I will be with them in trouble,
              I will rescue them and bring them to honour.

16   'With long life I will satisfy them:
          and show them my saving power.'

Psalm 121

1   I lift up my eyes to the hills:
          but where shall I look for help?

2   My help comes from the Lord:
          who has made heaven and earth.

3   The Lord will not let your foot stumble:
          the one who guards you will not sleep.

4   The one who keeps watch over this people:
          shall neither doze nor sleep.

5   The Lord is the one who will guard you:
          the Lord at your right hand will be your defence,

6   so that the sun shall not strike you by day:
          nor yet the moon by night.

7   The Lord shall preserve you from all evil:
          yes it is the Lord who will keep you safe.

8   The Lord shall take care of your going out,
              and your coming in:
          from this time forth and for ever.

Prayer Before a Funeral

This service may be used by a minister with the family and friends of the person who has just died. It may be used in the house, or at the church or marae, or elsewhere at the time of viewing of the body as a preparation for the funeral itself; or when the coffin is brought to the church or marae before a funeral; or at any other appropriate time.

The minister shall greet those present with words of holy Scripture such as the following.

Jesus said,
'I am the resurrection and the life;
even in death,
anyone who believes in me, will live.'

John 11:25

The minister may say

God is with us;
God's love unites us,
God's purpose steadies us,
God's Spirit comforts us.

Blessed be God forever.

The minister continues

Merciful and compassionate God,
we bring you our grief in the loss of N
and ask for courage to bear it.
We bring you our thanks
for all you give us in those we love;
and we bring you our prayers for peace of heart
in the knowledge of your mercy and love,
in Christ Jesus.
Amen.

Other prayers from pages 855-863 may be used.

One or more of the following or other psalms or canticles may be used.

The Song of Simeon

Lord now you let your servant go in peace:
    your word has been fulfilled.
My own eyes have seen the salvation:
    which you have prepared in the sight of every people,
a light to reveal you to the nations:
    and the glory of your people Israel.

Glory to the Father, and to the Son,
    and to the Holy Spirit:
as it was in the beginning, is now,
    and shall be for ever. Amen.

Verses from one or both of the following may be read.

Psalm 27   Psalm 139

*The following or some other appropriate **Reading** may follow.*

Romans 8:31b -39

The minister may stand beside the body and say

We commend *N* to God,
as *s/he* journeys beyond our sight.
God of all consolation,
in your unending love and mercy you turn
the darkness of death
into the dawn of new life.

Your Son, our Lord Jesus Christ,
by dying for us, conquered death,
and by rising again, restored life.

May we not be afraid of death but desire to be with Christ,
and after our life on earth,
to be with those we love,
where every tear is wiped away and all things are made new.
We ask this through Jesus Christ.
Amen.

The Lord's Prayer is said in one of the following forms or in the form on page 817.

Gathering all our prayers into one,
as our Saviour has taught us, we pray

Our Father in heaven,
 hallowed be your name,
 your kingdom come,
 your will be done,
  on earth as in heaven.
Give us today our daily bread.
Forgive us our sins
 as we forgive those who sin against us.
Save us from the time of trial
 and deliver us from evil.

For the kingdom, the power, and the glory are yours
 now and for ever.   Amen.

Kia kotahi tatou i te Inoi a te Ariki

E to matou Matua i te rangi
 Kia tapu tou Ingoa.
 Kia tae mai tou rangatiratanga.
 Kia meatia tau e pai ai
  ki runga ki te whenua,
   kia rite ano ki to te rangi.
Homai ki a matou aianei
 he taro ma matou mo tenei ra.
Murua o matou hara,
  Me matou hoki e muru nei
   i o te hunga e hara ana ki a matou.
Aua hoki matou e kawea kia whakawaia;
  Engari whakaorangia matou i te kino:
Nou hoki te rangatiratanga, te kaha,
 me te kororia,
  Ake ake ake.   Amine.

The minister may say

Now to the One who can keep us from falling
and set us in the presence of the divine glory,
jubilant and above reproach,
to the only God our Saviour,
be glory and majesty, might and authority,
through Jesus Christ our Lord,
before all time, now and for evermore.
Amen.

Or

A priest may give a blessing.

The Funeral Service

The congregation is invited to read this before the service begins.

The service we use today expresses our close relationship with God and with one another. The minister and family have selected what is suitable for this occasion.

Christians have always believed that there is hope in death as in life, and that there is renewed life, in Christ, after death.

God's love and power extend over all creation. Every life, including our own, is precious to God.

*Even those who share this faith find that there is a real feeling of loss at the death of a loved one. The living need our support and consolation. The whole congregation has an important part in giving this help; one way in which we can do this is by joining in those parts printed in **bold type**.*

In the Service

We begin by remembering the person who has died, and offering comfort to those who mourn.

We say the Lord's Prayer.

We hear God's word of hope and consolation.

We give thanks for Christ's victory over death.

We pray for a deeper faith, for ourselves and all who mourn.

*We make our farewells to the deceased in a commendation to God's mercy and love, and conclude with **The Blessing of Peace**.*

*The committal of the body may take place at the graveside or the crematorium or during the service, before **The Blessing of Peace**.*

The Greeting

All standing, the minister may greet the people.

The minister then says

We have come together
to remember before God the life of *N*,
to commend *her/him* to God's keeping,
to commit *her/his* body to be *buried/cremated*,
and to comfort those who mourn
with our sympathy and with our love;
in the hope we share
through the death and resurrection
of Jesus Christ.

The following may be said.

The Lord be with you.
    Kia noho a Ihowa ki a koutou.
The Lord bless you.
    Ma Ihowa koe e manaaki.

The Love of God

The minister says some or all of the following.

Hear the words of Jesus Christ our Saviour:

> Ko ahau te aranga, me te ora: ko ia e whakapono ana ki ahau,
> ahakoa kua mate, e ora ano: e kore ano hoki e mate
> ake ake ake nga tangata katoa e ora ana,
> a e whakapono ana ki ahau.
> *Hoani 11:25*

I am the resurrection and the life;
even in death,
anyone who believes in me, will live.
John 11:25

Set your troubled hearts at rest.
Trust in God always;
trust also in me.
John 14:1

Come to me all who labour and are heavy laden
and I will give you rest.

Matthew 11:28

> Haere mai ki ahau, e koutou katoa e mauiui ana, e taimaha
> ana, a maku koutou e whakaokioki.

Matiu 11:28

God so loved the world that he gave his only Son
that whoever believes in him should not perish
but have eternal life.

John 3:16

> Koia ano te aroha o te Atua ki te ao, homai ana e ia tana
> Tama kotahi, kia kahore ai e mate te tangata e whakapono
> ana ki a ia, engari kia whiwhi ai ki te oranga tonutanga.

Hoani 3:16

The minister continues

Therefore, although we have been parted from N
none of us need ever be separated
from the love of God.

> Ahakoa, na te mate tatou i wehe i a *Ingoa*
> kia mahara, e kore tatou e motuhia
> i te aroha noa o te Atua.

The people may kneel.

The minister says

Let us pray *(saying together)*

God our Comforter,
you are a refuge and a strength for us,
a helper close at hand in times of distress.
Help us so to hear the words of our faith
that our fear is dispelled,
our loneliness eased and our hope reawakened.
May your Holy Spirit lift us
above our natural sorrow,
to the peace and light of your constant love;
through Jesus Christ our Lord.
Amen.

The Remembrance

The minister continues

In a time of silence,
let us make our personal thanksgiving to God
for all that *N* has meant to us.

Silence is kept, concluded by one of the following

For *her/his* life and our memories
we give thanks.

Or

God our Father,
we thank you that you have made each of us
in your own image,
and given us gifts and talents
with which to serve you.
We thank you for *N*,
the years we shared with *her/him*,
the good we saw in *her/him*,
the love we received from *her/him*.
Now give us strength and courage,
to leave *her/him* in your care,
confident in your promise of eternal life
through Jesus Christ our Lord.
Amen.

One of the following prayers is used.

Almighty God,
you judge us with infinite mercy and justice
and love everything you have made.
We rejoice in your promises of pardon, joy and peace
to all who love you.
In your mercy turn the darkness of death
into the dawn of new life,
and the sorrow of parting into the joy of heaven;
through our Saviour Jesus Christ
who died, who rose again,
and lives for evermore.
Amen.

Or

Lord Jesus Christ,
you took children into your arms
and blessed them.
Keep this child in your loving care
and bring us all to the heavenly kingdom,
where you live and reign
with the Father and the Holy Spirit now and for ever.
Amen.

The minister says

With faith and hope, we pray

Our Father in heaven,
 hallowed be your name,
 your kingdom come,
 your will be done,
  on earth as in heaven.
Give us today our daily bread.
Forgive us our sins
 as we forgive those who sin against us.
Save us from the time of trial
 and deliver us from evil.

For the kingdom, the power, and the glory are yours
 now and for ever.   Amen.

I runga i te whakapono me te tumanako,
ka inoi tatou

E to matou Matua i te rangi
 Kia tapu tou Ingoa.
 Kia tae mai tou rangatiratanga.
 Kia meatia tau e pai ai
  ki runga ki te whenua,
   kia rite ano ki to te rangi.
Homai ki a matou aianei
 he taro ma matou mo tenei ra.

Murua o matou hara,
   Me matou hoki e muru nei
      i o te hunga e hara ana ki a matou.
Aua hoki matou e kawea kia whakawaia;
   Engari whakaorangia matou i te kino:
Nou hoki te rangatiratanga, te kaha,
   me te kororia,
      Ake ake ake.   Amine.

The Ministry of the Word

The Psalms

One or more psalms may be said or sung.

Particularly suitable psalms are to be found on pages 841-846.

The Readings

A reading or readings, including one from the New Testament, follows.

The minister may pray

Lord, help us to accept and understand your gospel,

**so that we may find light in our darkness,
faith in our doubts
and comfort for one another.   Amen.**

The Address

A minister may speak to the people.

The Prayers

The minister may use some of the prayers on pages 855-863, or other prayers, in addition to the following.

The minister invites the people to pray.

FIRST FORM

The minister says

Let us pray that God
will grant comfort
and strength to all who mourn.

God our loving Father,
draw near to (*N* and) all who mourn today.
Make your love known to them,
that they may turn to you
and receive comfort and strength.

Help them
to put their trust in you,
and their hope in your grace and compassion.

The people respond

**Use us, Father,
as bearers of your love
to support them in their grief;
this we ask through Christ our Lord. Amen.**

Let us pray for a growing faith in Jesus Christ.

**God,
the strength of all who believe in you,
increase our faith and trust
in your Son,
that we may live victoriously
now and for ever. Amen.**

Let us pray for that hope which only God can give.

Almighty God,
give us such a vision of your purpose,
and such an assurance of your love and power,
that we may ever hold fast the hope
which is in Jesus Christ.   Amen.

Additional prayers may be said and may conclude as on page 835.

SECOND FORM

The minister prays

God our Father,
we pray for the family and friends of N,
that they may know the comfort of your love.
Lord, hear our prayer.

We pray that you will use us
as bearers of your love,
to support them in their grief.
We also remember before you
all who mourn and all who suffer.
Lord, hear our prayer.

Give us patience and faith
in this time of our loss,
so that we may come to understand
the wonder of your mercy,
and the mystery of your love.
Lord, hear our prayer.

Increase our faith and trust
in your Son, Jesus Christ,
that we may live victoriously.
Lord, hear our prayer.

Give us such a vision of your purpose,
and such an assurance of your love and power,
that we may ever hold fast the hope
which is in Jesus Christ, our Lord.
Lord, hear our prayer.

FURTHER PRAYERS

One of these prayers of thanksgiving for Christ's victory over death may be used.

God of grace,
we thank you for sending your Son, Jesus Christ,
who by his death has destroyed the power of death,
and by his glorious resurrection
has opened the kingdom of heaven to all believers.
Grant us to know that because Christ lives,
we shall live also,
and that neither death nor life
shall be able to separate us from your love.
Amen.

God of all that lives and dies,
we thank you that Jesus is risen from the dead,
offering us the hope of new life.
Because Jesus lives, nothing can separate us from your love,
which unites us now with those we mourn.
Amen.

We thank you, God of life and death:
Christ facing death on the cross gives us courage;
Christ rising from the dead brings us hope.
The dawn breaks and gives us light for the new day.
Amen.

God,
you sent Jesus to share our earthly life.
We thank you for Christ's victory over death.
Help us to share that victory,
and give us the hope to look forward again.
Amen.

Now to God who is able to do immeasurably more
than all we can ask or conceive,
by the power which is at work among us,
be glory in the Church and in Christ Jesus
throughout all ages.
Amen.

The Commendation

The minister may ask the congregation to stand.

The minister says one or both of the following sentences.

There is nothing in death or life,
in the world as it is,
or the world as it shall be,
nothing in all creation,
that can separate us
from the love of God
in Jesus Christ our Lord.

Romans 8:38,39

    E kore te mate, e kore te ora,
    e kore nga anahera, e kore nga rangatira,
    e kore nga kaha, e kore nga mea onaianei,
    e kore nga mea e puta mai a mua,
    e kore te tiketike, e kore te hohonu,
    e kore tetahi atu mea hanga,
    e kaha ki te momotu i a tatou i te aroha o te Atua,
    i tera i roto nei i a Karaiti Ihu i to tatou Ariki.

Roma 8:38,39

Blessèd be the God and Father of our Lord Jesus Christ,
by whose great mercy
we have been born anew into a living hope
by the resurrection of Jesus Christ from the dead.

1 Peter 1:3

    Kia whakapaingia te Atua,
    te Matua o to tatou Ariki, o Ihu Karaiti.
    Na tana mahi tohu tatou i whanau hou ai,
    ki te tumanako ora,
    i a Ihu Karaiti
    ka ara ake nei i te hunga mate.

1 Peta 1:3

The minister says one of the following commendations.
A form of commendation in Maori is found on pages 840-841.

God alone is holy and just and good.
In that confidence, therefore,
we commend you, *N*,
to God's judgment and mercy,
to God's forgiveness and love.
Blessed be God the Father,
who has caused the light of Christ
to shine upon you.

Go forth from this world:
in the love of God the Father
who created you,
in the mercy of Jesus Christ
who redeemed you,
in the power of the Holy Spirit
who strengthens you.
In communion with all the faithful,
may you dwell this day in peace.
Amen.

Or

Gracious God,
by your mighty power you gave us life,
and in your love you have given us new life in Christ.
We now entrust *N* to your keeping,
in the faith of Jesus Christ
who died and rose again,
and now lives and reigns with you and the Holy Spirit
in glory for ever.
Amen.

*The service continues with **The Committal** or **The Blessing of Peace**
(page 838).*

The Committal

*If **The Committal** takes place immediately, the minister says one of the following.*

Now therefore, *N*,
we commit your body to be *buried / cremated*,
earth to earth,
ashes to ashes,
dust to dust;
in the sure and certain hope
of the resurrection to eternal life
in Jesus Christ our Lord.
Amen.

Or

Since the earthly life of *N*
has come to an end,
we commit *her/his* body to be *buried / turned to ashes;*
   [earth to earth,
   ashes to ashes,
   dust to dust;]
in the sure and certain hope
of the resurrection to eternal life
through Jesus Christ our Lord.
Amen.

The minister may then say

Blessed are the dead who die in the Lord,
for they rest from their labours.

The minister says

We have been parted from *N*,
but none of us need ever be separated
from the love of God.

Heavenly Father,
you have given us a true faith and a sure hope
in your Son Jesus Christ;
help us to live as those who believe and trust
in the communion of saints,
the forgiveness of sins,
and the resurrection to eternal life.

Strengthen this faith and hope in us
as long as we live;
so that we in turn
may not be afraid to die.
You are Lord of heaven and earth;
your goodness never fails.
Have mercy on your people who need your strength
and bless us now and evermore.
Amen.

The Blessing of Peace

The minister may say

Go forth into the world in peace,
be strong and of good courage,
hold fast that which is good.
Love and serve the Lord with singleness of heart,
rejoicing in the power of the Spirit;
and the peace of the Lord
be always with you.
Amen.

Or

The grace of our Lord Jesus Christ
and the love of God and the fellowship
of the Holy Spirit be with us all.
Amen.

Or

A priest may give a blessing.

If a separate committal takes place at the crematorium or at the graveside, the following form is used.

A Form of Committal at a Graveside or Crematorium

The following sentences may be read.

Blessed be the God and Father
of our Lord Jesus Christ,
a gentle Father,
and the God of all consolation,
who comforts us in our sorrows,
so that we can offer others, in their sorrows,
the consolation that we ourselves have received from God.

2 Corinthians 1:3-4

The eternal God is your refuge,
and underneath are the everlasting arms. *Deuteronomy 33:27*

Further sentences are to be found on pages 853-855.

The minister says one of the following forms of committal.

God alone is holy and just and good.
In that confidence we have commended you, *N*,
to God's judgment and mercy,
God's forgiveness and love.
Now therefore, we commit your body
to the ground / to be cremated,
earth to earth,
ashes to ashes,
dust to dust;
in the sure and certain hope
of the resurrection to eternal life
in Jesus Christ our Redeemer.
Amen.

Or

We have entrusted our *brother/sister, N,*
into the hands of God;
we now commit *her/his* body *to the ground / to be turned to ashes*
  [earth to earth,
  ashes to ashes,
  dust to dust;]
having our whole trust and confidence
in the mercy of our heavenly Father
and in the victory of Jesus Christ,
who himself died, was buried and rose again for us,
and is alive and reigns for ever and ever.
Amen.

Further prayers may be added.

*The minister may conclude with **The Grace** or a priest may give a **Blessing.***

Alternative Commendation and Committal

*The following form in Maori may be used in place of **The Commendation** and
The Committal.*

Ko Ihowa anake e tapu ana, e tika ana,
e marama ana.
I runga i tenei whakapono
ka tukua atu koe e *Ingoa,*
ki tana whakawa me ana mahi tohu;
ki tana murunga hara, me tona aroha.
Kia whakapaingia te Atua, te Matua,
nana nei i mea kia tiaho te maramatanga
o te Karaiti ki a koe.

Whakangaro i te ao,
i runga i te aroha o te Atua Matua,
nana nei koe i hanga;
i runga i nga mahi tohu a Ihu Karaiti,
nana nei koe i hoko;
i runga i te mana o te Wairua Tapu,
e whakakaha nei i a koe.
Whakauru atu ki te kahui o te hunga pono;
noho mai i runga i te rangimarie.

Waihoki, ka tukua to tinana *ki te oneone/kia tahuna*
he oneone ki te oneone,
he pungarehu ki te pungarehu,
he puehu ki te puehu;
me te tino tumanako atu ki te
aranga ake ki te ora tonu;
Ko Ihu Karaiti hoki to matou Ariki.
Amine.

Psalms

Psalm 23

1   The Lord is my shepherd:
        therefore can I lack nothing.

2   You Lord make me lie down in green pastures:
        and lead me beside the waters of peace.

3   You revive my spirit:
        and guide me in right pathways
            for your name's sake.

4   Though I walk through the valley of the shadow of death,
            I will fear no evil:
        for you are with me,
            your rod and your staff are my comfort.

5   You spread a table for me
            in the sight of my enemies:
        you have anointed my head with oil,
            and my cup is overflowing.

6   Surely your goodness and mercy shall follow me
            all the days of my life:
        and I will dwell in the house of the Lord for ever.

**Glory to the Father, and to the Son,
    and to the Holy Spirit:
as it was in the beginning, is now,
    and shall be for ever. Amen.**

Waiata 23

1 Ko Ihowa toku hepara:
     e kore ahau e hapa.

2 Ko ia hei mea kia takoto ahau i nga wahi tarutaru hou:
     e arahi ana ia i ahau i te taha o nga wai ata rere.

3 Ko ia hei whakahoki ake i toku wairua:
     e arahi ana ia i ahau i nga ara o te tika,
       he whakaaro hoki ki tona ingoa.

4 Ae, ahakoa haere ahau i te awaawa o te atarangi o te mate,
     kahore he kino e wehi ai ahau:
       no te mea kei toku taha koe; ko tau rakau, ko tau tokotoko,
         ko ena hei oranga ngakau moku.

5 E taka ana e koe he tepara ki toku aroaro
     i te tirohanga ano o oku hoa-riri:
       e whakawahia ana e koe toku matenga ki te hinu,
         purena tonu taku kapa.

6 He pono, e aru i ahau te pai me te atawhai i nga ra katoa
     e ora ai ahau:
       a ka noho ahau ki te whare o Ihowa ake tonu atu.

Kororia ki a koe, e te Ariki.

Psalm 121

1 I lift up my eyes to the hills:
     but where shall I look for help?

2 My help comes from the Lord:
     who has made heaven and earth.

3 The Lord will not let your foot stumble:
     the one who guards you will not sleep.

4 The one who keeps watch over this people:
     shall neither doze nor sleep.

5 The Lord is the one who will guard you:
     the Lord at your right hand will be your defence,

6 so that the sun shall not strike you by day:
     nor yet the moon by night.

7   The Lord shall preserve you from all evil:
        yes it is the Lord who will keep you safe.

8   The Lord shall take care of your going out,
            and your coming in:
        from this time forth and for ever.

    Glory to the Father, and to the Son,
        and to the Holy Spirit:
    as it was in the beginning, is now,
        and shall be for ever. Amen.

Waiata 121

1   Ka anga atu oku kanohi ki nga maunga:
        kei hea hoki te awhina moku?

2   No Ihowa te awhina moku:
        no te Kai-hanga i te rangi, i te whenua.

3   E kore ia e tuku i tou waewae kia nekehia:
        e kore tou Kai-tiaki e moe.

4   Ina, e kore te Kai-tiaki o Iharaira:
        e parangia, e moe.

5   Ko Ihowa tou Kai-tiaki:
        ko Ihowa tou whakamarumaru i tou ringa matau.

6   E kore koe e pakia e te ra i te awatea:
        e te marama ranei i te po.

7   Ma Ihowa e tiaki tou haerenga atu, me tou haerenga mai:
        aianei a ake tonu atu.

    Kororia ki a koe, e te Ariki.

Psalm 130

1   Out of the depths have I called to you O Lord:
        give heed O Lord to my cry.

2   Let your ears consider well:
        the plea I make for mercy.

3   If you should keep account of what is done amiss:
        who then O Lord could stand?

4   But there is forgiveness with you:
        therefore you shall be revered.

5   I wait for you Lord with all my soul:
        and in your word is my hope.

6   My soul waits for you O Lord:
        more than those who watch by night
            long for the morning,
        more I say than those who watch by night
            long for the morning.

7   Wait in hope for the Lord,
        for with the Lord there is love unfailing:
        and with the Lord there is ample redemption.

8   The Lord will redeem you:
        from all your many sins.

Glory to the Father, and to the Son,
    and to the Holy Spirit:
as it was in the beginning, is now,
    and shall be for ever. Amen.

Waiata 130

1   I karanga atu ahau ki a koe, e Ihowa:
        i roto i nga hohonu.

2   E te Ariki, whakarongo mai ki toku reo:
        kia anga mai ou taringa ki toku reo inoi.

3   Me i maharatia e koe nga kino, e Ihowa:
        ko wai, e te Ariki, e tu?

4   Otira he muru hara tau:
        e wehingia ai koe.

5   E tatari ana ahau ki a Ihowa:
        e tatari ana toku wairua e tumanako
            atu hoki ahau ki tana kupu.

6   Te taringa o toku wairua ki te Ariki,
        nui atu i to te hunga e whanga ana ki te ata:
        ae, i to te hunga e whanga ana ki te ata.

7 Kia tumanako a Iharaira ki a Ihowa,
    kei a Ihowa hoki te mahi tohu:
    kei a ia te hokonga nui.

8 A mana a Iharaira e hoko:
    i roto i ona hara katoa.

Kororia ki a koe, e te Ariki.

Psalm 139:1-11

1 Lord you have searched me out and known me:
    you know when I sit down and when I stand up,
      you discern my thoughts from afar.

2 You mark my path, and the places where I rest:
    you are acquainted with all my ways.

3 Even before there is a word on my tongue:
    you Lord know it altogether.

4 You guard me from behind and before:
    and cover me with your hand.

5 Such knowledge is too wonderful for me:
    so high that I cannot attain to it.

6 Where shall I go from your spirit:
    or where shall I flee from your presence?

7 If I climb up to heaven you are there:
    if I make my bed in the grave you are there also.

8 If I take the wings of the dawn:
    and alight at the uttermost parts of the sea,

9 even there your hand will lead me:
    and your right hand will hold me fast.

10 If I say, 'Let the darkness cover me:
    and my day be turned to night,'

11 the darkness is no darkness with you,
    but the night is as clear as the day:
    for darkness and light to you are both alike.

Glory to the Father, and to the Son,
    and to the Holy Spirit:
as it was in the beginning, is now,
    and shall be for ever. Amen.

Waiata 139:1-11

1 E Ihowa kua tirotirohia mai ahau,
    kua mohiotia ano hoki e koe:
  e matau ana i oku nohoanga iho,
    ki oku whakatikanga ake;
    mohio ana koe ki oku whakaaro i tawhiti.

2 Toku ara, me taku takotoranga iho kitea putia e koe:
  oku huarahi katoa, matau tonu i a koe.

3 Kahore rawa hoki te kupu i toku arero:
  i toe i a koe te mohio, e Ihowa.

4 Kua hanga a muri, a mua, oku e koe:
  kua pa mai ano tou ringa ki ahau.

5 He mea whakamiharo rawa,
    kei tawhiti atu hoki i ahau, tenei matauranga:
  kei runga noa atu, e kore e taea atu e ahau.

6 Me haere ahau ki hea i tou Wairua:
  me oma ranei ki hea i tou aroaro.

7 Ki te kake atu ahau ki te rangi, kei reira koe:
  ki te wharikitia e ahau toku moenga i roto i te rua
    tupapaku, na, kei reira ano koe.

8 Ki te tango ahau i nga pakau o te ata:
  a noho ana ki nga wahi whakamutunga mai o te moana.

9 Kei reira ano hoki tou ringaringa hei arataki i ahau:
  tou ringaringa matau, hei pupuri i ahau.

10 Ki te mea ahau, Tera ahau e ngaro i te pouri:
  marama noa te po i tetahi taha oku, i tetahi taha.

11 Ae, e kore te pouri e pouri ki a koe,
    engari rite tahi te po me te ao te marama:
  ki a koe, rite tahi te pouri me te marama.

Kororia ki a koe, e te Ariki.

A Service
for the Funeral of a Child

*The death of a child brings a specially devastating grief to the family. **The
Funeral Service** may be used with appropriate options, but this shorter
service will often be preferred.*

*Its simplicity and concern for the needs of the bereaved reveals Christ's
care for little children.*

The following form may be supplemented at the discretion of the minister.

All standing, the minister may greet the people.

The minister says

NN, *(Parents)*,
we have come here today
to commend *N* to our heavenly Father;
and to commit *her/his* body to be *buried/cremated*;
to assure you of God's everlasting love,
to share in your sorrow
and to offer you comfort and support.

The Lord will tend the flock like a shepherd;
embracing the lambs together and nursing them.   *Isaiah 40:11*

Jesus said, 'Let the little children come to me, do not stop them;
for it is to such as these that the kingdom of God belongs.'

Mark 10:14

The minister prays

Heavenly Father,
your Son took little children
into his arms and blessed them.
Grant to us now the assurance that *N* is encircled
by those arms of love.
In the midst of our grief
strengthen our faith and hope
in your Son, Jesus Christ our Lord.
Amen.

A Reading *from the Scriptures may follow.*

The following, or another appropriate **Psalm**, *may be said.*

Psalm 23

1   The Lord is my shepherd:
　　therefore can I lack nothing.

2   You Lord make me lie down in green pastures:
　　and lead me beside the waters of peace.

3   You revive my spirit:
　　and guide me in right pathways
　　　for your name's sake.

4   Though I walk through the valley of the shadow of death,
　　　I will fear no evil:
　　for you are with me,
　　　your rod and your staff are my comfort.

5   You spread a table for me
　　　in the sight of my enemies:
　　you have anointed my head with oil,
　　　and my cup is overflowing.

6   Surely your goodness and mercy shall follow me
　　　all the days of my life:
　　·　and I will dwell in the house of the Lord for ever.

Glory to the Father, and to the Son,
   and to the Holy Spirit:
as it was in the beginning, is now,
   and shall be for ever. Amen.

The Address

The minister may speak to the people.

The Prayers

One of the following prayers is said.

The minister says

Let us pray

God of all compassion,
you make nothing in vain
and love all you have created.
Comfort *(these)* your servants *(NN)*
whose hearts are weighed down by grief and sorrow.
Lift them up,
and grant that they may so love and serve you in this life,
that together with *N*,
your child and theirs,
they may obtain the fulness of your promises
in the age to come;
through Jesus Christ our Lord.
Amen.

Or

Loving Father,
we thank you for the gift of *N (this child)*,
and for the blessing *s/he* brought to our lives.
Help us now to entrust *her/him*
to your never-failing care and love,
and bring us all to your heavenly kingdom;
through Jesus Christ our Redeemer.
Amen.

The Commendation

Into God's loving care and compassion,
into the arms of that infinite mercy,
we commend N *(this child)*
in the assurance that *s/he* will share
in the risen life of Jesus Christ, our Saviour.
Amen.

*The service continues with **The Committal** or **The Lord's Prayer**.*

The Committal

*If **The Committal** takes place immediately, the minister says*

The Lamb who is at the heart of the throne
will be their shepherd
and will guide them to the springs of the water of life;
and God will wipe all tears from their eyes.   *Revelation 7:17*

The minister says

We have entrusted N to God's merciful keeping,
and we now commit *her/his* body to be *buried / cremated*,
earth to earth,
ashes to ashes,
dust to dust;
in the sure and certain hope
of the resurrection to eternal life;
through Jesus Christ our Lord.
Amen.

The minister prays for the family.

Loving God,
be with us as we face the mystery of life and death.
Strengthen the bonds of this family
as they bear their loss.

Help them to go from here
with courage and confidence in your care and love;
through our Redeemer, Jesus Christ.
Amen.

The Lord's Prayer *is said in one of the following forms,
or in the form on page 863.*

With faith and hope we pray

Our Father in heaven,
hallowed be your name,
your kingdom come,
your will be done,
on earth as in heaven.
Give us today our daily bread.
Forgive us our sins
as we forgive those who sin against us.
Save us from the time of trial
and deliver us from evil.

For the kingdom, the power, and the glory are yours
now and for ever.   Amen.

I runga i te whakapono me te tumanako,
ka inoi tatou

E to matou Matua i te rangi
   Kia tapu tou Ingoa.
   Kia tae mai tou rangatiratanga.
   Kia meatia tau e pai ai
     ki runga ki te whenua,
      kia rite ano ki to te rangi.
Homai ki a matou aianei
   he taro ma matou mo tenei ra.
Murua o matou hara,
   Me matou hoki e muru nei
     i o te hunga e hara ana ki a matou.
Aua hoki matou e kawea kia whakawaia;
   Engari whakaorangia matou i te kino:
Nou hoki te rangatiratanga, te kaha,
   me te kororia,
     Ake ake ake.   **Amine.**

The priest concludes with the following or some other appropriate blessing.

May Christ the Good Shepherd
enfold you with love,
fill you with peace,
and lead you in hope,
this day and all your days.
Amen.

*(A lay minister says the prayer using 'us' instead of 'you',
and 'our' instead of 'your').*

Sentences, Prayers, Readings and Hymns for the Funeral Liturgies

Sentences

1   The eternal God is your refuge,
     and underneath are the everlasting arms.   *Deuteronomy 33:27*

2   In my heart I know that my redeemer lives,
     and at last will stand upon the earth;
     and from my flesh I shall look on God
     whom I shall see with my own eyes,
     I myself and no other.   *Job 19:25-26*

3   Call to remembrance, O Lord, your tender care
     and the unfailing love
     which you have shown from of old.

     Do not remember the sins and offences of my youth:
     but according to your mercy
     remember me, Lord, in your goodness.

     You O Lord are upright and good
     therefore you show the path to those who go astray.

     You guide the humble to do what is right,
     and those who are gentle you teach your way.

     All your ways are loving and sure
     to those who keep your covenant
     and your commandments.   *Psalm 25:5-9*

4   God is our refuge and strength:
     a very present help in trouble.   *Psalm 46:1*

5   You are full of compassion and mercy:
     slow to anger and rich in kindness.

     You will not always be chiding:
     nor do you keep your anger for ever.

You have not dealt with us according to our sins:
nor punished us according to our wickedness.

For as the heavens are high above the earth,
so great is your mercy over those who fear you.

As far as the east is from the west,
so far have you put away our sins from us.

As parents have compassion on their children,
so do you Lord have compassion on those who fear you.

For you know what we are made of:
you remember that we are but dust.

Our days are like the grass:
we flourish like a flower of the field.

But as soon as the wind goes over it, it is gone:
and its place shall know it no more.

But your merciful goodness O Lord
extends for ever toward those who fear you,
and your righteousness to children's children,

when they are true to your covenant
and remember to keep your commandments.

Psalm 103:8-18

6   The steadfast love of the Lord never ceases;
God's mercies never come to an end;
they are new every morning;
your faithfulness, O Lord, is great.   *Lamentations 3:22-23*

7   How blest are the sorrowful;
they shall find consolation.   *Matthew 5:4*

8   Jesus said, 'Set your troubled hearts at rest.
Trust in God always; trust also in me.

There are many dwelling places in my Father's house;
if it were not so I should have told you;
for I am going there on purpose to prepare a place for you.
And if I go to prepare a place for you,
I shall come again and receive you to myself,

so that where I am, you may be also;
and my way there is known to you.

I am the way; I am the truth and I am the life;
no one comes to the Father except by me.'   *John 14:1-4, 6*

9   No one of us lives,
and equally no one of us dies,
for self alone.
If we live, we live for the Lord;
and if we die, we die for the Lord.
This is why Christ died and came to life again,
to establish his lordship over dead and living.   *Romans 14:7-9*

10   No eye has seen, no ear has heard, no mind has conceived,
what has been prepared for those who love God.

1 Corinthians 2:9

11   Blessèd be the God and Father of our Lord Jesus Christ,
by whose great mercy
we have been born anew into a living hope
by the resurrection of Jesus Christ from the dead.   *1 Peter 1:3*

12   The Lamb who is at the heart of the throne
will be their shepherd and will guide them
to the springs of the water of life;
and God will wipe all tears from their eyes.   *Revelation 7:17*

Additional Prayers

FOR A CHILD

1   Heavenly Father,
the strength of all who believe in you,
comfort this family in their sorrow
at the death of *(their child)* N.
May they find hope in your steadfast love;
through Jesus Christ our Lord.
Amen.

2   Creator of all,
      we thank you for the gift of life you gave to *N*.
      In our confusion and grief
      help us to remember the joy
      which *s/he* brought us in the short time that *s/he* lived,
      and guide us through our present darkness
      to the light of your unfailing love,
      through Jesus Christ our Lord.
      Amen.

3   Father, the death of *N* brings an emptiness into our lives.
      We are separated from *her/him*
      and feel broken and disturbed.
      Give us confidence that *s/he* is safe
      and *her/his* life complete with you.
      Help us by your constant presence to know
      that Jesus bridges the gap
      between death and life.
      This we ask through Jesus Christ our Lord.
      Amen.

4   We commend into your keeping, heavenly Father,
      this your child,
      whose life on earth we wanted to share.
      Unite us with *her/him* in your unending love,
      through Jesus Christ our Saviour.
      Amen.

FOR A STILL-BORN CHILD

5   God our Creator,
      from whom all life comes,
      comfort this family,
      grieving for the loss of their hoped-for child.
      Help them to find assurance
      that with you nothing is wasted or incomplete,
      and uphold them with your love,
      through Jesus Christ our Saviour.
      Amen.

AFTER RELEASE FROM SUFFERING

6   We thank you loving Father
      for taking *N* from sickness into health,
      and from suffering into joy.
      Grant that those whom *s/he* has left
      may be strengthened
      by your continuing presence,
      and share with *her/him* your gift of eternal life.
      Amen.

AFTER A SUDDEN DEATH

7   Jesus our Saviour,
      comfort us with the great power of your love
      as we mourn the sudden death of *N*.
      Give us a patient faith in this time of darkness
      and help us to understand and know your ways.
      Strengthen us in our faith that *s/he* is with you for ever.
      We ask this through Jesus Christ our Lord.
      Amen.

8   Compassionate God,
      we ask you to receive *N*,
      who has died by *her/his* own hand.
      Grant that the knowledge of your love and mercy
      may comfort those who grieve for *her/him*,
      strengthen our assurance of your redeeming purpose
      for all your children,
      through Jesus Christ your Son.
      Amen.

9   God of hope,
      we come to you in shock and grief and confusion of heart.
      Help us to find peace
      in the knowledge of your loving mercy
      to all your children,
      and give us light to guide us out of our darkness
      into the assurance of your love.
      Amen.

WHEN NO BODY HAS BEEN RECOVERED

10 Almighty God,
   your love embraces all people;
   to you we commend your servant *N*,
   whom we have lost in death.
   Grant us a firm faith in your loving purpose,
   and the comfort of your presence,
   now and always.
   Amen.

FOR USE WITH CHILDREN

11 Lord Jesus,
   we ask you to be close to the children of this family,
   whose lives have been changed by sorrow.
   Give them courage to face their loss,
   and comfort them with your unchanging love.
   Amen.

12 Please listen, God,
   while we talk to you about *N* who has died.
   Take care of *her/him*, and please take care of us too.
   Thank you for the times we had together.
   Thank you for Jesus, who shows us your love.
   He is close to *N*, and he is close to us.
   Thank you, God.
   Amen.

PRAYERS FOR GENERAL USE

13 Father of all,
   we pray to you for those we love but see no longer.
   We thank you
   for the peace and light you bestow upon them;
   in your loving wisdom and almighty power
   continue to work in them
   the good purpose of your perfect will,
   through Jesus Christ our Lord.
   Amen.

14   God of all comfort,
       we pray to you for those we love but see no longer.
       Grant them your peace;
       let light perpetual shine upon them;
       and in your loving wisdom and almighty power
       work in them the good purpose of your perfect will,
       through Jesus Christ our Lord.
       Amen.

15   Living God,
       we rejoice in your promises of blessing
       to those who die in the Lord;
       so strengthen our understanding of the light and peace
       which they now enjoy in Christ,
       that we may find consolation in our sorrow,
       through Jesus Christ our Lord.
       Amen.

16   Support us, Lord, all the day long of this troubled life,
       until the shadows lengthen, and the evening comes,
       the busy world is hushed,
       the fever of life is over, and our work is done.
       Then, Lord, in your mercy, give us safe lodging,
       a holy rest, and peace at the last.
       Amen.

17   You have ordered this wondrous world, O God,
       and you know all things in earth and heaven;
       so fill our hearts with trust in you that by day and by night,
       at all times and in all seasons,
       we may without fear commit those who are dear to us
       to your never failing love,
       for this life and the life to come,
       through Jesus Christ our Lord.
       Amen.

18 Merciful God,
    we remember those who have gone before us,
    who have stood by us and helped us,
    who have cheered us by their sympathy
    and strengthened us by their example;
    help us so to live, that in dying,
    we may rejoice with them in the promise
    of a glorious resurrection;
    through your Son our Redeemer.
    Amen.

19 Jesus, our friend and Redeemer,
    on the first Easter Day you stood among your disciples
    as the conqueror of sin and death,
    and spoke to them of your peace.
    Come to us in your risen power
    and make us glad with your presence;
    and so breathe your Holy Spirit into our hearts
    that we may be strong to serve you,
    for the glory of your great name.
    Amen.

20 Father in heaven,
    your Son Jesus Christ wept at the grave of Lazarus;
    show your compassion now to those who mourn.
    Supply their needs,
    and help them to trust for ever in your fatherly care.
    Amen.

21 Risen Saviour,
    you comforted your disciples when you were going to die;
    now set our troubled hearts at rest and banish our fears.
    You are the way to the Father:
    help us to follow you.
    You are the truth:
    bring us to know you.
    You are the life:
    give us that life with you, now and for ever.
    Amen.

22 God of heaven and earth,
help us to entrust our loved ones to your care.
When sorrow darkens our lives, teach us to look to you.
May we on earth always rejoice in your presence,
and share with them the rest and peace you give,
in Jesus Christ our Lord.
Amen.

23 Glorious God,
with your whole Church we offer you our thanks and praise
for all you have done for humanity through Jesus Christ.
By giving him to live and die for us
you have disclosed your gracious plan for the whole world,
and shown that your love has no limit.
By raising Jesus from the dead you have promised
that those who trust in him will share his resurrection life.
For the assurance and hope of our faith,
and for the saints you have received into eternal joy,
we thank you heavenly Father.
And especially now we lift up our hearts in thanksgiving
for the life of *N*, now gone from us;
for all your goodness to *her/him* through many days,
for all that *s/he* was to those who loved *her/him*
and for everything in *her/his* life
that reflected your goodness and love,
blessed be your name, O God.
Amen.

24 Gracious God,
surround us and all who mourn this day
with your continuing compassion.
Do not let grief overwhelm your children,
or be unending,
or turn them against you.
May we travel more peacefully because of today,
and come at last, in the fellowship of all your people,
to the haven where we long to be;
through Jesus Christ our Lord.
Amen.

25   Almighty God,
          from whom neither life nor death
          can separate those who trust in your love,
          and whose love holds in its embrace
          your children in this world and the next;
          so unite us to yourself,
          that in our fellowship with you
          we may always be united to our loved ones.
          Give us courage, constancy and hope;
          through him who died and was buried and rose again for us,
          Jesus Christ our Saviour.
          Amen.

26   God of mercy,
          as we mourn the death of *N*
          and thank you for *her/his* life,
          we also remember times
          when it was hard for us to understand,
          to forgive, and to be forgiven.
          Heal our memories of hurt and failure,
          and bring us to forgiveness and life.
          Amen.

BLESSINGS

27   God grant to the living, grace;
          to the departed, rest;
          to all the world, peace and concord;
          and to us and to every faithful servant, life everlasting:
          and the blessing of God almighty,
          Father, Son, and Holy Spirit,
          be with you and remain with you for ever.
          Amen.

28   The God of peace,
          who by the blood of the eternal covenant
          brought again from the dead our Lord Jesus Christ,
          that great shepherd of the sheep,
          make you perfect in every good work,

working in you that which is pleasing and good,
through Jesus Christ, to whom be glory for ever and ever.
Amen.

29 To God's gracious mercy and protection we commit you;
the Lord bless you and keep you;
the Lord make his face to shine upon you
and be gracious to you;
the Lord lift up the light of his countenance upon you
and give you peace:
and the blessing of God almighty,
the Father, the Son, and the Holy Spirit,
be with you, now and always.
Amen.

30 To God's gracious mercy and protection we commit you;
God bless you, keep you and be gracious to you;
The Lord's face shine upon you;
the light of God's countenance lift you up
and give you peace.
Amen.

A FORM OF THE LORD'S PRAYER

31 Our Father, which art in heaven,
hallowed be thy Name,
thy kingdom come,
thy will be done,
in earth as it is in heaven.
Give us this day our daily bread.
And forgive us our trespasses,
as we forgive them
that trespass against us.
And lead us not into temptation,
but deliver us from evil.

For thine is the kingdom, the power, and the glory
for ever and ever. **Amen.**

Readings and Psalms suitable for Funeral Liturgies

PASSAGES FROM THE OLD TESTAMENT AND THE APOCRYPHA

Proverbs 31 *verses may be selected*	In praise of a good woman
Ecclesiastes 3:1-14	A time for everything
Isaiah 25:6a, 7-9	Death shall be swallowed up in victory
Isaiah 40:28-31	The Lord is an everlasting God
Lamentations 3:(17-21)22-26	The steadfast love of the Lord
2 Esdras 2:42-48	The faithful are exalted in heaven
Wisdom 3:1-6 (7,8), 9	The souls of the righteous are in the hands of God
Wisdom 4:7-9 (10-12), 13-15	Age is not length of time

PASSAGES FROM THE PSALMS

Selected verses may be used from the following.

Psalms   23;   25;   27;   46;   103;   121;   130;   139.

PASSAGES FROM THE EPISTLES AND REVELATION

Romans 6:1-11 *or: 3,4,8,9 for a child*	Dead to sin but alive in Christ
Romans 8:31b-39	God's love in Jesus Christ
1 Corinthians 13	Faith, hope and love remain
1 Corinthians 15:12-19	The assurance of a resurrection
1 Corinthians 15:20-22, 35-38 42-44, (53-58)	Our resurrection
1 Corinthians 15:20-27a	Our resurrection
1 Corinthians 15:51-58	Our resurrection
2 Corinthians 1:3-5	Consolation in Christ
2 Corinthians 4:7-14	Perplexed, but not in despair
2 Corinthians 4:13 - 5:10	At home with the Lord
Philippians 3:8-21	Our citizenship is in heaven
Philippians 3:20 - 4:1, 4-7	Rejoice in the Lord
1 Thessalonians 4:13,14,(15-18) *also suitable for a child*	Raised with Jesus

1 Peter 1:3-9	A living hope
Revelation 7:9-17	The great company of the
also suitable for a child	redeemed
Revelation 21:1-7	A new heaven and a new earth
also suitable for a child	

PASSAGES FROM THE GOSPELS

Matthew 5:3-10	True happiness
Mark 10:13-16	Let the little children come to me
Luke 15:11-32	The parable of the lost son
Luke 23:44-49; 24:1-7	The death and resurrection of Jesus
Luke 24:13-19 (20-26), 27-35	Jesus known in the breaking of bread
John 5:19-29	Eternal life in Christ
John 6:36-40	Nothing lost
John 6:46-58	Jesus the bread of life
John 10:1-15 (or:11-16)	The good shepherd
John 11:(17-20), 21-27	The resurrection and the life
John 12:23-26	Where I am, there shall my servant be
John 14:1-6	Jesus the way to the Father

Hymns suitable for Funeral Liturgies

Abide with me
All creatures of our God and King
Blessed assurance
Blest are the pure in heart
Christ the Lord is risen again
For the beauty of the earth
Guide me, O thou great Redeemer
He who would valiant be
How great thou art
How sweet the name of Jesus sounds

Immortal, invisible, God only wise
Jesu, lover of my soul
Jesu, son of Mary
Jesu, the very thought of thee
Jesus lives! thy terrors now
Just as I am
Lead us, heavenly Father
Let saints on earth in concert sing
Lord it belongs not to my care
Lord of the living
Love divine, all loves excelling
My faith looks up to thee
Ma te marie
Now thank we all our God
O God our help in ages past
Piko nei te Matenga
Praise, my soul, the King of heaven
Rock of ages, cleft for me
Te Ariki hei au koe noho ai
The Church's one foundation
The day thou gavest
The king of love my shepherd is
The Lord's my shepherd
The strife is o'er, the battle done
Thine be the glory
Thine for ever, God of love
Think, O Lord, in mercy
Through all the changing scenes of life
Through the night of doubt and sorrow
Whakarongo ki te kupu
When all thy mercies

Additional Directions

Arrangements for the Funeral

In general, a church or a marae is the appropriate place for the funeral of a Christian.

It may be helpful if the minister, having visited the family at home, meets the chief mourners at the entrance to the church or wherever the service will be held, and accompanies them to their places.

*The service on pages 826-838 provides for the whole funeral to be in the church or on the marae, with **The Committal** as the conclusion, either in the church or at the hearse.*

*However, provision is made in the rubrics for the committal to take place elsewhere. In this case, the service in church or on the marae concludes with **The Commendation**, and **The Blessing of Peace;** and the form of committal on page 839 is then used. Alternatively, the whole service may be used at the graveside or in the crematorium chapel.*

*When the coffin is brought to the church or marae before a funeral the minister may meet the coffin at the entrance, and may read one of the psalms from pages 841-846 while it is carried to its place. If prayers are to be used, suitable ones will be found under **Additional Prayers**, from pages 855-863.*

During the Service

*Optional sections are noted by the use of the word 'may' in the rubrics. In **The Committal**, sections may be omitted at the graveside when the weather is inclement.*

Phrases in any of these services which are inappropriate in particular circumstances may be omitted or varied at the discretion of the minister.

Where there is provision in the service for the use of the name of the person who has died, the minister may substitute 'our brother' or 'our sister', if it seems more appropriate, although their name (not necessarily the whole name) should be used at least once.

Words printed in italics in the text indicate pronouns and other words that may require to be changed according to the circumstances.

Suitable places for hymns are

> *Before **The Readings** - page 831*
> *Before or after **The Address** - page 831*
> *After **The Blessing of Peace** - page 838*

On appropriate occasions the minister may invite another person to speak.

*Non-liturgical farewells may take place after the blessing at the end of **The Committal**, or at some other appropriate point.*

If the Funeral Service is used with a Liturgy of the Eucharist the following order is recommended

> *– **The Funeral Service** up to and including **The Prayers**;*
>
> *– the Eucharist from **The Ministry of the Sacrament**;*
>
> *– when the **Prayer after Communion** has been completed, **The Funeral Service** continues with **The Commendation**.*

When children are among the mourners, it may be suitable to ask them to place flowers either on the coffin during the service or into the grave after the committal, or on the coffin at the crematorium.

When the committal takes place at sea, the minister shall substitute for the words

> to the ground . . . dust to dust

the following

> to the sea, to be turned again to its elements.

*When the ashes are disposed of at sea, the minister concludes **The Committal** with the words,*

> and we commit the ashes of *her/his* mortal body to their resting place in the deep.

A Memorial Service

For a service of remembrance when the body of the person who has died is not present, one of the following orders may be used

> **The Funeral Service** *without* **The Committal;**
>
> *a* **Liturgy of the Eucharist** *with appropriate prayers;*
>
> **The Funeral Service** *combined with a* **Liturgy of the Eucharist** *as directed above, without* **The Committal;**
>
> **Morning or Evening Worship** *with appropriate prayers.*

A lighted candle or other symbol may be placed where the coffin would usually stand.

Prayers and readings from pages 853-865 may be used.

Those parts of the service providing for actual burial or cremation should be omitted.

In particular, in **The Funeral Service** *the following may be substituted for* **The Greeting** *on page 827*

> We have come together
> to remember before God the life of *N*,
> to give thanks for all *s/he* has meant to us,
> to commend *her/him* to God *her/his* creator,
> and to affirm our faith in the saving power
> of the death and resurrection of our Redeemer Jesus Christ.

Te Tikanga Karakia mo te Takahi Whare

Prayers in a House after Death

Returning to a house after the death of a family member can be a painful experience for a family. Friends may support them by accompanying them and sharing in a meal.

In this service the Church marks the family's return home. It reflects the continuing care for their well-being as they take up their life again. In **Te Takahi Whare** and the meal, the house is re-hallowed for the now smaller family. This is marked by a formal entry into the house.

The service takes place at the earliest possible time after **The Funeral Service**. Where possible, every room is visited, either by the minister alone or by the minister leading the bereaved family and friends.

In this service the English parallels rather than translates the Maori text.

This service is normally conducted by a priest. A duly authorised lay person may take the service.

If it is the custom of the people concerned that the house should be sprinkled with water, the water should be sanctified before the service. (The form of sanctifying is given at the conclusion of this service.)

This service may be adapted as appropriate for use in other places.

Ka ahei ma te Pirihi ma te Reimana ranei e whakahaere tenei Karakia.

Te Tomohanga

I runga i te Ingoa o te Atua,
te Matua, te Tama me te Wairua Tapu.
Amine.

Kia tau mai te rangimarie o te Atua to tatou Matua i te rangi,
te rangimarie o Ihu Karaiti, te puna o te rangimarie,
te rangimarie o te Wairua Tapu, te Kai-whakamarie
ki runga ki tenei whare
me te hunga e noho ana i konei.

Hei konei ka tomo atu te Pirihi me nga tangata ki roto i te whare,
me te ki a te Pirihi

Huakina, e te Atua, te tatau o tenei whare;
tomo mai ki roto, a tukua kia tiaho tou marama
hei whakakahore atu i nga mea katoa o te pouri;
ko Ihu Karaiti hoki to matou Ariki.
Amine.

Kua ara mai a te Karaiti i te mate,
Kua waiho hei mataamua mo te hunga kua moe.

Na te tangata nei hoki te mate,
Waihoki na te tangata te aranga mai o te hunga mate.

I roto hoki i a Arama ka mate katoa nga tangata,
Waihoki i roto i a te Karaiti, ka whakaorangia katoatia.

Kia whakakororiatia te Matua, te Tama,
    me te Wairua Tapu.
Ko te ritenga ia i te timatanga, a tenei ano inaianei,
    a ka mau tonu iho, a ake ake ake. Amine.

Where possible, the service should begin outside the house.

The Entry

The priest says

In the name of God,
Father, Son and Holy Spirit.
Amen.

The peace of God our heavenly Father,
and of Jesus Christ, the source of peace,
and of the Holy Spirit, the comforter,
come upon this house
and all who live here.

The priest and people now enter the house, the priest saying

Open, O God, the door of this house;
enter it and let your light shine here,
to drive away all darkness;
through Jesus Christ our Lord.
Amen.

Christ has been raised from the dead,
the first fruits of those who have fallen asleep.

For as by a man came death,
by a man has come also the resurrection of the dead.

For as in Adam all die,
so also in Christ shall all be made alive.

Glory to the Father, and to the Son,
    and to the Holy Spirit:
as it was in the beginning, is now,
    and shall be for ever. Amen.

E Ihowa, tohungia matou,
E te Karaiti, tohungia matou,
E Ihowa, tohungia matou.

E to matou Matua i te rangi
 Kia tapu tou Ingoa.
 Kia tae mai tou rangatiratanga.
 Kia meatia tau e pai ai
  ki runga ki te whenua,
   kia rite ano ki to te rangi.
Homai ki a matou aianei
 he taro ma matou mo tenei ra.
Murua o matou hara,
  Me matou hoki e muru nei
   i o te hunga e hara ana ki a matou.
Aua hoki matou e kawea kia whakawaia;
 Engari whakaorangia matou i te kino:
Nou hoki te rangatiratanga, te kaha,
 me te kororia,
  Ake ake ake.   **Amine.**

Mehemea ko te tikanga a te iwi me ruirui te whare ki te wai, me whakatapu te wai i te tuatahi i mua atu i te ruiruinga.

Hei konei ka haere te Pirihi ki ia wahi i roto, i waho ranei o te whare ka rui haere i te wai, me te mea

Ka ruiruia e tatou tenei wahi,
hei horoi atu i nga mea poke,
a te rewera a te tangata ranei,
i runga i te Ingoa o te Matua,
o te Tama, o te Wairua Tapu.
Amine.

Lord, have mercy.
Christ, have mercy.
Lord, have mercy.

Our Father in heaven,
 hallowed be your name,
 your kingdom come,
 your will be done,
  on earth as in heaven.
Give us today our daily bread.
Forgive us our sins
 as we forgive those who sin against us.
Save us from the time of trial
 and deliver us from evil.

For the kingdom, the power, and the glory are yours
 now and for ever.   Amen.

If water is to be used the priest shall visit various places, inside and outside the house, and sprinkle water, saying

We sprinkle this place
to wash away the effects of all evil,
whether of people, or of spiritual powers,
in the name of the Father,
and of the Son, and of the Holy Spirit.
Amen.

Nga Inoi Whakamutunga

Pirihi

E te Ariki, e Ihu Karaiti,
na tau Apotoro tapu nei te whakahau
kia kaua e whakarite ki te hunga tumanako-kore
te pouri mo te hunga e moe ana i roto i a koe;
e inoi atu ana matou ki a koe
kia awhinatia e koe i runga i te aroha,
te hunga e tangi ana mo te hunga kua mate,
mukua atu nga roimata katoa i o ratou kanohi:
tena koe te ora nei, te kingi tahi nei
me te Matua, me te Wairua Tapu,
kotahi ano Atua a ake tonu atu.
Amine.

E Ihowa, ko koe te Matua o nga mahi tohu
te Atua hoki o nga whakamarietanga katoa;
he inoi atu tenei na matou ki a koe,
kia titiro iho koe me te aroha, me te atawhai ano
ki enei pononga au, e nui nei to ratou pouri;
whakamamangia nga taimahatanga
kei runga i o ratou tinana me o ratou hinengaro;
araia atu i a ratou nga rauhanga a te wairua kino;
meinga te marama o tou kanohi
kia whiti mai ki runga i a ratou,
a, tukua mai ki a ratou te tino rangimarie;
kia whakaaro hoki koe ki nga mahi wawao
a to matou Ariki, a Ihu Karaiti.
Amine.

Ka ahei he Himene ki konei.

Kia noho a Ihowa ki a koutou.
Ma Ihowa koe e manaaki.

Kia haere atu tatou i konei i runga i te rangimarie.
I runga i te Ingoa o te Ariki.

Concluding Prayers

The priest prays

Lord Jesus Christ,
by your holy apostle you have taught us
that our sorrow should not be without hope
for the dead that rest with you;
visit with your compassion
those who mourn the loss of their loved ones,
and wipe away all tears from their eyes;
for you live and reign with the Father and the Holy Spirit,
one God, for ever and ever.
Amen.

God,
the Father of mercies and giver of all comfort,
look down in pity and compassion
upon your sorrowing servants;
lighten the burdens
which weigh them down in soul and body;
shelter from the forces of evil;
let the light of your presence shine upon them
and give them perfect peace;
through Jesus Christ our Lord.
Amen.

A hymn may be sung.

The Lord be with you.
The Lord bless you.

Be at peace.
Thanks be to God.

Pirihi

Ma te Atua o te rangimarie,
nana nei i whakahoki mai i roto i te hunga mate
to tatou Ariki, a Ihu, taua Hepara nui o nga hipi,
he meatanga na nga toto o te kawenata mutungakore;
mana *koutou* e mea kia tino tika i runga i nga mahi pai katoa,
kia mahia ano e *koutou*
te mea e ahuareka ana ki tana titiro,
i roto ano i a Ihu Karaiti;
waiho atu i a ia te kororia ake ake.
Amine.

(Kauaka te reimana e mea 'koutou', engari 'tatou'.)

Me mau mai ki te Pirihi he wai, i roto i te ipu tika, ka mea ai te Pirihi.

E te Atua Kaha rawa, ora tonu,
i whakatapua e koe te wai
hei hakarameta mo te horoi i te hara,
tenei matou te inoi atu nei ki a koe,
he nui nei hoki tou aroha,
kia whakatapua tenei wai
i runga i te Ingoa o te Matua,
o te Tama, o te Wairua Tapu.
Amine.

The God of peace,
who by the blood of the eternal covenant
brought again from the dead our Lord Jesus,
that great shepherd of the sheep,
make you perfect in every good work,
working in you that which is pleasing and good;
through Jesus Christ, to whom be glory for ever and ever.
Amen.

When water is to be sanctified, the priest shall say

Almighty and everliving God,
in baptism you give water a holy use to wash away sin:
sanctify this water
as a sign of cleansing from all the powers of evil;
through Jesus Christ our Lord,
who triumphed over evil on the cross,
and now lives and reigns with you for ever.
Amen.

The Committal of Ashes

After a cremation, the family may wish to mark the reverent disposal of the ashes in a dignified way. It can be a significant moment in a time of bereavement, a final letting-go of the one who has died. It is therefore an act which is rightly accompanied by the prayers of the Church. This service provides a means of doing this.

When all are gathered together, the minister shall say one or more of the following sentences.

Jesus said,
'I am the resurrection and the life;
even in death,
anyone who believes in me, will live.'

John 11:25

'Set your troubled hearts at rest.
Trust in God always,
trust also in me.
There are many dwelling places in my Father's house;
if it were not so, I should have told you;
for I am going there on purpose
to prepare a place for you.
And if I go to prepare a place for you,
I shall come again and receive you to myself,
so that where I am, you may be also.'

John 14:1-3

Saint Paul said, 'I am convinced
that there is nothing in death or life,
in the realm of spirits or superhuman powers,
in the world as it is
or the world as it shall be,
in the forces of the universe,
in the heights or depths -
nothing in all creation
that can separate us from the love of God
in Christ Jesus, our Lord.'

Romans 8:38,39

The following may be said.

God our Father,
we thank you for N,
the years we shared with *her/him*,
the good we saw in *her/him*,
the love we received from *her/him*.
We thank you that *s/he* is in your care
and trust in your promise of eternal life
through Jesus Christ our Lord.
Amen.

The Lord's Prayer *is said in one of the following forms,
or in the form on page 863.*

With faith and hope we pray

Our Father in heaven,
hallowed be your name,
your kingdom come,
your will be done,
on earth as in heaven.
Give us today our daily bread.
Forgive us our sins
as we forgive those who sin against us.
Save us from the time of trial
and deliver us from evil.

For the kingdom, the power, and the glory are yours
now and for ever.   Amen.

I runga i te whakapono me te tumanako
ka inoi tatou

E to matou Matua i te rangi
Kia tapu tou Ingoa.
Kia tae mai tou rangatiratanga.
Kia meatia tau e pai ai
ki runga ki te whenua,
kia rite ano ki to te rangi.

Homai ki a matou aianei
   he taro ma matou mo tenei ra.
Murua o matou hara,
     Me matou hoki e muru nei
        i o te hunga e hara ana ki a matou.
Aua hoki matou e kawea kia whakawaia;
   Engari whakaorangia matou i te kino:
Nou hoki te rangatiratanga, te kaha,
   me te kororia,
     Ake ake ake.   Amine.

The Committal of Ashes

The minister prays

We thank you, loving Creator,
that we have been able to entrust *N*
into your keeping.
Through Christ's victory we have hope in life eternal.
So now, we commit the ashes of *her/his* mortal body
to the ground/to their final resting place.
Amen.

For a committal at sea the minister says

to their resting-place in the deep.

The ashes are placed in their resting place.

The Prayers

The minister says one or both of the following and/or other appropriate prayers.

Father,
accept our praise and thanksgiving
for the lives of all your faithful people
who have served you on earth and are now at rest.
Grant that we too may dedicate ourselves to your service,
following their good examples,
and share with them your heavenly kingdom;
through Jesus Christ our Lord.
Amen.

Merciful Father,
to all who mourn, grant faith and courage
to meet the days to come with steadfastness and patience,
not sorrowing as those without hope,
but in thankful remembrance of your goodness in the past,
and in the sure expectation
of sharing in the resurrection of Jesus Christ our Lord.
Amen.

A priest says

The peace of God which passes all understanding
keep your hearts and minds in Christ Jesus;
and the blessing of God almighty,
the Father, the Son and the Holy Spirit,
be with you now and for ever.
Amen.

Or

The minister and people together say

**The grace of our Lord Jesus Christ,
and the love of God,
and the fellowship of the Holy Spirit
be with us all. Amen.**

Te Tikanga Karakia mo te Hura Kohatu me te Whakatapu Tohu Whakamaharatanga

The Unveiling of a Memorial

For many people the final resting place focuses a family's grieving, and their memory of the one who has died. The memorial stone placed there may be their only tangible link with that person.

Te Hura Kohatu *marks the placing of the stone, and brings the family together again to renew their bond once more. It is a symbol of a new beginning.*

It normally takes place about a year after the death.

In this service the English parallels rather than translates the Maori text.

Ka ahei ma te Pirihi	This service is normally
ma te Reimana	conducted by a priest.
ranei e whakahaere	A duly authorised
tenei Karakia.	lay person may take
	the service.

'There is a season for everything.'
Ecclesiastes 3:1

Ma te Pirihi e arahi atu te iwi ki te wahi kei reira te tohu whakamaharatanga,
a, ka tae atu, ka mea ia

I runga i te Ingoa
o te Atua, o te Matua, o te Tama, o te Wairua Tapu.
Amine.

Kua hanga a muri, a mua, oku e koe:
kua pa mai ano tou ringa ki ahau.

Ki te kake atu au ki te rangi, kei reira koe:
Ki te wharikitia e ahau toku moenga i roto i te rua tupapaku,
na, kei reira ano koe.

E Ihowa, tohungia matou.
E te Karaiti, tohungia matou.
E Ihowa, tohungia matou.

E to matou Matua i te rangi
   Kia tapu tou Ingoa.
   Kia tae mai tou rangatiratanga.
   Kia meatia tau e pai ai
     ki runga ki te whenua,
      kia rite ano ki to te rangi.
Homai ki a matou aianei
   he taro ma matou mo tenei ra.
Murua o matou hara,
   Me matou hoki e muru nei
     i o te hunga e hara ana ki a matou.
Aua hoki matou e kawea kia whakawaia;
   Engari whakaorangia matou i te kino:
Nou hoki te rangatiratanga, te kaha,
   me te kororia,
     Ake ake ake.   Amine.

Approach

The priest shall lead the people to the memorial and then say

In the name of God,
the Father, the Son and the Holy Spirit.
Amen.

Lord, you guard me from behind and before me.
You cover me with your hand.

If I climb up to heaven, you are there.
If I make my bed in the grave you are there also.

The priest says

Lord, have mercy.
Christ, have mercy.
Lord, have mercy.

Our Father in heaven,
hallowed be your name,
your kingdom come,
your will be done,
on earth as in heaven.
Give us today our daily bread.
Forgive us our sins
as we forgive those who sin against us.
Save us from the time of trial
and deliver us from evil.

For the kingdom, the power, and the glory are yours
now and for ever.   Amen.

Nga Inoi

Ka mea te Pirihi

E te Atua Kaha rawa,
na tou mana, me tou aroha,
i whakatapua ai i tika ai nga mea katoa;
kia aroha mai koe, a manaakitia matou;
tukua kia whakapumautia
te mahi a o matou ringaringa:
ko Ihu Karaiti hoki to matou Ariki.
Amine.

E te Matua i te rangi,
awhinatia matou ki te tuku atu ki tou atawhai
te hunga e arohatia ana e matou;
i nga wa e pehia ai matou e te pouri,
akona matou ki te anga atu ki a koe
me te mahara ano ki te kapua nui
o nga whakaatu e karapoti nei i a matou:
tukua matou e ora nei, kia whiwhi me ratou,
ki te okiokinga me te rangimarie e homai e koe,
ara e tau Tama, e to matou Ariki, e Ihu Karaiti.
Amine.

Hei konei ka tango ai i te arai o te tohu whakamaharatanga, a ka mea te Pirihi

I runga i te Whakapono o Ihu Karaiti,
ka whakatapua e tatou *tenei Kohatu/Tohu Whakamaharatanga*,
hei whakamaharatanga ki *tana* pononga ki a *Ingoa* ,
i runga i te Ingoa o te Matua, o te Tama, o te Wairua Tapu.
Amine.

Ka mutu te Inoi Whakatapu, ka ahei me panui nga kupu i runga i taua Tohu Whakamaharatanga.

Prayers

The priest prays

Almighty God,
by your power and love
all things are sanctified and made perfect.
Be merciful to us and bless us.
Let your face shine upon us
and prosper the work of our hands,
through Jesus Christ our Lord.
Amen.

Heavenly Father,
help us to entrust our loved ones to your care;
when sorrow darkens our lives,
teach us to look to you,
remembering the cloud of witnesses
by whom we are surrounded.
Grant that we on earth may share with them
the rest and peace which you give
through your Son, our Lord Jesus Christ.
Amen.

The veil is removed and the priest says

In the faith of Jesus Christ,
we dedicate this *stone/memorial* in memory of his servant *N*,
in the name of the Father, and of the Son, and of the Holy Spirit.
Amen.

The words on the memorial may be read.

Te Inoi mo te Hunga Tapu

E te Atua kaha rawa,
i te mea e kotahi ana te hunga tapu ki a koe
i roto i te tinana tapu o te Karaiti o to matou Ariki,
meinga matou kia aru i a ratou i roto i te aroha
me te piri pono kia tae rawa atu matou
ki te kainga kua whakaritea mai nei e koe
mo te hunga e aroha ana ki a koe,
i roto i te kotahitanga pai
o te Wairua Tapu, ake ake.
Amine.

Ka ahei te korero i konei etahi atu inoi e tika ana.

Ka ahei he himene i konei.

Kia noho a Ihowa ki a koutou.
Ma Ihowa koe e manaaki.

Ma te Atua o te rangimarie,
nana nei i whakahoki mai i roto i te hunga mate
to tatou Ariki, a Ihu Karaiti, taua Hepara nui o nga hipi,
he meatanga no nga toto o te Kawenata mutungakore;
mana *koutou* e mea kia tino tika i runga i nga mahi pai katoa,
kia mahia ano e *koutou* te mea e ahuareka ana ki tana titiro,
i roto ano i a Ihu Karaiti;
waiho atu i a ia te kororia ake ake.
Amine.

Haere i runga i te aroha. Haere i runga i te rangimarie.
Amine. Ka haere matou i runga i te ingoa o te Karaiti.

The Collect for All Saints' Day

Almighty God,
your saints are one with you
in the mystical body of Christ;
give us grace to follow them
in all virtue and holiness
until we come to those inexpressible joys
which you have prepared for those
who truly love you;
through Jesus Christ our Lord.
Amen.

Other appropriate prayers may be said.

A hymn may be sung.

A priest may give a blessing or the following may be said.

The God of peace,
who by the blood of the eternal covenant
brought again from the dead our Lord Jesus,
that great shepherd of the sheep,
make you perfect in every good work,
working in you that which is pleasing and good;
through Jesus Christ, to whom be glory for ever and ever.
Amen.

Go now to love and serve the Lord. Go in peace.
Amen. We go in the name of Christ.

Ordination
Liturgies

Concerning these Services

The provision of an ordained ministry, to serve the local congregation in the name of Christ and the universal Church, is one of the responsibilities of the apostolic Church. These services provide for the ordination of such ministry.

The Ordination Liturgies follow a common pattern and are based on a common understanding of ministry. In each service of ordination the words used at the introduction to the presentation of the candidates acknowledge that all Christians have a ministry by virtue of their baptism, and that some members of the baptised community are also called and empowered to fulfil an ordained ministry, and to enable the total mission of the Church.

Within the ordained ministry there are three orders: deacons, priests (also called presbyters) and bishops. Each order is equally important; yet those in the various orders differ in the tasks they do on behalf of the whole Church. The description of these tasks is set out at The Presentation and The Commitment.

The assent of the people that the candidate should be ordained is an integral part of the service.

The set readings highlight the biblical understanding of ministry, and in the sermon the preacher proclaims the enabling power of the Holy Spirit to provide the appropriate gifts of ministry.

In The Commitment, the candidates affirm their standard of faith and their willingness to minister within the discipline and authority of the Church. They express their spiritual lifestyle and their dependence on God for their gifts of ministry.

The Invocation is followed by The Ordination.

The whole ordination is set within a Liturgy of the Eucharist, using any of the authorised forms.

These services, allowing for an appropriate definition of the role of each order in ordained ministry, affirm the understanding of the Church that all ministry has its source in Christ's ministry, and is part of the response to the command of Christ to the Church to fulfil its apostolic mission.

The Ordination of Deacons

The Gathering of the Community

All standing, the bishop greets the congregation.

The bishop says

Glory to God,
Creator, Redeemer and Giver of life,
who is, who was, and is to come.

Grace and peace to you from God.
 Kia tau ki a koutou, te atawhai me te rangimarie o te Atua.

God fill you with truth and joy.
 Ma te Atua koe e whakau, ki te pono me te hari.

A hymn of praise, waiata or a psalm may be sung,
or the following is said or sung.

Glory to God in the highest,
 and peace to God's people on earth.

Lord God, heavenly King,
almighty God and Father,
 we worship you, we give you thanks,
 we praise you for your glory.

Lord Jesus Christ, only Son of the Father,
Lord God, Lamb of God,
you take away the sin of the world:
 have mercy on us;
you are seated at the right hand of the Father:
 receive our prayer.

For you alone are the Holy One,
you alone are the Lord,
you alone are the Most High,
 Jesus Christ,
 with the Holy Spirit,
 in the glory of God the Father. Amen.

The bishop says

God has promised forgiveness
to all who truly repent,
turn to Christ in faith
and are themselves forgiving.

In silence we call to mind our sins.

Silence

Let us confess our sins.

**Merciful God,
we have sinned
in what we have thought and said,
in the wrong we have done
and in the good we have not done.
We have sinned in ignorance:
we have sinned in weakness:
we have sinned through our own deliberate fault.
We are truly sorry.
We repent and turn to you.
Forgive us, for our Saviour Christ's sake,
and renew our lives to the glory of your name.   Amen.**

The Absolution *is declared by the bishop.*

Through the cross of Christ,
God have mercy on you,
pardon you
and set you free.
Know that you are forgiven
and be at peace.
God strengthen you in all goodness
and keep you in life eternal.
Amen.

Glory to God in the highest *may be said or sung here, all standing.*

All sit.

The Presentation

The bishop says

E te whanau a te Karaiti / People of God,
we have come to ordain a *deacon / deacons*
in Christ's holy Church.
Christ is head of the Church;
he alone is the source of all Christian ministry.
Through the ages it is Christ
who has called men and women to serve.

By the Holy Spirit all who believe and are baptised
receive a ministry to proclaim Jesus as Saviour and Lord,
and to love and serve the people with whom they live and work.
In Christ they are to bring redemption,
to reconcile and to make whole.
They are to be salt for the earth; they are to be light to the world.

After his resurrection and ascension
Christ gave gifts abundantly to the Church.
Some he made apostles, some prophets, some evangelists,
some pastors and teachers; to equip God's people
for their work of ministry and to build up the body of Christ.

We stand within a tradition
in which there are deacons, priests and bishops.
They are called and empowered to fulfil an ordained ministry
and to enable the whole mission of the Church.
Our authority is in Scripture
and in the Church's continuing practice through the ages.

Therefore let us welcome *NN*, who *come/s* to be ordained deacon.

Each candidate is presented by a priest and a layperson.

The priest says

Bishop *N*, we present *N*. Those responsible for *her/his* selection and
training believe *her/him* ready to be ordained deacon in the Church
of God.

The layperson says

We believe that *s/he* will serve Christ well in this ministry.

Deacons in the Church of God serve in the name of Christ,
and so remind the whole Church
that serving others is essential to all ministry.

They have a special responsibility to ensure that those in need
are cared for with Christlike compassion and humility.

When called upon to do so, they may baptise,
preach and give instruction in the faith.

When the people are gathered for worship,
deacons are authorised to read the Holy Scriptures,
lead the prayers,
and distribute the bread and wine of Holy Communion.

Do you believe that you are called to the office and work
of a deacon? *N* ?

Each candidate responds   Yes, I do.

All standing, the bishop says to the people

E te whanau / People of God,
are you willing that *NN* should be ordained deacon?

People   **We are.   Thanks be to God.**

The bishop prays

Holy and living God,
you call men and women
to bring us your creative and redeeming Word.
Equip your people
for their work of ministry
and give to *these your servants*,
now to be ordained,
the gifts of grace *they* need.
Amen.

The Collect of the Day *may follow.*

The congregation sits.

The Proclamation

The Readings

The readings are selected from the following

OLD TESTAMENT
Isaiah 6:1-8
Isaiah 42:1-7
Sirach (Ecclesiasticus) 39:1-8

PSALM
84
119:33-40

EPISTLE
Romans 12:1-13
Romans 16:1-2
1 Timothy 3:8-13
1 Peter 4:7-11
Acts 6:2-6

GOSPEL
Luke 12:35-40
Luke 22:24-27
John 12:20-26

The reader first says

A reading from ... (chapter ... beginning at ...)

Silence may follow each reading.

After each reading, the reader may say

Hear what the Spirit is saying to the Church.
Thanks be to God.

A psalm, hymn or anthem may follow each reading.

*Then, all standing, a deacon reads the **Gospel**, first saying*

The Holy Gospel according to ... (chapter ... beginning at ...)
Praise and glory to God.

After the Gospel, silence may be kept.

The reader says

This is the Gospel of Christ.
Praise to Christ, the Word.

The Sermon

***The Sermon** is preached here.*

The Affirmation of Faith

The Nicene Creed is said, all standing.

We believe in one God,
　　the Father, the Almighty,
　　maker of heaven and earth,
　　of all that is,
　　seen and unseen.

We believe in one Lord, Jesus Christ,
　　the only Son of God,
　　eternally begotten of the Father,
　　God from God, Light from Light,
　　true God from true God,
　　begotten, not made,
　　of one being with the Father;
　　through him all things were made.
　　For us and for our salvation
　　　　he came down from heaven,
　　　　was incarnate of the Holy Spirit and the Virgin Mary
　　　　and became fully human.
　　　　For our sake he was crucified under Pontius Pilate;
　　　　he suffered death and was buried.
　　　　On the third day he rose again
　　　　in accordance with the Scriptures;
　　　　he ascended into heaven
　　　　and is seated at the right hand of the Father.
　　　　He will come again in glory to judge
　　　　　　the living and the dead,
　　　　and his kingdom will have no end.

We believe in the Holy Spirit,
　　the Lord, the giver of life,
　　who proceeds from the Father and the Son,
　　who in unity with the Father and the Son
　　　　is worshipped and glorified,
　　and has spoken through the prophets.
　　We believe in one holy catholic and apostolic Church.
　　We acknowledge one baptism for the forgiveness of sins.
　　We look for the resurrection of the dead,
　　　　and the life of the world to come.　　Amen.

All are seated except the candidates who stand before the bishop.

The Commitment

The bishop addresses the candidates who respond individually or together

NN, you have declared your faith in God.
We believe God is calling you to serve as a deacon.
We now ask you to declare
your commitment to Christ in his Church.

Bishop   Do you believe that the Bible contains all
that is essential for our salvation,
and reveals God's living word in Jesus Christ?

Candidate   Yes, I do.
God give me understanding in studying the Scriptures.
May they reveal to me the mind and heart of Christ,
and shape my ministry.

Bishop   Do you hold to the doctrines of the faith
as this Church understands them?

Candidate   Yes, I do.
My duty and my joy will be to witness
to Christ crucified and risen.

Bishop   Will you be constant in prayer and study?

Candidate   I will. God give me imagination and perseverance.

Bishop   Will you accept the order and discipline of this Church
and the guidance and leadership of your bishop?

Candidate   Yes, I will.
And God give me grace to work in partnership
with my sisters and brothers in Christ's service.

Bishop	Will you so live the gospel that you challenge us with the demands of love?
Candidate	I will. God give me strength and humility.
Bishop	Will you seek the lost and lonely, caring for all God's people whatever their need?
Candidate	I will. My concern will be to show love, care and compassion. God give me courage to strive for justice and peace among all people. I commit myself fully to this ministry.

*The Bishop says to **each** candidate in turn*

N, will you then give glory to God,
the holy and blessed Trinity?

Each candidate responds

Glory to God on high, God of power and might.
You are my God.
I can neither add to your glory
nor take away from your power.
Yet will I wait upon you daily in prayer and praise.

The bishop then continues

NN, we praise God for your commitment
to serve Christ in the order of deacons.
To search and to serve
is the priceless contribution God calls you to make;
by this you will bring enthusiasm and encouragement to others.
Work with all who labour for the kingdom.
As your hands care for the needy
may they witness to Christ your Master;
he took a towel and a basin;
he came among us as one who serves.

The candidates and the congregation kneel.

The Invocation

After a pause, the bishop continues

Like the first disciples waiting for your coming,
empowering Spirit, we watch and pray.

The congregation prays in silence for the candidates.

Silence

A hymn invoking the Holy Spirit may be sung.

Bishop   Holy Spirit of God,
             meet us in this moment
             as you met the apostles of old.
             Be with us, Holy Spirit,
People   **bring faith and hope, we pray.**

Bishop   Come Holy Spirit,
People   **be present in your power.**

*After a pause, the bishop continues with **The Ordination.***

The Ordination

Then the bishop, facing those being ordained says this prayer of consecration.

All present join with the bishop in saying the concluding part of the prayer.

Blessed are you,
God our creator, God in history, God in revelation;
throughout the ages your unchanging purpose
has created a people to love and serve you.

Blessed are you in Christ Jesus,
your Incarnation, our Servant Lord,
who by death overcame death.

Through his resurrection and ascension,
through the gift of the Holy Spirit,
you have given life and order to your Church,
that we may carry out the ministry of love.
We thank you for calling *these your servants*
to share this ministry as *deacon(s)*.

*The bishop then lays hands on the head of each candidate in turn,
saying after silence*

God of grace, through your Holy Spirit,
gentle as a dove, living, burning as fire,
empower your servant *N*
for the office and work of a deacon in the Church.

At the conclusion of the laying on of hands, the bishop continues

May every grace of ministry rest on *these your servants*.
Keep *them* strong and faithful,
steadfast in Jesus Christ, our Saviour.
Amen!
May *they* proclaim the good news,
inspire our prayers,
and show us Christ, the Servant.

The new deacons stand.

The bishop gives each of them a New Testament, saying

N, here are the Gospels of Christ;
read from them,
and proclaim the good news.

The new deacon may now be vested and symbols of ministry may be given.

The congregation stands and the new deacons may be presented to the Church.

The Peace

The Eucharist *continues at* **The Peace***, during which the bishop may share
the sign of peace with the newly ordained, who then greet their families and the
congregation.*

The Ordination of Priests
[also called Presbyters]

The Gathering of the Community

All standing, the bishop greets the congregation.

The bishop says

Glory to God,
Creator, Redeemer and Giver of life,
who is, who was, and is to come.

Grace and peace to you from God.
Kia tau ki a koutou, te atawhai me te rangimarie o te Atua.

God fill you with truth and joy.
Ma te Atua koe e whakau, ki te pono me te hari.

A hymn of praise, waiata or a psalm may be sung,
or the following is said or sung.

Glory to God in the highest,
and peace to God's people on earth.

Lord God, heavenly King,
almighty God and Father,
we worship you, we give you thanks,
we praise you for your glory.

Lord Jesus Christ, only Son of the Father,
Lord God, Lamb of God,
you take away the sin of the world:
have mercy on us;
you are seated at the right hand of the Father:
receive our prayer.

For you alone are the Holy One,
you alone are the Lord,
you alone are the Most High,

Jesus Christ,
with the Holy Spirit,
in the glory of God the Father. Amen.

The congregation kneels.

The bishop says

God has promised forgiveness
to all who truly repent,
turn to Christ in faith
and are themselves forgiving.

In silence we call to mind our sins.

Silence

Let us confess our sins.

Merciful God,
we have sinned
in what we have thought and said,
in the wrong we have done
and in the good we have not done.
We have sinned in ignorance:
we have sinned in weakness:
we have sinned through our own deliberate fault.
We are truly sorry.
We repent and turn to you.
Forgive us, for our Saviour Christ's sake,
and renew our lives to the glory of your name.   Amen.

The Absolution *is declared by the bishop.*

Through the cross of Christ,
God have mercy on you,
pardon you
and set you free.
Know that you are forgiven
and be at peace.
God strengthen you in all goodness
and keep you in life eternal.
Amen.

Glory to God in the highest may be said or sung here, all standing.

All sit.

The Presentation

The bishop says

E te whanau a te Karaiti / People of God,
we have come to ordain a *priest / priests* in Christ's holy Church.
Christ is head of the Church;
he alone is the source of all Christian ministry.
Through the ages it is Christ
who has called men and women to serve.

By the Holy Spirit all who believe and are baptised receive a
ministry to proclaim Jesus as Saviour and Lord,
and to love and serve the people with whom they live and work.
In Christ they are to bring redemption,
to reconcile and to make whole.
They are to be salt for the earth; they are to be light to the world.

After his resurrection and ascension
Christ gave gifts abundantly to the Church.
Some he made apostles, some prophets, some evangelists,
some pastors and teachers; to equip God's people
for their work of ministry and to build up the body of Christ.

We stand within a tradition
in which there are deacons, priests and bishops.
They are called and empowered to fulfil an ordained ministry
and to enable the whole mission of the Church.
Our authority is in scripture
and in the Church's continuing practice through the ages.

Therefore let us welcome *NN*, who *come/s* to be ordained priest.

Each candidate is presented by a priest and a layperson.

Bishop *N*, we present *N*.
Those responsible for *her/his* training
believe *her/him* ready to be ordained priest
in the Church of God.

The layperson says

We give thanks for *N*'s ministry as a deacon.
We believe that *s/he* will serve Christ well as a priest.

The bishop says to the candidates

Priests in the Church
are called to build up Christ's congregation,
to strengthen the baptised,
and to lead them
as witnesses to Christ in the world.

To do this they are called to be pastors.
They are to share people's joys and sorrows,
encourage the faithful, recall those who fall away,
heal and help the sick.

Above all they are to proclaim God's word
and take their part in Christ's prophetic work,
to declare forgiveness through Jesus Christ,
to baptise,
to preside at the Eucharist,
to administer Christ's holy sacraments.

Do you believe that you are called to the office and work
of a priest? *N*?

Each candidate responds

I believe that God and the Church are calling me to this ministry.
I thank God for this call, and the Church for its encouragement.

All standing, the bishop says to the people

E te whanau / People of God,
are you willing that *NN* should be ordained priest?

People **We are. Thanks be to God.**

The bishop prays

Holy and living God,
you call men and women
to bring us your creative and redeeming Word.
Equip your people
for their work of ministry
and give to *these your servants*,
now to be ordained,
the gifts of grace *they need*.
Amen.

The Collect of the Day *may follow.*

The congregation sits.

The Proclamation

The Readings

The readings are selected from the following

OLD TESTAMENT	PSALM
Numbers 11:16-17, 24-25b	43
Jeremiah 1:4-9	145:1-7, 21
Ezekiel 33:1-9	

EPISTLE	GOSPEL
2 Corinthians 4:1-7	Matthew 9:35-38
Ephesians 4:1-16 (1-7,11-16)	John 10:11-18
2 Timothy 4:1-5	John 21:15-19
1 Peter 5:1-4	

The reader first says

A reading from ... (chapter ... beginning at ...)

Silence may follow each reading.

Hear what the Spirit is saying to the Church.
Thanks be to God.

The Holy Gospel according to … (chapter … beginning at …)
Praise and glory to God.

This is the Gospel of Christ.
Praise to Christ, the Word.

The Sermon

The Affirmation of Faith

We believe in one God,
    the Father, the Almighty,
    maker of heaven and earth,
    of all that is,
    seen and unseen.

We believe in one Lord, Jesus Christ,
    the only Son of God,
    eternally begotten of the Father,
    God from God, Light from Light,
    true God from true God,
    begotten, not made,
    of one being with the Father;
    through him all things were made.
    For us and for our salvation
        he came down from heaven,
        was incarnate of the Holy Spirit and the Virgin Mary
        and became fully human.
        For our sake he was crucified under Pontius Pilate;
        he suffered death and was buried.
        On the third day he rose again
        in accordance with the Scriptures;
        he ascended into heaven
        and is seated at the right hand of the Father.
        He will come again in glory to judge
            the living and the dead,
        and his kingdom will have no end.

We believe in the Holy Spirit,
    the Lord, the giver of life,
    who proceeds from the Father and the Son,
    who in unity with the Father and the Son
        is worshipped and glorified,
    and has spoken through the prophets.
    We believe in one holy catholic and apostolic Church.
    We acknowledge one baptism for the forgiveness of sins.
    We look for the resurrection of the dead,
        and the life of the world to come.   Amen.

All are seated except the candidates who stand before the bishop.

The Commitment

The bishop addresses the candidates who respond individually or together.

NN, you have declared your faith in God.
We believe God is calling you to serve as a priest.
We now ask you to declare
your commitment to Christ in his Church.

Bishop   Do you believe that the Bible contains all
that is essential for our salvation,
and reveals God's living word in Jesus Christ?

Candidate   Yes, I do.
God give me understanding in studying the Scriptures.
May they reveal to me the mind and heart of Christ,
and shape my ministry.

Bishop   Will you set forth the doctrines of the faith
as this Church has received them?

Candidate   Yes, I will.
My duty and my joy will be to witness
to Christ crucified and risen.

Bishop   Will you accept the order and discipline of this Church
and the guidance and leadership of your bishop?

Candidate   Yes, I will.
And God give me grace to work in partnership
with my sisters and brothers in Christ's service.

Bishop   Will you seek the lost and lonely,
caring for all God's people whatever their need?

Candidate   I will.
My concern will be to show love, care and compassion.
God give me courage
to strive for justice and peace among all people.

Bishop	Will you so live the gospel that you challenge us with the demands of love?
Candidate	I will. God give me strength and humility.
Bishop	Will you be constant in prayer and study?
Candidate	I will. God give me imagination and perseverance.
Bishop	Will you do all in your power to build up the body of Christ?
Candidate	I will. I commit myself fully to this ministry. I will proclaim the word of God and celebrate the sacraments of the new covenant.

*The bishop says to **each** candidate in turn*

N, will you then give glory to God,
the holy and blessed Trinity?

Each candidate responds

Glory to God on high, God of power and might.
You are my God.
I can neither add to your glory
nor take away from your power.
Yet will I wait upon you daily in prayer and praise.

The bishop then continues

NN, we praise God for your commitment to serve Christ
in the order of priests.
Serve patiently and cheerfully,
remembering that the work you are called to do is God's work;
it is in God's hand, and it is done in God's name to God's glory.
Follow Christ whose servant you are.
Share the burden of those whose cross is heavy.

You are marked as a person who proclaims
that among the truly blessed are the poor, the troubled,
the powerless, the persecuted.
You must be prepared to be what you proclaim.
Serve Christ simply and willingly,
and let your joy in Christ overcome all discouragement.
Have no fear; be humble and full of hope.

The candidates and congregation kneel.

Those priests assisting at the laying on of hands join the bishop.

The Invocation

After a pause, the bishop continues

Like the first disciples waiting for your coming,
empowering Spirit, we watch and pray.

The congregation prays in silence for the candidates.

Silence

A hymn invoking the Holy Spirit may be sung.

Bishop	Holy Spirit of God,
	meet us in this moment
	as you met the apostles of old.
	Be with us, Holy Spirit,
People	**bring faith and hope, we pray.**

Bishop	Come Holy Spirit,
People	**be present in your power.**

After a pause, the bishop continues with **The Ordination.**

The Ordination

The assisting priests then stand beside the bishop, who, facing those being ordained, says this prayer of consecration.

All present join with the bishop in saying the concluding part of the prayer.

Blessed are you,
God our creator, God in history, God in revelation;
throughout the ages your unchanging purpose
has created a people to love and serve you.

Blessed are you in Christ Jesus,
your Incarnation, our Servant Lord,
who by death overcame death.

Through his resurrection and ascension,
through the gift of the Holy Spirit,
you have given life and order to your Church,
that we may carry out the ministry of love.
We thank you for calling *these your servants*
to share this ministry as priests.

The bishop, and the assisting priests, lay hands on the head of each candidate in turn, with the bishop saying after silence

God of grace, through your Holy Spirit,
gentle as a dove, living, burning as fire,
empower your servant *N*
for the office and work of a priest in the Church.

At the conclusion of the laying on of hands, the bishop continues

May every grace of ministry rest on these your servants.
Keep them strong and faithful,
steadfast in Jesus Christ, our Saviour.
Amen!
May *they* herald the joy of your kingdom,
bring freedom rather than bondage,
serve rather than be served;
through the sacraments *they minister*
let your grace abound.

The new priests stand.

The bishop gives each of them a Bible, saying

N, here are the Holy Scriptures;
learn from them
and proclaim Christ, the living Word.

The new priests may now be vested and symbols of ministry may be given.

The congregation stands and the new priests may be presented to the Church.

The Peace

The Eucharist *continues at* **The Peace** *during which the bishop may share the sign of peace with the newly ordained who then greet their families and the congregation.*

The Ordination of Bishops

The Gathering of the Community

All standing, the presiding bishop greets the congregation.

The bishop says

Glory to God,
Creator, Redeemer and Giver of life,
who is, who was, and is to come.

Grace and peace to you from God.
> Kia tau ki a koutou, te atawhai me te rangimarie o te Atua.

God fill you with truth and joy.
> **Ma te Atua koe e whakau, ki te pono me te hari.**

*A hymn of praise, waiata or a psalm may be sung,
or the following is said or sung.*

Glory to God in the highest,
> **and peace to God's people on earth.**

Lord God, heavenly King,
almighty God and Father,
> **we worship you, we give you thanks,**
> **we praise you for your glory.**

Lord Jesus Christ, only Son of the Father,
Lord God, Lamb of God,
you take away the sin of the world:
> **have mercy on us;**
you are seated at the right hand of the Father:
> **receive our prayer.**

For you alone are the Holy One,
you alone are the Lord,
you alone are the Most High,
> **Jesus Christ,**
> **with the Holy Spirit,**
> **in the glory of God the Father. Amen.**

The bishop says

God has promised forgiveness
to all who truly repent,
turn to Christ in faith
and are themselves forgiving.

In silence we call to mind our sins.

Silence

Let us confess our sins.

**Merciful God,
we have sinned
in what we have thought and said,
in the wrong we have done
and in the good we have not done.
We have sinned in ignorance:
we have sinned in weakness:
we have sinned through our own deliberate fault.
We are truly sorry.
We repent and turn to you.
Forgive us, for our Saviour Christ's sake,
and renew our lives to the glory of your name.   Amen.**

The Absolution *is declared by the bishop.*

Through the cross of Christ,
God have mercy on you,
pardon you
and set you free.
Know that you are forgiven
and be at peace.
God strengthen you in all goodness
and keep you in life eternal.
Amen.

Glory to God in the highest *may be said or sung here, all standing.*

All sit.

The Presentation

The presiding bishop says

E te whanau a te Karaiti / People of God,
we have come to ordain a bishop in Christ's holy Church.
Christ is head of the Church;
he alone is the source of all Christian ministry.
Through the ages it is Christ
who has called men and women to serve.

By the Holy Spirit all who believe and are baptised
receive a ministry to proclaim Jesus as Saviour and Lord,
and to love and serve the people with whom they live and work.
In Christ they are to bring redemption,
to reconcile and to make whole.
They are to be salt for the earth; they are to be light to the world.

After his resurrection and ascension
Christ gave gifts abundantly to the Church.
Some he made apostles, some prophets, some evangelists,
some pastors and teachers; to equip God's people
for their work of ministry and to build up the body of Christ.

We stand within a tradition
in which there are deacons, priests and bishops.
They are called and empowered to fulfil an ordained ministry
and to enable the whole mission of the Church.
Our authority is in Scripture
and in the Church's continuing practice through the ages.

Therefore let us welcome *N*, now presented to us,
to be ordained bishop.

The bishop-elect, in rochet or alb, is presented by a layperson, a priest and a bishop.

They say

We present *N*, who has been chosen by the Diocese of…, and the Anglican Church in Aotearoa, New Zealand and Polynesia, in accordance with the Constitution, to be a bishop in the Church. We believe that *s/he* will serve Christ well as a bishop.

Bishops are sent to lead by their example
in the total ministry and mission of the Church.
They are to be Christ's shepherds
in seeking out and caring for those in need.
They are to heal and reconcile,
uphold justice and strive for peace.

Bishops are to exercise godly leadership
in that part of the Church committed to their care,
and to maintain wise discipline within its fellowship.
The Church looks to them to promote peace and unity
among all God's people,
and to encourage their obedience to God's word.
They are to keep the Church true to its faith,
as found in Scripture and the Creeds,
to teach this faith and proclaim it.

Bishops are to ensure that an episcopal ministry is maintained.
They are to ordain, send forth and care for the Church's pastors,
and to preside over its worshipping life.

N, do you believe that you are called to the office and work of a bishop?

The bishop-elect responds

I believe that God and the Church are calling me to this ministry.
I thank God for this call, and the Church for its encouragement.

All standing, the presiding bishop says to the people

E te whanau / People of God,
are you willing that *N* should be ordained bishop?

People   **We are. Thanks be to God.**

The presiding bishop prays

Holy and living God,
you call men and women
to bring to us your creative and redeeming Word.
Equip your people
for their work of ministry
and give to this your servant,
now to be ordained,
the gifts of grace *s/he* needs.
Amen.

The Collect of the Day may follow.

The congregation sits.

The Proclamation

The Readings

The readings are selected from the following

OLD TESTAMENT
Numbers 27:15-20,22-23
Isaiah 61:1-4(5-8)
Ezekiel 34:11-16

PSALM
40:1-17
99

EPISTLE
Acts 20:17-32
1 Timothy 3:1-7
2 Timothy 1:6-14

GOSPEL
John 13:2-17
John 17:1-9,18-21
John 21:15-19

The reader first says

A reading from ... (chapter ... beginning at ...)

Silence may follow each reading.

After each reading, the reader may say

Hear what the Spirit is saying to the Church.
Thanks be to God.

A psalm, hymn or anthem may follow each reading.

*Then, all standing, a deacon reads the **Gospel**, first saying*

The Holy Gospel according to ... (chapter ... beginning at ...)
Praise and glory to God.

After the Gospel, silence may be kept.

The reader says

This is the Gospel of Christ.
Praise to Christ, the Word.

The Sermon

The Sermon *is preached here.*

The Affirmation of Faith

The Nicene Creed is said, all standing.

We believe in one God,
    the Father, the Almighty,
    maker of heaven and earth,
    of all that is,
    seen and unseen.

We believe in one Lord, Jesus Christ,
    the only Son of God,
    eternally begotten of the Father,
    God from God, Light from Light,
    true God from true God,
    begotten, not made,
    of one being with the Father;
    through him all things were made.
    For us and for our salvation
        he came down from heaven,
        was incarnate of the Holy Spirit and the Virgin Mary
        and became fully human.
        For our sake he was crucified under Pontius Pilate;
        he suffered death and was buried.
        On the third day he rose again
        in accordance with the Scriptures;
        he ascended into heaven
        and is seated at the right hand of the Father.
        He will come again in glory to judge
            the living and the dead,
        and his kingdom will have no end.

We believe in the Holy Spirit,
        the Lord, the giver of life,
    who proceeds from the Father and the Son,
    who in unity with the Father and the Son
        is worshipped and glorified,
    and has spoken through the prophets.
    We believe in one holy catholic and apostolic Church.
    We acknowledge one baptism for the forgiveness of sins.
    We look for the resurrection of the dead,
        and the life of the world to come.   Amen.

All are seated except the bishop-elect who stands before the presiding bishop.

The Commitment

The presiding bishop addresses the bishop-elect.

N, you have declared your faith in God.
We believe God is calling you to serve as a bishop.
We now ask you to declare again
your commitment to Christ in his Church.

Presiding Bishop	Do you believe that the Bible contains all that is essential for our salvation, and reveals God's living word in Jesus Christ?
Bishop-elect	Yes, I do. God give me understanding in studying the Scriptures. May they reveal to me the mind and heart of Christ, and shape my ministry.
Presiding Bishop	Will you maintain the doctrines of the faith as this Church has received them?
Bishop-elect	Yes, I will. My duty and my joy will be to witness to Christ crucified and risen.
Presiding Bishop	Will you uphold the authority of the General Synod and the Constitution of the Anglican Church in Aotearoa, New Zealand and Polynesia?
Bishop-elect	Yes, I will. I am under that authority, and will exercise it in partnership with my sisters and brothers in Christ.

Presiding Bishop	Will you oversee with compassion and patience the people of God committed to your care? Will you give encouragement to all, and labour to strengthen the Church's witness and mission?
Bishop-elect	I will. God give me grace to listen, grace to be fair and merciful, courage and boldness to proclaim the gospel.
Presiding Bishop	In selecting, training and ordaining, will you be thorough and discerning?
Bishop-elect	I will. God grant me wisdom to care for those ordained.
Presiding Bishop	Will you lead God's people in seeking the lost and lonely, in healing the sick and ministering to all, whatever their needs? Will you build up the Church in faith, and challenge us with the demands of love?
Bishop-elect	I will. My concern will be to show love and compassion. God give me courage to strive for justice, wholeness and peace among all people.
Presiding Bishop	As a bishop in the Church of God, will you help us to share in the life of the world-wide Christian community?
Bishop-elect	Yes, I will. I will promote the unity and mission for which Christ prayed.
Presiding Bishop	Will you pray faithfully and expectantly, alone and with the whole Church?

Bishop-elect	Yes, I will.
	Prayer will inspire my ministry.
	I will constantly seek the Lord
	and celebrate God's presence with joy.
Presiding Bishop	Will you then give glory to God, the holy and blessed Trinity?
Bishop-elect	Glory to God on high, God of power and might.
	You are my God.
	I can neither add to your glory
	nor take away from your power.
	Yet will I wait upon you daily in prayer and praise.

The presiding bishop says

N, we praise God for your commitment
to serve Christ as a bishop in the Church.
A bishop is given authority to speak and act
as the Church's representative,
to be a focus of unity for the diocese.

Remember, the work to which we are called is God's work.
It is in God's hand, and it is done in God's name to God's glory.
We must serve humbly and cheerfully.

People look to us as bishops to make decisions and to speak with
authority, whether or not we can do so. In the exercise of your
office do not be arrogant or overbearing.
Let us have the same mind as Christ Jesus.

N, do not allow the burdens and anxieties of your office to blunt
your purpose or cloud your vision, but strive always to be pure in
heart, to be Christ's servant, to follow Jesus.

May the vision of God enlighten your understanding.
May God's continuing call sustain your walk with Christ,
and keep you joyful.

The bishop-elect and the congregation kneel.

The other bishops join the presiding bishop.

The Invocation

After a pause, the presiding bishop continues

Like the first disciples waiting for your coming,
empowering Spirit, we watch and pray.

The congregation prays in silence for the bishop-elect.

Silence

A hymn invoking the Holy Spirit may be sung.

| Presiding Bishop | Holy Spirit of God, meet us in this moment as you met the apostles of old. Be with us, Holy Spirit, |
| People | **bring faith and hope, we pray.** |

| Bishop | Come, Holy Spirit, |
| People | **be present in your power.** |

After a pause, the presiding bishop continues with **The Ordination.**

The Ordination

The assisting bishops then stand on either side of the presiding bishop who, facing the bishop-elect, says this prayer of consecration.

All present join with the presiding bishop in saying the concluding part of the prayer.

Blessed are you,
God our creator, God in history, God in revelation;
throughout the ages your unchanging purpose
has created a people to love and serve you.

Blessed are you in Christ Jesus,
your Incarnation, our Servant Lord,
who by death overcame death.
Through his resurrection and ascension,
through the gift of the Holy Spirit,
you have given life and order to your Church,

that we may carry out the ministry of love.
We thank you for calling this your servant
to share this ministry as a bishop.

The presiding bishop and the other bishops lay hands on the head of the
bishop-elect, the presiding bishop saying after silence

God of grace, through your Holy Spirit,
gentle as a dove, living, burning as fire,
empower your servant *N*
for the office and work
of a bishop in the Church.

At the conclusion of the laying on of hands the presiding bishop continues

May every grace of ministry rest on this your servant
Keep *her/him* strong and faithful,
steadfast in Jesus Christ, our Saviour.
Amen!
May *s/he* **point us to Christ, the Living Way,**
feed us with Christ, the Bread of Life,
and unite us in Christ,
rejoicing!

The new bishop stands. The presiding bishop gives her/him a Bible, saying

N, here are the Holy Scriptures;
learn from them,
teach them,
live by them,
and proclaim Christ, the living Word.

The new bishop may now be vested and symbols of ministry may be given.

The Greeting

All standing, the new bishop may be welcomed by the other bishops and the
whole congregation.

The new bishop may respond.

The Peace

The Eucharist *continues at the* **Peace** *during which the bishop may greet*
her/his family.

Additional Directions

Ordinations of priests and deacons shall take place on a day appointed by the bishop. The ordination of a bishop shall take place on a day appointed by the Primate.

The bishop conducting the ordination shall direct what shall be worn by those participating.

*The candidates for the orders of deacon, and priest shall make the declarations required by the Constitution and Canons before the **Service of Ordination**.*

It is important that a rehearsal be held at the direction of the presiding bishop.

*The full name of each person being ordained shall be used at **The Presentation**, and thereafter the name by which s/he is known.*

The presenters for deacons and priests shall be chosen by the candidates in consultation with the bishop.

The priest and lay representative who present the bishop-elect shall be appointed by the Standing Committee of the Diocese/Amorangi Whaiti of the Hui Amorangi concerned. The bishop who takes part in the presentation shall, after consultation with the bishop-elect, be appointed by the presiding bishop on behalf of the Anglican Church in Aotearoa, New Zealand and Polynesia. These three presenters shall satisfy themselves that the Primate has issued a mandate for the ordination of the bishop.

At ordinations of deacons or priests when there is more than one candidate the presentation of each candidate may be made either by separate presenters for each candidate, or by a priest and a layperson who present all the candidates.

At ordinations, when it is necessary to ordain deacons and priests in one service, the following should be noted:

(i) *At **The Presentation** the deacons are presented first (pages 890-891) concluding with the response 'We are. Thanks be to God', and then the priests are presented (page 900) beginning*

(ii)   After the deacons have been ordained, the candidates for priesthood come forward for **The Commitment** (page 905) and **The Ordination**.

Hymns, waiata, anthems, fanfares, and other music are appropriate at various places in the service, some of which are suggested in the rubrics.

The sermon shall include description of the work which a deacon, priest or bishop may be called to do, its setting in the Church's life, and its links with Christ's ministry.

At least some of the priests present shall join with the bishop in the laying on of hands at the ordination of a priest.

At least two other bishops shall join the presiding bishop at the laying on of hands of every bishop.

Symbols of ministry may be presented to the newly ordained provided they do not obscure the prime significance of what is prescribed in the service.

In any of the ordinations, the following tasks may be assigned.

– *the newly ordained may assist at* **The Preparation of the Gifts** *and the distribution of* **Communion**.
– *the newly ordained may lead the* **Prayer after Communion** *and* **The Dismissal**.
– *the newly ordained bishop may give a concluding blessing.*

It may be appropriate for the newly ordained priests or the newly ordained bishop to be associated with the presiding priest or bishop during the Eucharist, but this should not include vocal participation in **The Great Thanksgiving**.

The family of the ordained may be recognised either at **The Peace**, *or at the distribution of the Communion.*

At the Eucharist

The variations to **The Great Thanksgiving**, *and the* **Seasonal Sentences, Prayers and Blessings for use after Communion** *for Pentecost are suitable for use.*

The following prayer may be added before the blessing.

Go before us, Lord, in all our doings
with your most gracious favour
and further us with your continual help;
that in all our works begun, continued,
and ended in you,
we may glorify your holy name
now and always.

A Catechism

He Katikihama

Concerning this Catechism

This catechism is a teaching resource expressing the basic Christian beliefs and cast in the traditional question and answer form for ease of reference. Each answer can be used as an introduction to deeper and wider understanding. It includes a commentary on the Apostles' Creed but is not to be regarded as a complete statement of belief or practice.

A further use of this Catechism is to provide a summary of the teaching of the Church for an enquirer.

It may also be used selectively in liturgical worship.

Human Nature
To Te Tangata Ahua

1. *What is our nature as human beings?*

    We are part of God's creation, made in God's image: male and female we are created.

2. *What does it mean to be made in the image of God?*

    We are free to reflect God's own nature, to make choices: to love, to create, to reason, and to live in harmony with God and all creation. However we are also free to disobey, or deny the reality of God.

3. *Why is there so much disharmony in our world and in human lives?*

    From the beginning we have misused our freedom. We work against God and put ourselves in the place of God. We sin, we fall.

4. *What help is there?*

    God has acted in Jesus to bring us back to a loving and forgiven relationship. In that action all humanity is offered re-creation and wholeness.

God
Te Atua

5. *How do we become aware of God?*

    By God's initiative in our thinking and understanding: by
    experiencing and reflecting on the wonder and mystery of
    creation, birth and death, love, guilt and the need to find
    meaning and worth beyond ourselves.

6. *Where do we learn about God?*

    Christians learn about God in the Bible, in the teaching of the
    Church summed up in the Apostles' and Nicene Creeds, and
    through sharing in the living community of faith.

7. *What do we learn about God?*

    God is eternal, earth maker, pain bearer, life giver; source of
    all that is and shall be; father and mother of us all. We learn
    that God is one, yet revealed as Father, Son, and Holy Spirit -
    a Holy Trinity.

God as Father
Te Atua Matua

8. *What does the Church teach about God as Father?*

    There is one God the Father Almighty, creator of heaven and
    earth, of all that is, seen and unseen.

9. *What does this mean?*

    God creates all the worlds that are, and is sovereign over all.
    God is in all and through all, and all that God creates is good.

10. *What does this mean about our place in the universe?*

    It means that the world belongs to its creator; and that we are
    called to enjoy it and to care for it in accordance with God's
    purposes.

11. *What does this mean about human life?*

It means that all people are worthy of respect and honour because all are created in the image of God, and all can respond to the love of God.

God the Son
Te Atua Tama

12. *What does the Church teach about Jesus?*

Jesus is the only Son of God, conceived by the Holy Spirit and born of the Virgin Mary. He suffered under Pontius Pilate, was crucified, died, was buried. On the third day he rose again. He ascended into heaven, and is seated at the right hand of the Father.

13. *What does this mean?*

Jesus is the promised Saviour or Christ, God with us. Uniquely conceived by God's power and born as a human, Jesus lived lovingly and obediently. In the time of Pontius Pilate, Roman governor of Judea, he died unjustly by crucifixion. Jesus was raised from death and now lives and reigns in glory.

14. *What does Christ's death and resurrection mean?*

Through Christ's death and resurrection we are offered forgiveness and oneness with God.

15. *What is the nature of God revealed in Jesus?*

God is love.

16. *Why did Jesus, the Son of God, share our human nature?*

So that we might enter into a restored relationship or covenant with God and live as children and heirs of God's Kingdom.

17. *What did Jesus teach about our new relationship with God?*

Jesus taught that we are to love God with all our heart, mind, soul and strength: we are to love our neighbours as ourselves.

18. *What did Jesus teach about the Kingdom of God?*

The Kingdom of God is God's rule in the world, the presence of God's love, justice and peace. The Kingdom has come with Jesus, continues to come among us, and will finally come in fulness.

God the Holy Spirit
Te Atua Wairua Tapu

19. *What does the Church teach about the Holy Spirit?*

The Holy Spirit is God at work in the world and in the Church now, the giver of life and truth.

20. *How does the Holy Spirit reveal the truth?*

The Holy Spirit reveals God's truth through human experience, in the Bible, and in the witness of the Church.

21. *How is the Holy Spirit active in people's lives today?*

The Holy Spirit enfolds, nurtures and strengthens us in the love of God. By the power of the Holy Spirit people enter into the new life of the kingdom, receive Jesus as Lord of life and become disciples. They grow into love and harmony with God, their neighbours, themselves and all creation.

22. *How is the Holy Spirit active in the Church today?*

The Holy Spirit gives a variety of gifts to the people of God, produces fruit in their lives, and equips them for ministry in the world.

23. *What is the fruit of the Holy Spirit?*

The fruit of the Holy Spirit includes love, joy, peace, patience, kindness, goodness, faithfulness, gentleness, and self-control.

The Bible
Te Paipera Tapu

24. *What is the Bible?*

The Bible, or Holy Scripture, is a library of books divided into the Old and New Testaments.

25. *What is the Old Testament?*

The Old Testament consists of books written by the people of the Old Covenant before the birth of Christ to show how God was at work in nature and in the history of Israel.

26. *What is the New Testament?*

The New Testament consists of books written by the people of the New Covenant to set forth the life and teaching of Jesus and the Apostles, the growth of the early Church, and the good news of the kingdom for all people.

27. *Why does the Church value the Holy Scriptures?*

Because the Holy Spirit inspired their human authors and through the Scriptures God's word continues to speak to the Church.

28. *How do we best understand the Bible?*

We understand the meaning of the Bible, the Church's book, with the help of the Holy Spirit, who guides the people of God in interpretation and understanding.

29. *What is the Apocrypha?*

It is a collection of books written by the people of the Old Covenant and sometimes read in church, but not used to establish doctrine.

The Church
Te Haahi

30. How is the Church described in the New Testament?

The Church is described as the body of which Christ is the head, and all baptised persons are members. It is called the people of God, a holy nation, a royal priesthood, a community of faith and the fellowship of the Holy Spirit.

31. How is the Church described in the Creeds?

The Church is described as one, holy, catholic and apostolic.

It is one because it is one body, under one head, Jesus Christ.

It is holy because the Holy Spirit dwells in its members and guides it in mission.

It is catholic because it seeks to proclaim the whole faith to all people to the end of time.

It is apostolic because it presents the faith of the apostles and is sent to carry Christ's mission to all the world.

32. What is the mission of the Church?

To proclaim the good news of God's Kingdom, to make disciples, to work for justice and peace; and to strive for reconciliation and healing in a broken world.

33. How does the Church carry out its mission?

Through the ministry of its members.

Ministry
Minitatanga

34. Who are the ministers of the Church?

They are the lay persons, deacons, priests, bishops; all the baptised.

35. *What is the ministry of lay persons?*

From baptism, their vocation is to witness to Christ in the world using the gifts the Spirit gives them. Within the Church they share in the leadership of worship and in government.

36. *What is the ministry of a deacon?*

The ministry of a deacon is to be a servant, both within the Church and in the wider community.

37. *What is the ministry of a priest?*

The ministry of a priest is to build up the Body of Christ in the world through the ministry of Word and Sacrament, pastoral care and teaching.

38. *What is the ministry of a bishop?*

The ministry of a bishop is to be a pastor and shepherd of Christ's flock, a teacher of the faith and a focus of the Church's unity and mission in the world.

39. *What is the purpose of ministry?*

It is to continue Jesus' servant ministry in the world by witnessing to God's reconciling love, to bring in the Kingdom of God, to build up the body of Christ, and to glorify God's holy name.

The Sacraments
Nga Hakarameta

40. *What are the Sacraments?*

They are outward and visible signs of inward and spiritual grace, given by Christ to the Church.

41. *What is grace?*

Grace is God's freely-given love for people, forgiving sins, enlightening minds, stirring hearts and strengthening wills. Through grace we are given strength to live as loving sons and daughters of God.

42. *What are the two sacraments of the Gospel?*

The two sacraments given by Christ to the Church are Holy Baptism and the Holy Eucharist.

43. *What is Holy Baptism?*

Baptism is the sacrament by which we are made children of God, members of Christ's body the Church, and heirs of the Kingdom of God.

44. *What is the outward and visible sign of Baptism?*

Water, by which a person is baptised in the name of the Father, Son and Holy Spirit.

45. *What is the inward and spiritual grace of Baptism?*

The gift of union with Christ in his death and resurrection, birth into God's family the Church, forgiveness of sins, and new life in the Holy Spirit.

46. *What is required of those seeking Baptism?*

That they renounce evil and turn from sin to Christ as the Way, the Truth and the Life.

47. *Why are infants baptised?*

When infants are brought for Baptism, the Church acknowledges that children can share in the community of faith, enter the new Covenant, and experience the renewing spirit of God. As a response to baptism such children are called to profess faith in Christ for themselves and to receive the laying on of hands in Confirmation.

48. *What is the Eucharist?*

The Eucharist is the sacrament of thanksgiving given by Christ for the continual recalling of his life, death and resurrection. It is the family meal of the Church in which we are strengthened in our union with the living Christ and with one another for service in the world.

49. *What is the outward and visible sign in the Eucharist?*

Bread and wine, given, shared and received as Christ commanded.

50. *What is the inward and spiritual grace?*

The life of Christ, the body and blood, given by Christ and received by faith.

51. *How are we to come to the Eucharist?*

We come trusting in God's forgiving love, having examined our lives and with goodwill towards others. We come to make thanksgiving, expecting to meet Christ, to be filled with new life.

52. *What other sacramental actions does the Church provide?*

Reconciliation of a Penitent; Anointing, for healing and wholeness; Christian Marriage; Confirmation, or commissioning for Christian witness and service; Ordination of Deacons, Priests and Bishops.

Prayer
To Te Inoi Ahua

53. *What is prayer?*

Prayer is our response to God's love. We pray in the name of Christ and by the power of the Holy Spirit.

54. *What are the different ways of prayer?*

We can pray with or without words, by ourselves or with others. The main kinds of prayer include adoration, praise, thanksgiving, confession of sins, intercession to God for others and for ourselves. The prayer of listening to God is called meditation or contemplation.

55. *What is a helpful way for us to begin?*

We can realise God's presence with us by being quiet and still, and by recognising God's love within us and around us.

56. *How can the Bible be used in prayer?*

We can use a passage or verse of the Bible to reflect on God. Through the words of the Bible God is able to challenge, give guidance, strength and peace for daily living.

57. *What prayer does Christ give us?*

Our Father in heaven,
   hallowed be your name,
   your kingdom come,
   your will be done,
     on earth as in heaven.
Give us today our daily bread.
Forgive us our sins
   as we forgive those who sin against us.
Save us from the time of trial
   and deliver us from evil.

For the kingdom, the power, and the glory are yours
   now and for ever. Amen.

E to matou Matua i te rangi
   Kia tapu tou Ingoa.
   Kia tae mai tou rangatiratanga.
   Kia meatia tau e pai ai
     ki runga ki te whenua,
       kia rite ano ki to te rangi.
Homai ki a matou aianei
   he taro ma matou mo tenei ra.
Murua o matou hara,
   Me matou hoki e muru nei
     i o te hunga e hara ana ki a matou.
Aua hoki matou e kawea kia whakawaia;
   Engari whakaorangia matou i te kino:
Nou hoki te rangatiratanga, te kaha, me te kororia,
   Ake ake ake.   Amine.

The Anglican Church
Te Haahi Mihinare

58. *What is the Anglican Communion?*

It is a world-wide fellowship of self-governing churches holding the doctrine and ministry of the one, holy, catholic and apostolic church, and in communion with the Archbishop of Canterbury. It initially grew from the historic faith of the English speaking peoples but is now present in many different cultures and languages.

59. *What part of the Anglican Communion is this Church?*

It is the Anglican Church in Aotearoa, New Zealand, and Polynesia/te Haahi Mihinare, made up of Te Pihopatanga o Aotearoa, the dioceses in New Zealand, and the Diocese of Polynesia. In character this Church is multi-racial and multi-cultural.

60. *How does the Anglican Church in New Zealand understand the relationship bteween Maori and Pakeha?*

The Church recognises a special bi-cultural partnership, founded upon the principles of the Treaty of Waitangi, and seeks to express this in its life.

61. *How does the Anglican Church regard other Christians?*

Anglicans see other Christians as sisters and brothers in Christ, and pray and work for the unity which is Christ's will for the Church.

62. *How does the Anglican Church regard members of other faiths?*

Anglicans believe that all people are created in God's image and need to find meaning and purpose beyond themselves. All living faiths witness in some way to the reality of God, but in Jesus Christ God's revelation is unique.

63. *How does the Anglican Church respond to secular philosophies?*

There is much we can learn from them in the common search for meaning of life, but Anglicans believe only God can satisfy the deepest human needs.

64. *How does the Anglican Church regard the scientific advances of our age?*

Anglicans welcome those scientific advances that add to our knowledge of creation, and all technological developments that improve the quality of human life, and thank God for them .

Christian Lifestyle
Te Kawe A Te Karaitiana

65. *What is the lifestyle of a Christian?*

By the grace of God it is to die to sin and rise with Christ to the new life of the Kingdom.

66. *How may we live this life?*

By prayer, by regular worship and by using our time, talents and money to serve Christ in the world.

67. *What values characterise the followers of Christ?*

Followers of Christ seek to be loving in all relationships, honest, thankful, generous and forgiving. They seek to honour marriage and the importance of family, to work for peace and justice, and to be responsible stewards of God's creation.

68. *How is the Christian life possible?*

Following Christ is demanding and costly but Christians have the support of their brothers and sisters in Christ and are strengthened and encouraged by God's grace.

Christian Hope
To Te Karaitiana Tumanako

69. *What is the hope of a Christian?*

The Christian hope is that nothing, not even death, shall separate us from the love of God which endures and prevails forever.

70. *What does the Church believe about the last things?*

That God in Christ will come in glory to judge the living and the dead, in the fulness of time. We look to resurrection life and participation with the saints in glory.

71. *How are we to live in this hope?*

We anticipate the coming of Christ and we live now in the newness of eternal life which the Spirit gives: we work for the fulfilment of God's purpose for the whole creation.

Table to Regulate Observances

Table to Regulate Observances when Two Feasts or Holy Days Fall on the Same Day

When two Feasts or Holy Days fall on the same day, there shall be said the whole Service proper to the Day in the left hand column of the following Table; and the Service of the Day in the right-hand column shall be either praetermitted, or transferred as directed.

First Sunday in Advent	St Andrew, transferred to Tuesday
Fourth Sunday in Advent	St Thomas, transferred to Monday
St Stephen, St John the Ev., The Holy Innocents, The Naming of Jesus (Or St Stephen, St John, Ev., The Holy Innocents may be transferred to their alternative dates of 3 August, 6 May, 16 February)	First Sunday after Christmas
The Epiphany	Second Sunday after Christmas
The Conversion of St Paul *	Third Sunday after Epiphany
The Presentation of Jesus *†	Fourth Sunday after Epiphany Septuagesima, Sexagesima, Quinquagesima
Septuagesima or Sexagesima	The Conversion of St Paul, transferred to Monday

* The Collect of the Sunday will follow that of the Day.

† The Sunday may take precedence over the Feast if desired, in which case the Feast is transferred to Tuesday.

Septuagesima, Sexagesima, Quinquagesima, Ash Wednesday, First Sunday in Lent	The Holy Innocents (alternate date) transferred to the next day
Sexagesima, Quinquagesima, Ash Wednesday, Sundays in Lent	St Matthias, transferred to the next day
Third, Fourth or Fifth Sunday in Lent	Annunciation to the Blessed Virgin Mary transferred to Monday
Palm Sunday to Low Sunday	Annunciation, St Mark, St Philip and St James, transferred to Tuesday after Low Sunday
St Mark*, St Philip and St James*†, St John the Ev. (alternate date)*	Second, Third, Fourth, or Fifth Sunday after Easter
Ascension Day	St Philip and St James, St John the Ev.(alternate date), transferred to Friday
Sunday after the Ascension	St John the Ev. (alternate date) transferred to Tuesday
Pentecost to Trinity Sunday	St Barnabas transferred to Tuesday after Trinity Sunday
St Peter and St Paul and all other Feasts and Holy Days in **bold type** in Section 2 A,B,C *	Sundays after Pentecost
St Barnabas and all other Feasts and Holy Days in light type*†	Sundays after Pentecost

On Principal Feasts and Holy Days, the Collect of the Feast or Holy Day is the only Collect used.

The Vigil of a transferred Feast shall lapse.

When any other Feast is observed on a Monday, then Evening Worship on Sunday is celebrated as the first Evening Worship of the

* The Collect of the Sunday will follow that of the Day.

† The Sunday may take precedence over the Feast if desired, in which case the Feast is transferred to Tuesday.

Feast, the Collect of the Sunday being added after that of the Feast. Except that on Christmas Eve or the Eve of the Epiphany only the Collect for the Feast is said.

If any other Feast falls on a Saturday, except those before the First Sunday in Advent or the Fifth or Sixth Sundays in Lent, Evening Worship on Saturday is celebrated as the second Evening Worship of the Feast, the Collect of the Sunday being added after that of the Feast.

If any Feast falls on the Saturday before the First Sunday in Advent or the Fifth or Sixth Sundays in Lent, Evening Worship on Saturday is celebrated as the first Evening Worship of Sunday, a Collect for the Feast being added after the Collect for the Sunday.

When any Feast is observed on the day after Ash Wednesday, then Evening Worship on Wednesday is that of Ash Wednesday, the Collect of the Feast being added after that of Ash Wednesday.

When a Feast falls on the day before Ascension Day, then Evening Worship on Wednesday is celebrated as the First Evening Worship of the Ascension without any additional Collect for the Feast. When any Feast is observed on the day after Ascension Day, then Evening Worship on Thursday is celebrated as the second Evening Worship of the Ascension.

If any other Commemoration falls upon a Holy Day, then the Service of the Holy Day shall take precedence, but the Collect of the Commemoration may be added after the Collect of the Holy Day, unless it be a Principal Feast or Holy Day or one of the days from Palm Sunday to Low Sunday inclusive.

The Collect for Christmas Day and the Feast of Pentecost, shall be used on the six days following, and the Collect for the Epiphany and Ascension Day on the seven days following; except where other provision is made, and in that case the Collect of the Feast shall be added after the Collect of the Day.

One of the Collects appointed for every Sunday, or for any Feast or Holy Day that has a Vigil or Eve, shall be said at the Evening Service before it.

In Advent a Collect for Advent Sunday may be said after any other appointed Collect until Christmas Eve inclusive.

In Lent a Collect for Ash Wednesday may be said until Maundy Thursday inclusive.

A Table to Find Movable

YEAR OF OUR SAVIOUR	SUNDAY LETTER	ORDINARY SUNDAYS BEFORE SEPTUA-GESIMA	SEPTUAGESIMA SUNDAY (EPIPHANY 7)	ASH WEDNESDAY	EASTER DAY
1989	A	2	22 Jan	8 Feb	26 Mar
1990	G	5	11 Feb	28 Feb	15 Apr
1991	F	2	27 Jan	13 Feb	31 Mar
1992	ED	5	16 Feb	4 Mar	19 Apr
1993	C	4	7 Feb	24 Feb	11 Apr
1994	B	3	30 Jan	16 Feb	3 Apr
1995	A	5	12 Feb	1 Mar	16 Apr
1996	GF	4	4 Feb	21 Feb	7 Apr
1997	E	2	26 Jan	12 Feb	30 Mar
1998	D	4	8 Feb	25 Feb	12 Apr
1999	C	3	31 Jan	17 Feb	4 Apr
2000	BA	6	20 Feb	8 Mar	23 Apr
2001	G	5	11 Feb	28 Feb	15 Apr
2002	F	2	27 Jan	13 Feb	31 Mar
2003	E	5	16 Feb	5 Mar	20 Apr
2004	DC	4	8 Feb	25 Feb	11 Apr
2005	B	2	23 Jan	9 Feb	27 Mar
2006	A	5	12 Feb	1 Mar	16 Apr
2007	G	4	4 Feb	21 Feb	8 Apr
2008	FE	1	20 Jan	6 Feb	23 Mar
2009	D	4	8 Feb	25 Feb	12 Apr
2010	C	3	21 Jan	17 Feb	4 Apr
2011	B	6	20 Feb	9 Mar	24 Apr
2012	AG	4	5 Feb	22 Feb	8 Apr
2013	F	2	27 Jan	13 Feb	31 Mar

Feasts and Holy Days

ASCENSION DAY	PENTECOST	ORDINARY SUNDAY CORRESPONDING TO PENTECOST 2	SUNDAYS AFTER PENTECOST * (EXCL. LAST)	ADVENT SUNDAY	YEAR OF OUR SAVIOUR
4 May	14 May	8	25	3 Dec	1989
24 May	3 Jun	11	22	2 Dec	1990
9 May	19 May	9	24	1 Dec	1991
28 May	7 Jun	12	21	29 Nov	1992
20 May	30 May	11	22	28 Nov	1993
12 May	22 May	10	23	27 Nov	1994
25 May	4 Jun	11	22	3 Dec	1995
16 May	26 May	10	23	1 Dec	1996
8 May	18 May	9	24	30 Nov	1997
21 May	31 May	11	22	29 Nov	1998
13 May	23 May	10	23	28 Nov	1999
1 Jun	11 Jun	12	21	3 Dec	2000
24 May	3 Jun	11	22	2 Dec	2001
9 May	19 May	9	24	1 Dec	2002
29 May	8 Jun	12	21	30 Nov	2003
20 May	30 May	11	22	28 Nov	2004
5 May	15 May	9	24	27 Nov	2005
25 May	4 Jun	11	22	3 Dec	2006
17 May	27 May	10	23	2 Dec	2007
1 May	11 May	8	25	30 Nov	2008
21 May	31 May	11	22	29 Nov	2009
13 May	23 May	10	23	28 Nov	2010
2 Jun	12 Jun	13	20	27 Nov	2011
17 May	27 May	10	23	2 Dec	2012
9 May	19 May	9	24	1 Dec	2013

* The number given is that of the Sunday after Pentecost which falls between 13 and 19 November.

General Index

This general index should be read in conjunction with the Contents pages v-vii, the Index of Songs of Praise, Hymns and Waiata on page 946, and the Table of Seasonal Material on page 947.

Songs of Praise, Hymns, and Waiata

Before the ending of the day *176*
Glory to you, my God, this night *175*
God be in my head *178*
God that madest earth and
heaven *178*
Hail, gladdening light *175*

WAIATA, HIMENE

Poi Chant *154*
Waiata 23 *842*
Waiata 121 *843*

Waiata 130 *844*
Waiata 139: 1- 11 *846*
Te Waiata a te Haahi *45*
Te Waiata a Hakaraia *40*
Te Waiata a Himiona *47*
Te Waiata a te Puhi Tapu a Meri *42*
Ko te Karaiti te hepara pai *478*
Ko te Karaiti te Waiora *477*
Kororia ki te Atua i runga rawa *494,502*
Tama ngakau marie *174*
Ma te marie a te Atua *177*

Table of Seasonal Material
Liturgies of the Eucharist

	Theme Sentences Collects Readings		Seasonal Variants	Sentences Prayers and Blessings
	2 year	3 year		
Advent	550-554	692-693	431,440,474,491	525-526
Ascension Day	601	704	432,441,475,492	539-540
Ash Wednesday	573-574	696	*as for* Lent	
Christmas	555-559	694-695	431,440,474,491	527-528
Easter	591-601	701-704	432,441,475,492	536-538
Epiphany	560-572	695,707-711	431,440,474,491	529-531
Good Friday	587-589	700	*as for* Passiontide	
Holy Week	582-586	700	*as for* Passiontide	533-536
Lent	574-581	696-699	431,440,474,491	531-533
Passiontide	579-581	698	431,440,474,492 *also as for* Lent	
Pentecost	604	705	433,441,475,493	541-542
After Pentecost	606-640	710-723		542-543
Saints	642-690		435,441,475,493	544
Trinity	606-607	706	433,441	544

Note: In the Liturgies of the Word appropriate Songs of Praise may be found on pages 96-103 and Sentences on pages 30-34. Collects for these Liturgies are chosen from those listed above.

Acknowledgements

The Commission wishes to acknowledge with gratitude the liturgical heritage of the past into which they entered and which was their own formation in worship and prayer. Adaptions and echoes from such sources will be obvious to readers. So, too, will be the overwhelming influence of words, phrases and sentences from the many translations of the Old and New Testaments which are current in our times.

The Commission also thanks members of the Anglican Communion and other Christian Churches throughout the world, who are engaged on the common journey of expressing liturgy for their generation. The tradition is for mutuality in the sharing of resources and for this we are grateful.

It may be that the Commission has found a treasure in the vast numbers of prayers and services now available to us all, and brought it forth from the memory without realising its source. We acknowledge with thankfulness such treasures, and ask for understanding if any recognise some part of this work as springing from their own which the publishers have not acknowledged formally. In future editions we would wish to correct our error if we are informed of the same.

Our purpose in all things is to glorify God and we acknowledge especially the inspiration, grace and guidance of the Holy Spirit.

Kororia ki te Atua.

Permission to quote from the following copyright sources is acknowledged with thanks*:

Prayers in *Liturgies of the Word:* Sunday Evening, Saturday Morning; *Prayers* in *Liturgies of the Eucharist:* Epiphany C, D, Lent C, D, Holy Week D, E, Easter D, Ascension C, Pentecost C; *Thanksgiving:* For a child (755, 756); For the mother after the delivery (758); *Collect* for St Simon and St Jude D: (some adapted) from *The Book of Alternative Services of the Anglican Church of Canada*, copyright © 1985 by the General Synod of the Anglican Church of Canada.

Blessings in *Liturgies of the Eucharist:* Christmas B, C, Easter D, Ascension B: from *Alternative Prayer Book 1984*, © copyright 1984 the General Synod of the Church of Ireland, Collins.

Blessings in *Liturgies of the Eucharist:* Advent C, Christmas B, Lent B, Holy Week D, Easter E, F, G, Pentecost B, Trinity Sunday, Saints A, B, General A, D; *Prayers* in *Liturgies of the Eucharist:* Most merciful Lord (425), We do not Presume, Father of all (428); Prayer for natural parents (758); *Dialogue* in *Marriage Liturgies* (789, et al); *Collects:* Visitation, St Stephen A, Missionary A, Any Saint A, Holy Cross A and Sentence, All Souls A; *Baptism, the words at signing:* reproduced from or adapted from, *The Alternative Service Book, 1980*, by permission of The Central Board of Finance of the Church of England.

* The letters A, B, C etc refer in order to the prayers given at this place.
Numbers in brackets refer to pages in this book.

Prayers in *Liturgies of the Word:* Morning (50), Evening (51B); *Salvator Mundi;
Collects:* Christmas C, Epiphany 3 C, Epiphany 5 A, Lent 1 B, Lent 3 B, Easter 4 A,
Pentecost 3 A, Pentecost 21 B, Pentecost 23 A, Pentecost 25 A: adapted from *The Daily
Office Revised*, ed. Ronald Jasper, © The Joint Liturgical Group, by permission of SPCK.

Prayer in *Liturgies of the Word:* Friday Morning, © copyright 1979 Church Hymnal
Corporation.

Alternative Blessing in *Liturgies of the Eucharist* (545), © copyright Gail Ramshaw.

English translation of the *Benedictus* (39) and of the *Magnificat* (41) by the International
Consultation on English Texts 1975, adapted.

English translation of the *Te Deum* (44), originally prepared by the First Consultation
on English texts, and revised in 1987 by the English Language Liturgical Consultation,
adapted.

English translation of the *Nunc Dimittis* (47) by International Consultation on English
Texts, 1975.

*Our Father, Lord have mercy, Glory be to God in the highest, Nicene Creed, Apostles Creed,
Sanctus and Benedictus, Agnus Dei, Glory to the Father:* English translation originally
prepared by International Consultation on English Texts and revised in 1987 by the
English Language Liturgical Consultation. Adapted.

Evening Collect (95), *The Minister's Prayer Book*, ed. John W Doberstein, Collins.

Extract from the English translation of the *Rite of Penance*, © 1974; Prayer in *Liturgies of
the Word*, Sunday Morning, from *Liturgy of the Hours* © 1974; Prayer in *Liturgies of the
Eucharist*, Christmas C, from *The Roman Missal* © 1973; International Committee on
English in the Liturgy, Inc. All rights reserved. Altered with permission.

Midday Prayer: Opening Invocation, Prayers 1, 2, 3, Concluding Response, from *Prayer
in the Day* by Jim Cotter; *Night Prayer:* a substantial portion has been taken from *Prayer
at Night* by Jim Cotter; introduction (167) from Foreward to *Prayer at Night* by Mother
Jane of the Sisters of the Love of God, Fairacres, Oxford, England: both publications
available from Cairns Publications, 47 Firth Park Avenue, Sheffield S5 6HF, England.

Song to the Holy Spirit (157), Song to the Lord God (160), from James K Baxter, *Collected
Poems*, Oxford University Press.

Extract (160) from *Murder in the Cathedral*, by T.S. Eliot, published by Faber and Faber.

'The Lake of Beauty' (157), from *Towards Democracy*, by Edward Carpenter, published
by Unwin Hyman Limited.

Prayer to be said by the couple (803), Prayer 8 (857), from *The Pastor's Prayerbook* by
Robert N Rodenmayer, copyright © 1960 Oxford University Press, Inc.

Prayers 2 in *Marriage Liturgies (799)*, and in *The Funeral Service* (828), from C. Micklem,
Contemporary Prayers for Public Worship, adapted, SCM Press, 1967.

Marriage Blessing C, lines 6-10, from The Methodist Service Book, 1975, Methodist
Publishing House, Peterborough.

The Blessing of the God of Sarah (761) by Lois Wilson, Canada, from *No Longer Strangers*,
ed. Iben Gjerding and Katherine Kinnamon, p.45, © 1983; quotations (379, 403) from
Baptism, Eucharist and Ministry, © 1982; World Council of Churches Publications,
Geneva, Switzerland.

The Blessing of a Home draws material from *The Occasional Services Book*, The Episcopal
Church of America.

Quotations from scripture have been reprinted, or adapted, from a number of translations, especially:

Extracts from *Revised Standard Version of the Bible*, copyright 1946, 1952, 1971, by the Division of Christian Education of the National Council of Churches in the USA. Used by permission.

Extracts from *New English Bible* © 1961, 1970, by permission of Oxford and Cambridge University Presses.

Extracts adapted from the *Good News Bible*, published by the Bible Societies and Collins, © American Bible Society 1966, 1971, 1976; used by permission.

Extracts from *New International Version of the Holy Bible*, copyright © 1973, 1978, 1984, by International Bible Society: Deuteronomy 33:26,27*; Isaiah 33:2, 33:5,6*, 41:8,9*, 45:8, 49:10*, 51:3*, 51:11; Jeremiah 16:19-21*; Lamentations 5:19; Micah 7:7*; Matthew 21:9; John 1:47; Acts 1:3*; Colossians 1:12*; 1 Thessalonians 4:14; James 1:18*. * indicates that certain verbal changes have been made: these in no sense indicate any intention of the copyright owners to change the actual text of New International Version. Reproduced by kind permission of Hodder & Stoughton Publishers.

ILLUSTRATIONS

The following artists have contributed original work to the illustration of this book:

Cover Archbishop Brian Davis
Half Title Ross Hemera
Calendar Michael Smither
Liturgies of the Word Marilynn Webb
Psalms for Worship Ralph Hotere
Liturgies of Baptism Ross Hemera
Liturgies of the Eucharist Nigel Brown
Sentences, Prayers and Readings Marilynn Webb
Pastoral Liturgies Claudia Pond Eyley
Marriage Liturgies Maurice Conly
Funeral Liturgies Ross Hemera
Ordination Liturgies Michael Smither
Catechism Ross Hemera
Design in footline on Maori parallel pages Ross Hemera